Why Do You Need This New Edition?

If you're wondering why you should buy this new edition of *The Writer's World*, here are 10 good reasons!

1 New "Visualizing (the mode)" Feature: Chapters 6 to 14 now include a new feature that illustratively represents each of the nine patterns/modes so you can visually grasp how they are used in everyday writing situations! "Visualizing (the mode)" helps you "see" how to use each of the nine modes/patterns.

2 Expanded Writer's Exchange Activities: The first edition contained Writer's Exchange activities at the beginnings of each essay pattern chapter in Part II. This feature has been expanded into Part III in the new edition. Thus, you are getting more and better practice at every turn and preparing yourself for success!

3 Report Writing Success: Chapter 18 now includes expanded coverage about writing reports. Both a film (*Avatar*) and a novel (Hemingway) are discussed and modeled.

4 New Essay Models and Practices: New and more engaging essay models and essay writing prompts! In fact, to make the content more topical and appealing, roughly 30 percent of the book's content has been updated. You will notice new sample essays, examples, practices, and writing prompts throughout.

5 New MLA Updates: Chapter 16, The Research Essay, contains updated information from the Seventh Edition of the *MLA Handbook*. Material in the chapter has been streamlined and revised with topical examples and references. The final student essay about energy drinks has a detailed Works Cited page and the chapter ends with a practice related to the sample essay.

6 New Media Writing Activities: Chapters 6 to 14 now end with a newly modified Media Writing activity. You are asked to view a television program, film, or online video and use the content as writing prompts that will help you sharpen your overall writing skills.

7 Getting Motivated: Cooperative Learning Teaching Tips appear throughout the book and can be used by your instructor to promote peer-to-peer interaction, share knowledge, solve a problem, negotiate, and reflect. These activities will help prepare you for the workplace!

8 Your World: You spend your day texting friends and family, checking Facebook and Twitter, and listening to music on your iPod. New teaching suggestions help your instructors to incorporate more activities that include these cutting edge devices. For example, in Chapter 11, you can look on Facebook and categorize types of friends or the features of the social networking site. In Chapter 12, you can compare and contrast two online shopping sites.

9 New Readings: Chapters 6 to 14 include a wide selection of new essays, including student samples about imprisonment and rehabilitation, goth culture, and discrimination of those with physical disabilities. Chapter 40 has six provocative and appealing new readings that relate to the grammar themes. For example, David Leonhardt examines theories about success in "Chance and Circumstance," and Maya Angelou reflects on a life-changing event in "Guy."

10 New Chapter Objectives & MyWritingLab Prompts: Each chapter in *The Writer's World: Essays* now opens with a listing of chapter objectives and ties them into the most powerful online writing tool on the planet with Pearson's **MyWritingLab** (www.mywritinglab.com). Now you can truly grasp chapter content and test your understanding of that content with MyWritingLab in a more meaningful way!

PEARSON

What are the diverse needs of your students?

- ✔ *For many of my students, English is a second language.*
- ✔ *I have many visual learners in my classes.*
- ✔ *My students have varying skill levels.*

Students differ in many ways, and each brings his or her own set of needs to the writing classroom. It is the great variety of those needs that poses a major challenge for writing instructors. Lynne Gaetz and Suneeti Phadke, the authors of *The Writer's World*, understand this dynamic from their numerous years of teaching students how to improve their writing, preparing them for success. They understand that there are many types of writers, all with unique strengths and weaknesses, circumstances, and goals. Therefore, *The Writer's World* is designed to help you reach as great a number of students as possible by meeting the needs of those students. The following pages detail how *The Writer's World* helps learners with varying needs come together and excel at becoming stronger, more consistent, and more creative writers.

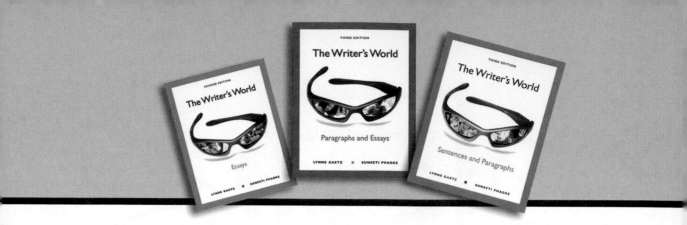

Do you have students for whom English is a second language?

"For my ESL students I find the chapters in the grammar section are what I use the most. I REALLY appreciate the box "Hints" that I can refer my students to as a reminder of something that often pertains to their writing."

—Patrice Plummer, *Bakersfield College*

With Lynne Gaetz's and Suneeti Phadke's expertise in teaching nonnative speakers of English, ESL material is a strength of *The Writer's World* texts.

- **ESL Teaching Tips:** *The Writer's World: Essays, Second Edition,* contains ESL Teaching Tips in the margins of the Annotated Instructor's Edition. Many of these teaching tips are derived from the authors' first-hand experience teaching nonnative speakers in their classrooms, while others have been suggested by users of *The Writer's World* and experts in the field of English language training.

  - Expanded subject–verb agreement ESL tips and overall content has been added in order to meet the needs of instructors who have a growing mixture of nonnative and native speakers in the classroom.

- **Seamless Integration of ESL Topics:** *The Writer's World* weaves traditional ESL topics throughout the text, often in "Hint" boxes. By identifying ESL topics only in the Annotated Instructor's Edition (and not the student edition), this important material can benefit both native and nonnative speakers.

- **Vocabulary Boost:** One important skill for nonnative speakers is improved vocabulary. This edition of *The Writer's World* introduces Vocabulary Boosts throughout Part II to prompt students to review and improve their own writing. Designed to help enhance student vocabulary, Vocabulary Boost helps ESL and non-ESL students alike!

> **ESL**
> **Teaching Tip:**
> Encourage your nonnative speakers to write about culture-specific topics because other students will enjoy learning something new or exotic.

> **vo•cab•u•lar•y BOOST**
>
> Some words have neutral, positive, or negative associations. Look at each set of words and categorize each as neutral, positive, or negative. Do this with a partner.
>
> 1. thin, cadaverous, lean, emaciated, wiry, skinny, slender
> 2. home, shack, cottage, slum, stomping ground, dump, sanctuary
> 3. dainty, delicate, finicky, fussy, prissy, fragile, elegant, frail
> 4. honest, coarse, crude, open, gross, straightforward
> 5. brat, child, sweetheart, cutie, munchkin, delinquent, heir, mama's boy

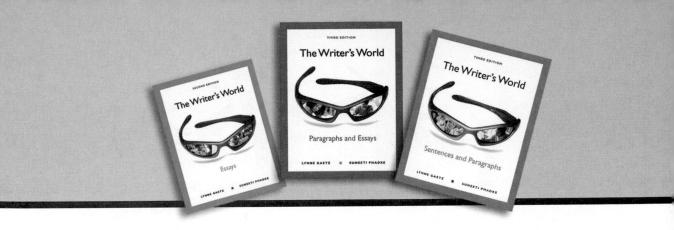

Do you have visual learners?

"The overall design, graphics, and visuals are absolutely phenomenal."
—Yolanda Nieves, *Wilbur Wright College*

"With pop culture as it is and media's huge impact on our students, I think all of my students have been raised to pull cues from visual prompts. They require visual aids/elements to help them understand what they are learning and The Writer's World *offers a good balance between being visually appealing and being stimulating."*
—Patrice K. Johnson, *Eastfield College*

The authors have utilized visuals throughout the text to illustrate key writing concepts. These visual cues help students retain information by providing it to them in an additional format.

- **Visuals to Illustrate Concepts:** *The Writer's World* uses numerous visuals throughout the text to illustrate concepts, including tables and charts, chapter-opening photos, and the new Visualizing the Mode feature.

- **Visual Writing Prompts:** Topics and ideas for essay writing can come from a number of different sources. In addition to reading essays, *The Writer's World* encourages students to take inspiration from examining photos, watching movies, and engaging in all kinds of new media. These visual prompts, found at the end of each writing chapter and thematic unit, give students varied and engaging options for finding an essay topic.

- **Open and Inviting Text Design:** *The Writer's World* layout grabs students' attention and draws them into the material. The text has just the right mix of exciting visual and design elements to help stimulate readers' interest without being cluttered.

- **New e-Text for *The Writer's World*:** Students now have access to the interactive andvisually appealing e-Text via MyWritingLab.

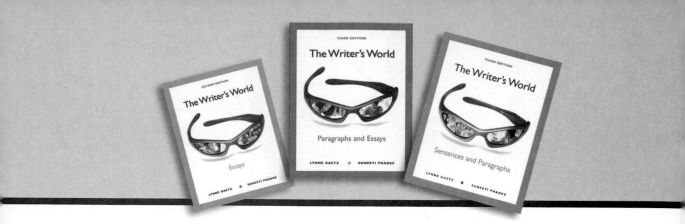

Do you have students with varying skill levels?

"I use the Final Review exercises of the grammar chapters as homework, group practice, or in-class exercises to check student's understanding before they take an assessment of the material. The thing I like the most about these reviews is that they are in passages rather than in individual sentences . . . so this format gives them more authentic practice."

—Lory Conrad, *University of Arkansas, Fort Smith*

- **Thematic Grammar Chapters:** This unique way of presenting grammar concepts thematically makes the material more engaging. The more engaging grammar is, the more likely students will retain key concepts and comprehend material overall.

- **Using MyWritingLab with** *The Writer's World* **and making it part of the curriculum enhances the student experience with the material and offers an opportunity for vast overall improvement in skill building.** It is the first complete learning system that will truly help students become better writers.

  - **A Comprehensive Writing Program:** MyWritingLab houses over 9,000 exercises in grammar, writing process, essay development, and research.

  - **Diagnostic Testing:** MyWritingLab includes groundbreaking diagnostic testing that thoroughly assesses students' skills in grammar. Based on the results, students receive a study plan that reflects the areas where they need help the most and those areas that they have mastered.

  - **Recall, Apply, and Write Exercises:** These activities, the heart of MyWritingLab, are designed to move students from literal comprehension to critical comprehension to demonstrating concepts in their own writing. This recursive learning process, not available in any other online resource, enables students to master the skills and concepts they need to be successful writers.

- Students now have automatic access to the e-Text version of the printed text when they register for and use *The Writer's World* with MyWritingLab!

For tips on integrating MyWritingLab into your course, see pages I–9 through I–12.

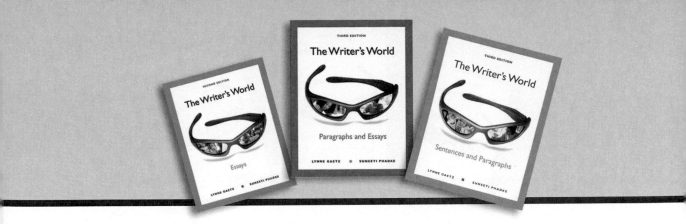

What are the diverse needs of instructors?

The Writer's World: Essays, Second Edition

INSTRUCTOR SUPPORT:

- **Annotated Instructor's Edition.** The AIE contains the answers to all of the exercises in the text and over 150 teaching tips in the margins for instructors. (ISBN: 0-205-78173-X)

- **Instructor's Resource Manual.** For each chapter in the text, this resource provides PowerPoint slides, summaries, and additional chapter quizzes. Also included are sample syllabi and a textbook answer key for those instructors who wish to distribute exercise answers to their students. (ISBN: 0-205-78174-8)

- **User Community Notes.** The AIE now includes comments from instructors across the country detailing how they utilize *The Writer's World* in their courses.

- *The Writer's World* **on Facebook.** Correspond with fellow users of *The Writer's World* to exchange ideas or just become a fan of the book series!

ADDITIONAL RESOURCES
THE PEARSON WRITING PACKAGE

Pearson is pleased to offer a variety of support materials to help make teaching writing easier for teachers and to help students excel in their coursework. Many of our student supplements are available free or at a greatly reduced price when packaged with *The Writer's World*. Additionally, there are many instructor supplements available upon adoption for experienced and first-time instructors alike. Visit www.pearsonhighereducation.com, contact your local Pearson sales representative, or review a detailed listing of the full supplements package in the Instructor's Resource Manual for more information.

User Community

"The topics (in Classification) include universals such as clothing and jobs. Reading and discussing the prompts, the students can see how to organize for classification."
—Sandra Block
CENTURY COLLEGE

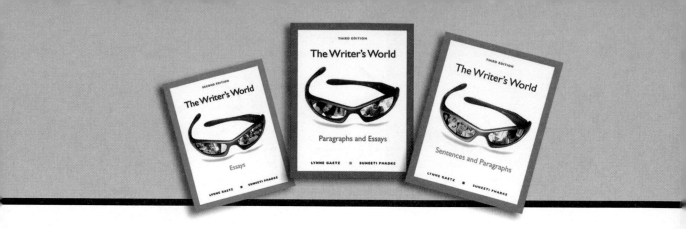

The growing *Writer's World* community

With now over 300 colleges and 90,000 students using *The Writer's World* in its first year alone, *The Writer's World* community is growing rapidly. We rely on that community to continually improve the series, and those improvements can be seen here and in the revisions of the *Paragraphs and Essays*, *Sentences and Paragraphs*, and *Essays* texts.

The authors and Pearson Prentice Hall would like to thank the following instructors who reviewed the completed first editions and not only told us what they liked but also made specific comments for improvements. Some of these reviewers were asked to provide specific feedback on an entire text, others responded specifically to the ESL material, and yet others were asked how best to use *The Writer's World* in the classroom. We are most grateful for their comments.

Annette Aagard, Grossmont College
Angela Adams, Loyola University College
Linda S. Anderson, Washington University*
Maria Assif, Truman College
Linda Austin, Glendale Community College
Craig Bartholomaus, Metropolitan Community College–Penn Valley
Scott Bauman, Orangeburg–Calhoun Technical College
Timothy Benell, Hunter College*
Mary Anne Bernal, San Antonio College
Sandra Block, Century College
Kay Blue, Owens Community College
Christian Blum, Bryant and Stratton College
Frances Boyd, Columbia University*
Nellie Boyd, Texas Southern University
Brent Bryant, Edgecombe CC
Christina Bumgardner, Minnesota School of Business
Bryce R. Campbell, Victor Valley College
Lorraine Caplan, IADT Pittsburgh
Karen Carlson, Jamestown Business College
Jessica Carroll, Miami-Dade College

Sharon Cavusgil, Georgia State University*
Sandra Chumchal, Blinn College
Cynthia Clark, Belmont Technical College
Lory Conrad, University of Arkansas–Fort Smith
Jodi Crandall, University of Maryland–Baltimore County*
Kennette Crockett, Malcolm X College
Marjorie Dernaika, Southwest TN CC
Jonathan Dewberry, Gibbs College
Candace Dismuke, Texas Southern University
Connie Duke, Keiser University
Tyson Dutton, Chemeketa CC
Kevin Dvorak, Keiser University
Crystal Echols, Sinclair Community College
Donna Estill, Alabama Southern Community College
Beth Flanagan, Tennessee Career College
Christine Foster Meloni, Northern Virginia Community College*
Paul T. Gallagher, Red Rocks CC
Sally Gearhart, Santa Rosa Junior College*
Cindy L. Geiswein, Ivy Tech CC–Terre Haute

Jennifer Georgen, Missouri College
Anne Gervasi, DeVry University
Charles Gonzalez, Central Florida Community College
Wendy Goodwin, Miami-Dade College
Lois Gould, Kaplan Career Institute
Bill W. Hall, St. Petersburg College
Martha Hall, The New England School of English*
Carin Halper, Fresno City College
Beth Hammett, College of the Mainland
Barbara Hampton, Rend Lake College
Isabel Hansen, Black Hawk College
Carrie Harrison, Pittsburgh Technical Institute
Laraine Herring, Yavapai College
Amy Hickman, Collins College
Sara K. Holzberlein, Spring International Language Center*
Steve Horowitz, Central Washington University*
Judith A. Huber, Ivy Tech–Bloomington
Sharyn Hunter, Sinclair CC

*ESL Expert

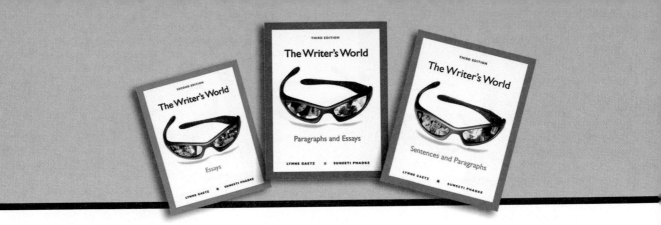

Greg Jewell, Drexel University*
Doreen Johnson, Rochester Community and Technical College
Patrice K. Johnson, Eastfield College
Aleyenne Johnson-Jonas, The Art Institute of California
Laura Kingston, South Seattle CC
Teresa Kozek, Housatonic Community College
Julie Kratt, Cowley County Community College
Trudy Krisher, Sinclair Community College
Deonne Kunkel, City College of San Francisco
Michael Lackey, William R. Harper College
Michelle Lockett, Lincoln College of Technology
John Luukkonen, TCI College of Technology
Carole MacClennan, Sinclair Community College
Elizabeth McCaffrey, St. Francis College
Alice McDonough, College of Technology
Sara McLaughlin, Texas Tech University
Tara Mills, DeVry University
Aubrey Moncrieffe, Jr., Housatonic CC
Kelley Montford, Colorado Technical University
Miriam P. Moore, Lord Fairfax CC
Debbie Naquin, North Virginia CC
Mary Needle, Cuyahoga Community College
David Nelson, Glendale CC
Caryn Newburger, Austin Community College
Sarah Nichter, Sullivan University
Yolanda Nieves, Wilbur Wright College
David Norman, South University
Ellen Olmstead, Montgomery College
Angela Parrino, Hunter College School of Continuing Education*
Jeff Partridge, Capital Community College
Ronald Peacock, Edgecombe CC
Patrice Plummer, Bakersfield College
Kim Rickard, Sinclair Community College
Doug Rigby, Lehigh Carbon Community College

Esther Robbins, Prince George's Community College*
Nina Rosen, Santa Rosa Junior College*
Marybeth Ruscica, St. John's University
Karin Russell, Keiser University
Martha Sacks, Johnson & Wales U
Lynn Saul, Pima Community College
Basudha Sengupta, Diablo Valley College
Kathy Sherak, San Francisco State University*
Erica Smith, Berkeley College
Theresa Sternat, Eastfield College
Sharon Tash, Saddleback Community College
Roseann Torsiello, Berkeley College
James Trick, Newport Business Institute
Christine M. Tutlewski, University of Wisconsin-Parkside
Chris Twiggs, Florida Community College at Jacksonville
Mary Verbout, Yavapai College
Rhonda Wallace, Cuyahoga Community College
Arlene Weaver, Wilbur Wright College
Dale Weinbach, Miami International University of Art and Design
Joette Whims, Barstow CC and Victor Valley College
Tunya Whitaker, Westwood College
Elizabeth Wurz, Columbus State College
George Q. Xu, Clarion University of Pennsylvania*

REVIEWER SUMMIT PARTICIPANTS AND CONTRIBUTORS

Brent Bryant, Edgecombe Community College
Mary Ward, Cuyahoga Community College
Yolanda Nieves, Wilbur Wright College
Kelley Montford, Colorado Technical University
Barbara Hampton, Rend Lake College
Sharyn Hunter, Sinclair Community College

Erica Smith, Berkeley College
Barbara Monaghan, Berkeley College
Ellen Olmstead, Montgomery College

If you or your students would like to participate in *The Writer's World* Review or Reviewer Summit, please e-mail matthew.wright@pearson.com.

We also would like to thank the original members of *The Writer's World* community—those who reviewed manuscript and attended focus groups before the original publication of the series in August 2005.

Karin Alderfer, Miami Dade College
Paul Bellwoar, Harper College
Nellie Boyd, Texas Southern University
Beverly Braniff, Carl Sandburg University
Donald Brotherton, DeVry University
Lina Brotherton, Oakton Community College
Barbara Brown, Olive Harvey College
Mary Coleman, San Diego Community College
David Critchett, Community College of Rhode Island
Sandra Cusak, Heald University
Robin Daniel, Broward Community College
Patsy Daniels, Lane College
Nancy Davies, Miami Dade College
Rita Delude, New Hampshire Technical College
Curt Duffy, Los Angeles Pierce College

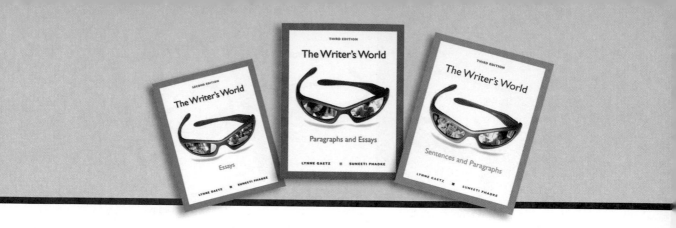

Bettie Estes, Ozarka College
Ray Foster, Scottsdale Community College
Maria Garcia-Landry, Palm Beach
Community College
Anne Gervasi, DeVry University
Casey Gilson, Broward Community College
Kate Gleason, Interboro Institute
Joyce Henna, Honolulu Community College
Todd Heyden, Pace University
Lorena Horton, San Jacinto College
Cari Kenner, Texas State Technical College
Deonne Kunkel, Diablo Valley College
Paulette Longmore, Essex County
Community College
Teri Maddox, Jackson State Community
College
Robin Madieros, Community College
of Rhode Island
Peter Marcoux, El Camino College
Sara McLaughlin, Texas Tech University
Alpha McMath, Triton College
Caryn Newburger, Austin Community
College
Virginia Nugent, Miami Dade College
Patrick Parks, Elgin Community College
Bruce Peppard, El Camino College
Dara Perales, Palomar College
Patricia Pullenza, Mesa Community College
Marcia Rogers, Orange Coast College
Bonnie Ronson, Hillsborough Community
College
Harvey Rubenstein, Hudson County
Community College
Anna Marie Schlender, Austin Community
College
Jeffrey Siddal, College of DuPage
Karen Sidwell, St. Petersberg College
Marcie Sims, Green River Community
College
Virginia Smith, Carteret Community College
Marc Sonnenfeld, Broward Community
College

Carmen Subryan, Howard University
Mitchell Summerlin, Calhoun Community
College
Lisa Tittle, Harford Community College
Danielle True, Florida Gulf Coast University
Donald Weasenforth, Collin County
Community College
Sally Wheeler, Georgia Perimeter College
Evelyn Wilson, Tarrant County Community
College
David Winsper, Springfield Technical College
Beverly Winters, Florida Community College
Arnold Wood, Florida Community College
Wendy Wright, El Camino College
Gary Zacharias, Palomar College
Donna Accardo, Los Angeles Pierce College
Jeanette Adkins, Tarrant County College
Pam Arterburn, Mount San Antonio College
Michelle Banks, Pasadena City College
Nicholas Bekas, Valencia Community College
Jennifer Black, McLennan Community
College
Frank Cronin, Austin Community College
Patricia Dungan, Austin Community College
Joan Eberle, Shasta College
Heather Elko, Brevard College
Karen Feldman, Seminole Community
College
Linda Fields, Broward Community College
Chriss Foster, Merrit College
Laura Foster-Eason, Collin County
Community College
Gladys Garcia, California State
University–Long Beach
Maria Garcia-Landry, Palm Beach
Community College
Casey Gilson, Broward Community College
Barbara Goldberg, Humboldt State University
Sally Good, South Plains College
Traci L. Gourdine, American River College
Liza Greenberg, Miami Dade College

Dr. Susan Guzman-Trevino, Temple College
Carmen Hall, St. Petersburg College
Carin Halper, Fresno City College
Judy Harris, Tomball College
Gisela Herrera, East Los Angeles College
Alex Immerblum, East Los Angeles College
Diana Jones, Anglo-American University
Catherine Lally, Brevard Community College
Rebecca Loya, El Camino College
Alexandra Maeck, Los Angeles City College
Mimi Markus, Broward Community College
Karen McCafferty, Fresno City College
Joseph McDade, Houston Community
College
Suzanne Morales, Central Texas College
Linda Nugent, San Joaquin Delta College
Sandra Offiah-Hawkins, Daytona Beach
Community College
Cindy Okamura, Riverside Community
College
Joan Perillo, Hillsborough Community
College
Neil Plackcy, Broward Community College
Patricia Plasket-Oslerman, Palm Beach
Community College
Valerie Russell, Valencia Community College
Margaret Rustick, California State
University–Hayward
Mickey Schafer, University of Florida
Marjorie Smith, Ventura College
Marie Theodore-Pharel, Broward Community
College
Stacey Thompson, Austin Community
College
Denton Tulloch, Miami Dade College
Wendy Ward, Miami Dade College
Donna Willingham, Tomball College
Anne Ysunza, Santa Rosa Junior College

MyWritingLab™ and Your Course: The Basics

Results Show That Students Overwhelmingly Support MyWritingLab

Students who thought MyWritingLab was easy to use

- Agree
- Neutral
- Disagree

What do students think of MyWritingLab?

A recent survey of 531 students who used MyWritingLab for at least one semester (3/2007) revealed extremely positive results. The graph at left shows how easy students found the system to use.

What is MyWritingLab?

MyWritingLab from Pearson Education is the first online learning system built from the ground up to help low-literacy learners improve their writing skills. MyWritingLab combines established pedagogy with an easy-to-use online platform.

The Pedagogy

- **Diagnostics:** MyWritingLab first diagnoses students on their writing strengths and weaknesses.

- **Study Plan:** The diagnostics lead to a Study Plan that is unique to each student. The Study Plan provides access to the exercises students need to work on to improve their skills.

- **Step-by-Step Exercises:** A team of educators created exercises — Recall, Apply, and Write — to challenge students at the Knowledge, Application, and Synthesis levels of the cognitive domain. More than ten thousand questions help your students move beyond the recall of grammatical facts to the ability to express themselves in written form.

The Platform

The best pedagogy in the world is worthless if hidden behind confusing Web pages. A team of instructional designers, writing teachers, and students worked together tirelessly to put all this pedagogy behind an intuitive, easy-to-use platform. Our guiding principles:

- **The "3 Tab Rule":** Devoid of confusing drop down menus, busy pages, or unnecessary images, the pages include 3 simple tabs at the top to guide students.

- **Most Important Information Up Front:** The content in the four panels on the homepage changes depending on what the student needs to do next.

- **Use the Simplest Language at All Times:** Every word of instruction has been carefully scrutinized for reading comprehension.

www.mywritinglab.com

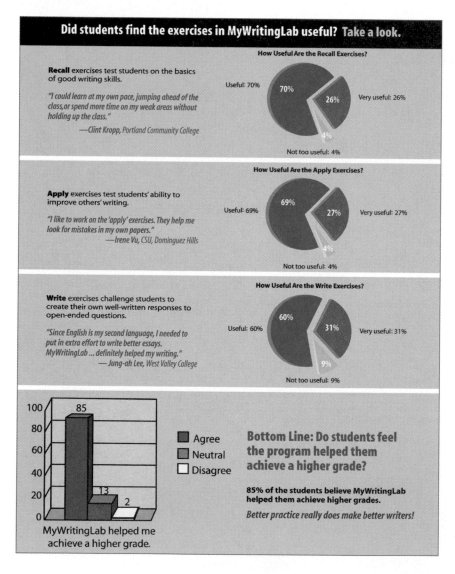

MyWritingLab™ and Your Course: Student Success

Did students find the exercises in MyWritingLab useful? Take a look.

How Useful Are the Recall Exercises?

Recall exercises test students on the basics of good writing skills.

"I could learn at my own pace, jumping ahead of the class, or spend more time on my weak areas without holding up the class."

—*Clint Kropp, Portland Community College*

Useful: 70%
70%
26% Very useful: 26%
4%
Not too useful: 4%

How Useful Are the Apply Exercises?

Apply exercises test students' ability to improve others' writing.

"I like to work on the 'apply' exercises. They help me look for mistakes in my own papers."

—*Irene Vu, CSU, Dominguez Hills*

Useful: 69%
69%
27% Very useful: 27%
4%
Not too useful: 4%

How Useful Are the Write Exercises?

Write exercises challenge students to create their own well-written responses to open-ended questions.

"Since English is my second language, I needed to put in extra effort to write better essays. MyWritingLab ... definitely helped my writing."

—*Jung-ah Lee, West Valley College*

Useful: 60%
60%
31% Very useful: 31%
9%
Not too useful: 9%

100
85
80
60
40
20
13
2
0

■ Agree
■ Neutral
□ Disagree

MyWritingLab helped me achieve a higher grade.

Bottom Line: Do students feel the program helped them achieve a higher grade?

85% of the students believe MyWritingLab helped them achieve higher grades.

Better practice really does make better writers!

MyWritingLab™ and Your Course: Assessment

Comprehensive, detailed reporting provides both instructors and students with progress tracking for the skill work in MyWritingLab. At a glance, an instructor can see details such as student mastery, individual progress, time on task, topic averages, diagnostic details, alerts to indicate students who are struggling, and more!

PEARSON TUTOR SERVICES

With MyWritingLab, students receive complimentary access to Pearson Tutor Services, powered by SMARTTHINKING, Inc. Students can submit a specified number of papers or essays each semester to Smartthinking's highly qualified e-structors™, who provide detailed feedback on how to improve the essay. Feedback is usually returned within 24 hours.

www.mywritinglab.com

MyWritingLab™ and Your Course: Integration

MyWritingLab is incredibly flexible and can be used in several useful ways in your classroom. Students can use it to focus on their individual areas of weakness, or the instructor can choose the MWL course that matches the table of contents of *The Writer's World*.

To find out how other instructors have integrated MyWritingLab into their course, visit our Faculty Advocate page on our Web site at www.mywritinglab.com/facultyadvocates.html. There you will find teaching tips, their syllabi with MyWritingLab integrated, and more!

Here are what some of the Faculty Advocates have to say . . .

"In order to avoid slowing the whole class down, I have found it very useful to assign elements of MWL to those students who are having particular ESL difficulties other students are not experiencing. MWL has also helped in reinforcing comments I make on students' papers."

—Ona Seaney
Southern Methodist University

You can also check out the Success Stories tab at www.mywritinglab.com to read white papers and various reports/case studies filled with realdata confirming the positive impactMyWritingLab has had on developing writers!

"It helps me monitor student progress anytime and from anywhere. It instantly tells me what students are struggling with."

—Pamela Smith
Macon State College

"MyWritingLab enhances a student's understanding of terms and concepts in the textbook that need to be reinforced."

—Donna Lucas
Lawson State Community College–Bessemer

www.mywritinglab.com

LYNNE GAETZ
Lionel Groulx College

SUNEETI PHADKE
St. Jerome College

The Writer's World

Essays

SECOND EDITION

Prentice Hall

Boston   Columbus   Indianapolis   New York   San Francisco   Upper Saddle River
Amsterdam   Cape Town   Dubai   London   Madrid   Milan   Munich   Paris   Montreal
Toronto   Delhi   Mexico City   Sao Paulo   Sydney   Hong Kong   Seoul   Singapore   Taipei   Tokyo

Senior Acquisitions Editor: Matthew Wright
Senior Development Editor: Katharine Glynn
Senior Marketing Manager: Thomas DeMarco
Senior Media Producer: Stefanie Liebman
Project Coordination, Text Design, and Electronic Page Makeup: Laserwords
Cover Art Director: Anne Nieglos
Cover Designer: Ximena Tamvakopolous
Cover Illustration: Sunglasses: Thorsten Rust/Shutterstock Images; Left image: © Ken Skeet/Corbis Premium/Alamy;
   right image: © MBI/Alamy
Photo Researcher: Katharine S. Cebik
Permissions Researcher: Beth K. Keister
Senior Manufacturing Buyer: Mary Ann Gloriande
Printer and Binder: Quad Graphics-Dubuque
Cover Printer: Lehigh-Phoenix Color Corporation-Hagerstown

For permission to use copyrighted material, grateful acknowledgment is made to the copyright holders on pages 615–616, which
are hereby made part of this copyright page.

1 2 3 4 5 6 7 8 9 10—QGD—14 13 12 11

Student Edition ISBN-13:
978-0-205-78171-3
Student Edition ISBN-10:
0-205-78171-3
Annotated Instructor s Edition ISBN-13:
978-0-205-78173-7
Annotated Instructor s Edition ISBN-10:
0-205-78173-X

Prentice Hall
is an imprint of

www.pearsonhighered.com

Contents

PART 1 — The Writing Process   2

CHAPTER 1 — Exploring   3

CHAPTER 2 — Developing the Main Idea   16

CHAPTER 3 — Developing the Essay Plan   30

CHAPTER 4 — Developing the First Draft   41

CHAPTER 5 — Revising and Editing   57

PART **II** — Essay Patterns   76

Classification   169

 **Comparison
and Contrast**   192

 Cause and Effect   210

 Argument   228

III — More College and Workplace Writing   248

 IV — Editing Handbook   310

SECTION I   **Effective Sentences** ▪ *Section Theme* **CONFLICT**

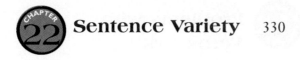

Sentence Variety 330

SECTION 2 Common Sentence Errors ▪ *Section Theme* URBAN DEVELOPMENT

Fragments 340

Run-Ons 350

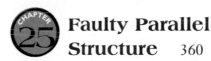

Faulty Parallel Structure 360

Mistakes with Modifiers 367

SECTION 3 Verbs ▪ *Section Theme* COMMERCE AND MARKETING

Subject–Verb Agreement 375

SECTION 7   Editing

Editing Practice   519

Why Bother Editing?   519

— Reading Strategies and Selections   526

From Reading to Writing   527

Appendices

Readings Listed by Rhetorical Mode

Welcome to the Second Edition of *The Writer's World: Essays*

Thank you for making the first edition of *The Writer's World* a resounding success. We are delighted that the book has been able to help so many students across the country. This new edition, too, can help your students produce writing that is technically correct and richly detailed whether your classes are filled with students who have varying skill levels, whether students are native or nonnative speakers of English, or whether they learn better through the use of visuals. When we started the first edition, we set out to develop practical and pedagogically sound approaches to these challenges, and we are pleased to hear that the book is helping students succeed in their writing courses.

For those new to the book, here is some background information to give a more complete picture.

A Research-Based Approach

We began with the idea that this project should be a collaboration with other developmental writing teachers. So we met with more than forty-five instructors from around the country, asking for their opinions and insights regarding (1) the challenges posed by the course, (2) the needs of today's ever-changing student population, and (3) the ideas and features we were proposing in order to provide them and you with a more effective teaching and learning tool. Prentice Hall also commissioned dozens of detailed manuscript reviews from instructors, asking them to analyze and evaluate each draft of the manuscript. These reviewers identified numerous ways in which we could refine and enhance our key features. Their invaluable feedback was incorporated throughout *The Writer's World*. The text you are seeing is truly the product of a successful partnership between the authors, publisher, and well over one hundred developmental writing instructors.

How We Organized *The Writer's World*

The Writer's World is separated into five parts for ease of use, convenience, and ultimate flexibility.

Part I: The Writing Process teaches students (1) how to formulate ideas (Exploring); (2) how to expand, organize, and present those ideas in a piece of writing (Developing); and (3) how to polish writing so that they convey their message as clearly as possible (Revising and Editing). The result is that writing a paragraph or an essay becomes far less daunting because students have specific steps to follow.

Part II: Essay Patterns gives students a solid overview of the patterns of development. Using the same easy-to-understand process (Exploring, Developing, and Revising and Editing), each chapter in this section explains how to convey ideas using one or more writing patterns. As they work through the practices and write their own essays, students begin to see how using a writing pattern can help them fulfill their purpose for writing.

Part III: More College and Workplace Writing covers topics ranging from the letter and résumé to the research essay. This section also explains how to respond to films and literary works, and how to prepare for essay exams.

Part IV: The Editing Handbook is a thematic grammar handbook. In each chapter, the examples correspond to a theme, such as popular culture, college life, and work. As students work through the chapters, they hone their grammar and editing skills while gaining knowledge about a variety of topics. In addition to helping build interest in the grammar practices, the thematic material provides a spark that ignites new ideas that students can apply to their writing.

Part V: Reading Strategies and Selections offers tips, readings, and follow-up questions. Students learn how to write by observing and dissecting what they read. The readings relate to the themes found in Part IV: The Editing Handbook, thereby providing more fodder for generating writing ideas.

How *The Writer's World* Meets Students' Diverse Needs

We created *The Writer's World* to meet your students' diverse needs. To accomplish this, we asked both the instructors in our focus groups and the reviewers at every stage not only to critique our ideas but to offer their suggestions and recommendations for features that would enhance the learning process of their students. The result has been the integration of many elements that are not found in other textbooks, including our **visual program, coverage of nonnative speaker material, and strategies for addressing the varying skill levels students bring to the course.**

The Visual Program

A stimulating, full-color book with more than 80 photos, *The Writer's World* recognizes that today's world is a visual one, and it encourages students to become better communicators by responding to images. Chapter-opening visuals in Parts I, II, and III help students to think about the chapter's key concept in a new way.

The visuals in Part II provide students with another set of opportunities to write in response to images, with Photo Writing and Media Writing activities that encourage them to respond using particular paragraph and essay patterns.

Throughout *The Writer's World*, words and images work together to encourage students to explore, develop, and revise their writing.

Seamless Coverage for Nonnative Speakers

Instructors in our focus groups noted the growing number of nonnative/ESL speakers enrolling in writing courses. Although some of these students have special needs relating to the writing process, many of you still have a large portion of native speakers in your courses whose more traditional needs must also be satisfied. In order to meet the challenge of this rapidly changing dynamic, we have carefully implemented and integrated content throughout to assist these students.

The Writer's World does not have separate ESL boxes, ESL chapters, or tacked-on ESL appendices. Instead, information that traditionally poses a challenge to nonnative speakers is woven seamlessly throughout the book. In our extensive experience teaching writing to both native and nonnative speakers of English, we have learned that both groups learn best when they are not distracted by ESL labels. With the seamless approach, nonnative speakers do not feel self-conscious and segregated, and native speakers do not tune out detailed explanations that may also benefit them. Many of these traditional problem areas receive more coverage than you would find in other textbooks, arming the instructor with the material to effectively meet the needs of nonnative speakers. Moreover, the Annotated Instructor's Edition provides over seventy-five ESL Teaching Tips designed specifically to help instructors better meet the needs of their nonnative speaking students.

Issue-Focused Thematic Grammar

In surveys, many of you indicated that one of the primary challenges in teaching your course is finding materials that are engaging to students in a contemporary context. This is especially true in grammar instruction. **Students come to the course with varying skill levels,** and many students are simply not interested in grammar. To address this challenge, we have introduced **issue-focused thematic grammar** into *The Writer's World*.

Each chapter centers on a theme that is carried out in examples and activities. These themes include topics related to conflict, urban development, business and commerce, nature, and human development. The thematic approach enables students to broaden their awareness of subjects important to American life, such as understanding advertising and consumerism. The thematic approach makes reading about grammar more engaging. And the more engaging grammar is, the more likely students will retain key concepts—raising their skill level in these important building blocks of writing.

We also think that it is important to teach grammar in the context of the writing process. Students should not think that grammar is an isolated exercise. Therefore, **each grammar chapter includes a warm up writing activity.**

What Tools Can Help Students Get the Most from *The Writer's World?*

Overwhelmingly, focus group participants and reviewers asked that both a larger number and a greater diversity of exercises and activities be incorporated into *The Writer's World*. In response, we have developed and tested the following learning aids in *The Writer's World*. We are confident they will help your students become better writers.

Hints   In each chapter, **Hint** boxes highlight important writing and grammar points. Hints are useful for all students, but many will be particularly helpful for nonnative speakers. For example, in Chapter 14, one Hint encourages students to state an argument directly and a second Hint points out the need to avoid circular reasoning. In Chapter 22, a Hint discusses word order in embedded questions. Hints include brief discussions and examples so that students will see both concept and application.

Vocabulary Boost   Throughout Part II of *The Writer's World*, Vocabulary Boost boxes give students tips to improve their use of language and to revise and edit their word choices. For example, a Vocabulary Boost in Chapter 6 asks students to replace repeated words with synonyms, and the one in Chapter 8 explains how to use vivid language. These lessons give students concrete strategies and specific advice for improving their diction.

The Writer's Desk   Parts I, II, and III include **The Writer's Desk** exercises that help students get used to practicing all stages and steps of the writing process. As the chapter progresses, students warm up with a prewriting activity, and then use specific methods for developing, organizing (using paragraph and essay plans), drafting, and finally, revising and editing to create a final draft.

Essay Patterns at Work   To help students appreciate the relevance of their writing tasks, Chapters 6–14 highlight an authentic writing sample from work contexts. Titled **Illustration at Work, Narration at Work,** and so on, this feature offers a glimpse of how people use writing patterns in different workplace settings.

The Writer's Room   The Writer's Room contains writing activities that correspond to general, college, and workplace topics. Some prompts are brief to allow students to freely form ideas while others are expanded to give students more direction.

There is something for every student writer in this end-of-chapter feature. Students who respond well to visual cues will appreciate the photo and media writing prompts in **The Writer's Room** in Part II: Essay Patterns. To help students see how grammar is not isolated from the writing process, there are also **The Writer's Room** activities at the end of sections 1–6 in Part IV: The Editing Handbook.

The Writer's World e-Text   Accessed through MyWritingLab (www.mywritinglab .com), students now have the e-text for *The Writer's World* at their fingertips while completing the various exercises and activities within MyWritingLab. Students can highlight important material and add notes to any section for further reflection and/or study throughout the semester.

New to the Second Edition

Visualizing the Mode

Chapters 6 to 14 cover the nine essay patterns. To help students visualize how to use each pattern, they do a practice called "Visualizing." For example, Chapter 8, "Visualizing Description," includes a thesis statement about unhealthy fashion trends and photos of a corset, wig, and a pair of high heels. Chapter 9, "Visualizing Process," has a thesis statement about the steps to take when planning a trip. Students see photos of a passport, vaccination clinic, and suitcase.

These visual examples help students get an overview of the essay mode.

Updated High-Interest Essay Models and Practices

Throughout the book you will notice new examples, sample paragraphs, writing practices, Writer's Desk topics, and grammar practice exercises. In fact, to make the content more topical and appealing, roughly 30 percent of the book's content has been updated.

Cooperative Learning Teaching Tips

New to this edition are cooperative learning teaching tips. Cooperative learning, which promotes peer interaction, helps students share knowledge, problem-solve, and negotiate. Students are responsible for their contribution to a team effort. Jigsaw activities, Roundtable Writing, Nonstop Talking, and Pair & Share help make routine lessons interesting and enjoyable. These communicative and interactive activities are especially useful for nonnative speakers.

Media Writing

Chapters 6 to 14, which cover the nine essay patterns, now end with a Media Writing activity. Students are invited to view a television program, film, or online video and to use the content as a writing prompt.

Expanded Writer's Exchange Activities

The first edition contained Writer's Exchange activities at the beginnings of each essay pattern chapter in Part II. The feature has been expanded to Part III. Chapters 15 to 19 now begin with a Writer's Exchange. The collaborative learning activities help students build confidence about their knowledge before having to apply it in writing. Such activities, which are useful for auditory, tactile, and visual learners, initiate them to the chapter's content.

Updated Chapter on Research

Chapter 16, The Research Essay, contains updated information from the Seventh Edition of the *MLA Handbook*. The final student essay about energy drinks has a detailed Works Cited page, and the chapter ends with a practice related to the sample essay.

APA Coverage in the Appendix

American Psychological Association guidelines, which previously appeared in Chapter 16, are now in Appendix 5. Sample citations have been updated with information from the Sixth Edition of the APA Publication Manual.

More Comprehensive Coverage of Report Writing

Chapter 18 now includes reports about both a film and a novel. The first model essay is a student's response to James Cameron's *Avatar*. The second model essay is a student's response to an Ernest Hemingway novel.

Tech Tips

New to this edition are some teaching tips that incorporate everyday technology. Students in this digital age spend their days texting, checking their Facebook page, and listening to music on their iPods. The Tech Tips help students learn while using the technology that they are familiar with. For example, in Chapter 1, students are invited to choose a random text message on their cell phones and do freewriting about it.

New Readings

Chapters 6 to 14 contain a wide selection of new essays. New student samples include a narrative essay about imprisonment and rehabilitation, a definition essay about Goth culture, and a classification essay about the discrimination faced by people with physical disabilities. Chapter 40 has five provocative and appealing new readings that relate to the grammar themes. For example, David Leonhardt examines theories about success in "Chance and Circumstance," and Maya Angelou reflects on a life-changing event in "Guy."

Acknowledgments

Many people have helped us produce *The Writer's World*. First and foremost, we would like to thank our students for inspiring us and providing us with invaluable feedback. Their words and insights pervade this book.

We also benefited greatly from the insightful comments and suggestions from over two hundred instructors across the nation, all of whom are listed in the opening pages of the Annotated Instructor's Edition. Our colleagues' feedback was invaluable and helped shape *The Writer's World* series content, focus, and organization.

We are indebted to the team of dedicated professionals at Prentice Hall who have helped make this project a reality. They have boosted our spirits and have believed in us every step of the way. Special thanks to Katharine Glynn for her careful job in polishing this book and to Matthew Wright for trusting our instincts and enthusiastically propelling us forward. Also thanks to Beth Keister and Kate Cebik for their dedication and hard work. We owe a deep debt of gratitude to Yolanda de Rooy, whose encouraging words helped ignite this project. Karen Berry's attention to detail in the production process kept us motivated and on task and made *The Writer's World* a much better resource for both instructors and students.

Finally, we would like to dedicate this book to our husbands and children who supported us and who patiently put up with our long hours on the computer. Manu, Octavio, and Natalia continually encouraged us. We especially appreciate the help and sacrifices of Diego, Becky, Kiran, and Meghana.

Lynne Gaetz and Suneeti Phadke

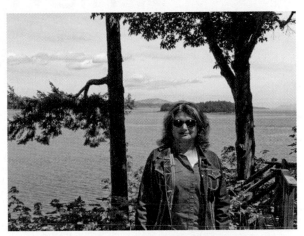

Suneeti Phadke on Salt Spring Island, British Columbia.

A Note to Students

Your knowledge, ideas, and opinions are important. The ability to clearly communicate those ideas is invaluable in your personal, academic, and professional life. When your writing is error-free, readers will focus on your message, and you will be able to persuade, inform, entertain, or inspire them. *The Writer's World* includes strategies that will help you improve your written communication. Quite simply, when you become a better writer, you become a better communicator. It is our greatest wish for *The Writer's World* to make you excited about writing, communicating, and learning.

Enjoy!

Lynne Gaetz & Suneeti Phadke
writingrewards@pearson.com

Call for Student Writing!

Do you want to be published in *The Writer's World*? Send your paragraphs and essays to us along with your complete contact information. If your work is selected to appear in the next edition of *The Writer's World*, you will receive an honorarium, credit for your work, and a copy of the book!

Lynne Gaetz and Suneeti Phadke
writingrewards@pearson.com

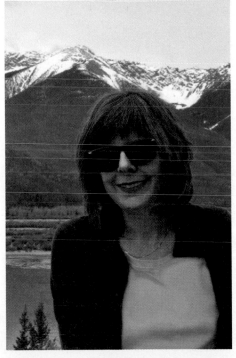

Lynne Gaetz in the Rocky Mountains.

The Writing Process

The writing process is a series of steps that most writers follow to advance from thinking about a topic to preparing the final draft. Generally, you should follow the process step by step. However, sometimes you may find that your steps overlap. For example, you might do some editing before you revise, or you might think about your main idea while you are prewriting. The important thing is to make sure that you have done all the steps of the process before preparing your final draft.

Before you begin the next chapters, review the steps in the writing process.

Exploring
Chapter 1

Step 1 Think about your topic.

Step 2 Think about your audience.

Step 3 Think about your purpose.

Step 4 Try exploring strategies.

Developing
Chapters 2, 3, 4

Step 1 Express your main idea.

Step 2 Develop your supporting ideas.

Step 3 Make a plan or an outline.

Step 4 Write your first draft.

Revising and Editing
Chapter 5

Step 1 Revise for unity.

Step 2 Revise for adequate support.

Step 3 Revise for coherence.

Step 4 Revise for style.

Step 5 Edit for technical errors.

Exploring

Before planting seeds or shrubs, a gardener might look for ideas in magazines, on the Internet, or in nurseries. Similarly, a writer uses various prewriting strategies to explore topics for writing.

Visualizing the Paragraph and the Essay

A **paragraph** is a series of sentences that are about one central idea. Paragraphs can stand alone, or they can be part of a longer work such as an essay, a letter, or a report. A paragraph contains a **topic sentence**, which expresses the main idea, and **body sentences** that develop that idea. Most paragraphs end with a **concluding sentence** that brings the paragraph to a satisfactory close.

Sample Paragraph

The **topic sentence** introduces the subject of the paragraph and shows the writer's attitude toward the subject.

People learn negotiation skills through sports. Children playing informally at recess must decide what game to play and what rules to follow. They must negotiate with the other children about game boundaries. Every day, my daughter comes home from school and tells me that she and her friends have invented a new game. The children make up the rules of the new game by bargaining with one another. In team sports, athletes must make choices about who will play a certain position or which player will play for how much time. Such decisions require negotiation skills, which help people in other areas of their lives.

The **body of the paragraph** contains details that support the topic sentence.

The paragraph ends with a **concluding sentence**.

An **essay** contains several paragraphs that revolve around one central idea. The introductory paragraph includes a **thesis statement** expressing the main idea of the essay. **Body paragraphs** support the thesis statement. Finally, the essay closes with a **concluding paragraph** that wraps up the main ideas the writer has presented throughout the paper.

Sample Essay

The **title** gives a hint about the essay's topic.

Sports: A Vital Necessity

The **introductory paragraph** introduces the essay's topic and contains its thesis statement.

The **thesis statement** contains the essay's topic and its controlling idea.

Humans have been playing sports since the beginning of civilization. Cave art in France and Africa depicts people playing archery, wrestling, and racing horses. Indigenous North Americans engaged in team sports such as lacrosse. The ancient Greeks, Romans, Chinese, and Egyptians also enjoyed many physical activities. Similarly, most people enjoy sports today. Young girls and boys play in soccer leagues, or they may play a baseball game during recess. Adults, too, play or watch sports. Athletic activities are very necessary to people's well-being. Sports help people to develop good character by learning many life skills.

Each **body paragraph** begins with a topic sentence that supports the thesis statement.

First, when people play games, they learn how to make friends. In the United States, according to the National Center for Health Statistics, 24 percent of adults engage in some form of physical activity three or more times a week, and approximately 67 percent of high school students participate in some type of physical activity. Whether it is by exercising informally or playing a team sport, people interact with strangers. Going to the gym, participating in a hiking club, and playing in a team sport bring different people into close personal contact with each other. These strangers all have something in common. They like to engage in the same activity, so most people end up developing friendships.

Second, people learn negotiation skills through sports. Children playing informally at recess must decide what game to play and what rules to follow. They must negotiate with the other children about game boundaries. Every day, my daughter comes home from school and tells me that she and her friends have invented a new game. The children make up the rules of the new game by bargaining with one another. In team sports, athletes must make choices about who will play a certain position or which player will play for how much time. Such decisions require negotiation skills, which help people in other areas of their lives.

Finally, players learn how to deal with disappointments and pressure. For example, many Olympic athletes are very discouraged when they lose, but most continue training to become even better. Players on high school and college teams also learn to win and lose. For example, my neighbor's son plays on the volleyball team. His team had a winning streak, but the team lost in the semi-finals. All the players on the team were extremely disappointed but vowed to play better in the next season. Sports teach people how to win and lose gracefully. Such a lesson is invaluable in life.

People build character through sports. In fact, they learn many valuable life lessons, including social skills. They learn practical skills such as how to negotiate. As Jeff Kemp, in his article "A Lesson in Humility," says, "In fact, sports teach important moral lessons that athletes can apply on and off the playing field." So don't just sit around at home; go participate in a sport.

*Each **body** paragraph contains details that support the topic sentence.*

*The **concluding** paragraph brings the essay to a satisfactory close.*

Essay-length prose is the backbone of written communication in and out of college. Throughout your life, you will use principles of essay writing in various written communications, including research papers, e-mails, reports, formal letters, newsletters, and Web pages. Essays help you explore ideas and share those thoughts with others. By reading through this text and completing the many helpful writing practices in it, you will significantly improve your chances of getting more out of your courses and jobs. Enjoy the journey!

Key Steps in Exploring

Perhaps you recently received a writing assignment and have been staring at the blank page, thinking, "I don't know what to write." Well, it is not necessary to write a good essay immediately. There are certain things that you can do to help you focus on your topic.

Understand Your Assignment

As soon as you are given an assignment, make sure that you understand your task. Answer the following questions about the assignment.

- How many words or pages does the assignment require?
- What is the due date for the assignment?
- Are there any special qualities my writing should include? For example, should my writing be double-spaced? Should I include a list of works cited?

After you have thought about your assignment, consider the following four key steps in the exploring stage of the writing process.

EXPLORING		
STEP 1	➤	**Think about your topic.** Determine what you will write about.
STEP 2	➤	**Think about your audience.** Consider your intended readers and what interests them.
STEP 3	➤	**Think about your purpose.** Ask yourself why you want to write.
STEP 4	➤	**Try exploring strategies.** Experiment with different ways to generate ideas.

Teaching Tip:
If you prefer, you can substitute the word "subject" for "topic."

Teaching Tip:

Cooperative Learning (Jigsaw) Place students in groups of three or four. Their goal is to write a short letter of apology because they have to cancel a meeting or an outing. Ask each group to write for a different audience: a child, a boss, a client, a friend, and a grandmother. Then have students read their letters out loud. Students can discuss how the tone varies depending on the audience.

Topic

Your **topic**, or **subject**, is what you are writing about. When an instructor gives you a writing topic, narrow the topic and find an angle that interests you. When you think about your topic, ask yourself the following questions.

- What special knowledge do I have about the topic?
- What subtopics are most relevant to me?
- What aspect of the topic do I care deeply about?

Audience

Your **audience** is your intended reader. In your personal, academic, and professional life, you will often write for a specific audience. You can keep your readers interested by adapting your tone and vocabulary to suit them.

Tone shows your general attitude or feeling toward a topic. You might write in a tone that is humorous, sarcastic, or serious. For example, imagine that you are preparing an invitation to an event. To determine the design and phrasing, you need to know important information about your recipients. What are their ages and lifestyles? Are they mainly male or female? Would they prefer printed invitations, e-mails, or text messages? Questions like these help you connect with your audience.

Knowing your reader is especially important when you are preparing academic or workplace documents. When you consider your audience, ask yourself the following questions.

- Who will read my essay? Will my instructor be my only reader, or will others also read it?
- What does my audience already know about the topic?
- What information will my readers expect?
- Should I use formal or informal language?
- How should I adjust my vocabulary and tone to appeal to my readers?

Hint **Instructor as the Audience**

Your instructor represents a general audience. Such an audience of educated readers will expect you to use correct grammar and to reveal what you have learned or understood about the topic. Your ideas should be presented in a clear and organized manner. Also, do not leave out information because you assume that your instructor is an expert in the field.

Purpose

Your **purpose** is your reason for writing. Sometimes you may have more than one purpose. When you consider your purpose, ask yourself the following questions.

- Is my goal to **entertain**? Do I want to tell a personal story or anecdote?
- Is my goal to **persuade**? Do I want to convince readers that my point of view is the correct one?
- Is my goal to **inform**? Do I want to explain something or present information?

Hint **General and Specific Purpose**

Your **general purpose** is to entertain, inform, or persuade. Your **specific purpose** is your more precise reason for writing. For example, imagine that you are writing about music. You can have the following general and specific purposes.

> **General purpose:** to inform
> **Specific purpose:** to explain how to become a better musician.

Teaching Tip:

Cooperative Learning (Sharing Circle) Bring in different types of writing samples. For instance, bring in a postcard, a business letter, a letter to the editor, an e-mail from a family member, a Facebook page printout, a text message, and an advertisement. Ask groups to analyze each item and determine the audience and purpose of each selection. As an additional activity, you could ask students to take one of the messages, choose a different audience, and rewrite the message.

Teaching Tip:
Group Work
Students can do
Practice 1 in pairs
or groups, and they
can compare
answers.

Teaching Tip:
Ask students to
translate e-mail A
into standard
English. The full text
reads: Dear
professor, Do you
remember me? I'm
in your English class.
How are you? Can
you help me with
my essay? What is
the number of
words? Also, can
you tell me the
deadline? Thanks,
and I will see you in
class. I have to go.
Taylor.

PRACTICE 1   As you read the following messages, consider the differences in both the tone and the vocabulary the writer uses. Then answer the questions that follow.

E-Mail A

Yo prof,
remember me im in ur english
class. how ru? can u help wth
my essay? whats the # words also deadline. :)
thanx and cu in class
gtg Taylor

E-Mail B

Dear Professor Sanchez,
I'm in your Tuesday morning English class. I
have started working on my essay and have
prepared an essay plan, but I am not sure if my
thesis statement is focused enough. Can you
please let me know if I'm on the right track?
Thanks,
Damon

1. Why is the language inappropriate in the first instant message?

    The instructor might not understand the abbreviations and might not

    appreciate the symbols. The language is too informal.

2. What judgments, based on the messages, might the instructor make about the two students?

    Taylor doesn't show respect and treats the instructor like a peer.

    Damon uses standard English and is respectful.

Teaching Tip:
Group Work
Students can do
Practice 2 in pairs
or groups. Discuss
how the language
style is adapted for
the different
audiences.

PRACTICE 2   The following selections are all about food; however, each excerpt has a different purpose, has been written for a different audience, and has been taken from a different source. Read each selection carefully. Then underline any language clues (words or phrases) that help you identify the selection's source, audience, and purpose. Finally, answer the questions that follow each selection.

EXAMPLE:

slang ➤
slang ➤
slang, informal tone ➤

I just made my very first dessert. It looks awesome. I hope it tastes alright. I almost freaked out when I realized I forgot to turn the oven on. My instructor is super, and he's got a great sense of humor with me and the other students. Next, I am going to try to make a more complicated dessert.

What is the most likely source of this paragraph?

a. Web site article   b. *personal journal*   c. textbook   d.   memoir

What is its primary purpose? ___*to inform*___

Who is the audience? ___*friend or family member*___

1. I never <u>mastered the art of the thump</u>. Whether the melon is ripe or not, the thump sounds the same to me. Each one I cut, however, <u>seems to be at its pinnacle—toothy crispness, audacious sweetness</u>. . . . Sitting on the stone wall, sun on my face, big slice of watermelon—<u>I'm seven again, totally engrossed in shooting seeds between my fingers and spooning out circles from the dripping quarter moon of fruit.</u>

   What is the most likely source of this paragraph?

   a. Web site article   b. personal journal   c. textbook   *d. memoir*

   What is its primary purpose? ___*to entertain*___

   Who is the audience? ___*general readers of nonfiction*___

2. <u>Eat regularly.</u> Eating is one of life's great pleasures, and it is important to take time to stop, relax, and enjoy mealtimes and snacks. By scheduling eating times, people do not miss meals. People may not get adequate nutrients if they miss a meal, and they might not be able to compensate for a lack of nutrients by eating a subsequent meal. So eating meals regularly is especially important for school-age children, adolescents, and older adults.

   What is the most likely source of this paragraph?

   a. Web site article   b. personal journal   c. textbook   d. memoir

   What is its primary purpose? ___*to persuade*___

   Who is the audience? ___*a general audience interested in health and nutrition*___

3. About 5,000 years ago, <u>another revolution in technology was taking place in the Middle East, one that would end up changing the entire world</u>. This was the discovery of agriculture, <u>large-scale cultivation using plows harnessed to animals or more powerful energy sources.</u> So important was the invention of the animal-drawn plow, along with

Teaching Tip:
The paragraphs in Practice 2 came from the next sources:
1) *Under the Tuscan Sun* by Frances Mayes (Broadway Books: New York, 1997, p. 62).
2) "Adult Nutrition" from the European Food Information Council site (www .eufic.org/en/ quickfacts/adult_ nutrition.htm).
3) *Sociology* (11th ed.) by John J. Macionis (Pearson: Upper Saddle River, 2007, p. 95).

other breakthroughs of the period—<u>including irrigation, the wheel,</u> <u>writing, numbers, and the use of various metals</u>—that this moment in history is often <u>called "the dawn of civilization."</u>

What is the most likely source of this paragraph?

a. Web site article   b. personal journal   (c. textbook)   d. memoir

What is its purpose? _to inform_

Who is the audience? _students who are learning about human_ _civilization_

Exploring Strategies

After you determine your topic, audience, and purpose, try some **exploring strategies**—also known as **prewriting strategies**—to help get your ideas flowing. Four common strategies are *freewriting*, *brainstorming*, *questioning*, and *clustering*. It is not necessary to do all of the strategies explained in this chapter. Find the strategy that works best for you.

You can do both general and focused prewriting. If you have writer's block and do not know what to write about, use **general prewriting** to come up with possible writing topics. Then, after you have chosen a topic, use **focused prewriting** to find an aspect of the topic that is interesting and that could be developed in your essay.

> ⟨*Hint*⟩   **When to Use Exploring Strategies**
>
> You can use the exploring strategies at any stage of the writing process:
> • To find a topic
> • To narrow a broad topic
> • To generate ideas about your topic
> • To generate supporting details

Narrow Your Topic

An essay has one main idea. If your topic is too broad, you might find it difficult to write a focused essay about the subject. For example, imagine that you are given the topic "mistakes." If the topic is not narrowed, it will lead to a meandering and unfocused essay. To narrow the topic, think about types of errors, examples of errors, or people who make errors. A more focused topic could be "mistakes newlyweds make" or "mistakes first-year college students make." Find one aspect of the topic that you know a lot about and that you personally find interesting. If you have a lot to say and you think the topic is compelling, chances are that your reader will also like your topic.

Review the following examples of general and narrowed topics.

Topic	Narrowed Topic
jobs	preparing for a job interview
music	protest songs from the past and present

To help narrow and develop your topic, you can use the following exploring strategies: freewriting, brainstorming, questioning, and clustering.

Freewriting

Freewriting gives writers the freedom to write without stopping for a set period of time. The goal of this exercise is to record the first thoughts that come to mind. If you run out of ideas, don't stop writing. Simply fill in the pause with phrases like "blah blah blah" or "What else can I write?" As you write, do not be concerned with word choice, grammar, or spelling. If you use a computer, let your ideas flow and do not worry about typing mistakes. You could try typing without looking at the screen.

Alicia's Freewriting

College student Alicia Parera thought about mistakes college students make. During her freewriting, she wrote down everything that came to mind.

> Mistakes students make? Not doing the homework. Not asking for help when they need it. I sometimes feel shy to speak up when I don't understand something. What else? Some college students leave college early. Why do they leave? Tim. He only stayed for one semester. I don't think he was ready for college life. He treated college like high school and always came late. Goofed off. Cut class. What else? What about Amanda who had that family crisis? She had to leave when her mother was sick. Of course, finances. It's tough. Sometimes I go crazy trying to keep up with my job, friends, schoolwork . . . it's really hard.

Brainstorming

Brainstorming is like freewriting, except that you create a list of ideas and you can take the time to stop and think when you create your list. As you think about the topic, write down words or phrases that come to mind. Do not worry about grammar or spelling; the point is to generate ideas.

Teaching Tip: Reassure students that their freewriting (and other exploring strategies) can be messy and will not necessarily be graded for errors in mechanics.

Alicia's Brainstorming

Topic: Mistakes that college students make

- party too much
- not doing homework
- feeling too shy to speak with instructors when they have problems
- getting too stressed
- choosing the wrong career path
- don't know what they want to do
- feeling intimidated in class

Questioning

Another way to generate ideas about a topic is to ask yourself a series of questions and write responses to them. The questions can help you define and narrow your topic. One common way to do this is to ask yourself *who, what, when, where, why,* and *how* questions.

Alicia's Questioning

What kinds of mistakes do college students make?
— not doing homework, missing classes, partying too much

Who makes the most mistakes?
— first-year students because they aren't always prepared for college life

Why do some students miss classes?
— feel as if there are no consequences, don't feel interested in their program

When do most students drop out?
— administrators say that November is the most common month that students drop out

How should colleges encourage students who are at risk of dropping out?
— give more financial aid
— offer career counseling

Where can students get help?
— guidance counselors, instructors, friends, family, professionals doing students' dream jobs

Why is this topic important?
— new students can learn about pitfalls to avoid, administrators can develop strategies for helping students

Clustering

Clustering is like drawing a word map; ideas are arranged in a visual image. To begin, write your topic in the middle of the page and draw a box or a circle around it. That idea will lead to another, so write the second idea and draw a line connecting it to your topic. Keep writing, circling, and connecting ideas until you have groups, or "clusters," of them on your page.

Alicia's Clustering

Teaching Tip:

Cooperative Learning (Jigsaw) With the whole class, brainstorm some writing ideas for the topic "consumer culture." Then, divide the class into four groups. Assign a specific focused prewriting strategy to each group. (You can ask the entire class to work on one focused topic or assign different topics to each group.) Each team works together using an exploring strategy. Team A members use cooperative freewriting on the topic, Team B members use brainstorming, Team C members use clustering, and Team D members use questioning. Teams can write their strategy on the board or read it aloud.

Writer's Desk   **Exploring**

Explore the next three topics. Use a different exploring strategy for each topic. You can choose to do freewriting, brainstorming, questioning, or clustering.

a risky decision   consumer culture   volunteer work

Journal and Portfolio Writing

Keeping a Journal

You may write for work or school, but you can also practice writing for pleasure. One way to practice your writing is to keep a journal. A **journal** can be a book, computer file, or even a blog where you record your thoughts, opinions, ideas, and impressions.

Journal writing gives you a chance to practice your writing without worrying about the audience and what they might think about it. It also gives you a source of material when you want to write about a topic of your choice.

In your journal, you can write about any topic that appeals to you. Here are some possible topics for journal writing.

- Anything related to your personal life, such as your feelings about your career goals, personal problems and solutions, opinions about your college courses, reflections about past and future decisions, or feelings about your job
- Your reactions to controversies in your family, neighborhood, college, city, or country, or in the world
- Your reflections on the opinions and philosophies of others, including those of your friends or of people whom you read about in your courses

Keeping a Portfolio

A **writing portfolio** is a place (a binder or an electronic file folder) where you keep samples of all of your writing. The purpose of keeping a portfolio is to have a record of your writing progress. In your portfolio, keep all the drafts of your writing assignments. When you work on new assignments, review your previous work in your portfolio. Identify your main problems, and try not to repeat the same errors.

The Writer's Room

Writing Activity 1: Topics

Choose one of the following topics, or choose your own topic. Then generate ideas about the topic. You may want to try the suggested exploring strategy.

General Topics

1. Try freewriting about people who have helped you succeed.
2. Brainstorm a list of thoughts about different types of fear.
3. Create a cluster diagram about problems with technology.
4. Ask and answer questions about voting.

College and Work-Related Topics

5. Try freewriting about a mistake you made at work or at college. Include any emotions or details that come to mind.
6. Brainstorm a list of ideas about noisy work environments.
7. Ask and answer questions about bosses.
8. Create a cluster diagram about different types of students.

Writing Activity 2: Photo Writing

Use questioning to generate ideas about the following image. Ask and answer *who*, *what*, *when*, *where*, *why*, and *how* questions.

 EXPLORING

When you explore a topic, ask yourself these questions.

☐ What is my **topic**? Consider what you will write about.

☐ Who is my **audience**? Think about your intended reader.

☐ What is my **purpose**? Determine your reason for writing.

☐ Which exploring strategy will I use? You could try one strategy or a combination of strategies.

> **Freewriting** is writing without stopping for a limited period of time.
> **Brainstorming** is making a list.
> **Questioning** is asking and answering a series of questions.
> **Clustering** is drawing a word map.

mywritinglab To check your progress in meeting this chapter's objectives, log in to **www.mywritinglab.com**, go to the **Study Plan** tab, click on **The Writing Process** and choose **Exploring** from the list of subtopics. Read and view the resources in the **Review Materials** section, and then complete the **Recall, Apply,** and **Write** sets in the **Activities** section.

Teaching Tip:
Students can use their favorite exploring strategy in the Writer's Room activities. They do not have to use the suggested strategy.

Teaching Tip:

Cooperative Learning (Ask & Learn) Ask students to review the chapter and identify anything that they are not completely clear about. All students should write two questions on a sheet of paper. Then in teams, students can ask other members their questions and share answers.

Teaching Tip:
Writer's World Competition Please advise students that they can submit their paragraphs and essays for possible publication to www .pearsonhighered .com/essayrewards/ writingrewards.html

Developing the Main Idea

Faced with so many plant and flower varieties, a gardener narrows down which ones are most appropriate for his or her garden. Similarly, a writer considers many ideas before choosing a main idea for an essay.

Key Steps in Developing the Main Idea

In Chapter 1, you learned how to consider your reading audience and your purposes for writing. You also practiced using exploring strategies to formulate ideas. In this chapter, you will focus on developing a main idea that can be expanded into a complete essay. There are two key steps in this process.

DEVELOPING THE MAIN IDEA

STEP 1	➤	**Write a thesis statement.** Write a statement that expresses the main idea of the piece of writing.
STEP 2	➤	**Develop the supporting ideas.** Find facts, examples, or anecdotes that best support your main idea.

Writing a Thesis Statement

Your **thesis** is the main idea that you want to express. A clear thesis statement presents the topic of the essay, and it includes a **controlling idea** that expresses the writer's opinion, attitude, or feeling about the topic. The controlling idea can appear at the beginning or end of the thesis statement.

topic   controlling idea

Art courses should be compulsory in all high schools.

controlling idea   topic

School districts should stop funding **art courses.**

PRACTICE 1   Circle the topic and underline the controlling idea in each thesis statement.

EXAMPLE: Starting college is a stressful time for many students.

1. There are diverse reasons why youths join gangs.

2. Employers can use several strategies for creating harmony in the workplace.

3. There are three types of common job interviews.

4. A telescam is not just a silly prank; it is an illegal moneymaking scheme by fraudulent telemarketers.

5. Watching the rock concert was an exhilarating experience for me.

6. Border guards should be trained to recognize and prevent smuggling activities.

Teaching Tip:
Discuss the types of essays the thesis statements could develop. If your students are already familiar with writing patterns (rhetorical modes), you might ask them what pattern the thesis statements suggest. Possible answers are:
1. cause and effect
2. process
3. classification
4. definition
5. description
6. argument

Writing an Effective Thesis Statement

When you develop your thesis statement, ask yourself the following questions to help you avoid thesis statement errors.

1. **Is my thesis a complete statement?**
    Make sure that your thesis does not express an incomplete idea or more than one idea. A thesis statement should reveal one complete thought.

Incomplete:	Allergies: so annoying.
	(This is not a complete statement.)
More than one idea:	There are many types of allergens, and allergies affect people in different ways.
	(This statement contains two distinct ideas. Each idea could become an essay.)
Thesis statement:	Doctors suggest several steps people can take to relieve symptoms related to pet allergies.

2. **Does my thesis statement have a controlling idea?**
    Rather than announcing the topic, your thesis statement should make a point about the topic. It should have a controlling idea that expresses your attitude or feeling about the topic. Avoid phrases such as *My topic is* or *I will write about*.

Announces:	I will write about computers.
	(This sentence says nothing relevant about the topic. The reader does not know what the point of the essay is.)
Thesis statement:	When Microsoft develops a new operating system, there are political, financial, and environmental consequences.

3. **Can I support my thesis statement in an essay?**
    Your thesis statement should express an idea that you can support in an essay. If it is too narrow, you will find yourself with nothing to say. If it is too broad, you will have an endless composition.

Too broad:	There are many childless couples in our world.
	(This topic needs a more specific and narrow focus.)
Too narrow:	The average age of first-time mothers is approximately twenty-six years old.
	(It would be difficult to write an entire essay about this fact.)
Thesis statement:	Many couples are choosing to remain childless for several reasons.

    Teaching Tip: Demonstrate that the thesis statement about couples who remain childless can be supported with several points. Ask students to brainstorm reasons that people choose not to have children.

4. **Does my thesis statement make a valid and interesting point?**
    Your thesis statement should make a valid point. It should not be a vaguely worded statement or an obvious and uninteresting comment.

Vague:	Censorship is a big problem.
	(For whom is it a big problem?)
Obvious:	The Internet is important.
	(So what? Everyone knows this.)
Invalid:	The Internet controls our lives.
	(This statement is difficult to believe or prove.)
Thesis statement:	The Internet has become a powerful presence in our personal, social, and working lives.

PRACTICE 2   Examine each statement.

- Write **TS** if it is an effective thesis statement.
- Write **I** if it is an incomplete idea.
- Write **M** if it contains more than one complete idea.
- Write **A** if it is an announcement.

EXAMPLE: This essay is about spousal abuse.   _A_

1. The high price of gas.   _I_

2. My college has a great sports stadium, but it needs to give more help to female athletes.   _M_

3. Nursing is extremely demanding.   _TS_

4. My subject is the torture of war prisoners.   _A_

5. There are many excellent commercials on television, but some are too violent.   _M_

6. The loss of a job can actually have positive effects on a person's life.   _TS_

PRACTICE 3   Examine each statement.

- Write **TS** if it is a complete thesis statement.
- Write **V** if it is too vague.
- Write **O** if it is too obvious.

EXAMPLE: Americans are more nationalistic.   _V_

1. New York has a large population.   _O_

2. We had a major problem.   _V_

3. Some adult children have legitimate reasons for moving back into their parents' homes.   _TS_

4. The roads are very crowded during holiday periods.   _O_

Teaching Tip:
You can give students the next examples and ask them to explain why the sentences are invalid. Examples:

No one can afford to attend college anymore.

Republicans and Democrats will never agree on issues.

Children are becoming too violent.

Teaching Tip:
Pair Work
You could ask students to do Practice 2 with a partner. They can then choose three weak statements and create better thesis statements.

5. There are several ways to do this.   _v_

6. Children in our culture are changing.   _v_

PRACTICE 4   Examine each pair of sentences.

- Write **B** if the sentence is too broad.
- Write **TS** if the sentence is an effective thesis statement.

EXAMPLE: _B_ Plants can help people.

   _TS_ Learning to care for plants gave me unexpected pleasure.

1. _B_ Music is important around the world.

   _TS_ Some simple steps can help you successfully promote your music.

2. _TS_ My neighborhood is being transformed by youth gangs.

   _B_ Violence is a big problem everywhere.

3. _B_ My life has been filled with mistakes.

   _TS_ My jealousy, insecurity, and anger ruined my first relationship.

4. _TS_ The car accident transformed my life.

   _B_ Everybody's life has dramatic moments.

PRACTICE 5   Examine each pair of sentences.

- Write **N** if the sentence is too narrow.
- Write **TS** if the sentence is an effective thesis statement.

EXAMPLE: _N_ I grow coriander in my garden.

   _TS_ Learning to care for plants gave me unexpected pleasure.

1. _N_ Our roads are very icy.

   _TS_ Driving in the winter requires particular skills.

2. _N_ Carjacking rates have increased by 20 percent in our city.

   _TS_ You can avoid being a carjacking victim by taking the next steps.

3. _TS_ I hurt myself in various ways during my three days on the beach.

   _N_ There are many sharp pieces of shell on the local beach.

4. _TS_ Identical twins who are raised together have distinct personalities.

   _N_ My twin sisters have similar birthmarks on their necks.

Revising Your Thesis Statement

A thesis statement is like the foundation that holds up a house. If the thesis statement is weak, it is difficult to construct a solid and compelling essay. Most writers must revise their thesis statements to make them strong, interesting, and supportable.

When you plan your thesis, ask yourself if you can support it with at least three ideas. If not, you have to modify your thesis statement. To enliven a dead-end statement, ensure that your thesis can answer the *why, what,* or *how* questions. Sometimes, just by adding a few words, you can turn a dead-end statement into a supportable thesis.

Poor thesis: Many students drop out of college.

(How could you develop this into an essay? It is a dead-end statement.)

Better thesis: Students drop out of college **for several reasons**.

(You could support this thesis with at least three ideas. This thesis statement answers the question "Why?")

 Writing a Guided Thesis Statement

Give enough details to make your thesis statement interesting. Your instructor may want you to guide the reader through your main points. To do this, mention your main and supporting ideas in your thesis statement. In other words, your thesis statement provides a map for the readers to follow.

Weak: My first job taught me many things.

Better: My first job taught me about the importance of responsibility, organization, and teamwork.

PRACTICE 6   The next thesis statements are weak. First, identify the problem with the statement (write *vague, obvious, incomplete, announces,* and so on) and ask yourself questions to determine how you might be able to revise it. Then revise each statement to make it more forceful and focused.

EXAMPLE: Spousal abuse is a big problem.

Comments: *Obvious. Vague. For whom is it a problem? How is it a problem?*

Revision: *Our state government should provide better support for victims of spousal abuse.*

1. Environmental damage is causing global problems.

   Comments: _Broad / Vague. What kind of environmental damage and what sort of problems?_

   Revision: _Answers will vary._

2. I made a difficult decision.

   Comments: _Vague. What decision? Why was it difficult?_

   Revision: _Answers will vary._

3. Exercise is important.

   Comments: _Vague / Obvious. Why is it important?_

   Revision: _Answers will vary._

4. Telecommuting means that employees do their work from home.

   Comments: _Obvious / No controlling idea. What is important about it?_

   Revision: _Answers will vary._

5. I will explain about home schooling.

   Comments: _Announces. Has no controlling idea._

   Revision: _Answers will vary._

Overview: Writing a Thesis Statement

To create a forceful thesis statement, you should follow the next steps.

Step 1

Find your topic. You can use exploring strategies to get ideas.

General topic: Traditions

Brainstorming:
- Commercialization of holidays
- My family traditions
- Important ceremonies
- Why do we celebrate?
- Benefits of traditions
- Initiation ceremonies

Step 2

Narrow your topic. Decide what point you want to make.

Narrowed topic: Initiation ceremonies

Point I want to make:
Initiation ceremonies can help people make the transition from childhood to adulthood.

Step 3

Develop a thesis statement that you can support with specific evidence. You may need to revise your statement several times.

Initial thesis statement:
Initiation ceremonies serve a valuable function.

Revised thesis statement:
Meaningful initiation ceremonies benefit individuals, families, and communities.

Writer's Desk **Write Thesis Statements**

Write a thesis statement for each of the next topics. If you explored these topics in Chapter 1, you can use those ideas to help you write your thesis statement. If you have not explored these topics yet, then spend a few minutes exploring them. Brainstorm some ideas for each topic to help you define and narrow it. Then develop a thesis statement that makes a point and is not too broad or too narrow.

bullying   consumer culture   volunteer work

EXAMPLE: Topic: Mistakes students make

Narrowed topic: *Reasons students drop out*

Thesis statement: Students may drop out of college because they are unprepared, have financial problems, or experience an emotional crisis.

1. _____

_____

2. _____

_____

3. _____

_____

Teaching Tip:

Cooperative Learning (Pair & Share) Have students work with a partner. Ask pairs of students to brainstorm thesis statements for the three Writer's Desk topics. They should write their thesis statements on a sheet of paper. Then ask students to exchange their sheets of paper with another pair. On the exchanged sheet, students can circle the topic and underline the controlling idea of each topic sentence.

Developing the Supporting Ideas

The next step in essay writing is to plan your supporting ideas. Support is not simply a restatement of the thesis. The body paragraphs must develop and prove the validity of the thesis statement.

Each body paragraph has a **topic sentence** that expresses the main idea of the paragraph. Like a thesis statement, a topic sentence must have a controlling idea. Details and examples support the topic sentence. In the following illustration, you can see how the ideas flow in an essay. Topic sentences support the thesis statement, and details bolster the topic sentences. Every idea in the essay is unified and helps to strengthen the essay's thesis.

PRACTICE 7   Write a thesis statement for each group of supporting ideas. Make sure that your thesis statement is clear, makes a point, and is not too broad or too narrow.   Answers will vary.

EXAMPLE: Thesis: *When you buy a car, make an informed decision.*

    a. Ask family members what type of car they would prefer.

    b. Research on the Internet or in car guides to find information about specific models that interest you.

    c. Keeping your budget in mind, compare new and used cars.

1. Thesis: *Politicians should impose curfew laws on adolescents.*

    a. First, keeping teens off the street at night will ensure that they do not become victims of crime.

    b. Next, requiring adolescents to remain at home will prevent them from committing delinquent acts.

    c. Finally, parents won't need to worry about the whereabouts of their children after dark.

2. Thesis: *To dramatically improve school success rates, educators should seriously consider dividing students according to gender.*

    a. When boys are in all-male classrooms, teachers can modify their activities to keep the boys' attention.

    b. All-female classrooms permit the female students to focus on the material and show their intelligence.

    c. Unlike co-education classrooms, same-gender classrooms are easier for teachers to control.

3. Thesis: <u>*To make an outstanding sales presentation, you should know*</u>
    <u>*your sales pitch, use appropriate body language, and involve the customer.*</u>

    a. First, internalize and believe in your sales pitch.

    b. Speak softly, and do not scare the customer with a commanding voice
        or aggressive mannerisms.

    c. Finally, involve the customer in your sales presentation.

PRACTICE 8   Read the full essay in this practice and then do the
following.   Answers will vary.

1. First, determine the topic of each body paragraph. Then write a topic
    sentence for each body paragraph. Your topic sentence should have a
    controlling idea and express the main point of the paragraph.
2. Next, ask yourself what this essay is about. Finally, compose a thesis
    statement that sums up the main point of the essay. You might look in
    the concluding paragraph to get some ideas.

> **(Introduction)** Paparazzi are photographers who take pictures of celebrities.
> Paparazzi do whatever it takes to get the job done. They exploit celebrities,
> and they don't care about the consequences of their actions.
>
> **Thesis statement:** <u>*The actions of paparazzi cause their subjects a lot*</u>
> <u>*of harm.*</u>
>
> **(Body 1)** Topic Sentence: <u>*When the paparazzi ambush celebrities,*</u>
> <u>*there can often be tragic results.*</u>
>
> When people read gossip magazines, or even watch TV channels like
> *VH1*, they always see paparazzi surrounding the stars. They also see
> celebrities jumping into cars and trying to get away from the
> photographers. This type of behavior can cause serious accidents. The
> most famous case was the death of Princess Diana. Trying to escape
> from paparazzi, she died in a car crash in 1997.
>
> **(Body 2)** Topic Sentence: <u>*Paparazzi cause more harm than good*</u>
> <u>*because they invade people's privacy.*</u>
>
> Some paparazzi stalk celebrities and take photos from trees, rooftops,
> helicopters, or boats. For instance, Jennifer Hudson, a former *American
> Idol* contestant, lived through a great personal tragedy. Her mother,
> brother, and nephew were murdered. Photographers and reporters
> were seen hounding Hudson with questions and taking photographs of
> her during this misfortune.

Teaching Tip:
Group Work
Students can work
in teams. Ask teams
to write their thesis
statement and topic
sentences on the
board. You can ask
them to decide
which statements
are most
appropriate.

Teaching Tip:

**Cooperative
Learning
(Sharing Circle)**
Ask students to do
Practice 8 in teams
of three or four.
Advise them to read
the body paragraphs
before they attempt
to write the thesis
statement and topic
sentences. Teams
can then share
their answers with
the class.

(Body 3) Topic Sentence: *Celebrities are also harmed when their families become the targets of paparazzi.*

Magazine covers regularly display photographs of celebrities' spouses and children. The family members may not want or appreciate the attention. For example, the children of Brad Pitt and Angelina Jolie are exposed to scrutiny, criticized for their clothing choices, and occasionally ridiculed. Several years ago, Pierce Brosnan's wife was mocked for gaining weight.

(Conclusion) Paparazzi hurt people rather than help them. It is almost sickening to think of what a photographer is willing to do to get a story. The public should stop buying gossip magazines so photographers will not be able earn a living by committing gross invasions of privacy.

Generating Supporting Ideas

When you develop supporting ideas, make certain that they all focus on the central point that you are making in the thesis statement. To generate ideas for body paragraphs, you could use the exploring strategies (brainstorming, freewriting, questioning, or clustering) that you learned in Chapter 1.

Review the process that student Alicia Parera went through. First, she created a list to support her thesis statement. Then she reread her supporting ideas and removed ideas that she did not want to develop in her essay. She also grouped together related ideas.

Teaching Tip:
Ask students to discuss why Alicia crossed out the last idea. Point out that college can be useful for students who want to start a business. Also, starting a business is not a common reason for students to drop out.

Initial Ideas

Draft thesis statement: Students drop out of college for many reasons.

Supporting ideas:
- can't adapt to college life
- feel confused about career goals ⟩ — A
- don't have study skills
- can't afford tuition
- part-time job takes time away from schoolwork ⟩ — B
- financial problems
- lose a family member
- undergo an emotional crisis such as a breakup ⟩ — C
- ~~want to start their own business~~

After critically examining her supporting ideas, Alicia chose three that could become body paragraphs. She evaluated each set of linked ideas and summarized the connections between ideas in the set. These sentence summaries then became her topic sentences.

Revised Thesis and Supporting Points

Thesis Statement: Students may drop out of college because they are unprepared, have financial problems, or experience an emotional crisis.

Topic Sentence: Many students are unable to adapt to college life.

Topic Sentence: Some students face overwhelming financial burdens.

Topic Sentence: Furthermore, students may undergo an emotional crisis.

Hint **Look Critically at Your Supporting Ideas**

After you have made a list of supporting ideas, look at it carefully and ask yourself the next questions.

• **Which ideas could I develop into complete paragraphs?** Look for connections between supporting ideas. Group together ideas that have a common thread. Then create a topic sentence for each group of related ideas. In Alicia's example, three of her ideas became topic sentences.

• **Does each idea support my thesis?** Choose ideas that directly support the thesis statement, and drop any ideas that might go off topic. In Alicia's example, the last idea, "Want to start their own business," didn't support her thesis, so she crossed it out.

PRACTICE 9   Brainstorm three supporting ideas for the next thesis statements. Find ideas that do not overlap, and ensure that your ideas support the thesis. (You can brainstorm a list of ideas on a separate sheet of paper, and then add the three best ideas here.)   Answers will vary.

EXAMPLE: Driving in the city is very stressful.

— *pedestrians and cyclists are careless*

— *poor street planning has led to larger traffic jams*

— *other drivers act in dangerous and erratic ways*

Teaching Tip:
If you have started to discuss writing patterns with your students, discuss what types of essays the statements in Practice 9 would generate.

1. Losing a job can have some positive consequences.

    _____

    _____

    _____

2. There are several concrete steps that you can take to help preserve the environment.

    _____

    _____

    _____

3. When young people move away from home, they quickly learn the next lessons.

    _____

    _____

    _____

Writer's Desk Generate Supporting Ideas

Brainstorm supporting ideas for two or three of your thesis statements from the previous Writer's Desk. Look critically at your lists of supporting ideas. Ask yourself which supporting ideas you could expand into body paragraphs, and then drop any unrelated ideas.

The Writer's Room   Topics to Develop

Writing Activity 1

Choose one of the Writer's Room topics from Chapter 1 and write a thesis statement. Using an exploring strategy, develop supporting ideas for your thesis.

Writing Activity 2

Narrow one of the following topics. Then develop a thesis statement and some supporting ideas.

General Topics

1. good hygiene
2. annoying rules
3. delaying childbirth
4. traditions

College and Work-Related Topics

5. pressures students face
6. credit cards
7. creative teaching
8. benefits of extracurricular activities

✓ THESIS STATEMENT AND TOPIC SENTENCES

When you write a thesis statement, ask yourself these questions.

☐ Is my thesis a complete sentence?

☐ Does it contain a narrowed topic and a controlling idea?

☐ Is my main point clear and interesting?

☐ Can the thesis be supported with several body paragraphs? (Verify that the topic is not too narrow, or you will hit a dead end with it. Also check that the topic is not too broad. Your essay requires a clear focus.)

☐ Can I think of details, examples, and other ideas to support the thesis?

☐ Is my thesis forceful and direct, and not too vague or obvious?

☐ Does my thesis make a valid point?

☐ Do I have good supporting ideas?

☐ Does each topic sentence have a controlling idea and support the thesis statement?

Teaching Tip:

Cooperative Learning (Quick Review) Divide the class into groups of three or four. Assign one main section of Chapter 2 to some groups and the other main section to the other groups. The main sections are (1) Writing a Thesis Statement and (2) Developing Supporting Ideas. Ask each group to review the information in the section and to generate two questions about that information. Then you can ask teams to read the questions aloud. Anybody in the class can answer a question. Or, as an alternative, you can ask teams to exchange questions and to answer another team's questions.

Teaching Tip: Writer's World Competition Please advise students that they can submit their paragraphs and essays for possible publication to www .pearsonhighered .com/essayrewards/ writingrewards.html

mywritinglab To check your progress in meeting this chapter's objectives, log in to **www.mywritinglab.com**, go to the **Study Plan** tab, click on **The Writing Process** and choose **Developing the Main Idea** from the list of subtopics. Read and view the resources in the **Review Materials** section, and then complete the **Recall**, **Apply**, and **Write** sets in the **Activities** section.

Developing the Essay Plan

Like gardens, essays require careful planning. Some ideas thrive while others do not. Writers develop essay plans to help them decide which ideas support the main idea most effectively and where to place those ideas so that readers can understand them.

Key Steps in Developing the Essay Plan

In the previous chapters, you learned how to use exploring strategies to formulate ideas and narrow topics. You also learned to develop main ideas for essays. In this chapter, you will focus on the third stage of the essay writing process: developing the essay plan. There are two key steps in this process.

DEVELOPING THE ESSAY PLAN

STEP 1 ➤ **Organize your supporting ideas.** Choose an appropriate method of organization.

STEP 2 ➤ **Write an essay plan.** Place your main and supporting ideas in an essay plan.

Organizing Supporting Ideas

Once you have a list of main ideas that will make up the body paragraphs in an essay, you need to organize those ideas in a logical manner using time, space, or emphatic order.

Time Order

To organize an essay using **time order (chronological order)**, arrange the details according to the sequence in which they occurred. Time order can be effective for narrating a story, explaining how to do something, or describing an event.

first   then   after that

When you write essays using time order, you can include the following transitional expressions to help your readers understand when certain events happened. (There is a more extensive list of transitions on page 64 in Chapter 5.)

after that	first	last	next
eventually	in the beginning	meanwhile	suddenly
finally	later	months after	then

PRACTICE 1   The writer uses time order to organize supporting ideas for the following thesis statement.

THESIS STATEMENT: My one and only ferry ride was a disaster.

1. To begin with, the only available seat was in a horrible location near the back of the boat.

2. Next, the rain began, and the passengers on deck rushed inside.

3. After that, the ferry began to rock, and some passengers became ill.

One paragraph from the essay also uses time order. Underline any words or phrases that help show time order.

Teaching Tip:

Cooperative Learning (Jigsaw) Divide the class into three teams. One team will learn about emphatic order, one about time order, and one about space order. (If you have a class of more than fifteen students, then divide each large team into two smaller teams.) Students in the "Time Order" section must brainstorm and write a thesis statement with three supporting ideas that use time order. Students in the "Space Order" and "Emphatic Order" sections do the same thing. Then ask representative students from each section to explain their organization strategy to the class.

Next, the rain began, and the passengers on deck started to move inside. Suddenly, a sprinkle became a downpour. I was in the middle of the crowd, and water was running in rivulets down my face and down the back of my neck. Then, those behind me got impatient and began to shove. The doorway was narrow, and many people were jostling for position. I was pushed to the right and left. Meanwhile, I was soaked, tired, and cranky. The crowd squeezed me more and more. Finally, I was pushed through the door; I stumbled and tried not to fall. The inner cabin was so crowded that I had to stand in the aisle holding on to the back of one of the seats.

Space Order

Organizing ideas using **space order** helps the reader to visualize what you are describing in a specific space. For example, you can describe someone or something from top to bottom or bottom to top, from left to right or right to left, or from far to near or near to far.

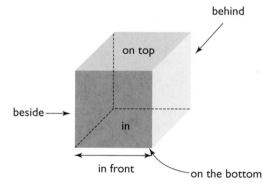

Help readers find their way through your essay by using the following transitional expressions.

above	beneath	nearby	on top
behind	closer in	on the bottom	toward
below	farther out	on the left	under

PRACTICE 2   The writer uses space order to organize supporting ideas for the following thesis statement.

THESIS STATEMENT: Spending very little money, local students helped turn a tiny old house into a vibrant youth center.

1. Working outdoors, two students cleared the yard.

2. Focusing on the exterior surfaces of the building, a second team of students painted and made minor repairs.

3. Inside the house, some students turned the living room into a recreation and meeting place.

One paragraph from the essay also uses space order. Underline any words or phrases that indicate space order.

> Working outdoors, two students cleared the yard. <u>At the front edge of the property</u>, there were paper bags, fast-food wrappers, and broken bottles. Wearing gloves, the students picked up the mess and put the items in the garbage. <u>In the center of the yard</u>, some of the grass was dying, so the students planted new grass seeds. <u>Leading up to the front of the house</u> was a stone walkway. The students repaired the paving stones. <u>Under the front windows</u> were two empty flower boxes. The boxes were gray with peeling paint. One student sanded the boxes, and the other repainted them. When they finished their work, the yard looked inviting.

Emphatic Order

To organize the supporting details of an essay using **emphatic order**, arrange them in a logical sequence. For example, you can arrange details from the least to the most important, from general to specific, from the least appealing to the most appealing, and so on.

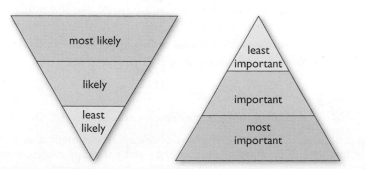

Here are some transitional expressions that help readers understand which ideas you want to emphasize the most or the least in the body paragraphs of an essay.

above all	first	moreover	principally
clearly	in particular	most importantly	the least important
especially	last	of course	the most important

Using Emphatic Order

When you organize details using emphatic order, use your own values and opinions to determine what is the most or the least important, upsetting, remarkable, and so on. Another writer may organize the same ideas in a different way.

PRACTICE 3   The writer uses emphatic order to organize support-ing ideas for the following thesis statement.

THESIS STATEMENT: In our city, some types of public transportation are more dependable and pleasant than others.

1. First, subways can be uncomfortable and even frightening.

2. Of course, bus trips can have certain drawbacks.

3. Clearly, the most pleasant and reliable way to travel is the suburban train.

One paragraph from the essay also uses emphatic order. Underline any words or phrases that help show emphatic order.

> <u>First</u>, subways can be uncomfortable and even frightening. Subway riders must deal with crowds. In front of the tracks, there is very little seating room, so people line the walls. <u>Moreover</u>, the lighting is usually terrible, so ordinary people look sad and even sinister under the fluorescent tubes. Feeling uncomfortable and unattractive, they avoid eye contact. <u>Above all</u>, for those who feel claustrophobic, being in a subway can feel like being in a grave. Passengers cannot see the sunlight, sky, or outdoors for the entire duration of the journey. Passengers can only stare at the sullen faces of the other travelers. <u>Clearly</u>, the entire subway experience can be unpleasant and disturbing.

Hint   **Combining Time, Space, and Emphatic Order**

You will probably use more than one type of organizational method in an essay. For example, in a time order essay about a journey, one paragraph might be devoted to a particular place that you visited, and in that paragraph, you might use space order to describe the scene.

Teaching Tip:
As an additional activity, ask students to add transitional words or phrases to the topic sentences in Practice 4. Their transitions should help clarify the type of order.

PRACTICE 4   Read each list of supporting ideas, and number the items in a logical order. Then write *time*, *space*, or *emphatic* to indicate the organization method.   Answers will vary.

EXAMPLE: Thesis Statement: Painting a picture can be a rewarding experience.

___1___ Choose a location that you find particularly peaceful.

___3___ Add colors to your sketch that best represent the mood you are feeling.

___2___ Settle in and make a preliminary sketch of the place.

Order: ___*time*___

1. Thesis Statement: Overexposure to the sun can have terrible consequences.

   ___1___ The skin cells lose elasticity, and wrinkles set in earlier.

   ___3___ Some people develop cancers that can lead to premature death.

   ___2___ Brown spots can develop on parts of the face.

   Order: *emphatic*

2. Thesis Statement: Over the course of American history, some presidents have made decisions that profoundly affected the nation.

   ___2___ Franklin D. Roosevelt, as a result of the Great Depression, reformed the economy and helped the poor with his New Deal.

   ___1___ During the Civil War, Abraham Lincoln faced conflict when he resolved to end slavery.

   ___3___ George W. Bush, in response to terrorist attacks of September 11, 2001, committed the nation to ongoing wars.

   Order: ___*time*___

3. Thesis Statement: For an important interview, dress conservatively.

   ___3___ Employers may notice every detail, so pay attention to your footwear.

   ___1___ If possible, invest in a good haircut a few days before the interview.

   ___2___ Wear a suit jacket and matching pants or a skirt.

   Order: ___*space*___

Developing an Essay Plan

A contractor would never build a house without making a drawing or plan of it first. In the same way, an essay plan can help you organize your ideas before you write the first draft. Planning your essay actually saves you time because you have

Teaching Tip:

Pair Work
Ask students to work in pairs to create an essay plan for one of the readings in Chapter 40.

already figured out your supporting ideas and how to organize them so your readers can easily follow them. To create an essay plan, follow the next steps.

- Looking at the list of ideas that you created while prewriting, identify the ones that most effectively support your thesis statement.
- Next, write topic sentences that express these main supporting ideas.
- Finally, add details under each topic sentence.

A formal essay plan uses Roman numerals and letters of the alphabet to identify main and supporting ideas. A formal plan also contains complete sentences. The basic structure is shown below.

Thesis Statement: _____

    I. _____

        A. _____

        B. _____

   II. _____

        A. _____

        B. _____

Concluding Idea: _____

In the planning stage, you do not have to develop your introduction and conclusion. It is sufficient to simply write your thesis statement and an idea for your conclusion. Later, when you write your essay, you can develop the introduction and conclusion.

Teaching Tip:
Before you assign essay plans, specify whether you prefer informal or formal essay plans. Explain that an informal plan can include phrases instead of complete sentences and that it doesn't require Roman numerals.

Alicia's Essay Plan

Alicia Parera wrote topic sentences and supporting examples and organized her ideas into a plan. Notice that she begins with her thesis statement, and she indents her supporting ideas. Also notice that she uses emphatic order.

Thesis statement: Students may drop out of college because they have financial problems, experience an emotional crisis, or are unprepared for college life.

    I. Some students face overwhelming financial burdens.

        A. They may have a part-time job to pay for such things as tuition and rent.

        B. Moreover, a part-time job leaves little time for studying and homework.

        C. Also, transportation may be expensive and beyond a student's means.

II. Furthermore, some students are faced with life-changing
   events and must leave college to cope.
   A. A pregnancy and childbirth consume energy and
      attention.
   B. Also, a serious illness or death in the family can cause
      a student to miss classes, and it becomes too difficult to
      catch up.
   C. Of course, a broken relationship can cause a student to
      feel emotionally fragile and unable to concentrate.
III. Finally, they may be unprepared for college life.
   A. They might have poor study skills.
   B. Furthermore, some students cannot respect schedules.
   C. The increased freedom in college causes some students
      to skip too many classes.
   D. Additionally, many students feel confused about career
      goals and decide to leave college.

PRACTICE 5   Read the following essay plan. Brainstorm and
develop three supporting ideas for each topic sentence.   Answers will vary.

THESIS STATEMENT: Each generation has produced influential musical
icons.

Topic Sentence: In the 1960s, some amazing singers and bands
influenced their generation.

Motown singers such as The Supremes popularized soul music.

The Beatles brought their style of pop music to America.

The Rolling Stones made gritty rock and roll popular.

_____

Topic Sentence: During the 1980s, certain musical stars made lasting
impressions.

Madonna started her career in the early 1980s.

Michael Jackson's album, Thriller, became a huge success.

Prince and Whitney Houston also had strong careers.

_____

Teaching Tip:

**Cooperative
Learning
(Pair & Share)**
Divide the class into
pairs. Ask half the
class to do Practice
5 and the other half
to do Practice 6.
After pairs have
brainstormed lists
of supporting ideas,
they can join pairs
who did the other
practice. The groups
of four can share
answers and make
suggestions for
improvement.

Topic Sentence: From 2000 to 2010, a wide variety of music styles became popular.

Hip-hop artists sold millions of CDs.

American Idol produced popular singers such as Kelly Clarkson and Carrie Underwood.

Indie rockers and rappers also affected the music scene.

PRACTICE 6   Read the following essay plan. Brainstorm and develop three supporting ideas for each topic. Include specific anecdotes. Answers will vary.

THESIS STATEMENT: I learned valuable life lessons in primary and secondary school.

Topic Sentence: Through various activities, I learned to get along with others.

I shared food during lunch hours.

I did schoolwork in teams.

Sports activities such as baseball taught me to cooperate.

Topic Sentence: I learned about the importance of knowledge.

My second-grade teacher helped me appreciate good stories.

I learned to do math at school.

I loved learning about American history from my fifth-grade teacher.

Topic Sentence: Finally, I learned self-discipline.

I had to wake up on time for school.

I learned to do my homework without prodding.

When my friend Blake made me angry, I learned to use words instead of my fists.

Writer's Desk **Write an Essay Plan**

Brainstorm ideas for an essay on a separate piece of paper. You can choose ideas that you developed in Chapter 2. Then do the following.

1. Highlight at least three ideas from your list that you think are the most compelling and most clearly illustrate the point you are making in your thesis statement. These three ideas will make up your body paragraphs.

2. Group together any related ideas with the three supporting ideas.

3. Organize your ideas for the body paragraphs using time, space, or emphatic order.

4. Create a complete essay plan.

Teaching Tip:

Cooperative Learning (Question Cards) Place students in teams of three or four. Using index cards or paper cut into four sections, the teams brainstorm four questions about the chapter's key concepts. They write the question on one side of the paper and the answer on the other side. Then teams can exchange cards with another team. They can look at each question, answer it as a group, and then check the answer.

The Writer's Room   Topics to Develop

Writing Activity 1

Choose one of the Writer's Room topics from Chapter 2, and create an essay plan. Using an exploring strategy, develop supporting ideas for your thesis.

Writing Activity 2

Create a list of supporting ideas for one of the next thesis statements. Then develop an essay plan.

General Topics

1. Single people should (or should not) have the right to adopt children.
2. The three talents I would most like to have are . . .
3. Noise pollution is increasing in our homes and neighborhoods.
4. There are good reasons to postpone marriage.

College and Work-Related Topics

5. New employees make three types of common mistakes.
6. An elected official should have the following characteristics.
7. I do (or do not) vote for the following reasons.
8. (Choose a story, novel, or film) has important lessons for all of us.

Teaching Tip:
Writer's World
Competition
Please advise
students that they
can submit their
paragraphs and
essays for possible
publication to www
.pearsonhighered
.com/essayrewards/
writingrewards.html

✔ **CHECKLIST: ESSAY PLAN**

When you develop an essay plan, ask yourself these questions.

☐ Does my thesis statement express the main idea of the essay?

☐ In my plan, does each body paragraph contain a topic sentence?

☐ Does each topic sentence support the thesis statement?

☐ In each body paragraph, do the sentences support the topic sentence?

☐ Are my ideas well organized?

PEARSON
mywritinglab To check your progress in meeting this chapter's objectives, log in to **www.mywritinglab.com,** go to the **Study Plan** tab, click on **The Writing Process** and choose **Developing the Essay Plan** from the list of subtopics. Read and view the resources in the **Review Materials** section, and then complete the **Recall, Apply,** and **Write** sets in the **Activities** section.

Developing the First Draft

By preparing the soil and planting seeds and shrubs, a gardener creates a landscape's basic foundation. In the same way, a writer plans the main idea, develops the plan, and then prepares the first draft of a writing assignment.

Key Steps in Developing the First Draft

In previous chapters, you learned how to develop a thesis statement, support it with ideas, and create an essay plan. To develop a first draft, follow the next five steps.

DEVELOPING THE FIRST DRAFT

STEP 1 ➤ **Write an introduction.** Try to attract the reader's attention in the first paragraph of your essay.

STEP 2 ➤ **Write complete body paragraphs.** Expand each supporting idea with specific details.

STEP 3 ➤ **Write a conclusion.** Bring your essay to a satisfactory close.

STEP 4 ➤ **Title your essay.** Sum up your essay topic in a few words.

STEP 5 ➤ **Write the first draft.** Tie the introduction, body paragraphs, and conclusion into a cohesive essay.

Writing an Introduction

The **introductory paragraph** establishes the subject of your essay and contains the thesis statement. A strong introduction will capture the reader's attention and make him or her want to read on. Introductions may have a lead-in, and they can be developed in several different ways.

The Lead-In

Teaching Tip:
Tell students that they do not always need to have a lead in.

The point of writing an essay is to have people read it. Your essay should entertain, inform, or persuade readers. So, you can try to grab your readers' attention in the first sentence. There are three common lead-ins:

- a quotation
- a surprising or provocative statement
- a question

Introduction Styles

You can develop the introduction in several ways. Experiment with any of the following introduction styles.

- **Give general or historical background information** that gradually leads to your thesis. For example, in an essay about gender stereotypes in movies, you might begin by discussing some classic films.
- **Tell an interesting anecdote** or a story that leads to your thesis statement. For example, you might begin your essay about film violence by describing how aggressive your younger brother and his friends became after they watched the movie *Dark Knight*.
- **Describe something in vivid detail,** and then state your thesis. For example, you might begin your essay about the beauty myth by describing a cosmetic surgery procedure.
- **Define a term,** and then state your thesis. For example, in an essay about ways to avoid marital conflicts, you can begin by defining a happy marriage.

- **Present a contrasting position,** which is an idea that is the opposite of the one you will later develop, and then offer your thesis. Your readers will not expect you to present one side and then to argue for the other side. For example, in an essay about abortion, you might begin by presenting the arguments of those who would not agree with your particular point of view on the debate.
- **Pose several questions,** and end with a thesis statement. The purpose may be to engage your readers by inviting them to think about the topic. You might also ask questions that you will answer in your essay. For instance, in an essay about lotteries, you might ask, *Have you ever bought a lottery ticket? Why do so many people play lotteries?*

The next example presents the structure of a typical introduction.

Have good manners disappeared? In past centuries, a gentleman would spread his cloak over a muddy road so that his lady wouldn't dirty her feet. Twenty years ago, an elderly man or woman would never have to stand in a bus because other passengers would offer up their seats. Times have certainly changed. Today, many people lack consideration for others. **Parents and schools should teach children basic good manners.**

◅ Lead-in

◅ Historical background information

◅ Thesis statement

PRACTICE I   Read the following introductions. Underline each thesis statement, and determine what introduction style the writer used.

1. One of the most important developments of the eighteenth century was the invention of an African American language. An English traveler during the 1770s complained he could not understand Virginia slaves who spoke "a mixed dialect between Guinea and English." But such a language made it possible for country-born and "saltwater" Africans to communicate. The two most important dialects were Gullah and Geechee, named after two of the African peoples most prominent in the Carolinas and Georgia low country. <u>These creole languages were a transitional phenomenon, gradually giving way to distinctive forms of black English.</u>

    —John Mack Faragher et al., *Out of Many*

    a. Underline the thesis statement.
    b. What is the introduction style? Indicate the best answer.

    __X__ historical background   _____ anecdote

    _____ definition   _____ contrasting position

2. Adolescent males are dangerous. They join gangs, and they are responsible for most of the crime in our society. They drive too fast, causing accidents on our highways. They all experiment with drugs, and they annoy others with their loud music. But is such a portrayal of our nation's young men really fair? <u>In fact, most stereotypes about adolescent males are incorrect and misleading.</u>

—Abeer Hamad, student

a. Underline the thesis statement.

b. What type of lead-in did the writer use?

_____ quotation   _____ question   __X__ surprising statement

c. What is the introduction style? Indicate the best answer.

_____ historical background   _____ anecdote

_____ definition   __X__ contrasting position

3. Where did you buy that blouse? I heard the question every time I wore it. It was a truly lovely designer model that had been marked down to $40. It was pale blue with swirling tiny flower buds running down each front panel. The little buttons were topped with imitation pearls. Unfortunately, the middle button kept coming undone. People at a certain angle to my left could peek in and view the lace eyelets on my brassiere. When I wore the blouse, my head kept bobbing down, looking to see if I was exposing myself. <u>Over the years, I have had several humorous and embarrassing wardrobe and makeup malfunctions.</u>

—Catalina Ortega, student

a. Underline the thesis statement.

b. What type of lead-in was used?

_____ quotation   __X__ question   _____ surprising statement

c. What is the introduction style? Indicate the best answer.

_____ general background   _____ anecdote

_____ definition   __X__ description

4. The term *cool jazz* refers to modern jazz that tends to be softer and easier than the bebop of Charlie Parker and Dizzy Gillespie. Cool jazz avoids roughness and brassiness. The term *cool jazz* has been

applied to the music of saxophonist Lester Young and some of the musicians whom he and Count Basie influenced. Though musicians inspired by Basie and Young were found in almost all regions of America, many of them were based in California during the 1950s. <u>The West Coast became one center of innovation in cool jazz.</u>

—Mark C. Gridley, Concise Guide to Jazz

a. Underline the thesis statement

b. What is the introduction style? Indicate the best answer.

_____ general background   _____ anecdote

__X__ definition   _____ contrasting position

5. "All the men were frightened," Julius Matthews said. On June 6, 1944, he, along with other young men, landed on the French beach. German bullets were flying all around him. He ran as fast as he could towards the cliffs, but his heavy boots sank into the sand, slowing him down. He saw men around him fall to the ground as bullets penetrated their bodies. <u>On that day, many of the best-laid military plans went awry</u>.

—Niles Logan, journalist

a. Underline the thesis statement.

b. What type of lead-in was used?

__X__ quotation   _____ question   _____ surprising statement

c. What is the introduction style? Indicate the best answer.

_____ general background   __X__ anecdote

_____ definition   _____ questions

6. Why do some hip-hop artists embed jewels and gold in their teeth? Are the grills meant to impress others, or do the grills fit some deep need on the part of the artists to show that they matter? Is the hip-hop artist who shows off his "bling" any different from the accountant who buys a BMW to show that she has succeeded, or the corporate executive who marries a beautiful trophy wife? Showing off one's wealth is not new. <u>In fact, throughout history, people have found extravagant ways to flaunt their wealth</u>.

—Jamal Evans, student

Teaching Tip:

Cooperative Learning (Jigsaw)
Place students in groups of five. Assign one of the introductions in Practice I to each team. They should rewrite the introduction using a different style. Then ask students in each team to assign themselves a number between one and five. Ask the ones, the twos, the threes, etc. to get together and form new teams. The new teams can share their new introductions and ask other members to guess the style.

a. Underline the thesis statement.

b. What type of lead-in was used?

_____ quotation   _X__ question   _____ surprising statement

c. What is the introduction style? Indicate the best answer.

_____ general background   _____ anecdote

_____ definition   __X__ questions

PRACTICE 2   Write interesting lead-ins (opening sentences) for the next topics. Use the type of lead-in that is indicated in parentheses.
Answers will vary.

EXAMPLE: Video games (question)

How many people have developed a serious addiction to video games?

1. Television commercials   (a question)

_____

_____

2. College sports   (a provocative statement)

_____

_____

3. Homelessness   (a surprising fact or idea)

_____

_____

Teaching Tip:
Collaborative Learning (Sharing Circle)
Write a thesis statement on the board such as *There are three common mistakes people make on the first date.* Then place students in teams. Ask each team to prepare an introduction using a different style. Team members can read their introductions out loud. Then the class can show, with applause, which introductions are the most powerful.

PRACTICE 3   Choose *one* of the next thesis statements. Then write three introductions using three different introduction styles. Use the same thesis statement in each introduction.   Answers will vary.

1. Physical education courses should be compulsory for college students.

2. American films and television shows do not reflect the cultural diversity of the nation.

3. Censorship is sometimes necessary for the welfare of society.

You can choose any three of the following introduction styles:

- General or historical background
- Anecdote
- Description

- Definition
- Contrasting position
- Series of questions

Writer's Desk **Write Two Introductions**

In Chapter 3, you prepared an essay plan. Now, on a separate piece of paper, write two different styles of introductions for your essay. Use the same thesis statement in both introductions. Later, you can choose the best introduction for your essay.

Writing Complete Body Paragraphs

In your essay plan, you developed supporting ideas for your topic. When you prepare the first draft, you must flesh out those ideas. As you write each body paragraph, make sure that it is complete. Do not offer vague generalizations, and do not simply repeat your ideas. Provide evidence for each topic sentence by inserting specific details. You might include examples, facts, statistics, anecdotes, or quotations.

Examples are people, places, things, or events that illustrate your point. To support the view that some local buildings are eyesores, the writer could give the following examples.

> The car dealership on Labelle Boulevard is run down.
>
> The gray block apartment buildings that line Main Street are monotonous.
>
> The Allen Drive mini-mall has tacky signs and cracked store windows.

Facts are objective details that can be verified by others. **Statistics** are facts that are expressed in numbers. (Make sure that your statistics are from reliable sources.) To support the view that transportation costs are too high for students, you could give the following facts and statistics as evidence.

> A one-way bus ticket now costs $3.50 for students.
>
> The monthly subway pass just increased to $260 for students.
>
> In a college survey of four hundred students, 70 percent expressed concern about the recent rate increases in public transportation.

Anecdotes are true experiences that you or someone else went through. An anecdote tells the story of what happened. **Quotations** are somebody's exact words, and they are set off in quotation marks. To support the view that lack of sleep can have dangerous consequences, you could include the following anecdote and quotation as evidence.

> When Allen Turner finished his night shift, he got into his car and headed home. On Forest Drive, he started to nod off. Luckily, a truck driver in another lane noticed that Turner's car was weaving, and the trucker honked. Turner said, "My eyes snapped open and I saw a wall

Teaching Tip:
Many students have problems providing sufficient examples and details in their body paragraphs. After students read this section, ask them to evaluate one of their previous essays and analyze whether or not they included well-supported paragraphs.

Teaching Tip:
Point out the difference between an opinion or observation and a fact. Give students these examples.

Opinion: The children are too young to be left alone. Fact: Evan is nine, and Tracy is just six.

Observation: The local economy is booming. Fact: The local employment center reports that fewer people are looking for work this year.

Teaching Tip:
Ask students to look again at Alicia's essay plan in Chapter 3 on pages 36–37. Ask students to brainstorm what type of specific evidence could help make the essay more complete. A draft of the essay about college dropouts appears in Chapter 5.

growing larger in front of me. I slammed on my brakes just before smashing into it."

Essay with Sample Body Paragraphs

Read the next body paragraphs. Notice how they are fleshed out with specific evidence.

Thesis Statement:

> For personal and financial reasons, a growing number of adult children are choosing to live with their parents.

Body Paragraphs

The cost of education and housing is very high, so it is more economical to live at home. First, rents have increased dramatically since the 1990s. In *The Daily Journal*, Anna Reinhold states that rents tripled in the past ten years. During the same period, student wages have not risen as much as the rents. In fact, the minimum wage is still $6.15 an hour. Also, college fees are increasing each year. Tuition and fees at four-year public colleges rose $344, or 6.3 percent this year, to an average of $5,836, according to the College Board's annual "Trends in College Pricing" report.

fact →

fact →
statistic →

Many young people want to build a nest egg before moving out of the family home. If they remain at home, they can save income from part-time jobs. "I've saved $14,000 by staying in my parents' place," says Kyle Nehme, a twenty-four-year-old student at the University of Texas. Such students do not need to worry about student loans. According to financial analyst Raul Gomez, "Students who stay in the family home reap significant financial benefits."

quotation →

quotation →

Students who remain in their parents' home have a much more relaxed and comfortable lifestyle. Often, the parents do the shopping and housework. For example, Liz Allen, a twenty-six-year-old marketing student, moved back in with her parents last May. She discovered how much more convenient it was when someone else did the vacuuming, laundry, and cooking. Moreover, such students feel more secure and safe in the cocoon of their parents' home. In a *Daily Journal* survey of ninety adults who live at home, 64 percent cited "comfort" as their major reason.

anecdote →

statistic →

 Using Research to Support Your Point

Your instructor might ask you to back up your ideas with research. You can investigate several resources, including books, magazines, and the Internet, for relevant quotations, statistics, and factual evidence. For more information about doing research, see Chapter 16, The Research Essay.

Teaching Tip:
If Practice 4 is done in class, ask students to use anecdotes, facts, and examples as support. If you assign this practice as homework, you could ask students to do some research and find statistics or quotations to support the topic.

PRACTICE 4 Make the next body paragraphs more complete by adding specific examples. You can include the following:

- examples
- anecdotes from your own life or from the lives of others
- quotations (for this exercise, you can make up punchy quotations)
- facts, statistics, or descriptions of events that you have read about or seen

Do not add general statements. Check that the details you add are very specific. Answers will vary.

THESIS STATEMENT: Prospective pet owners should become informed before buying an animal.

Body Paragraph 1 First, when families choose a dog, they should consider the inconvenience and possible dangers. Some breeds of dogs can become extremely aggressive. _Rottweilers and pit bulls, for example, have been known to act erratically. There have been many documented cases of dog attacks on humans. Last year a Michigan pet owner expressed shock and sadness when her beloved pit bull suddenly attacked her grandson. "My dog is usually so gentle," the owner said._ Moreover, dog owners must accept that dogs require a lot of time and attention. _Dogs need to be walked daily, so owners should expect to devote at least half an hour per day to that activity. Dogs also require attention. New Jersey pet owner Susan Dover said, "My dog chews the arms of my sofa when I leave her alone for too long."_ Furthermore, it is very expensive to own a dog. _Vaccinations can cost thousands of dollars. Dog food is costly, and large dogs require a lot of food._

Body Paragraph 2 Some new pet owners decide to buy exotic pets. However, such pets come with very specific problems and require particular environments. _Snakes need terrariums with particular heat and light requirements. Lizards can die if they are not kept in the proper conditions. Other exotic pets such as lion cubs require outdoor enclosures that provide them with the room to roam._ Also, some exotic pets seem interesting when they are young, but they can become distinctly annoying or dangerous when they reach maturity.

Teaching Tip:
If your student essays lack well-supported body paragraphs, suggest that students prepare a very detailed essay plan before they write their next essay. They can add specific quotations, examples, statistics, and other references directly into their plan.

Sarah Jorba bought a cute baby chimpanzee, but said her animal became

"very aggressive and destructive" when it reached maturity. Owners of baby

alligators end up with animals that they cannot maintain.

> ### Hint ⟩ **Making Detailed Essay Plans**
>
> You can shorten the time you spend developing the first draft if you make a very detailed essay plan. In addition to your main ideas, your plan can include details for each supporting idea. Notice the detailed evidence in the following excerpt from an essay plan.
>
> **Thesis Statement:** For personal and financial reasons, a growing number of adult children are choosing to live with their parents.
>
> I. **Topic Sentence:**   The cost of education and housing is very high.
>   A. Rents have increased dramatically in the past ten years.
>   Evidence: *The Daily Journal* states that rents tripled in the past ten years.
>   B. Student wages have not risen as much as the rents.
>   Evidence: The minimum wage is still $6.15 an hour.
>   C. Tuition fees are very high.
>   Evidence: Tuition and fees at four-year public colleges rose $344, or 6.3 percent this year, to an average of $5,836, according to the College Board's annual "Trends in College Pricing" report.

fact ➤ (A.)
fact ➤ (B.)
statistic ➤ (C.)

Writer's Desk   Make Complete Body Paragraphs

In Chapter 3, you prepared an essay plan. Now write complete body paragraphs for your essay. Make certain that each body paragraph contains specific details.

Writing a Conclusion

The **concluding paragraph** gives you one last chance to impress the reader and to make your point clear. A good conclusion makes the essay seem complete. One common and effective way to conclude a composition is to summarize the main ideas. The essay then comes full circle, and you remind the reader of your strongest points.

To make your conclusion more interesting and original, you could also close with a prediction, a suggestion, a quotation, or a call to action.

Linking the Conclusion to the Introduction

- One effective way to conclude an essay is to continue an idea that was introduced in the introduction.
- If you began an anecdote in the introduction, you can finish it in the conclusion.
- If you posed some questions in the introduction, you can answer them in the conclusion.
- If you highlighted a problem in the introduction, you might suggest a solution in the conclusion.

Look at the concluding paragraph to an essay about etiquette in our technological age.

> Do not hide behind technology as your excuse for displaying rude or annoying behavior. You can turn off your cell phone when you are with someone you care about. If someone is writing an e-mail, do not read over his or her shoulder. Also, never send nor accept chain e-mails that promise wealth, happiness, or cures for cancer.

The last sentence in the essay could be one of the following.

Prediction: If you follow the basic rules of etiquette, you will ensure that your friends and colleagues maintain their respect for you.

Suggestion: The next time someone forwards you a nasty chain letter asking you to send it to at least ten people or else, return it to the sender ten times.

Quotation: As the French author Colette once said, "It is wise to apply the oils of refined politeness to the mechanism of friendship."

Call to Action: To help the next generation learn good manners, offer to teach a class to local high school students about etiquette in the technological age.

PRACTICE 5 Read the following conclusions and answer the questions.

A. It doesn't have to be this way. Germany and Japan, because of a combination of government and corporate policies, suffered far

Teaching Tip:
For an enjoyable activity, ask students to print out the introductions and conclusions to one of their essays. Mix up the selections, and then give either an introduction or a conclusion to each student. Ask students to wander around the class matching the introductions with the conclusions.

less worker dislocation in the recession than the U.S. Until we begin to value our workers and understand the critical importance of employment to a thriving economy, we will continue to see our standards of living decline.

—Bob Herbert, "Sin and Shame"

1. What method does the author use to end the conclusion? ___*prediction*___

    B. Mr. Mishra arrived alone in New York in July, and was later joined by two of his sisters. He had been bracing for "serious cultural shock," he said, but his fears evaporated when he walked into the building. "The moment I'm about to enter my apartment, there were dozens of Bhutanese around me," he recalled. "Some looked like my mother, and some looked like my father. They said, 'You will be O.K.'"

—Kirk Semple, "Bhutanese Refugees Find a Toehold in the Bronx"

2. What method does the author use to end the conclusion? ___*quotation*___

    C. In this new millennium, let's put the concept of IQ to rest, once and for all. Stop giving IQ tests. Stop all the studies on IQ and birth order, IQ and nutrition, or IQ and Mozart. Let's find newer, more fluid, and more fair ways to debate and enable human potential. Let's use our heads for a change.

—Dorothy Nixon, "Let's Stop Being Stupid About IQ"

3. What method does the author use to end the conclusion? ___*call to action*___

Hint   **Avoiding Conclusion Problems**

In your conclusion, do not contradict your main point, and do not introduce new or irrelevant information. Also, avoid ending your essay with a rhetorical question, which is a question that cannot be answered, such as "When will humans stop having wars?"

Writer's Desk **Write a Conclusion**

Write a conclusion for the essay you've been preparing in the previous Writer's Desk exercises.

Choosing an Essay Title

Think of a title *after* you have written your essay because you will have a more complete impression of your essay's main point. The most effective titles are brief, depict the topic and purpose of the essay, and attract the reader's attention.

 Capitalizing Titles

Place your title at the top center of your page. Capitalize the first and last words of your title. Also capitalize the main words except for prepositions (*in, at, for, to,* etc.) and articles (*a, an, the*). Leave about an inch of space between the title and the introductory paragraph.

Descriptive Titles

Descriptive titles are the most common titles in academic essays. They depict the topic of the essay clearly and concisely. Sometimes, the writer takes key words from the thesis statement and uses them in the title. Here are two examples of descriptive titles.

> Etiquette in the Technological Age
> Avoiding Mistakes in the First Year of College

Titles Related to the Writing Pattern

You can also relate your title directly to the writing pattern of your essay. Here are examples of titles for different writing patterns.

Illustration:	Problems with Internet Dating
Narration:	My Worst Nightmare
Description:	The Anniversary Party
Process:	How to Handle a Workplace Bully
Definition:	The Meaning of Tolerance
Classification:	Three Types of Fathers
Comparison and Contrast:	Fads Versus Timeless Fashions
Cause and Effect:	The Reasons People Pollute
Argument:	Why Writing Matters

Hint **Avoiding Title Pitfalls**

When you write your title, watch out for problems.

- Do not view your title as a substitute for a thesis statement.
- Do not write a really long title because it can confuse readers.
- Do not put quotation marks around the title of your essay.

PRACTICE 6   Read the next introductions, and underline the thesis statements. Then write titles for each essay.   Answers will vary.

1. Some people fear mistakes more than others fear snakes. Perfectionism refers to self-defeating thoughts and behaviors aimed at reaching excessively high, unrealistic goals. Unfortunately, nobody is perfect. <u>In fact, there are many problems associated with the desire to be perfect.</u>

    Title: _____

2. Gang life, once associated with large urban centers in the United States, has become a common part of adolescent experience in towns and rural areas. Many of the gang members have no strong role models at home, and their gang affiliation makes them feel like part of a powerful group. <u>To combat the problems associated with youth gangs, adults need to give adolescents more responsibilities.</u>

    Title: _____

3. "A person who is not initiated is still a child," says Malidoma Somé. Somé is from the Dagara Tribe in West Africa, and he underwent a six-week initiation ceremony. Left alone in the bush with no food or clothing, he developed a profound appreciation of nature and of magic. When he returned to his village, everyone welcomed him and other initiates with food and dancing. Somé had passed from childhood into adulthood and was expected to assume adult responsibilities. The ceremony helped Somé and the other initiates feel that they were valued participants in village life. <u>Our culture should have formal initiation ceremonies for adolescents.</u>

    Title: _____

PRACTICE 7   Read the next body paragraphs of a short essay. First, highlight the topic sentence in each body paragraph. Then, on a separate sheet of paper, develop a title, a compelling introduction, and a conclusion.   Answers will vary.

Add a title

Add an introduction

Body 1   <u>First, family communication suffers when a television is present.</u> The TV is turned on from morning to night. Families install televisions in the kitchen, living room, and bedrooms. Thus, in locations where families traditionally congregated to talk, they now sit mutely—sometimes next to each other—staring at the screen. Instead of reading a bedtime story together, families deposit children in front of the television to watch a bedtime video. Fourteen-year-old Annie Wong says, "When I get home from school, I head straight for my bedroom. I watch my shows in my room, and my brother watches the TV in the living room. I never have to talk to him."

Body 2 — Too often, when people do communicate, their discussions revolve around television shows. It is common to hear people quoting Dr. Phil or Oprah, and water cooler conversations often revolve around the latest hot series. Thirty-year-old William and his friend Jay love nothing more than to reminisce about their favorite programs. They are big fans of *Glee* and discuss each episode in detail. They also love theme songs. "I know the songs for about fifteen television shows," William says, as he proceeds to do the *Fresh Prince of Bel-Air* rap. Jay admits that his conversations with William rarely stray beyond the lightness of the television world.

Body 3 — Most importantly, the health of children has changed since the introduction of television. Before televisions existed, children played outdoors and spent most of their free time doing physical activities. Today, most children pass hours sitting or lying down as they stare at the television screen. According to Anna Franklin, a researcher at the Mayo Clinic, such inactivity is contributing to the obesity epidemic in our nation. Ben Tyler, a 10-year-old from Fort Lauderdale, admits that he watches between six and eight hours of television each day. "I can watch whatever I want," he says proudly. But Ben is also overweight and suffers from asthma.

Add a conclusion

Writing the First Draft

After arranging the supporting ideas in a logical order, and after creating an introduction and conclusion, you are ready to write your first draft. The first draft includes your introduction, several body paragraphs, and your concluding paragraph.

Teaching Tip:

Cooperative Learning (Jigsaw) Ask all students to read the body paragraphs in Practice 6. The class can have a discussion to find the best thesis statement for the essay. Then place students in groups of three or four. Ask each team to write an introduction using one of the listed introduction styles on pages 42–43. Teams can then share their introductions with the class, or they can regroup and share their introductions with their new teammates. If you have enough time, you can also ask teams to write the conclusion for the essay.

Writer's Desk **Write the First Draft**

In the previous Writer's Desk exercises, you wrote an introduction, a conclusion, and an essay plan. Now write the first draft of your essay.

Teaching Tip:

Cooperative Learning (Ask & Learn) Ask students to review the chapter and identify any content that they are not completely clear about. Then each student should write down two questions about the unclear topic. Finally, working in teams, students can ask other members their questions and share answers.

The Writer's Room   Topics to Develop

Writing Activity I

Choose an essay plan that you developed for Chapter 3, and write the first draft of your essay.

Writing Activity 2

Write the first draft of an essay about one of the following thesis statements.

General Topics

1. In divorce cases, grandparents should receive visitation rights.
2. Movies and television shows glorify crime and criminals.
3. Lying is appropriate in certain situations.
4. I would like to improve three of my traits.

College and Work-Related Topics

5. People go to college for the following reasons.
6. Getting fired can be a liberating experience.
7. Compare learning from experience versus learning from books.
8. I do (or do not) have the skills to be a salesperson.

Teaching Tip:
Writer's World Competition
Please advise students that they can submit their paragraphs and essays for possible publication to www.pearsonhighered.com/essayrewards/writingrewards.html

✔ CHECKLIST: FIRST DRAFT

When you develop the first draft, ask yourself these questions.

☐ Do I have a compelling introduction?

☐ Does my introduction lead into a clear thesis statement?

☐ Do my body paragraphs contain interesting and sufficient details?

☐ Do the body paragraphs support the idea presented in the thesis statement?

☐ Do I have an interesting title that sums up the essay topic?

☐ Does my conclusion bring my essay to a satisfactory close?

mywritinglab To check your progress in meeting this chapter's objectives, log in to **www.mywritinglab.com**, go to the **Study Plan** tab, click on **The Writing Process** and choose **Developing the First Draft** from the list of subtopics. Read and view the resources in the **Review Materials** section, and then complete the **Recall, Apply**, and **Write** sets in the **Activities** section.

Revising and Editing

CHAPTER 5

Revising and editing are similar to adding the finishing touches to a garden. A gardener adds new plants or transplants flowers and shrubs to enhance a garden. Similarly, a writer revises details and edits errors to improve an essay.

Key Steps in Revising and Editing

The revising and editing stage is the final step in the writing process. When you **revise**, you modify your writing to make it stronger and more convincing. To revise, read your first draft critically and look for faulty logic, poor organization, and poor sentence style. Then reorganize and rewrite the draft, making any necessary changes. When you **edit**, you proofread your final draft for errors in grammar, spelling, punctuation, and mechanics.

There are five key steps to follow during the revising and editing stage.

REVISING AND EDITING

STEP 1 ➤ **Revise for unity.** Make sure that all parts of your work relate to the main idea.

STEP 2 ➤ **Revise for adequate support.** Determine that your details effectively support the main idea.

STEP 3 ➤ **Revise for coherence.** Verify that your ideas flow smoothly and logically.

STEP 4 ➤ **Revise for style.** Make sure that your sentences are varied and interesting.

STEP 5 ➤ **Edit for technical errors.** Proofread your work, and correct errors in grammar, spelling, mechanics, and punctuation.

Revising for Unity

Teaching Tip: Explain that every idea in an essay must move in the same direction, just as this road goes straight ahead. There should be no forks in the road.

Unity means that the ideas in an essay clearly support the focus of the essay. All information heads in the same direction, and there are no forks in the road. If an essay lacks unity, then some ideas drift away from the main idea a writer has expressed in the essay. To check for unity in an essay, consider the following:

- Make sure that all topic sentences in the body paragraphs support the thesis statement of the essay.
- Make sure that all sentences within a body paragraph support the topic sentence of that paragraph.

Essay Without Unity

The next essay plan looks at the reasons for deforestation. The third topic sentence veers away from the writer's central focus that deforestation has implications for the quality of life.

Thesis Statement: Deforestation in the Amazon has tremendous implications for people's quality of life.

Topic Sentence 1: First, logging, mining, and agriculture displace the indigenous population in the Amazon.

Topic Sentence 2: Also, scientists believe that deforestation in the Amazon will lead to a rapid increase in global climate change, which will affect people worldwide.

Topic Sentence 3: Many development experts are trying to find methods to have sustainable development in the Amazon.

◄ This topic sentence strays from the thesis of this essay.

PRACTICE I   The following thesis statements have three supporting points that can be developed into body paragraphs. Circle the point that does not support the thesis statement.

1. North Americans have created a throw-away culture.
   a. First, waste from disposable containers and packaging has increased during the last one hundred years.
   b. Old appliances can be recycled.
   c. Consumers throw away about 40 percent of edible food.

2. Thesis Statement: International adoptions should be banned.
   a. Too many celebrities have adopted internationally.
   b. An internationally adopted child will often lose contact with his or her culture.
   c. By adopting from poor countries, wealthy Westerners contribute to the exploitation of mothers who cannot afford to keep their babies.

Teaching Tip:
Ask students to think of three points that argue in favor of international adoptions.

Paragraph Without Unity

Not only must your essay have unity, but each body paragraph must have unity. The details in the paragraph must support the paragraph's topic sentence. In the next paragraph, which is part of a larger work, the writer drifted away from his main idea. Some sentences do not relate to the topic sentence. If the highlighted sentences are removed, then the paragraph has unity.

Americans should not fear the practice of outsourcing by businesses. First, outsourcing is the same practice as subcontracting. In the past, many companies subcontracted work to companies within the same country. Now, businesses simply subcontract to companies in other nations. Furthermore, outsourcing usually leads to higher profits because the product or service is produced more cost effectively. Therefore, the head company's profit margin increases. The company can then reinvest in domestic markets. In addition, when a company increases its profit, not only do the stockholders benefit, but so do the employees of the company. The stockholders receive more value for their stock, and the employees receive more salaries and benefits. But my sister is against outsourcing. She worked in computers, and her job became obsolete when her company outsourced the work to India. Now my sister is devastated. Thus, with more disposable income, people can help the domestic economy by buying more products.

The writer ➤ detours here.

Teaching Tip: Remind students that the topic sentence must be supported by everything else in the paragraph.

PRACTICE 2   Paragraphs A and B contain problems with unity. In each paragraph, underline the topic sentence and cross out any sentences that do not support the controlling idea.

Paragraph A

Academic performance of students weakens if they are sleep deprived. Therefore, our college should implement a few rules to help students get enough sleep. First, the college should actively promote physical exercise for students. People who exercise regularly find it easier to fall asleep at night. I am a member of the badminton team. This year, I am coaching the new team members. Classes could also start one hour later to give students an extra hour to sleep. Or students could have an hour free in the afternoon. Some students would take advantage of this free period to take a nap. Finally, the college could offer seminars and sleep clinics to educate students about the consequences of too little sleep. If the college implements these small changes, students' grades may improve.

Paragraph B

The electric car is not as good for the environment as many people think. First, many people buy electric cars thinking that such vehicles produce no carbon dioxide emissions. Consumers forget how electricity is produced. Most electricity plants generate power by burning coal, oil, or diesel fuel. In fact, burning coal releases many contaminants into the air, which creates a great deal of air pollution. Moreover, electric car batteries contain toxic ingredients. If these are not properly recycled, they could contaminate landfill sites. My friend is in the market for a car, and we are going to test-drive a few on the weekend. He is considering both new and used cars. So think carefully about environmental concerns before buying your next car.

Revising for Adequate Support

An arch is built using several well-placed stones. Like an arch, an essay requires **adequate support** to help it stand on its own.

ESL
Teaching Tip:
In many cultures, people use circular reasoning because they believe that stating a point directly is rude or aggressive. Explain to the class that it is important to express a point upfront and to support it with clear evidence.

When revising an essay for adequate support, consider the following:

- Make sure that your thesis statement is broad enough to be supported by several points. You may need to revise the thesis statement to meet the length requirements of the essay.
- When you write the body paragraphs of the essay, insert specific details and try to include vivid descriptions, anecdotes, examples, facts, or quotations.

Avoid Circular Reasoning

Circular reasoning means that a paragraph restates its main point in various ways but does not provide supporting details. Like a driver aimlessly going around and around a traffic circle, the main idea never seems to progress. Avoid using circular reasoning by directing your paragraph with a clear, concise topic sentence and by supporting the topic sentence with facts, examples, statistics, or anecdotes.

Paragraph with Circular Reasoning

The following paragraph contains circular reasoning. The main point is repeated over and over. The writer does not provide any evidence to support the topic sentence.

> Traveling is a necessary educational tool. Students can learn a lot by visiting other countries. Many schools offer educational trips to other places for their students. Students may benefit from such cultural introductions. Clearly, traveling offers students an important educational opportunity.

◄ This writer leads the reader in circles.

In the second version of this paragraph, the paragraph contains specific examples that help to illustrate the main point.

Revised Paragraph

Traveling is a necessary educational tool. Students can learn a lot by visiting other places. Many schools and colleges offer educational trips. On such trips, students visit museums, art galleries, and historical sites. For example, the art department of our college sponsored a trip to Washington, D.C., and the students visited the Smithsonian. Other travel programs are work programs. Students may travel to another region or country to be involved in a community project. Students in the local high school, for example, helped build a community center for children in a small town in Nicaragua. The students who participated in this project all said that they learned some very practical lessons, including organizational and construction skills. Clearly, traveling offers students an important educational opportunity.

Anecdotes and examples provide ➤ *supporting evidence.*

PRACTICE 3   Read the following paragraphs, and write OK next to the ones that have adequate support. Underline the specific details in those paragraphs. Then, to the paragraphs that lack adequate support, add details such as descriptions, examples, quotations, or anecdotes. Use arrows to indicate where you should place specific details.   Answers will vary.

The next example is from an essay. In the first paragraph, the writer was repetitive and vague. After the writer added specific examples and vivid details, the paragraph was much more interesting.

Weak Support

To become a better dresser, follow the next steps. First, ask friends or family members what colors suit you. Also, don't be a slave to the latest fashion. Finally, spend money on a few good items rather than filling your closet with cheap outfits. My closet is half-full, but the clothing I have is of good quality.

Better Support with Details

To become a better dresser, follow the next steps. First, ask friends or family members what colors suit you. *I love green, for instance, but when I wore an olive green shirt, a close friend said it brought out the green in my skin and made me look ill.* Also, don't be a slave to the latest fashion. *Although tank tops and low-rise jeans were popular for several years, I didn't have the right body type for that fashion because my belly spilled over the tops of my jeans. Instead, I wore longer shirts with my jeans, so I looked stylish but not ridiculous.* Finally, spend money on a few good items rather than filling your closet with cheap outfits. My closet is half-full, but the clothing I have is of good quality.

1. **Many cyclists are inconsiderate.** Some think that they don't have to obey traffic rules and that traffic signs are just for car drivers. Also, some cyclists are pretty crazy and do dangerous things and risk their lives or the lives of others. People have ended up in the hospital after a run-in with these two-wheeled rebels. Cyclists should take safety courses before they ride on public roads.

   Write OK or add details
   Cyclists don't stop at stop signs. Last week I saw a rider cycling the wrong way on a one-way street.

   They weave in and out of traffic. I have been nearly run off the sidewalk by frantic bicycle couriers.

2. **During my first job interview, I managed to overcome my fright.** I sat in a small, brightly lit room in front of four interviewers. A stern woman stared at me intently and curtly asked me why I wanted the job. <u>Perspiration dripped into my eyes as I stammered that I had seen an advertisement.</u> She smirked and asked me to be more specific. <u>Feeling that I didn't have a chance anyway, I relaxed and stopped worrying about the faces gazing at me.</u> <u>I spoke about my first experience in a hospital, and I described the nurses who took care of me and the respectful way the orderlies treated me. I expressed my heartfelt desire to work as an orderly,</u> and I got the job.

   Write OK or add details
   OK

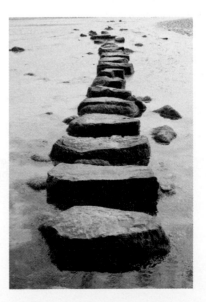

Revising for Coherence

Make your writing as smooth as possible by using expressions that logically guide the reader from one idea to the next. When revising an essay for **coherence**, consider the following:

- Ensure that sentences within each body paragraph flow smoothly by using transitional expressions.
- Ensure the supporting ideas of an essay are connected to each other and to the thesis statement by using paragraph links.

Teaching Tip:
Remind students
that transitional
expressions are
followed by a
comma. If they are
placed between
two independent
clauses, then they
are preceded by a
semicolon. Read the
following examples:

*Therefore, fast-food
chains should list
product ingredients.*

*I love eating fast food;
however, I haven't
gone to a fast-food
restaurant in months.*

ESL

Teaching Tip:

**Cooperative
Learning
(Sharing Circle)**
If you have a large
number of
nonnative speakers
in your class, do the
following. Give
students one minute
to underline words
or expressions that
they do not fully
understand. If some
students say, "I
understand all of
the words," then
designate them as
experts. Create
teams that are
mixed with native
and nonnative
speakers. Those
who understand the
terms can teach
the others by using
the terms in
sentences.

Transitional Expressions

Just as stepping stones can help you cross from one side of the water to the other, **transitional expressions** can help readers cross from idea to idea in an essay. Here are some common transitional expressions.

Function	Transitional Word or Expression		
Addition	again also besides finally first (second, third)	for one thing furthermore in addition in fact	last moreover next then
Comparison and contrast	as well equally even so however	in contrast instead likewise nevertheless	on the contrary on the other hand similarly
Concession of a point	certainly even so	indeed of course	no doubt to be sure
Effect or result	accordingly as a result consequently	hence otherwise then	therefore thus
Emphasis	above all clearly first especially in fact	in particular indeed least of all most important	most of all of course particularly principally
Example	for example for instance in other words	in particular namely	specifically to illustrate
Reason or purpose	because for this purpose	for this reason the most important reason	
Space	above behind below beneath beside beyond closer in	farther out inside near nearby on one side/the other side on the bottom	on the left/right on top outside to the north/east/ south/west under
Summary or conclusion	in conclusion in other words in short generally	on the whole therefore thus	to conclude to summarize ultimately
Time	after that at that time at the moment currently earlier eventually first (second, etc.) gradually	immediately in the beginning in the future in the past later meanwhile months after now	one day presently so far subsequently suddenly then these days

> ⟨*Hint*⟩ **Use Transitional Expressions with Complete Sentences**
>
> When you add a transitional expression to a sentence, make sure that your sentence is complete. Your sentence must have a subject and a verb, and it must express a complete thought.
>
> **Incomplete:** For example, violence on television.
>
> **Complete:** For example, violence on television <u>is very graphic</u>.

Adding Transitional Words Within a Paragraph

The next paragraph shows transitional words linking sentences within a paragraph.

GRAMMAR LINK

For more practice using transitions in sentences, see Chapter 21, Sentence Combining.

Have you ever started a workout program and after a few weeks stopped doing it? There are several steps that you can take to stay motivated. **First**, try activities that you like to do. For example, if you hate exercising on machines, you could try swimming. **Next**, schedule your exercise activities in advance. Choose a time and plan other activities around your workout times. **In addition**, participate in a variety of exercises. If you keep doing the same activity all the time, you will get bored and lose your motivation. **Finally**, promise yourself a little treat after you have completed your workout. A little self-indulgence is a good motivator, so reward yourself.

PRACTICE 4 Add appropriate transitional expressions to the following paragraph. Choose from the following list, and use each transitional word once. There may be more than one correct answer. Answers will vary.

in addition	therefore	in fact	for instance
first	then	for example	moreover

Counterculture is a pattern of beliefs and actions that oppose the cultural norms of a society. _____*First,*_____ hippies are the best-known countercultural group in the recent past, and they are known for rebelling against authority. _____*For instance,*_____ they rejected the consumer-based capitalist society of their parents in favor of communal living arrangements. _____*Moreover,*_____ the hippie generation valued peace and created a massive antiwar movement. _____*In fact,*_____ there were mass protests against the Vietnam War. _____ *Also,* _____ small religious groups belong to the countercultural current. These groups live with other like-minded people and turn away from widely accepted ideas on lifestyle. _____ *For example,* _____ the Amish reject modern technology. _____ *In addition,* _____ militant groups and anarchist groups reject conventional laws. Some of these groups want to eliminate legal, political, and social institutions. There will always be countercultural movements in society.

PRACTICE 5   The next paragraph lacks transitional expressions. Add appropriate transitional expressions wherever you think they are necessary.   Answers will vary.

First,

People in our culture tend to idolize notorious gangsters. Al Capone operated during Prohibition, selling alcohol and building a criminal empire. He *Then,* became infamous, and his name is instantly recognizable. The Gotti family's patriarch was the head of a large and vicious crime family in New Jersey. The family members are celebrities, and one of the daughters, Victoria Gotti, had *Moreover,* her own reality television show. Filmmakers contribute to the idealization of *For example,* criminals. Movies such as *The Godfather* and *Live Free or Die Trying* celebrate gangsters and criminals. Gangsters appear to have exciting and glamorous lives. It is unfortunate that our culture elevates criminals to heroic status.

Making Links in Essays

To achieve coherence in an essay, try the following methods to move from one idea to the next.

1. **Repeat words or phrases from the thesis statement in the topic sentence of each body paragraph.** In this example, *giftedness* and *ambiguity* are repeated words.

Thesis Statement:	Although many schools offer a program for gifted children, there continues to be ambiguity concerning the definition of gifted.
Body Paragraph 1:	One ambiguity is choosing the criteria for assessing the gifted.
Body Paragraph 2:	Another ambiguity pertains to defining the fields or areas in which a person is gifted.

2. **Refer to the main idea in the previous paragraph, and link it to your current topic sentence.** In the topic sentence for the second body paragraph, the writer reminds the reader of the first point (*insomnia*) and then introduces the next point.

Thesis Statement:	Sleeping disorders cause severe disruption to many people's lives.
Body Paragraph 1:	Insomnia, a common sleep disorder, severely limits the sufferer's quality of life.
Body Paragraph 2:	The opposite condition of insomnia, narcolepsy also causes mayhem as the sufferer struggles to stay awake.

Teaching Tip:
Students may overuse transitional words. Remind students to use transitions only when they think a reader might need further guidance to navigate from one idea to the next.

3. **Use a transitional word or phrase to lead the reader to your next idea.**

Body Paragraph 3:	Moreover, when sufferers go untreated for their sleep disorders, they pose risks to the people around them.

Revising for Style

When you revise for sentence **style**, you ensure that your essay has concise and appropriate language and sentence variety. You can ask yourself the following questions.

- Have I used a variety of sentence patterns? (To practice using sentence variety, see Chapter 22.)
- Are my sentences parallel in structure? (To practice revising for parallel structure, see Chapter 25.)
- Have I used exact language? (To learn about slang, wordiness, and overused expressions, see Chapter 33.)

Alicia's Revision

In Chapter 3, you read Alicia's essay plan about college dropouts. After writing her first draft, she revised her essay. Look at her revisions for unity, support, coherence, and style.

Add title. ➤

Dropping Out of College

I live in a small coastal town on the Atlantic. The town attracts tourists from all over the country. Because of its beautiful beach. My college roommate, Farrad, works as a cook at the local pizza stand. Last year, Farrad started working a few hours per week, but because of his efficiency, his boss increased Farrad's hours. My roommate then joined a growing group of people. He became a

Thesis ➤
statement

college dropout. **Students may drop out of college because they lack financial support, experience an emotional crisis, or are unprepared.**

Add transition. ➤

First, some
~~Some~~ students drop out because they face overwhelming
^

financial burdens. Like Farrad, they may have a part-time job to

According to an Indiana government Web site, Investment Watch, "Teenagers and young adults often find themselves in high debt with little knowledge of basic savings and budgeting concepts. About 40 percent of Americans spend 110 percent of their income."

Add detail. ➤

help pay for tuition and rent. If the job requires students to work for
^

many hours, they might not have time to study or to do homework.

Add detail. ➤

The number of hours is overwhelming and she may drop out of college.
Nadia, for exemple, works in the computer lab four nights a week.
^

Clarify pronoun. ➤

Some students
~~They~~ also drop out because they live far from campus.

Transportation may be too expensive or inconvenient.

Combine ➤
sentences.

events, and they
Furthermore, some students undergo life-changing events. ~~They~~

In an interview with CNN, Dr. William Pepicello, president of the University of Phoenix, stated that one reason that students drop out is "life gets in the way."

must leave college. A college student may get married, or a
^

female student may become pregnant and taking care of a

Revise for unity. ➤

baby may consume all of her time and energy. ~~There are public and private daycare centers. But parents must choose very carefully.~~

Add transition. ➤

In addition, an
~~An~~ illness in the family may cause a student to miss too many

classes. A student may feel emotionaly fragile because of a broken relationship. The student may not be able to cope with their feelings and wanted to leave college.

adapt to

Moreover, some students may be unable to ~~get into~~ ◄ Find better word.

college life. Some have poor study skills and fall behind in homework assignments. Students may not be able to organize there time. Or a student might be unused to freedom in college and skip too many classes. For instance, my lab partner has missed about

In addition, not

six classes this semester. ~~Not~~ every student has career plans. ◄ Add transition.

According to the National Academic Advising Association (NACADA) Web site, 75 percent of first-year students do not have clear career goals.

Those who are unsure about their academic futur may drop ◄ Add detail.

For instance, my cousin realized she did not want to be an engineer, so she left school until she could figure out what she really wanted to do.

out rather than continue to study in a field they do not enjoy. ◄ Add detail.

Even though students drop out of college for many good

For example,

reasons, some decide to return to college life. Farrad hopes to ◄ Add transition.

finish his studies next year. *He knows he would have to find a better balance* ◄ Improve conclusion.
between work and school to succeed, but he is motivated to complete his education.

Hint   **Enhancing Your Essay**

When you revise, look at the strength of your supporting details. Ask yourself the following questions.

- Are my supporting details interesting, and will they grab my reader's attention? Should I use more vivid vocabulary?
- Is my concluding sentence appealing? Could I end the paragraph in a more interesting way?

Editing for Errors

When you **edit**, you reread your writing to make sure that it is free of errors. You focus on the language, and you look for mistakes in grammar, punctuation, mechanics, and spelling.

There is an editing guide on the inside back cover of this book. It contains some common error codes that your instructor may use. It also provides you with a list of errors to check for when you proofread your text.

GRAMMAR LINK
To practice your editing skills, try the practices in Chapter 39.

Editing Tips

The following tips will help you to proofread your work more effectively.

- Put your text aside for a day or two before you do the editing. Sometimes, when you have been working closely with a text, you might not see the errors.
- Begin your proofreading at any stage of the writing process. For example, if you are not sure of the spelling of a word while writing the first draft, either you could highlight the word to remind yourself to verify it later, or you could immediately look up the word in the dictionary.
- Use the grammar and spelling checker that comes with your word processor. However, be vigilant when accepting the suggestions. Do not always choose the first suggestion for a correction. For example, a grammar checker cannot distinguish between when to use *which* and *that*. Make sure that suggestions are valid before you accept them.
- Keep a list of your common errors in a separate grammar log. When you finish a writing assignment, consult your error list and make sure that you have not repeated any of those errors. After you have received each corrected assignment from your instructor, you can add new errors to your list. For more information about a grammar and spelling log, see Appendix 6.

Teaching Tip:
If your students are familiar with grammatical terms, you might ask them to identify the types of errors in the paragraph. (Types are fragment, spelling, tense shift, pronoun shift, and punctuation.)

Alicia's Edited Essay

Alicia edited her essay about college dropouts. She corrected errors in spelling, punctuation, and grammar.

Dropping Out of College

I live in a small coastal town on the Atlantic. The town attracts tourists from all over the country. ~~Because~~ *country because* of its beautiful beach. My college roommate, Farrad, works as a cook at the local pizza stand. Last year, Farrad started working a few hours per week, but because of his efficiency, his boss increased Farrad's hours. My roommate then joined a growing group of people. He became a college dropout. Students may drop out of college because they lack financial support, experience an emotional crisis, or are unprepared.

First, some students drop out because they face overwhelming financial burdens. Like Farrad, they may have a part-time job to help pay for tuition and rent. According to an Indiana government Web site, *Investment Watch*, "Teenagers and young adults often find themselves in high debt with little knowledge of basic savings and budgeting concepts. About 40 percent of Americans spend 110 percent of their income." If the job requires students to work for many hours, they might not have time to study or to do homework. Nadia, for ~~exemple~~ *example*, works in the computer lab four nights a week. The number of hours is overwhelming, and she may drop out of college. Some students also drop out because they live far from campus. Transportation may be too expensive or inconvenient.

Furthermore, some students undergo life-changing events, and they must leave college. In an interview with CNN, Dr. William Pepicello, president of the University of Phoenix, stated that one reason that students drop out is "life gets in the way." A college student may get married, or a female student may become pregnant and taking care of a baby may consume all of her time and energy. In addition, an illness in the family may cause a student to miss too many classes. A student may also feel ~~emotionaly~~ *emotionally* fragile because of a broken relationship. The student may not be able to cope with ~~their~~ *his or her* feelings and ~~wanted~~ *want* to leave college.

Moreover, some students may be unable to adapt to college life. Some have poor study skills and fall behind in homework assignments. Also, students may not be able to organize ~~there~~ *their* time. Or a student might not be used to freedom in college and skip too many classes. For instance, my lab partner has missed about six classes this semester. In addition, not every student has career plans. According to the National Academic Advising Association (NACADA) Web site, 75 percent of first-year students do not have clear career goals. Those who are unsure about their academic ~~futur~~ *future* may drop out rather than continue to study in a field they do not enjoy. For instance, my cousin realized she did not want to be an engineer, so she left school until she could figure out what she really wanted to do.

Even though students drop out of college for many good reasons, some decide to return to college life. Farrad, for example, hopes to finish his studies next year. He knows he ~~would~~ *will* have to find a better balance between work and school to succeed, but he is motivated to complete his education.

Writer's Desk   Revise and Edit Your Paragraph

Choose an essay that you have written for Chapter 4, or choose one that you have written for another assignment. Carefully revise and edit the essay. You can refer to the Revising and Editing checklists on the inside covers.

Peer Feedback

After you write an essay, it is useful to get peer feedback. Ask a friend, family member, or fellow student to read your work and give you comments and suggestions on its strengths and weaknesses.

Offer Constructive Criticism

When you peer edit someone else's writing, try to make your comments useful. Phrase your comments in a positive way. Look at the examples.

Instead of saying . . .   **You could say . . .**
You repeat the same words.   Maybe you could find synonyms for some words.
Your paragraphs are too short.   You could add more details here.

Teaching Tip:
Draw attention to this hint. Students should encourage each other by offering constructive criticism.

You can use this peer feedback form to evaluate written work.

Peer Feedback Form

Written by _____   Feedback by _____

Date: _____

1. What is the main point of the written work? _____
   _____
   _____

2. Which details effectively support the thesis statement? _____
   _____
   _____

3. What, if anything, is unclear or unnecessary? _____
   _____
   _____

4. Give some suggestions about how the work could be improved. _____
   _____
   _____

5. What is the most interesting feature of this written work? _____
   _____
   _____

Writing the Final Draft

When you have finished making revisions on the first draft of your essay, write the final draft. Include all the changes that you have made during the revising and editing phases. Before you submit your final draft, proofread it one last time to make sure that you have caught any errors.

Writer's Desk   Write Your Final Draft

You have developed, revised, and edited your essay. Now write the final draft.

Hint   Spelling, Grammar, and Vocabulary Logs

- **Keep a Spelling and Grammar Log.** You probably repeat, over and over, the same types of grammar and spelling errors. You will find it very useful to record your repeated grammar mistakes in a Spelling and Grammar Log. You can refer to your list of spelling and grammar mistakes when you revise and edit your writing.
- **Keep a Vocabulary Log.** Expanding your vocabulary will be of enormous benefit to you as a writer. In a Vocabulary Log, you can make a list of unfamiliar words and their definitions.

See Appendix 6 for more information about spelling, grammar, and vocabulary logs.

Teaching Tip:
To verify that students understand the essay-writing process, you can suggest that they write an essay explaining the essay-writing process.

The Writer's Room   Essay Topics

Writing Activity 1

Choose an essay that you have written for this course or for another course. Revise and edit that essay, and then write a final draft.

Writing Activity 2

Choose any of the following topics, or choose your own topic, and then write an essay. Remember to follow the writing process.

General Topics

1. online shopping
2. a problem in politics
3. unfair gender roles
4. making the world better

College and Work-Related Topics

5. something you learned in college
6. bad work habits
7. unpleasant jobs
8. a funny co-worker

✔ CHECKLIST: REVISING AND EDITING

When you revise and edit your essay, ask yourself the following questions.

☐ Does my essay have **unity**? Ensure that every paragraph relates to the main idea.

☐ Does my essay have **adequate support**? Verify that there are enough details and examples to support your main point.

☐ Is my essay **coherent**? Try to use transitional expressions to link ideas.

☐ Does my essay have good **style**? Check for varied sentence patterns and exact language.

☐ Does my essay have any errors? **Edit** for errors in grammar, punctuation, spelling, and mechanics.

☐ Is my **final draft** error-free?

Teaching Tip:
Writer's World Competition
Please advise students that they can submit their paragraphs and essays for possible publication to www.pearsonhighered.com/essayrewards/writingrewards.html

mywritinglab To check your progress in meeting this chapter's objectives, log in to **www.mywritinglab.com,** go to the **Study Plan** tab, click on **The Writing Process** and choose **Revising and Editing** from the list of subtopics. Read and view the resources in the **Review Materials** section, and then complete the **Recall, Apply,** and **Write** sets in the **Activities** section.

Essay Patterns

What Is an Essay Pattern?

A pattern or mode is a method used to express one of the three purposes: to inform, to persuade, or to entertain. Once you know your purpose, you will be able to choose which writing pattern to use.

Patterns may overlap. You can combine writing patterns. You may use one predominant pattern, but you can also introduce other patterns in supporting material.

Illustration
to illustrate or prove a point using specific examples

Narration
to narrate or tell a story about a sequence of events that happened

Process
to inform the reader about how to do something, how something works, or how something happened

Description
to describe using vivid details and images that appeal to the reader's senses

Definition
to explain what a term or concept means by providing relevant examples

Classification
to classify or sort a topic to help readers understand different qualities about that topic

Comparison and Contrast
to present information about similarities (compare) or differences (contrast)

Cause and Effect
to explain why an event happened (the cause) or what the consequences of the event were (the effects)

Argument*
to argue or to take a position on an issue and offer reasons for your position

*Argument is included as one of the nine patterns, but it is also a purpose in writing.

Illustration

Health clubs advertise a variety of activities that customers can do to get in shape. In the same way, writers have a better chance of persuading readers when they illustrate their ideas using examples.

Writers' Exchange

Work with a partner. You have three minutes to list as many words as you can that are examples of the following. For example, bungee jumping is a dangerous sport.

annoying habits   dangerous sports   comfort food

Teaching Tip: In Chapters 6–14, the Writer's Exchange, What Is Illustration? and Visualizing the Modes help students with different learning styles (auditory, tactile, and visual) understand the particular mode.

EXPLORING

What Is Illustration?

Illustration writing includes specific examples that help readers acquire a clearer, deeper understanding of an essay's subject. You illustrate or give examples each time you explain, analyze, narrate, or express an opinion. Examples might include something that you have experienced or observed, or they may include factual information, such as a statistic.

People use illustration every day. At home, a parent might list ways that a child's room is becoming messy. At college, classmates may share examples of how they have been given too much homework. At work, an employee could list examples of ways for the company to save money.

Visualizing Illustration

PRACTICE I   Brainstorm supporting ideas for the following thesis statement. List examples on the lines provided.   Answers will vary.

THESIS STATEMENT: The average person's diet contains too much junk food.

sugar and lard in pies

mystery meat in hot dogs

salty and buttery popcorn

pizza with sausage

sugar-filled cake

fatty burgers

greasy fries

The Illustration Essay

There are two effective ways to exemplify your main point and support your body paragraphs in an illustration essay.

1. Use a **series of examples**. When writing an essay about innovative commercials, you might list things that some directors do, such as using bizarre camera angles, introducing hilarious scenarios, adding amusing jingles, or creating catchy slogans.

2. Use an **extended example**, such as an anecdote or a description of an event. When writing about problems faced by first-year college students, you might tell a story about a specific student's chronic lateness.

Illustration at Work

Portland Bolt and Manufacturing Company requires a large sales force. In the following excerpt from a job announcement on the company's Web site, there is a list of examples showing what a sales associate must do. These examples give job seekers a clear understanding of the responsibilities expected of sales associates.

Sales Associate Duties

- Estimating the costs associated with manufacturing bolts.
- Assigning appropriate profit margins to estimates.
- Selling bolts and fasteners primarily via the telephone to an established customer base made up of contractors, steel fabricators, and other construction-related companies.
- Tracking and following up a small quantity of specific construction projects.
- Making sales order entries.
- Doing a limited amount of prospecting.
- (Optional) Limited selling in both the local and regional marketplace.

A Student Essay

Read the student essay, and answer the questions that follow.

Priceless Euphoria
by Lisa Monique

1   The Beatles recorded a song, satirically titled *Money,* in which they sing, "The best things in life are free." Undoubtedly, the best things in life are free. Although costs might be associated, these "things" are not purchased items. The best things are a common thread among all people regardless of sex, race, religion, or nationality. In fact, the best things in life are not things but are precious segments in time involving and engaging us in experiences, emotions, and various states of being.

2   Nature provides us with many priceless treasures of breathtaking scenery. We might view a cascading waterfall, a brilliant sunset casting a serene, pink glow on the mountain jags and peaks, or the glistening beauty of a fresh, undisturbed snowfall. Each location we visit stimulates the senses. A day at the beach allows us to listen to crashing waves, watch a school of dolphins play, splash in the shallow water, or bury our feet in the gushy, wet sand. The desert is also a smorgasbord of sensations. Marvels include the mighty Saguaro cacti, the ethereal haze of the Palo Verde trees, and the grace and gentleness of a passing butterfly.

3   Emotional experiences, as well, are often the best "things" in life. Falling in love, viewing the birth of a child, having the first kiss, laughing and conversing with an old friend, and watching the klutzy steps of a puppy are some simple delights in life. Emotional experiences can occur with loved ones, but they can also be kindled in natural environments. A day at the beach is renewing and refreshing. Hiking in the desert helps us to feel wild, free, and reckless. The purity of a fresh snowfall makes us feel childlike and innocent.

4   Similarly, states of being bring great satisfaction, which is, yet again, a great thing. Good health after a prolonged illness or even after a short bout of the flu is a greatly appreciated state of being. Invaluable gratification is derived from meeting a deadline, winning a race, nurturing a garden, sculpting a creation, giving a gift, receiving a gift, dispensing good advice, accepting good advice, planning a successful event, helping someone in need, and achieving a well-earned goal.

5   Money does directly buy cars, jewelry, furs, vacations, large homes, designer clothing, or French perfume. Purchases are not the best "things" in life. It is true that crayons and paper are purchased, but coloring is free. Writing, dancing, laughing, loving, and learning are all beneficial activities with peripheral costs. The value is found in each experience. Consequently, "the best things in life are free" is not just a simple song lyric, but also a rather complex and admirable human philosophy.

Teaching Tip:
The Writer's Desk activities, the first of which appears on the next page, provide students with an opportunity to develop a topic through all stages of the writing process using the illustration rhetorical mode. In the Warm Up, they begin by exploring various topics and examples for illustration. Those topics then carry on throughout the chapter.

PRACTICE 2

1. Who is the intended audience? _____*General audience*_____

2. Highlight the essay's thesis statement.

3. Highlight the topic sentence in each body paragraph.

4. In body paragraphs 2, 3, and 4, what does the writer use?
   (a.) series of examples
   b. extended examples

5. In paragraph 4, what does the writer mean by *states of being*? Using your own words, explain her point.

   She means having good health or doing activities that make a person

   feel satisfied.

6. What organizational strategy does the writer use?
   a. time order   b. space order   (c.) emphatic order

7. Add one more example to each body paragraph.   Answers will vary.

   nature _____

   _____

   emotional experiences _____

   _____

   states of being _____

   _____

Explore Topics

In the Writer's Desk Warm Up, you will try an exploring strategy to generate ideas about different topics.

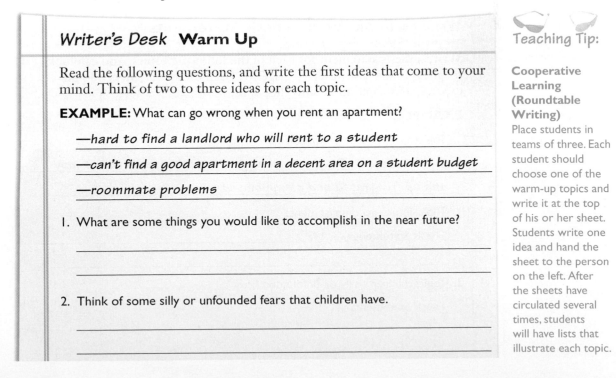

Writer's Desk **Warm Up**

Read the following questions, and write the first ideas that come to your mind. Think of two to three ideas for each topic.

EXAMPLE: What can go wrong when you rent an apartment?

—*hard to find a landlord who will rent to a student*

—*can't find a good apartment in a decent area on a student budget*

—*roommate problems*

1. What are some things you would like to accomplish in the near future?

   _____

   _____

2. Think of some silly or unfounded fears that children have.

   _____

   _____

Teaching Tip:

Cooperative Learning (Roundtable Writing)
Place students in teams of three. Each student should choose one of the warm-up topics and write it at the top of his or her sheet. Students write one idea and hand the sheet to the person on the left. After the sheets have circulated several times, students will have lists that illustrate each topic.

3. What are some status symbols in today's society?

_____

_____

DEVELOPING

The Thesis Statement

The thesis statement of the illustration essay is a general statement that expresses both your topic and your controlling idea. To determine your controlling idea, think about what point you want to make. Remember to express an attitude or point of view about the topic.

topic   controlling idea

Newlyweds often have misconceptions about married life.

controlling idea   topic

I am unable to control **the mess in my work space.**

Writer's Desk **Write Thesis Statements**

Write a thesis statement for each of the following topics. You can look for ideas in the Warm Up on page 81. Each thesis statement should express your topic and controlling idea.   Answers will vary.

EXAMPLE:

Topic: apartment rental problems

Thesis Statement: *Students who want to rent an apartment may end up frustrated and disappointed.*

1. Topic: future accomplishments

    Thesis Statement: _____

    _____

2. Topic: children's silly or unfounded fears

    Thesis Statement: _____

    _____

3. Topic: status symbols in our society

Thesis Statement: _____

_____

The Supporting Ideas

After you have developed an effective thesis statement, generate supporting ideas.

- Use prewriting strategies to generate a list of examples. Brainstorm a series of examples and extended examples that will best illustrate your main point.
- Choose the best ideas. Use either a series of examples or extended examples.
- Organize your ideas. Choose the best organizational method for this essay pattern.

Writer's Desk   Generate Supporting Ideas

Choose one of your thesis statements from the previous Writer's Desk. List three or four examples that support the thesis statement.

EXAMPLE:

Thesis Statement: _Students who want to rent an apartment may end up frustrated and disappointed._

    Supports: —_can't find an affordable place_

    —_landlords might be hesitant to rent to them_

    —_roommates may be immature_

    —_not enough housing for students_

    —_only available housing is in dangerous neighborhood_

Thesis Statement:

_____

_____

    Supports:

_____

_____

_____

_____

ESL
Teaching Tip:
Encourage students from other countries to discuss culture-specific status symbols. Ask them to share thesis statements and ensure that the statement expresses a point and an attitude or point of view. For instance, you could ask them to compare the following two thesis statements. Discuss how the second statement is more specific and expresses a point of view.

There are many status symbols in our culture.

In the business world, status symbols are very superficial.

Teaching Tip:
For extra practice, ask students to develop supporting ideas for all three Writer's Desk topics. The topics are listed in the previous Writer's Desk.

Teaching Tip:
Ask students to
generate specific
details that could
flesh out the first
draft of the sample
essay. For example,
under II A, "They
have limited
choices," details
could be *The student
housing on Maple
Street has only fifty
units.*

Teaching Tip:
Ask students to
keep their essay
plans and attach
them to the final
draft. You can then
determine how
the students have
developed their
ideas.

The Essay Plan

When writing an outline for an illustration essay, make sure that your examples are valid and relate to the thesis statement. Also, include details that will help clarify your supporting examples and organize your ideas in a logical order.

THESIS STATEMENT: <u>Students who want to rent an apartment may end up frustrated and disappointed</u>.

    I. Landlords often hesitate to rent to students.
       A. Young people might be irresponsible.
       B. They don't have credit ratings.
    II. Students have money problems.
       A. They have limited choices.
       B. They cannot apply for nicer apartments because many are too expensive.
       C. They must settle for dives and dumps.
    III. Sharing a place with another student can end badly.
       A. The roommate might be very messy.
       B. The roommate might be a party guy or girl.
       C. There could be financial disputes over unpaid rent and bills.
    IV. Some students choose to rent alone but have other problems.
       A. They may feel lonely.
       B. People living alone may feel unsafe.

Writer's Desk **Write an Essay Plan**

Refer to the information you generated in previous Writer's Desks, and prepare a detailed essay plan. Consider the order in which you list details.

The First Draft

After outlining your ideas in a plan, write the first draft using complete sentences. Also, include transitional words or expressions to help your ideas flow smoothly. Here are some transitional expressions that can help you introduce an example or show an additional example.

To introduce an example		To show an additional example	
for example	namely	also	in addition
for instance	specifically	first (second)	in another case
in other words	to illustrate	furthermore	moreover

Writer's Desk **Write the First Draft**

In the previous Writer's Desk, you developed an essay plan. Now write the first draft of your illustration essay. Remember to include details such as specific names, places, facts, or statistics to flesh out each body paragraph.

vo•cab•u•lar•y BOOST

Here are some ways to vary sentences, which will help you avoid boring readers with repeated phrases.

1. Underline the opening word of every sentence in your first draft. Check to see if some words are repeated.
2. If you notice every sentence begins the same way, try introducing the sentence with an adverb, such as *usually, generally,* or *luckily,* or a prepositional phrase such as *With his help* or *Under the circumstances.* In the following example, *They* is repeated too many times.

Repeated first words

People make many mistakes with their finances. They want luxuries that they cannot afford. They buy items on credit. They do not consider the high interest rates that credit card companies charge.

Variety

People make many mistakes with their finances. Desiring luxuries that they cannot afford, consumers buy items on credit. Sadly, many do not consider the high interest rates that credit card companies charge.

REVISING AND EDITING

Revise and Edit an Illustration Essay

When you finish writing an illustration essay, review your work and revise it to make the examples as clear as possible to your readers. Make sure that the order of ideas is logical, and remove any irrelevant details. Before you work on your own essay, practice revising and editing a student essay.

A Student Essay

Read the essay, and then answer the questions that follow. As you read, correct any errors that you find and make comments in the margins.

Teaching Tip:
The activity of revising and editing a student essay should help your students understand the important link between the writing process and the grammar chapters.

Finding an Apartment
by Shannon Nolan

1   Renting an apartment for the first time is one of the defining rites of passage that marks the transition from adolescence to young adulthood. Many young people have a dream of what their first apartment will be like, whether it is the boho chic flat in a trendy neighborhood, the immaculate penthouse in the heart of downtown, or the ultimate party pad with a gang of best friends for roommates. Unfortunately, it is often harder to find that perfect apartment than it is to daydream about it. Students who want to rent an apartment may end up frustrated and disappointed.

2   Finding an apartment—any apartment—can be hard enough. Landlords are often hesitant to rent to students for the very reasons students want an apartment. Young renters do not have credit ratings with banks, and they haven't proved that they're capable of handling responsability. They throw parties, make noise, and never stay in one place very long. Landlords usually require a reference from a former landlord and a security deposit, if not the co-signature of a parent or relative. However, landlords are far from the sainted beings their high standards might indicate. The ones who don't ask for references are usually equally lax about fixing blocked drains or leaking ceilings, and the ones who do demand references aren't necessarily any better.

3   Money is another common issue when you are renting a place. A student budget in most cases is fairly limited. Rent, bills, and tuition must be paid, on a part-time salary at best. Often after one weekend of apartment hunting, the dream of the perfect apartment goes up in smoke. The place advertised as a "spacious studio" turns out to be a sort of basement mausoleum with grime-covered slats for windows, more appropriate as the setting for a horror movie than a romantic year of independence. "One bedroom" means "walk-in closet." A trend emerges—if the price is right, everything else is wrong.

4   To reduce expenses, many people opt to share a place, but the joys of shared housekeeping can turn overnight into a disaster. Students quickly wonder why did they want a roommate in the first place. A certain amount of messiness can be expected from first-time renters, but some people take this to an extreme. No one wants to end up rooming with the guy who starts a biology lab in the kitchen—studying the growth patterns of breakfast cereal mold (especially when he is a sociology major). Similarly, students who are serious about their studies do not want to live with a party-guy or -girl who is out all night, every night, and who seems to come home only for about five minutes at a time to puke in the sink.

5   Some students, unhappy with their experiences sharing a closet-sized bedroom in a <u>dorm decide</u> to rent a bachelor or studio apartment, <u>prefering</u> to pay a little more in exchange for peace of mind. Sandra, a second-year student, took this route and found that a whole new problem confronted her. "I couldn't believe how lonely I was the first few months," she said. "Even though I hated my roommate, I actually missed her. I spent so much time studying in coffee shops that I might as well have stayed in res." Besides loneliness, safety is another problem for those living alone. Many students, especially women, are worried about the risks of walking home alone.

6   The first year or so of independence can be a vulnerable time, and not just emotionally. Finding apartments is tough, and renting can be expensive. Sharing can be a solution—unless roommates become a nightmare. Then <u>there is the dangers</u> of being lonely and depressed or of having something bad happen with no one there to offer support. It might seem like the pitfalls of apartment renting outweigh the benefits. But the first step into true independence has its rewards as well, and after all, it's a step everyone must take.

PRACTICE 3

Revising

1. Highlight the thesis statement.

2. Highlight the topic sentence in paragraphs 2 and 4.

3. In paragraph 2, the writer veers off course. Cross out the sentences that do not support the topic sentence.

4. Paragraph 3 is missing a topic sentence. Which sentence best sums up the main point of paragraph 3?

   a. Many apartments are small and ugly.

   b. Landlords do not rent to students easily.

   c. Because students have limited budgets, they must settle for small, run-down apartments.

   d. Apartments are often not as nice as they are described in the advertisements.

5. Paragraph 5 is also missing a topic sentence. Which sentence best sums up the main point of paragraph 5?

   a. Furthermore, students who can afford to live alone might have problems.

   b. There are safety issues when renting an apartment.

   c. Sandra had her own studio apartment.

   d. Sometimes students who live alone feel lonely.

6. Which paragraph contains an extended example? ___5___

GRAMMAR LINK

See the following chapters for more information about these grammar topics:
Embedded Questions,
    Chapter 22
Commas, Chapter 35
Spelling, Chapter 34
Subject–Verb
    Agreement,
    Chapter 27

Editing

7. Paragraph 4 contains an embedded question error. (For information about embedded questions, see the Grammar Hint following this practice.)

   Underline and correct the error.

   Correction: _Students quickly wonder why they wanted a roommate in_

   the first place.

8. Paragraph 5 contains a comma error. Underline and correct the error.

   Correction: _bedroom in a dorm, decide_

9. This essay contains misspelled words in paragraphs 2 and 5. Underline and correct them.

   Corrections: _responsibility_   _preferring_

10. Underline and correct a subject–verb agreement error in paragraph 6.

    Correction: _There are the dangers_

Grammar Hint   **Writing Embedded Questions**

When a question is part of a larger sentence, do not use the question word order. View the next examples.

   Error: I wondered how would I pay the rent.
   Correction: I wondered how I would pay the rent.

Writer's Desk **Revise and Edit Your Essay**

Revise and edit the essay that you wrote for the previous Writer's Desk. You can refer to the revising and editing checklists at the end of this chapter and on the book's inside front and back covers.

A Professional Essay

Matt Richtel is a journalist for the *New York Times*. In the next essay, he examines the development of some inventions.

"Edison . . . Wasn't He the Guy Who Invented Everything?"
by Matt Richtel

Teaching Tip:
Like many essays,
"Edison" includes
elements of other
writing patterns,
such as argument
and comparison and
contrast. If you are
planning to show
other modes, you
might ask students
to identify the
writer's main
arguments. Or you
might ask students
in which paragraphs
the writer uses
comparison of
successful and
unsuccessful
inventors.

1   Invention may be mothered by necessity. But determining the father can require a paternity test. Take sound recording. Researchers said last week that they had discovered a recording of a human voice, made by a little-known Frenchman two decades before Thomas Edison's invention of the phonograph. Is it an unusual case of innovation misconception? Hardly. The reality is that the "Aha" moments of industrial creation are preceded by critical moments far less heralded.

2   Behind and beside every big-name inventor are typically lots of others whom history forgot, or never knew. "It's rare that you've got a major breakthrough that wasn't developed by multiple people at about the same time," said Mark Lemley, professor of intellectual property at Stanford Law School. For instance, on February 14, 1876, both Alexander Graham Bell and Elisha Gray filed papers with the United States Patent Office to register their competing telephone technologies. Years earlier, the Italian immigrant Antonio Meucci devised his own version of the telephone but ultimately couldn't afford the patent application process to defend his innovation. History remembers Bell, while his rivals are footnotes known mostly by aficionados of intellectual-property trivia. "It's not that we wouldn't have had the telephone. Not only would we have had it, we would have had it the same day," Mr. Lemley said, adding, "The people who aren't the winners in the historical dispute sort of fade into obscurity."

3   Édouard-Léon Scott de Martinville has certainly been obscure, at least until now. Researchers say that in April 1860, the Parisian tinkerer used a device called a phonautograph to make visual recordings of a woman singing "Au Clair de la Lune." That was 17 years before Thomas Edison received a patent for the phonograph, and 28 years before his technology was used to capture and play back a piece of a section of a Handel oratorio.

4   Whom we credit with an invention often has less to do with who came up with an idea, and more to do with who translated it into something usable, accessible, or commercial. Garages and laboratories, workbenches and scribbled napkins are filled with brilliant ideas unmatched with determination, resources, and market sensibilities, said Jack Russo, a Silicon Valley intellectual-property lawyer. "People run out of money, or they can't find someone to manufacture for them. There are a gazillion reasons why it doesn't work out," Mr. Russo said.

5   A patent doesn't hurt, especially the right one. Edison also gets credit for the light bulb, though he got help from the Supreme Court, which in 1895 ruled that his technology did not infringe on a patent the court ruled

was too broad, filed by competing (and now forgotten) innovators. The Wright Brothers held a critical patent for an early airplane, and history rewards them for it. But lots of other innovators were making significant advances in the technology, Mr. Lemley noted.

6   <u>Some part of the alchemy of anointing inventors has nothing to do with the innovator at all but with the rest of us—as audience and consumer.</u> Sometimes we're finally receptive to an idea—whether it is a political one like civil rights as proffered by the Rev. Dr. Martin Luther King Jr., or an online auction site, like eBay. Great ideas, while perhaps not novel, are delivered to us in palatable packaging just as we're hungry for them.

7   Oddly, by the time such a tipping point happens, the innovators of the original spark may find the ideas outdated. "People come out of the woodwork and get a patent for something fundamental that the others in the field will think is trivial, understood, and expected," said Dennis Allison, a lecturer in electrical engineering at Stanford University. He has a bit of personal experience both with innovation and watching others get credit for it. In the early and mid-1970s, he was a co-founder of the PCC—People's Computer Company—which published papers and magazines describing essential early design and technology that begat the computer and then Internet revolution. "Maybe I have a little bit of a claim—I and the people I was working with—to having invented the personal computer."

8   The names we remember are Gates and Jobs, and to a lesser extent Jobs's early partner, Steve Wozniak. They had an entrepreneurial zeal, marketing genius, and a capacity and desire to translate the language of geeks into the products of the common people—just as our lifestyles and work styles and pocketbooks were ready to open up. Mr. Allison, one among many of the early Silicon Valley innovators whose names seem not destined to be recorded by history, is peaceful with his relative obscurity. "I have my contribution," he said. "The people who I care about know what my role was."

PRACTICE 4

1. Underline the thesis statement.

2. Underline the topic sentences in paragraphs 2, 3, 4, 5, and 6.

3. In which paragraph does the writer use an extended example?

    paragraph 7

4. According to the author, what factors are necessary for an invention to be successful?

   The invention should be patented. The invention also needs to arouse

   the interest of the audience or consumer. Also, the inventor needs

   marketing savvy and capital.

5. Who are some people the writer mentions that have not received credit for an invention? List their names and the inventions they are associated with.

   Elisha Gray, Antonio Meucci—telephone

   Édouard-Léon Scott de Martinville—phonautograph

   Dennis Allison—personal computers

6. List some examples of expert opinion the writer uses to support his ideas.

   Mark Lemley, professor of Intellectual Property at Stanford Law School

   Jack Russo, Silicon Valley intellectual-property lawyer

   Dennis Allison, professor at Stanford University

READING LINK

More Illustration Readings

"Weird Weather" by Pamela D. Jacobsen (page 571)

"Songs of Insects" by Sy Montgomery (page 581)

The Writer's Room

Writing Activity 1: Topics

Write an illustration essay about one of the following topics, or choose your own topic.

General Topics

1. rude behavior
2. favorite objects
3. mistakes that newlyweds make
4. great or horrible films
5. bad habits

College and Work-Related Topics

6. things people should know about my college
7. examples of successful financial planning
8. qualities of an ineffective manager
9. mistakes students make
10. examples of obsolete jobs

WRITING LINK

More Illustration Writing Topics

Chapter 20, Writer's Room topic 1 (page 317)

Chapter 24, Writer's Room topic 1 (page 358)

Chapter 36, Writer's Room topic 1 (page 496)

Chapter 37, Writer's Room topic 1 (page 510)

Writing Activity 2: Photo Writing

Imagine that you must create an essay for a time capsule. In one hundred years, your descendants will read what you have written. How would you describe the world you are living in today? Give examples to show that our world has positive or negative points.

Writing Activity 3: Media Writing

Watch a popular television show or movie that focuses on helping others. Examples are movies such as *The Blind Side*, *The Soloist*, and *Crazy Heart*. The television shows *The Doctors*, *The Biggest Loser*, and *Super Nanny* also focus on helping others. Also look on *YouTube* for videos about people helping other people. Write an essay and provide examples showing how the main characters help others.

CHECKLIST: ILLUSTRATION ESSAY

After you write your illustration essay, review the essay checklist on the inside front cover. Also ask yourself the following questions.

☐ Does my thesis statement include a controlling idea that I can support with examples?

☐ Do I use a series of examples or an extended example in each body paragraph?

☐ Does each body paragraph support the thesis statement?

☐ Does each body paragraph focus on one idea?

☐ Do I have sufficient examples to support my thesis statement?

☐ Do I logically and smoothly connect paragraphs and supporting examples?

Teaching Tip:
Writer's World Competition
Please advise students that they can submit their paragraphs and essays for possible publication to www .pearsonhighered .com/essayrewards/ writingrewards.html

mywritinglab To check your progress in meeting this chapter's objectives, log in to **www.mywritinglab.com,** go to the **Study Plan** tab, click on **Essay Patterns** and choose **Illustration** from the list of subtopics. Read and view the resources in the **Review Materials** section, and then complete the **Recall, Apply,** and **Write** sets in the **Activities** section.

Narration

When investigating a story, a reporter must try to find answers to the questions who, what, when, where, why, *and* how. *You answer the same questions when you write a narrative essay.*

Teaching Tip:

Collaborative Learning (Nonstop Talking) The Writers' Exchange activity can help your students understand narration. Also ask students to describe what happened during a recent newsworthy event.

Writers' Exchange

Try some nonstop talking. First, sit with a partner and come up with a television show or movie that you have both seen. Then, starting at the beginning, describe what happened in that episode or film. Remember that you must speak without stopping. If one of you stops talking, the other must jump in and continue describing the story.

EXPLORING

What Is Narration?

Narrating is telling a story about what happened. You generally explain events in the order in which they occurred, and you include information about when they happened and who was involved in the incidents.

People use narration in everyday situations. For instance, at home, someone might explain how a cooking accident happened. At college, students tell stories to explain absences or lateness. At work, a salesperson might narrate what happened on a business trip.

Hint   **Value of Narration**

Narration is useful on its own, but it also enhances other types of writing. For example, student writer Bruno Garcia had to write an argument essay about traffic laws. His essay was more compelling than it might otherwise have been because he included a story about his grandmother's eyesight and her driving accident.

👓 Visualizing Narration

PRACTICE 1   Brainstorm supporting ideas for the following thesis statement.

Teaching Tip:
Ask students to work on the Visualizing practice with a partner.

THESIS STATEMENT:

The 2010 oil rig explosion in the Gulf of Mexico was a horrible disaster.

- mistakes made	- oil gushed out	- oil hit beaches
- rig caught fire	- efforts made to fix it	- wildlife threatened
- explosion	- many efforts failed	- jobs affected

The Narrative Essay

When you write a narrative essay, consider your point of view.

Use **first-person narration** to describe a personal experience. To show that you are directly involved in the story, use *I* (first-person singular) or *we* (first-person plural).

> When **we** landed in Boston, **I** was shocked by the white landscape. **I** had never seen so much snow.

Use **third-person narration** to describe what happened to somebody else. Show that you are simply an observer or storyteller by using *he, she, it* (third-person singular), or *they* (third-person plural).

> Drivers waited on the highway. **They** honked their horns and yelled in frustration. **They** did not understand what was happening.

Narration at Work

After real-estate agent Francine Martin has shown a home, she records the client's reactions. Here is an excerpt from one of her client records. Keeping records of what her clients like and dislike helps Ms. Martin do her job efficiently and effectively.

Clients: The Nguyens

Needs: The Nguyens have twin sons, and Mrs. Nguyen works at home. They would like a three-bedroom house and prefer two bathrooms or a full bath and powder room. A garage is unnecessary. They will accept townhouses, but cannot spend more than $150,000, which limits their possibilities in this region. They are not willing to view other municipalities.

March 14: We visited 114 Philippe Street. Their first impressions were not favorable. The master bedroom was too small. Cracks in the wall near the ceiling worried them. (Discuss repair of cracks with owner.) They were pleased with the view. They liked the main floor and especially appreciated the kitchen, which may sell the house. The price is in their range. Suggest a second visit.

A Student Essay

Read the essay and answer the questions that follow.

Rehabilitation
by Jack McKelvey

1   I am the sum of all my experiences. I take away lessons from my failures and disappointments. These memories shape my view of my

existence. Many individual experiences, from my first day of school to my first love, have changed me. However, one experience overshadows the rest: prison. Although being in prison was not pleasant, the experience has made me a much better person today.

2   Before I was convicted and shipped off to jail, I was not a good person. I sold drugs, I lied, and I stole. If I thought I could get away with something, I would try. I had no respect for anyone, including myself. I harbored no ambitions or desires. I just wanted to sell drugs, spend money, and smoke pot. In April of 2003, that would all change.

3   On April 11, I was on the return leg of my usual trip to Grand Rapids for two pounds of marijuana. Flashing lights blinded me through the rearview mirror. I pulled over, and the lights followed. I had been making this trip every week or so for almost two years without incident. That day, I didn't even hide my illegal cargo. I knew the officer was going to smell the marijuana I was smoking. I knew he would find the large black trash bag on my back seat. I thought about running, but that never seems to end up well for the people who try it on television. Resigned to my fate, I enjoyed one last cigarette before I was shoved into the back of a royal blue state police cruiser.

4   "I sentence you to twenty-four to sixty months in the Michigan Department of Corrections." I had never heard a more sinister cluster of words. My stomach turned, and a single cold drop of sweat trickled from my armpit. My ears must not have been working correctly. The judge had just used the word prison. The worst images from prison documentaries flashed through my mind like lightning. I am five foot nothing and a buck thirty soaking wet, so how was I going to survive incarceration?

5   The first day of prison was not as I had imagined. I was expecting to see someone running with a knife sticking out of his ribs or to hear someone screaming as he was being raped. Bad things did occur but not on that first day. What did happen was nothing—just silence—and that, I believe, was even worse. Alone, I relived every mistake I had made that led to prison. As the months progressed, I thought most often of freedom and what I wanted to do the day I was released. I also thought of odd things I came to miss: adjusting the water temperature in the shower, opening a refrigerator door, and sleeping in a dark room. I also thought of how I had spent my life so far, and how little I had accomplished. I began to feel as if my life were over, and the best years of my life were sliding by. Although most inmates considered me a short timer, I felt as if my sentence was timeless eternity.

6   Two years into my incarceration, I realized that my release was on the horizon, and I became motivated to change. I began tearing through books with a vengeance. I took every college course available at the institution, and I even enrolled in a vocational skills program. I was going to have a

Teaching Tip:
If your students have studied description, ask them to highlight examples of descriptive imagery in the student essay.

Teaching Tip:
Students may question why *were* is used in the sentence, "I began to feel as if my life were over. . . ." Point out that such conditional sentences require *were* in the *if* clause. For more information about conditional forms, students can refer to page 408 in Chapter 29.

second chance, and soon. Although I was doing all I could intellectually to prepare myself for my release, I was most anxious to begin repairing the relationships I had labored to destroy. I often thought of what I would say to everyone I had disappointed and hurt. I soon realized that words would not prove that I had changed from the person I was before prison. I was going to have to show them, and that is exactly what I planned to do. For the first time since my early teen years, I was optimistic about my future.

7   After three years, two months, six days, eleven hours, and twenty-two minutes, I left prison. Euphoria fails to describe the feeling, and fails miserably. After readjusting to freedom, I found work at a landscaping company, one of the few places that will hire a felon with no degree, and I stayed out of trouble. Over the next year, I would spend a great deal of time with my family. I am proud to say that our relationship now is the best it has ever been. I have come to realize that life is about those we care about. Being imprisoned was what it took for me to realize what I was truly missing in life. The time we have is fleeting, even when it appears to be standing still. I don't plan to waste another second.

Teaching Tip:
Ask students to list the main events in "Rehabilitation." They may come up with only five or six sentences. Point out that the power of this narrative is in the details. The descriptions help involve the reader in the story. Also solicit answers about the narrative's message. You can discuss how a narrative becomes more powerful when it makes a point.

PRACTICE 2

1. Highlight the thesis statement.

2. Underline the topic sentences in paragraphs 2, 5, and 6.

3. Using your own words, sum up what happened in paragraphs 3 and 4.

    Paragraph 3: _Answers will vary._ _While transporting drugs, he was stopped and arrested._

    Paragraph 4: _Scared, he listened as the judge sentenced him to a long period in prison._

4. In paragraphs 3, 4, and 5, the narrative is simple: a man is arrested and jailed. Yet the power of the narrative is in the details: readers can see, hear, feel, and smell what happened. What are some of the most striking descriptions? _Answers will vary._

    Paragraph 3 _flashing lights, smell of marijuana, large black trash bag on the back seat, royal blue state police cruiser_

    Paragraph 4: _a single drop of sweat, a buck thirty soaking wet_

    Paragraph 5: _silence, adjusting water temperature, opening a refrigerator door, sleeping in a dark room_

5. Why did Jack McKelvey write about his experience? What are some messages in this essay?   Answers will vary.

It is a horrible idea to deal drugs and break the law because there are

serious consequences. People should focus on honest work and on their

close relationships.

Explore Topics

In the Writer's Desk Warm Up, you will try an exploring strategy to generate ideas about different topics.

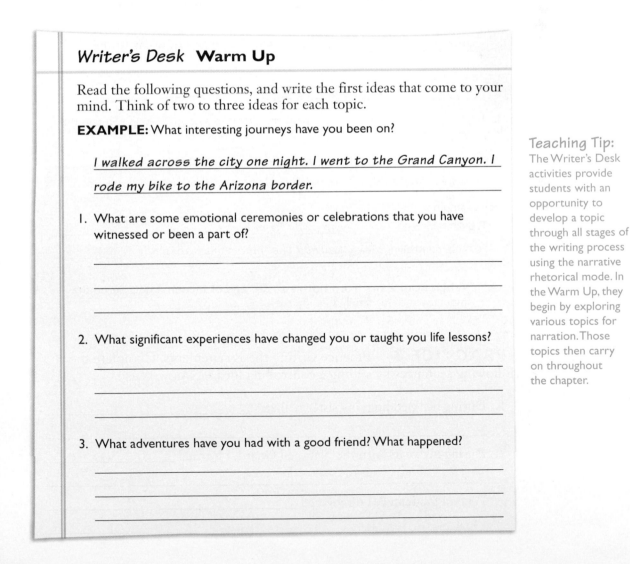

Writer's Desk **Warm Up**

Read the following questions, and write the first ideas that come to your mind. Think of two to three ideas for each topic.

EXAMPLE: What interesting journeys have you been on?

I walked across the city one night. I went to the Grand Canyon. I

rode my bike to the Arizona border.

1. What are some emotional ceremonies or celebrations that you have witnessed or been a part of?

2. What significant experiences have changed you or taught you life lessons?

3. What adventures have you had with a good friend? What happened?

Teaching Tip:
The Writer's Desk activities provide students with an opportunity to develop a topic through all stages of the writing process using the narrative rhetorical mode. In the Warm Up, they begin by exploring various topics for narration. Those topics then carry on throughout the chapter.

DEVELOPING

The Thesis Statement

When you write a narrative essay, choose a topic that you personally find very interesting, and then share it with your readers. For example, very few people may be interested if you simply list what you did during your recent vacation. However, if you write about a particularly moving experience during your vacation, you can create an entertaining narrative essay.

Ensure that your narrative essay expresses a main point. Your thesis statement should have a controlling idea.

topic   controlling idea

The day I decided to get a new job, <u>my life took a dramatic turn.</u>

controlling idea   topic

<u>Sadie's problems began</u> **as soon as she drove her new car home.**

 Hint   **How to Make a Point**

In a narrative essay, the thesis statement should make a point. To help you find the controlling idea, you can ask yourself the following questions:

- What did I learn?
- How did I change?
- How did it make me feel?
- What is important about it?

For example:

Topic: *ran away from home*

Possible controlling idea: *learned the importance of family*

topic   controlling idea

When I ran away from home at the age of fifteen, I discovered the importance of my family.

PRACTICE 3   Practice writing thesis statements. Complete the following sentences by adding a controlling idea.   Answers will vary.

1. During her wedding, my sister realized _____

   _____

2. During my years with the National Guard, I learned _____

   _____

3. When I graduated, I discovered _____

   _____

Writer's Desk Write Thesis Statements

Write a thesis statement for each of the following topics. You can look for ideas in the Warm Up on page 99. Each thesis statement should mention the topic and express a controlling idea.

EXAMPLE: Topic: An interesting journey

Thesis statement: *I went on an exciting hike in the Grand Canyon.*

1. Topic: An emotional ceremony

   Thesis statement: _____

   _____

2. Topic: A significant experience

   Thesis statement: _____

   _____

3. Topic: An adventure with a friend

   Thesis statement: _____

   _____

Teaching Tip: Point out that the Warm Up example's thesis statement is modified later in this chapter. Remind students that they can modify their thesis statements as they develop their essays.

The Supporting Ideas

A narrative essay should contain specific details so that the reader understands what happened. To come up with the details, ask yourself a series of questions and then answer them as you plan your essay.

- **Who** is the essay about?
- **What** happened?
- **When** did it happen?
- **Where** did it happen?
- **Why** did it happen?
- **How** did it happen?

When you recount a story to a friend, you may go back and add details, saying, "Oh, I forgot to mention something." However, when you write, you have the opportunity to clearly plan the sequence of events so that your reader can easily follow your story. Organize events in chronological order (the order in which they occurred). You can also begin your essay with the outcome and then explain what happened that led to the outcome.

$\left(\text{Hint}\right)$ **Narrative Essay Tips**

Here are some tips to remember as you develop your narrative essay.

• Do not simply recount what happened. Reflect on why the event is important.

• Consider the main source of tension in your narrative. Descriptions of conflict or tension can help engage the reader.

• To make your essay more powerful, use descriptive language that appeals the senses. For more information on using descriptive imagery, see pages 115–116 in Chapter 8.

Writer's Desk   **Develop Supporting Ideas**

Choose one of your thesis statements from the previous Writer's Desk on page 101. Then generate supporting ideas. List what happened.

EXAMPLE: An interesting journey   Topic: _____

— hitchhiked to the canyon   _____

— descended five miles   _____

— met a crazy man at the ranch   _____

— saw a sheep on a narrow ledge   _____

— was worn out during the final climb   _____

Teaching Tip:
For extra practice, ask students to develop supporting ideas for all three Writer's Desk topics. The topics are listed in the previous Writer's Desk.

The Essay Plan

Before you write a narrative essay, make a detailed essay plan. Write down main events in the order in which they occurred. To make your narration more complete, include details about each event.

THESIS STATEMENT: My hike in the Grand Canyon was an exhausting adventure.

    I. On the first day, my condition rapidly deteriorated as I walked down the trail.

        A. The soles of my boots ripped.

        B. I got blisters.

        C. My backpack hurt my shoulders.

II. Eventually, I reached Phantom Ranch at the bottom of the canyon.
    A. A slow talker poked a piece of wood.
    B. He described tragedies in the canyon.
    C. His stories shocked and depressed me.
III. On the way back up, I came face to face with trouble.
    A. I encountered a bighorn sheep.
    B. We were both on a narrow ledge, with room for just one of us to pass.
    C. The sheep suddenly went straight up.
    D. I was able to pass.
IV. Near the end of my hike, I had no drive left.
    A. The rock face kept getting steeper and the air significantly thinner.
    B. Whenever I felt that I was at the top, another area opened up above me.
    C. I didn't want to take another step.

Concluding idea: My journey showed me that there is nothing that can stop me.

Writer's Desk **Write an Essay Plan**

Refer to the information you generated in previous Writer's Desks, and prepare a detailed essay plan. Include details for each supporting idea.

The First Draft

After you outline your ideas in a plan, you are ready to write the first draft. Remember to write complete sentences and to use transitions to help readers understand the order in which events occur or occurred. Here are some transitions that are useful in narrative essays.

To show a sequence of events

afterward	finally	in the end	meanwhile
after that	first	last	next
eventually	in the beginning	later	then

Enhancing Your Essay

One effective way to enhance your narrative essay is to use dialogue. A **direct quotation** contains the exact words of an author, and the quotation is set off with quotation marks. When you include the exact words of more than one person in a text, you must make a new paragraph each time the speaker changes.

> "Who did this?" my mom shrieked, as my brother and I stood frozen with fear.

> "Mark did it," I assured her shamelessly, as I pointed at my quivering brother.

An **indirect quotation** does not give the author's exact words, but it keeps the author's meaning. It is not set off by quotation marks.

> As Mark and I stood frozen with fear, our shrieking mother asked who had done it. I assured her shamelessly that Mark had done it, as my finger pointed at my quivering brother.

Grammar Hint   **Using Quotations**

When you insert a direct quotation into your writing, capitalize the first word of the quotation, and put the final punctuation inside the closing quotation marks.

• Place a comma after an introductory phrase.

> Zsolt Alapi said, "Everyone was terrified."

• Place a colon after an introductory sentence.

> Zsolt Alapi described the atmosphere: "Everyone was terrified."

See Chapter 37 for more information about using quotations.

Writer's Desk **Write the First Draft**

In the previous Writer's Desk, you developed an essay plan. Carefully review your essay plan, make any necessary changes to the details or chronology, and then write the first draft of your narrative essay.

Teaching Tip:

REVISING AND EDITING

Revise and Edit a Narrative Essay

When you finish writing a narrative essay, carefully review your work and revise it to make the events as clear as possible to your readers. Check that you have organized events chronologically, and remove any irrelevant details. Before you revise and edit your own essay, practice revising and editing a student essay.

A Student Essay

Read the essay, and then answer the questions that follow. As you read, correct any errors that you find, and make comments in the margins.

My Journey Down the Grand Canyon
By Andrew Wells

1   Twenty years old, on a break from studies, I decided to set out backpacking to see where it would take me. After staying in a youth hostel in Flagstaff, Arizona, I spontaneously decided to see the Grand Canyon. From the upper ridge to the Colorado River at the base, and back up again. I told no one of my plans, and I did not register with authorities. What I didn't realize was that this sort of hiking is not a simple test of aerobic fitness or personal desire. No, it's a type of brutal self-destruction. My hike in the Grand Canyon left me dazed and depleted.

2   After walking and hitchhiking from Flagstaff, I descended five miles into the canyon. The next morning, I set out towards the river, and my physical condition rapidly deteriorated. First, the soles of my boots gave out, partially tearing from the seams and flapping against the pads of my feet with every step I took. My feet were raw and peeling. My blisters ached continuously. The straps from my backpack tore into my shoulder blades, and pain ran down my spine. But the dull pounding of my boots against the rocky terrain drowned out my thoughts. My focus remained on the path in front of me. I knew that if I lost concentration, at any point I can trip and fall over the edge. At least the awe-inspiring surroundings made it easier to forget the pain.

3   Eventually, I reached Phantom Ranch at the bottom of the canyon. The isolated ranch serves as a rest-stop, it is so popular that people reserve years ahead of time. I spoke with the man working the canteen desk. He was a calm, slow talker in his early thirties, tall and thin, with ear-length tangled hair and a dull, emotionless expression. While poking at a block of wood with a steel pick, he droned on and on about all the people he knew about who had died in the canyon. "Once, some parents let their three-year old girl walk alone, and she just walked right off the edge" he said. "Another time a couple tried to hike in from the far west, ran out

Cooperative Learning (Roundtable Writing) Ask students to write the names of two well-known celebrities at the top of a sheet of paper. All students should write two lines of dialogue on their sheets. Then each student should pass his or her sheet to the person on the left. That person adds another two lines of dialogue. After sheets have rotated several times, all students will have a sheet with dialogue. Ask students to add a variety of introductory phrases such as *She said* or *He replied*. They should punctuate the dialogue correctly. Then teams can read their dialogues to teammates or to the class.

Teaching Tip:
The activity of revising a student essay should help your students understand the important link between the writing process and the grammar chapters.

Teaching Tip:
If your students have descended the Grand Canyon, they might have had very different experiences from the writer's. You can discuss how a narrative essay is a very personal writing form.

Teaching Tip:
After students identify the thesis statement, ask them to review how the thesis has evolved in this chapter. They can look at the examples of this essay's thesis in the Writer's Desk: Write Thesis Statements on page 101 and in the sample essay plan on pages 102–103. Remind students that they can modify their thesis statements and topic sentences as they develop their essays.

of water, and expired." He kept tapping the wood with his pick. He continued, "Then there was the guy who was knocked off the edge by one of the sheep." In my head I screamed for him to stop!

4   On my climb back up, I encountered a bighorn sheep on a narrow ledge. ~~I also saw a California condor gliding in the open air.~~ The sheep wanted to go where I was, and I wanted to go where it was, but there was no room to pass. For minutes on end the sheep and I engaged in a stare-down. Then all of a sudden it got bored with me and climbed up an 85-degree sheer rock face! I was stunned. It was so smart, and as soon as I passed, it climbed back down, turned and looked at me, and walked on.

5   After several hours of non-stop hiking, I had <u>absolutly</u> no drive left. The rock face kept getting steeper and the air significantly thinner. Each layer of the canyon above me was hidden behind the nearest sheet of towering sandstone. Whenver I felt that I was at the top, a <u>hole</u> new area opened up above me. At certain points, I felt like saying "That's it. I'm living the rest of my life on this ledge. I'm not moving." Then I started making deals with myself, planning what I was going to do with my life once I got out, just to motivate myself to keep going.

6   When I reached the top, I looked down into the bowels of the canyon and felt relieved that I had done it. Hiking the Grand Canyon is something that does not need to be done more than once. I can retain the knowledge of what I have accomplished. I have come out believing that there's nothing that can stop me, and there's no greater feeling.

PRACTICE 4

Revising

1. Highlight the thesis statement.

2. What type of narration is this?
    (a.) first person   b. third person

3. Paragraph 3 lacks a topic sentence. An appropriate topic sentence for paragraph 3 could be:
    a. Phantom Canyon is at the bottom of the canyon, and it is a very popular place.
    (b.) At Phantom Ranch, I met a strange man who told gruesome stories.
    c. Many people die in the Grand Canyon.
    d. Sheep can knock people off ledges in the Grand Canyon.

4. Paragraph 4 lacks unity. One sentence adds a description, but it doesn't support the paragraph's topic. Strike through that sentence.

Editing

5. A fragment is an incomplete sentence. Underline a fragment in paragraph 1, and then write the correction on the line below.

    Correction: *I would travel from the upper ridge to the . . .*

6. Paragraph 2 contains a tense shift. A verb tense changes for no logical reason. Underline the sentence with the tense shift, and write a correction on the line below.

    Correction: *. . . I could trip and fall over the edge*

7. Paragraph 3 contains a run-on sentence. Underline the error, and show three ways to correct the sentence.

    Corrections: *. . . a rest-stop, and it is so popular that . . .*

    . . . a rest-stop. It is so popular that . . .

    . . . a rest-stop; it is so popular that . . .

8. There is a missing comma in paragraph 3. Circle where the comma should be placed and write the correction here.

    Correction: *edge," he said*

9. Underline two spelling errors in paragraph 5. Write the corrections here.

    Corrections: *absolutely*   *whole*

Writer's Desk Revise and Edit Your Essay

Revise and edit the essay that you wrote for the previous Writer's Desk. You can refer to the revising and editing checklists at the end of this chapter and on this book's inside covers.

---

vo•cab•u•lar•y BOOST

Writers commonly overuse words. To make your writing more vivid and interesting, identify five common and overused verbs in your essay. Replace each verb with a more vivid and specific verb.

First draft: We walked to the edge of the cliff and looked at the sea.

Revision: We strolled to the edge of the cliff and gazed at the sea.

GRAMMAR LINK

See the following chapters for more information about these grammar topics:
Fragments,
  Chapter 23
Run-Ons, Chapter 24
Verb Consistency,
  Chapter 29
Spelling and
  Commonly
  Confused Words,
  Chapter 34
Commas,
  Chapter 35

Teaching Tip:

Cooperative Learning (Pair & Share) First, ask students to read the essay silently. As they read, they should circle any mistakes that they find. Then place students in pairs. They can share what they have found and answer the revising and editing questions together. As a possible third step, pairs can share their answers with other pairs of students.

A Professional Essay

In his memoir, *Cockeyed*, Ryan Knighton, an author and teacher, describes his slow descent into blindness. In the following excerpt, he narrates what happened.

Out of Sight
by Ryan Knighton

ESL
Teaching Tip:
Pair nonnative speakers with native speakers to do the vocabulary boost. You might suggest that each pair use a thesaurus. Students can peer edit each other's essays.

eradicate:
remove completely

1   On my 18th birthday, my first retina specialist, a man who delivered his bedside manner like napalm, informed me that I would be blind within a few years. "No cure," he said. "Sorry." The specialist told me the name of the condition, retinitis pigmentosa. He described how it would soon **eradicate** my remaining night vision, limit me to tunnel vision, and eventually blinker me altogether. The whole scene took less than ten minutes.

2   For four years, I had exhibited clumsy behaviour nobody could account for. As a warehouse worker during summer vacations, I drove a forklift and ran over nearly everything possible, including one of my co-workers. True, I hated him and his insistence that we play nothing but Iron Maiden on the shipping area stereo, but it wasn't in my character to crush him.

3   But the real giveaway came when I drove my father's Pontiac into a ditch. Lots of friends crashed their parents' cars, but my accident stood out. I did my teenaged duty at roughly five miles per hour. How do you miss a turn at that speed unless your eyes are closed? After sundown, mine might as well have been.

4   When I reported to my mother that, as a new driver, I was having trouble on rainy nights, she said they gave everybody trouble and told me not to worry. I was on my way out the door, about to drive to work. "But do you use the **cat's eyes** sometimes?" I asked.

cat's eyes:
raised glass circles that mark the center of the road by reflecting light

5   "Sure," she said. "That's what they're for, reflecting light when it's hard to see the yellow line."

6   "No, I mean do you use them? Do you drive on them?"

7   When I couldn't see the yellow line, I had taken to steering onto the cat's eyes. This, I found, helped position me on the road. I was a little close to the middle, maybe, but better than anything I could determine on my own. The clunk clunk clunk of the reflectors under my tires let me know where I was. I suppose I drove Braille.

8   "You drive on the cat's eyes?" my mother asked.

9   "Well, only at night." I would wager my mother called for my first ophthalmological appointment by the time I had shut the front door behind me.

10   Retinitis pigmentosa is the loss of photoreceptors associated with pigmentary changes in the retina. Another way to put it is that my retina is scarring itself to death. I've enjoyed the slow loss of all peripheral and

night vision. By my own estimate, I have a year to go until that tiny pinhole of clarity in which I live will consume itself, and the lights will go out. To know what's filling up my little tunnel, I rely mostly on context.

11 Once I asked a red-headed waitress for directions to the washroom. I didn't know she was a waitress by the colour of her hair, of course—the bit of it I saw—but by the smell of coffee, which was quickly overwhelmed by a perfumy fog.

12 "Would you like more coffee?"

13 "I'd love coffee," I said, "but I'd love to be in the men's room even more."

14 "Um, okay, the men's room is over that way."

15 I stared vacantly ahead while she, I imagine, continued to point "that way." Then I heard the pleasant sound of coffee being poured.

16 "I'm sorry," I said, "but I don't know what *that way* means." I plucked my white cane from the bag beside me. "I guess it wasn't obvious, and I forgot to—"

17 "Oh my God, I'm sorry, I didn't know you're blind! You didn't look—you don't look—not at all—I mean really."

18 I smiled with that warm sensation you get when you are sixteen and someone says you look like you're in your twenties. "Thanks. That is very kind. Where did you say the washroom is?"

19 "At the back."

20 "Which way is back?"

21 "It's over there," she said, and walked away.

22 All I wanted were specific directions. Instead, my waitress gave me a demonstration of the fact that, along with vision, parts of language disappear into blindness. The capacity of language to guide me has atrophied. Not even Braille can substitute for some words. *This way. Right here, in front of you. No, there. Right there, under your nose.* Such directional cues have lost their meaning. Who would have guessed that a disease can alter language as it alters the body, disabling parts of speech—that language is, in this way, an extension of the body and subject to the same pathologies.

23 "EXCUSE ME."

24 My waitress was back, not a second too soon. I really did need to use the facilities.

25 "I don't mean to intrude," she said, "but didn't you go to Langley Secondary School?"

26 "Yes, I did."

27 "It's Ryan, right? I'm Danielle! We were in drama class together. God, I didn't recognize you at all. You look so different now," she said.

28 I braced myself. "I'm not sure what it is. Maybe it's—" *The fierce squint? The white cane? The expression of perpetual disorientation?*

29 "It's—well. I know!" She put a hand on my head with daring compassion. "You shaved your hair off. When did you do that?"
30 Now I was free to burn with embarrassment at my self-centeredness. Just because it's a sighted world doesn't mean blindness is the first thing people notice about me, nor the first thing that comes to mind. Along with mutant celebrity and meaningless words, I suppose paranoia is another side effect. "A couple of years ago, I guess," I replied.
31 "Looks cool."
32 "Thanks."
33 "I remember in high school your hair used to be long," she said. "Really long. It was down to here, right?"

PRACTICE 5

1. What type of narration is this text?
    a. first person   b. third person

2. The thesis of this essay is not stated directly, but it is implied. Using your own words, write the thesis of this essay.
    Answers will vary. *Becoming blind affected me in various ways.*

3. Knighton divides his essay into two time periods. What are they?
    before his diagnosis of blindness   *after his diagnosis*

4. How does Knighton realize that he is losing his sight? In two or three sentences, explain what happens.
    He drives on the cat's eyes because he can't see well at night. He mentions this fact to his mother, and she gets him an appointment with an eye specialist.

Teaching Tip:
Point out that Ryan Knighton uses the "definition" writing pattern in paragraph 10. He also explains the cause and effects of his blindness. You can discuss how an essay with one overall pattern can still incorporate elements of other writing patterns.

5. In which paragraph is there a definition of a term? ____ *Paragraph 10*

6. Describe what happens during Knighton's encounter with the waitress. Use your own words.
    Knighton asks the waitress for directions to the men's room. Her directions are only useful for someone with sight. She points and says, "Over there." Eventually, he realizes that he went to high school with the waitress.

7. Write down one example of an indirect quotation from the essay.
    I asked a red-haired waitress for directions to the men's room.

8. Write down one example of a direct quotation from the essay.

   Answers will vary.

9. Narrative writers do more than simply list a series of events. Knighton explains why the events were meaningful. What did he learn?

   He learned that losing sight also entails losing language. Many words

   became meaningless. He also learned to feel less paranoid about the way

   people perceive him.

The Writer's Room

Writing Activity 1: Topics

Choose any of the following topics, or choose your own topic, and write a narrative essay.

General Topics

1. a breakup
2. a lie or a mistake
3. a personal ritual
4. a thrilling or frightening moment
5. a news event that affected you

College and Work-Related Topics

6. a fearful moment at college
7. a sudden realization at school or work
8. an uncomfortable incident at work
9. a positive or negative job interview
10. a difficult lesson at work or school

Writing Activity 2: Photo Writing

Write about a physical or spiritual journey that you have been on. Describe what happened.

Teaching Tip:

Cooperative Learning (Sharing Circle) Ask students to work in groups of three or four. They should review the chapter and identify the three most important points that all students should remember about narration. They should write their ideas on a sheet and then share them with the class.

Tech

Teaching Tip: Ask students to create a blog by going to Blogger at www.blogger .com/start or another starter blog site. They can write a blog about one of the suggested Writer's Room topics, or they can write about a topic that interests them. Have students read and respond to each other's blog. Students can also peer-edit grammar errors particular to this grammar chapter.

READING LINK

More Narrative Readings

"Naming Good Path Elk" by Kenneth M. Kline (page 542)

"My African Childhood" by David Sedaris (page 546)

WRITING LINK

More Narrative Writing Topics

See the next grammar sections for more narrative writing topics.

Chapter 21, Writer's Room topic 1 (page 328)

Chapter 27, Writer's Room topic 1 (page 386)

Chapter 28, Writer's Room topic 1 (page 402)

Chapter 31, Writer's Room topic 1 (page 440)

Writing Activity 3: Media Writing

Watch a popular television show or movie that describes how someone overcame an obstacle to be successful. Examples are movies such as *Precious*, *Dream Girls*, and *Milk*, or television shows such as *House*, *Grey's Anatomy*, and *Ugly Betty*. Also look on *YouTube* for videos about ordinary people who achieved surprising success. Write an essay and describe what happened to the main character(s).

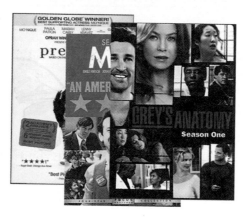

✔ CHECKLIST: NARRATIVE ESSAY

After you write your narration essay, review the checklist on the inside front cover. Also ask yourself these questions.

☐ Does my thesis statement clearly express the topic of the narration?

☐ Does my thesis statement contain a controlling idea that is meaningful and interesting?

☐ Does my essay answer most of the following questions: who, what, when, where, why, how?

☐ Do I use transitional expressions that help clarify the order of events?

☐ Do I include details to make my narration more vivid?

Teaching Tip:
Writer's World Competition
Please advise students that they can submit their essays for possible publication to www .pearsonhighered .com/essayrewards/ writingrewards.html

mywritinglab To check your progress in meeting this chapter's objectives, log in to **www.mywritinglab.com,** go to the **Study Plan** tab, click on **Essay Patterns** and choose **Narration** from the list of subtopics. Read and view the resources in the **Review Materials** section, and then complete the **Recall, Apply,** and **Write** sets in the **Activities** section.

Description

LEARNING OBJECTIVES

Painters add details in their work to express their artistic vision. Similarly, writers use the tools of descriptive writing to create images that readers can visualize in their mind's eye.

Writers' Exchange

Choose one of the objects from the following list. Then, brainstorm a list of descriptive words about the object. Think about the shape, texture, smell, taste, color, and so on. List the first words that come to your mind.

For example: cake   *gooey, sweet, chocolate, smooth, pink icing, layered*

ostrich   dump truck   baby blanket   toddler   strawberry

Teaching Tip: The Writers' Exchange activity can help your students understand description. Write some of their ideas on the board. As an extra activity, you could ask students to choose three of the words and construct a paragraph.

EXPLORING

What Is Description?

Description creates vivid images in the reader's mind by portraying people, places, or moments in detail. Here are some everyday situations that might call for description.

People use description every day. At home, family members might describe the style of their new apartment to a friend. At college, students could describe the results of a chemistry experiment to their classmates. At work, employees may describe a retirement party to an absent colleague.

👓 Visualizing Description

PRACTICE 1   Brainstorm supporting ideas for the following thesis statement. Write some descriptive words or phrases on the lines.

THESIS STATEMENT: Historically, there have been some very unhealthy fashion trends.

corsets

tall wigs

extremely high heels

corsets	tall wigs	extremely high heels
difficulty breathing	itchy	may develop bunions
uncomfortable	difficult to put on	not good for posture
stiff	hot	shorten calf muscles

Teaching Tip:
Ask students which
details appeal to the
reader's senses.

Description at Work

To help hikers plan camping trips effectively, the Web site http://www
.americansouthwest.net describes hiking trails in Zion National Park.

The trail descends quite steeply, close to the course of the South Fork of
Taylor Creek, and soon reaches the main stream. Here, the canyon is deep but
wide and V-shaped, with red rocks and sandy soils, quite densely covered by
trees, bushes, and cacti. The path follows the valley upstream, at first on the
south side but later on either side as it crosses the creek several times. The
water is fast flowing but shallow and easily forded.

The Descriptive Essay

When you write a descriptive essay, focus on three main points.

1. **Create a dominant impression.** The dominant impression is the overall
   atmosphere that you wish to convey. It can be a strong feeling, mood, or image.
   For example, if you are describing a casual Sunday afternoon party, you can
   emphasize the relaxed ambience in the room.

2. **Express your attitude toward the subject.** Do you feel positive or negative
   toward the subject? For instance, if you feel pleased about your last vacation,
   then the details of your essay might convey the good feelings you have about
   it. If you feel tense during a business meeting, then your details might express
   how uncomfortable the situation makes you feel.

3. **Include concrete details.** Details will enable a reader to visualize the person,
   place, or situation that you are describing. You can use active verbs, adjectives,
   and adverbs so that the reader imagines the scene more clearly. You can also
   use **imagery,** which is description using the five senses. Review the following
   examples of imagery.

Tech
Teaching Tip:
Place students in
pairs. In a computer
lab, they should go
to a photo Web site
such as *flickr.com*
and choose a very
interesting image.
Ask students to
brainstorm a list of
sensory details
about the image.

Sight:	A Western Tiger Swallowtail dipped by my face. About three inches across, its lemon yellow wings were striped improbably and fluted in black. They filliped into a long forked tail with spots of red and blue. (Sherman Apt Russell, "Beauty on the Wing")
Sound:	The tree outside is full of crows and white cranes who gurgle and screech. (Michael Ondaatje, *Running in the Family*)
Smell:	I think it was the smell that so intoxicated us after those dreary months of nostril-scorching heat, the smell of dust hissing at the touch of rain and then settling down, damply placid on the ground. (Sara Suleri, *Meatless Days*)

Touch: The straps from my backpack tore into my shoulder blades, and
pain ran down my spine.
(Andrew Wells, "My Journey Down the Grand Canyon")

Taste: Entirely and blessedly absent are the cloying sweetness, chalky
texture, and oily, gummy aftertaste that afflict many mass-
manufactured ice creams.
(R.W. Apple Jr., "Making Texas Cows Proud")

A Student Essay

Read the following student essay, and answer the questions that follow.

The House with the Brown Door
by Judith Lafrance

1   In the little village of St. Lin, there is a house with a brown front door.
It has beautiful awnings on the windows and huge grounds. When I was
a child, the house was sold and a strange couple moved in. The man
and woman stayed in their house, never going outside except to work.
Furthermore, I never saw anyone visiting them. When they first moved into
my neighborhood, I thought they were malicious or unpleasant. In reality, I
have come to know them better, and everything scary that happened
behind the brown door one fateful evening was nothing but coincidence.

2   When I was seven years old, a moving van rumbled down the street. I
was excited and curious. I watched four men unload the van. They carried
in a refrigerator, a black sofa, two beds, and boxes of various sizes and
shapes. As I was looking at the movers, a woman parked her shiny green
car behind the truck. Tall and impressive, she had big blue eyes and long
auburn hair, and she was wearing a red dress. In her hands, she held a
huge pink purse that I imagined was full of cosmetics because the aging
skin on her face was heavily made up. Even so, she was beautiful. A very
tall muscular man stepped out of the driver's seat. He had blond hair and
wore a gray suit. They must have unpacked quickly because empty boxes
were piled by the street two days later.

3   My friend Mary Lou and I were curious, so after school, we decided to
spy on the new neighbors. We crept behind their house. The first few times,
we had fun imagining their conversations as they gestured behind the
windows. However, one cool autumn afternoon, we were frightened by
what we heard. As we peered from behind a bush, we heard a loud bang
and some shrieking coming from inside the house. Terrified, we rushed to
leave. In our haste, we forgot to stay clear of the rose bushes, so thorns
scratched our skin and snagged on our clothing. Mary Lou and I decided
that we wouldn't go there anymore.

4   When I arrived home, I saw my brother Karl in the kitchen. I could smell the bacon sizzling on the stove. I told him what I had heard and said that my spying days were over. He chuckled and replied that I was so young and delicate. Feeling insulted, I shouted angrily, "I am not so young! I'll go with you to the house tonight." I hoped he wouldn't accept my idea, but he did.

5   That evening, after dinner, we snuck into our neighbors' garden. I pretended to be brave, but my skin was covered in goosebumps. As we peered at the house, we heard a loud cracking noise. Then the sounds of yelling, crying, and suffering came from the house. I turned white. Karl said we should go closer to find out what had happened. We crept up to the house and peered through the kitchen window. There was no one there, but I saw a big shadow coming from the bedroom. I tried to yell, but no sound came from my mouth. Karl saw the same shadow. We looked at each other, let go of the window sill, and turned around. A large man was standing in the darkness right behind us. My imagination went wild. I thought, "This big ugly man is going to kill us. He doesn't like children, and he thinks we are too curious." Then I fainted.

6   Parents want their children to have great lives full of love, peace, and joy. That's why, when I was a child, my mother always told me, "Don't talk to strangers." That's also why, the night that my older brother and I decided to spy on our new neighbors, my father followed us to make sure we would not get into mischief. He was the man who was standing in front of us. He wanted to punish us for our inquisitiveness, but I had briefly lost consciousness. When I opened my eyes, I saw my brother and father arguing. Hearing the commotion, the man living in the house came outside. He was surprised to see the three of us in his backyard. He asked if I was okay and then said that he was a doctor. He examined me and told my father I would be fine after a couple hours of sleep. He asked why we were in his backyard. My brother sheepishly admitted that we were spying on the man and his wife. Instead of being angry, the man laughed and said that it was normal for children to be curious.

7   The neighbor introduced himself: "By the way, my name is Martin Champagne. I am very pleased to meet you and your family." He was so gentle that my brother and I felt shy. However, I asked him about the screaming I had heard. He answered, "My wife and I love horror films. We turn the sound up high to get the full effect of the movie. Maybe that is what you heard." His wife then appeared and introduced herself.

8   This story happened ten years ago. Since then, our families have become close friends. They still live in the same house near us, and we see

Teaching Tip:

Cooperative Learning (Jigsaw)
You can continue with the same topic such as *the college cafeteria*. Divide the class into five teams. Team A must write two to four sentences about the place using imagery that appeals to sight. Team B writes using imagery that appeals to sound, Team C about smell, Team D about touch, and Team E about taste. Give teams a few minutes to write their sentences. Then teams can share their sentences with the class. Or, if you have time, you can number students in each team from one to six (depending on how many are in the team). The ones can get together, the twos, threes, and so on. The new teams, which include people from all "sense" groups, share ideas and construct a text with imagery that appeals to the five senses.

each other often. With time, they had a baby, and I am their babysitter. I love them as if they were my aunt and uncle. I should have gotten to know them before judging them.

PRACTICE 2

1. Underline the thesis statement.

2. The writer recounts the story using description that appeals to the senses. Find imagery from the essay.   Answers will vary.

    a. Sight: *Tall and impressive, she had big blue eyes and long auburn hair,*

        and she was wearing a red dress.

    b. Sound: *a moving van rumbled down the street*

    c. Touch: *thorns scratched our skin*

    d. Smell: *I could smell the bacon sizzling on the stove.*

Teaching Tip:
Encourage all students to use a thesaurus to enhance their vocabulary when they are writing descriptions.

3. What dominant impression does the writer create in this essay? Underline examples in the essay to support your answer.

    Answers will vary. Possible answers are fear and shock.

Explore Topics

In the Writer's Desk Warm Up, you will try an exploring strategy to generate ideas about different topics.

Writer's Desk **Warm Up**

Read the following questions, and write the first ideas that come to your mind. Think of two or three ideas for each topic.

EXAMPLE: List some memorable trips you have taken.

    —*my trip to Africa*

    —*the time I stayed with my grandmother in Seattle*

    —*a field trip to the Natural History Museum*

1. Who are your best friends?

_____

_____

_____

2. What are some unattractive fashion trends?

_____

_____

_____

3. List some memorable trips that you have taken.

_____

_____

_____

Teaching Tip:
The Writer's Desk activities provide students with an opportunity to develop a topic through all stages of the writing process using the descriptive rhetorical mode. In the Warm Up, they begin by exploring various topics. Those topics then carry on throughout the chapter.

DEVELOPING

When you write a descriptive essay, choose a subject that lends itself to description. You should be able to describe images or objects using some of the five senses. To get in the frame of mind, try thinking about the sounds, sights, tastes, smells, and feelings you would experience in certain places, such as a busy restaurant, a hospital room, a subway car, a zoo, and so on.

The Thesis Statement

In the thesis statement of a descriptive essay, you should convey a dominant impression about the subject. The dominant impression is the overall impression or feeling that the topic inspires.

ESL
Teaching Tip:
Encourage your nonnative speakers to write about culture-specific topics. Let them know that others in the class will appreciate descriptive details about an unfamiliar topic.

         topic   controlling idea

The photograph of me as a ten-year-old has an embarrassing story behind it.

      controlling idea   topic

Feeling self-satisfied, **Odysseus Ramsey started his first day in public office.**

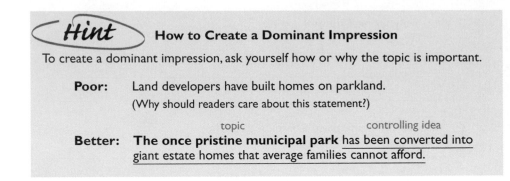

Hint   How to Create a Dominant Impression

To create a dominant impression, ask yourself how or why the topic is important.

Poor: Land developers have built homes on parkland.

(Why should readers care about this statement?)

                  topic   controlling idea

Better: **The once pristine municipal park** has been converted into giant estate homes that average families cannot afford.

Writer's Desk Thesis Statements

Write a thesis statement for each of the following topics. You can look for ideas in the Warm Up on pages 118–119. Each thesis statement should state what you are describing and contain a controlling idea.

EXAMPLE: Topic: a memorable trip

   Thesis Statement: *My first day in Ghana left me enthralled but exhausted.*

1. Topic: a close friend

   Thesis Statement: _____

   _____

2. Topic: unattractive fashion trends

   Thesis Statement: _____

   _____

3. Topic: a memorable trip

   Thesis Statement: _____

   _____

The Supporting Ideas

After you have developed an effective thesis statement, generate supporting details.

- Use prewriting strategies such as freewriting and brainstorming to generate ideas.

- Choose the best ideas. Most descriptive essays use imagery that describes the person or scene.
- Organize your ideas. Choose the best organizational method for this essay pattern.

Show, Don't Tell

Your audience will find it more interesting to read your written work if you show an action of a person or a quality of a place rather than just state it.

Example of Telling: Mr. Leon was a very kind man.

Example of Showing: Our neighbor, Mr. Leon, a grim-faced, retired seventy-year-old grandfather, always snapped at the neighborhood children, telling us not to play street hockey, not to make so much noise, and not to throw the ball near his roses. When it came to important matters, however, he was always supportive of us. Mr. Leon taught all the local youths to ride bikes. He used to walk along beside us holding on to the cycle as we wobbled down the sidewalk. One day, we learned that Mr. Leon had been donating fifty bicycles to the local children's charity annually for many years.

PRACTICE 3   Choose one of the following sentences, and write a short description that shows—not tells—the quality or action.
Answers will vary.

1. Today was a perfect day.

2. I was frightened as I walked down the street.

3. The weather did not cooperate with our plans.

Use Different Figurative Devices

When writing a descriptive essay, you can use other figurative devices (besides **imagery**) to add vivid details to your writing.

- A **simile** is a comparison using *like* or *as*.

    My thoughts ran as fast as a cheetah.

    Let us go then you and I,
    When the evening is spread out against the sky
    Like a patient etherised upon a table;
    (from "The Love Song of J. Alfred Prufrock" by T.S. Eliot).

- A **metaphor** is a comparison that does not use *like* or *as*.

    Life is sweet-and-sour soup.

    Love is a temple.
    (from "One" by U2)

Teaching Tip:

**Cooperative
Learning
(Roundtable
Writing)**
Give your students
a list of one-line
sentences such as
*The doctor was
cranky, The building is
rundown,* or *The train
station was noisy.*
Place students in
teams and ask them
to expand on the
description by
writing a paragraph
that shows the
quality. Then teams
can share what they
have written with
the class. Another
activity is to ask
students to write
one sentence at the
top of a sheet. Then
team members
rotate their sheets
around their group,
adding ideas to each
sheet that they
receive.

▪ **Personification** is the act of attributing human qualities to an inanimate object or an animal.

> The chocolate cake winked invitingly at us.
> Life has a funny way of helping you out.
> (from "Ironic" by Alanis Morrissette).

PRACTICE 4   Practice using figurative language. Use a simile, metaphor, or personification to describe each numbered item below. If you are comparing two things, try to use an unusual comparison.   Answers will vary.

EXAMPLE: toddler: *The toddler was like a monkey, climbing up and down with great agility. (simile)*

1. mountain: *Overcoming my shyness was like climbing the highest mountain. (simile)*

2. hair: *Her hair was cotton candy. (metaphor)*

3. ocean: *On that scorching day, the ocean generously invited us in. (personification)*

---

vo•cab•u•lar•y BOOST

Use Vivid Language
When you write a descriptive essay, try to use vivid language. Use specific action verbs and adjectives to create a clear picture of what you are describing.

                    livid
My boss was ~~angry.~~   Use a more vivid, specific adjective.

                    whimpered
The child ~~cried.~~   Use a more vivid, specific verb or image.

Think about other words or expressions that more effectively describe these words: *laugh, talk, nice, walk.*

Teaching Tip:
The Vocabulary
Boost activity helps
all students,
especially nonnative
speakers, expand
their vocabulary.
Ask students to
brainstorm words
that are overused.
Examples are *nice,
beautiful, good, bad,*
and *happy.*

Writer's Desk **List Sensory Details**

Choose one of your thesis statements from the previous Writer's Desk, and make a list of sensory details. Think about images, impressions, and feelings that the topic inspires in you.

EXAMPLE: Topic: a memorable trip

—*colorful clothes*

—*bright, warm sand*

—*appetizing smell of food*

—*putrid odor of sewers*

—*a cool breeze*

—*powerful drumbeat of music*

—*bodies moving to a beat*

Your topic: _____

Your list of sensory details: _____

_____

_____

_____

_____

The Essay Plan

An essay plan helps you organize your thesis statement, topic sentences, and supporting details before you write a first draft. When you make an essay plan, remember to include concrete details and to organize your ideas in a logical order. If you want to emphasize some descriptive details more than others, arrange them from least affecting to most affecting. If you want your readers to envision a space (a room, a park, and so on), arrange details using spatial order.

THESIS STATEMENT: My first day in Ghana left me enthralled but exhausted.

   I.   I was overwhelmed by my surroundings.
      A. People wore traditional African clothing.
      B. Some walked balancing objects on their heads.
      C. Mothers carried babies tied to their backs.
      D. I could smell different types of food.
  II. The beach was unlike any other beach I'd seen.
      A. I felt a cool breeze and saw orange sand.
      B. I sat in the shade and had a cold beverage.
      C. People were swimming and dancing.

Teaching Tip:
Ask students to keep their essay plans and then attach them to their final draft. You can then determine how the students have developed their ideas.

III. The scenery of the countryside was breathtaking.
- A. There were mud huts with straw roofs.
- B. People were cooking on open fires.
- C. Many animals roamed, including dogs and goats.
- D. I saw immense anthills.

Writer's Desk Write an Essay Plan

Choose one of the ideas that you have developed in previous Writer's Desks and prepare an essay plan. Remember to use vivid details and figurative language to help create a dominant overall impression.

The First Draft

After you outline your ideas in a plan, you are ready to write the first draft. Remember to write complete sentences. Also, as you write, think about which transitions can effectively help you lead your readers from one idea to the next. Descriptive writing often uses space order. Here is a list of transitions that are useful for describing the details in space order.

To show place or position

above	beyond	in the distance	outside
behind	closer in	nearby	over there
below	farther out	on the left/right	under
beside	in front	on top	underneath

Writer's Desk Write the First Draft

In the previous Writer's Desk, you developed an essay plan. Now write the first draft of your descriptive essay. Before you write, carefully review your essay plan and make any necessary changes.

REVISING AND EDITING

Revise and Edit a Descriptive Essay

When you finish writing a descriptive essay, review your work and revise it to make the description as vivid as possible to your readers. Check that you have organized your ideas, and remove any irrelevant details. Before you work on your own essay, practice revising and editing a student essay.

Teaching Tip:
The activity of revising a student essay should help your students understand the important link between the writing process and the grammar chapters.

 Using Adjectives and Adverbs

When you revise your descriptive essay, check that you have used adjectives and adverbs correctly. For example, many people use *real* when the adjective is actually *really*.

> *really*
> My brother, Magnus, is ~~real~~ tall and powerful.

See Chapter 32 for more information about adjectives and adverbs.

A Student Essay

Read the essay, and then answer the questions that follow. As you read, correct any errors that you find and make comments in the margins.

African Adventure
by Natalia MacDonald

1   My trip to Africa began with a twenty-hour journey filled with boring flights and long layovers. When I <u>finaly</u> arrived in Ghana, it was 9:00 P.M. local time, and I was exhausted. I went straight to my hotel to get some rest for the long day I had ahead of me. My first day in Ghana left me enthralled but exhausted.

2   <u>Kwame, the coordinator of my volunteer program picked me up to accompany me for the day.</u> As I left the hotel, I was overwhelmed by the heat and the surroundings. Although many people dressed in Western-style clothing, the majority wore traditional African dress. The colors were vibrant: bright blues, purples, and yellows. Men, women, and children alike walked by carrying incredible amounts of goods balanced on their heads with amazing grace and poise. <u>Mothers also carried their babies in a way you had never seen before</u>, tied to their backs with colorful scarves in almost a piggy-back position with the babies' little feet sticking out at either side. As we hurried through the center, I noticed the strong smells of

food being cooked by street vendors, fruit being sold in baskets, and of course the not-so-pleasant smell of the open sewers lining the roads. After getting to the bank and cashing my traveler's checks, it was off to the beach.

3   Everything, from the sand to the activities people were doing, was unique. The first thing I felt was the much-needed cool breeze from the ocean brushing against my face as I approached. After the hustle and bustle of the capital, I felt relaxed as I walked on the beach. I wiggled my toes in the rich, dark, orange sand. I then took a seat in the shade to enjoy a cold beverage and observe my surroundings. Some people were swimming and sunbathing, and others were dancing. There was a particular group of young boys dressed in colorful loincloths dancing to traditional music. The powerful drumbeat of the music was moving. The boys moved their bodies with such a natural fluidity along with the music that I was completely captivated. I was thoroughly enjoying myself, but it was time to catch my bus.

4   The bus was a large white van that left from a station not too far from the beach. As we drove out of the city and onto the dirt road, the scenery was breathtaking. We drove past many different types of villages along the way. Some of the villages were large and had schools, stores, and houses while others were much smaller and more basic and consisted of a circle of around twenty little mud huts with straw roofs with people cooking over an open fire in the middle of the circle. Along the road there were many animals walking around, such as dogs, mules, and small goats. A month later I went to visit a national park to see wild animals. The road itself was the same rich, dark orange color that the sand had been at the beach. One of the most incredible sights were the numerous huge anthills that were formed from the dark orange dirt. They stood about four feet high! After driving through some rain, we finally arrived in Manya Krobo, my new home.

5   My first full day in Ghana was one filled with new discoveries and adventure. In a mere matter of hours, I saw things that I had only read about in books and seen in movies. In one day, I had gone from the snowy minus 18-degree weather of Montreal to the humid 90 degrees of Ghana. My long planned and awaited adventure in Africa was finally a reality.

PRACTICE 5

Revising

1. Highlight the thesis statement.

2. Highlight the topic sentences in paragraphs 2 and 4.

3. Paragraph 3 lacks a topic sentence. One possible topic sentence could be:
   a. I went to the beach that evening.
   (b.) La Pleasure beach was unlike any other beach I had ever seen.
   c. There were many people at La Pleasure beach.
   d. Everyone goes to La Pleasure beach in Ghana.

4. What overall dominant impression does the writer convey in the essay? Underline examples in the essay to support your answer.

   Surprise and awe.   Answers will vary.

5. In paragraph 4, cross out the sentence that does not support the topic sentence.

Editing

6. Paragraph 1 contains a spelling mistake. Underline and correct the mistake. Correction: *finally*

7. Paragraph 2 contains a pronoun shift. Underline and correct the error.

   Correction: *Mothers also carried their babies in a way I had never seen before . . .*

8. Underline and correct a comma error in paragraph 2. *In the morning, Kwame, the coordinator of my volunteer program, picked me up . . .*

9. Underline and correct one subject–verb agreement error in paragraph 4.

   Correction: *One of the most incredible sights was the numerous huge anthills that were formed from the dark orange dirt.*

GRAMMAR LINK

See the following chapters for more information about these grammar topics:
Subject–Verb Agreement, Chapter 27
Pronouns, Chapter 31
Spelling, Chapter 34
Commas, Chapter 35

Teaching Tip: For question 9, explain that the subject is "one," thus the verb must be singular.

Writer's Desk **Revise and Edit Your Essay**

Revise and edit the essay that you wrote for the previous Writer's Desk. You can refer to the revising and editing checklists at the end of this chapter and on this book's inside covers.

A Professional Essay

Lucie L. Snodgrass, a regular contributor to *Vegetarian Times*, is a passionate gardener and a college teacher. She is also the author of *Green Roof Plants: A Resource and Planting Guide*. In the following essay, she reflects on the importance of bees.

Teaching Tip:

Cooperative Learning (Jigsaw)
With students, generate a thesis statement or choose a thesis statement from this chapter's Writer's Desk. Place students in groups of five. One group should write an introduction for that thesis statement. Three groups should write separate body paragraphs, and a fifth group should write a concluding paragraph. (Ask each person in the group to write the same paragraph.) After about ten minutes, ask one representative from each team to stand up. In order, they should read the intro, body paragraphs, and conclusion. If you have time, number students from one to five. The ones get together, the twos get together, and so on. The new teams can revise and edit their essays.

Living Among the Bees
by Lucie L. Snodgrass

1   Scattered along a gently sloping hill on our farm is a series of white wooden boxes that resemble fallen tiles from a game of giant dominos. The boxes arrived one spring six years ago in an old pickup truck driven by Ed Yoder, a longtime neighbor and beekeeper who sells his honey at local supermarkets. Always searching for open land in this county of dwindling farms, Ed approached my husband and me, asking whether we would mind having some hives on our property. Since we didn't, twenty of them—home to about a million bees—came to share our 135 acres. At least that's how we described it initially. In reality, we've come to understand, it is the bees who have consented to share their workspace with us, and we, clumsy and often inadvertently destructive humans, are the better for it.

2   Our coexistence did not get off to an auspicious start. Shortly after the bees moved in, I began, as I always do in spring, spending most of my free time in the vegetable garden—tilling the raised beds, pulling early weeds, and carrying out flats of plants started in the greenhouse some fifty feet away. The bees, I quickly learned, disapproved of my activity. They had claimed this formerly quiet area as their own. They had chosen well, packed as the garden was with nectar-dripping flowers and fruit trees in brilliant bloom, a veritable juice bar that they frequented from early to late.

3   Each of my trips into the garden brought an angry protest as dozens of them dive-bombed my head, just as barn swallows do to cats when their territory is encroached upon. I had always found that funny, but being the victim myself was eminently less amusing. I tried varying the hours that I gardened; I tried apologizing to the bees each time I walked in; I even tried singing to them—all to no avail. Whether I was early or late, contrite or in song, the bees were piqued to see me, a fact made clear by the number of welts on various parts of my body. After six stings, I'd had enough.

4   "Ed," I complained on the beekeeper's next visit, "every time I go into the vegetable garden, your bees sting me. Something's got to give." He returned my gaze, his sympathy evident. "Of course they sting you," he said after a long silence. "You're walking right into their flight path."

5   And so my real experience began of living with the bees and their fiercely protective keeper. I quickly learned that Ed's devotion was complete, his concern solely for them. Implicit in his reply was the suggestion that I, and not the bees, was at fault for getting stung. Only after I pointed out that the garden had been there longer than the hives and that it wasn't feasible to move the orchard did he agree to move the hives that were closest to the garden—a concession I'm sure he secretly regrets even today.

6   That was the only disagreement we've ever had, and perhaps if I had avoided the garden for a while, as Ed bluntly suggested, the problem would have resolved itself. In retrospect, perhaps the bees, like people moving into a new neighborhood, needed some time to settle in without the threat of interference. In any event, they have long since accepted my presence, whether I am picking raspberries, walking on the road back to our nursery—a trip that takes me within ten feet of some of the hives—or simply sitting beside a hive for long stretches, watching the bees come and go. I've never again been stung, not when I've scooped some into my hand to rescue them from drowning in the birdbath or when I've picked them up, so covered with pollen they couldn't fly, to avoid someone trampling them. Ed says that the bees have come to trust me, and I believe that I, in turn, have given them my trust.

7   As wonderful as watching the bees is watching Ed, who is an old-fashioned suitor. He visits the bees almost every day, wooing them with presents, fixing things, delighting in the offerings they give back to him. When he has to disturb the bees, he calms them first, moving among them with his smoker like a priest with incense burners. **Loquacious** by nature, Ed can spend the day talking about his charges: waxing on about their cleanliness, their loyalty to their queen, and their industriousness. Ed's love is infectious. We felt no small amount of pride when he told us after the first year's harvest that their honey production increased dramatically after the bees moved to our farm, certain that our unsprayed fields and flower gardens were responsible. We mourned with him when he lost many of his colonies to mites several years ago and others to a harsh winter. And we have done things that we would never have contemplated, like plowing up a few acres to plant clover because Ed told us that the bees would love it.

loquacious: talkative

8   As with any good teachers, the bees have made me see things in a new light. About a half a mile from the hives is a small, perpetually muddy bog with a boardwalk of old heart pine running through it. In early spring, when the skunk cabbage blooms, I find bees there by the thousands, humming happily and drinking greedily. It is, I now know, their first source of nectar in spring. I am glad, and wiser, to know that the skunk cabbages, which always make my nose wrinkle, are to bees what poached strawberries are to me: both a delectable perfume and a welcome harbinger of spring.

9   The bees' contributions to the farm are everywhere. Berry bushes that bore modestly before the bees' arrival now hang heavy with fruit; my vegetable plants produce an embarrassing abundance of heirloom squash, cucumbers, and runner beans. Even seemingly barren fruit trees, far from the house and orchard in what were once cow pastures, have suddenly begun producing again. And, of course, there is the honey itself,

velvety brown and perfectly sweet, dissolving in my tea and rippling across my bread. None of this is my work; it is all the bees' doing, and in their labor I have found wonder, gratitude, and a welcome sense of my own very modest place in the world.

Teaching Tip:

Cooperative Learning (Ask & Learn) Ask students to review the chapter and identify anything that they are not completely clear about. All students should write three questions on a paper. Then in teams, students can ask other members their questions and share answers.

PRACTICE 6

1. What is the writer's attitude toward the subject? Circle the best answer.
   a. positive   b. negative   c. neutral

2. Highlight the thesis statement.

3. How has the relationship between the writer and the bees changed? Explain, using your own words.   *The bees and the writer have learned to trust each other. The bees no longer sting her.*

4. The writer describes her life with the bees. Highlight some of the most effective examples of imagery.   Answers will vary.

5. A simile is a comparison using *like* or *as*. Highlight one simile in paragraph 6 and another in paragraph 7.

6. Circle some examples where the writer personifies, or attributes human qualities to, the bees.   Answers will vary.

7. Throughout the essay, the writer shows how the bees have had a positive influence on her life. In your own words, give some examples of how the bees have helped the writer.

   Answers will vary.

   The bees have produced more honey after moving to the writer's farm. The bees teach her to appreciate things in nature that she has not appreciated before, like the skunk cabbage. The bees have helped pollinate her orchard and vegetable garden. They have produced quality honey that she likes to eat.

 The Writer's Room

Writing Activity 1: Topics
Write a descriptive essay about one of the following topics, or choose your own topic.

General Topics

1. a music concert
2. the day _____ went to the _____
3. your dream house
4. a night out
5. an exciting sports event

College and Work-Related Topics

6. a beautiful building or area on campus
7. a frustrating day
8. an eccentric professor
9. a new person I have met
10. an exciting event

WRITING LINK

More Descriptive Writing Topics

Chapter 25, Writer's Room topic 1 (page 366)

Chapter 27, Writer's Room topic 1 (page 386)

Chapter 29, Writer's Room topic 1 (page 416)

Chapter 31, Writer's Room topic 1 (page 440)

Chapter 38, Writer's Room topic 1 (page 518)

Writing Activity 2: Photo Writing

Describe an interesting area in your city or a nearby town. You could describe streets, parks, and buildings. Include details that appeal to the senses.

READING LINK

More Descriptive Readings

"Into Thin Air" by Jon Krakauer, page 578

"Guy" by Maya Angelou, page 598

Writing Activity 3: Media Writing

Watch a popular television show or movie that describes a past era. For example, you can watch movies such as *The Hurt Locker*, *Young Victoria*, or *Malcolm X*. Some television shows such as *Mad Men* also describe the past. You can also check on *YouTube* for video clips from past eras. In an essay, describe the setting. Use imagery that appeals to the senses.

Teaching Tip: For Writing Activity 2, you could ask students to discuss in groups a strange or unusual event that they have seen or heard about.

Teaching Tip: Have students read one of the essays in the Reading Link. They could discuss the effectiveness of the imagery.

Teaching Tip:
**Writer's World
Competition**
Please advise
students that they
can submit their
essays for possible
publication to www
.pearsonhighered
.com/essayrewards/
writingrewards.html

CHECKLIST: DESCRIPTIVE ESSAY

After you write your descriptive essay, review the essay checklist on the inside front cover. Also ask yourself these questions.

☐ Does my thesis statement clearly show what I will describe in the essay?

☐ Does my thesis statement have a controlling idea that makes a point about the topic?

☐ Does my essay have a dominant impression?

☐ Does each body paragraph contain supporting details that appeal to the reader's senses?

☐ Do I use vivid language?

mywritinglab To check your progress in meeting this chapter's objectives, log in to **www.mywritinglab.com,** go to the **Study Plan** tab, click on **Essay Patterns** and choose **Description** from the list of subtopics. Read and view the resources in the **Review Materials** section, and then complete the **Recall, Apply,** and **Write** sets in the **Activities** section.

Process

Every industry uses processes. For example, to make pottery, an artists needs to shape, fire, and glaze the pot. Along similar lines, not only do writers have to follow the writing process, but sometimes they need to be able to explain processes to their readers as well.

Writers' Exchange

Choose one of the following topics, and have a group or class discussion. Describe the steps you would take to do that process.

- How to discipline a child
- How to deal with the flu
- How to get rich quickly
- How to parallel park

Teaching Tip:

Cooperative Learning (Nonstop Talking) The Writers' Exchange activity helps students understand process. Place students in small groups. Taking turns, students speak without stopping. Give them about 40 seconds to speak, and flick the lights every time you want the speakers to change. As an additional activity, you can then ask the team to write a group paragraph about one of the topics in the Writers' Exchange.

EXPLORING

What Is Process?

A **process** is a series of steps usually done in chronological order. In process writing, you explain how to do something, how an incident took place, or how something works.

People explain processes every day. At home, parents might explain to their children how to cook spaghetti. At college, a professor may explain to students how they could become tutors. At work, an employer could describe to newly hired interns how to perform their daily responsibilities.

Visualizing Process

PRACTICE I   Brainstorm supporting ideas for the following thesis statement. Write a few words to show each step.   Answers will vary.

THESIS STATEMENT: When you are traveling to a tropical destination, there are some important steps to follow.

Find out what travel
  documents you need.
Get passport well
  ahead of trip.
Find out about visas
  or other travel
  permits.

Get vaccinations.
Remember to take
  along prescription
  medication.
Pack bandages,
  lotions, and creams.

Don't overpack.
Pack wrinkle-free and
  easy-to-wash clothes.
Take a good pair of
  walking shoes.

Teaching Tip:
Ask students to identify the steps in the process.

Process at Work
Frank Morelli is a mechanic who specializes in repairing sports cars. In this pamphlet excerpt, he advises customers on how to buy a car.

First, decide if you want a new or used car. There are some advantages and disadvantages for both. A new car will be more expensive, but you can buy an extended warranty, and a new car will probably not incur expensive repairs. A used car is, of course, more economical. However, if the previous owner has not properly maintained the car, you may have to pay for costly repairs, and the car may not last for very long.

Next, research the safety record of the car that you want to buy. Some types of cars offer extensive safety features such as dual airbags and a reinforced frame. To find information about the safety statistics of the car you want to buy, consult the car insurance Web sites or read some consumer magazines that deal with cars.

The Process Essay

Before planning a process essay, you need to determine your purpose. Do you want to tell readers how to complete a process or how to understand a process?

1. **Complete a process.** This type of essay contains directions for completing a particular task. For example, a writer might explain how to change a flat tire, how to decorate a room, or how to use a particular computer program.
2. **Understand a process.** This type of essay explains how something works or how something happens. For example, a writer might explain how the admissions process at a college works or how food goes from the farm to the table.

A Student Essay

Read the essay and answer the questions that follow.

Learning Good Finances
by Tony Ruiz

1   Every year, when you apply for more student aid, it takes a toll on your fiscal confidence. No matter how well you think you have curbed your spending, you always find yourself staring at your W-2 tax return form in disbelief. Your humble living standards do not reflect the overwhelming

discrepancy between your alleged total earnings and your most recent bank statement. Students can begin making smart financial decisions today and help reduce the financial burden they are likely to experience after graduation.

2   Students should avoid spending money on unnecessary gadgets. For example, the iPod is a terrible investment for students who are trying to save money. Besides paying around $150 for the iPod nano and more than $500 for the iPad, consumers end up buying crucial trendy accessories. An FM transmitter that will let listeners wire their iPod through a car's sound system costs around $30. For those who want to listen to FM radio while walking to class, the FM Radio Remote costs about $45. And before long, the iPod's dead battery will have to be replaced for about $30 (plus shipping and handling). Some students might even be tempted to buy a newer model of iPod. Meanwhile, an impressive iTunes library costs about $1 for every song and $3 for every episode of *Glee* that could be watched on television at no cost.

3   Another common mistake students make is adopting expensive daily regimens. They should reduce "treat" spending by half. For the sluggish, a $4.50 personalized Starbucks coffee is the only way to function. Jamba Juice is the formidable, health-conscious counterpart. Replacing the designer drink every day with generic coffee or fruit juice would amount to substantial savings. Skipping the Chai Latte or the Mocha Cappuccino Delight three days out of five is painless but effective.

4   Students can earn more money by investing carefully. Setting aside even as little as $500 every year toward student debt means that after a four-year period, they will have $2,000 less to worry about paying off. The elimination of interest charges will generate pocket change in the long term as well. Furthermore, student loans also offer a unique advantage. Since students will not feel the cost until graduation, they should make that money work for them. Those who are absolutely sure that they will not need a certain amount of money until graduation can lock up the money in a certificate of deposit and let it earn interest typically higher than those of savings and money market accounts.

5   Nobody expects students to invest all of their time and money in scholarly endeavors. Everybody needs to have some leisure activities. But they should be reasonable. New gadgets and expensive habits are unnecessary indulgences.

PRACTICE 2

1. Highlight the thesis statement.

2. Highlight the topic sentence in each body paragraph.

3. Who is the audience for this essay? __*College students*__

4. For each of the body paragraphs, list some supporting details the writer gives.

Paragraph 2: _iPod nano = $150. iPad = more than $500; FM Radio_
Remote = about $45

Paragraph 3: _Starbucks coffee; Jamba Juice; $4.50 per specialized_
drink

Paragraph 4: _Saving $500 a year will lead to $2,000 after two years._
Lock the money into a certificate of deposit.

Explore Topics

In the Writer's Desk Warm Up, you will try an exploring strategy to generate ideas about different topics.

Teaching Tip:
The Writer's Desk activities, such as the one below, provide students with an opportunity to develop a topic through all stages of the writing process using the process rhetorical mode. In the Warm Up, they begin by exploring various topics. These topics then carry on throughout the chapter.

Writer's Desk Warm Up

Read the following questions, and write the first ideas that come to your mind. Think of two or three ideas for each topic.

EXAMPLE: Imagine that you are starting college tomorrow. What are some steps that you would take to make your first day of class successful?

—start to get organized the day before

—try to make a good first impression

—don't stress out; try to relax

1. What are some ways to save money?

_____

_____

_____

2. What can you do to fall out of love?

_____

_____

_____

3. How can you become a better friend?

_____

_____

_____

DEVELOPING

When you write a process essay, choose a process that you know something about. For example, you might be able to explain how to become more environmentally conscious; however, you might not know how to reduce nuclear waste.

The Thesis Statement

In a process essay, the thesis statement states what process you will be explaining and what readers will be able to do after they have read the essay.

topic   controlling idea

Remaining attractive to your spouse can help keep your relationship exciting.

controlling idea   topic

Consistency, patience, and time are essential **to becoming a good parent**.

Writer's Desk **Thesis Statements**

Write a thesis statement for each of the following topics. You can look for ideas in the Warm Up on page 137. Each thesis statement should state the process and contain a controlling idea.

EXAMPLE: Topic: how to prepare for the first day of class

Thesis Statement: *To have a good first day of class, follow the next steps.*
_____

1. Topic: how to save money

   Thesis Statement: _____

   _____

2. Topic: how to fall out of love

   Thesis Statement: _____

   _____

3. Topic: how to become a better friend

   Thesis Statement: _____

   _____

The Supporting Ideas

A process essay contains a series of steps. When you develop supporting ideas for a process essay, think about the main steps that are necessary to complete the process.

- Use prewriting strategies such as freewriting and brainstorming to generate ideas.
- Choose the best ideas. Clearly explain the steps of the process.
- Organize your ideas. Choose the best organizational method for this essay pattern. Process essays generally use chronological (time) order.

Hint   **Give Steps, Not Examples**

When you explain how to complete a process, describe each step. Do not simply list examples of the process.

Topic: How to Plan an Interesting Vacation

List of Examples
- going to a tropical island
- riding a hot air balloon
- swimming with the sharks
- touring an exotic city

Steps in the Process
- decide what your goal is
- research possible locations
- find out the cost
- plan the itinerary according to budget

Teaching Tip:
Go over these examples with students. Make sure that they see the difference between a list of examples of an interesting vacation and a process explaining how *to plan* an interesting vacation.

Writer's Desk   **List the Main Steps**

Choose one thesis statement from the previous Writer's Desk. List the main steps to complete the process.

EXAMPLE:

Thesis Statement: *To have a good first day of classes, follow the next steps.*

1. *Get your final preparations done the day before classes begin.*

2. *Make a good impression with professors and other students.*

3. *Remember to relax.*

Thesis Statement: _____

Teaching Tip:
For extra practice, ask students to develop supporting ideas for all three Writer's Desk topics. The topics are listed in the Warm Up.

Steps to complete the process:

_____

_____

_____

_____

_____

Teaching Tip:
Some students may find it easier to plan their essays if they include their three points in their thesis statements.

Tech
Teaching Tip:
Ask students to find a topic on the eHow Web site by going to www.ehow .com. They can review the top-ten list. Place students in pairs or groups, and ask them to choose the clearest or most interesting process samples in the top-ten list. You can also ask students to post their own "how to" paragraphs on the site.

The Essay Plan

An essay plan helps you organize your thesis statement, topic sentences, and supporting details before you write a first draft. Decide which steps and which details your reader will really need to complete the process or understand it.

THESIS STATEMENT: To have a good first day of classes, begin preparations the day before classes start, focus on making a good first impression, and remember to relax.

   I. Immediately get all your final preparations done.
     A. Buy remaining school supplies.
     B. Gas up your car.
     C. Find nice clothes.
     D. Get a good night's sleep.
  II. Make a good first impression.
     A. Set your alarm clock early.
     B. Get to your class on time.
     C. Impress classmates with your preparedness.
 III. Remember to relax.
     A. Relaxing will help you take everything one step at a time.
     B. If you are not relaxed, you may have a meltdown.

Teaching Tip:
Ask students to keep their essay plans and then attach them to their final draft. You can then determine how the students have developed their ideas.

Writer's Desk **Write an Essay Plan**

Refer to the information you generated in previous Writer's Desks, and prepare a detailed essay plan. Add details and examples that will help to explain each step.

The First Draft

As you write your first draft, explain the process in a way that would be clear for your audience. Address the reader directly. For example, instead of writing "You should scan the newspaper for used cars," simply write "Scan the newspaper for used cars." Also, remember to use complete sentences and transitions to smoothly string together the ideas from your essay plan. Here are some time-order transitions that are useful for explaining processes.

Teaching Tip:

To begin a process	To continue a process		To end a process
(at) first	after that	later	eventually
initially	afterward	meanwhile	finally
the first step	also	second	in the end
	furthermore	then	ultimately
	in addition	third	

  Avoid Sentence Fragments

Ensure that you do not use sentence fragments to list the steps of the process. A sentence must have a subject and a verb to express a complete idea.

Consider your airline's carry-on luggage requirements. First, the weight of
                                                         ^check
your suitcase.

See Chapter 23 for more information about sentence fragments.

Writer's Desk **Write the First Draft**

In the previous Writer's Desk, you developed an essay plan. Now, carefully review your essay plan, make any necessary changes, and write the first draft of your process essay.

REVISING AND EDITING

Revise and Edit a Process Essay

When you finish writing a process essay, carefully review your work and revise it to make the process as clear as possible to your readers. Check to make sure that you have organized your steps, and remove any details that are not relevant to

Cooperative Learning (Jigsaw) Working with the class, generate a thesis statement or choose a thesis statement from this chapter's Writer's Desk. Place students in groups of five. Ask one group to write an introduction for that thesis statement. Ask three groups to write separate body paragraphs, and a fifth group to write a concluding paragraph. (Ask each person in the group to write the same paragraph.) After about ten minutes, invite one representative from each team to stand up and in correct order read the intro, body paragraphs, and conclusion. If you have time, number students from one to five. The ones get together, the twos get together, and so on. The new teams can revise and edit their work.

being able to complete or understand the process. Before you revise and edit your own essay, practice revising and editing a student essay.

A Student Essay

Read the essay, and then answer the questions that follow. As you read, correct any errors that you find and make comments in the margins.

Steps to Help Out Your First Day of Classes
by Justin Sanders

1   Summer vacation was fun; you played hard and saw too much sun. As soon as you realize that classes start tomorrow, the reality of summer vacation shatters instantly like a window being hit by a baseball. You begin to pull your hair out from anxiety about and anticipation for the following morning. Fear not; I have a few helpful tips to aid you through your first day of classes. Pull out your highlighter, your notebook, your laptop, and your calculator and take careful notes. Ready? To have a good first day of classes, begin preparations the day before classes begin, focus on making a good first impression, and remember to relax.

2   You might think that since classes do not start until tomorrow, you have one more day to play. Use today to get all your final preparations done. Otherwise, tomorrow could be a bad day. Write down all the school supplies that you have and don't have. Figure out how long it will take you to buy the remaining supplies. If you're like me, you will remember to buy at least twenty pencils so that you can end tomorrow with at least one of them. You never know who might need one or how many you will accidentally leave behind in a class as you nervously run off to your next class. Schedule time for your most expensive activity: putting a few gallons of gas in your tank. Stop by your local clothing store, and pick up something new and in style. To replace those moth-eaten rags you have been wearing over the vacation. It would be a fashion disaster to wear the same outfit twice in the first week. Think hard. Make sure that you consider every last thing you could possibly need, and make time to get it. You will need to plan for your bedtime. If you want to be alert and ready for your classes the next day, get a good night's sleep.

3   Tomorrow is now today. Classes begin. You should have set your alarm early enough to get ready and to make sure you get to class on time. Making a good first impression can have a big impact on the entire semester. If you are on the instructor's good side, he or she might be more lenient with due dates, offer extra credit, give extra help on assignments,

and probably more. ~~Now, granted, there are instructors that are as hard as rocks and are so indifferent that it doesn't matter what you do because it won't help.~~ Also, during your first day, there are other areas where you will want to make a good impression. During some of your classes, you may find yourself seated next to an attractive person. <u>Impress them with your incredible preparedness by loaning one of your pencils</u>. In such a situation, you really hope you woke up on time, you wore a matching outfit, and you showered. If you smell like the gym socks you left in the locker room over the summer and look like a three-year-old dressed you, it might be a little hard to ask out or be asked out by this person. Impressions are important, so take your time and make a good one.

4   Relaxation will allow you to take everything one step at a time. Not relaxing can result in a major breakdown. <u>If you fall apart, I sincerely hope you made a really good first impression on your instructors before the meltdown, that way you will survive the semester.</u>

5   If you follow these simple steps, you will have a great first day of classes. You are now in with your instructors, you may have a date, and you won't fall into a bottomless hole of depression from stress and anxiety. I hope this gives you a pleasant enough outlook on the future to encourage you to repeat these steps many times for the next eternity, or at least until graduation. Good luck and remember that school does end . . . some year.

PRACTICE 3

Revising

1. Highlight the thesis statement.

2. Highlight the topic sentences for paragraphs 2 and 3. (Remember that a topic sentence may not always be the first sentence in the paragraph.)

3. Paragraph 2 lacks transitions. Add at least three transitions to link the sentences.   Answers will vary.

_____   _____   _____

4. In paragraph 3, cross out the sentence that does not support the topic sentence.

5. Which of the following would make an effective topic sentence for paragraph 4?
   a. With all the stress and tensions of school, remember one key thing: relax.
   b. Becoming nervous is not a good idea.
   c. All students get stressed on the first day of classes.

6. Paragraph 4 lacks adequate support. Think of a detailed example that would help flesh out the paragraph.   Answers will vary.

_____

_____

GRAMMAR LINK

See the following chapters for more information about these grammar topics:
Fragments,
    Chapter 23
Run-Ons, Chapter 24
Pronouns,
    Chapter 31

Editing

7. Underline a sentence fragment in paragraph 2. Then correct it.

Correction: _Stop by your local clothing store, and pick up something_
new and in style to replace those moth-eaten rags you have been
wearing over the vacation.

8. Underline a pronoun error in paragraph 3. Write the correction below.

Correction: _Impress him or her with your incredible preparedness by_
loaning one of your pencils.

9. Underline the run-on sentence in paragraph 4. Then correct it here.

Correction: _If this happens, I sincerely hope you made a really good first_
impression on your instructors before the breakdown. That way you will
survive the semester.

Writer's Desk Revise and Edit Your Process Essay

Revise and edit the essay that you wrote for the previous Writer's Desk. You can refer to the revising and editing checklists at the end of this chapter and on this book's inside covers.

---

vo•cab•u•lar•y BOOST

Look at the first draft of your process essay. Underline the verb that you use to describe each step of the process. Then, when possible, come up with a more evocative verb. Use your thesaurus for this activity.

A Professional Essay

Journalist Stacey Colino specializes in health and family issues and has written for *The Washington Post*, *Parenting*, and *Shape*. In the next essay, she writes about how to become a happier person.

Do You Have What It Takes to Be Happy?
by Stacey Colino

1   If you add up money, beauty, fame and admiration, you've got the formula for a lifetime of bliss, right? Wrong. The truth is, your financial status, external circumstances, and life events account for no more than 15 percent of your happiness quotient, studies show. What elements do make a difference? Surprisingly simple internal factors such as having healthy self-esteem, a sense of optimism and hope, gratifying relationships, and meaning and purpose in your life have the most influence, according to recent studies on what researchers call "subjective well-being."

2   If that sounds like a tall order, here's the good news: Even if they don't come naturally, many of the attitudes and thought patterns that influence happiness can be cultivated, which means you can boost your capacity for happiness today—and in the future. "Studies with twins reveal that happiness is somewhat like a person's cholesterol level—it's genetically influenced, but it's also influenced by some factors that are under our control," explains David Myers, Ph.D., a social psychologist at Hope College in Holland, Michigan, and author of *The Pursuit of Happiness* (Harper-Collins, 1993). In other words, while your genetically determined temperament has a fairly strong influence on your happiness quotient, you can nudge it upward with the attitudes and approaches you bring to your life. To develop a sunnier disposition, use the simple strategies outlined below, and you'll be on your way to a richer, more satisfying life, starting now!

3   Develop an upbeat attitude. No, you don't want to become a Pollyanna who overlooks problems and thinks everything is peachy even when it isn't. But you do want to consciously focus on what's positive in your life because this can engender a sense of optimism and hope. And research has found that happy people are brimming with these key ingredients. In one study at Southern Methodist University in Dallas, happy subjects were more hopeful about their wishes than their less **sanguine** peers. It's not that their wishes came true more often, but the happy people expected them to come true. How? They do it by expecting to have a joyful summer every day, not just when they're on vacation, by identifying negative thoughts and countering them with positive or neutral ones, and by embracing challenges (such as parasailing or public speaking) instead of fearing them. Such people realize that challenges will help them grow as a person.

sanguine: optimistic

4   Hang out with your favorite people. It's as simple as this: Carving out as much time as you can to spend with people you value gives you a sense of connection, as well as a support system for when your luck heads south. Research at the University of Illinois at Urbana–Champaign found that people who are consistently very happy have stronger romantic and social relationships than unhappy people. "We're social creatures by nature,"

says Louis H. Janda, an associate professor of psychology at Old Dominion University in Norfolk, Virginia. "When you're involved with others, it gives you a sense of belonging and lets you engage in mutually enjoyable activities, all of which can buffer you from stress."

5   Infuse your life with a sense of purpose. If you want to be happy, it is important to give your life meaning: Research at Middle Tennessee State University in Murfreesboro found that having a sense of purpose is a significant predictor of happiness and life satisfaction. To create a vision of what's meaningful to you, ask yourself, "What activities make me feel excited or enthusiastic? What do I want to be remembered for? What matters most to me?" If you can articulate these desires to yourself, you can set specific goals to help you fulfill them. If you realize that your strongest desire is to become an influential teacher and role model, for example, you might set a goal of volunteering to help disadvantaged kids or of going back to school to get your teaching degree.

6   Count your blessings, not your burdens. When people keep a gratitude journal, in which they jot down a daily list of what they appreciate in their lives, they experience a heightened sense of well being, according to research at the University of California, Davis, and the University of Miami in Florida. "There's a natural tendency to take things for granted, but if you stop and think of all the ways you are blessed, it doesn't take long for the mind to use that as the new baseline for perceiving how happy you are," explains study co-author Michael E. McCullough, Ph.D., an associate professor of psychology and religious studies at the University of Miami.

7   Recharge your energy and your spirits. Sure, exercise can work wonders in keeping your mood buoyant, but so can getting some simple R & R. "Happy people lead active, vigorous lives yet reserve time for restorative sleep and solitude," Myers says. Short-change yourself of the shut-eye you need, and it's hard to enjoy much of anything when you're exhausted. In a recent study involving more than nine hundred women, researchers assessed how happy women were based on their daily activities and found that sleep quality had a substantial influence over how much the women enjoyed life, even when they engaged in plenty of pleasurable activities like sex and socializing.

8   Put on a happy face! If you act as if you're on cloud nine—by smiling with your mouth and eyes, speaking in a cheerful voice, and walking confidently—going through the motions can trigger the actual emotion. There's even science to prove it: A study at Fairleigh Dickinson University in Teaneck, New Jersey, found that when people forced themselves to smile or laugh, they experienced a substantial boost in mood afterward.

9   So start off by acting as if you're walking on the sunny side of the street—even if it's cloudy. Chances are, you'll begin to feel a little happier after just a few steps!

R & R:
rest and relaxation

PRACTICE 4

1. What is the writer's specific purpose? *To show people how to be happy*

2. Highlight the thesis statement. It may not be in the first paragraph.

3. Find the topic sentence of each body paragraph. Highlight the verbs in each topic sentence.

4. In each topic sentence, the subject is implied but not stated. What is the subject?
    The subject is "you."

5. In paragraph 5, list the examples the writer gives to support the topic sentence.
    Give your life meaning, ask yourself questions to find what is meaningful
    in your life, and set goals to achieve that meaning.

6. The writer supported her main ideas with many specific examples. Identify and underline six research studies that the writer refers to.

7. Circle the names of three experts that the writer quotes.

8. The writer uses no transitional words or phrases to link the steps of the process. Add a transitional word or expression to the beginning of at least four body paragraphs.
    Answers will vary.

Teaching Tip:

Cooperative Learning (Question Cards) Place students in teams of three or four. Using index cards or paper cut into four sections, each team brainstorms six questions about the chapter's key concepts. The teams write the question on one side of the paper and the answer on the other side. Then teams can exchange cards with another team. They can look at each question, answer it as a group, and then check the answer.

The Writer's Room

Writing Activity 1: Topics

Write a process essay about one of the following topics, or choose your own topic.

General Topics

How to . . .

1. buy a used car
2. become a good driver
3. communicate more effectively with family members
4. win a _____
5. do an activity or a hobby

College and Work-Related Topics

How to . . .

6. look for a new job
7. assemble a _____
8. become a better manager or supervisor
9. change a law
10. make a good impression at an interview

WRITING LINK

More Process Writing Topics

Chapter 21, Writer's
   Room topic 2
   (page 328)
Chapter 25, Writer's
   Room topic 2
   (page 366)
Chapter 26, Writer's
   Room topic 1
   (page 374)
Chapter 30, Writer's
   Room topic 1
   (page 425)

READING LINK

More Process Readings

"The Rich
   Resonance of
   Small Talk" by
   Roxanne
   Roberts
   (page 567)
"The Rules of
   Survival" by
   Laurence
   Gonzales
   (page 573)

Teaching Tip:
Have students read
one of the essays in
the Reading Link
and discuss the
main ideas. Also
ask students what
characteristics the
reading has that
classify it as a
process essay.

Writing Activity 2: Photo Writing

What are some steps people can take to have an enduring personal relationship?

Writing Activity 3: Media Writing

Watch a television show or movie about training an animal. For example, watch the television show *The Dog Whisperer*, the channel *Animal Planet*, or a movie such as *The Horse Whisperer* or *Seabiscuit*. You might also look on *YouTube* for videos about animal training. In an essay, explain how to train a dog, horse, cat, bird, or other animal.

✔ **CHECKLIST: PROCESS ESSAY**

As you write your process essay, review the checklist on the inside front cover. Also ask yourself these questions.

☐ Does my thesis statement make a point about the process?

☐ Do I include all of the steps in the process?

☐ Do I clearly explain each step so my reader can accomplish the process?

☐ Do I mention all of the supplies that my reader needs to complete the process?

☐ Do I use transitions to connect all of the steps in the process?

PEARSON mywritinglab To check your progress in meeting this chapter's objectives, log in to **www.mywritinglab.com,** go to the **Study Plan** tab, click on **Essay Patterns** and choose **Process** from the list of subtopics. Read and view the resources in the **Review Materials** section, and then complete the **Recall, Apply,** and **Write** sets in the **Activities** section.

Teaching Tip:
You could ask students to brainstorm together and come up with ways to achieve wealth, happiness, notoriety, education, or love.

Teaching Tip:
Writer's World Competition
Please advise students that they can submit their essays for possible publication to www .pearsonhighered .com/essayrewards/ writingrewards.html

Definition

To help patients understand a diagnosis, doctors may define the illness itself or explain related medical terms. Similarly, you may write an entire essay in which you define a term. Or, you may need to define only a few terms within an essay to ensure that your readers understand specific concepts.

Writers' Exchange

Brainstorm some common slang expressions. Think about words you use to express pleasure or disgust. You can also consider words describing a specific type of person. Choose one expression and define it without using a dictionary. Make your definition clear so that a nonnative speaker will understand the word.

EXPLORING

What Is Definition?

When you define, you explain the meaning of a word. Some terms have concrete meanings, and you can define them in a few words. For example, a *town* is "a small city." Other terms, such as *values*, *faith*, or *human rights*, are more abstract and require more detailed definitions. It is possible to write a paragraph, an essay, or even an entire book about such concepts.

People often try to define what they mean. For example, at home, parents might explain to their children what it means to be *reliable*. At college, a professor may ask students to define the term *poverty*. At work, a colleague could tell her coworkers that their business presentation *needs improvement*, and then she could explain what she means.

Visualizing Definition

PRACTICE 1   Brainstorm supporting ideas for the following thesis statement.

Answers may vary.

THESIS STATEMENT: A home is not just wood, plaster, and shingles; it is a place where one feels safe.

invite friends

celebrate special occasions

relax

bond over board games

share meals with the family

meet with friends

create strong bonds

Teaching Tip:
The Writers' Exchange activity can help your students understand definition. This activity can be done in small groups or as a class discussion. Write students' definitions on the board. You might draw their attention to the types of definitions students use (definition by synonym, category, or negation). Place nonnative speakers with native speakers.

Teaching Tip:
Remind students that abstract nouns such as *beauty* and *friendship* can often be misunderstood. Students should support their definitions by using concrete nouns, which are clearer.

The Definition Essay

When you write a definition essay, try to explain what a term means to you. For example, if someone asks you to define *overachiever*, you might give examples of overachievers and what you think those people do that goes beyond the limits. You may also explain what an overachiever is not. Also, remember the next two points.

1. **Choose a term that you know something about.** You need to understand a term to say something relevant and interesting about it.
2. **Give a clear definition.** Write a definition that your reader will easily understand, and support your definition with examples.

Definition at Work

In the following excerpt, Anthony Mullen, 2009 National Teacher of the Year, defines one characteristic of an exceptional teacher.

Passion is the noblest of the trio because it ignites a flame too bright to be ignored by students. A teacher must project passion in the classroom because this powerful emotion sparks the learning process in children and motivates them to remember key concepts and ideas. Students can feel the energy, enthusiasm, and creativity radiating from a teacher and realize that what is being taught is important and worthwhile.

Hint ❯ **Consider Your Audience**

Consider your audience when you write a definition essay. You may have to adjust your tone and vocabulary, depending on who will be reading the essay. For example, if you write a definition essay about cloning for your political science class, you may have to explain concepts using basic, nontechnical terms. If you write the same essay for your biology class, you may be able to use more technical terms.

A Student Essay

Read the student essay and answer the questions that follow.

Journalists Are History's Record Keepers
by Lindsey Davis

1   When you want to find research for that paper on World War II for class, you hit the books in the library, looking for the historian who summed up the events or the political scientist who offered critical insight as to why it happened. But when you want to find out what is happening in the world right now, you pick up the *Los Angeles Times* or log onto your computer and browse the **plethora** of news sites. Journalists play multiple roles in society. From acting as a check on government and business to hosting a forum for free and open debate, the **Fourth Estate** plays a crucial role in society. But beyond this, journalists are historians. They are the note takers and storytellers who document today's activities and events and preserve them for a record of history.

2   First, different types of media are crucial for preserving historical records. Newspapers, news Web sites, and television news programs are the only places you can find the latest developments concerning what is happening in Washington, what reforms Governor Jerry Brown is planning, the status of the war in Afghanistan, and the crucial stats of the last NFL playoff game. Before it goes into the history books, that information goes into the newspaper. Before you can find it in the library, you can find it in the news.

3   Moreover, journalists are the record keepers for the community. They will give you the plain and simple facts. They will find out how much those tickets were selling for at the Rose Bowl. They will tell you who won the basketball games and what the upcoming baseball season looks like. But beyond simple facts, they will record the emotions of a Rose Bowl defeat. How about those new movies and CDs that are coming out next week? They will give you the scoop of what's good and what's bad. They will tell you what you can't miss in Los Angeles. You can find the thoughts and analyses of a vast array of differing voices.

4   Furthermore, journalists are also crucial to preserving the spirit of the times. It is within the media that you'll find the record of the year's events. But this history won't be complete unless it includes your voice, your opinion, and your perspective on events. Tell the journalists what's going on and what you would like to see covered. Send them an e-mail. Talk to reporters and tell them what you think. The media will never be able to create an accurate record of history unless you help gather all the facts by saying what you know or what you saw. Do you think something was wrongly covered? Let the media know. Do you disagree with a column you have read? Send a letter to the editor, and make sure your viewpoint is printed and recorded as well.

plethora: a large amount
Fourth Estate: the entire press, including newspapers, television news programs, magazines, etc.

5   Journalists are committed to ensuring that whatever happens is recorded forever. Some people say that journalists write the first rough draft of history. But they strive to report accurately enough that their record of history will be the final draft. Their dedication ensures that you get the news and ensures that history is recorded. All they ask is that you read to keep the history alive.

PRACTICE 2

1. What is the specific purpose of this essay? *It is to inform the reader about the importance of the press for recording history.*

2. Highlight the thesis statement.

3. Highlight the topic sentence of each body paragraph.

4. What introductory style is used? Circle the best answer.
   a. anecdote
   b. historical
   c. contrasting position
   d. general background

5. In your own words, list some of the specific examples in each body paragraph.   Answers will vary.

   Paragraph 2: newspapers, television, Web sites give latest development in news and sports

   Paragraph 3: cost of tickets, who won game, new CDs

   Paragraph 4: record of year's events, letters to the editor, interactions between the public and the media

6. Circle the transitional expressions that link the body paragraphs.

Explore Topics

In the Writer's Desk Warm Up, you will try an exploring strategy to generate ideas about different topics.

Teaching Tip:
Writer's World Competition
The Writer's Desk activities, such as the one below, provide students with opportunities to develop a topic through all stages of the writing process using the definition rhetorical mode. In the Warm Up, they begin by exploring various topics. Those topics then carry on throughout the chapter.

Writer's Desk **Warm Up**

Read the following questions, and write the first ideas that come to your mind. Think of two or three ideas for each topic.

EXAMPLE: What is a Goth? Think of some characteristics of a Goth.

—*wear black*

—*people stare at them*

—*not mainstream*

—*listen to Goth metal*

1. What is a fame junkie?

2. What is the American dream?

3. What is a religion?

---

vo•cab•u•lar•y BOOST

Some words have neutral, positive, or negative associations. Look at each set of words and categorize each as neutral (=), positive (+), or negative (–). Do this with a partner.

1. thin, cadaverous, lean, emaciated, wiry, skinny, slender

2. home, shack, cottage, slum, stomping ground, dump, sanctuary

3. dainty, delicate, finicky, fussy, prissy, fragile, elegant, frail

4. honest, coarse, crude, open, gross, straightforward

5. brat, child, sweetheart, cutie, munchkin, delinquent, heir, mama's boy

ESL
Teaching Tip:
Pair native and nonnative speakers in mixed groups to do the Vocabulary Boost. Nonnative speakers may not understand all of the connotations.

DEVELOPING

The Thesis Statement

A clear thesis statement for a definition essay introduces the term and provides a definition. There are three basic ways to define a term.

Definition by Synonym

Providing a definition by synonym is useful if the original term is difficult to understand, and the synonym is a more familiar word.

term   +   synonym

He is a neophyte,   which means he is a beginner or novice.

Definition by Category

When you define by category, you determine the larger group to which the term belongs. Then you determine what unique characteristics set the term apart from others in that category.

term   +   category   +   detail

A forest ranger   is a worker   who is trained to protect
                                            wildlife in national parks.

Definition by Negation

When you define by negation, you explain what a term does not mean. You can then include a sentence explaining what it does mean.

term   +   what it is not   +   what it is

Obsession   is not an eccentricity;   it is a mental illness.

 Using Semicolons

You can join two related and complete ideas with a semicolon, as the writer has done in this example of a definition.

> **EXAMPLE:** Marriage is not the end of your freedom; it is the beginning of a shared journey.

See Chapter 21 for more information about using semicolons.

Making a Point

Defining a term by synonym, category, and negation is only a guideline for writing thesis statements for a definition essay. Keep in mind that your essay will be more interesting if you express your attitude or point of view in your thesis statement.

No point: Avarice means greed.

Point: Avarice, or greed, invariably leads to tragedy.

PRACTICE 3   Write thesis statements by defining the following terms using your own words. Try to make definitions by synonym, category, and negation. Remember to indicate your controlling idea in the thesis statements.   Answers will vary.

EXAMPLE: Road rage *is not a momentary lapse of judgment; it is serious*

criminal behavior.

1. A meltdown _____

_____

2. Helicopter parents _____

_____

3. Public opinion _____

_____

4. Youthful _____

_____

5. The school of hard knocks _____

_____

Hint   **Be Precise!**

When you write a definition essay, it is important to use precise words to define the term. Moreover, when you define a term by category, make sure that the category for your term is correct.

Anorexia nervosa is the <u>inability</u> to eat.
(Anorexia nervosa is not an ability or an inability.)

Anorexia nervosa is <u>when</u> you want to be thin.
(*When* refers to a time, but anorexia nervosa is not a time.)

Anorexia nervosa is <u>where</u> it is hard to eat properly.
(*Where* refers to a place, but anorexia nervosa is not a place.)

Now look at a better definition of this illness.

Anorexia nervosa is a tragic **eating disorder** characterized by the desire to become very thin.

Teaching Tip:
Ask students to compare the following examples. Which sentence in each pair clearly indicates a point of view or attitude? (1) He is a critic, which means he states his opinion; He is a controversial critic, stating opinions that jar people from their comfort zone; (2) Westerns are films set in the North American frontier; Set in the North American frontier, Westerns are films that raise audience passions and longings; (3) A statesman is not a politician but a leader; A statesman is not an ordinary politician but a skilled and farsighted leader.

ESL
Teaching Tip:
Group Work
For Practice 3, pair nonnative speakers with native speakers. Students should also discuss if they have defined the term using a synonym, category, or negation. If they do not remember the types of definitions, refer them to page 156.

PRACTICE 4   Revise each sentence using precise language.
Answers will vary.

EXAMPLE: Multitasking is when you do many activities at once.

Multitasking is doing many activities at once.

1. A spin doctor is when public opinion is influenced by manipulating information.

   A spin doctor manipulates information to influence public opinion.

2. A poor loser is the inability to accept defeat graciously.

   A poor loser is a person who is unable to accept defeat graciously.

3. Brain candy is someone having an enjoyable experience associated with fluffy entertainment.

   Brain candy is an enjoyable experience associated with fluffy entertainment.

Teaching Tip:
Explain to students that word connotations are important for revealing their attitude toward the subject of their text.

Writer's Desk   Write Thesis Statements

Write a thesis statement in which you define each of the following topics. You can look for ideas in the previous Writer's Desk. Remember to make a point in your thesis statement.

EXAMPLE: Topic: Goth

Thesis Statement: *Goth is a complete lifestyle that embraces attitude, culture, and fashion.*

1. Topic: a fame junkie

   Thesis statement: _____

   _____

2. Topic: the American dream

   Thesis statement: _____

   _____

3. Topic: a religion

   Thesis statement: _____

   _____

   _____

The Supporting Ideas

After you have developed an effective thesis statement, generate supporting ideas. In a definition essay, you can give examples that clarify your definition. To develop supporting ideas follow these three steps:

- Use prewriting strategies to generate ideas. Think about facts, anecdotes, and examples that will help define your term.
- Choose the best ideas. Use examples that clearly reveal the definition of the term.
- Organize your ideas. Choose the best organizational method for this essay pattern.

Teaching Tip:
You can make the Writer's Desk activity more challenging by asking students if they have defined by synonym, category, or negation.

Writer's Desk Generate Supporting Ideas

Choose one of your thesis statements from the previous Writer's Desk. List three or four ideas that most effectively illustrate the definition.

EXAMPLE: Thesis Statement: *Goth is a complete lifestyle that embraces attitude, culture, and fashion.*

—*must have self-confidence*

—*must believe in the culture*

—*introspective music is important*

—*black colors and theatrical fashions are critical*

Thesis Statement: _____

_____

Supports: _____

_____

_____

_____

_____

Teaching Tip:
As an additional
activity, ask students
to develop
supporting ideas for
all three Writer's
Desk topics. The
topics are listed in
the Warm Up.

The Essay Plan

An essay plan helps you organize your thesis statement and supporting details
before you write the first draft. A definition essay includes a complete definition
of the term and provides adequate examples to support the central definition.
When creating a definition essay plan, make sure that your examples provide
varied evidence and do not just repeat the definition. Organize your ideas in a
logical sequence.

THESIS STATEMENT: Goth is a complete lifestyle that embraces attitude,
culture, and fashion.

    I. What makes a real Goth is the attitude he or she shows.
        A. Confidence is key.
        B. A Goth must feel that he or she does not fit into
           mainstream culture.
        C. Outsiders often misunderstand Goth culture.
   II. Music is important to Goths.
        A. Goth started in the late 1970s.
        B. Music was introspective with dark lyrics.
        C. It had elements of horror and the supernatural.
  III. Fashion is crucial to their way of life.
        A. They love medieval or Victorian styles with velvet and
           lace.
        B. They sometimes wear religious symbols.
        C. They often wear black and dye their hair black.

Teaching Tip:
Ask students to keep their essay plans and then attach them to their final draft. You can then determine how the students have developed their ideas.

Writer's Desk **Write an Essay Plan**

Refer to the information you generated in previous Writer's Desks and prepare a detailed essay plan.

The First Draft

Your essay plan is the backbone upon which you can build your first draft. As you write, remember to vary your sentence structure and to write complete sentences. Also include transitional words or expressions to help your ideas flow smoothly. Here are some transitional expressions that can help you show different levels of importance in a definition essay.

To show the level of importance

clearly	next
first	one quality . . . another quality
most important	second
most of all	undoubtedly

Writer's Desk **Write the First Draft**

Carefully review the essay plan you prepared in the previous Writer's Desk. Make any necessary changes to the definition or its supporting details, and then write your first draft.

REVISING AND EDITING

Revise and Edit a Definition Essay

When you finish writing a definition essay, carefully review your work and revise it to make the definition as clear as possible to your readers. You might have to adjust your definition and supporting ideas to suit their knowledge. Also keep in

Teaching Tip:

Cooperative Learning (Jigsaw)
With students, generate a thesis statement or choose a thesis statement from this chapter's Writer's Desk. Place students in groups of five. One group should write an introduction for that thesis statement. Three groups should write separate body paragraphs, and a fifth group should write a concluding paragraph. Then teams can read their paragraphs aloud.

mind the tone of your essay. Certain words have either negative or positive connotations. Finally, check that you have organized your ideas logically and remove any irrelevant details. Before you revise and edit your own essay, practice revising and editing a student essay.

A Student Essay

Read the essay, and then answer the questions that follow. As you read, correct any errors that you find and make comments in the margins.

Welcome to My World
By Marie-Pier Joly

1   A woman passes by wearing a long black dress. Her pale face, dark eyeliner and lipstick, and jet-black hair are objects of attention. Whether its a single horror-filled glance or a full stop to stare in shock, people react to Goths in surprising ways. A Goth's appearance clearly attracts scrutiny. However, being Goth is not just about clothes; it is a complete lifestyle that embraces attitude, culture, and fashion.

2   Be it, breath it, live it, and believe it. What makes someone a real Goth is the attitude he or she shows. Confidence is the key. Without it, people will not remain in the Goth scene for very long. For example, if someone is extremely shy and has very low self-esteem, he will not tolerate people's stares. Also, Goths must believe in their culture. Most Goths feel that they do not fit into mainstream society, and their outsider status binds them. Being a Goth is risky because of the misconceptions that the public has, so Goths must be strong. For instance, people incorrectly believe that the Columbine killers were Goths; thus, Goths are associated with violence. ~~The 2002 film *Bowling for Columbine* is about this tragedy.~~ Violence is not part of the Goth **creed**, so good Goths have to trust themselves. Most importantly, they have to demonstrate that they have self-composure.

creed:
belief system

3   Goth music culture started in the late 1970s within the punk subculture. The elder Goths appreciated bands such as <u>Siouxsie & the banshees</u> and Bauhaus. The music was introspective and had dark lyrics. It had elements of horror, morbidity, and the supernatural. But it was also tongue in cheek. Performers would dress in campy outfits. Current Goths listen to a variety of music styles, including Goth metal and industrial music.

4   <u>Fashion is not just a passing fad for Goths it is crucial for their way of life.</u> They have a sense of drama and love theatrical clothing. For

example, romantic Goths like velvet and lace and are inspired by Victorian or medieval styles. They sometimes wear religious symbols such as crucifixes. Both males and females may dye their hair black, paint their fingernails black or dark purple, and wear dark eyeliner. People who wear dark trench coats and white face makeup are not necessarily Goths.

5   Finaly, Goth is an entire lifestyle that may be very demanding. There is a special image to maintain and music to buy. Goths must also have the right attitude. Goths draw a lot of attention, not all of it positive. So those who plan to be Goths must believe in themselves.

Teaching Tip:
The activity of revising a student essay should help your students understand the important link between the writing process and the grammar chapters.

PRACTICE 5

Revising

1. Highlight the thesis statement.

2. What type of definition does the thesis statement have? Circle the best answer.

    a. synonym   b. category   c. negation

3. Highlight the topic sentences in paragraphs 2 and 4.

4. Cross out one sentence in paragraph 2 that does not support the topic sentence.

5. Paragraph 3 does not have a topic sentence. Which sentence would be an effective topic sentence for that paragraph? Circle the best answer.

    a. Goths listen to punk music.
    b. Goths listen to a lot of music.
    c. Music is an important element in the Goth subculture.
    d. All Goth music has its origins in the 19th century.

6. What type of definition is the topic sentence in paragraph 4?

    a. synonym   b. category   c. negation

Editing

7. In paragraph 1, there is an apostrophe error. Underline and correct the error.

    Correction: _it's_ _____

8. In paragraph 3, there is a capitalization error. Underline and correct the error.

    Correction: _Siouxsie & the Banshees_ _____

GRAMMAR LINK

See the following chapters for more information about these grammar topics:
Run-Ons, Chapter 24
Spelling, Chapter 34
Apostrophes, Chapter 36
Capitalization, Chapter 37

9. In paragraph 4, there is a run-on sentence. Underline and correct the run-on.

   Correction: *Fashion is not just a passing fad for Goths; it is crucial for their way of life.*

10. There is a spelling mistake in paragraph 5. Underline and correct the error.

   Correction: *Finally*

Writer's Desk Revise and Edit Your Essay

Revise and edit the essay that you wrote for the previous Writer's Desk. You can refer to the revising and editing checklists at the end of this chapter and on this book's inside covers.

A Professional Essay

Dorothy Nixon, a freelance writer, has written for *Salon.com*, *Chatelaine*, and *Today's Parent* magazine. In the following article, Nixon ponders the meaning of genius.

On Genius
by Dorothy Nixon

1   When Albert Einstein was chosen as *Time* magazine's Man of the Century, I was not surprised. Our society is simply obsessed with the idea of genius, and no man embodies that concept in this scientific age better than Albert Einstein, with his godlike grasp of mathematics and his messy mad-scientist hair.

2   Around the same time, a group of Canadian researchers were grabbing headlines. The researchers, while analyzing Einstein's brain, had discovered some extra connections in the famous physicist's grey matter. They theorized that Einstein's brain held the secret to the man's genius. "I held Einstein's brain, and I was in awe," said a researcher, revealing the fact that the research was not entirely objective on his part. After all, *awe* is usually a feeling reserved for religious experiences.

3   Rationally speaking, holding Einstein's brain cannot feel too differently from holding a chimp's brain or a Vegas chorus girl's brain. Still, everyone understood what he meant: he was moved by the idea of Einstein's genius, which seems almost mystical in nature and therefore something to be "in awe of." The question remains, why were the scientists trying to quantify Einstein's genius by locating it somewhere in his brain in the first place? Genius is not quantifiable. Genius cannot be captured in a butterfly net or put in a bottle. Genius is not even that mysterious, really: it exists all around us, almost always in unrecognized form.

4   Societies tend to value some forms of genius over others. In the Renaissance, artists, sculptors, and architects were esteemed above all. In sixteenth century Vienna, musicians were revered. Today, mathematicians and scientists are lauded. Da Vinci, Mozart, and Einstein arose from these environments.

5   Genius has to be given a chance; it has to be **nurtured.** It has to be rigorously trained, too. (Remember, genius is one percent inspiration and ninety-nine percent perspiration, according to Thomas Edison.) Genius has to have good timing, or it is liable to be labeled lunacy. Above all, it has to be recognized for what it is.

nurtured: encouraged

6   A while back, I was sitting on the Montreal–Toronto train. To my dismay, the grandmotherly woman beside me wanted to talk. I don't normally like talking on trains, but within minutes I was truly mesmerized by the old woman's story. In broken English, the old woman told me about her life; how she had grown up in a poor country and spent only a few years in school; how she had eloped to Canada with a hardworking young man from her village; how she had helped out her husband with his landscaping business "doing the money part" until they had enough cash scraped together to buy a small apartment building. She told me how her husband had died soon thereafter and left her with three young boys, and how, with good business "luck" (for she had never remarried), she made enough money to put all her boys through graduate school. Indeed, she was on her way this minute to visit her youngest son and his wife, both law school professors.

7   She felt sorry for young people these days, she said. They were all so busy juggling careers and kids that they found it so hard to cope. That is why she often visited her sons' homes to help out. While there, she cooked all the meals, mostly Italian specialties (as she described them my mouth watered uncontrollably), and even whipped up some outfits for the kids.

8   By modern definitions, this woman was not a genius: she did not discover a new element or the reason the stars stay up in heaven. She had not even been to high school. But as I got off the train, I felt that I had been

in the presence of someone very special; someone with extraordinary gifts who had lived and was continuing to live a full and balanced life.

9   If that is not pure genius, what is?

PRACTICE 6

1. Highlight the thesis statement of the essay.

2. According to the writer, what four things does genius need to flourish?

   It needs to be given a chance, to be nurtured, to be trained, and to be

   recognized.

3. According to the writer, how has the definition of genius changed over time?

   Today's society values science, whereas in previous eras, society

   recognized arts and music.

4. Highlight the topic sentence of paragraph 6. Remember that it may not always be the first sentence of the paragraph.

5. The old woman tells the writer her life story. What can you infer (conclude) about the old woman's personality from this tale?

   She is hardworking, caring, loyal, and persevering.

6. The writer acknowledges that society recognizes Einstein as a genius. But why does the writer think that the old woman is also a good example of genius?

   The old woman has led a well-balanced and responsible life. She has taken

   care of her children, and she also helps to take care of her grandchildren.

   She has made a positive contribution to society through her actions.

7. In paragraph 6, why does the writer place quotation marks around "doing the money part" and "luck"?

   The author is indicating that she doesn't really believe the woman simply

   had luck. She thinks the woman worked very hard. Also, maybe the writer

   is directly quoting the old woman.

The Writer's Room

Writing Activity 1: Topics

Write a definition essay about any of the following topics, or choose your own topic.

General Topics

1. a soul mate
2. meltdown
3. culture of entitlement
4. family
5. a good sport

College and Work-Related Topics

6. teamwork
7. poor workplace communication
8. equal opportunity
9. good education
10. healthy competition

Writing Activity 2: Photo Writing

The Irish writer Oscar Wilde once said that all art is useless. Is art only paintings and sculptures, or does it also include folk art, advertising, comics, posters, and fashion? Does art have to be original, or can it include something that is copied? Does the definition of art depend on a person's background, such as his or her ethnicity? Write an essay in which you define what art means to you.

READING LINK

More Definition Readings

"Slum Tourism" by Eric Weiner (page 556)

"Chance and Circumstance" by David Leonhardt (page 591)

WRITING LINK

More Definition Writing Topics

Chapter 23, Writer's Room topic 1 (page 348)

Chapter 29, Writer's Room topic 2 (page 416)

Chapter 33, Writer's Room topic 1 (page 462)

Chapter 36, Writer's Room topic 2 (page 496)

Teaching Tip: **Writer's World Competition** Please advise students that they can submit their essays for possible publication to www .pearsonhighered .com/essayrewards/ writingrewards .html.

Writing Activity 3: Media Writing

Define "common sense." Watch a television show such as *Dr. Phil* or *The Dr. Oz Show*. You can also watch a movie such as *It's Complicated*, *Juno*, or *Up in the Air*. In an essay, define the term "common sense" and support your definition with examples or anecdotes from the media.

✔ CHECKLIST: DEFINITION ESSAY

As you write your definition essay, review the checklist on the inside front cover. Also ask yourself the following set of questions.

☐ Does my thesis statement contain a definition by synonym, category, or negation?

☐ Do I use concise language in my definition?

☐ Do I make a point in my thesis statement?

☐ Do all of my supporting paragraphs relate to the thesis statement?

☐ Do the body paragraphs contain enough supporting details that help define the term?

PEARSON **mywritinglab** To check your progress in meeting this chapter's objectives, log in to **www.mywritinglab.com,** go to the **Study Plan** tab, click on **Essay Patterns** and choose **Definition** from the list of subtopics. Read and view the resources in the **Review Materials** section, and then complete the **Recall, Apply,** and **Write** sets in the **Activities** section.

Classification

To make shopping easier for consumers, many shoe stores display footwear according to different styles and purposes, such as sandals, sneakers, and boots. Similarly, when writing a classification essay, you divide a topic into categories to help your readers understand your ideas.

Writers' Exchange

Work with a partner or group. Divide the next words into three or four different categories. What are the categories? Why did you choose those categories?

art	studio	medicine
construction	stethoscope	workshop
doctor	paintbrush	hospital
hammer	welder	sculptor

Teaching Tip: Cooperative Learning (Sharing Circle) The Writers' Exchange activity can help your students understand classification. Students might classify the words in different ways. Ask them what unites their categories (the classification principle).

EXPLORING

What Is Classification?

When you classify, you divide a large group into smaller and more understandable categories. For instance, if a bookstore simply put books randomly on shelves, you would have a hard time finding the book that you need. Instead, the bookstore classifies according to subject area. In classification writing, each of the categories must be part of a larger group, yet they must also be distinct. For example, you might write an essay about the most common types of hobbies and sort those into board games, sports, and crafts.

People use classification in their everyday lives. For instance, at home you classify laundry into piles on the basis of fabric or color. At college, the administration classifies subjects into arts, sciences, and so on. A workplace such as an office might classify employees as managers, sales staff, and secretaries.

👓 Visualizing Classification

PRACTICE I Brainstorm supporting ideas for the following thesis statement. Divide each category into subcategories.
Answers will vary.

THESIS STATEMENT:

The best Olympic sports require strength and graceful movements.

Track and Field

dash

marathon

high jump

Gymnastics

balance beam

parallel bars

trampoline

Aquatics

diving

relay race

water polo

The Classification Essay

To find a topic for a classification essay, think of something that you can sort or divide into different groups. Also, determine a reason for classifying the items. When you are planning your ideas for a classification essay, remember the following points.

Teaching Tip:
Ask students to brainstorm categories for each classification principle. For example, "outsourced jobs" might include those in textiles, those in telephone technical support, and those in toy manufacturing.

1. **Use a common classification principle.**

   A **classification principle** is the overall method that you use to sort the subject into categories. To find the classification principle, think about one common characteristic that unites the different categories. For example, if your subject is "jobs," your classification principle might be any of the following:

   - jobs in which people work with their hands
   - dangerous jobs
   - outsourced jobs

2. **Sort the subject into distinct categories.**
   A classification essay should have two or more categories.

Topic: jobs

Classification principle: dangerous jobs

Category 1	**Category 2**	**Category 3**
public security	construction	hazardous materials

3. **Say something meaningful.**

   Your essay should not simply divide a topic into categories; it should say something meaningful. For instance, you can divide cars into small, medium, and large sizes. If you simple describe those categories, you will not be giving the reader any valuable information because everyone knows those three sizes exist. Instead, justify why each category is significant. For example, you can describe what the size of a car tells us about the owner. Or you can categorize cars according to specific life stages (the ideal dating car, family car, and retirement car). Always consider what point you are trying to make.

   In an essay about dangerous jobs, your point can be: "The public should express more gratitude to those people who work in dangerous fields."

Teaching Tip:
Ask students to
identify the
categories of
the Web site.

Classification at Work

Ahmad Bishr is a Web design consultant. In the next excerpt from an e-mail to a client, he makes suggestions about classifying a Web site.

The second thing you need to do is decide how to divide your site. The opening page should contain only the most pertinent information about the cottage you are trying to rent. For instance, include the number of rooms, the location, the most spectacular traits of the cottage, and so on. Each subcategory will become a link. Because you are trying to rent your cottage, I suggest that one link contain photos of the interior, with details about each room. You will also need a link that includes a rental calendar and rates. A third section might contain information about local attractions. Remember that too many categories will confuse the viewer. You'll want a simple, uncluttered site. Keep the divisions down to four or five pages at the most.

A Student Essay

Read the student essay and answer the questions that follow.

Discrimination in the 21st Century
by Victoria Johnson

1   When the topic of discrimination is discussed, it is usually described in terms of racial, religious, or gender offenses. These types of discrimination are undeniable, but the disabled community is rarely mentioned. In 1990, Congress passed the Americans with Disabilities Act. The ADA mandated that buildings be accessible and job modifications be made to accommodate the disabled. Although this policy was a welcome beginning for people with disabilities, in practical terms, the disabled still face challenges. The disabled, specifically those in electric wheelchairs, are discriminated against in personal relationships, transportation options, and public venues.

2   Disabled people have more difficulties establishing relationships with others. I use an electric wheelchair, and a hard part of my life is not having a lot of friends. When I was little, I had friends because the other children thought it was cool to push me or to ride in my wheelchair. However, by the time I was ten, the situation had changed. As people grow up, they begin doing more and more activities; they no longer just want to go over to someone's house to play. For people in electric wheelchairs, this is a problem. I cannot go to a friend's house unless there is a way to get

inside. During my adolescence, I usually couldn't go to parties because there was no ramp. Because I was not able to take part in weekend activities like roller-skating or sports, the kids started to forget me. They saw me only at school and did not think to include me in the after-school activities. Unfortunately, people are uncomfortable around the disabled.

3   Transportation is another problem for people in electric wheelchairs because they need vans with ramps. Anyone can drive a van, but many hesitate to do so. The disabled cannot just get into any car and go to lunch. Friends need to make arrangements to take disabled people in a special van. This extra planning causes problems. Since many disabled people cannot drive and go where they want when they want, they become frustrated. In most localities, the bus system has only a few buses with wheelchair lifts, so people in wheelchairs are dependent on others to get where they want to go. The lack of independence can lead to a lack of self-esteem. People with disabilities feel they are bothering others when they ask for transportation help, and it becomes easier to stay at home.

4   People without disabilities think that things are so much better now because buildings are accessible. Of course, gaining access to buildings is important, but what happens once I am inside? Public venues often do not meet the needs of the handicapped. Whenever I go to a sports event or a concert, I have to sit near the top, and I cannot see a thing. For example, when the Clay Center in Charleston, West Virginia, was built, handicapped seating was placed in the back row instead of throughout the theater. Shopping malls are also a problem. Although the entrance is easily accessible, actual shopping is difficult. In some stores, the aisles are so narrow that the chair hits everything. Stores place too many clothes on the racks, and wheelchairs cannot get between them. The dressing rooms are also too small. The bigger department stores will have one handicapped dressing room, but usually it is filled with boxes. Grocery stores place items too high to reach. The clerks are helpful, but it is still annoying to have to ask for help.

5   For people in wheelchairs, doing activities for and by themselves is difficult. Whether the discrimination in personal relationships, transportation, and building accommodations is intentional or not, it still serves to divide people. It has been nineteen years since the Americans with Disabilities Act was passed. The disabled should not be complacent about the steps that have been taken to improve their lives because discrimination is still a problem. Unfortunately, it may take years for the handicapped population to truly become a part of the community.

PRACTICE 2

1. Highlight the thesis statement.

2. Highlight the topic sentence in each body paragraph. Remember that the topic sentence is not always the first sentence in the paragraph.

3. State the three categories that the writer discusses, and list some details about each category.   Answers will vary.

   a. _discrimination by friends_

      Details: _Small children like to push wheelchairs but not older kids._
      Friends' homes do not have ramps. Friends stop inviting the
      handicapped.

   b. _discrimination in transportation options_

      Details: _Disabled need special vans, which friends may be reluctant to_
      drive. There are very few buses with wheelchair lifts. Disabled lose sense
      of independence.

   c. _discrimination in public venues_

      Details: _Handicapped seating is in the back with poor views. Store_
      aisles are crowded and difficult for a wheelchair to maneuver in.
      Changing rooms are too small.

4. Which introductory style does this essay use? Circle your answer.

   a. anecdote   c. historical
   b. definition   d. opposing position

Teaching Tip:
The Writer's Desk
activities, such as
the one below,
provide students
with opportunities
to develop a topic
through all stages
of the writing
process using
the classification
rhetorical mode. In
the Warm Up, they
begin by exploring
various topics that
can be divided for a
classification essay.
Those topics then
carry on throughout
the chapter.

Explore Topics

In the Writer's Desk Warm Up, you will try an exploring strategy to generate ideas about different topics.

Writer's Desk **Warm Up**

Read the following questions, and write the first ideas that come to your mind. Think of two to three ideas for each topic.

EXAMPLE: What are some types of lawbreakers?

—_petty thieves (pickpockets, scam artists)_

—_people who break traffic laws_

—_violent criminals like carjackers and terrorists_

1. What are some different categories of families?

_____

_____

_____

2. What are some different types of sports fans?

_____

_____

_____

3. What are some types of heroes that people have at different times in their lives?

_____

_____

_____

Making a Classification Chart

A **classification chart** is a visual representation of a main topic and its categories. Making a classification chart can help you to identify the categories more clearly so that you will be able to write more exact thesis statements.

When you classify items, remember to find a common classification principle. For example, you can classify sports according to their benefits, their degree of difficulty, or their costs.

Classification Principle: psychological benefits

You can also use a pie chart to help you classify items.

Psychological Benefits of Sports

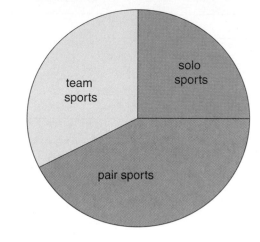

> ## Hint   Make a Point
>
> To make interesting classification essays, try to express an attitude, opinion, or feeling about the topic. For example, in an essay about discipline, your classification principle might be types of discipline methods; however, the essay needs to inform readers of something specific about those methods. You could write about discipline methods that are most effective, least effective, ethical, unethical, violent, nonviolent, and so on.

PRACTICE 3   In the following classification charts, a subject has been broken down into distinct categories. The items in the group should have the same classification principle. Cross out one item in each group that does not belong. Then write down the classification principle that unites the group.

EXAMPLE

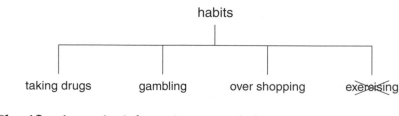

habits

taking drugs   gambling   over shopping   ~~exercising~~

Classification principle: *dangerous habits*

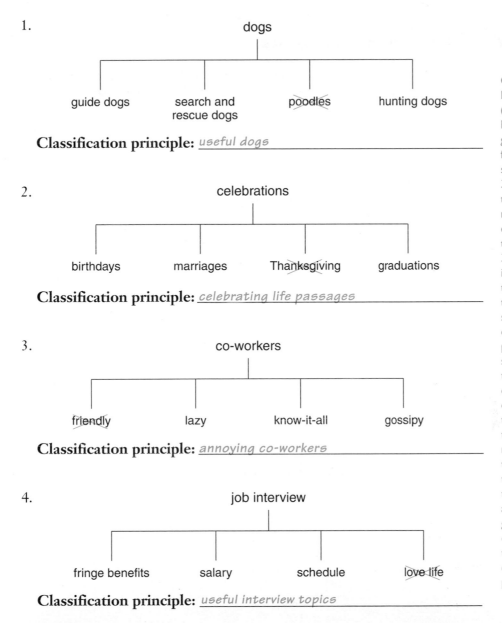

1.

dogs

guide dogs | search and rescue dogs | ~~poodles~~ | hunting dogs

Classification principle: _useful dogs_

2.

celebrations

birthdays | marriages | ~~Thanksgiving~~ | graduations

Classification principle: _celebrating life passages_

3.

co-workers

~~friendly~~ | lazy | know-it-all | gossipy

Classification principle: _annoying co-workers_

4.

job interview

fringe benefits | salary | schedule | ~~love life~~

Classification principle: _useful interview topics_

Teaching Tip:

Cooperative Learning (Jigsaw)
Place students in groups of three to five. First, they should do Practice 3. Then ask groups to brainstorm two more classification charts that look like the items in Practice 3. They should include one example that doesn't fit in their charts. They should also figure out the classifying principle. Then ask students to number themselves from one to five. Ask the ones, the twos, the threes, etc. to get together and form new teams. The new team members can take turns reading their lists. They can ask the others to guess which item doesn't belong and to determine the classification principle.

Hint **Categories Should Not Overlap**

When sorting a topic into categories, make sure that the categories do not overlap. For example, you would not classify *roommates* into aloof, friendly, and messy because a messy roommate could also be aloof or friendly. Although the categories share something in common, each category should be distinct.

Writer's Desk Find Distinct Categories

Break down the following topics into three distinct categories. Remember to find categories that do not overlap. You can look for ideas in the Writer's Desk Warm Up on pages 174–175.

EXAMPLE:

lawbreakers

pedestrians   cyclists   drivers

Classification principle: __*people who break traffic laws*_____

1.

families

_____   _____   _____

Classification principle: _____

2.

sports fans

_____   _____   _____

Classification principle: _____

3.

heroes

_____   _____   _____

Classification principle: _____

Teaching Tip:
Remind students
not to list just types,
but to list three
distinct categories.
For example, ask
what is wrong with
the following. Topic:
unhealthy foods;
categories: *sugary
snacks, fried foods,*
and *ice cream.*
Students should
notice that ice
cream is also a
sugary snack.

DEVELOPING

The Thesis Statement

The thesis statement in a classification essay clearly indicates what you will classify. It also includes the controlling idea, which is the classification principle.

topic   controlling idea

Several types of coworkers can completely destroy a workplace environment.

You can also mention the types of categories in your thesis statement.

topic   controlling idea

Gossipy, lazy, and know-it-all coworkers can completely destroy a workplace environment.

Writer's Desk **Write Thesis Statements**

Write clear thesis statements. You can refer to your ideas in previous Writer's Desks. Remember that your thesis statement can include the different categories you will be discussing.

EXAMPLE: Topic: lawbreakers

Thesis Statement: *Pedestrians, cyclists, and drivers regularly break the rules of the road.*

1. Topic: families

   Thesis statement: _____

   _____

2. Topic: sports fans

   Thesis statement: _____

   _____

3. Topic: heroes

   Thesis statement: _____

   _____

The Supporting Ideas

After you have developed an effective thesis statement, generate supporting ideas. In a classification essay, you can list details about each of your categories.

- Use prewriting strategies to generate examples for each category.
- Choose the best ideas.
- Organize your ideas. Choose the best organizational method for this essay pattern.

You can prepare a traditional essay plan. You can also illustrate your main and supporting ideas in a classification chart such as the one that follows.

The public should be grateful to those who perform dangerous jobs in three particular areas.

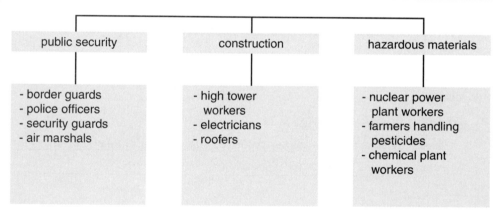

public security	construction	hazardous materials
- border guards - police officers - security guards - air marshals	- high tower workers - electricians - roofers	- nuclear power plant workers - farmers handling pesticides - chemical plant workers

Writer's Desk Develop Supporting Ideas

Choose one of the thesis statements from the previous Writer's Desk on page 179, and list supporting ideas.

Thesis statement: _____

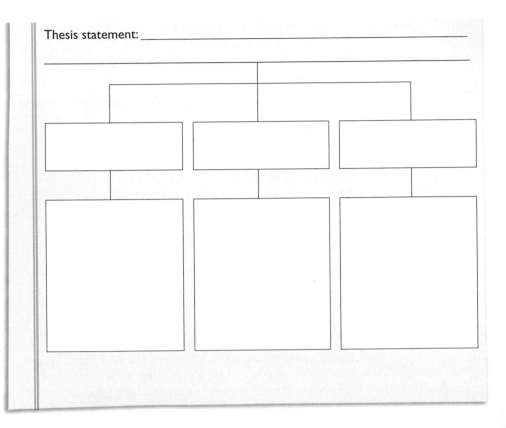

Teaching Tip:
For extra practice, ask students to develop supporting ideas for all three Writer's Desk topics. The topics are listed in the Warm Up.

The Essay Plan

Before you write a classification essay, make a detailed essay plan. Add supporting details for each category.

THESIS STATEMENT: <u>Pedestrians, cyclists, and drivers regularly break the rules of the road.</u>

I.   Pedestrians are supposed to obey traffic rules, but most do not.
    A. Many cross between intersections instead of at corners.
    B. A lot of pedestrians walk on the road.
    C. Some people disobey walking signals.

II. Cyclists frequently break traffic laws.
    A. Many cyclists don't wear bicycle helmets.
    B. Some don't put proper reflectors on their bikes.
    C. It is common to see cyclists going through lights and stop signs.
    D. There are even bike riders who go the wrong way on one-way streets.

III. Drivers are the most dangerous lawbreakers.
    A. Speeding is common on roads and highways.
    B. Some people drive on the shoulders of roads.
    C. Many drivers disobey traffic signs.

Teaching Tip:
You can ask students to keep their essay plans and then attach them to their final draft. You can then determine how the students have developed their ideas.

Writer's Desk **Make an Essay Plan**

Refer to the information you generated in previous Writer's Desks, and prepare a detailed essay plan. Arrange the supporting details in a logical order.

The First Draft

After you outline your ideas in a plan, you are ready to write the first draft. Weave together the ideas you have in your essay plan. Remember to write complete sentences and to include transitional words or expressions to help your ideas flow smoothly. Here are some transitions that can help you express which category is most important and to signal a movement from one category to the next.

To show importance	**To show types of categories**
above all	one kind . . . another kind
clearly	the first/second kind
most of all	the first/second type
the most important	the last category
particularly	

Writer's Desk **Write the First Draft**

Carefully review the classification essay plan you prepared in the previous Writer's Desk and make any necessary changes. Then, write the first draft of your classification essay.

REVISING AND EDITING

Revise and Edit a Classification Essay

When you finish writing a classification essay, carefully review your work and revise it to make sure that the categories do not overlap. Check to make sure that you have organized your essay logically, and remove any irrelevant details. Before you work on your own essay, practice revising and editing a student essay.

A Student Essay

Read the essay, and then answer the questions that follow. As you read, correct any errors that you find and make comments in the margins.

Breaking Traffic Laws
by Lonzell Courtney

1   Ask most people, and they will insist they are law-abiding. Dig a little deeper, though, and the hidden criminal emerges. Stand on any street corner for a few hours, and you will probably observe all types of honest people who break traffic laws. Pedestrians, cyclists, and drivers regularly break the rules of the road.

2   There are many traffic laws that pedestrians ignore. For example, jaywalking. When people arrive at a crossing with traffic lights, they are supposed to wait for the walk signal. They should also cross the street at corners and proper crossings, and they should not walk on the road. Yet most people be breaking these rules. Armando Guzman, an exterminator from Florida, is an unapologetic jaywalker. When him and I go for a walk, he crosses between intersections rather than make the long walk to the corner. Kate Shapiro, a hairdresser, admits that she always crosses when the "Don't Walk" signal is blinking if there is no traffic. "It is ridiculous to wait when I know I can cross safely," she argues. Some pedestrians are also very rude. They push through crowds, knock people over, and are basically very unpleasant.

3   Most cyclists would say they are law-abiding, yet they break traffic laws. For example, many municipalities have bicycle helmet laws, but most bike riders disobey the laws. Also, cyclists ignore signs and ride on sidewalks, on lawns, and walking paths. They zoom past stop signs and red lights, and they go the wrong way on one-way streets. Thus, cyclists break the law too.

4   Drivers, of course, are the worse offenders. They can harm or even kill others, yet virtually every driver has occasionally broken a traffic law. Who hasn't gone over the speed limit, for example? Many people believe that the maximum speed limit sign really means, "I can go twenty miles

Teaching Tip:
The activity of revising a student essay should help your students understand the important link between the writing process and the grammar chapters.

Teaching Tip:

Cooperative Learning (Pair & Share) First, ask students to read the essay silently. As they read, they should circle any mistakes that they find. Then place students in pairs. They can share what they have found and answer the revising and editing questions together.

per hour over that limit." Drivers also change lanes without signaling, they drive on the shoulder to pass slow traffic, and they allow children to ride without seatbelts. For instance, in 2006, while driving, Britney Spears placed her infant on her lap.

5   Most lawbreakers are unrepentant, and some of them have original excuses for ignoring traffic rules. They claim that everyone else does it. Some people condemn seatbelt and helmet laws as infringements on their rights.

PRACTICE 4

Revising

1. Highlight the thesis statement and three topic sentences.

2. In paragraph 2, one of the examples is not a valid support. Cross it out. Explain why it is not valid. _The example is not about lawbreakers. Being_ _rude is not breaking the law._

3. This essay does not have a concluding sentence. Write a concluding sentence in the space. _Answers will vary._

Editing

GRAMMAR LINK

See the following chapters for more information about these grammar topics:
Fragments,
      Chapter 23
Parallel Structure,
      Chapter 25
Verb Tenses,
      Chapter 28
Pronouns,
      Chapter 31
Adjectives,
      Chapter 32

4. A fragment lacks a subject or a verb and is an incomplete sentence. Underline one fragment in paragraph 2. Then write a correct sentence here.

    Correction: _For example, many people are jaywalkers._

5. Paragraph 2 contains a verb-tense error. Underline the error and correct it.

    Correction: _Yet most people break these rules._

6. The writer uses a pronoun incorrectly in paragraph 2. Underline and correct the error.

    Correction: _he and I_

7. In paragraph 3, there is a parallel structure error. Underline and correct the error. (For more information about parallel structure, see the Grammar Hint on the next page.) _Answers will vary._

    Correction: _ride on sidewalks, on lawns, and on walking paths_

    (or remove the second and third repetitions of "on")

8. In paragraph 4, there is an error with the superlative form of an adjective. Underline the error and correct it.

Correction: <u>*worst*</u>

Grammar Hint   **Parallel Structure**

Use parallel structure when words or phrases are joined in a series. The groups of items should be balanced.

Some annoying sales methods include calling customers on the phone,

leaving
putting pop-up ads on the Internet, and ~~when they leave~~ text messages.

Writer's Desk **Revise and Edit Your Essay**

Revise and edit the essay that you wrote for the previous Writer's Desk. You can refer to the revising and editing checklists at the end of this chapter and on this book's inside covers.

---

vo•cab•u•lar•y BOOST

Writers commonly overuse the same vocabulary. To make your writing more vivid and interesting, look at your first draft and underline at least ten repeated nouns and verbs. (Remember that a noun is a person, place, or thing.) Then add details or specific descriptions to five of the nouns and write more vivid verbs. Here is a brief example of how you might avoid repetition of nouns and verbs.

Dull, repetitive:	Patrice likes cycling. Patrice often cycles to work at his bookstore. Often Patrice is reckless and cycles without a helmet.
Detailed, uses synonyms:	**Patrice** likes **cycling** and **commutes** to work on his **bike**. Although **the 30-year-old bookstore owner** knows better, **he** often **recklessly rides** without a helmet.

A Professional Essay

Frank Schmalleger is director of the Justice Research Association, a private consulting firm that focuses on issues relating to crime and justice. The following excerpt is from his book *Criminal Justice Today*.

Types of Correctional Officers
by Frank Schmalleger

1   Prison staff culture, in combination with naturally occurring personality types, gives rise to a diversity of officer types. Correction staff can be classified according to certain distinguishing characteristics. Among the most prevalent types are the dictator, the friend, the merchant, the turnkey, the climber, and the reformer.

The Dictator

Teaching Tip:
To practice vocabulary, ask students to brainstorm synonyms for the following terms. They should read the terms in context to guess the meanings.

-prevalent (paragraph 1)
-omnipotence (paragraph 3)
-affability (paragraph 5)
-substantially (paragraph 7)
-argot (paragraph 9)
-apt (paragraph 10)
-consternation (paragraph 11)
-unsolicited (paragraph 12)
-supplanted (paragraph 13)

2   Some officers go by the book; others go beyond it, using prison rules to reinforce their own brand of discipline. The guard who demands signs of inmate subservience, from constant use of the word *sir* or *ma'am* to frequent free shoeshines, is one type of dictator. Another goes beyond legality, beating or "macing" inmates even for minor infractions or perceived insults. Dictator guards are bullies.

3   Dictator guards may have sadistic personalities and gain ego satisfaction through feelings of near omnipotence, which come from the total control of others. Some may be fundamentally insecure and employ a false bravado to hide their fear of inmates. Officers who fit the dictator category are the most likely to be targeted for vengeance should control of the institution temporarily fall into the hands of the inmates.

The Friend

4   Friendly officers try to fraternize with inmates. They approach the issue of control by trying to be "one of the guys." They seem to believe that they can win inmate cooperation by being nice. Unfortunately, such guards do not recognize that fraternization quickly leads to unending requests for special favors—from delivering mail to bending "minor" prison rules. Once a few rules have been bent, the officer may find that inmates have the upper hand through the potential for blackmail.

5   Many officers have amiable relationships with inmates. In most cases, however, affability is only a convenience that both sides recognize can quickly evaporate. "Friendly officers," as the term is being used here, are *overly* friendly. They may be young and inexperienced. On the other

hand, they may simply be possessed of kind and idealistic personalities built on successful friendships in free society.

The Merchant

6   Contraband could not exist in any correctional facility without the merchant officer. The merchant participates in the inmate economy, supplying drugs, pornography, alcohol, and sometimes even weapons to inmates who can afford to pay for them.

7   Probably only a very few officers consistently perform the role of merchant, although a far larger proportion may occasionally turn a few dollars by smuggling some item through the gate. Low salaries create the potential for mercantile corruption among many otherwise "straight-arrow" officers. Until salaries rise substantially, the merchant will remain an institutionalized feature of most prisons.

The Turnkey

8   The turnkey officer cares little for what goes on in the prison setting. Officers who fit this category may be close to retirement, or they may be alienated from their jobs for various reasons. Low pay, the view that inmates are basically "worthless" and incapable of changing, and the monotonous ethic of "doing time" all combine to numb the professional consciousness of even young officers.

9   The term *turnkey* comes from prison argot where it means a guard who is there just to open and shut doors and who cares about nothing other than getting through his or her shift. Inmates do not see the turnkey as a threat, nor is such an officer likely to challenge the status quo in institutions where merchant guards operate.

The Climber

10   The climber is apt to be a young officer with an eye for promotion. Nothing seems impossible to the climber, who probably hopes eventually to be warden or program director or to hold some high-status position within the institutional hierarchy. Climbers are likely to be involved in schooling, correspondence courses, and professional organizations. They may lead a movement toward unionization for correctional personnel and tend to see the guard's role as a profession that should receive greater social recognition.

11   Climbers have many ideas. They may be heavily involved in reading about the latest confinement or administrative technology. If so, they will suggest many ways to improve prison routine, often to the consternation of complacent staff members. Like the turnkey, climbers turn a blind eye

toward inmates and their problems. They are more concerned with improving institutional procedures and with their own careers than they are with the treatment or day-to-day control of inmates.

The Reformer

12   The reformer is the "do-gooder" among officers, the person who believes that prison should offer opportunities for personal change. The reformer tends to lend a sympathetic ear to the personal needs of inmates and is apt to offer armchair counseling and suggestions. Many reformers are motivated by personal ideals, and some of them are highly religious. Inmates tend to see the reformer guard as naive but harmless. Because the reformer actually tries to help, even when help is unsolicited, he or she is the most likely of all the guard types to be accepted by prisoners.

13   Correctional officers have generally been accorded low occupational status. Historically, the role of prison guard required minimal formal education and held few opportunities for professional growth and career advancement. Such jobs were typically low paying, frustrating, and often boring. Growing problems in our nation's prisons, including emerging issues of legal liability, however, increasingly require a well-trained and adequately equipped force of professionals. As correctional personnel have become better trained and more proficient, the old concept of guard has been supplanted by that of correctional officer. Thus, many states and a growing number of large-city correctional systems make efforts to eliminate individuals with potentially harmful personality characteristics from correctional officer applicant pools.

PRACTICE 5

1. What is the topic of this essay? _types of prison guards_

2. What are the main characteristics of the following types of guards?

    a. the dictator _bossy, demands subservience, intimidating, bullying, may be sadistic_

    b. the friend _tries to be one of the guys, may bend prison rules, usually young and inexperienced_

    c. the merchant _out to make a profit, supplies contraband, corrupt_

d. the turnkey _indifferent, only there to do the job, not personally_
invested in the job

e. the climber _has goals and wants to be promoted, probably takes_
courses, gets involved, may try to change things

f. the reformer _idealistic, sympathetic and listens to inmates, may have_
strong personal ideals or religious beliefs, naive

3. What is the writer's purpose? Circle your answer.
   a. to entertain   b. to persuade   c. to inform

4. Consider the order in which the guards are listed. Think of another effective way to organize the guards, and list them in order here.
   Answers will vary.

   Organizational method: _____

   a. _____   c. _____   e. _____

   b. _____   d. _____   f. _____

The Writer's Room

Writing Activity 1: Topics

Choose any of the following topics, or choose your own topic, and write a classification essay. Determine your classification principle, and make sure that your categories do not overlap.

General Topics

Types of . . .

1. computer users
2. politicians
3. weight-loss methods
4. neighbors
5. games

College and Work-Related Topics

Types of . . .

6. electronic modes of communication
7. help professions
8. success
9. work environments
10. customers

Teaching Tip:
Brainstorm ideas for question 4 with students. For instance, they might organize guards according to their level of naiveté, helpfulness to prisoners, or level of corruption.

Teaching Tip:
Pair Work
Have students read one of the essays in the Reading Link. In pairs, they can discuss what the classification principle is. Also, discuss if the categories overlap or are distinct.

Teaching Tip:
For writing topic 9, ask pairs to brainstorm ideas. Discuss stereotypes about scientists, artists, musicians, librarians, mechanics, and so on.

READING LINK
More Classification Readings
"Types of Rioters" by David Locher (page 537)
"Living Environments" by Avi Friedman (page 553)

WRITING LINK

More Classification Writing Topics

Chapter 22, Writer's Room topic 1 (page 339)

Chapter 26, Writer's Room topic 2 (page 374)

Chapter 34, Writer's Room topic 1 (page 477)

Chapter 37, Writer's Room topic 2 (page 510)

Teaching Tip: To help students come up with ideas for Writing Activity 3, you could brainstorm with them. Ideas can be FBI, CIA, and police officers. They can also write about petty criminals, white-collar criminals, and violent criminals. Types of crimes could be shoplifting, fraud, and murder or mugging, home invasion, and bank robbery. You can even engage students in a discussion about justifiable crimes such as self-defense, speeding to get to a hospital, and so on.

Writing Activity 2: Photo Writing

Examine this photo of a man doing tai chi, and think about some classification topics. For example, you might write about types of athletes, attitudes toward exercise, fitness programs, places to work out, or healthy activities. Determine a classification principle, and then follow the writing process to write a classification essay.

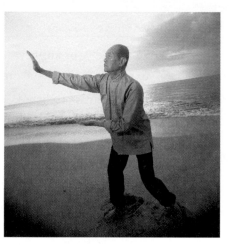

Writing Activity 3: Media Writing

Watch a television show or movie that deals with crime. There are many possible television programs, such as *CSI*, *Bones*, *NCIS*, or *The Good Wife*. Examples of crime movies are *The Informant*, *Sherlock Holmes*, and *The Godfather*. In an essay, divide crime fighters or criminals into categories or describe different types of crimes. Use examples to support your ideas.

Teaching Tip:

Cooperative Learning (Ask & Learn)
Ask students to review the chapter and identify any content that they are not completely clear about. Then each student should write down two questions about the unclear topic. Finally, working in teams, students can ask other members their questions and share answers.

✔ CHECKLIST: CLASSIFICATION ESSAY

After you write your classification essay, review the checklist on the inside front cover. Also, ask yourself these questions.

☐ Does my thesis statement explain the categories that I will discuss?

☐ Do I use a common classification principle to unite the various items?

☐ Do I offer sufficient details to explain each category?

☐ Do I arrange the categories in a logical manner?

☐ Does all of the supporting information relate to the categories that I am discussing?

☐ Do I include categories that do not overlap?

☐ Does my essay make a point and say something meaningful?

Teaching Tip:
Writer's World Competition
Please advise students that they can submit their essays for possible publication to www.pearsonhighered.com/essayrewards/writingrewards.html

To check your progress in meeting this chapter's objectives, log in to **www.mywritinglab.com,** go to the **Study Plan** tab, click on **Essay Patterns** and choose **Classification** from the list of subtopics. Read and view the resources in the **Review Materials** section, and then complete the **Recall, Apply,** and **Write** sets in the **Activities** section.

CHAPTER 12
Comparison and Contrast

When you plan to move to a new place, you compare the features of different houses or apartments to help you make a decision. When you write a comparison and contrast essay, you examine two or more items or issues to help yourself and your readers make conclusions about them.

Teaching Tip:
The Writers' Exchange activity can help your students understand comparison and contrast. When students write some ideas on the board, you can demonstrate point-by-point or topic-by-topic comparisons.

Writers' Exchange

What were your goals as a child? What are your goals as an adult? Think about work, money, and family. Compare your answers with those of a partner, and discuss how childhood goals are different from adult goals.

EXPLORING

What Is Comparison and Contrast?

When you want to decide between options, you compare and contrast. You **compare** to find similarities and **contrast** to find differences. The exercise of comparing and contrasting can help you make judgments about things. It can also help you to better understand familiar things.

People use comparison and contrast in their daily lives. For instance, at home, you might explain to your father why a laptop is more useful than a desktop computer. At college, students often compare two courses. In workplaces, salespeople compare their new products with competing products to highlight the differences.

Visualizing Comparison and Contrast

PRACTICE I Brainstorm supporting ideas for the following thesis statement. Write some benefits of each type of sport on the lines provided. Answers will vary.

Teaching Tip: Ask students to work on the Visualizing practice with a partner.

THESIS STATEMENT: Team sports provide different benefits than solo sports.

Team sports	Solo sports
- learn to cooperate	- learn discipline
- share wins and losses	- learn to persevere
- learn to communicate	- gain self-confidence

Teaching Tip:
Tell students that
instructors
sometimes use
compare to mean
both compare and
contrast.

The Comparison and Contrast Essay

In a comparison and contrast essay, you can compare and contrast two different subjects, or you can compare and contrast different aspects of a single subject. When you write using this essay pattern, remember to think about your specific purpose.

- Your purpose could be to make judgments about two items. For example, you might compare and contrast two cars to convince your readers that one is preferable.
- Your purpose could be to describe or understand two familiar things. For example, you might compare two movies to help your readers understand their thematic similarities.

Comparison and Contrast at Work

Eric Hollymead works in public relations. In the next memo, he compares two job candidates. To respect each person's privacy, he has numbered the candidates.

Teaching Tip:
Ask students to
identify other
instances in the
workplace where
people would use
comparison and
contrast.

Although both candidates have the required education, I suggest that we go with Candidate 1. Her experience is more relevant to this industry. I also believe she will be a better fit for the sales department because her energy level is high, and she seems like a real team player. Candidate 2, although highly competent, is less experienced in sales. He was quite nervous in the interview, and I sense he may be less at ease with clients. On the other hand, his questions were thoughtful, and he seemed interested in the business. I also appreciated his sense of humor. Perhaps we should keep his résumé on file should we have future positions that are more suitable to his skills.

Comparison and Contrast Patterns

Comparison and contrast essays follow two common patterns.

Point by Point   Present one point about Topic A and then present the same point about Topic B. Keep following this pattern until you have a few points for each topic. Go back and forth from one side to the other like tennis players hitting a ball back and forth across a net.

Topic by Topic   Present all of your points about one topic, and then present all of your points about the second topic. Offer one side and then the other side, just as opposing lawyers would do in the closing arguments of a court case.

Teaching Tip:

Cooperative Learning (Sharing Circle) Place students in small groups. Ask groups to compare and contrast two fast-food restaurants. Some of the groups should use the "point-by-point" method, and the others should use the "topic-by-topic" method. Then the students can share their responses with classmates.

Marina's Example

Marina is trying to decide whether she would prefer a part-time job in a clothing store or in a restaurant. Marina can organize her information using a topic-by-topic pattern or a point-by-point method.

THESIS STATEMENT: <u>The clothing store is a better place to work than the restaurant.</u>

Point-by-Point Comparison

Topic sentence: Salaries
   Job A
   Job B

Topic sentence: Working hours
   Job A
   Job B

Topic sentence: Working environments
   Job A
   Job B

Topic-by-Topic Comparison

Topic sentence: Job A
- salary
- hours
- working environment

Topic sentence: Job B
- salary
- hours
- working environment

A Student Essay

Read the student essay, and answer the questions that follow.

Swamps and Pesticides

by Corey Kaminska

1   Having had many jobs in my twenty-two years, I have realized some jobs are a good experience, but many jobs turn into a horrible nightmare. I have also realized that every job has some good points. My favorite all-time job was working as a mosquito abater, and my worst was being a Crystal Hot Springs campground janitor.

2   In my best job, I worked for the Box Elder Mosquito Abatement District, and I had a very exciting routine. This may sound like an odd job, and I would not blame anyone for thinking so. I began my day by walking into the modern abatement building. I drooled over the fancy trucks and four-wheelers that would be mine for the summer. Each morning, the abatement crew met in the conference room to discuss the day's duties. We were then set free to protect the citizens of Box Elder County.

3   Being a mosquito abater was a laid-back and pleasant job. I could work alone while enjoying the outdoors and having fun at the same time. Each day, I gathered my pesticides and supplies. I tossed the chemicals into my 2005 Chevy extended cab, and then I traveled the vast countryside for the day. Pulling my new Honda Rancher on the trailer behind, I

searched for a spot where mosquito larva might be. Then I unloaded my four-wheeler off the trailer and drove through the mucky swamp looking for the perfect spot to start treating the unpleasant larva-infested water. When I finally found the tiny worm-like creatures swimming on top of the water, the fun began. I turned on my hopper, which spread sand-like granules into the water and killed the larva. Bogging through the swampy water on the four-wheeler was something I would have done for fun, but now I was getting paid for it.

4   On the other hand, my job as a Crystal Springs campground janitor was horrible in almost every way. As a janitor, I would begin my day by waking up exceptionally early. Arriving at Crystal Springs, the first thing I had to do was clean out the empty pools and hot tubs. That was a nasty experience. Cleaning up human filth that lingers in the pools until evening and then sticks to the walls as the pool drains is not an appealing task. Scrubbing the walls of the pool for hours is a boring nightmare. The only thing that made it worse was the constant smell from the dairy farm directly across the street. After cleaning out the pools and refilling them with fresh water, I was required to clean out the men's and women's locker rooms. During the cleaning, I often found disgusting items. The work was boring, and the pay was horrible.

5   Although there were drastic differences between my best and my worst job, I discovered some surprising similarities. Both jobs taught me that work is work and money is money. In each job, I helped other people and made their lives just a little bit more enjoyable. I also learned that life is not always about me. Although I was not really appreciated in either job, I learned to recognize my own value. If the job had not been done, people would have suffered the consequences. They would have lived with more mosquitoes, and they would have seen the filth in the pool, hot tubs, and locker rooms.

PRACTICE 2

1. Highlight the thesis statement.

2. Highlight the topic sentences in paragraphs 2, 3, and 4.

3. What pattern of comparison does the writer follow in the entire essay?
   a. point by point   b. topic by topic

4. In paragraphs 2, 3, and 4, what does the writer focus on?
   a. similarities   b. differences

5. List the main advantages of the mosquito abater job.
   It had a pleasant routine. It was laid-back. He worked outdoors. It was fun.

Answers will vary.

6. List reasons why the janitor job was horrible.   Answers will vary.

   He woke up too early. The pool was filthy. The work was boring. There

   were horrible smells. The locker rooms had disgusting items.

7. In the conclusion, the writer mentions some similarities. Use your own
   words to list the main similarities.   Answers will vary.

   Both jobs provided him with money and a sense of personal value, and

   he knew he was helping others.

Explore Topics

In the Writer's Desk Warm Up, you will try an exploring strategy to generate
ideas about different topics.

Writer's Desk Warm Up

Read the following questions, and write the first ideas that come to your
mind. Think of two to three ideas for each topic.

EXAMPLE: What are some key differences between girls' and boys' toys?

girls' toys	boys' toys
—pastel colors	—noisy
—stuffed animals	—toy cars, trucks, fire engines
—dolls with clothes	—action figures

1. Think of two recent events that were widely reported in the news. What
   happened?

Event 1	Event 2
_____	_____
_____	_____
_____	_____

2. What are the key features of your generation and your parents' generation?

your generation	your parents' generation
_____	_____
_____	_____
_____	_____

Teaching Tip:
The Writer's Desk
activities provide
students with an
opportunity to
develop a topic
through all stages
of the writing
process using the
comparison and
contrast rhetorical
mode. In the Warm
Up, they begin by
exploring various
topics. Those topics
then carry on
throughout the
chapter.

3. What are some key features of a celebrity and a hero?

celebrity   hero

_____   _____

_____   _____

_____   _____

DEVELOPING

The Thesis Statement

In a comparison and contrast essay, the thesis statement indicates what you are comparing and contrasting, and it expresses a controlling idea. For example, the following thesis statement indicates that the essay will compare the myths and reality of mold to prove that it does not seriously threaten human health.

> Common household mold is not as dangerous as many people believe.

PRACTICE 3

Read each thesis statement, and then answer the questions that follow. State whether the essay would focus on similarities or differences.

1. The weather in our region is more extreme than it was in the past.
   a. What is being compared? _____weather in the past and today_____
   b. What is the controlling idea? _weather is more extreme today_____
   c. What will the essay focus on? _____ similarities   _X__ differences

2. The new stadium is as beautifully designed as the old one was.
   a. What is being compared? _____new and old stadiums_____
   b. What is the controlling idea? _both are beautiful_____
   c. What will the essay focus on? __X__ similarities   _____ differences

3. Before marriage, people expect to feel eternally lustful toward their "soul mate," but the reality of married life is quite different.
   a. What is being compared? _____ideals and reality of marriage_____
   b. What is the controlling idea? _expectations or situations change_____
      _____after marriage_____
   c. What will the essay focus on? _____ similarities   _X__differences

ESL
Teaching Tip:
Nonnative speakers may not be aware that many different prefixes mean *not*. You could give them the following rules, but note that there are exceptions. Use *il* before most words beginning with *l* (*illegal*, *illogical*). Use *im* before most words beginning with *m* or *p* (*impossible*).

vo•cab•u•lar•y BOOST

Some prefixes mean "not" and give words opposite meanings. Examples are *il-, im-, in-, dis-, un-,* and *ir-.* Create opposites by adding prefixes to the following words.

EXAMPLE: available   *unavailable*

1. legal   *illegal*
2. polite   *impolite*
3. toxic   *nontoxic*
4. appropriate   *inappropriate*
5. approve   *disapprove*
6. considerate   *inconsiderate*

7. reliable   *unreliable*
8. harmed   *unharmed*
9. reversible   *irreversible*
10. necessary   *unnecessary*
11. patient   *impatient*
12. agree   *disagree*

Writer's Desk Write Thesis Statements

For each topic, write a thesis statement that includes what you are comparing and contrasting and a controlling idea.

EXAMPLE: Topic: girls' and boys' toys

Thesis statement: *Both girls' and boys' toys reinforce gender stereotypes.*

1. Topic: two events in the news
   Thesis statement: _____

2. Topic: two generations
   Thesis statement: _____
   _____

3. Topic: a celebrity versus a hero
   Thesis statement: _____
   _____

The Supporting Ideas

After you have developed an effective thesis statement, generate supporting ideas. In a comparison and contrast essay, think of examples that help to clarify the similarities or differences, and then incorporate some ideas in your final essay plan.

To generate supporting ideas, you might try using a Venn diagram. In this example, you can see how the writer draws two circles to compare traditional boys' and girls' toys and how some ideas fall into both categories.

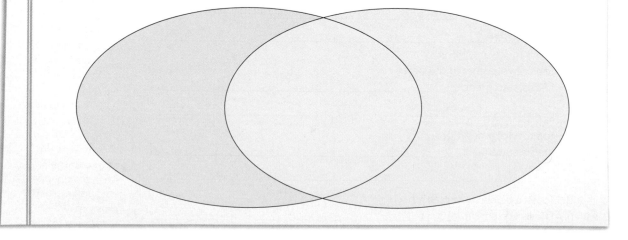

Boys
Bold red and black
Fighting figures
Uniforms, weapons
Hard plastic
Animals
Toy guns

Both
Human figure toys
Active toys such as
  balls, hacky sacks,
  skateboards
Video games
Blocks

Girls
Pastel colors
Baby-like dolls
Doll fashions
Stuffed animals
Bake ovens

Writer's Desk   **Develop Supporting Ideas**

Choose one of your thesis statements from the previous Writer's Desk. List some similarities and differences.

The Essay Plan

Before you write a comparison and contrast essay, make a detailed essay plan. Decide which pattern you will follow: point by point or topic by topic. Then add supporting details. Make sure that each detail supports the thesis statement. Also think about the best way to organize your ideas.

THESIS STATEMENT: <u>Both girls' and boys' toys reinforce gender stereotypes.</u>

Point by Point

A/B Girls' toys focus on activities in the home, whereas boys' toys focus on outside activities.

Details: Girls have dollhouses and baking ovens whereas boys have carpenter sets and racecars.

A/B Girls' toys focus on physical appearance, and boys' toys focus on heroic fighters.

Details: Girls dress their Barbie dolls, and they put on child-friendly makeup. Boys have action figures such as GI Joes and superheroes.

Topic by Topic

A Girls' toys reinforce the importance of looks, body image, and fashion.

Details: They receive fashion dolls with clothing, shoes, and other accessories.

A Girls' toys encourage nurturing by focusing on home and the family.

Details: They have dolls with baby bottles, baking ovens, toy vacuums, and shopping carts.

B Boys' toys prepare them for creative careers and activities outside the home.

Details: Boys have little workshops, lego sets, and toy cars and trucks.

B Boys' toys encourage boys to be heroes in their fantasy games.

Details: Boys receive action figures such as GI Joe, X-Men, and Superman.

Teaching Tip: As an additional activity, ask students to develop supporting ideas for all three Writer's Desk topics, which are listed in the Warm Up. They can try using Venn diagrams when they develop ideas for the other two Warm Up topics.

Writer's Desk **Write an Essay Plan**

Refer to the information you generated in previous Writer's Desks, and prepare a detailed essay plan using a point-by-point or topic-by-topic pattern. You can use the letters A and B to indicate which side you are discussing in your plan. Include details about each supporting idea.

Teaching Tips: You might ask students to keep their essay plans and then attach them to the final draft. You can then determine how the students have developed their ideas.

Tech
Teaching Tip:
Ask students to
compare and
contrast two online
shopping sites such
as *kijiji.com* and
craigslist.com. They
should determine
which site is more
visually pleasing and
easy to use. Then
pairs can create
Venn diagrams or
lists of supporting
ideas to show the
similarities and
differences.

The First Draft

After you outline your ideas in an essay plan, you are ready to write the first draft. Remember to follow the topic-by-topic or the point-by-point pattern you used in your plan. Write complete sentences and use transitions to help your ideas flow smoothly. The following transitions can be helpful for guiding readers through a comparison and contrast essay.

To show similarities		To show differences	
additionally	in addition	conversely	nevertheless
at the same time	in the same way	however	on the contrary
equally	similarly	in contrast	then again

Writer's Desk **Write the First Draft**

Write the first draft of your comparison and contrast essay. Before you write, carefully review your essay plan to see if you have enough support for your points and topics. Flesh out each body paragraph with specific details.

REVISING AND EDITING

Teaching Tip:
The activity of
revising a student
essay should help
your students
understand the
important link
between the writing
process and the
grammar chapters.

Revise and Edit a Comparison and Contrast Essay

When you finish writing a comparison and contrast essay, carefully review your work and revise it to make sure that the comparison or contrast is as clear as possible to your readers. Check that you have organized your essay logically, and remove any irrelevant details. Before you work on your own essay, practice revising and editing a student essay.

A Student Essay

Read the essay, and then answer the questions that follow. As you read, correct any errors that you find, and make comments in the margins.

Gender and Toys
by Ashley Lincoln

1   As a young mother, I try to avoid gender stereotyping my children. I encourage my five-year-old daughter to play sports, and I bought my son a baby doll when he asked for one. My friends <u>been saying</u> they have the same concerns about gender roles. But insulating children from male or female role expectations is almost impossible. Most parents, in spite of their best efforts, reinforce gender stereotypes every time they shop for toys.

2   Girls' toys reinforce the importance of looks, body image, and fashion. Parents can buy their daughters makeup sets that include child-friendly lipstick, blush, and eye shadow. Barbies and other fashion dolls fill store shelves. Hanging next to the dolls are packages with tiny clothing. Of course, none of the dolls are pudgy, pimply, large-boned, or just plain unattractive. When girls play with these toys, they are taught that beauty and the right clothes and makeup are very important.

3   If <u>a little girl</u> does not like fashion toys, <u>they</u> will surely enjoy baby dolls with their fake bottles of milk, soft little blankets, and strollers. Girls' toys encourage nurturing by focusing on the home and the family. At a very young age, girls learn to be competent mothers when they change the little diapers of their dolls. Girls can learn to cook with their Easy-Bake ovens, and they learn to shop with tiny shopping carts and cash registers. My daughter and her friends love playing "house" with one child acting as the mother. They shop, pull the "cry" strings on their dolls, and feed their "babies." Girls learn about the importance of parenting <u>quicker</u> than boys do.

4   Boys' toys, on the other hand, stress jobs and activities outside the home. My son begged for, and received, a miniature workshop complete with a plastic saw, drill, screwdriver, and wrench. Lego sets prepare boys for creative occupations such as architecture and auto design. Computer and video games prepare boys for jobs in the high-tech industries. Finally, <u>there is a lot of toy cars</u>, trucks, and racetracks to remind boys that cars are very important to their identities.

5   Toys aimed at young males also permit boys to be the heroes in their fantasy games. In the boys' aisle of the toy store, there are rows of action figures. The GI Joes fight soldiers from other armies. Batman, Superman, and the X-Men fight fantasy villains. Curiously, the X-Men figures include female characters such as Storm, but the toys <u>are not call</u> "X-People." Aimed predominantly at boys, fighting action figures bolster ideas boys have about rescuing others. In their fantasy lives, boys learn early on that they are the heroes and the saviors.

6   Some suggest that it is useless to fight against the male and female roles. They point out that girls in previous centuries made their own dolls out of straw and rags, and boys made weapons out of tin cans and wood. While that is true, toy stores take the stereotyping to extremes. One solution is to try to buy gender-neutral toys such as modeling clay, painting supplies, or balls and other sporting equipment.

PRACTICE 4

Revising

1. Highlight the thesis statement.

2. Highlight the topic sentence in each body paragraph.

3. Circle a transitional word or phrase in the topic sentence of paragraph 4. Then add transitional words or phrases to the other topic sentences. Answers will vary.

4. What pattern does the writer use to organize this essay? Circle your response.

   a. point by point   (b.) topic by topic

5. The student writer uses the word "reinforce" at the end of the introduction and in the first sentence of the second paragraph. To avoid repeating the same word, what synonym could the student use?

   Answers will vary. *emphasize, strengthen, bolster, highlight*

Editing

6. Underline the verb error in the introduction. Write the correction on the line.

   Correction: *have been saying*

7. Underline and correct the pronoun-antecedent error in paragraph 3.

   Correction: *little girls/they*

8. Underline and correct a comparative form error in paragraph 3. (For more information about comparative errors, see the Grammar Hint on the next page.)

   Correction: *Girls learn about the importance of parenting more quickly than boys do.*

9. Underline and correct the subject–verb agreement error in paragraph 4.

   Correction: *there are a lot of toy cars*

10. Underline and correct the passive verb that has been incorrectly formed in paragraph 5.

    Correction: *are not called*

GRAMMAR LINK

See the following chapters for more information about these grammar topics:
Subject–Verb Agreement, Chapter 27
Passive Voice, Chapter 28
Verbs, Chapter 29
Pronouns, Chapter 31
Adjectives and Adverbs, Chapter 32

Comparing Adjectives and Adverbs

When comparing or contrasting two items, ensure that you have correctly written your comparative forms. For instance, never put *more* with an adjective ending in *-er*.

City life is ~~more~~ better than country life.

If you are comparing two actions, remember to use an adverb instead of an adjective.

more easily
Children learn lessons ~~easier~~ when they are treated with respect.

Writer's Desk Revise and Edit Your Essay

Revise and edit the essay that you wrote for the previous Writer's Desk. You can refer to the revising and editing checklists at the end of this chapter and on this book's inside covers.

A Professional Essay

Writer and translator Naomi Louder has published poetry in *The Fiddlehead Review* and *The New Quarterly*, among other publications. In the following essay, she uses the comparison and contrast pattern. Read the essay and answer the questions that follow.

The Dating World
by Naomi Louder

1   Dating has changed a lot over the years. Many people, post millennium, can't help associating the word "date" with a more innocent time and scenarios involving ice-cream sodas, varsity jackets, and drive-in movies. In smaller and more traditional communities, vestiges of this association remain, and high school sweethearts who paired up early on wind up getting married straight out of school. Compared to previous generations, today's singles have a new dating ethic that involves flying straight into a whirlwind affair.

2   The most obvious difference between the past and the present is in dating methods. In the 1950s and 1960s, potential sweethearts met at

school dances, the lunch-line at the school cafeteria, or at school sports events. There were certain formal rules of etiquette to be followed, down to the "base" system, dictating when, where, and how the relationship was to progress to its logical conclusion. People were concerned, after a date, with whether "first base"—a kiss—was attained. Nowadays, it is more common to obsess over the other party's sexual history, his or her expectations, and whether a relationship might be a possibility. The "base" system has been supplanted, in junior high or even elementary school, by the "gummy" trend, where cheap rubber bracelets, coded by color, announce the sexual experience or willingness of the wearer.

3   In a traditional dating context, couples worried primarily about pregnancy, and—mainly in the case of the girls—about losing their reputations. An ill-timed boast on the part of a boy could jeopardize a girl's dating career, while a pregnancy could result in the ultimate shame to the girl and her family or a rushed and gossiped-over wedding. In a contemporary urban center, these worries seem naïve. Early sexual relationships are more the norm than before, and the concerns are sexually transmitted infections, date rape, and abortion or adoption versus single parenthood. Of course, some young people have rejected the ethic of sexual freedom and chosen to make chastity pledges. However, the majority of teens and young adults are more determined than ever to fulfill their sexual and emotional needs, sometimes before they are clearly aware of the consequences.

4   Both the traditional and the new dating methods have downsides. The new generation, with all its scorn of traditional and prudish dating etiquette, finds itself lost and lonelier than ever. The old-fashioned courtship ritual has been condensed to a witty remark, a compliment or two, and an animal assault on a balcony, on a street corner, or in a taxi. Once the deed is done, people often find that they have no idea who they're dating. On the other hand, using the traditional method, people may try to represent themselves dishonestly, behaving with courtesy, unselfishness, or generosity that they would never bother with if they weren't trying to impress. The person's true personality—perhaps that of a slob or a diva—may only be unveiled when a commitment has been made. Advocates of casual encounters argue that when the formalities are dispensed with, people show themselves as they truly are.

5   There are pitfalls to both of these ways of dating, but the fact is, most people are looking for a partner in life, and the only way to find one is to trust somebody. A high school sweetheart or the best-looking person at a party is not necessarily the ideal partner. For the most part, relationships succeed because there is a sounder basis to them than passion or romance. If a true friendship is possible between two people, when passion and excitement fade, there will still be a reason to stay together.

PRACTICE 5

1. Highlight the thesis statement.

2. Highlight the topic sentence in paragraphs 2 and 4.

3. Paragraph 3 does not have a topic sentence. Which sentence best expresses the implied point?

   a. In the past, women worried about losing their reputations.

   b. Dating is difficult.

   c. Dating anxieties have also changed over the years.

   d. Today, there is a revival of religious values among young people.

4. In this essay, what pattern of comparison does the writer follow? Circle the correct answer.

   a. point by point   b. topic by topic

5. Using your own words, sum up the main subjects in this essay.

   Paragraph 2: *dating rules*

   Paragraph 3: *dating anxieties*

   Paragraph 4: *disadvantages of both methods*

6. Does this essay mainly focus on similarities or differences? Circle the correct answer.

   a. similarities   b. differences

Teaching Tip:

Cooperative Learning (Ask & Learn)
Ask students to review the chapter and identify any content that they are not completely clear about. Then each student should write down two questions about the unclear topic. Finally, working in teams, students can ask other members their questions and share answers.

The Writer's Room

Writing Activity 1: Topics

Choose any of the following topics, or choose your own topic, and write a comparison and contrast essay.

General Topics

Compare or contrast . . .

1. two types of music
2. an early bird and a night owl
3. a true friend and an acquaintance
4. two characters from film or fiction
5. two common phobias

College and Work-Related Topics

Compare or contrast . . .

6. courage versus recklessness
7. living on campus versus living off campus
8. being self-employed versus working for others
9. online classes and traditional classes
10. expectations about a job versus the reality of the job

READING LINK

More Comparison and Contrast Readings

"The Untranslatable Word 'Macho'" by Rose del Castillo Guilbault (page 587)

"The Happiness Factor" by David Brooks (page 594)

WRITING LINK

More Comparison and Contrast Writing Topics

Chapter 20, Writer's Room topic 2 (page 317)

Chapter 23, Writer's Room topic 2 (page 348)

Chapter 27, Writer's Room topic 2 (page 386)

Chapter 32, Writer's Room topic 1 (page 452)

Chapter 38, Writer's Room topic 2 (page 518)

Teaching Tip:
Pair Work

Have students read one of the essays in the Reading Link. Then, in pairs, they can list the main comparisons or contrasts.

Writing Activity 2: Photo Writing

Examine the photo, and think about things that you could compare and contrast. You can focus on something in the photo, or use it to spark ideas about related topics. You can compare two neighborhoods or two small towns. You can also compare a downtown area with a suburb. Brainstorm ideas and then write a comparison and contrast essay.

Writing Activity 3: Media Writing

Compare and contrast two characters or two life stages. Watch a television soap opera or a drama such as *Brothers and Sisters* or *Glee* or a movie such as *The Kite Runner*, *The Social Network*, or *Dreamgirls*. In an essay, you can compare and contrast two life stages, such as childhood and adulthood or adolescence and old age. You can also choose to compare and contrast two characters in the television show or movie.

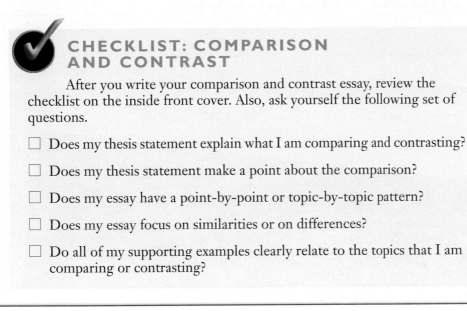

CHECKLIST: COMPARISON AND CONTRAST

After you write your comparison and contrast essay, review the checklist on the inside front cover. Also, ask yourself the following set of questions.

☐ Does my thesis statement explain what I am comparing and contrasting?

☐ Does my thesis statement make a point about the comparison?

☐ Does my essay have a point-by-point or topic-by-topic pattern?

☐ Does my essay focus on similarities or on differences?

☐ Do all of my supporting examples clearly relate to the topics that I am comparing or contrasting?

Teaching Tip:
Writer's World Competition
Please advise students that they can submit their essays for possible publication to www .pearsonhighered .com/essayrewards/ writingrewards.html

mywritinglab To check your progress in meeting this chapter's objectives, log in to **www.mywritinglab.com,** go to the **Study Plan** tab, click on **Essay Patterns** and choose **Compare and Contrast** from the list of subtopics. Read and view the resources in the **Review Materials** section, and then complete the **Recall, Apply,** and **Write** sets in the **Activities** section.

Cause and Effect

When a flood occurs, people ask themselves, "How did this happen?" and "What is the extent of the damage?" Writers use the cause and effect pattern to explain the answers to these types of questions.

Teaching Tip: Cooperative Learning (Sharing Circle) The Writers' Exchange activity can help your students understand cause and effect. Try this activity as a class discussion, and list ideas on the board.

Writers' Exchange

Work with a group of students. Each group has two minutes to brainstorm as many reasons as possible to explain why people follow fashion fads. Then, each team will have two minutes to explain the effects of following fashion fads. The team with the most causes and effects wins.

EXPLORING

What Is Cause and Effect?

Cause and effect writing explains why an event happened or what the consequences of such an event were. A cause and effect essay can focus on causes, effects, or both.

People often analyze the causes or effects of something. At home, a teenager might explain to her parents why she had a car accident. At college, an administrator may be asked to give reasons for the lack of student housing on campus. At work, a boss might clarify the reasons for company downsizing to employees.

Visualizing Cause and Effect

PRACTICE I   Brainstorm supporting ideas for the following thesis statement. Write some details on the lines provided.

THESIS STATEMENT: A shopping addiction has some serious effects.

accumulate debt

pay high interest

declare bankruptcy

_____

waste time shopping

accumulate useless

  items

have clutter

argue about money

disagree about bills

cause marital

  problems

The Cause and Effect Essay

When you write a cause and effect essay, focus on two main tasks.

1. **Indicate whether you are focusing on causes, effects, or both.** If you do decide to focus on both causes and effects, make sure that your thesis statement indicates your purpose to the reader.

2. **Make sure that your causes and effects are valid.** You should determine real causes and effects and not simply list things that happened before or after the event. Also, verify that your assumptions are logical.

Illogical: Our furnace stopped working because the weather was too cold.

(This is illogical; cold weather cannot stop a furnace from working.)

Better: Our furnace stopped working because the filters needed replacing and the gas burners needed adjusting.

Cause and Effect at Work

In this community newsletter about safety, the writer explains about the causes and effects of computer-related injuries.

Musculoskeletal disorders (MSDs) are a family of painful disorders affecting tendons, muscles, nerves, and joints in the neck, upper and lower back, chest, shoulders, arms, and hands. They include repetitive strain injuries (RSIs), which may take years to develop. Recovery can be difficult and may even require surgery in extreme cases.

MSDs are the scourge of the computerized workplace. Workers can develop chronic pain if their workstations are set up without proper attention to ergonomics. A small change, such as repositioning the screen or keyboard or using an adjustable chair, can often eliminate the problem.

Teaching Tip:
Ask students to list causes and effects in these paragraphs.

A Student Essay

Read the student essay and answer the questions that follow.

College Students and the Challenge of Credit Card Debt
by Katie Earnest

1   Did you know that most college students carry credit card debt? In fact, according to a Nelli Mae study, three out of four students have an outstanding balance of $2,200. My son maxed out three different credit cards by the time he was in the second semester of his junior year. He couldn't keep up with his monthly payments to the credit card companies anymore, even though he had a part-time job on campus and a part-time job off campus. Students get into credit card debt for a variety of reasons.

2   Credit card companies have clever ways to promote their products to students. Anyone who is at least eighteen years old can get a credit card without parental consent or any source of income. According to the *Daily Emerald*, one of the many ways that major credit card companies take advantage of this situation is to offer universities generous monetary donations in exchange for the full rights to market their cards on campus.

Credit card companies distribute brochures or flyers around campus, and set up a booth offering free gifts to college students if they fill out a card application. Another way that credit card companies target college students is by calling them four to five times a month or continuously mailing them card applications.

3   While most college students obtain a credit card with the intention of using it only for emergencies, it doesn't always work out that way. Students start off using their credit card to buy gas, purchase a few groceries, catch a movie, or grab a late night pizza. However, before they know it, they have reached their credit card limit. College students don't realize that fees or penalties will grow because of high interest rates. After maxing out the first credit card, many people will sign up for another credit card, still telling themselves that it will be for emergencies only. The credit card debt spirals out of control. There have been two widely reported cases of college students who took their lives because of their excessive accumulation of credit card debt. According to the *College Student Journal*, one of the students was a twenty-year-old with a debt of $10,000, and the other was a nineteen-year-old with a debt of $2,500.

4   Furthermore, students don't realize how difficult it can be to pay credit card bills. A part-time job may result in lower than expected salary. Living expenses may be higher than expected. Thus, it is challenging for students to make their monthly payments on time. For example, my son could not keep up with his monthly payments even though he had a job. His debt accumulated quickly

In conclusion, credit cards have become a fact of life on college campuses. They continue to be a temptation for students. College students who carry a high level of credit card debt face financial stress just as my son did. If I had known that card companies solicited students on campus, I would have educated my son about credit card usage, and I would have warned him about the challenges that he would face if he accumulated a large amount of debt.

PRACTICE 2

1. What introductory style does the writer use?
    a. general background   c. definition
    (b.) anecdote   d. contrasting position

2. Underline the thesis statement.

3. Does the thesis statement express causes, effects, or both?

    only causes

Teaching Tip:
The Writer's Desk activities, such as the one below, provide students with opportunities to develop a topic through all stages of the writing process using the cause and effect rhetorical mode. In the Warm Up, they begin by exploring various topics. Those topics then carry on throughout the chapter.

4. Highlight the topic sentences in paragraphs 2, 3, and 4.

5. Using your own words, sum up the causes for student credit card debt.

   -Credit card companies make it easy for students to acquire credit cards.

   -College students find it tempting to use credit cards. They may even get

   another credit card because they have maxed out their first credit card.

   -College students sometimes don't earn enough money to cover costs, so

   they quickly get into credit card debt.

6. What does the writer think she should have done to help her son?

   She says that she would have educated him better about credit card debt

   and would have taught him how to use his credit cards more wisely.

Explore Topics

In the Writer's Desk Warm Up, you will try an exploring strategy to generate ideas about different topics.

Writer's Desk **Warm Up**

Read the following questions, and write the first ideas that come to your mind. Think of two or three ideas for each topic.

EXAMPLE: Why are reality television shows so popular?

—*voyeurism*

—*people are bored with sitcoms and other regular television programs*

—*a large variety for every taste*

1. What are some causes and effects of workplace romances?

   _____

   _____

   _____

2. What are some causes and effects of the social networking culture?

   _____

   _____

   _____

3. Why do couples live together without marriage? What are the effects of living together without marriage?

_____

_____

_____

DEVELOPING

The Thesis Statement

When writing a thesis statement for a cause and effect essay, clearly demonstrate whether the focus is on causes, effects, or both. Also, make sure that you state a controlling idea that expresses your point of view or attitude.

    controlling idea (causes)   topic
There are many reasons for **global warming.**

    topic   controlling idea (effects)
Global warming may have a profound influence on our lifestyles.

    topic   controlling idea (causes and effects)
Global warming, which has developed for many reasons, may have a profound influence on our lifestyles.

PRACTICE 3   Look carefully at the following thesis statements. Decide if each sentence focuses on the causes, effects, or both. Look at the key words that give you the clues and circle the best answer.

1. Poverty persists in developing countries because of lack of education, scarcity of jobs, and political corruption.
     (a.) causes   b. effects   c. both

2. In our college, the high student dropout rate, which is triggered by the tourist industry, results in long-term problems for the community.
     a. causes   b. effects   (c.) both

3. The Haitian earthquake has created many problems for the environment, as well as in people's mental and physical health.
     a. causes   (b.) effects   c. both

Grammar Hint   **Affect and Effect**

Use *affect* as a verb and *effect* as a noun. *Affect* means "to influence or change" and *effect* means "the result."

verb

How does the ban on fast food in public schools <u>affect</u> children's health?

noun

What <u>effects</u> will the ban on fast food in public schools have on children's health?

You can also use *effect* as a verb that means "to cause or to bring about a change or implement a plan."

verb

Health care professionals lobbied to <u>effect</u> changes in public school lunch menus.

See Chapter 34 for more information about commonly confused words.

Writer's Desk   **Write Thesis Statements**

Write a thesis statement for each of the following topics. You can look for ideas in the previous Writer's Desk. Determine if you will focus on the causes, effects, or both in your essay.

EXAMPLE: Topic: popularity of reality shows

Thesis Statement: *Reality television shows have become increasingly popular for several reasons.*

1. Topic: workplace romance

   Thesis Statement: _____

   _____

2. Topic: social networking culture

   Thesis Statement: _____

   _____

3. Topic: living together without marriage

   Thesis Statement: _____

   _____

The Supporting Ideas

After you have developed an effective thesis statement, generate supporting ideas. In a cause and effect essay, think of examples that clearly show the causes or effects. To develop supporting ideas follow these three steps:

- Use prewriting strategies such as freewriting and brainstorming to generate ideas.
- Choose the best ideas. Use examples that clearly reveal the causes and effects.
- Organize your ideas. Choose the best organizational method for this essay pattern.

Hint **Do Not Oversimplify**

Avoid attributing a simple or general cause to a very complex issue. When you use expressions such as *it appears that* or *a possible cause is,* it shows that you are aware of the complex factors involved in the situation.

Oversimplification: Global warming is caused by cars.

Better: One possible cause of global warming is the CO_2 emissions from cars.

Identifying Causes and Effects

Imagine that you had to write a cause and effect essay on gambling. You could brainstorm and think of as many causes and effects as possible.

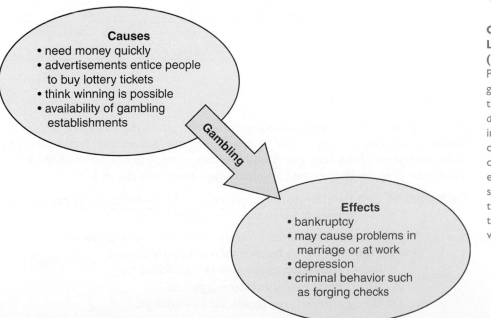

Causes
- need money quickly
- advertisements entice people to buy lottery tickets
- think winning is possible
- availability of gambling establishments

Gambling

Effects
- bankruptcy
- may cause problems in marriage or at work
- depression
- criminal behavior such as forging checks

Writer's Desk Identify Causes and Effects

Choose the topic of one of the thesis statements from the previous Writer's Desk. Then write some possible causes and effects.

EXAMPLE: Topic: _Popularity of reality television programs_

Causes	Effects
new television concept	become TV junkie
empathize with the contestants	contestants become famous
each episode has a hook ending	take pleasure in others' humiliation
feel superior to contestants	live vicariously through others

Focus on: _causes_

Topic: _____

Causes	Effects

Focus on: _____

Teaching Tip:
Pair Work
Ask students to discuss their answers for the Writer's Desk activity with a partner. Together, they will help each other come up with more ideas.

The Essay Plan

In many courses, instructors ask students to write about the causes or effects of a particular subject. Take the time to plan your essay before you write your first draft. Also, think about how you would logically arrange the order of ideas. As you make your plan, make sure that you focus on causes, effects, or both.

THESIS STATEMENT: Reality television shows have become increasingly popular for several reasons.

I. Many situation comedies and movies of the week are no longer innovative, so people turn to reality shows.
    A. Some television comedies retell old jokes.
    B. Characters are often stereotypical.
    C. Many shows have predictable endings.

II. Reality television programs cater to a variety of tastes.
   A. Some shows focus on family dynamics.
   B. Some shows focus on romance.
   C. Other shows focus on extreme situations.
III. Home audiences live vicariously through contestants.
   A. Audiences may feel superior to contestants.
   B. An audience member can empathize with a contestant.
   C. Audience members think they can become famous like the contestants.

Teaching Tip:
As an additional activity, ask students to develop supporting ideas for all three Writer's Desk topics. The topics are listed in the Warm Up.

Writer's Desk Write an Essay Plan

Choose one of the ideas that you have developed in previous Writer's Desks, and prepare an essay plan. If you think of new details that will explain your point more effectively, include them in your plan.

The First Draft

After you have developed and organized your ideas in your essay plan, write the first draft. Remember to write complete sentences and to use transitional words or expressions to help your ideas flow smoothly. Most writers arrange cause and effect essays using emphatic order, which means that they place examples from the most to the least important or from the least to the most important. The following transitional expressions are useful for showing causes and effects.

To show causes
for this reason
the first cause
the most important cause

To show effects
accordingly
as a result
consequently

Writer's Desk Write the First Draft

Carefully review and, if necessary, revise your essay plan from the previous Writer's Desk, and then write the first draft of your cause and effect essay.

Teaching Tip:
Ask students to keep their essay plans and then attach them to their final draft. You can then determine how the students have developed their ideas.

ESL
Teaching Tip:
Pair nonnative
speakers with native
speakers when
doing the
Vocabulary Boost.
Possible answers
are *friend, man,
child, relax, items or
products, criminal.*

---

vo•cab•u•lar•y BOOST

Using inappropriate vocabulary in a particular context can affect the way people respond to you. For example, you would not use street language in a business meeting. Replace the following words with terms that can be used in academic or professional writing.

buddy   guy   kid   chill   stuff   crook

Teaching Tip:
The activity of
revising a student
essay should help
your students
understand the
important link
between the writing
process and the
grammar chapters.

REVISING AND EDITING

Revise and Edit a Cause and Effect Essay

When you finish writing a cause and effect essay, review your work and revise it to make the examples as clear as possible to your readers. Check that you have organized your ideas logically, and remove any irrelevant details. Before you work on your own essay, practice revising and editing a student essay.

A Student Essay

Read the essay, and then answer the questions that follow. As you read, correct any errors that you find, and make comments in the margins.

Reality Television Is Here to Stay
by Ivan Pogrebkov

1   Matt is a twenty-one-year-old college student. Each Thursday evening, he and his friends get together to watch television. They are hooked on reality shows, which have changed the television landscape since they first arrived on the screen a few years ago. These television shows have become increasingly popular for several reasons.

2   First, the traditional situation comedies have become repetitive; therefore, bored viewers are looking for more innovative programming that will hold their attention. For example, many weekly comedy programs have the same mind-numbing plot in which the parents have to deal with their children getting into superficial trouble. The jokes are the same, and the endings are predictable. The parents help the children solve the problem, and everybody learn a valuable life lesson. Most viewers are tired of a format in which family problems can be solved in thirty minutes. Some comedies in the past were very good, though. *Seinfeld* was a great situation comedy that was very popular and ran for a decade. Reality

television is more interesting than run-of-the mill television shows because ordinary people can react in unexpected ways.

3   <u>There are reality shows that focus on family dynamics, shows concentrating on romance, and on extreme situations</u>. Although reality shows are somewhat scripted, they do provide viewers with a degree of suspense and unpredictability. One never knows who is going to <u>loose</u> the competition. This factor attracts audiences who keep watching to find out the outcome for each participant.

4   Finally, reality shows are <u>all the rage</u> because audiences can relate to the situations and participants on some level. Most of the people appearing on reality shows are ordinary citizens as opposed to glamorous stars with expensive hairdos and clothes. Spectators' emotions may range from empathy for the participants to feeling superior to them. Because they are just like the participants, viewers enjoy envisioning themselves doing the same things and achieving fifteen minutes of fame. And, if the reality show is a contest, the winner usually wins money, prizes, and some amount of recognition.

5   People are loyal to reality shows because they offer variety, humor, and suspense. In fact, these programs are today's new soap operas. Although many critics find reality shows uninspiring, those programs are probably going to continue to be popular for a long time.

PRACTICE 4

Revising

1. Does the essay focus on causes, effects, or both? *causes* _____

2. Each body paragraph lacks adequate details. List some examples that could support the main idea of each body paragraph.
   Answers will vary. Students should give examples from specific reality shows.

   Paragraph 2 _____

   _____

   Paragraph 3 _____

   _____

   Paragraph 4 _____

   _____

3. Highlight the topic sentence in paragraph 2, and then cross out any sentences that do not support the topic sentence.

Teaching Tip:
Encourage students to list examples of particular reality shows. Discuss how examples would strengthen the essay.

4. Choose an appropriate topic sentence for paragraph 3.

   a. Reality programs, unlike most sitcoms, soap operas, and made-for-TV movies, cater to a variety of tastes.

   b. Contestants of reality shows must follow a script, so they are not "real."

   c. Reality shows are unpredictable.

   d. Not everyone likes reality shows because most of the shows are boring.

5. What is the introductory style of this essay? _____ *anecdote* _____

6. How does the writer conclude the essay?

   a. with an observation   b. with a prediction   c. with a suggestion

Editing

GRAMMAR LINK

See the following chapters for more information about these grammar topics:
Parallel Structure, Chapter 25
Subject–Verb Agreement, Chapter 27
Exact Language, Chapter 33
Spelling, Chapter 34

7. In paragraph 2, there is a subject–verb agreement error. Underline and correct the error.

   Correction: *everybody learns*

8. In paragraph 3, a sentence has faulty parallel structure. Underline and rewrite the sentence.

   Correction: Answers will vary. *There are shows that focus on family dynamics, on romance, and on extreme situations.*

9. Underline and correct the misspelled word in paragraph 3.

   Correction: _____ *lose* _____

10. Change a slang expression or cliché in paragraph 4 into standard English.

    Correction: *all the rage = very popular*

Writer's Desk Revise and Edit Your Essay

Revise and edit the essay that you wrote for the previous Writer's Desk. You can refer to the revising and editing checklists at the end of this chapter and on this book's inside covers.

A Professional Essay

Ellen Goodman is a Pulitzer Prize–winning columnist for the *Boston Globe*, and her articles appear in more than 370 newspapers. She has also written several books, including *Value Judgments* and *Keeping in Touch*. In the next essay, she examines why North Americans are becoming more isolated socially.

Friendless in North America
by Ellen Goodman

1   Lynn Smith-Lovin was listening in the back seat of a taxi when a woman called the radio talk-show hosts to confess her affairs with a new boyfriend and a not-yet-former husband. The hosts, in their best therapeutic voices, offered their on-air opinion, "Give me an S, give me an L, give me a U," You can spell the rest. It was the sort of exchange that would leave most of us wondering why anyone would share her intimate life story with a radio host. Didn't she have anyone else to talk with? Smith-Lovin might have been the only one in the audience with an answer to the question: Maybe not.

2   The Duke University sociologist is co-author of one of those blockbuster studies that makes us look at ourselves. This one is labeled "Friendless in America." A face-to-face study of 1,467 adults turned up some disheartening news. One-fourth reported that they have nobody to talk to about "important matters." Another quarter reported they are just one person away from nobody. But this was the most startling fact. The study is a replica of one done twenty years ago. In only two decades, from 1985 to 2004, the number of people who have no one to talk to has doubled. And the number of confidants of the average person has gone down from three to two.

3   The people to whom we are closest form our own informal safety net. They're the ones who see us through a life crisis, lend us their spare bedroom, or pick up our kids at school in a pinch. Social isolation is as big a risk factor for premature death as smoking. Robert Putnam has already chronicled the erosion of the ties that bind in *Bowling Alone*. But we've paid less attention to "coping alone" or "suffering alone." Imagine if some other piece of the social safety net had frayed that furiously. Imagine if income had gone down by a third or divorce doubled or the medical system halved. We would be setting up commissions and organizing rallies.

4   Not everything in the study was gloomy. Deep in the data is the suggestion that families—husbands and wives, parents and adult children—might be closer. Spouses who call each other "my best friend" might be right. We might have fewer intimates, but we're more intimate with them. On average, we see them more than once a week and have

Teaching Tip:

Cooperative Learning (Jigsaw)
With students, generate a thesis statement or choose a thesis statement from this chapter's Writer's Desk. Place students in groups of five. One group should write an introduction for the thesis statement. Three groups should write separate body paragraphs, and a fifth group should write a concluding paragraph. (Ask each person in the group to write the same paragraph.) After about ten minutes, ask one representative from each team to stand up. In order, they would read the intro, body paragraphs, and conclusion. If you have time, number students from one to five. The ones get together, the twos get together, and so on. The new teams can revise and edit their essays.

known them seven years. Nevertheless, the big news is that circles have tightened, shrunk, and gone nuclear. As Smith-Lovin says, "Literally nothing takes the place of family." The greatest loss has been in neighbors and friends who will provide help, support, advice, and connections to a wider world.

5   There is no shortage of speculation about why our circle of friends is eroding. The usual suspect is the time crunch. It's knocked friendship off the balancing beam of life as we attend to work and family. It's left less time for the groups and associations that bind us. But in the past twenty years, technology has changed the way we use our "relationship time." Walk along any city street and people talking on cell phones are more common than pigeons. Go into Starbucks and a third of the customers are having coffee dates with their laptops. "It could be that talking to people close to us on cell phones has caused our social circle to shrink," says Smith-Lovin. It could be that we are both increasingly in-touch and isolated. It's become easier to keep extensive relationships over time and distance but harder to build the deep ones in our backyard. In the virtual neighborhood, how many have substituted email for intimacy, contacts for confidants, and Facebook for face to face?

6   A few years ago, when my friend Patricia O'Brien and I wrote a book on the power of friendship in women's lives, we noted that there was no official status for friends, no pro-friendship movement, no cultural or political support system for friends. Yet this voluntary relationship can be the most sustaining one of life.

7   Now we are living in smaller, tighter circles. We are ten degrees of separation from each other and one or two people away from loneliness. And many now outsource intimacy from friends to professional therapists and *gawd* help us, talk shows. Who can we talk to about important matters? Who can we count on? As we search for tools to repair this frayed safety net, we can take poor, paradoxical comfort from the fact that if we are feeling isolated, we are not alone.

PRACTICE 5

1. Who is the audience for this essay? *General audience*

2. The thesis of this essay is not stated directly, but it is implied. Using your own words, write the thesis of this essay.   Answers will vary.

    The increasing use of technology is leading North Americans to become

    more and more isolated.

3. Circle the type of introduction Goodman uses.

   a. historical background   (b.) anecdote   c. general background

4. In your own words, how have the socialization habits of North Americans changed in the past twenty years?

   The circle of intimates has become smaller. We have lost closeness with

   neighbors and friends.

5. What specific reasons does Goodman give for this social change?

   Goodman says technology, such as cell phones and online

   communications, have contributed to social change.

6. Goodman writes, "It could be that we are both increasingly in-touch and isolated." What does she mean?

   New technology gives us the means to communicate with people who are

   far from us, but it also discourages us from having face-to-face meetings

   with those near us.

 The Writer's Room

Writing Activity 1: Topics

Write a cause and effect essay about one of the following topics, or choose your own topic.

General Topics

Causes and/or effects of

1. playing a sport
2. getting married
3. a fear of _____
4. road rage
5. a natural phenomenon

College and Work-Related Topics

Causes and/or effects of

6. changing a career
7. becoming successful
8. giving somebody a second chance
9. learning a skill
10. a hostile workplace

Teaching Tip:
Discuss Goodman's essay with your students. Suggest that they write a response. They can discuss the reasons they have certain friends or the effects of friendship on their lives.

ESL
Teaching Tip:
Encourage your nonnative speakers to write about the causes or effects of moving to the United States.

Teaching Tip:
Pair Work
Ask students to read one of the suggested essays in the Reading Link. Then, in pairs, they can outline the essay and list the main causes or effects.

READING LINK
More Cause and Effect Readings
"The CSI Effect" by Richard Willing (page 533)
"Nature Returns to the Cities" by John Roach (page 584)

**WRITING
LINK**

**More Cause and
Effect Writing
Topics**

Chapter 22, Writer's
Room topic 2
(page 339)

Chapter 28, Writer's
Room topic 2
(page 402)

Chapter 30, Writer's
Room topic 2
(page 425)

Chapter 33, Writer's
Room topic 2
(page 462)

Chapter 35, Writer's
Room topic 1
(page 489)

Writing Activity 2: Photo Writing

Why do people gossip? What are the causes or effects of gossip?

Writing Activity 3: Media Writing

Watch a medical show or movie that deals with health issues. You could watch *House*, *Nip/Tuck*, or *Trauma*. You can also watch movies such as *Erin Brockovich*, *The Soloist*, *The Elephant Man*, or *Philadelphia*. Write an essay describing the causes or effects of a physical or mental ailment, and use examples to support your point.

Teaching Tip:

**Cooperative
Learning
(Ask & Learn)**
Ask students to
review the chapter
and identify anything
that they are not
completely clear
about. All students
should write two
questions on a
sheet of paper. Then
in teams, students
can ask other
members their
questions and share
answers.

Teaching Tip:
**Writer's World
Competition**
Please advise
students that they
can submit their
essays for possible
publication to www
.pearsonhighered
.com/essayrewards/
writingrewards.html

✔ CHECKLIST: CAUSE AND EFFECT ESSAY

As you write your cause and effect essay, review the checklist on the inside front cover. Also, ask yourself the following questions.

☐ Does my thesis statement indicate clearly that my essay focuses on causes, effects, or both?

☐ Do I have adequate supporting examples of causes and/or effects?

☐ Do I make logical and valid points?

☐ Do I use the terms *effect* and/or *affect* correctly?

mywritinglab To check your progress in meeting this chapter's objectives, log in to **www.mywritinglab.com,** go to the **Study Plan** tab, click on **Essay Patterns** and choose **Cause and Effect** from the list of subtopics. Read and view the resources in the **Review Materials** section, and then complete the **Recall, Apply,** and **Write** sets in the **Activities** section.

CHAPTER 14

Argument

LEARNING OBJECTIVES

Medical practitioners often use argument to convince colleagues about the best treatment for a patient. In the same way, you use argument writing to convince readers to see issues from your point of view.

Teaching Tip:

Cooperative Learning (Nonstop Talking) The Writers' Exchange activity helps students understand argument. Give them 30 seconds to speak; flick the lights when speakers should switch.

Writers' Exchange

For this activity, you and a partner will take turns debating an issue. To start, choose which one of you will begin speaking. The first speaker chooses one side of any issue listed below, and then argues about that issue without stopping. When your instructor makes a signal, switch speakers. The second speaker talks nonstop about the opposing view. If you run out of ideas, you can switch topics when it is your turn to speak. Possible topics:

Technology has improved our lives.   Technology has hurt our lives.
It is better to be an only child.   It is better to have brothers and sisters.
Adolescence is the best time of life. Adolescence is the worst time of life.

EXPLORING

What Is Argument?

When you use **argument,** you take a position on an issue, and you try to prove or defend your position. Using effective argument strategies can help you convince somebody that your point of view is a valid one.

Argument is both a writing pattern and a purpose for writing. In fact, it is one of the most common aims, or purposes, in most college and work-related writing. For example, in Chapter 10, there is an essay called "On Genius," in which the writer uses definition as the predominant pattern. At the same time, the author uses argument to convince the reader that true genius exists all around us. Therefore, in most of your college and work-related writing, your purpose is to persuade the reader that your ideas are compelling and legitimate.

People use argument in their daily lives. For instance, at home, you might argue about the distribution of housework, providing examples to support your point. At college, students argue for better equipment in the computer lab or art department. At work, salespeople make well-planned arguments to convince customers to buy a product or service.

⌖ Visualizing Argument

PRACTICE I   Brainstorm supporting ideas for the following thesis statement. Write some details on the lines provided.   Answers will vary.

THESIS STATEMENT: All college students should learn a second language.

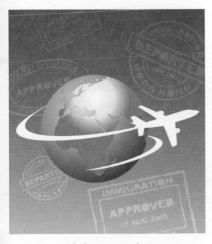

- visit countries

- communicate

- speak to customers

- find work

- learn about other
  cultures

- develop tolerance

Teaching Tip:
Ask students to work on the Visualizing practice with a partner.

Teaching Tip:
You may wish to explain how argument can be both a writing pattern (rhetorical mode) and a purpose.

Teaching Tip:
Ask students if they can think of other places where they might see, read, or hear argument being used. Examples: letters of protest, political campaigns, commercials, pop-up ads, promotional flyers, and editorials.

Teaching Tip:
If you teach your
students about
ethos, logos, and
pathos, you could
point out that point
3 is about logos and
point 4 is about
ethos. Information
about logos and
pathos appears in
"The Supporting
Ideas" section.

The Argument Essay

When you write an argument essay, remember four key points.

1. **Consider your readers.** What do your readers already know about the topic? Will they be likely to agree or disagree with you? Do they have specific concerns? Consider what kind of evidence would be most effective with your audience.

2. **Know your purpose.** In argument writing, your main purpose is to persuade the reader to agree with you. Your specific purpose is more focused. You may want the reader to take action, you may want to support a viewpoint, you may want to counter somebody else's argument, or you may want to offer a solution to a problem. Ask yourself what your specific purpose is.

3. **Take a strong position, and provide persuasive evidence.** Your thesis statement and your topic sentences should clearly show your point of view. Then back up your point of view with a combination of facts, statistics, examples, and informed opinions.

4. **Show that you are trustworthy.** Respect your readers by making a serious argument. If you are condescending, or if you try to joke about the topic, your readers may be less inclined to accept your argument. You can also help your readers have more respect for your ideas when you choose a topic that you know something about. For example, if you have been in the military or know people in the military, you might be able to make a very convincing argument about the lack of proper equipment for soldiers.

Argument at Work

Network administrator Octavio Pelaez uses argument writing in this excerpt from a memo to his director.

We need to invest in a new e-mail server. First, the slow speed and unreliability of the present equipment is becoming a serious inconvenience. While the cost of replacing the server and the accompanying software will be very high, the cost of not doing so is going to be much higher in lost time and productivity. It would not be an exaggeration to say that for the last three months, we have lost more than a thousand billable hours as a result of the poor condition of our equipment. The average hourly rate per user is $30; thus, those lost hours of productivity have cost the company more than $30,000. Also, consider the impact on our company's reputation when the clients have problems communicating with us. We cannot afford to wait any longer to invest in new equipment and technology. In fact, over the long term, replacing the e-mail server will actually increase productivity and profitability.

Teaching Tip:
Ask students to list
the main point and
the supporting
arguments in this
excerpt.

A Student Essay

Read the student essay and answer the questions that follow.

Changing Face of Cosmetic Surgery
by Kate Howell

1   Many people who undergo cosmetic surgery are regarded as vapid, shallow, and lacking in self-esteem. The phrases "Be happy with who you are" and "God made you perfect as is" are thrown around to provide assurance. For instance, a woman who attempts to change her appearance is told that such an act signals a level of dishonesty toward herself, her family, and possibly her creator. The stigma associated with plastic surgery clearly exists—note the negative connotation of the word "plastic." However, such attitudes ignore reality. Anyone who uses cosmetic surgery to enhance his or her appearance should be applauded, not condemned.

2   Cosmetic surgery has become popular on TV, in the office, and all around campus. TV shows such as *Extreme Makeover* have become hits. Prices for all kinds of procedures, from eyelifts to liposuction, have gone down, so more and more people can afford them. The age of plastic surgery recipients has also gone down, with college-aged girls opting for breast implants and nose jobs.

3   It is not just women who are body-obsessed. According to *HealthDay News*, men are the newest arrivals to the cosmetic surgery party. In 2000, there was a 16 percent increase in body-altering procedures performed on males. Competition in the business world is fierce, and men are looking for any advantage they can find. Bags under the eyes and a weak chin just won't cut it when there is an army of young bucks with MBAs gunning for every job. The idea that men are not supposed to care about their personal appearance is outdated and unfortunate. We do not live in a society of cattle ranchers and frontier explorers anymore. The beaten-up faces and callused hands of **yore** are no longer necessary tools of the trade; in today's society, they have been replaced by cheek lifts and palm scrubs, and that is not necessarily a bad thing.

yore:
a long time ago

4   There remains a degree of disapproval of plastic surgery, yet the importance of personal appearance is everywhere. Consumers spend billions of dollars each year on makeup, haircuts, tanning salons, manicures, and pedicures. Studies show that good-looking people tend to get hired for jobs. In the movies, some distinct qualities belong to the majority of the stars: trim bodies, immaculate grooming, and gleaming teeth. Science tells us we are attracted to certain features, and it is ridiculous to deny that fact. Appearance certainly isn't everything, but to downplay its importance is self-righteous hypocrisy.

5   If, as is widely believed, it is what is on the inside that matters, then people should not get in such a huff about altering one's outside. If a person feels unattractive, he or she should not be held back from making a change because friends or family cling to some half-hearted notion of

"playing the cards one has been dealt." If people desire to remake their body as they see fit, then more power to them. In this time of laziness and apathy, at least these people are taking steps to try to improve their lot in life. As humans, we adapt to our society, and ours is now one of aesthetics. To borrow an oft-used phrase from hip-hop: Don't hate the player, hate the game.

PRACTICE 2

1. Highlight the thesis statement.

2. What introduction style does the author use?
   a. an anecdote
   b. a definition
   c. a contrasting position
   d. a description

3. Highlight the topic sentence in paragraphs 2 and 4.

4. The topic sentence in paragraph 3 is implied but is not stated directly. Choose the most effective topic sentence for this paragraph.
   a. Men are obsessed with their bodies.
   b. In 2000, the percentage of males getting cosmetic surgery increased.
   c. Men no longer want to have wrinkled, beaten-up faces and callused hands.
   d. To gain an advantage in the competitive workplace, men are increasingly opting to have cosmetic surgery.

5. What is the author's specific purpose? _To counter the idea that plastic surgery is bad_

6. In your own words, sum up the writer's main point about cosmetic surgery. Answers will vary.

   She points out that cosmetic surgery has become a standard part of our culture. She also conveys the idea that looks are important and that they help people succeed in the workplace.

Teaching Tip:
The Writer's Desk activities, such as the one on the next page, provide students with an opportunity to develop a topic through all stages of the writing process using the argument mode. In the Warm Up, they begin by exploring various controversial topics. Those topics then carry on throughout the chapter.

Explore Topics

In the Writer's Desk Warm Up, you will try an exploring strategy to generate ideas about different topics.

Writer's Desk **Warm Up**

Read the following questions, and write the first ideas that come to your mind. Think of two or three ideas for each topic.

EXAMPLE: Does age matter in a relationship?

I don't know. Love is love, but there could be problems. What if the older person doesn't

want children?

1. Should children be in beauty pageants? Why or why not?

_____

_____

_____

2. Should the custom of tipping for service be abolished? Why or why not?

_____

_____

_____

3. What are some of the major controversial issues in your neighborhood, workplace, college, state, or country? List some issues.

_____

_____

_____

DEVELOPING

The Thesis Statement

In the thesis statement of an argument essay, state your position on the issue.

topic   controlling idea (the writer's position)

Many corporate executives are overpaid for very substandard work.

ESL
Teaching Tip:
Some nonnative
speakers may feel
reluctant to share
their thoughts in a
forceful and direct
manner. In many
cultures, it is
considered rude or
arrogant to question
elders or those in
authority or to
debate.

Teaching Tip:

Cooperative
Learning
(Jigsaw)
Place students in
groups of three.
First, they should
complete Practice 3.
Then ask groups to
brainstorm three
more sentences for
the practice. They
should write a fact,
an opinion, and an
argument. When
they have finished,
ask students to
number themselves
from one to three.
All of the ones get
together as well as
the twos and the
threes. The new
team members can
take turns reading
their new sentences
and asking the
others to guess
which sentence is a
fact, which is an
opinion, and which
is an argument.

A thesis statement should be debatable; it should not simply be a fact or a statement of opinion.

Fact:	Toyota had to recall more than two million cars.
	(This is a fact. It cannot be debated.)
Opinion:	I think that car companies should act immediately when safety issues arise.
	(This is a statement of opinion. Nobody can deny that you feel this way. Therefore, do not use phrases such as *In my opinion, I think*, or *I believe* in your thesis statement.)
Argument:	When safety issues arise, car companies should be obligated to inform the public immediately.
	(This is a debatable statement.)

> ### *Hint* Be Direct
>
> Many students feel reluctant to take a stand on an issue. They may feel that it is too personal or impolite to do so. However, in academic writing, it is perfectly acceptable, and even desirable, to state an argument in a direct manner and then support it.

PRACTICE 3   Evaluate the following statements. Write F for a fact, O for an opinion, or A for an argument.

1. I think that dogs make wonderful companions.   _O_

2. Many Americans spend too much money pampering their pets.   _A_

3. The Doggy Boutique charges $150 for doggie boots.   _F_

4. Oil companies should not be permitted to drill in deep oceans.   _A_

5. I don't think it is safe to drill in deep ocean waters.   _O_

6. Many Internet sites have pop-up advertising.   _F_

7. In my opinion, country music is predictable and repetitive.   _O_

8. Parents should pay when their children commit acts of vandalism. _A_

> ### *Hint* Making a Guided Thesis Statement
>
> Your instructor may want you to guide the reader through your main points. To do this, mention your main and supporting ideas in your thesis statement. In other words, your thesis statement provides a map for the readers to follow.
>
> High school students should receive art education because it promotes their creativity, enhances their cultural knowledge, and develops their analytical skills.

Writer's Desk **Write Thesis Statements**

Write a thesis statement for the next topics. You can look for ideas in the Warm Up on page 233. Make sure that each thesis statement clearly expresses your position on the issue.

EXAMPLE: Topic: age in relationships

Thesis statement: *Age matters in relationships.*

1. Topic: children in beauty pageants

   Thesis statement: _____

   _____

2. Topic: tipping customs

   Thesis statement: _____

   _____

3. Topic: a controversial issue

   Thesis statement: _____

   _____

The Supporting Ideas

To make a logical and reasoned argument, support your main point with facts, examples, and statistics. (For details about adding facts, examples, and statistics, see page 47 in Chapter 4.)

You can also include the following types of support.

- **Quote informed sources.** Sometimes experts in a field express an informed opinion about an issue. An expert's thoughts and ideas can add weight to your argument. For example, if you want to argue that people are becoming complacent about AIDS, you might quote an article published by a respected national health organization.
- **Consider logical consequences.** When you plan an argument, think about long-term consequences of a proposed solution to a problem. For instance, maybe you oppose a decision to drill for oil off the coast of California. A long-term consequence could be an environmental disaster if there is an earthquake near the rig.

Teaching Tip:

Cooperative Learning (Jigsaw)
With the class, generate a thesis statement such as *People should stop wearing certain horrible fashions,* or choose a thesis statement from this chapter's Writer's Desk. Place students in groups. Ask one group to write an introduction for that thesis statement. Ask three groups to write separate body paragraphs. (Ask each person in the group to write the same paragraph.) After about ten minutes, invite one representative from each team to stand up and in correct order read the intro and body paragraphs. As a group, the class can brainstorm a conclusion.

Teaching Tip:
Ask students to think about the opposing viewpoints for the following arguments: *The sale of cigarettes should be banned. Daycares should be closed.*

- **Acknowledge opposing viewpoints.** Anticipating and responding to opposing views can strengthen your position. For instance, if you argue that school uniforms should be mandatory, you might address those who feel that students need freedom to express themselves. Try to refute some of the strongest arguments of the opposition.

Making an Emotional Appeal

Generally, an effective argument appeals to the reader's reason, but it can also appeal to his or her emotion. For example, you could use certain words or descriptions to encourage a reader's sense of justice, humanity, or pride. However, use emotional appeals sparingly. If you use **emotionally charged words** such as *wimp* or *thug*, or if you appeal to base instincts such as fear or cowardice, then you may seriously undermine your argument. Review the next examples of emotional appeals.

Overemotional: Crazy women such as the "Octomom" go to fertility clinics, have multiple births, and then feed off the state like leeches. The innocent premature infants, facing chronic illness and blindness, can end up needing lifelong medical care.

Reasonable and more neutral: Women visiting fertility clinics may underestimate potential problems. If a multiple birth results, the parents can face financial difficulties. Additionally, premature infants can suffer from a variety of long-term medical problems.

> ### *Hint* Avoid Common Errors
>
> When you write your argument essay, avoid the following pitfalls.
>
> **Do not make generalizations.** If you begin a statement with *Everyone knows* or *It is common knowledge*, then the reader may mistrust what you say. You cannot possibly know what everyone else knows or does not know. It is better to refer to specific sources.
>
> **Generalization:**   American children are spoiled brats.
>
> **Better:**   Parents should not overindulge their children for several reasons.
>
> **Do not make exaggerated claims.** Make sure that your arguments are plausible.
>
> **Exaggerated:**   If marijuana is legalized, drug use will soar in schools across the nation.
>
> **Better:**   If marijuana is legalized, drug use may increase in schools across the nation.

PRACTICE 4   You have learned about different methods to support a topic. Read each of the following thesis statements, and think of a supporting idea for each item. Use the type of support suggested in parentheses.
Answers will vary.

Teaching Tip:

Cooperative Learning (Jigsaw)
Before you discuss emotional arguments, generalizations, and exaggerated claims, do the following activity. Place students in teams of up to five students. Give them a controversial sentence such as *Abortion should be legal* or *Guns should be banned*. Ask teams to brainstorm some detailed arguments either for or against the topic. After all teams have a list of arguments, students should number themselves from one to five. All of the ones should form a new team. The twos, threes, and so on, should do the same thing. The new team members should analyze each other's statements and check to see if there are emotional arguments, generalizations, or exaggerated claims.

1. Volunteer work should be mandatory in all high schools.

   (Logical consequence) _____

   _____

2. Online dating is a great way to meet a potential mate.

   (Acknowledge an opposing view) _____

   _____

3. Children should not be spanked.

   (Emotional appeal) _____

   _____

4. The college dropout rate is too high in our state.

   (Logical consequence) _____

   _____

---

vo•cab•u•lar•y BOOST

Some words can influence readers because they have positive or negative connotations, which are implied or associated meanings. The meaning often carries a cultural value judgment with it. For example, *macho* may have negative connotations in one country and positive connotations in another country. For the word *thin*, synonyms like *skinny* or *skeletal* have negative connotations, while *slender* and *svelte* have positive ones.

Using a thesaurus, try to come up with related terms or descriptions that have either positive or negative connotations for the words in bold.   Answers will vary.

Gloria is **large.** *big boned, fat, overweight, plump, curvy, robust, a "real" woman*

Calvin is **not assertive.** *weak, a wimp, girly, shy, sweet, attentive*

Mr. Wayne **expresses his opinion.** *is loud-mouthed, overbearing, strong-willed, forceful, confident*

Franklin is a **liberal.** *left-wing nut, bleeding heart, open-minded, inclusive*

Identify terms you chose that might be too emotionally loaded for an argument essay.

ESL
Teaching Tip:
Pair native and
nonnative students
to do the
Vocabulary Boost.

Tech
Teaching Tip
Give a topic such as
tax cuts or *global
warming,* or choose a
recent controversy.
Ask students to
compare how
different Web sites
discuss the topic.
They can go to the
Fox News Web site
or the *PBS* or
MSNBC Web sites.
Students can analyze
if the writers have
expressed strong
biases by using
emotional
arguments,
generalizations, and
exaggerations.

Teaching Tip:
As an extra activity,
you can give
students a selection
of topics and ask
them to brainstorm
for and *against*
arguments.

Teaching Tip:
To give students
more practice, you
can ask them to
develop supporting
ideas for all three
Writer's Desk
topics, which are
listed in the Warm
Up on page 233.

Consider Both Sides of the Issue

Once you have decided what issue you want to write about, try to think about both sides of the issue. Then you can predict arguments that your opponents might make, and you can plan your answer to the opposition. Here are examples.

Topic: Age matters in relationships

For	Against
• People have different levels of maturity.	• Love is love and age doesn't matter.
• The desire to have children is strong at certain ages.	• People can adapt to each other.
• Such relationships will probably not last when one person gets ill.	• Other factors (finances, culture) may be more important than age.
• Society condemns couples with large age differences.	• People must be free to choose their own partners.

Writer's Desk **Consider Both Sides of the Issue**

Choose one of the topics from the previous Writer's Desk, and write arguments showing both sides of the issue.

Topic: _____

For	Against
_____	_____
_____	_____
_____	_____
_____	_____

 Strengthening an Essay with Research

In some courses, your instructors may ask you to include supporting ideas from informed sources to strengthen your essays. You can find information in a variety of resources, including textbooks, journals, newspapers, magazines, or the Internet. When researching, make sure that your sources are from legitimate organizations. For example, for information about the spread of AIDS, you might find statistics on the World Health Organization Web site. You would not go to someone's personal rant or conspiracy theory site.

For more information about evaluating and documenting sources, refer to Chapter 16, The Research Essay.

The Essay Plan

Before you write your argument essay, outline your ideas in a plan. Include details that can help illustrate each argument. Make sure that every example is valid and relates to the thesis statement. Also think about your organization. Many argument essays use emphatic order and list ideas from the least to the most important.

THESIS STATEMENT: <u>Age matters in a relationship.</u>

    I. Two people with a large age difference may have conflicting values and cultural experiences.
        A. Music, movies, politics, etc. change over time.
        B. People raised in different generations may see gender roles differently.
        C. Such differences can lead to breakups (Rick and Barbara example).
    II. People's goals change as they age.
        A. One person may want to retire when the other doesn't.
        B. The younger partner may want children, but the older partner already has kids.
        C. The younger partner might still want to party when the older partner is more career oriented.
    III. Other people judge such couples.
        A. Young wives are called "trophy wives" and "gold diggers."
        B. Older men are called "sugar daddies."
        C. Older women are called "cougars."
        D. Anna Nicole Smith was laughed at when she married an old man.
    IV. Couples break up when the older one starts getting frail.
        A. People get more fragile and unhealthy as they age.
        B. The younger partner may not want to become a nursemaid.
        C. Barbara and Rick broke up after Rick had a stroke.

Concluding idea: People should look for age-appropriate partners.

Writer's Desk Write an Essay Plan

Choose one of the ideas that you have developed in the previous Writer's Desk, and write a detailed essay plan.

Teaching Tip:
Ask students to keep their essay plans and then attach them to the final draft. You can then determine how the students have developed their ideas.

The First Draft

Now that you have a refined thesis statement, solid supporting details, and a roadmap of your arguments and the order in which you will present them, you are ready to write the first draft. Remember to write complete sentences and to include transitional words or expressions to lead readers from one idea to the next. Here are some transitions that introduce an answer to the opposition or the supporting ideas for an argument.

To answer the opposition	To support your argument
admittedly	certainly
however	consequently
nevertheless	furthermore
of course	in fact
on one hand/on the other hand	obviously
undoubtedly	of course

Writer's Desk **Write the First Draft**

Write the first draft of your argument essay. Include an interesting introduction. Also, add specific details to flesh out each body paragraph.

Teaching Tip:
The activity of revising a student essay should help your students understand the important link between the writing process and the grammar chapters.

REVISING AND EDITING

Revise and Edit an Argument Essay

When you finish writing an argument essay, carefully review your work and revise it to make the supporting examples as clear as possible to your readers. Check that the order of ideas is logical, and remove any irrelevant details. Before you revise and edit your own essay, practice revising and editing a student essay.

A Student Essay

Read the essay, and then answer the questions that follow. As you read, correct any errors that you find and make comments in the margins.

Age Matters

by Chloe Vallieres

1   In 2003, *The American Association of Retired Persons* (AARP) published a study revealing that 34 percent of women over forty were dating younger men. Having a younger spouse is becoming more and more popular.

However, statistics also demonstrate that couples separate more often when the age gap between the two lovers exceeds ten years. Important age gaps in relationships can lead to considerable conflicts; therefore, age matters in a relationship.

2   Two people with a large age difference may have conflicting values and cultural experiences. Your views about religion and gender roles may differ. Also, politics, music, and movies change with time, so it may be hard to find topics to talk about if partners grew up in different eras. They might not have none of the same tastes. Imagine that a forty-year-old woman is dating a sixty-year-old man. The woman loves hip hop. She was raised to believe that her job is as important as her spouse's job and that childrearing should be shared. Her older partner might hate her musical tastes, and he could assume that his wife should be the primary caretaker of their children. Our family friends Rick and Barbara had this experience. Barbara, who is much younger than Rick, often complained about his chauvinism. He hated her clothing styles and music. Their fifteen-year relationship ended last year.

3   Partners with an age gap are likely to have different goals. When Rick turned sixty-two, he retired, but Barbara still had professional ambitions. He wanted to travel every winter, she hoped to build her career. Damon and Sherrie, another May–December couple, disagree about having children. Damon, who is in his fifties, already has three adult children, but Sherrie, who is just thirty-five, wants to have a baby. Even younger couples can have problems. A twenty-five-year-old woman who has finished university might want to settle down and focus on her career, but her younger partner might still want to party.

4   Couples with age differences have to face other people's bad opinions. "Cougar" and "dirty old man" are common negative terms. There are other unflattering stereotypes: The girl dates the older man (her "sugar daddy") to get her hands on his money, and the mature man marries his young girlfriend (his "trophy wife") to have sexual favors and to appear virile. For example, Anna Nicole Smith. She was publicly ridiculed when she married a man in his nineties. Her legal fight to inherit his wealth contributed to the perception that younger women marry older men for their money.

5   Finally, some couples break up when the older partner develops health problems. Bone injuries or a weak heart. For example, Rick has high blood pressure, and, three years ago, he suffered a minor stroke. Barbara recently left the marriage, confiding to my mother that she did not want to spend the next years being a nursemaid for an old man.

6   Those who proclaim that love can overcome everything are naïve airheads. Age matters and people should look for age-appropriate partners. When spouses have huge age differences, the relationship is

Teaching Tip:
You can ask students to write an opposing argument for this essay or for any other essay in this chapter.

Teaching Tip:

Cooperative Learning (Pair & Share)
First, ask students to read the essay silently. As they read, they should circle any mistakes that they find. Then place students in pairs. They can share what they have found and answer the revising and editing questions together. As an extra activity, you can ask students to think of extra examples for the body paragraphs.

doomed. Dave, a popular blogger on the Intro2u Web site, writes, "It's elements like maturity and life experience, which tend to correlate with age, that can make or break a relationship's long-term potential."

PRACTICE 5

Revising

1. Highlight the thesis statement.

2. Highlight the topic sentences in paragraphs 2, 3, 4, and 5.

3. In the margins next to the essay, add transitional words or expressions to each topic sentence in paragraphs 2 to 4.   Answers will vary.

4. In the concluding paragraph, the writer uses emotionally charged words and exaggerates. Give examples of these two problems.

    Emotionally charged language: *. . . are naïve airheads*

    Exaggeration: *When spouses have huge age differences, the relationship*

    is doomed.

Teaching Tip:
Point out that this type of essay would normally include a Works Cited page. You can ask students to identify sources that should be properly cited.

Editing

5. Paragraph 2 contains a pronoun-antecedent error. (See the explanation in the Grammar Hint on the next page.) Circle the incorrect pronoun and write your correction here.   Answers will vary.

    Their views about religion and gender roles may differ.

6. Paragraph 2 contains a double negative. Underline it and correct it here.
    Answers will vary.

    They might have none . . . / They might not have any . . .

GRAMMAR LINK

See the following chapters for more information about these topics:
Fragments,
    Chapter 23
Run-Ons,
    Chapter 24
Double Negatives,
    Chapter 29
Pronouns,
    Chapter 31

7. Paragraph 3 contains a run-on sentence. Two complete ideas are incorrectly joined. Underline the run-on sentence and correct it on the lines provided.   Answers will vary.

    He wanted to travel every winter, but she hoped to build her career.

8. Identify fragments in paragraphs 4 and 5 and correct them here.

    Paragraph 4: *For example, Anna Nicole Smith was publicly . . .*

    Paragraph 5: *. . . health problems such as bone injuries or a weak heart.*

Grammar Hint   **Keeping Pronouns Consistent**

In argument writing, make sure that your pronouns do not switch between *they*, *we*, and *you*. If you are writing about specific groups of people, use *they* to refer to those people. Change pronouns only when the switch is logical.

Many hunters argue that they need large collections and varieties of guns. Yet

they

why would ~~you~~ need a semi-automatic to go hunting?

See Chapter 31 for more information about pronoun usage.

Writer's Desk **Revise and Edit Your Essay**

Revise and edit the essay that you wrote for the previous Writer's Desk. You can refer to the revising and editing checklists at the end of this chapter and on this book's inside covers.

A Professional Essay

Melonyce McAfee is an editorial assistant at *Slate* magazine. She has written for a variety of publications including the *San Diego Union-Tribune*. In this essay, she argues for the abolition of Administrative Professionals Day. Read the essay and answer the questions that follow.

Keep Your Roses
by Melonyce McAfee

1   Here's a plot line for the writers at NBC's *The Office*: It's April 26. Paper salesman Jim presents a bouquet of tulips to his office crush, Pam, the receptionist. The accompanying card reads, "For all you do. Happy Secretaries Day." Competitive and cringe-inducing boss Michael, until now oblivious to the holiday, sees the card and orders a garish bouquet, large enough to blot out Pam's head and overshadow Jim's arrangement. The bouquet arrives at 4:49 p.m. Eyes roll. Administrative Professionals Day is the Hallmark holiday that leads to interoffice jealousy, discomfort, and not much else.

NSA:
National
Secretaries
Association

2   The National Secretaries Association got the ball rolling with Professional Secretaries Week in 1952. The holiday was renamed Administrative Professionals Week in 2000, but I prefer the tell-it-like-it-is Secretaries Day. The **NSA** (now, naturally, the International Association of Administrative Professionals) claims the day is meant to enhance the image of administrative workers, promote career development, and encourage people to enter the field. But does it really do any of the above?

3   In my first job out of college, I worked as a typist at a title company, a job akin to cryptography. I pecked my way toward carpal tunnel syndrome to turn chicken scratch into property reports. Typists served the entire office, but title officers also had personal secretaries. On Secretaries Day, we typists sucked our teeth at the bouquets on the secretaries' desks. At my next corporate job, I had gained an "assistant" title. But along with the other assistants, I was still left empty-handed. The office professionals chipped in for a bouquet for the division secretary, who regularly pawned off duties on us assistants and huffed when asked to, well, work. "I can't believe they got *her* flowers," we hissed.

4   My mother, a former hospital administrative assistant, was surprised with three greeting cards and a gorgeous scarf last Secretaries Day. She wasn't aware of the holiday and was touched that the nurses in her department took the opportunity to thank her for working hard on special projects. But she also had to listen to a chorus of "*I* didn't get anything" from other administrators. She says that didn't diminish her pleasure, but it does prove my point. When the holiday makes someone feel appreciated, it almost invariably leaves others out in the cold.

5   <u>Maybe part of the problem is that in the fifty years since the holiday began, the duties of a secretary have been farmed out across the office, and the job definition is no longer clear.</u> A secretary used to be the woman who answered phones, took dictation, typed, picked up dry cleaning, and stole the boss's husband, if she was really good. Now she (or he) might give PowerPoint presentations or build a Web site. Meanwhile, someone else might do the typing and filing.

6   The confusion over who qualifies as a secretary creates social anxiety about either overcelebrating the holiday or undercelebrating it. One Secretaries Day, a former advertising-sales assistant and co-worker of mine got lovely plants from colleagues who rushed to point out that they'd gotten her a gift even though she wasn't really a secretary. She got the impression they thought she might be offended by being lumped in with the administrative staff. The holiday forces workers, like it or not, to evaluate how they stack up. Mail-room guy, copy clerk, typist, receptionist, administrative secretary, executive assistant—are they low enough on the totem pole to merit a gift? Or are they too low?

7   Perhaps my impatience with Secretaries Day springs from job dissatisfaction, as an executive assistant at a New York-based magazine suggested when we mused about why the holiday creates bitterness. True—in my mind, I should be the boss. And I resent being reminded of my slow progress up the chain of command every April 26. Those of us who yearn to be professionals, not administrative professionals, tend to bristle at the idea that we're just boosters for the big boys and girls.

8   Some bosses feel compelled to take their secretary, assistant, or whoever out to lunch on Secretaries Day. It's a nice gesture, but who wants to sit through that awkward meal? Anyone who has seen the *Curb Your Enthusiasm* episode in which Larry David takes his maid on a squirm-worthy lunch date at his country club knows the potential disaster of forced boss–employee **conviviality.** Instead of Secretaries Day, why not just chip in for a big cake on the Friday before Labor Day and toast everyone in the office. Wouldn't that be kinder, not to mention easier? I'd much prefer that to a holiday that's a catch-all for "attagirl," "I'm sorry for being an insufferable employer," and "we should talk about that raise."

conviviality:
friendliness

PRACTICE 6

1. Highlight the thesis statement.

2. What technique does the writer use to introduce the topic?
    a. historical background   (b.) anecdote   c. a definition

3. What synonyms does McAfee use for "secretary" in this essay?

    Possible answers: executive assistant, administrative assistant,

    administrative professional, typist

4. In which paragraphs does the writer acknowledge an opposing viewpoint?   *2, 4*

5. Which sentence best sums up the writer's implied argument in paragraph 3?
    a. Typists and assistants are secretaries.
    b. The writer worked as a typist in a small company for many years, and then she became an executive.
    c. Typists do a lot of hard work but are not appreciated.
    (d.) Many people in offices, such as typists and assistants, feel resentful when they are not rewarded on Secretaries Day.

6. Underline the topic sentence in paragraph 5.

7. Which sentence best sums up the writer's implied argument in paragraph 7?

   a. Administrative assistants really do the work of the bosses.

   b. Honestly, most administrative assistants dislike their jobs.

   c. Secretaries Day reminds administrative assistants that they have not advanced on the career ladder.

   d. Most administrative assistants want to be professionals.

8. Using your own words, sum up McAfee's main supporting arguments.

   Secretaries Day is not fair to other employees.

   In many workplaces, it is difficult to know who the secretary is.

   It reminds the secretary of his or her lowly status.

Teaching Tip:

Cooperative Learning (Ask & Learn) Ask students to review the chapter and identify anything that they are not completely clear about. All students should write two questions on a paper. Then in teams, students can ask other members their questions and share answers.

The Writer's Room

Writing Activity 1: Topics

Choose any of the following topics, or choose your own topic, and write an argument essay. Remember to narrow your topic and to follow the writing process.

General Topics

1. value of graffiti
2. dependence on computers
3. tax rates for the wealthy
4. value of home schooling
5. legalization of same-sex marriage

College and Work-Related Topics

6. usefulness of college programs
7. working while going to college
8. stereotypes at work
9. cheating in college
10. an under-appreciated profession

READING LINK

Argument
"Medicating Ourselves" by Robyn Sarah (page 560)
"Brands R Us" by Stephen Garey (page 564)

Writing Activity 2: Photo Writing

Examine the photo and think about arguments that you might make, such as controversies related to sex selection, sperm donors, international adoptions, foster care, and celebrity adoptions. For instance, you could argue that the children of sperm donors should or should not receive information about their biological fathers. Then write an argument essay.

Writing Activity 3: Media Writing

Watch a television show or movie that deals with war. You can watch television shows such as *V* or movies such as *The Hurt Locker*, *Saving Private Ryan*, *Avatar*, *Brothers*, or *Green Zone*. Find a controversial issue online or in a program or movie, and write an argument essay.

Teaching Tip:
Suggest that students read one of the essays in the Reading Link. They can analyze the writer's arguments.

WRITING LINK

See the next grammar sections for more argument writing topics.

Chapter 24, Writer's Room topic 2 (page 358)

Chapter 26, Writer's Room topic 1 (page 374)

Chapter 31, Writer's Room topic 2 (page 440)

Chapter 32, Writer's Room topic 2 (page 452)

Chapter 34, Writer's Room topic 2 (page 477)

Chapter 35, Writer's Room topic 2 (page 489)

✔ CHECKLIST: ARGUMENT ESSAY

After you write your argument essay, review the checklist on the inside front cover. Also, ask yourself the following set of questions.

☐ Does my thesis statement clearly state my position on the issue?

☐ Do I make strong supporting arguments?

☐ Do I include facts, examples, statistics, and logical consequences?

☐ Do my supporting arguments provide evidence that directly supports the thesis statement?

☐ Do I acknowledge and counter opposing arguments?

☐ Do I use valid arguments? (Do I avoid making broad generalizations? Do I restrain any emotional appeals?)

☐ Do I use a courteous tone?

Teaching Tip:
Writer's World Competition
Please advise students that they can submit their essays for possible publication to www .pearsonhighered .com/essayrewards/ writingrewards.html

mywritinglab To check your progress in meeting this chapter's objectives, log in to **www.mywritinglab.com,** go to the **Study Plan** tab, click on **Essay Patterns** and choose **Argument** from the list of subtopics. Read and view the resources in the **Review Materials** section, and then complete the **Recall, Apply,** and **Write** sets in the **Activities** section.

More College and Workplace Writing

In the next chapters, you will learn about college and workplace writing. Chapters 15 and 16 guide you through the process of synthesizing material and researching.

When you apply for a job, the ability to present yourself in a professional manner is important; thus, Chapter 17 gives you some important workplace writing strategies.

Chapter 18 focuses on responses to film and literature. Finally, Chapter 19 provides valuable information about writing essay exams.

Source: *Understanding Music* by Jeremy Yudkin, Fifth Edition, 2008, Prentice Hall, Upper Saddle River, New Jersey

Page 411. "Jazz singers also deliberately make use of unusual sounds. A special kind of singing in which the vocalist improvises with nonsense syllables . . . is known as 'scat' singing."

423: bebop uses "nonsense syllables used in scat singing." Different from swing—not as predictable.

MLA Style

Single-space your identification information.

Leonard J. Bukowski
Professor Donald E. Crawford, PhD.
AMH 2020
May 31, 2006

Bukowski 1

Double-space throughout the body of the essay.

The Free Jazz Movement and Black Nationalism

Jazz has been termed a truly unique American music. It shares much of the emotions and strengths of America and has affected and been affected by social and political changes and turmoil.

In the 1960's American society and politics would be confronted by a determined desire among African Americans for their rights and political power, sometimes sought to be obtained violently. Jazz would be confronted by an abandoning of traditional musical forms, such as melody, harmony, and rhythm, as musicians found a method of producing sounds relevant in their minds to the discord of the times.

In many respects, the music called jazz is a representation of the atmosphere of American life. A music that was the result of the mixture of races in the North American continent, it borrowed freely from the Western musical tradition of melody and harmony while transporting rhythms from Africa and elsewhere. As jazz evolved, it became a unique method of expression.

CHAPTER 17   The Résumé and Letter of Application   303

A Sample Résumé

Include contact information but NOT your birth-place, birth-date, nationality, or a personal photo.

Francesca Benaroya
33 Winsted Road
Atlanta, GA 30322
(987) 654-3210
email: fbenaroya@gmail.com

Specify what job you are applying for or state the general field that interests you.

Objective	Entry-level position as a costume designer
Education	Diploma in Theater Studies, June 2008
	Emory College, Atlanta, Georgia
	Certificate of Completion, Fine Arts Institute
	Cincinnati, Ohio, May 2005

Put the most recent schooling first. If you have more than a high school education, it is not necessary to list your high school.

Outline your most recent job experience. If you have not had any paying jobs, you could mention any volunteer work that you have done.

For each job that you list, mention the tasks that you completed and the aptitudes you developed.

Employment	**2006–Present**
	Camp Discovery, Atlanta
	• Organize a variety of summer sports activities for ten-year-olds.
	• Negotiate disagreements and lead children with gentle authority.
	• Act as a big sister to several children with special needs.
	2004–2006
	Hancock Fabrics, Bell's Shopping Center
	• Cut and sorted fabric.
	• Greeted customers.
	• Learned about fabric suppliers.
	• Developed the ability to discern fabric quality, which has been useful in my costume design courses.

Mention any special abilities that you have. Do you have artistic talent? Are you bilingual or trilingual? Do you have computer skills?

Skills	Fluent in English, Italian, and Spanish
	Familiar with Photoshop and Microsoft Office
	Winner of first-place prize for oil painting in the Garden Artists' Society

| References | Available on request |

If past teachers or past employers have agreed to recommend you, you can include their names and phone numbers. Otherwise, you can write "Available on request."

Sample Letter of Application
Review the parts of the next letter.

Sender's Address

Francesca Benaroya
33 Winsted Road
Atlanta, GA 30322
(404) 654-3210
email: fbenaroya@gmail.com

Date
Put a comma between the full date and the year.

April 5, 2008

Recipient's address
Capitalize each word in a company name.

Raymond Montafur
Aurora Theater Company
70 South Clayton Street
Lawrenceville, GA 30045

Salutation
The best way to address someone is to use his or her name followed by a colon.
If you do not know the name of the recipient, write the following:
• Dear Sir or Madam
• Attention: Personnel Department

Subject: Position of Costume Designer

Dear Mr. Montafur:

In response to your advertisement in the *Weekly Shout* newspaper, I am applying for the position of junior costumer designer at your theater. I have enjoyed your productions for many years and believe that I can be a valuable addition to your design team.

Body
Sell yourself. Summarize your skills and experience.

For three years, I studied set and costume design at Emory College. Having finished my program last spring, I am anxious to begin working in this field. I was principal costume designer for our school's production of *Sweet Charity* and also worked extensively on costumes for *Gypsy* and *Cabaret*.

Please see the enclosed résumé with further details about my experience and some sketches and photos of costumes that illustrate my creativity. I am hard-working and energetic. Moreover, I am excited about beginning my career in the theater!

Closing
Some possible closings are Yours truly, Respectfully yours, or Many thanks. Notice that only the first word is capitalized. After the closing, add your handwritten signature followed by your typed name.

I would appreciate the opportunity to speak with you in detail about my qualifications. I am available for an interview at your convenience and could start work immediately. Thank you for your consideration.

Sincerely yours,

F. Benaroya

Francesca Benaroya

Answer both parts A and B. You will have two hours to complete th

Part A   Define two of the following terms. (5 points each)
1. democracy
2. electorate
3. communism
4. industrial revolution
5. gerrymandering

Part B   Write a well-structured essay on one of the following top (20 points)

1. Explain what is panic versus mass hysteria. Can governments ev from either of these phenomena?
2. Evaluate the usefulness of sanctions that western nations impose nations such as North Korea.
3. Trace the rise of National Socialism in Germany in the 1930s.

Paraphrasing and Summarizing

LEARNING OBJECTIVES

When a stylist cuts hair, the excess is trimmed away, and the essential style is revealed. In the same way, when you paraphrase or summarize, you write about key points and discard the details.

Writer's Exchange

Work with a partner. In a couple of minutes, describe the contents of an article or essay that you have read for this course. What were the key points?

GRAMMAR LINK

To find out more about using quotations, see Chapter 37.

Integrating Borrowed Information

During your college career, your instructor may ask you to support your essay ideas using quotations, paraphrases, or summaries. These useful strategies strengthen your research paper and make it more forceful and convincing.

A **quotation** permits you to use another person's exact language. A **paraphrase** lets you use your own words to present someone else's essential information or ideas. Finally, a **summary** allows you to use borrowed information because you present only the main points of one or several works in your own words. A summary is a shortened version of the original work.

All of these strategies are valid ways to incorporate research into your writing, as long as you give credit to the author or speaker.

Avoiding Plagiarism

Plagiarism is the act of using someone else's **words** or **ideas** without giving that person credit. Whether it is intentional or not, plagiarism is a very serious offense and can result in expulsion from a course or termination from work. Always acknowledge the source when you borrow material. The following actions are examples of plagiarism.

- Copying and pasting text from an Internet source without using quotation marks to properly set off the author's words
- Using ideas from another source without citing that source
- Making slight modifications to an author's sentences, but presenting the work as your own
- Buying another's work and presenting it as your own
- Using another student's work and presenting it as your own

The Internet has made it easier to plagiarize, but it is also easy for instructors to catch cheaters. To avoid plagiarism, always cite the source when you borrow words or ideas.

PRACTICE I   Read the original selection. Then determine if the paraphrase or summary is an example of plagiarism.

Original Selection

At a time when we Americans may abandon health care reform because it supposedly is "too expensive," how is it that we can afford to imprison people like Curtis Wilkerson? Mr. Wilkerson is serving a life sentence in California—for stealing a $2.50 pair of socks. As *The Economist* noted recently, he already had two offenses on his record (both for **abetting** robbery at age nineteen), and so the "three strikes" law resulted in a life sentence. This is unjust, of course. But considering

ESL

Teaching Tip:
In some cultures, borrowing ideas without citing sources is not considered to be plagiarism. For example, in many Asian cultures, referring to the ideas of an expert is often seen as a show of respect for someone who knows more about a subject than the student does. Emphasize to your students that they cannot borrow ideas without citing the sources.

abetting:
helping or encouraging

that California spends almost $49,000 annually per prison inmate, it's also an extraordinary waste of money.

—Kristof, Nicholas D. "Priority Test: Health Care or Prisons?"
New York Times. The New York Times Company, 19 Aug. 2009. Web.

Teaching Tip:
Pair Work
Ask students to complete Practice 1 with a partner. They can exchange ideas and discuss plagiarism.

1. **Paraphrase**

   In *The New York Times*, Kristoff writes that <u>Americans may abandon health care reform</u> because of the high costs, yet they will pay to keep nonviolent offenders in jail. Kristoff provides the example of Curtis Wilkerson, who <u>is serving a life sentence in California for stealing a pair of socks</u>. Taxpayers will spend $49,000 per year to keep him in jail, which is <u>an extraordinary waste of money</u>.

   Is this plagiarism?　　　Yes __X__

   　　　　　　　　　　　　No _____

   Why? *Exact phrases were used that were not put in quotation marks.*

2. **Paraphrase**

   According to Nicholas D. Kristof, California wastes money putting relatively harmless people in jail. He cites the example of Curtis Wilkerson, who stole some inexpensive socks. Wilkerson had two previous nonviolent robbery convictions; thus, his third conviction has put him in prison for life. Keeping him in prison will cost California taxpayers close to $50,000 a year.

   Is this plagiarism?　　　Yes _____

   　　　　　　　　　　　　No __X__

   Why? *It does not include any exact wording from the original text.*

3. **Summary**

   It is ridiculous for our nation to spend more on prison than on health care, especially when many people in prison are not dangerous. For instance, a California court has sentenced a sock thief to life in prison, and it will cost taxpayers $49,000 a year to keep him there.

   Is this plagiarism?　　　Yes __X__

   　　　　　　　　　　　　No _____

   Why? *The source is not mentioned.*

Paraphrasing

When you paraphrase or summarize, you restate someone's ideas using your own words. The main difference between a paraphrase and a summary is the length. While a paraphrase can be the same length as the original selection, a summary is much shorter.

Teaching Tip:
Ask students to read the example paragraphs aloud, line by line, alternating between the original selection and the paraphrase. They should notice how the language and sentence structure differ in the paraphrase.
   Point out that the paraphrase incorporates specialized terms such as *nicotine.* Synonyms are used for common words such as *women, teenagers, toxic,* and *nausea.* Also, the paraphrase contains different sentence structure and wording from the original selection.

How to Paraphrase

To paraphrase, do the following:

- Highlight the main ideas in the original text.
- Restate the main ideas using your own words. You can keep specialized words, common words, and names of people or places. However, find synonyms for other words, and use your own sentence structure.
- Use a dictionary or thesaurus, if necessary, to find synonyms.
- Maintain the original author's ideas and intent.
- Do not include your own opinions.
- After you finish writing, proofread your text.
- Acknowledge the author and title of the original text.

Remember that a paraphrase is roughly the same length as the original selection.

Original Selection

Although fewer Americans are smoking (down to about 25 percent from over 40 percent in the sixties), women and teenagers are actually smoking more than before. This is alarming news when one considers the toxic nature of nicotine: In the 1920s and 1930s, it was used as an insecticide and is considered to be highly toxic and fast acting.

—Ciccarelli, Saundra K. *Psychology*. Pearson: Upper Saddle River, 2009. Print.

Paraphrase

In *Psychology*, Ciccarelli states that the smoking rate has declined in the past fifty years. Nonetheless, nicotine addiction is up in females and adolescents. Exposing themselves to the highly dangerous chemicals, those groups are taking significant risks with their health. Ciccarelli points out the poisonous nature of nicotine, saying that, ninety years ago, farmers used it to kill insects.

PRACTICE 2   Paraphrase the next selections. Remember to cite the source and to use your own words.

1. The United States incarcerates people at nearly five times the world average. Of those sentenced to state prisons, 82 percent were convicted of nonviolent crimes, according to one study.

   —Kristoff, Nicolas D. "Priority Test: Health Care or Prisons."
   New York Times. The New York Times Company, 19 Aug. 2009. Web.

_____

_____

_____

_____

2. The Act Happy theory is that you get happier simply by going through the motions of contentment and joy. If you smile, laugh, hug, cheer or give someone a high five, you get the benefits of those feelings right back at you.

> —Neremberg, Albert. "Don't Worry, Act Happy."
> *Gazette*. Postmedia Publishing, 4 Oct. 2008. Web.

_____

_____

_____

_____

Summarizing

In most fields, you will be asked to summarize. For instance, your superiors may ask you to compress detailed information into its basic components so that managers can identify what action to take. In written summaries, readers should be able to understand the essential message. The complete document would contain details and examples, but readers would not require the original to make sense of the central ideas.

When you summarize, you condense a message to its basic elements. Do the following:

- Read the original text carefully because you will need a complete picture before you begin to write.
- Ask yourself *who, what, when, where, why*, and *how* questions to help you identify the central ideas of the text, and then write your summary.
- Reread your summary. Ensure that you have expressed the essential message in your own words.
- Keep your summary to a maximum of 30 percent of the original length.
- Cite the original source.

Here is a summary of the selection used in the example on page 252:

> In her book *Psychology*, Saundra Ciccarelli states that the smoking rate has decreased except among females and adolescents. The trend is worrisome because nicotine is so toxic.

PRACTICE 3 Summarize the next selections. Your summary should be much shorter than the original selection. Remember to cite the source and to use your own words.

1. Developing a friendship with a co-worker who has a work ethic and who can "keep it zipped" is a must-have. No matter how great your significant

Tech

Teaching Tip:
Ask students to go to a newspaper Web site and to find an article about a controversial topic. They can look on newspaper sites such as *nytimes.com*. Then, in pairs, students can summarize the article.

Teaching Tip:

Cooperative Learning (Jigsaw)
Place students in teams of four or five. Then assign a skills chapter to each team. (Choose chapters that you have already taught.) The team must identify the key concepts in the chapter and summarize it in one or two paragraphs. When students have finished, assign a number to each team member. Then the ones can get together, the twos, threes, and so on. The new teams can share what they have learned. Others can decide if the chapter's key ideas have been adequately summed up.

Teaching Tip:
To help students
write succinct
summaries about
longer works, ask
them to reduce
their summaries
from a page to a
paragraph and,
finally, to a sentence.

other, friends, and neighbors are at solving problems or listening to your
work concerns, they are not your best option. Why? Because they don't
work where you do. Only a co-worker can completely understand the
personalities and culture of your workplace.

—Goddard, Stephanie. "Top Ten Ways to Beat Stress at Work."
Work-Stress-Solutions.com. N.p., n.d. Web. 14 May 2010.

Summary

_____

_____

_____

_____

2. And credit-card companies have changed their lending policies in ways that
make credit more accessible—but also more complicated. . . . Instead of
charging everyone the same, companies adjust the interest rates according
to customers' credit scores. They also charge special fees for late payments,
purchases that exceed a credit limit, foreign-currency transactions, phone
payments, and so forth. This structure makes it profitable to extend credit
to high-risk borrowers, including those with low incomes.

—Postrel, Virginia. "The Case for Debt." *Atlantic* Nov. 2008: 44–47. Print.

Summary

_____

_____

_____

_____

Hint   Consider Your Audience

When you decide whether to paraphrase or summarize, think about your audience.

• Paraphrase if your audience needs detailed information about the subject.

• Summarize if the audience needs to know only general information.

PRACTICE 4   The following essay is from pages 192–193 of
Cultural Anthropology by Carol R. Ember and Melvin Ember. Read the essay
and then write a summary. To make summarizing a longer text a little easier,
follow these steps: Answers will vary.

- Read the complete article.
- Underline the main ideas in the text.
- Write the summary by answering *who*, *what*, *when*, *where*, *why*, and *how* questions.
- Write a first draft of the summary.
- Remove any unnecessary details.
- Ensure that you have not used the exact words or phrases from the original text.
- Reduce your writing to only a paragraph by revising and condensing your draft.
- Reread your summary to verify that you have stated the essential ideas of the text.

Why Street Gangs Develop

1   The street gangs of young people that we read and hear about so often are voluntary associations. They are a little like age-sets in that the members are all about the same age, but they are unlike age-sets in being voluntary, and they do not "graduate" through life stages together. Nobody has to join, although there may be strong social pressure to join the neighborhood gang. Gangs have a clear set of values, goals, roles, group functions, symbols, and initiations. Street gangs are also often like military associations in their commitment to violence in the defense of gang interests.

2   Violent street gangs are found in many U.S. cities, particularly in poor neighborhoods. But poverty alone does not appear sufficient to explain the existence of gangs. For example, there is plenty of poverty in Mexico, but gangs did not develop there. In Mexico there was a *palomilla* (age-cohort) tradition; age-mates hung out together and continued their friendship well into adulthood, but there were no gangs as we know them. Mexican American gangs did develop in the barrios of cities such as Los Angeles. When we realize that most youths in poor neighborhoods do not join gangs, it is clear that poor neighborhoods cannot explain gangs. It is estimated that only 3 to 10 percent of Mexican American young people join gangs.

3   But why do some young people join and not others? If we look at who joins a gang, we see that it seems to be those children who are subject to the most domestic stress. The gang "joiners" are likely to come from poor families, have several siblings, and have no father in the household. They seem to have had difficulty in school and have gotten into trouble early.

4   What about gangs appeals to them? Most adolescents in this country have a difficult time deciding who they are and what kind of people they want to be, but young people who join gangs seem to have more identity problems. One eighteen-year-old said he "joined the gang for my ego to go higher," reflecting a low self-esteem. Those who are raised in female-centered households seem to be looking for ways to show how "masculine" they are. They look up to the tough male street gang members and want to act like them.

Teaching Tip:
As an extra writing assignment, you can ask students to write a cause and effect essay explaining why youths join gangs. Their views may differ significantly from the textbook excerpt.

5   So, belonging to a gang may make some youths feel as if they belong to something important. This is a kind of psychological adjustment, but is it adaptive? Does being in a gang help such youth survive in a neighborhood where young men are often killed? Or are gang members less likely to survive? We really don't know the answers to those questions.

The Writer's Room

Writing Activity

Choose one of the following topics and write a summary.

1. Paraphrase a paragraph from a newspaper or magazine article.
2. Summarize the essay "Do You Have What It Takes to Be Happy?" from Chapter 9 (page 145).
3. Summarize Chapter 19, The Essay Exam.
4. Summarize the plot of a television program or movie.
5. Summarize a text that you have read for another course.

✓ CHECKLIST: PARAPHRASING AND SUMMARIZING

When you paraphrase or summarize, ask yourself these questions.

☐ In a paraphrase, have I kept the original intent of the author?

☐ In a summary, have I kept only the key ideas?

☐ Have I used my own words when paraphrasing or summarizing?

☐ Have I mentioned the source when paraphrasing or summarizing?

Teaching Tip:

Cooperative Learning (Ask & Learn)
Ask students to review the chapter and identify anything that they are not completely clear about. All students should write down three questions. Then in teams, students can ask other members their questions and share answers.

Teaching Tip:
Writer's World Competition
Please advise students that they can submit their essays for possible publication to www .pearsonhighered .com/essayrewards/ writingrewards.html

mywritinglab To check your progress in meeting this chapter's objectives, log in to **www.mywritinglab.com,** go to the **Study Plan** tab, click on **More College and Workplace Writing** and choose **Paraphrasing and Summarizing** from the list of subtopics. Read and view the resources in the **Review Materials** section, and then complete the **Recall, Apply,** and **Write** sets in the **Activities** section.

The Research Essay

CHAPTER 16

LEARNING OBJECTIVES

1. Planning a Research Essay (p. 258)
2. Gathering Information (p. 258)
3. Evaluating Sources (p. 262)
4. Taking Notes (p. 265)
5. Organizing Your First Draft (p. 269)
6. Incorporating Visuals (p. 270)
7. Citing Sources (p. 271)
8. Using MLA Style (p. 271)
9. Sample Research Essay (p. 278)

When cooking, you combine small amounts of specific ingredients to create an appetizing meal. When writing a research-supported essay, you cite other people's ideas and combine them with your own to make a more convincing paper.

Writer's Exchange

Work with a partner. Match the word in Column A with a word that has a similar meaning to a word in Column B. Then discuss the different meanings of each pair of words.

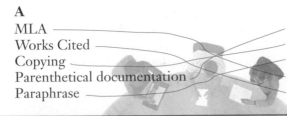

A	B
MLA	Footnote
Works Cited	Plagiarism
Copying	Indirect quotation
Parenthetical documentation	APA
Paraphrase	Bibliography

Teaching Tip:
Ask students to pair
the items in the
Writer's Exchange.
You might explain
the difference
between some
terms. For instance,
a bibliography lists
all works that were
consulted, and a
Works Cited page
lists only the
summarized or
quoted sources.
APA refers to
the American
Psychological
Association whereas
MLA refers to the
Modern Language
Association. You can
then ask students to
cross out terms that
you will not be
using in class.

Planning a Research Essay

Conducting **research** means looking for information that will help you better understand a subject. Knowing how to locate, evaluate, and use information from other sources is valuable in your work and day-to-day activities. It is also crucial in college writing because, in many of your assignments, you are expected to include information from outside sources. In this chapter, you will learn some strategies for writing a research paper.

Determining Your Topic

In some courses, your instructor will ask you to write a research paper about a specific topic. However, if you are not assigned one, then you will need to think about issues related to your field of study or to your personal interests.

The scope of your topic should match the size of the assignment. Longer essays may have a broader topic, but a short research essay (of three or four pages) must have a rather narrow focus. If you have a very specific focus, you will be able to delve more thoroughly into the topic. To help find and develop a topic, you can try exploring strategies such as freewriting, questioning, or brainstorming. (See Chapter 1 for more information about prewriting strategies.)

Finding a Guiding Research Question

The point of a research essay is not simply to collect information and summarize it; the idea is to gather information that relates directly to your guiding research question. To help you determine your central question, brainstorm a list of questions that you would like your research to answer. For example, Karine Maheu wants to write about energy drinks, so she asks herself some questions to narrow her topic.

Teaching Tip:
Please note that
updated APA
guidelines now
appear in Appendix
5, on pages
606–610.

How are energy drinks marketed?

What are the health effects of energy drinks?

How popular are energy drinks?

Who are the main consumers of energy drinks?

Karine's next step is to find a guiding research question that can become the focus of her essay.

What are the health effects of energy drinks?

Gathering Information

Once you know what information you seek, you can begin gathering ideas, facts, quotations, anecdotes, and examples about the research topic you have chosen. Before you begin to gather information, consider how to find it and how to sort the valid information from the questionable information.

Writer's Desk **Find a Research Topic**

Choose a general topic that you might like to write about.

Topic: _____

Now ask five or six questions to help you narrow the topic.

_____

_____

_____

_____

_____

Decide which question will become your guiding research question, and write it here.

_____

_____

_____

Consulting Library-Based Sources

Today's technological advances in both print and electronic publishing make it easier than ever to access information. For sources, you can consult encyclopedias, online catalogues in libraries, periodicals, and the Internet. Here are some tips for finding information about your topic through library resources.

- **Ask a reference librarian** to help you locate information using various research tools, such as online catalogues, CD-ROMs, and microfiches. Before meeting with the librarian, write down some questions that you would like the answers to. Possible questions might be *Can I access the library's online databases from my home computer?* and *Can you recommend a particular online database?*

- **Search the library's online holdings.** You can search by keyword, author, title, or subject. Using an online catalogue, student Lenny Bukowski typed in the keywords *jazz and social movements*. He found the following book about jazz.

Author	Goldstein, Avram
Title	Addiction: from biology to drug policy
Imprint	New York: Oxford University Press, 2001
Call Number	RC564.G66 2001
Location	NRG – Book Shelves
Status	Available
Description	353 p.; 24 cm.
ISBN	0195146638

Notice that the listing gives the call number, which helps you locate the book on the library shelves. If the catalogue is part of a library network, the online listing explains which library to visit. Because books are organized by topic, chances are good that you will find other relevant books near the one you have chosen.

▪ **Use online periodicals in libraries.** Your library may have access to *EBSCOhost®* or *INFOtrac*. By typing keywords into *EBSCOhost®*, you can search through national or international newspapers, magazines, or reference books. When you find an article that you need, print it or cut and paste it into a word processing file, and then e-mail the document to yourself. Remember to print or copy the publication data because you will need that information when you cite your source.

Searching the Internet

Search engines such as *Google* and *Yahoo!* can rapidly retrieve thousands of documents from the Internet. However, most people do not need as many documents as those engines can generate. Here are some tips to help make your Internet searches focused and efficient.

▪ **Choose your keywords with care.** Imagine you want information about new fuel sources for automobiles. If you type the words *alternative energy* in Google's keyword search space, you will come up with ten million entries (also known as "hits"). Think about more precise terms that could help you limit your search. For instance, if you are really interested in fuel sources for automobiles, you might change your search request to *alternative car fuel*. If you do not find information on your topic, think about synonyms or alternative ways to describe it.

▪ **Use quotation marks to limit the search.** Remember that you are driving the search, and you can control how many hits you get. By putting quotation

marks around your search query, you limit the number of sites to those that contain all of the words that you requested. For example, when you input the words *alternative car fuel* into Google, you will have more than three million hits. When the same words are enclosed within quotation marks, the number of hits is reduced significantly.

- **Use bookmarks.** When you find information that might be useful, create a folder where you can store the information in a "bookmark" or "favorites" list. Then you can easily find it later. (The bookmark icon appears on the toolbar of your search engine.)

- **Use academic search engines.** Sites such as *Google Scholar* (scholar .google.com) or *Virtual Learning Resources Center* (virtuallrc.com) help you look through academic publications such as theses, peer-reviewed papers, books, and articles. To find more academic sites, simply do a search for "academic search engines."

Conducting Interviews or Surveys

You can support your research essay with information from an interview. Speak to an expert in the field or someone who is directly affected by an issue. If you record the interview, ensure that your subject gives you permission to do so. Remember to plan the interview before you meet the person and list key questions that you would like answered. Include the person's complete name and qualifications in your research notes.

Another source of information can be a **survey,** which is an assessment of the views of many people. For example, if you are writing about a tuition fee increase, you can survey students to gather their opinions. When you plan your survey, follow some basic guidelines:

- **Determine your goal.** What do you want to discover?

- **Determine the age, gender, and status of the respondents** (people you will survey). For example, you might decide to survey equal-sized groups of males and females or those over and under twenty-five years of age.

- **Decide how many people you will survey.** Try to survey at least twenty people. If you are working with a partner or a team of students, you can increase that number.

- **Determine the type of survey you will do.** Will you survey people using the phone, e-mail, or written forms? Keep in mind that people are more likely to obscure the truth when asked questions directly, especially if the questions are embarrassing or very personal. For example, if you ask someone whether he agrees or disagrees with legalized abortion, he might present a viewpoint that he thinks you or nearby listeners will accept. The same person might be more honest in an anonymous written survey.

Teaching Tip:

Cooperative Learning (Jigsaw) List five different topics on the board such as *smoking, gambling, study habits,* and so on. Then ask teams to choose one of the topics. (Every team should have a different topic.) Teams should brainstorm six survey questions about their topic. Then one student should remain sitting and the others should spread out to different groups. Everyone can conduct the survey on the new teammates. Finally, the original teams can reform and compile results. The activity takes about thirty minutes. You could then ask students to do more detailed research about the topic, and they can include the survey results in their final research essay.

Teaching Tip:
Ask students in pairs
or teams to choose
a controversial
topic. Then, working
together, the group
can come up with
survey questions.
Each person on
the team can be
responsible for
surveying a set
number of people.
When students
mention the survey
in their essays, they
should mention
how many people
were surveyed.

- **Plan your survey questions.** If gender, age, marital status, or job status are important, place questions about those items at the beginning of your survey. When you form your questions, do not ask open-ended, essay-type questions because it will be difficult to compile the results. Instead, ask yes/no questions or provide a choice of answers. Sample questions:

What is your gender?   male _____   female _____

How often do you use the public transit system (the bus, subway, or train)?

_____ weekdays   _____ about once a week

_____ rarely or never   _____ about once a month

If you want to determine your respondents' knowledge about a topic, include an "I don't know" response. Otherwise, people will make selections that could skew your survey results.

Has Jackson Monroe done a good job as student union leader?

_____ yes   _____ no   _____ I don't know

Teaching Tip:
Ask students to find
a certain minimum
number of sources.
Request that at least
two sources be
from the library
so that students
practice using the
library for research.

Evaluating Sources

When you see sources published in print or online, especially when they are attention-grabbing with color or graphics, you may forget to question whether those sources are reliable. For instance, a company's Web site advertising an alternative cancer therapy might be less reliable than an article in a scientific journal by a team of oncologists (doctors who treat cancer).

Web Addresses

A Web address—also known as a URL—has the following parts.

protocol	host name	document path	specific topic

http://www.nytimes.com/2008/10/28/technology/28soft.html?ref=business

Sometimes you can determine what type of organization runs the Web site by looking at the last three letters of the Uniform Resource Locator (URL) address. However, it is easy to buy a *.com*, *.org*, *.biz*, or *.net* address, so make sure that you judge the content of the site with a critical eye.

Tech
Teaching Tip:
Ask students to go
online and to find
Web sites with
information about
the dangers of
Internet dating. They
should identify
three sites that
could be used in
an essay.

URL ending	Meaning	Example
.com	company	www.time.com
.edu	educational institution	www.fsu.edu
.gov	government	www.irs.gov
.org	organization	www.pbs.org

> ## _Hint_   **Questions for Evaluating a Source**
>
> Each time you find a source, ask yourself the following questions:
>
> • Will the information support the point that I want to make?
>
> • Is the information current? When was the site last updated? Ask yourself if the date is appropriate for your topic.
>
> • Is the site reliable and highly regarded? For instance, is it from a well-respected newspaper, magazine, or journal? Is the English grammatically correct?
>
> • Is the author an expert on the subject? (Many sites provide biographical information about the author.)
>
> • Does the writer present a balanced view, or does he or she clearly favor one viewpoint over another? Ask yourself if the writer has a political or financial interest in the issue.
>
> • Is there advertising on the site? Consider how advertising might influence the site's content.
>
> • Do different writers supply the same information on various sites? Information is more likely to be reliable if multiple sources cite the same facts.

PRACTICE 1   Imagine that you are conducting research about the safety of bottled water. Answer the questions by referring to the list of Web entries that follows the questions.

1. Write the letters of three Web hits that are **not** useful for your essay. For each one you choose, explain why.

   B. Water purifier site: the owners are trying to sell their product.

   C. It is a personal opinion posted on a site.

   E. It is about an incident in a Chinese city and is not relevant.

2. Write the letters of the three Web hits that you should investigate further. Briefly explain how each one could be useful.

   A. Organization's study presents both sides of the issue

   D. Presents an expert's opinion

   F. Shows results of a study

Teaching Tip: Engage students in a class discussion about the various sites. Ask them to evaluate which sites they would bother visiting and which sites they would ignore. Encourage them to look at the short blurbs _and_ the Web addresses before deciding if the Web site is relevant to their research.

A. Is Bottled Really Better? The NRDC Takes A Look At The Pros And . . .
The Natural Resources Defense Council (NRDC) Takes A Look At The Pros And Cons Of Bottled Water. July 25, 2007 | by Erin Petrun.
http://www.cbsnews.com/stories/2007/07/25/uttm/main3098492.shtml

B. There Can Be Dangers Of Drinking Bottled Water | Water Purifiers
22 Aug 2008 . . . Water is an excellent way to keep your mind sharp and your body
in excellent shape as most everyone in the world already knows.
http://www.home-water-distiller.com/waterpurifiers/drinking-
water/there-can-be-dangers-of-drinking-bottled-water-62/

C. Healthy Diet Info Zone: BOTTLED WATER - DANGER!!!
BOTTLED WATER - DANGER!!! Posted by Martin | 6:55 AM. Healthy Drinks ·
0 comments. Bottled water in your car . . . very dangerous, woman! . . .
http://health-diet-info.blogspot.com/2008/05/bottled-water-danger.html

D. Bottled vs. Tap
Is the extra cost of bottled water vs. tap water worth it? . . . "consumers should feel
confident of the safety of their water," says Stew Thornley, a water quality health
educator with the Minnesota Department of Health. . . .
http://pediatrics.about.com/cs/weeklyquestion/a/080702_ask_3.htm

E. City still in shock over water danger
City still in shock over water danger. By Qian Yanfeng (China Daily) ". . . but I'm
still drinking bottled water and only use tap water for washing," he said. . . .
http://www.chinadaily.com.cn/china/2009-02/23/content_7501020.htm

F. ABC News: Study: Bottled Water No Safer Than Tap Water
Bottled water users were twice as likely as others to cite health for their choice of
beverage, the study found. Fifty-six percent of bottled water users . . .
http://abcnews.go.com/Business/story?id=87558&page=

 Do Not Pay for Online Articles

Ignore Web sites that offer to sell articles or essays. There are many free online
journals, magazines, and newspapers that contain articles suitable for a research project.
Also find out if your college has access to extensive online databases such as EBSCO.

Writer's Desk Research Your Topic

Using the guiding research question that you developed in the previous Writer's Desk, list
some keywords that you can use to research your topic.

_____

_____

Using the library and the Internet, find some sources that you can use for your research
essay. You might also conduct interviews or prepare a survey. Print out relevant online
sources, and keep track of your source information.

Taking Notes

As you research your topic, keep careful notes on paper, on note cards, or in computer files. Do not rely on your memory! You would not want to spend several weeks researching, only to accidentally plagiarize because you had not adequately acknowledged some sources.

Look for sources that support your thesis statement. Each time you find a source that seems relevant, keep a detailed record of its publication information so that you can easily cite the source when you begin to write your research essay. You will find important information about preparing in-text citations and a Works Cited (MLA) list later in this chapter.

For example, Karine Maheu created the following note card after finding source material in the library.

Source: *Psychology* by Scott O. Lilienfeld et al., Upper Saddle River: Pearson, 2009. Print.

Page 432: Although most brain maturation occurs prenatally and in the first few years of life, the frontal lobes don't mature fully until late adolescence or early adulthood.

Finding Complete Source Information

Source information is easy to find in most print publications. It is usually on the copyright page, which is often the second or third page of the book, magazine, or newspaper. On many Internet sites, however, finding the same information can take more investigative work. When you research on the Internet, look for the home page to find the site's title, publication date, and so on. Record as much information from the site as possible.

Book, Magazine, Newspaper

author's full name
title of article
title of book, magazine, or
   newspaper
publishing information (name of publisher, city,
   and date of publication)
page numbers used

Web Site

author's full name
title of article
title of site
publisher of site
date of publication or update
date that you accessed the site
complete Web site address

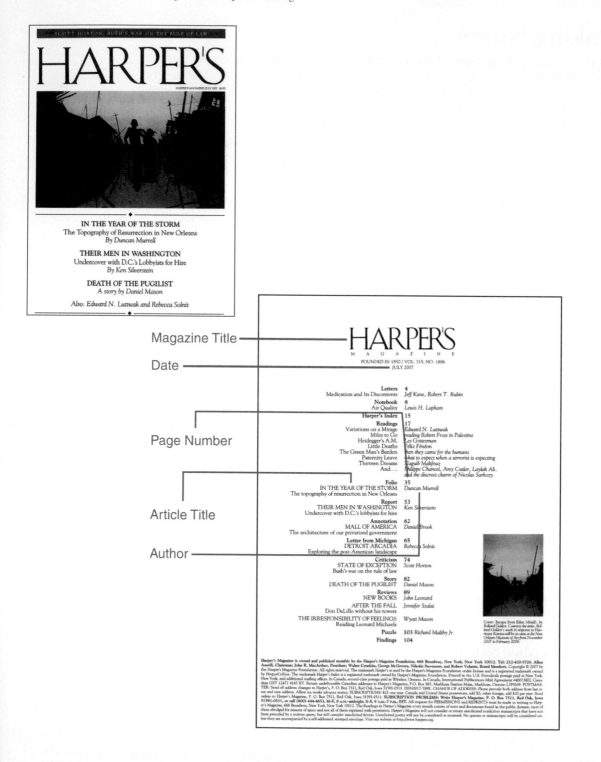

SCOTT HORTON: BUSH'S WAR ON THE RULE OF LAW

HARPER'S

HARPER'S MAGAZINE/JULY 2007 $6.95

IN THE YEAR OF THE STORM
The Topography of Resurrection in New Orleans
By Duncan Murrell

THEIR MEN IN WASHINGTON
Undercover with D.C.'s Lobbyists for Hire
By Ken Silverstein

DEATH OF THE PUGILIST
A story by Daniel Mason

Also: Edward N. Luttwak and Rebecca Solnit

Magazine Title ———

HARPER'S
M A G A Z I N E

Date ———

FOUNDED IN 1850 / VOL. 315, NO. 1886
JULY 2007

*Cover: Escape from Eden (detail), by
Roland Golden. Courtesy the artist. Roland Golden's work in response to Hurricane Katrina will be on view at the New
Orleans Museum of Art from November
2007 to February 2008.*

Harper's Magazine is owned and published monthly by the Harper's Magazine Foundation, 666 Broadway, New York, New York 10012. Tel: 212-420-5720. Allen Austill, Chairman; John R. MacArthur, President; Walter Cronkite, George McGovern, Nikolai Stevenson, and Robert Volante, Board Members. Copyright © 2007 by the Harper's Magazine Foundation. All rights reserved. The trademark *Harper's* is used by the Harper's Magazine Foundation under license and is a registered trademark owned by HarperCollins. The trademark *Harper's Index* is a registered trademark owned by Harper's Magazine Foundation. Printed in the U.S. Periodicals postage paid at New York, New York, and additional mailing offices. In Canada, second-class postage paid at Windsor, Ontario. In Canada, International Publications Mail Agreement #40013802. Canadian GST 12477 4167 RT. Return undeliverable Canadian addresses to Harper's Magazine, P.O. Box 885, Markham Station Main, Markham, Ontario L3P9H49. POSTMASTER: Send all address changes to Harper's, P. O. Box 7511, Red Oak, Iowa 51591-0511. ISSN0017-789X. CHANGE OF ADDRESS: Please provide both address from last issue and new address. Allow six weeks advance notice. SUBSCRIPTIONS: $21 one year. Canada and United States possessions, add $2; other foreign, add $20 per year. Send orders to Harper's Magazine, P. O. Box 7511, Red Oak, Iowa 51591-0511. SUBSCRIPTION PROBLEMS: Write Harper's Magazine, P. O. Box 7511, Red Oak, Iowa 51591-0511, or call (800) 444-4653, M–F, 8 A.M.–midnight, S–S, 9 A.M.–7 P.M., EST. All requests for PERMISSIONS and REPRINTS must be made in writing to Harper's Magazine, 666 Broadway, New York, New York 10012. The Readings in Harper's Magazine every month consist of texts and documents found in the public domain, most of them abridged for reasons of space and not all of them reprinted with permission. Harper's Magazine will not consider or return unsolicited nonfiction manuscripts that have not been preceded by a written query, but will consider unsolicited fiction. Unsolicited poetry will not be considered or returned. No queries or manuscripts will be considered unless they are accompanied by a self-addressed, stamped envelope. Visit our website at http://www.harpers.org.

Newspaper Title

Edition

Date

Page Number

Article Title

Author

Title of Site

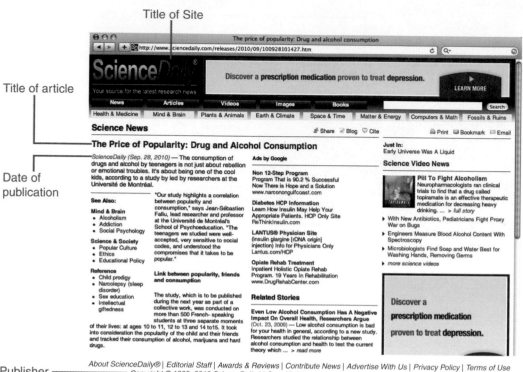

Title of article

Date of publication

Publisher

About ScienceDaily® | Editorial Staff | Awards & Reviews | Contribute News | Advertise With Us | Privacy Policy | Terms of Use
Copyright © 1995–2010 ScienceDaily LLC — All rights reserved — Contact: editor@sciencedaily.com
Note: This web site is not intended to provide medical advice, diagnosis or treatment.
Part of the *iVillage Your Total Health Network*

Teaching Tip:
Remind students that they must cite sources when they paraphrase, summarize, and quote. Some students mistakenly think it is acceptable to paraphrase or summarize without citing the source. Students can practice recognizing plagiarism by trying Practice 1 in Chapter 15.

 Avoid Plagiarism

Do not plagiarize. Plagiarism is using someone else's work without giving that person credit. Such an act is considered stealing and is a very serious offense. To eliminate your chances of inadvertently plagiarizing, ensure that your notes contain detailed and clear source information. Then, when you later quote, paraphrase, or summarize another's work, you can cite the source. For more information about plagiarism, paraphrasing, and summarizing, see Chapter 15.

Writer's Desk Take Notes

Use your topic from the previous Writer's Desk. Take notes from the sources that you have found. In your notes, include direct quotations, paraphrases, and summaries. Organize your sources and keep a record of your sources.

Organizing Your First Draft

For research essays, as for any other type of essay, planning is essential. After you have evaluated the material that you have gathered, decide how you will organize your material. Group your notes under the main points that you would like to develop. Then arrange your ideas in a logical order. You might choose to use spatial, chronological, or emphatic order.

Writing a Thesis Statement

After taking notes, plan your thesis statement. Your thesis statement expresses the main focus of your essay. You can convert your guiding research question into a thesis statement. For instance, Karine Maheu, the student mentioned earlier in this chapter, wrote the guiding research question *What are the health effects of energy drinks?* After researching and gathering material, she reworked her question to create a thesis statement.

> Energy drinks have serious side effects and are harmful when overused.

Creating an Outline

An **outline** or **plan** will help you organize your ideas. Write your main points, and list supporting details and examples. You can mention the sources you intend to use to support specific points. After looking at your preliminary outline, check if there are any holes in your research. If necessary, do more research to fill in those holes before writing your first draft. (For more samples of essay plans and for reminders about the writing process, see Chapters 1–5.)

Karine's Preliminary Outline

Thesis: Energy drinks have serious side effects and are harmful when overused.

1. The stimulants in energy drinks can be potentially harmful when consumed with alcoholic drinks.

   - Wake Forest University study about alcohol and energy drinks.
   - Energy drinks contain alcohol (Cloud 47)

2. If taken in excess, energy drinks can cause cardiovascular problems.

   - Blood pressure and energy drinks (Doheny)
   - Heart disease link (Tedmanson)

3. An ingredient in energy drinks called taurine might affect the brain.

   - Taurine can cause seizures (Merriman)
   - Age of consumers and developing brain (Lilienfeld 432)
   - Taurine's sedative properties ("Scientists")

Teaching Tip:
The sample outline is an informal one. Before students begin their papers, specify if you prefer a more formal format.

Writer's Desk **Make a Preliminary Plan**

Write a thesis statement for your essay. Then organize your topic and make a plan. In your preliminary plan, include source information. Remember that this is not a final plan. You can add or remove information afterward.

Incorporating Visuals

Visuals—such as charts, maps, graphs, photos, or diagrams—can help to clarify, summarize, emphasize, or illustrate certain concepts in research essays. For example, a graph showing the falling crime rate can be an effective way to support an argument that policing methods have become increasingly successful. Remember to use visuals sparingly and to cite them properly.

Most word processing programs offer templates for many visuals. For example, the toolbar in MS Word allows you to select *Chart* under *Insert* to create line, bar, pie, and other types of charts. Simply input your own data, and the program will create the chart for you. The following charts are standard templates from MS Word.

Other visuals can also be useful for illustrating concepts. Often, readers prefer seeing an object or idea in context rather than trying to understand it in writing. Basic diagrams, like the one shown here, can be especially useful for scientific and technical writing.

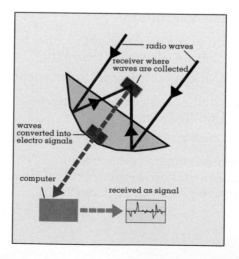

> ## Hint ▸ Using Visuals
>
> Here are some recommendations for using visuals in an academic research essay:
>
> - Ask your instructor whether you are permitted to use visuals in your essay and, if so, where you need to insert them (in the body of your essay or in an appendix).
> - Include a label above each visual to clearly identify it. For example, you can number figures and tables sequentially: *Fig. 1, Fig. 2,* or *Table 1, Table 2,* and so on.
> - Place a caption alongside or under the visual to help the reader understand it.
> - Acknowledge the source of any visual that you borrow.
> - Explain in the text how the visual supports a specific point. For example, in the body of your paper, you might write *Figure 2 illustrates how the crime rate has fallen steadily since the 1990s.*

Citing Sources

Each time you borrow someone's words, ideas, or images, you must **cite** or credit the source to avoid plagiarizing (see page 250 in Chapter 15). There are two places you need to cite sources in your research essays—in the essay and at the end of it. Use **in-text citations** (also known as **parenthetical citations**) as you incorporate quotations, paraphrases, or summaries. Then, cite the sources in an alphabetized list at the end of your essay. The title of this source list depends on the documentation style you choose. For example, the Modern Language Association (MLA) refers to the list as Works Cited and the American Psychological Association (APA) refers to it as References. For more information about where to find the most up-to-date guidelines and samples, see Appendix 5 (pages 606–610). You can also check each organization's Web site: www.mla.org or www.apastyle.org.

Teaching Tip: The guidelines in this chapter reflect changes in the *MLA Handbook for Writers of Research Papers, Seventh Edition.*

> ## Hint ▸ Choose a Documentation Style
>
> A **documentation style** is a method of presenting the material that you have researched. Three common sources for documenting style are the Modern Language Association (MLA), the American Psychological Association (APA), and *Chicago Manual of Style* (CMS). Before writing a research essay, check with your instructor about which documentation style you should use and where you can find more information about it.

Using MLA Style

MLA In-Text Citations

When you paraphrase, summarize, or quote, you must cite the source in the body of the essay. You must also cite the source in a Works Cited page at the end of your essay. See page 274 to view the Works Cited page for the following quotations.

There are two ways to show that you have borrowed an idea or quotation: cite the source in the sentence or cite the source in parentheses.

Source	Source cited in the sentence	Source cited in parentheses
Print	Mention the author's name in the sentence. Include the page number in parentheses. **Virginia Postrel** writes, "On the subject of credit, bad news sells" **(44)**.	Put the author's last name and the page number in parentheses. The crisis became a national obsession: "On the subject of credit, bad news sells" **(Postrel 44)**.
Internet	For online sources, mention just the author's name. No page number is necessary. **Michelle Singletary** mentions the misconception: "If you have a federal student loan, it can't be discharged in bankruptcy." If an online source does not provide an author's name, mention the article's title or the Web site title in the sentence. According to **"Student Debt Assistance,"** the student debt load is worrisome: "Undergraduates are carrying record-high credit card balances."	For online sources, put just the author's last name in parentheses. Students cannot simply refuse to pay a student loan from the federal government **(Singletary)**. If the online source does not provide an author's name, write a short form of the title in parentheses. The student debt load is worrisome: "Undergraduates are carrying record-high credit card balances" **("Student")**.

GRAMMAR LINK

To find out more about writing titles, see pages 506–507 in Chapter 37.

> **Hint** ⟩ **Quoting from a Secondary Source**
>
> Some works include quotations from other people. If an author is quoted in a secondary source, then put the abbreviation *qtd. in*, meaning "quoted in," in the parentheses.
>
> > Hillel Black describes a "consumer credit explosion that makes the population explosion seem small" (qtd. in Postrel).
>
> See Chapter 37 for more information about using quotations.

MLA: Preparing a Works Cited List

An MLA-style Works Cited list appears at the end of a research essay. It gives readers details about each source from which you have borrowed material to write your essay. Works Cited is not the same as a running bibliography, which lists all of the sources you consulted while you were researching your essay topic. In a Works Cited list, include only works that you have quoted, paraphrased, or summarized.

To prepare a Works Cited list, follow these basic guidelines.

1. A Works Cited list always starts on a new page. Put your name and page number in the upper-right hand corner, as you do on all other pages of the essay.
2. Write "Works Cited" at the top of the page and center it. Do not italicize it, underline it, or put quotation marks around it.
3. List each source alphabetically, using the author's last name.
4. Indent the second line and all subsequent lines of each entry five spaces.
5. Double space all lines.

Parts of a Works Cited Reference

Each Works Cited reference should have the following parts.

- **Name**

    Write the author's complete last name followed by a comma and then the first name.

- **Title**

    Add quotation marks around the titles of short works (Web site article, newspaper editorial, book chapter). Italicize the titles of longer works (newspaper, book, magazine, or Web site).

- **Place of Publication**

    When using a book as a source, look for the place of publication. Mention the name of the city but not the state.

- **Publisher's Name**

    Use a shortened form of the publisher's name. Omit *A*, *An*, or *The* from the beginning, and omit words such as *Co.*, *Corp.*, *Books*, *Press*, and *Publishers*. The short form for University Press is UP. On Internet sites, look for the publisher's or sponsor's name.

- **Date of Publication**

    Add the date that the item was published or placed online. With online sources, also include the date you accessed the site.

- **Medium of Publication**

    Mention the medium in which you found the content. Write *Print* for any paper source such as a book or newspaper. Write *Web* for all content found on the Internet. Other sources might be *CD*, *Performance*, *Television*, or *Film*.

EXAMPLE:

Davis, Ronald D. *The Gift of Dyslexia*. New York: Perigee, 1997. Print.

Teaching Tip:
The MLA recently revised the rules for citing sources. This book contains those recent changes. For example, it is no longer considered necessary to write the complete Web address. There has also been the introduction of the medium of publication (.Print, .Web, etc.). Finally, underlining is no longer accepted unless an essay is handwritten. Titles of complete works must be italicized.

Placement and Order of Works Cited

The Works Cited list should be at the end of the research paper. List sources in alphabetical order of the authors' last names. If there is no author, put the title in the alphabetized list. The example is a Works Cited page for the quotations listed on page 272.

Works Cited

Postrel, Virginia. "The Case for Debt." *Atlantic* Nov. 2008: 44–47. Print.

Singletary, Michelle. "The Color of Money." *Washington Post.* The Washington Post Company, 24 Sept. 2006. Web. 14 May 2010.

"Student Debt Statistics." *American Student Assistance.* American Student Assistance, 2009. Web. 15 May 2010.

Sample MLA-Style Works Cited Entries

The following are a few sample entries for various publications. The *MLA Handbook for Writers of Research Papers* has a complete list of sample entries. As you look at the samples, notice how they are punctuated.

Model Entries

Books

> Last name, First name. *Title of the Book.* Place of Publication: Publisher, Year. Print.

ONE AUTHOR   Write the author's last name followed by the first name.

> Krakauer, Jon. *Into Thin Air.* New York: Random, 1999. Print.

TWO OR THREE AUTHORS   Write the last name and first name of the first author. Follow with *and*, and then write the first and last name of subsequent authors. If the book is a second, third, or subsequent edition, write just the abbreviated form of the edition after the title.

> Bovée, Courtland, and John Thill. *Business Communication Essentials.* 2nd ed. Upper Saddle River: Prentice, 2006. Print.

FOUR OR MORE AUTHORS   Add *et al.*, which means "and others," after the first author's name.

> Ember, Carol R., et al. *Physical Anthropology and Archaeology.* Toronto: Pearson, 2006. Print.

EDITOR INSTEAD OF AN AUTHOR   Write the editor's name followed by *ed.*

> Gansworth, Eric, ed. *Sovereign Bones: New Native American Writing*. New York: Nation, 2007. Print.

TWO OR MORE BOOKS BY THE SAME AUTHOR   Write the author's name in the first entry only. In subsequent entries, type three hyphens followed by a period. Then add the title.

> Angelou, Maya. *I Know Why the Caged Bird Sings*. New York: Random, 1969. Print.

> ---. *Mother: A Cradle to Hold Me*. New York: Random, 2006. Print.

A WORK IN AN ANTHOLOGY   For articles or essays taken from an anthology or edited collection, mention the author and title of the article first. Then write the anthology's title followed by *Ed.* and the editor's name. End with the page numbers of the piece you are citing followed by *Print*.

> Weaskus, Jeanette. "A Ghost Dance for Words." *Sovereign Bones: New Native American Writing*. Ed. Eric Gansworth. New York: Nation, 2007. 129–134. Print.

A PREVIOUSLY PUBLISHED ARTICLE IN A COLLECTION   Some collections give information about a previously published article on the page where the article appears. When citing such sources, include information about the previous publication, and then add *Rpt. in* (which means "Reprinted in"). Then include the title of the collection.

> Buchwald, Art. "The Hydrogen Bomb Lobby." *Laid Back in Washington*. New York: G.P. Putman. 1981. Rpt. in *Controversy: Issues for Reading and Writing*. Ed. Judith J. Pula, Audrey T. Edwards, and R. Allan Dermott. 3rd ed. Upper Saddle River: Pearson, 2005. 178–180. Print.

A BOOK IN A SERIES   If the book is part of a series, then end your citation with the series name (but do not italicize it or set it off in any way).

> Fiorina, Morris P., Samuel J. Abrams, and Jeremy C. Pope, eds. *Culture War?*, 3rd ed. New York: Longman, 2011. Print. Great Questions in Politics.

ENCYCLOPEDIA AND DICTIONARY   When encyclopedias and dictionaries list items alphabetically, you can omit volume and page numbers. It is sufficient to list the edition and year of publication.

> "Democracy." *Columbia Encyclopedia*. 6th ed. 2005. Print.

> "Legitimate." *The New American Webster Handy College Dictionary*. 3rd ed. 2003. Print.

Teaching Tip:
Point out that there
is no punctuation
between the
magazine or
newspaper title
and the date.

Periodicals

Last name, First name. "Title of Article." *Title of the Magazine or Newspaper* Date: Pages. Print.

ARTICLE IN A MAGAZINE   Include the page numbers in magazine and newspaper sources.

Risen, Clay. "The Lightning Rod." *Atlantic* Nov. 2008: 78–87. Print.

ARTICLE IN A NEWSPAPER

Dugger, Celia W. "Clinton Helps Broker Deal for Medicine to Treat AIDS." *New York Times* 1 Dec. 2006: A9. Print.

EDITORIAL   If the editorial is signed, begin with the editor's name. If it is unsigned, begin with the title. Follow the title with the word *Editorial*.

"Tax Freedom Day Is Here." Editorial. *Gazette* 27 June 2006: A16. Print.

ARTICLE IN A JOURNAL

Seligman, Martin. "The American Way of Blame." *APA Monitor* 29.7 (1998): 97. Print.

Teaching Tip:
Point out the
punctuation in the
electronic source.
The publisher or
sponsor is followed
by a comma, but all
other items are
followed by periods.

Electronic Sources

Electronic sources include Web sites, information from subscription services, and reference databases. Electronic communications are frequently updated or moved, so keep track of the date you accessed a site. When using a source published on the Internet, include as much of the following information as you can find. Keep in mind that some sites do not contain complete information. Also, when you write the network address, break the address only at a slash mark. Only include the URL if your reader probably couldn't locate the source without it or if your instructor requires it.

Last name, First name. "Title of Article." *Title of Site or Online Publication.* Publisher or sponsor, Date of publication or most recent update. Web. Date of access (day, month, and year).

Note: If there is no clear publisher or sponsor, write n.p. If there is no clear publication date, write n.d.

ARTICLE ON A PERSONAL WEB SITE

Sacks, Oliver. "Uncle Tungsten." *Oliver Sacks.* Oliver Sacks, 2008. Web. 10 Apr. 2010.

ARTICLE IN AN ONLINE PERIODICAL   If the site mentions the volume or page reference, include it. If not, include as much information as you can find.

> Fortini, Amanda. "Little Darlings." *Salon*. Salon Media Group, 8 Nov. 2009. Web. 13 May 2010.

GOVERNMENT SITE (OR OTHER SITES WITHOUT AUTHOR INFORMATION)
If the author is not mentioned on the site, begin with just the title and include as much information as you can find.

> "Dangerous Jobs." *U.S. Department of Labor*. U.S. Bureau of Labor Statistics, 1997. Web. 28 May 2010.

Other Types of Sources

INTERVIEW THAT YOU CONDUCTED

> Kumar, Nantha. Personal interview. 14 Aug. 2010.

FILM OR VIDEO   Include the name of the film, the director, the studio, and the year of the film's release and the DVD's release.

> *Casablanca*. Dir. Michael Curtiz. 1942. Warner Brothers, 2003. DVD.

RADIO OR TELEVISION PROGRAM   Include the segment title, the program name, the network, and the broadcast date.

> "Global Warming." *Nightline*. ABC News. 27 June 2006. Television.

SOUND RECORDING   Include the name of the performer or band, the title of the song, the title of the CD, the name of the recording company, and the year of release.

> Nirvana. "About a Girl." *Unplugged in New York*. Geffen, 1994. CD.

PRACTICE 2   Imagine that you are using the following sources in a research paper. Arrange the sources for a works cited list using MLA style. Remember to place the items in alphabetical order.

- You consulted a magazine article called "Swamp Things" by Burkhard Bilger. Bilger's article appeared on April 20, 2009, on pages 80–89 in the *New Yorker*.
- You consulted an online article called "Service with a Snarl" by Joe Eskenazi. It appeared on *SF Weekly.com* on June 16, 2009. The site's publisher is SF Weekly. You accessed the site today.
- You consulted an online article called "Chimps Deserve Better." There is no listed author, but the article appeared on the Web site *The Humane Society*. The site sponsor is The Humane Society of the United States. The page was last updated on July 16, 2009. You accessed the site today.

■ You consulted a book called *Between the Species: A Reader in Human–Animal Relationships* by Arnold Arluke and Clinton Sanders. The book was published in 2009 by Allyn & Bacon in Boston.

Works Cited

Arluke, Arnold, and Clinton Sanders. *Between the Species: A Reader in*

　　Animal–Human Relationships. Boston: Allyn & Bacon, 2009. Print.

Bilger, Burkhard. "Swamp Things." *New Yorker* 20 Apr. 2009: 80–89.

　　Print.

"Chimps Deserve Better." *The Humane Society.* The Humane Society of the

　　United States, 16 July 2009. Web. Today's date.

Eskenazi, Joe. "Service with a Snarl." *SF Weekly.com.* SF Weekly, 16 June

　　2009. Web. Today's date.

Writer's Desk **Write a Research Essay**

Write your research essay. After you write your first draft, revise and edit it. Remember to double-space your essay and include a Works Cited page.

Sample Research Essay
Title Pages and Outlines

Although MLA does not insist on an outline for a research essay, your instructor may request one.

Outline

Thesis: Energy drinks have serious side effects and are harmful when overused.

I. The stimulants in energy drinks can be potentially harmful when consumed with alcoholic drinks.

    A. Wake Forest University studied alcohol and energy drinks.

    B. Energy drinks can mask a person's level of intoxication.

    C. Some companies mix energy drinks and alcohol.

II. Furthermore, if taken in excess, energy drinks can cause cardiovascular problems.

    A. The drinks can increase blood pressure.

    B. Heart disease is linked to energy drinks.

III. Taurine, an ingredient in energy drinks, might affect the brain.

    A. Taurine increases alertness but can seizures.

    B. Youths have developing brains.

    C. Taurine may act as a sedative.

The Research Essay

Maheu 1

◄ Write your last name and page number in the top right corner of each page.

Karyne Maheu

Professor Slater

English 102B

May 8, 2011

Double-space ➤ your identification information.

The Dangers of Energy Drinks

◄ Center the title without underlining, italics, quotation marks, or boldface type.

Red Bull, Monster, Rockstar, Burn, and Energy are all popular energy drinks. These products are an effective way to get coffee-like stimulation. People consume these products to wake up in the morning, to perform at work or school, to stay up late in clubs, and to perform in sports. Manufacturers point out that energy drinks contain natural ingredients such as herbs and vitamins. However, energy drinks also contain a lot of sugar and a concentration of caffeine that is almost ten times higher than the content in regular coffee. Some people have experienced illness and even death after consuming such drinks. Energy drinks have serious side effects and are harmful when overused.

Double-space ➤ throughout the body of the essay.

It is not ➤ necessary to document your common knowledge.

End your ➤ introduction with your thesis statement.

The stimulants in energy drinks can be potentially harmful, especially when consumed with alcohol. Scientists at Wake Forest University discovered that "students who consumed alcohol mixed with energy drinks were twice as likely to be hurt or injured . . . as were students who did not consume alcohol mixed with energy drinks" (Nauert). Another

Identify the source in ◄ parentheses.

Maheu 2

danger of mixing alcohol with energy drinks is that the
stimulant can make intoxicated students feel awake enough
to drive (Doheny). In *Time* magazine, John Cloud reports
that "a new generation of malt beverages also contains
stimulants" (47).

Include the page number of a print source.

Furthermore, if taken in excess, energy drinks can cause
cardiovascular problems. According to *WebMD*, many people
report increased blood pressure after consuming the drinks. In
Australia, researchers gave energy drinks to thirty university
students. Sophie Tedmanson and David Rose report that the
consequences on the heart were serious: "Australian researchers
said that after drinking one can, participants had shown a
cardiovascular profile similar to that of someone with heart
disease." Scott Willoughby, who works at the Cardiovascular
Research Center at the Royal Adelaide Hospital, says, "People
who have existing cardiovascular disease may want to talk to
their physician before they drink Red Bull" (qtd. in Tedmanson).
Thus, energy drinks, which can boost blood pressure and the
pulse rate, should be used with care.

Acknowledge sources of borrowed ideas.

Indentify the source in the phrase introducing the quotation.

Use "qtd. in" to show that the quotation appeared in a secondary source.

Finally, taurine, a key ingredient in energy drinks, might
affect the brain. Taurine increases intellectual alertness, so it's
active in the brain area. Researchers at St. Joseph's Hospital
and Medical Center in Phoenix found that energy drink

Maheu 3

consumption was related to seizures: "One patient, a previously healthy 25-year-old male, had been admitted to the emergency room for two seizure episodes four months apart. . . . The patient reported that he had consumed two 24-oz bottles of the energy drink Rockstar on an empty stomach approximately thirty to sixty minutes prior to both seizures" (Merriman).

Although only four people had related seizures, the possible link between energy drinks and brain injury is worrisome. Furthermore, most energy drink consumers are youths with undeveloped frontal lobes (Lilienfeld 432). Thus young people might suffer long-term effects when exposed to the stimulants and taurine in energy drinks. Also, taurine can have a "sedative effect" on the brain and "may play a role in the 'crash' people report after drinking these highly caffeinated beverages" ("Scientists").

In conclusion, energy drink ingredients such as caffeine, sugar, herbs, vitamins, and taurine have possibly dangerous side effects. These drinks, promoted heavily to youths, are not closely regulated for their medicinal qualities. Manufacturers of Red Bull and similar products should be forced to provide warnings. Consumers should use such drinks with moderation, and those with heart problems should avoid energy drinks completely.

Place ellipses after the period to show where irrelevant material has been removed.

Cite the source of summarized information.

If the author is not known, write the first words of the title in parentheses.

End with a quotation, prediction, or recommendation.

Maheu 4

Works Cited

Cloud, John. "Alcoholic Energy Drinks: A Risky Mix." *Time* 30

May 2008: 47. Print.

Doheny, Kathleen. "Energy Drinks: Hazardous to Your Health?"

WebMD. WebMD, 24 Sept. 2008. Web. 4 May 2011.

Lilienfeld, Scott O., et al. *Psychology*. Upper Saddle River:

Pearson, 2009. Print.

Merriman, John. "Do Stimulants in Energy Drinks Provoke

Seizures?" *Neurology Reviews.com*. Quadrant HealthCom,

June 2007. Web. 4 May 2011.

Nauert, Rick. "Energy Drinks + Alcohol = Danger."

PsychCentral. Psych Central, 5 Nov. 2007. Web. 4 May 2011.

"Scientists Close in on Taurine's Activity in the Brain." *Medical*

News Today. MediLexicon International Ltd., 18 Jan. 2008.

Web. 4 May 2011.

Tedmanson, Sophie, and David Rose. "Red Bull Gives You

Wings—and Heart Trouble?" *TimesOnline*. Times

Newspapers, 15 Aug. 2008. Web. 5 May 2011.

Double-space sources.

Place sources in alphabetical order.

Teaching Tip: Like most students, Maheu relied on the Internet for most of her research. Thus, the Works Cited page provides many examples of Internet citations.

Indent the second line when an entry runs over one line.

Teaching Tip:
Practice 3 provides
students with a
chance to analyze
the sample essay.
Ask students to
identify a magazine,
a book, and the Web
sites in the Works
Cited list. Also ask
them to identify a
source without an
author's name.

PRACTICE 3   Answer the following questions by referring to the research essay.

1. How many magazines or books were used as sources?   2

2. How many Internet articles were used as sources?   5

3. When the student used a quotation that appeared *as a quotation* in another source, how did she show that fact? (See the third paragraph.)

   She wrote "qtd. in" in parentheses.

4. In the Works Cited page, how many sources do not mention an author?   1

5. On the Works Cited page, are the sources listed in alphabetical order?

   yes _X_   no_____

Indicate if the following sentences are true (T) or false (F). Look at the Works Cited page to answer each question. If the sentence is false, write a true statement under it.

6. The second row of each citation should be indented.

   (T)   F

7. The title of articles should be set off with italics.

   T   (F)

   Use quotation marks. Use italics for the titles of Web sites.

8. Place periods after the author's first name and the title of the work.

   (T)   F

9. For Internet sources, no dates are necessary.

   T   (F)

   Put the date of publication and the date you accessed the site.

10. For Internet sources, always put "Web" at the very end.

   T   (F)

   Put "Web" between the two dates.

Teaching Tip:
If you would like
your students to
use APA Style
Guidelines, refer to
www.apastyle.org.
Students can view
tutorials on using
APA style.
Information on APA
style appears in
Appendix 5 at the
end of this book.

> ## Hint **APA Web Site**
>
> To get some general information about some basic style questions, you can view the APA's Web site at www.apastyle.org. Use the menu on the left side of the page to direct you to specific style questions and answers.
>
> On the same Web site, there is a link to information about online or "electronic" sources. Because the information about online sources is continually being updated, the site has comprehensive information about the latest citation methods. Visit www.apastyle.org.

The Writer's Room **Research Essay Topics**

Writing Activity 1

Write a research paper about one of the following topics. Ask your instructor what reference style you should use. Put a Works Cited page at the end of your assignment.

1. Write about a contemporary issue that is in the news.
2. Write about any issue in your career choice or field of study.

Writing Activity 2

Write a research paper about one of the following topics. First, brainstorm questions about your topic and find a guiding research question. Then follow the process of writing a research essay.

Abortion	Health-care reform
Affirmative action	Holistic healing
Assisted suicide	Home schooling
Attention-deficit disorder	Immigration
Body image	Legalization of marijuana
Censorship of the Internet	Mandatory drug testing
Childhood obesity	Prison reform
Consequences of war	Privacy and the Internet
Date rape	Same-sex marriage
Executive salaries	Technology and pollution (e-waste)
Fast food	Teen pregnancy
Foreign adoptions	Tobacco industry
Gambling	Violence in the media
Genetically modified food	Volunteer work
Government-sponsored gambling	Youth gangs

Teaching Tip:

Cooperative Learning (Question Cards) Place students in teams of three or four. Each team uses cards or cuts paper into six parts. Teams brainstorm questions about the chapter's key concepts. They write the question on one side of the paper and the answer on the other side. Teams should write about six questions. Then teams can exchange cards with another team. They can look at each question, answer it as a group, and then check the answer.

Teaching Tip:
Pair Work
Before students submit their essays, ask them to exchange essays with partners. Each student should evaluate his or her partner's essay to ensure that sources are cited properly.

Teaching Tip:
Writer's World Competition
Please advise your students that they can submit their essays for possible publication to www.pearsonhighered.com/essayrewards/writingrewards.html

CHECKLIST: RESEARCH ESSAY

When you plan a research essay, ask yourself these questions.

☐ Have I narrowed my topic?

☐ Have I created a guiding research question?

☐ Are my sources reliable?

☐ Have I organized my notes?

☐ Have I integrated source information using quotations, paraphrases, and summaries?

☐ Have I correctly documented my in-text or parenthetical citations?

☐ Have I correctly prepared and punctuated my Works Cited page?

To check your progress in meeting this chapter's objectives, log in to **www.mywritinglab.com,** go to the **Study Plan** tab, click on **More College and Workplace Writing** and choose **The Research Essay** from the list of subtopics. Read and view the resources in the **Review Materials** section, and then complete the **Recall, Apply,** and **Write** sets in the **Activities** section.

The Résumé and Letter of Application

CHAPTER 17

LEARNING OBJECTIVES

1. Preparing a Résumé (p. 288)
2. Writing a Letter of Application (p. 289)

When you apply for a job, you generally send a résumé and a letter of application. A résumé is like a professional version of your personal photo album. Each line is a snapshot of your education and work experience.

Writer's Exchange

Work with a partner and discuss your past work experience. Write down your job titles. Then brainstorm your duties, skills you developed, or accomplishments you achieved. You can use the list of action verbs to get ideas.

Example: Waiter—handled cash, interacted with customers, developed autonomy

Some action verbs

assembled	collaborated	facilitated	inspected	overhauled
advertised	compiled	forecasted	interacted	oversaw
assisted	coordinated	implemented	managed	resolved
budgeted	evaluated	handled	negotiated	served

Tech
Teaching Tip:
In a computer lab, ask students to compare job-hunting Web sites. Ask the class to choose the most useful job-hunting site in your region.

Preparing a Résumé

The word *résumé* comes from a French word meaning "to summarize." Essentially, a résumé is a short summary of your work-related experience. Review the parts of the résumé.

A Sample Résumé

Include contact information but not your birthplace, birth date, nationality, or a personal photo.

Summarize your most pertinent qualifications and skills.

Outline your most recent job experience. If you have not had any paying jobs, you could mention any volunteer work that you have done. For each job that you list, mention the tasks that you completed and the aptitudes you developed.

Ideally, your résumé should be only one page long. If you have extra space, you can end with Awards, Volunteer Work, or Activities.

Put the most recent schooling first. If you have more than a high school education, it is not necessary to list your high school.

It is not necessary to list references. Most employers ask for references at the interview stage.

Teana Butler
9001 Naples Drive
Jacksonville, FL 32211
Telephone: (904) 555-4567
E-mail: teana27@gmail.com

Objective   Position as a respiratory therapist in a long-term care facility

Qualifications Summary
Experience with senior citizens
Knowledge of hospitality management
Strong teamwork and leadership skills
Computer skills (Word and Excel)

Education   **Respiratory Therapy Diploma** June 2010
Concorde Career Institute
Jacksonville, FL

Relevant courses: Ventilator and Airway Management
Home Respiratory Care

Experience   **Nursing Home Cafeteria Manager** 2008 to present
Sunrise Center, Orlando
• Handle cash and calculate end-of-day sales
• Work well under high pressure
• Negotiate patiently with elderly residents
• Manage a team of three co-workers

Activities Coordinator, **Gray's Children's Camp**
Summer 2007
Wayson Drive, Orlando
• Organized a variety of summer sports activities for ten-year-olds
• Settled disagreements and led children with gentle authority
• Acted as big sister to several children with special needs

Activities   Volunteer driver for Meals on Wheels
Coach for a junior soccer team

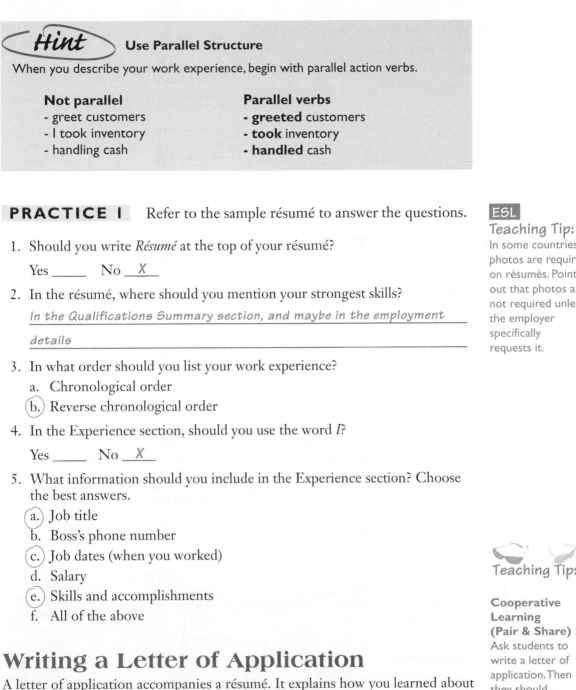

Hint > **Use Parallel Structure**

When you describe your work experience, begin with parallel action verbs.

Not parallel
- greet customers
- I took inventory
- handling cash

Parallel verbs
- **greeted** customers
- **took** inventory
- **handled** cash

PRACTICE 1   Refer to the sample résumé to answer the questions.

1. Should you write *Résumé* at the top of your résumé?

   Yes _____   No __X__

2. In the résumé, where should you mention your strongest skills?

   In the Qualifications Summary section, and maybe in the employment

   details

3. In what order should you list your work experience?
   a. Chronological order
   b. Reverse chronological order

4. In the Experience section, should you use the word *I*?

   Yes _____   No __X__

5. What information should you include in the Experience section? Choose the best answers.
   a. Job title
   b. Boss's phone number
   c. Job dates (when you worked)
   d. Salary
   e. Skills and accomplishments
   f. All of the above

Writing a Letter of Application

A letter of application accompanies a résumé. It explains how you learned about the position and why you are right for the job. It complements your résumé and doesn't repeat it. In your letter, include specific examples to demonstrate why you are right for the job. Maintain a direct and confident tone. Remember that the letter provides you with a chance to demonstrate your communication skills.

ESL
Teaching Tip:
In some countries, photos are required on résumés. Point out that photos are not required unless the employer specifically requests it.

Teaching Tip:

Cooperative Learning (Pair & Share)
Ask students to write a letter of application. Then they should exchange letters with a partner and edit their partner's work.

Sample Letter of Application

Review the parts of the next letter.

Teana Butler
9001 Naples Drive
Jacksonville, FL 32211
(904) 555-4567
teana27@gmail.com

July 5, 2010

Alexia Anders
Cedars Long-Term Care Facility
225 Meadowland Boulevard
Jacksonville, FL 32101

Subject: Position as a respiratory therapist

Dear Ms. Anders:

I am applying for the position of respiratory therapist that was posted in the *Florida Times-Union.* The three years I spent learning about respiratory care have prepared me for this challenge, and I am sure I can be a valuable asset to your nursing care team.

In my recently completed courses at the Concorde Career Institute, I learned about ECGs, arterial blood gas analysis, pulmonary function testing, and NICU monitoring. In addition, my experience at a nursing home has taught me to show patience and empathy when communicating with elderly patients. Furthermore, I have strong teamwork skills. For example, in a protracted dispute over shifts, I was able to negotiate an agreement between my colleagues and defuse an unhappy workplace atmosphere. Within weeks of being hired, I was rewarded with the manager's position.

I would appreciate the opportunity to speak with you in detail about my qualifications. I am available for an interview at your convenience and could start work immediately. Thank you for your consideration.

Sincerely yours,

Teana Butler

Teana Butler

Letter Basics

When you write a letter of application, remember the following points:

- Be brief! Employers may receive large numbers of applications. They will not appreciate long, detailed letters of application. Your letter should be no longer than four short paragraphs.

- Follow the standard business letter format. Most businesses use full block style, in which all elements of the letter are aligned with the left margin. Do not indent any paragraphs. Instead, leave an extra space between paragraphs.

- To make a favorable impression, ensure that your letter is free of grammar, spelling, or punctuation errors. Proofread your letter very carefully before you send it. If possible, ask someone else to look it over for you, too.

- If you e-mail your cover letter, you can send it as an attachment. You can also shorten it and then cut and paste it directly into your e-mail.

 Abbreviations for States

The following two-letter abbreviations are the standard ones used by the U.S. Postal Service (www.usps.com).

- Ten states have two-part names and are abbreviated by the first letter of each word.

   NC, ND, NH, NJ, NM, NY, RI, SC, SD, WV

- Nineteen states are abbreviated by their first two letters.

   AL, AR, CA, CO, DE, FL, ID, IL, IN, MA, MI, NE, OH, OK, OR, UT, WA, WI, WY

- Twelve states are abbreviated by the first and last letter in the state's name.

   CT, GA, HI, IA, KS, KY, LA, MD, ME, PA, VA, VT

- Nine states are abbreviated with two major letters.

   AK, AZ, MN, MO, MS, MT, NV, TN, TX

ESL
Teaching Tip:
Ask students to identify the states mentioned in the list of postal abbreviations. Students could do this as a competition.

ESL
Teaching Tip:
You can use the sample letter of application as a model. The punctuation and capitalization information is for the benefit of nonnative speakers because in many languages, words such as *street* are not capitalized.

ESL
Teaching Tip:
Your nonnative speakers may not know the differences between *Mrs., Miss,* and *Ms.* Point out the differences in meaning and in punctuation. Also, mention that in English, the word *dear* can be used in both personal and business letters. You could put the next examples on the board.

Dear Mr. Wong,
Dear Ms. Aziz,
Dear Sir or Madam:
Attention: Human Resources

PRACTICE 2 Answer the following questions. Refer to the sample letter of application if necessary.

1. Where should the date be placed? Circle your response.
   (a.) above the recipient's address
   b. below the recipient's address

2. If you do not know the name of the person in human resources, how should you address your letter of application?

   Attention: Human Resources Manager or Dear Sir or Madam

   _____

3. Should you place a comma at the end of each line in the recipient's address? Yes _____ No __X__

4. In a letter of application, why are the next closings inappropriate?
   a. Bye for now _____ *too informal* _____
   b. Please accept my most gracious sentiments _____ *too stiff and formal*

5. In the sample application letter, why would Teana avoid mentioning her job at the children's camp?

   She needs to keep her letter short and should include only the most important

   and relevant information. The job information appears on her résumé.

6. Write the two-letter postal abbreviations for each state.

a. Ohio	*OH*	d. West Virginia	*WV*
b. Maine	*ME*	e. Texas	*TX*
c. Vermont	*VT*	f. Kentucky	*KY*

ESL
Teaching Tip:
In some nations, letters of application are quite detailed, flowery, and overly formal. Remind your nonnative speakers that brevity and clarity are key requirements in American business writing.

PRACTICE 3 The next letter contains ten errors. Correct six punctuation errors and four capitalization errors.

Dr. Bakar Rahim

33 Winestead road,   [R above road; comma struck]

Cincinnati OH 45001

May 6, 2010

Fernanda Martinez

965 Slater street   [S above street]

Chicago, IL 65002

Subject: Project Assistant Position

Dear Ms. Martinez:

I have received your application for a position as a project assistant. Unfortunately, as a result of unforeseen circumstances, I did not receive the budget to fund this position. Please accept my apologies. Your education and experience appear exemplary.

On a brighter note, next January, I am hoping to receive the funding, which will allow me to begin accepting applications again. At that time, if you are still available, please contact me for a project assistant's position.

Respectfully Yours,

Dr. B. Rahim

Dr. Bakar Rahim

ESL
Teaching Tip:
In many languages, letter closings are extremely formal and elaborate; therefore, some students may try to directly translate elaborate closings from their native languages. Remind students that conventional closings such as *Sincerely* or *Yours truly* are preferable in American business letters.

The Writer's Room   **Résumé and Letter**

Find a job listing in the newspaper, at an employment center, or on the Internet. (Some Web sites are monster.com, usajobs.opm.gov, or careerbuilders.com. Also check your state's labor department Web site for job listings.) Look for a job that you feel qualified for, or find a job that you hope to have one day. Write a résumé and a letter of application.

ESL
Teaching Tip:
Suggest that each student peer-edit a partner's letter of application. If you have concerns about nonnative speakers needing some help with certain cultural or English-language conventions, try to pair them with native speakers.

CHECKLIST: THE RÉSUMÉ AND THE LETTER OF APPLICATION

When you write a résumé or letter of application, ask yourself these questions:

☐ Have I used correct spelling and punctuation?

☐ In my résumé, have I included my work experience and my education beginning with the most recent?

☐ In my letter of application, have I indicated the position for which I am applying and where or how I heard about the job?

☐ Is my letter concise?

☐ Have I used standard English?

 To check your progress in meeting this chapter's objectives, log in to **www.mywritinglab.com,** go to the **Study Plan** tab, click on **More College and Workplace Writing** and choose **The Résumé and Letter of Application** from the list of subtopics. Read and view the resources in the **Review Materials** section, and then complete the **Recall, Apply,** and **Write** sets in the **Activities** section.

The chapter number badge.

Responding to Film and Literature

CHAPTER 18

Critics who review musical performances are influenced by many factors. They consider the skill of the performer and the quality of the acoustics. They also notice the concert venue and the costumes. You take similar elements into consideration when you interpret works of film and literature.

Writer's Exchange

Work with a partner. Discuss films or stories that you love. Make a "top-five" list.

Tech
Teaching Tip:
Ask students to go
online and find a
video that helped
launch a person's
career. For instance,
there are videos
about Greyson
Chance, Susan
Boyle, and Justin
Bieber. (If there are
more recent viral
videos, you could
suggest them.) Then
students can create
a response to the
videos.

Teaching Tip:
Reassure students
that there are no
right answers.
Students should
focus on supporting
their reactions with
evidence from the
film, novel, or story.

Teaching Tip:
Ask students to
choose a particular
passage, quotation,
or scene from a
text or film and
discuss or write a
personal response
to it. Ask them, Why
did you choose it?
What emotions did
it arouse in you?

Responding to Film and Literature

As a college student, you are often asked to state your opinion, to interpret issues, and to support your ideas. In some of your courses, your instructors may ask you to write a personal response to a literary work or film. When writing a personal response, you use your knowledge and perspective to connect with the work you are analyzing.

Structuring Your Written Response

A basic written response has four parts: an introduction, a summary, some reactions, and a conclusion.

Introduction

For a story or novel, identify the author, title, and publication date. For a film, identify the title, director, and date of release. Then give some general background information about the film, story, or novel. For example, you might mention something about the director or author, the type of film or book, or the reception to the film or story.

Summary

Write a **brief synopsis** of the work. Include the main points and do not go into great detail about the work. Summarize the work so that readers can clearly understand the main storyline. At this point, do not make any personal value judgments about the work. Ensure that your summary is factual.

Reactions

Ask yourself the following questions to help you generate supporting ideas.

- Is the subject relevant to any of my academic studies? Does it relate to topics we have discussed in this class or in another course?
- Does the work give accurate, complete, or unbiased information about a subject? Does the author or filmmaker present the information in a balanced or a slanted way?
- Can I relate to the characters? What do they tell me about human nature?
- Does the work have technical merits? Does the author have a vivid writing style? Does the film have beautiful camera work or impressive special effects?
- What is the work's message? Has it changed my understanding about an issue? Is it related to a real-world problem?
- Would I recommend the work to other people? If so, why?

Note: Always support your reactions with specific examples.

Conclusion

Sum up your main points. End with a recommendation or a final thought.

Teaching Tip:
Group Work
Ask two or three
students to write a
personal response
to the same work.
Then have them
discuss their
responses with the
other students to
see the similarities
and differences in
their responses.

> (Hint) **Follow the Writing Process**
>
> When preparing your response, remember to follow the writing process. You can try exploring strategies to generate ideas. Organize your ideas and make a plan. Write a first draft and check for unity, adequate support, and coherence. Then edit your written work for errors.
>
> Give specific details to support your ideas and opinions. Include examples as well as direct and indirect quotations. Avoid using vague sentiments such as *I like this* or *I do not like that.* When you finish writing, refer to the checklist at the end of this chapter.

A Sample Response to a Film

College student Matt Fiorentino wrote the following response to one of his favorite films. Notice how he structured his response.

The World of *Avatar*

"They've sent us a message that they can take whatever they want. Well, we will send them a message. That this—this is our land!" cries Jake Sully at the height of a climactic battle scene in James Cameron's 2009 blockbuster *Avatar*. Using 3D technology, Cameron takes the "modern man among the natives" tale and includes a heart-warming romance. *Avatar* reminds viewers about the dangers of uncontrolled greed and exploitation of the environment.

As the films opens, we are introduced to the hero of the story, a paraplegic former Marine named Jake Sully. Sully decides to sign up for a paramilitary mission on the distant world of Pandora. He learns that greedy corporate figurehead Parker Selfridge intends to remove the native humanoid "Na'vi" from their homeland. The corporation wants the precious material known as unobtainium, which is scattered throughout the Na'vi's woodland. Selfridge states, "This is why we're here, because this little gray rock sells for twenty million a kilo." In exchange for the spinal surgery that will fix his legs, Jake gathers intelligence for a special military unit headed by Colonel Quaritch. Using an avatar identity, Jake infiltrates the Na'vi people. While Jake is bonding with the native tribe and falling in love with the beautiful alien Neytiri, the restless colonel prepares to invade Na'vi lands. Jake must take a stand and fight back in an epic battle for the fate of Pandora.

James Cameron's avatars are impressive. The director found a way for audiences to sympathize with the Na'vi, tall blue creatures with spotted faces. Young viewers like me are already familiar with avatars. We make graphic depictions of ourselves and pretend to be those characters in videogames or in online worlds such as Second Life. In the movie, the avatars are alien bodies that are controlled by human minds. Scenes of the floating avatar in a large tank are powerful and surprisingly realistic.

Introduction
The writer begins with general background information. He identifies the film's title, release date, and director.

Thesis statement
He expresses the main focus of the essay.

Summary
The writer briefly describes the film's main events. Notice that he uses the present tense to summarize the story.

Reaction
The writer relates to the film's avatars. He supports his ideas with specific examples.

Viewers believe that the sleeping Jake enters the alien's body and moves easily on a distant planet.

The planet Pandora is beautiful. The clues that we are "not in Kansas anymore," as we are told early on, can be seen in every aspect of life on the planet. Cameron's use of 3D technology shines, completely immersing the viewer in the alien landscape. Many animals on Pandora, such as the pterodactyl-like creatures that inhabit the skies, are a shocking neon blue. Another quality we do not expect from most living things is light. Yet on Pandora, light glows from bright ferns and from the pulsating white moss floating among the trees. Although Pandora is a fantasy world, it makes us realize that there is beauty in our own planet that we have not noticed or valued.

An important message in the film is that we need to show greater appreciation for the ecological world. One of the most impressive sequences in the film shows Jake Sully training among the Na'vi for three months. Jake learns to let himself fall from great heights, trusting that trees and bushes will save him. Jake also creates relationships with magnificent flying lizards. Most importantly, he learns about a sacred tree and its importance to the planet's inhabitants. After learning Na'vi customs and rituals, he understands the tribe's reverence for the living, breathing forest that surrounds them. Near the end of the film, viewers recoil when they see tanks destroy the sacred tree and burn the forest. After watching the film, I took a closer look at the natural world near my home, and I wished I understood more about nature. I don't know the names of trees, and I don't know what plants are edible. I feel horrible when I think of the ways humans are destroying our planet.

Avatar is a remarkable film that brilliantly depicts aliens in a distant land, and it makes us reflect on our environment. It also shows how wars are often fought for economic reasons. I would highly recommend the film especially because the message is very relevant. In the film, as we watch ignorant and greedy humans destroy Pandora, we remember how our Earth's forests, water, and mineral resources are being plundered. But as Jake Sully quietly says, "Eventually, you always have to wake up."

A Sample Response to a Novel

College student Diego Pelaez responded to the novel *For Whom the Bell Tolls*. Review how he structured his response.

Lessons from *For Whom the Bell Tolls*

Robert Jordan says to himself, "You have only one thing to do and you must do it" (45). He plans the strategic destruction of a bridge in Ernest Hemingway's novel *For Whom the Bell Tolls*. The story, published in 1940, contains a relevant message. The novel follows Robert Jordan, an American university teacher and weapons expert, as he fights with Spanish republican forces against the fascist army led by Francisco Franco. *For Whom the Bell Tolls* asks difficult, relevant questions about the necessity of war, and it graphically depicts the consequences.

The novel opens with Jordan planning a strategic demolition of a bridge. The rest of the novel explains the preparations required for the risky operation. Jordan is a cold military strategist. He falls in love with Maria, a beautiful young woman. She had been brutalized by fascist forces and was then rescued and nurtured back to health by the guerrilla band. Pablo, the previous leader of the band, makes it clear that he wants nothing to do with the blowing up of the bridge, and his refusal is considered a sign of cowardice. In the meantime, Jordan's love for Maria and his growing loyalty to the guerrillas make his mission more difficult. Knowing that the enemy forces are too numerous, Jordan's attack on the bridge becomes more and more doomed as the story progresses.

I was greatly moved and at times horrified by the honest depictions of war in the novel. For example, there is a description of an earlier attack by Pablo's band. Pablo orders all the fascists to be brutally whipped, and members of his band make fun of their fascist captives. "Should we send to the house for thy spectacles?" (115) the crowd asks Don Guillermo, one of the fascist sympathizers. Then they attack him with flails (instruments used for cutting down grain), and they throw him over a cliff. The scene shows the excessive brutality involved in war, even wars that can be justified.

I sympathized greatly with the characters in the novel, particularly the main character, Robert Jordan. At first, Jordan views the guerrilla band at his disposal as means to an end. His priority is the mission more than the well-being of the guerrillas. However, as the story progresses, Jordan becomes conflicted. His love for Maria grows, and he realizes that he has something to live for. While lying beside Maria, "he held her, feeling she was all of life there was" (253).

The other characters are also diverse and fascinating. Pablo's wife, Pilar, is a voice of conscience, and she strongly condemns the treatment Don Guillermo receives. She says, "Nobody can tell me that such things as the killing of Don Guillermo in that fashion will not bring bad luck" (117). Also, the guerrilla band is a very likeable group, with a wise-cracking gypsy and the honorable old Anselmo, among others. Pledging allegiance to the cause, Anselmo says, "I am an old man who will live until I die" (19). Despite Jordan's growing affection for the group, he keeps planning the dangerous mission knowing that a lot of his new friends could die while carrying it out.

For Whom the Bell Tolls shows the horrors of war. The desire to drive the fascists out is seen as a worthy goal, even if there will be many deaths.

Thesis statement
He expresses the main focus of the essay.

Summary
The writer briefly describes the book's main events. Notice that he uses the present tense to narrate actions that happen within the story.

Reaction
The writer responds to the book's depiction of war. The page of each direct quotation is indicated in parentheses.

Reaction
The writer responds to the characters.

Support
The writer provides specific examples to show that the characters are varied and interesting.

Reaction
The writer responds to one of the book's messages.

Conclusion
*The writer ends
with a final insight
about the book.* ➤

However, the futility of war is also shown. Robert Jordan's single-minded determination becomes eroded by his new-found love and desire for life. As his death approaches, Jordon thinks, "The world is a fine place and worth fighting for, and I hate very much to leave it" (440).

In the end, war is presented as neither good nor bad, but rather as a simple fact of life. In the final scene of the novel, after the attack on the bridge, Jordan falls and critically injures himself. He tells the rest of the group to move on. Jordan waits for the fascists to come up the path and tries to remain conscious long enough to go out in a blaze of glory. Jordan can "feel his heart beating against the pine needle floor of the forest" (444). Ultimately, this excitement is as much a reason for war as any ideals.

The Writer's Room Responding to Film and Literature

Write a response to a short story, novel, or film. Remember to include an introduction, a summary, and several paragraphs explaining your reaction to the work.

✔ CHECKLIST: RESPONSE TO A LITERARY WORK OR A FILM

After you write your response, review the checklist on the inside front cover. Also, ask yourself these questions:

☐ Have I considered my audience and purpose?

☐ In the introduction, have I identified the title, author, and date?

☐ Have I given a short summary of the plot?

☐ Have I described my reactions to the work?

☐ Have I integrated specific quotations and examples?

☐ Have I summed up my main arguments in the conclusion?

☐ Have I properly cited my sources?

Tech
Teaching Tip:
Ask students to go online and input "classic short stories" into the search bar. Students can browse a site and find a story that they like. The story can become the basis of a "response" essay.

Teaching Tip:
For film and television show topics, refer to the Media Writing Activity at the ends of Chapters 6–14.

Teaching Tip:
Please encourage your students to submit their best responses to a film or literary text for possible publication to www.pearsonhighered.com/essayrewards/writingrewards.html.

 To check your progress in meeting this chapter's objectives, log in to **www.mywritinglab.com,** go to the **Study Plan** tab, click on **More College and Workplace Writing** and choose **Responding to Film and Literature** from the list of subtopics. Read and view the resources in the **Review Materials** section, and then complete the **Recall, Apply,** and **Write** sets in the **Activities** section.

The Essay Exam

CHAPTER 19

LEARNING OBJECTIVES

1 Preparing for Exams (p. 302)

2 Writing Essay Exams (p. 303)

Just as athletes rigorously train to win an important race, successful students follow specific strategies to ace exams.

Writer's Exchange

Tell a partner about your study habits. Discuss the following questions.

1. When you are given an assignment, how do you react? Do you procrastinate or start working right away?

2. When you are told about a test, what do you do? Do you panic? Do you plan study times? Do you give yourself enough time to study?

3. How do you balance your college, home, and work lives? Do you put too much emphasis on your social life? Do you spend too much time at a part-time job?

After you discuss the questions, brainstorm a list of steps students can take to become successful at college.

Teaching Tip:

Cooperative Learning (Pair & Share) Ask students to do the Writer's Exchange with a partner. They can create a list of steps together. Then pairs can discuss their answers with another pair.

Preparing for Exams

In many of your college courses, you will be asked to write essay exams. You will be expected to show what you know in an organized and logical manner. To be better prepared for such exams, try the following strategies.

Take meaningful notes. In class, listen carefully and take notes about key points. Your instructor might signal important ideas with phrases such as "and most importantly." Also, remember to date your notes. You will want a record of when you wrote them during the semester. The dates might help you to know what to focus on while you are studying.

Hint   **Using Abbreviations**

Many abbreviations we use in English derive from Latin terms. Here are some abbreviations to help you take notes more efficiently.

Abbreviation	English	Latin
e.g.	for example	exempli gratia
etc.	and so on	et cetera
i.e.	in other words	id est
N.B.	important	nota bene
vs., v.	against	versus

Keep in mind that these abbreviations are useful for note taking. When you write an essay, use the complete English words, not the abbreviations.

Review course material. Cramming is an ineffective, short-term strategy for college success. Instead, reviewing your course material *regularly*, perhaps every second day or each week, will ensure that you know your subjects well. Choose regular study times, and always spend that time studying.

Ask questions. When you don't understand something in class, speak up. Chances are great that others in the class also have problems understanding the material. Also consider speaking with your instructors during their office hours. Prepare questions about concepts, that you do not understand. Waiting until the day before your exam will be too late.

Study with a classmate or friend. Set a particular time each week, which will motivate you to study during times when you want to do something else. Ask each other questions on key concepts, or proofread each other's written work.

Predict exam questions. Look for important themes in your course outline. Also review your notes and identify what information is of particular importance. Look over previous exams and answer those questions. Finally, predict what types of questions will be on the exam. Write down possible questions and practice answering them.

PRACTICE I   Imagine that your English instructor will give you an exam next week. The exam will cover material from the past three weeks. What types of questions might your instructor ask? Brainstorm some ideas here.   Answers will vary.

_____

_____

_____

_____

_____

Teaching Tip:
Ask students to work with a partner who is in the same program. Together, the students can predict exam questions for this course or for a specific course.

Writing Essay Exams

In many of your courses, you will have to answer exam questions with a paragraph or essay to reveal how well you understand information. Although taking any exam can be stressful, you can reduce exam anxiety and increase your chances of doing well by following some of the preparation and exam-writing strategies outlined in this chapter.

Schedule Your Time

Before you write the exam, find out exactly how much time you have, and then plan how much time you will need to answer the questions. For example, if you have a one-hour exam, and you have three questions worth the same value, try to spend no more than twenty minutes on each question.

Determine Point Values

As soon as you get an exam, scan the questions and determine which questions have a larger value. For example, you might respond to the questions with the largest point value first, or you might begin with those that you understand well. Then go to the more difficult questions. If you are blocked on a certain answer, skip to another question, and then go back to that question later.

Carefully Read the Exam Questions

In an exam question, every word counts. Here are two ways you can read actively.

1. **Identify key words and phrases.** When you read an exam question, underline or circle key words and phrases to understand exactly what you are supposed to do. In the next example of an essay question, the underlined words highlight two different tasks.

    Discuss cost-plus pricing, and analyze its importance to a company.

    1. Define the term.
    2. Explain why it is important.

2. **Pay attention to common question words.** Directions for exam questions often use specific verbs (action words). The following chart gives you several common words that you will find in essay-style questions.

Teaching Tip:
Ask students to
identify verbs that
relate to a specific
essay pattern.

Verb	Meaning
describe discuss review	Examine a subject as thoroughly as possible. Focus on the main points.
narrate trace	Describe the development or progress of something using time order.
evaluate explain your point of view interpret justify take a stand	State your opinion and give reasons to support your opinion. In other words, write an argument essay.
analyze criticize classify	Explain something carefully by breaking it down into smaller parts.
enumerate list outline	Go through important facts one by one.
compare contrast distinguish	Discuss important similarities and/or differences.
define explain what is meant by	Give a complete and accurate definition that demonstrates your understanding of the concept.
explain causes	Analyze the reasons for an event.
explain effects	Analyze the consequences or results of an event.
explain a process	Give the steps needed to do a task.
illustrate	Demonstrate your understanding by giving examples.
summarize	Write down the main points from a larger piece of work.

PRACTICE 2   Write the letter of the correct key word in the space provided.

Topic

1. Explain how the gross domestic product (GDP) of a country is calculated. __c__

2. Explain the events that led to the end of World War I. __e__

3. Illustrate alternative energy sources. __f__

Key Word

a. compare and contrast

b. define

c. explain a process

d. argue

4. Distinguish between universal health care and privatized medicine. __a__

5. Discuss whether euthanasia should be legalized. __d__

6. Explain what utilitarianism is. __b__

e. explain causes

f. give examples

PRACTICE 3   The following is an exam from a sociology course. Read the instructions and then answer the questions that follow the sample.

Answer both parts A and B. You will have two hours to complete the evaluation.

Part A   Define two of the following terms. (5 points each)
1. democracy
2. theocracy
3. fascism
4. communism

Part B   Write a 300-word essay about one of the following topics. (40 points)

1. How will economic development in low-income countries improve if women are given a higher social status? Explain your answer.
2. How does poverty in poor nations compare with poverty in the United States?
3. Some consider the United States a "middle-class society." Explain how true you believe this claim to be.
4. Trace the stages of economic development.

Teaching Tip:
In Practice 3, you can ask students to identify which essay topic is argument, comparison and contrast, and narration.

1. What is the total point value of the exam? _____ *50 points* _____

2. How many definitions should you write? *Two* _____

   How many essays should you write? *One* _____

3. Which part of the exam would you do first? Explain why. Answers will vary.

   _____

   _____

4. How much time would you spend on Part A and Part B? Explain why.

   Answers will vary.

   _____

   _____

Teaching Tip:
Point out that Practice 3 contains the entire exam, which has two parts.

Follow the Writing Process

Treat an essay exam as you would any other writing assignment by following the three main steps of the writing process.

Explore   Jot down any ideas that you think can help you answer the question. Try the prewriting activities suggested in Chapter 1 of this book, such as brainstorming or clustering. Prewriting will help you generate some ideas for your essay.

Develop   Use the exam question to guide your thesis statement and topic sentences. List supporting ideas, organize your ideas using an essay plan or outline, and then write an essay. Remember to include an introduction with a clear thesis statement and to use transitions such as *first*, *moreover*, or *in addition* to link your ideas.

Revise and Edit   Read over your essay to verify that all ideas support the thesis statement and to ensure that you have adequate details to support your topic sentences. Also check your spelling, punctuation, and mechanics.

Hint   **Writing a Thesis Statement**

In an essay exam, your thesis statement should be very clear. A good strategy is to write a guided thesis statement that includes details you will cover in the essay. Review the essay topic and sample thesis statement.

Essay topic: Explain the key pricing strategies that companies use.

Thesis statement: The most common pricing strategies are **cost-plus pricing**, **target pricing**, and **yield-management pricing**.

PRACTICE 4   Write thesis statements for the following exam questions.   Answers will vary.

EXAMPLE: Discuss the influences of the industrial revolution on class structure.

Thesis statement: _The industrial revolution caused a dramatic change in_

traditional class structure.

1. How does poverty in the United States compare with poverty in poor nations?

    _____

    _____

    _____

2. Explain social class structure in the United States.

_____

_____

_____

3. What are the causes of poverty in America's cities?

_____

_____

_____

PRACTICE 5   College student Seokman Chang wrote the following essay for an exam. Read the essay and answer the questions that follow.

1   Throughout human history, there have been migratory movements of people all over the world. The Polynesians journeyed to and stayed in the Hawaiian Islands, the Vikings found homes in Great Britain and Ireland, and the Moguls settled in India. Today, the migration trend continues. People migrate to different parts of the world for many reasons and often bring benefits to the host region or country.

2   First, many people go to different countries searching for better work opportunities. For example, many groups of professionals migrate to get higher-paying jobs. There are engineers, teachers, lawyers, and computer specialists who have come to this country to broaden their skills and work experience. One day, in a supermarket line, I had a conversation with a woman from China. She and her husband had just arrived in this country. They were both doctors and were preparing to take the qualifying exams. Unskilled laborers also come to North America because the pay for such jobs is higher than in their homeland. A factory worker usually earns more per hour in an industrialized country than in a developing country. Most skilled and unskilled economic migrants go to new lands seeking a better quality of life.

3   Second, sometimes immigrants leave their homelands unwillingly. They may be forced to leave their homes because of famine or war. For example, there are droughts in some nations and wars in Congo, Darfur, Somalia, and other areas. Furthermore, sometimes people are expelled from their homeland. In 1972, the Ugandan dictator Idi Amin expelled the Indian community. They had very little time to pack up and leave. China and other countries have expelled some political activists, while other activists have fled for their lives, claiming political refugee status.

4   Moreover, some people leave their native lands to join family members who have already emigrated. Such cases are especially true of new

Teaching Tip:
Group Discussion
Ask your nonnative speakers about their first experiences in this country. When did they arrive? Why did they immigrate? What were their first impressions? Also ask your native speakers if they would ever consider moving to another country. If so, which one and why? What adjustments would they have to make?

Thesis Statement: People migrate to different parts of the world for many reasons and often bring benefits to the host region or country.

Topic Sentence 1: First, people go to different countries searching for better work opportunities.

Details:
– engineers, teachers, lawyers, computer specialists, and unskilled laborers
– couple from China

Topic Sentence 2: Second, sometimes immigrants leave their homeland unwillingly.

Details:
– war and famine such as in Darfur, Congo, . . .
– political refugees such as East Indians from Uganda and political activists

immigrants. Often new immigrants arrive in the new country alone. When they have settled, they send for their immediate family members. My neighbor came from Vietnam about ten years ago. For the first few years, he was in this country alone. He worked during the day and took night courses. As soon as he got settled, he sent for his parents because they were getting older and had no one to take care of them in Vietnam. Now the family is together again.

5   The receiving country gains many advantages from immigrants. New groups add to the cultural diversity of the country. North American cities have a variety of ethnic restaurants, grocery stores, and cultural festivals. In addition, Western countries need immigrants to maintain or increase the population. The birthrates of most developed countries are falling, and immigrants are needed to maintain population rates. New immigrants also bring skills that are advantageous to the host country. New immigrants perform many varied jobs, from fruit pickers and waiters to doctors and engineers. Immigrants contribute to the economy of the host country.

6   People leave their homelands for a variety of reasons, and their adopted countries gain tremendously from migration. The immigrant usually finds a more stable and prosperous life. The adopted countries of new immigrants gain tremendously in social and economic areas. So the next time you eat at your favorite Italian restaurant, dance to Carlos Santana, or debate the political influence of former governor of California Arnold Schwarzenegger, remember that immigration made it all possible.

1. This student essay is an answer to which of the following questions? Circle the best possible answer.
   a. Distinguish the periods of immigration to North America, and describe the migrant groups.
   b. Evaluate the current immigration policy of the nation.
   c. Explain why people leave their countries, and describe some consequences of their migration.

2. Highlight the thesis statement in the introduction. Also highlight the topic sentences in body paragraphs 2–5.

3. On a separate sheet of paper or on the computer, create a plan for this essay. For the details, just use words or phrases.

The Writer's Room   **Essay Exam Topics**

1. Predict at least three essay exam questions for one of your courses. Then develop an informal essay plan for one of the questions.
2. Look at an exam that you completed previously. Write a paragraph explaining what you could have done to receive a higher mark.

✔ **CHECKLIST: AN ESSAY EXAM**

As you prepare for your essay exam, ask yourself the following questions.

☐ Have I taken clear notes during lectures?

☐ Have I reviewed my notes on a regular basis?

☐ Have I organized study time?

☐ Have I asked my instructor questions when I didn't understand a concept?

☐ Have I asked my instructor what material the exam will cover?

 To check your progress in meeting this chapter's objectives, log in to **www.mywritinglab.com,** go to the **Study Plan** tab, click on **More College and Workplace Writing** and choose **Becoming a Successful Student** from the list of subtopics. Read and view the resources in the **Review Materials** section, and then complete the **Recall, Apply,** and **Write** sets in the **Activities** section.

Topic Sentence 3: Moreover, some people leave their native lands to join family members who have already emigrated.

Details:
– true of new immigrants
– neighbor from Vietnam

Topic Sentence 4: The receiving country gains many advantages from immigrants

Details:
– restaurants, food stores, festivals
– helps offset declining population due to low birth rate
– bring skilled and unskilled labor force, which helps the economy

Teaching Tip:
Writer's World Competition
Please advise students that they can submit their paragraphs and essays for possible publication to www .pearsonhighered .com/essayrewards/ writingrewards.html

Editing Handbook

When you speak, you have tools such as tone of voice and body language to help you express your ideas. When you write, however, you have only words and punctuation to get your message across. If your writing includes errors in style, grammar, and punctuation, you may distract readers from your message, and they may focus, instead, on your inability to communicate clearly. You increase your chances of succeeding in your academic and professional life when you write in clear, standard English.

This Editing Handbook will help you understand important grammar concepts, and the samples and practices in each chapter offer interesting information about many themes. Before you begin working with these chapters, review the contents and themes shown here.

Identifying Subjects and Verbs

Section Theme **CONFLICT**

Is behavior learned or genetic? In this chapter, you will learn about the sources of aggressive behavior.

Identifying Subjects

A **sentence** contains one or more subjects and verbs, and it expresses a complete thought. The **subject** tells you who or what the sentence is about.

- Subjects may be **singular** or **plural**. A subject can also be a **pronoun.**

  Detective Marcos will interview the suspects.
  Many **factors** cause people to break laws.
  It is an important case.

- A **compound subject** contains two or more subjects joined by *and*, *or*, or *nor*.

  Reporters and **photographers** were outside the prison gates.

- Sometimes a **gerund** (*-ing* form of the verb) is the subject of a sentence.

    Listening is an important skill.

   Here and *There*

Here and *There* are not subjects. In sentences that begin with *Here* or *There*, the subject follows the verb.

   There are several **ways** to find a criminal.

   Here is an interesting **brochure** about the police academy.

How to Find the Subject

To find the subject, ask yourself *who* or *what* the sentence is about. The subject is the noun or pronoun or the complete name of a person or organization.

   The **Federal Bureau of Investigation** is a large organization. **It** has branches in every state.

When identifying the subject, you can ignore words that describe the noun.

$$\underbrace{\text{The pompous and rude}}_{\text{adjectives}} \underset{\text{subject}}{\textbf{sergeant}} \text{ left the room.}$$

PRACTICE 1   Circle the subject in each sentence. Be careful because sometimes there is more than one subject.

EXAMPLE: A behavioral (study) examines genetics and behavior.

1. Research psychiatrist (Carl E. Schwartz) works in the Department of Psychiatry at Massachusetts General Hospital.
2. (He) conducted a study to determine hereditary factors in behavior.
3. There were more than one hundred (children) in his study.
4. (Infants) and (toddlers) were classed into two groups.
5. (Objects), strange (people), and unfamiliar (settings) were used to test the children.
6. (Talking) was not permitted.

Prepositional Phrases

A **preposition** is a word that links nouns, pronouns, and phrases to other words in a sentence. It expresses a relationship based on movement or position. A **prepositional phrase** is made up of a preposition and its object (a noun or a pronoun).

ESL
Teaching Tip:
Remind students that the *-ing* form can be a noun or a verb. Ask them to explain the difference between two sentences:
Relaxing is important.
I am *relaxing* right now.

Teaching Tip:
Before doing the grammar sections, ensure that students understand the basic "Parts of Speech" vocabulary. As they do the following activity, they can look at the glossary of terms in Appendix 1 if they need help. Ask students to create sentences using the following parts of speech: noun, verb, pronoun, adjective, adverb, preposition, conjunction, and interjection.

Because the object of a preposition is a noun, it may look like a subject. **However, the object in a prepositional phrase is never the subject of the sentence.**

prepositional phrase   subject
With the parents' approval, the **experiment** began.

Common Prepositions

about	among	beside	during	into	onto	toward
above	around	between	except	like	out	under
across	at	beyond	for	near	outside	until
after	before	by	from	of	over	up
against	behind	despite	in	off	through	with
along	below	down	inside	on	to	within

ESL
Teaching Tip:
Ask nonnative speakers to underline prepositions that they do not understand. They can discuss the meanings of those prepositions with other students in the class.

To help you identify the subject, put parentheses around prepositional phrases, as shown below. Notice that a sentence can contain more than one prepositional phrase.

(In spite of the storm), **they** drove (to the hospital).

The **clinic**, (after 1971), expanded greatly.

(In the late 1990s), (during a period of cost cutting), high-tech **cameras** were placed in the room.

> ### Hint   Using *of the*
>
> In most expressions containing *of the*, the subject appears before *of the*.
>
> subject
> **Each** (of the parents) has agreed to participate.
>
> **One** (of the fathers) was uncomfortable with the process.

PRACTICE 2   Circle the subject in each sentence. Also add parentheses around any prepositional phrases that are near the subject.

EXAMPLE: (For many years), Schwartz has studied genetics and behavior.

1. (In Schwartz's study,) half (of the babies) were classified as shy. The others (in the group) were classified as outgoing. (In unfamiliar surroundings,) the shy and outgoing children reacted differently. (For example,) (in the presence of a stranger,) the shy toddlers would freeze. The outgoing toddlers would approach the stranger and interact.

2. One of the main differences in reactions was in the heart rate. Also, each of the shy children had higher levels of stress hormones than the outgoing children. Generally, the differences in the temperament of children persisted into adulthood.

Identifying Verbs

Every sentence must contain a verb. The **verb** expresses what the subject does, or it links the subject to other descriptive words.

An **action verb** describes an action that a subject performs.

> Detective Rowland <u>attended</u> a seminar. He <u>spoke</u> to some officials.

A **linking verb** connects a subject with words that describe it, and it does not show an action. The most common linking verb is *be*, but other common linking verbs are *appear*, *become*, *look*, and *seem*.

> Kim Rossmo <u>is</u> a former detective. His methods <u>seem</u> reliable.

When a subject performs more than one action, the verbs are called **compound verbs.**

> In 2003, Rossmo <u>wrote</u> and <u>spoke</u> about his methods.

Helping Verbs

The **helping verb** combines with the main verb to indicate tense, negative structure, or question structure. The most common helping verbs are forms of *be*, *have*, and *do*. **Modal auxiliaries** are another type of helping verb, and they indicate ability (*can*), obligation (*must*), and so on. For example, here are different forms of the verb *ask*, and the helping verbs are underlined.

<u>is</u> asking	<u>had</u> asked	<u>will</u> ask	<u>should have</u> asked
<u>was</u> asked	<u>had been</u> asking	<u>can</u> ask	<u>might be</u> asked
<u>has been</u> asking	<u>would</u> ask	<u>could be</u> asking	<u>could have been</u> asked

The **complete verb** is the helping verb and the main verb. In the following examples, the main verb is double underlined. In **question forms,** the first helping verb usually appears before the subject.

> Criminal profiling techniques <u>have been <u>spreading</u></u> across the continent.

> <u>Should</u> the detective <u>have <u>studied</u></u> the files?   <u>Do</u> you <u>agree</u>?

Interrupting words such as *often*, *always*, *ever*, and *actually* are not part of the verb.

> Rossmo <u>has</u> often <u>returned</u> to Vancouver.

> ⟨*Hint*⟩   **Infinitives Are Not the Main Verb**
>
> **Infinitives** are verbs preceded by *to*, such as *to fly*, *to speak*, and *to go*. An infinitive is never the main verb in a sentence.
>
> infinitive
> The network <u>wanted</u> **to produce** a show about geographic profiling.

Teaching Tip:
Draw attention to the hint about infinitives. Students often confuse the infinitive with the main verb.

PRACTICE 3   In each sentence, circle the subject and underline the complete verb. Hint: You can cross out prepositional phrases that are near the subject.

EXAMPLE: (According to Professor Saundra K. Ciccarelli,) many ⟨factors⟩ <u>contribute</u> to aggressive behavior.

Teaching Tip:
To make the practice more challenging, you can ask students to identify helping verbs (H) and linking verbs (L) as well.

1. The ⟨amygdala⟩ <u>is</u> near the base of the brain. ⟨Studies⟩ <u>have shown</u> the amygdala's role in fear responses. In a 1939 experiment, the temporal ⟨lobe⟩ <u>was removed</u> from the brains of several monkeys. The ⟨lobe⟩ <u>contains</u> the amygdala. After the surgery, the ⟨monkeys⟩ <u>showed</u> absolutely no fear of snakes and humans. This ⟨anecdote⟩ <u>illustrates</u> the role of the brain in fearful or aggressive behavior.

Teaching Tip:
Group Work
Groups of students could practice identifying subjects and verbs by looking at a reading in Part V. They could focus on one or two paragraphs in the reading.

2. Why <u>do</u> ⟨people⟩ <u>harm</u> others? In her book *Psychology*, ⟨Ciccarelli⟩ <u>discusses</u> the connection between the brain and aggressive behavior. In 1966, ⟨Charles Whitman⟩ <u>shot</u> and <u>killed</u> fourteen people. Before his death in a shootout with police, ⟨Whitman⟩ <u>wrote</u> a note and <u>asked</u> doctors to examine the state of his brain. In fact, a later ⟨examination⟩ <u>revealed</u> the presence of a tumor next to his amygdala.

3. There <u>are</u> also chemical ⟨links⟩ to aggression, according to Ciccarelli. ⟨Testosterone⟩, in high levels, <u>has been shown</u> to cause aggressive behavior. Also, certain ⟨substances⟩ <u>have</u> an impact on the brain. ⟨Alcohol⟩ <u>affects</u> the amount of some brain chemicals and <u>reduces</u> a person's inhibitions.

Teaching Tip:
You can use the final review as a test. Additional practice and test material appears in the Instructor's Resource Manual and on *MyWritingLab*.

FINAL REVIEW

Circle the subjects and underline the complete verbs in the following sentences.

EXAMPLE: The study (about role models) is fascinating.

1. There are many ways to modify a person's behavior. Young children can be influenced by aggressive characters on television. Young adults may be pressured or manipulated by peers. One of the most interesting influences on behavior is social roles.

2. In the autumn of 1971, psychologist Philip Zimbardo conducted an experiment at Stanford University. Seventy healthy middle-class students were recruited. Each of the young men was given the role of a prison guard or a prisoner. Volunteers with the role of prisoner were kept in cells. The student guards wore uniforms and were given batons.

3. Very quickly, students in both roles modified their behavior. The prisoners became meek and resentful. There were also noticeable differences in the guards' attitudes. On the second day, the prisoners revolted. The guards aggressively crushed the rebellion. Then, with increasing intensity, the guards humiliated and physically restrained the prisoners. The behavior of the young men had changed.

4. Zimbardo was forced to end the experiment early. Why did the guards act so cruelly? According to psychologists, a uniform and a specific social role can have powerful influences on people's behavior.

The Writer's Room   Topics for Writing

Write about one of the following topics. After you finish writing, identify your subjects and verbs.

1. List various ways in which social roles influence people's behavior. Support your points with specific examples.
2. Some experts suggest that personality traits are partly inherited. Are your character traits similar to a family member's traits? Compare and contrast yourself with someone else in your family.

✔ CHECKLIST: SUBJECTS AND VERBS

Review this chapter's main points.

☐ To identify **subjects,** look for words that tell you who or what the sentence is about.

☐ To identify **verbs,** look for words that do the following:

- **Action verbs** describe the actions that the subject performs.
- **Linking verbs** describe a state of being or link the subject with descriptive words.
- **Helping verbs** combine with the main verb to indicate tense, negative structure, or question structure.

☐ To identify **prepositional phrases,** look for words that consist of a preposition and its object. Note: the object of a prepositional phrase cannot be the subject of the sentence.

prepositional phrase   helping verb

subject ↓ verb

In spite of criticism, the police (chief) has released the suspect.

Teaching Tip:
Writer's World Competition
Please advise students that they can submit their paragraphs and essays for possible publication to www .pearsonhighered .com/essayrewards/ writingrewards.html

mywriting**lab** To check your progress in meeting this chapter's objectives, log in to **www.mywritinglab.com,** go to the **Study Plan** tab, click on **The Editing Handbook—Section 1** and choose **Identifying Subjects and Verbs** from the list of subtopics. Read and view the resources in the **Review Materials** section, and then complete the **Recall, Apply,** and **Write** sets in the **Activities** section.

Sentence Combining

LEARNING OBJECTIVES

1 Understanding Key Words (p. 319)

2 Making Compound Sentences (p. 320)

3 Making Complex Sentences (p. 324)

Section Theme **CONFLICT**

In this chapter, you will read about eyewitness testimony, profiling techniques, and wrongful convictions.

Understanding Key Words

When you use sentences of varying lengths and types, your writing flows more smoothly and appears more interesting. You can vary sentences and create relationships between ideas by combining sentences. Before you learn about the types of sentences, it is important to understand some key terms.

- A **phrase** is a group of words that is missing a subject, a verb, or both, and is not a complete sentence.

    in the morning   acting on her own   the excited witness

- A **clause** is a group of words that contains a subject and a verb. There are two types of clauses.

  - An **independent clause** is also called a simple sentence. It stands alone and expresses one complete idea.

    The victims asked for compensation.

  - A **dependent clause** has a subject and a verb, but it cannot stand alone. It "depends" on another clause to be complete. A dependent clause usually begins with a subordinator such as *after*, *although*, *because*, *unless*, and *when*.

    . . . because they had lost a lot of money.

Teaching Tip:
You might ask students to discuss how a person can be dependent. Help them visualize that an independent person needs no help whereas a dependent person must lean on someone else. They can then apply this visual to sentence structure.

PRACTICE I Write S next to each complete sentence. If the group of words is not a complete sentence—perhaps it is a phrase or a dependent clause—then write X in the blank.

EXAMPLE: Circumstantial evidence is discounted.   _S_
                Although it may be reliable.   _X_

1. Circumstantial evidence is often very reliable.   _S_

2. Blood, for example.   _X_

3. It may match with the DNA of the victim.   _S_

4. Pieces of clothing, hair fibers, and other types of evidence.   _X_

5. Unless somebody altered it.   _X_

6. Such evidence is usually very good.   _S_

7. A credit card may place a criminal at the crime scene.   _S_

8. Although the suspect may have an alibi.   _X_

Teaching Tip:
As an additional activity, ask students to make the incomplete sentences complete in Practice I.

Making Compound Sentences
Combining Sentences
Using Coordinating Conjunctions

Teaching Tip:
To help students remember the seven coordinators, suggest that they learn the acronym f.a.n.b.o.y.s.

A **coordinating conjunction** joins two complete ideas and indicates the connection between them. The most common coordinating conjunctions are *for*, *and*, *nor*, *but*, *or*, *yet*, and *so*.

Complete idea   **, coordinating conjunction**   complete idea.

The detective collected the evidence, **and** the lab analyzed it.

Review the following chart showing coordinating conjunctions and their functions.

Conjunction	Function	Example
and	to join two ideas	Anna went to school, **and** she became a forensics expert.
but	to contrast two ideas	The courses were difficult, **but** she passed them all.
for	to indicate a reason	She worked very hard, **for** she was extremely motivated.
nor	to indicate a negative idea	The work was not easy, **nor** was it pleasant.
or	to offer an alternative	She will work for a police department, **or** she will work for a private lab.
so	to indicate a cause and effect relationship	She has recently graduated, **so** she is looking for work now.
yet	to introduce a surprising choice	She wants to stay in her town, **yet** the best jobs are in a nearby city.

ESL
Teaching Tip:
This chart is useful for nonnative speakers.

Teaching Tip:

Cooperative Learning (Jigsaw)
Place students in teams of three to five. Assign each team a grammar concept from the chapter. Teams are responsible for teaching the class about their topic. They should summarize key ideas, give examples, and prepare some practice sentences. Then each team can present a short lesson to the class. Another option is to ask students to number themselves from one to five. All of the ones get together, the twos, the threes, and so on. Students can take turns teaching others what they have learned.

> *Hint* **Recognizing Compound Sentences**
>
> To be sure that a sentence is compound, place your finger over the coordinator, and then ask yourself if the two clauses are complete sentences. In compound sentences, always place a comma before the coordinator.
>
> **Simple:** The witness was nervous **but** very convincing.
>
> **Compound:** The witness was nervous, **but** she was very convincing.

PRACTICE 2 Insert coordinating conjunctions in the blanks. Choose from the following list, and try to use a variety of coordinators. (Some sentences may have more than one answer.)

> but   or   yet   so   for   and   nor

EXAMPLE: In 1969, the FBI introduced criminal profiling as an investigative strategy, _____***and***_____ it has been quite successful.

1. Kim Rossmo is a renowned geographic profiler, ___*but / and*___ he is also an excellent detective. Rossmo examines the movements of criminals, _____*and*_____ he searches for specific patterns. According to Rossmo,

criminals attack places they know, ___*but / yet*___ they generally don't work in their own neighborhoods. Most people don't want to travel long distances for their jobs, ___*for*___ they are lazy. Criminals work the same way, ___*so*___ they stay relatively close to home.

2. Rossmo developed a fascinating mathematical formula, ___*yet / but*___ many police departments were skeptical about his ideas. Basically, he inputs the addresses of suspects into a computer, ___*and*___ he also inputs details about the crime scenes. His program looks for a "hot" area. Suspects may live directly in the center of the hot area, ___*or*___ they may live within a few blocks. For example, in the late 1990s, there were several sexual assaults in a town in Ontario, Canada, ___*so*___ Rossmo and his associates created a profile map. One particular suspect's home was compared with the location of the crime scenes, ___*and*___ it was placed in Rossmo's computer program. Originally, the main offender's name was low on a list of 316 suspects, ___*but*___ it rose to number 6 on the list after the profiling. The suspect was eventually tried and convicted for the crimes, ___*so / and*___ he went to prison.

Combining Sentences Using Semicolons (;)

Another way to form a compound sentence is to join two complete ideas with a semicolon. The semicolon replaces a coordinating conjunction.

Teaching Tip:
Remind students that sentences containing *and*, *but*, etc. are not necessarily compound. To show the differences between simple and compound sentences, write a few examples on the board (without punctuation), and then ask students how to punctuate each sentence. Here is an example you can use:

You can study criminology or forensics.

You can study criminology, or you can study forensics.

GRAMMAR LINK

For more practice using semicolons, see Chapter 24, Run-Ons.

Complete idea   ;   complete idea.

The eyewitness was certain; she pointed at the suspect.

> ## Hint   Use a Semicolon to Join Related Ideas
>
> Use a semicolon to link two sentences when the ideas are equally important and closely related. Do not use a semicolon to join two unrelated sentences.
>
> **Incorrect:** Some eyewitnesses make mistakes; I like to watch criminal trials.
> (The second idea has no clear relationship with the first idea.)
>
> **Correct:** One eyewitness misidentified a suspect; the witness was not wearing contact lenses that day.
> (The second idea gives further information about the first idea.)

PRACTICE 3   Make compound sentences by adding a semicolon and another complete sentence to each simple sentence. Remember that the two sentences must have related ideas.   Answers will vary.

EXAMPLE: Last year, Eric joined a gang *; he regretted his decision.*

1. Eric rebelled against his parents _____

   _____

2. At age fifteen, he acted like other teens _____

   _____

3. His friends tried to influence him _____

   _____

4. Some people don't have supportive families _____

   _____

Teaching Tip:
Advise students to use semicolons sparingly. Some students overuse them.

Combining Sentences Using Transitional Expressions

A **transitional expression** links two complete ideas and shows how they are related. Most transitional expressions are **conjunctive adverbs** such as *however* or *furthermore*.

Some Transitional Expressions

Addition	Alternative	Contrast	Time	Example or Emphasis	Result or Consequence
additionally	in fact	however	eventually	for example	consequently
also	instead	nevertheless	finally	for instance	hence
besides	on the contrary	nonetheless	frequently	namely	therefore
furthermore	on the other hand	still	later	of course	thus
in addition	otherwise		meanwhile	undoubtedly	
moreover			subsequently		

   If the second clause begins with a transitional expression, put a semicolon before it and a comma after it.

Complete idea   **; transitional expression,**   complete idea

   Stephen Truscott was not guilty; **nevertheless,** he was convicted.

CHAPTER 21

ESL

Teaching Tip:
Group Work
Ask nonnative
speakers to
underline
transitional words
that they do not
understand. Then, in
groups, those who
understand the
term can teach the
others by using the
term in a sentence.
Ensure that
nonnative speakers
are placed in groups
with native
speakers.

PRACTICE 4   Combine sentences using the following transitional expressions. Choose an expression from the list, and try to use a different expression in each sentence.   Answers will vary.

in fact	~~frequently~~	however	thus
therefore	moreover	nevertheless	eventually

EXAMPLE: DNA evidence is useful. *; frequently, it* ~~It~~ has helped clear many innocent people.

1. In the early 1990s, a comparison of hair samples could deliver a
   ; eventually, scientists
   conviction. ~~Scientists~~ developed more sophisticated techniques.

2. Dr. Edward Blake is a leading authority on DNA evidence. *; thus, he* ~~He~~ often

   testifies at trials.

3. According to Dr. Blake, microscopic hair analysis is not precise. *; nevertheless, it* ~~It~~ has

   secured convictions in many cases.

4. Billy Gregory's hair matched a hair found at a crime scene. *; in fact, both* ~~Both~~ strands of

   hair appeared identical.

5. The strands of hair had exactly the same color and width. *; however, they* ~~They~~ were

   genetically different.

6. Today, conventional hair comparison evidence is no longer allowed in most
   ; therefore, it
   courtrooms. ~~It~~ may become an obsolete science.

Making Complex Sentences

When you combine a dependent and an independent clause, you create a **complex sentence.** An effective way to create complex sentences is to join clauses with a **subordinating conjunction.** "Subordinate" means secondary, so subordinating conjunctions—or subordinators—are words that introduce secondary ideas.

If you use a subordinator at the beginning of a sentence, put a comma after the dependent clause. Generally, if you use a subordinator in the middle of the sentence, you do not need to use a comma.

Main idea	**subordinating conjunction**	secondary idea

The police arrived **because** the alarm was ringing.

Subordinating conjunction	secondary idea	,	main idea

Because the alarm was ringing, the police arrived.

Teaching Tip:
Remind students that in most cases there is no comma before *because*.

Meanings of Subordinating Conjunctions

Subordinating conjunctions create a relationship between the clauses in a sentence.

Subordinating Conjunction	Indicates	Example
as, because, since, so that	a reason, cause, or effect	He paid a lot because he wanted a reliable alarm system.
after, before, since, until, when, whenever, while	a time	After he drove home, he parked on the street.
as long as, even if, if, provided that, so that, unless	a condition	The alarm won't ring unless someone touches the car.
although, even though, though	a contrast	Although the alarm began to wail, nobody looked at the car.
where, wherever	a location	Wherever you go, you will hear annoying car alarms.

Hint ⟶ **More About Complex Sentences**

Complex sentences can have more than two clauses.

        1   2

Although males commit most violent crimes, more and more females engage

       3

in violent acts after they have joined gangs.

You can also combine compound and complex sentences. The next example is a **compound-complex sentence.**

      complex

Although Alicia is tiny, she is strong, and she is a dedicated police officer.

                  compound

Teaching Tip:
You might write two short sentences on the board (example: *The defendant won her case. Her supporters cheered.*) and ask students to join them with different subordinating conjunctions. Point out that the verb in the sentence would have to change to accommodate some of the conjunctions.

PRACTICE 5   Add a missing subordinating conjunction to each sentence. Use each subordinating conjunction only once.   Answers will vary.

although	when	because	since
even though	if	after	whenever

1. _____Whenever_____ DNA evidence does not match a suspect's DNA, that person is usually released from custody. However, some people can have more than one type of DNA in their bodies. Chimeras are people with two types of DNA. _____Although_____ chimeras are rare, they do exist.

2. Lydia Fairchild separated from her partner _____because_____ they fought too much. To receive financial help from the government, Fairchild had to prove that she was the biological mother of her children. _____Even though_____ she had given birth to her two children, her DNA showed no link to them. Eventually, scientists discovered matching DNA _____after_____ they tested her internal organs.

3. Chimerism occurs _____when_____ two separate eggs fuse during the first few days of pregnancy. The judge in the Fairchild case expressed concern _____since_____ he often denies paternity rights to fathers based on DNA evidence. Also, _____if_____ a criminal is a chimera, his DNA will not necessarily match the evidence in a crime scene.

Teaching Tip:
You might suggest that students do Practice 5 in pairs.

PRACTICE 6   Combine the sentences by adding a subordinating conjunction. Use a different subordinating conjunction in each sentence. Properly punctuate your sentences.   Answers will vary.

EXAMPLE: He entered the courtroom. Photographers snapped photos.

As he entered the courthouse, photographers snapped photos.

Or   _The photographers snapped photos as he entered the courthouse._

1. Stephen was fourteen years old. He was arrested.

When Stephen was fourteen years old, he was arrested.

_____

2. He proclaimed his innocence. The police refused to believe him.

   Although he proclaimed his innocence, the police refused to believe him.

   _____

3. He was extremely nervous. He appeared to be guilty.

   Because he was extremely nervous, he appeared to be guilty.

   _____

4. He was in jail. He finished high school.

   While he was in jail, he finished high school.

   _____

5. New evidence surfaced. He was released.

   After new evidence surfaced, he was released.

   _____

FINAL REVIEW

The following paragraphs contain only simple sentences. When sentences are not varied, the essay is boring to read. To give the paragraphs more sentence variety, combine at least ten sentences. You will have to add some words and delete others. Answers will vary.

Teaching Tip:
You can use the final review as a test. Additional practice and test material appears in the Instructor's Resource Manual and on *MyWritingLab*.

             When the   *, she*

EXAMPLE: ~~The~~ witness is traumatized. ~~She~~ might not remember her

        assailant's face.

1. In 1986, Marvin Anderson was arrested for rape. At his trial, the rape

            , and she   *After*

   victim pointed at him. ~~She~~ identified him as her rapist. Anderson was

            , he

   convicted of the crime. ~~He~~ was sent to jail. Fifteen years later, another man

        , and

   confessed./ Anderson was released. Dr. Rod Lindsay is an expert on

             because he

   eyewitness testimony. Dr. Lindsay is worried. ~~He~~ does not trust the

   methods used to collect eyewitness testimony.

2. According to Dr. Lindsay, all crime scene photos should be shown

       When the   *, it*

   sequentially. ~~The~~ witness examines each photo. ~~It~~ can be compared to his

Teaching Tip:
Pair Work
You might ask students to do the final review with a partner. They can discuss possible combining options, and they can get ideas from each other.

Teaching Tip:

Cooperative Learning (Quick Review)
Divide the class into teams of three or four. Assign a part of the chapter to each team. Each team should review the information and generate three questions. Then ask teams to read the questions aloud. Anybody in the class can answer a question. Or, as an alternative, you can ask teams to exchange questions and to answer another team's questions.

Teaching Tip:

Pair Work
Each student can peer-edit a partner's work. Ask each pair to look specifically for places where sentences can be combined. Students can also determine whether compound and complex sentences are properly written and punctuated.

or her memory. Photos should also have similar color and lighting.

In the Anderson case, the police showed the rape victim a page with

six small photos. One photo was in color. *; the* ~~The~~ other photos were

black and white. The victim picked the color photo. *; but the* ~~The~~ man shown in the

color photo was not guilty.

3. Furthermore, police departments should use the "double-blind" procedure.

Sometimes, police officers know about the main suspect. *; therefore, they* ~~They~~ might cue

the witness unconsciously. The double-blind procedure ensures that the

person showing the photos does not know the main suspect.

4. *When* Dr. Lindsay contacted thirty-three police departments. *, only* ~~Only~~ six used the

double-blind procedure. Nine showed photos sequentially. In Dr.

Lindsay's opinion, many people are wrongfully convicted. *because witnesses* ~~Witnesses~~

misidentify them. It is unfortunate. *, but eyewitness* ~~Eyewitness~~ testimony can be seriously

flawed.

The Writer's Room

Write about one of the following topics. Include some compound and some complex sentences.

1. Do you watch crime shows or read about crime? Narrate what happened in your favorite crime show, movie, or book.
2. What can people do to reduce the risk of being robbed? List several steps that people can take.

✔ CHECKLIST: COMBINING SENTENCES

When you edit your writing, ask yourself these questions.

☐ Are my compound and complex sentences complete?

> *He was arrested because*
> ~~Because~~ of the scandal.

☐ Are my sentences correctly punctuated?

- In compound sentences, place a comma before the coordinator.
- In complex sentences, place a comma after a dependent introductory clause.

Comma:	The case was dismissed, and the suspect was freed.
Comma:	After she was released, she tried to find a job.
No comma:	She tried to find a job after she was released.

Teaching Tip:
Writer's World Competition
Please advise students that they can submit their paragraphs and essays for possible publication to www .pearsonhighered .com/essayrewards/ writingrewards.html

mywritinglab To check your progress in meeting this chapter's objectives, log in to **www.mywritinglab.com,** go to the **Study Plan** tab, click on **The Editing Handbook—Section 1** and choose **Sentence Combining** from the list of subtopics. Read and view the resources in the **Review Materials** section, and then complete the **Recall, Apply,** and **Write** sets in the **Activities** section.

Sentence Variety

Section Theme **CONFLICT**

In this chapter, you will read about crime and prisons.

What Is Sentence Variety?

In Chapter 21, you learned to write different types of sentences. In this chapter, you will learn to vary your sentences by consciously considering the length of sentences, by altering the opening words, and by joining sentences using different methods.

Consider the following example. The first passage sounds choppy because the sentences are short and uniform in length. When the passage is rewritten with sentence variety, it flows more smoothly.

Teaching Tip:
Ask students to discuss how the sentences have been modified in the version with sentence variety.

No Sentence Variety

The diamond necklace was in the cabinet. It was beautiful. Alberto picked the lock with expertise. He opened the glass door slowly. He held his breath. An alarm suddenly went off.

Sentence Variety

The diamond necklace, which was beautiful, was in the cabinet. With expertise, Alberto picked the lock. Opening the glass door slowly, he held his breath. Suddenly, an alarm went off.

Hint   **Be Careful with Long Sentences**

If your sentence is too long, it may be difficult for the reader to understand. Also, you may accidentally write run-on sentences. If you have any doubts, break up a longer sentence into shorter ones.

Long and complicated	In the eighteenth century, England sent convicts to the American colonies and to Australia, and the program was designed to rid Britain of undesirable criminals, but it also provided the colonies with a captive force of workers who would build roads, bridges, and housing.
Better	In the eighteenth century, England sent convicts to the American colonies and to Australia. The program was designed to rid Britain of undesirable criminals. It also provided the colonies with a captive force of workers who would build roads, bridges, and housing.

Teaching Tip: Read aloud each selection in the Hint box, and then point out that the second selection is much easier to understand.

PRACTICE 1   Combine the following sentences to provide sentence variety. Create some short and some long sentences.

Answers will vary.

There were many early punishment methods. One method was called a pillory. It had a hinge. It could lock a person's head and hands in place. An offender had to stand in the public square. He or she would feel humiliated. Citizens would see the person. They would yell at the offender. Sometimes they would throw eggs and tomatoes. The punishment method ended in 1905. Delaware was the last state to abandon it.

Varying the Opening Words

An effective way to make your sentences more vivid is to vary the opening words. Instead of beginning each sentence with the subject, you could try the following strategies.

Begin with an Adverb (-*ly* Word)

An **adverb** is a word that modifies a verb, and it often (but not always) ends in -*ly*. *Quickly* and *frequently* are adverbs. Non -*ly* adverbs include words such as *sometimes* and *often*.

> <u>Quickly</u>, the criminal left the scene.

Teaching Tip:

Cooperative Learning (Jigsaw)
Place students in teams of three to five. Assign each team a grammar concept from the chapter. Teams are responsible for teaching the class about the concept. They should summarize key ideas, give examples, and prepare some practice sentences. Then each team can present a short lesson to the class. Another option is to ask students to number themselves from one to five. All of the ones get together, the twos, the threes, and so on. Students can take turns teaching others what they have learned.

Begin with a Prepositional Phrase

A **prepositional phrase** is a group of words made up of a preposition and its object. *In the morning* and *at dawn* are prepositional phrases.

> <u>On the courtroom steps</u>, the defendant covered his head with his jacket.

Begin with a Present Participle (-*ing* Verb)

You can begin your sentence with a **present participle,** or -*ing* word. Combine sentences using an -*ing* modifier only when the two actions happen at the same time.

> <u>Reaching for her identification</u>, she asked the officer why she had been pulled over.

Begin with a Past Participle (-*ed* Verb)

You can begin your sentence with a **past participle,** which is a verb that has an -*ed* ending. There are also many irregular past participles such as *gone, seen,* and *known*.

> <u>Charged</u> with speeding, the woman received a ticket.

PRACTICE 2   Combine the sets of sentences using the indicated words.   Answers will vary.

EXAMPLE: The thief worked quickly.   (-*ing* verb)
              The thief broke into the car.

Working quickly, the thief broke into the car.

1. The woman watched the police cruiser arrive.   (-*ly* word)
    She was anxious.

    Anxiously, the woman watched the police cruiser arrive.

2. She spoke clearly.   (-*ing* verb)
   She described the thief.

   Speaking clearly, she described the thief.

3. The officer promised to help.   (prepositional phrase)
   He did this with a smile.

   With a smile, the officer promised to help.

4. The woman was raised to be polite.   (-*ed* verb)
   She thanked the officer.

   Raised to be polite, the woman thanked the officer.

5. The thief was arrested an hour later.   (-*ed* verb or -*ing* verb)
   The thief claimed to be innocent.

   *Arrested an hour later, the thief claimed to be innocent. OR Claiming
   to be innocent, the thief was arrested an hour later.*

Combining Sentences with an Appositive

GRAMMAR LINK

For a list of irregular past participles, see Appendix 2.

An **appositive** is a word or phrase that gives further information about a noun or pronoun. You can combine two sentences by using an appositive. In the example, the italicized phrase could become an appositive because it describes the noun *Mr. Zlatko*.

> **Two sentences:** Mr. Zlatko was *a middle-aged male*.
> He lost his savings.

You can place the appositive directly before the word that it refers to or directly after that word. Notice that the appositives are set off with commas.

> appositive
> **Combined:** A middle-aged male, **Mr. Zlatko** lost his savings.

> appositive
> **Mr. Zlatko**, a middle-aged male, lost his savings.

PRACTICE 3   Combine the following pairs of sentences. In each pair, make one of the sentences an appositive. Try to vary the position of the appositive.   Answers will vary.

EXAMPLE: The man ~~was~~ a thief. ~~He~~ was sentenced to three years in prison.

1. Adam Liptak is a journalist. He writes for the *New York Times*.

2. He writes about America. ~~It is~~ a place with the highest incarceration rate in the world.

3. The war on drugs is a major cause. ~~It~~ has contributed to the skyrocketing prison population.

4. Duval County jail is a prison in Jacksonville. ~~It~~ has too many inmates.

5. Sam Taylor was arrested on March 15. ~~It was~~ a day that changed his life.

6. Taxpayers spend a lot of money *, about $60 billion,* to maintain prisons. ~~They spend about $60 billion.~~

Combining Sentences with Relative Clauses

A **relative pronoun** describes a noun or pronoun. You can form complex sentences by using relative pronouns to introduce dependent clauses. Review the most common relative pronouns.

who   whom   whomever   whose   which   that

Which

Use *which* to add nonessential information about a thing. Generally use commas to set off clauses that begin with *which*.

> The crime rate, **which** peaked in the 1980s, has fallen in recent years.

That

Use *that* to add information about a thing. Do not use commas to set off clauses that begin with *that*.

> The car **that** was stolen belonged to a police officer.

Who

Use *who* (*whom, whomever, whose*) to add information about a person. When a clause begins with *who*, you may or may not need a comma. Put commas around the clause if it adds nonessential information. If the clause is essential to the meaning of the sentence, do not add commas. To decide if a clause is essential or not, ask yourself if the sentence still makes sense without the *who* clause. If it does, the clause is not essential.

ESL
Teaching Tip:
Draw attention to the spelling of *which*. It is a word that nonnative speakers commonly misspell.

GRAMMAR LINK

For more information about punctuating relative clauses, refer to Chapter 35.

The woman **who** committed the theft did not use a gun.
(The clause is essential. The sentence needs the "who" clause to make sense.)

The female thief, **who** spent a lot on legal fees, was sentenced to ten years in prison.
(The clause is not essential.)

> ## Hint ▸ Using *That* or *Which*
>
> Both *which* and *that* refer to things, but *which* refers to nonessential ideas. Also, *which* can imply that you are referring to the entire subject and not just a part of it. Compare the next two sentences.
>
> The shirts **that** had stains provided DNA evidence.
> (This sentence suggests that some shirts had no stains.)
>
> The shirts, **which** had stains, provided DNA evidence.
> (This sentence suggests that all of the shirts had stains.)

PRACTICE 4   Using a relative pronoun, combine each pair of sentences. Read both sentences before you combine them. Having the full context will help you figure out which relative pronoun to use.
Answers will vary.

EXAMPLE: Crime varies from culture to culture. ~~It~~ can force societies to change.
, which *,*

1. Sociologist Emile Durkheim was from France. ~~He~~ believed that deviant behavior can sometimes help societies.
, who *,*

2. Definitions of criminal behavior are agreed on by citizens. ~~The definitions~~ can change over time.
, which *,*

3. In many countries, people express their opinions about the government. ~~These people~~ are breaking the law.
who

4. Last year, some citizens in Iran criticized government policies. ~~They~~ were imprisoned.
who

5. In the 1960s, Americans broke Jim Crow laws. ~~They~~ were arrested.
who

Teaching Tip:
To help students understand essential versus nonessential information, give them the next sentences. Show them that some sentences can still be understandable without the *who* clause, whereas others can't. *The man who robbed me apologized. The man who torched the building was a dentist. Mr. Ray, who has two children, escaped from prison.*

Teaching Tip:
Remind students to put commas around *which* clauses. They should also be careful with *who* clauses; they should put commas around *who* clauses that contain nonessential information.

who

6. Sometimes activists are treated as criminals. ~~They~~ actually help change

   society.

CHAPTER 22

PRACTICE 5   Add dependent clauses to each sentence. Begin each clause with a relative pronoun (*who*, *which*, or *that*). Add any necessary commas.   Answers will vary.

EXAMPLE: The case **_that involved an adolescent boy_** was made into a documentary.

1. The boy _____ *who was in the store* _____ did not commit the crime.

2. His lawyers _____ *, who were unpaid,* _____ did not have all of the evidence.

3. The jury came to a conclusion _____ *that was not accurate.* _____

4. The judge sentenced the boy _____ *who was innocent* _____ to a long prison term.

5. Sometimes mistakes _____ *that could have been avoided* _____ can change the lives of individuals.

6. The case _____ *, which was widely publicized,* _____ brought attention to the wrongfully convicted.

Teaching Tip:
The specific distinction between *which* and *that* is complicated, but students sometimes ask to know the difference. Here is another example to help clarify the difference between *that* and *which*. Bears **that** have white fur live in the Arctic. Bears, **which** have white fur, live in the Arctic. (The second sentence incorrectly suggests that all bears have white fur.)

Writing Embedded Questions

It is possible to combine a question with a statement or to combine two questions. An **embedded question** is a question that is set within a larger sentence.

Question:
How old was the victim?

Embedded question:
The detectives wondered <u>how old the victim was.</u>

In questions, there is generally a helping verb before the subject. However, when a question is embedded in a larger sentence, remove the helping verb or place it after the subject. As you read the following examples, pay attention to the word order in the embedded questions.

1. **Combine two questions.**

   Separate: Why **do** people commit crimes? Do you know?

   (In both questions, the helping verb is *do.*)

   Combined: Do you know <u>why people commit crimes?</u>

   (The helping verb *do* is removed from the embedded question.)

2. **Combine a question and a statement.**

> **Separate:** How **should** society treat young offenders? I wonder about it.
>
> (In the question, the helping verb *should* appears before the subject.)
>
> **Combined:** I wonder <u>how society should treat young offenders</u>.
>
> (In the embedded question, *should* is placed after the subject.)

> *Hint* **Use the Correct Word Order**
>
> When you edit your writing, ensure that you have formed your embedded questions properly.
>
> Dr. Alvarez wonders why ~~do~~ people commit crimes. I asked her what
>
> *she thought*
>
> ~~did she think~~ about the issue.

PRACTICE 6 Edit six errors in embedded questions.

people can

EXAMPLE: The writer explains how ~~can people~~ become criminals.

the crime rate is

1. Many experts wonder why ~~is the crime rate~~ so high. Parents may ask how
role models are
~~are role models~~ a factor. Some blame icons in youth culture. For example,

a recent newspaper report linked the hateful words found in some gangsta

rap songs to youth crime.

people can

2. However, it is unclear how ~~can people~~ criticize only singers or other

celebrities from youth culture. In fact, they should really ask why ~~are~~ so many
are
"pillars" of society˄ deviant. For example, voters wonder why ~~do~~ politicians

cheat on their spouses and take bribes. Also, corporate executives have stolen

from shareholders, and prominent religious figures have promoted

intolerance and hatred. Perhaps reporters should question why ~~have~~ so many
have
people in highly regarded positions of authority˄ abused their power.

Teaching Tip:
Draw attention to problems with embedded questions. You might put extra examples on the board. For example, you could write a question such as *How old is he?* or *Why did he plead guilty?* and then ask the students to make the question embedded by adding *Do you know* or *I wonder*.

Teaching Tip:
Both native and nonnative speakers make embedded question errors, so draw special attention to the hint.

FINAL REVIEW

The next essay lacks sentence variety. Use the strategies that you have learned in this chapter, and create at least ten varied sentences.   Answers will vary.

, believing

EXAMPLE: Criminal profilers study crime scenes. ~~They believe~~ that they can determine the personality of the perpetrator.

who

1. Two people were at a bus stop. A large man ^ tried to take a woman's

    purse. ~~He~~ was very aggressive. An innocent bystander intervened. He

    Suddenly, the
    asked the man to leave the woman alone. ~~The~~ thief pushed the

    , which
    bystander. ~~This~~ caused the bystander to fall and crack his head

    on the pavement. The woman got onto the next bus.

    Thinking that the situation was under control, the

2. The police arrived. ~~The~~ witnesses left the scene. ~~They thought that the~~

    ~~situation was under control.~~ Susan Helenchild ~~is a prosecutor. She~~ has

    Remaining at the crime scene, they
    advice for witnesses. ~~They~~ should give their names and addresses to police

    Without evidence, a
    officers. ~~They should remain at the crime scene.~~ A court cannot easily

    convict a guilty person. ~~The court needs evidence.~~

    who

3. A girl ^ arrived after the crime had occurred. ~~She~~ was interviewed by the

    police. She said nothing important. The prosecutor asked the police to

    Earlier in the day, the
    interview her again. ~~The~~ girl had seen the thief ~~earlier in the day~~. He was

    drunk and aggressive. In court, the thief claimed to be calm and gentle.
    Blaming   , he
    ~~He blamed~~ the victim for the crime. ~~He~~ called the victim aggressive. The

    , which
    girl's testimony ^ helped the prosecution. ~~Her testimony~~ contradicted the

    words of the accused.

    Officers often wonder why

4. ~~Why do~~ witnesses leave crime scenes? ~~Officers often wonder.~~ Helenchild ^

    ~~feels~~ frustrated with such witnesses. ~~She~~ says that any evidence can help the prosecution. Witnesses should always give contact information to

police officers.

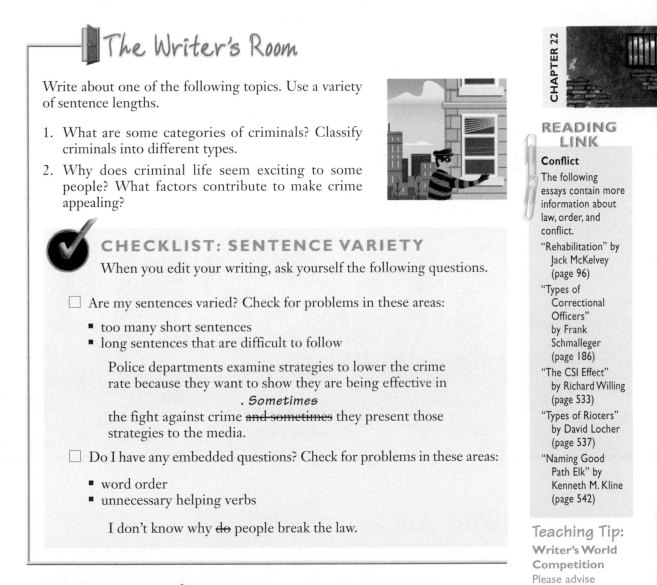

The Writer's Room

Write about one of the following topics. Use a variety of sentence lengths.

1. What are some categories of criminals? Classify criminals into different types.

2. Why does criminal life seem exciting to some people? What factors contribute to make crime appealing?

✔ CHECKLIST: SENTENCE VARIETY

When you edit your writing, ask yourself the following questions.

☐ Are my sentences varied? Check for problems in these areas:

- too many short sentences
- long sentences that are difficult to follow

  Police departments examine strategies to lower the crime rate because they want to show they are being effective in
  . Sometimes
  the fight against crime ~~and sometimes~~ they present those strategies to the media.

☐ Do I have any embedded questions? Check for problems in these areas:

- word order
- unnecessary helping verbs

  I don't know why ~~do~~ people break the law.

READING LINK

Conflict
The following essays contain more information about law, order, and conflict.

"Rehabilitation" by Jack McKelvey (page 96)

"Types of Correctional Officers" by Frank Schmalleger (page 186)

"The CSI Effect" by Richard Willing (page 533)

"Types of Rioters" by David Locher (page 537)

"Naming Good Path Elk" by Kenneth M. Kline (page 542)

Teaching Tip:
Writer's World Competition
Please advise students that they can submit their paragraphs and essays for possible publication to www.pearsonhighered.com/essayrewards/writingrewards.html

mywritinglab To check your progress in meeting this chapter's objectives, log in to **www.mywritinglab.com,** go to the **Study Plan** tab, click on **The Editing Handbook—Section I** and choose **Sentence Variety** from the list of subtopics. Read and view the resources in the **Review Materials** section, and then complete the **Recall, Apply,** and **Write** sets in the **Activities** section.

Fragments

Section Theme **URBAN DEVELOPMENT**

In this chapter, you will read about the development of suburbs and cities.

What Are Fragments?

A **fragment** is an incomplete sentence. It lacks either a subject or a verb, or it fails to express a complete thought. You may see fragments in newspaper headlines and advertisements (e.g., "Overnight Weight Loss"). You may also use fragments to save space when you are writing a text message. However, in college writing, it is unacceptable to write fragments.

> **Sentence:** More and more people are moving to urban centers.
>
> **Fragment:** In developing countries.

Phrase Fragments

Phrase fragments are missing a subject or a verb. In each example, the fragment is underlined.

No verb: <u>The history of cities</u>. It is quite interesting.

No subject: Ancient civilizations usually had one major city. <u>Specialized in trades</u>.

How to Correct Phrase Fragments

To correct phrase fragments, add the missing subject or verb, or join the fragment to another sentence. The following examples show how to correct the previous phrase fragments.

Join sentences: The history of cities is quite interesting.

Add words: Ancient civilizations usually had one major city. **The citizens in that city** specialized in trades.

Teaching Tip:

Cooperative Learning (Jigsaw)
Place students in teams of three to five. Assign each team a grammar concept from the chapter. Teams are responsible for teaching the class about their topic. They should summarize key ideas, give examples, and prepare some practice sentences. Then each team can present a short lesson to the class. Another option is to ask students to number themselves from one to five. All of the ones get together, the twos, the threes, and so on. Students can take turns teaching others what they have learned.

> ⬭ *Hint*   **Incomplete Verbs**
>
> The following example is a phrase fragment because it is missing a helping verb. To make this sentence complete, you must add the helping verb.
>
> **Fragment:** Modern cities growing rapidly.
>
> **Sentence:** Modern cities <u>are</u> growing rapidly.

PRACTICE I   Underline and correct eight phrase fragments.
Answers will vary.

It was founded
EXAMPLE: Damascus is one of the world's oldest cities. <u>~~Founded~~ in the third millennium B.C.E.</u>

1. The first cities began in ancient civilizations. <u>Mesopotamia, the Indus Valley, and China.</u> ~~Those~~ were large ancient civilizations. Early cities had only around 150,000 people. Eventually, ancient cities grew. Rome reached a population of one million. <u>Bhagdad.</u> ~~It~~ exceeded that number. London
   d
   became the largest city in the world. ~~D~~<u>uring the Middle Ages</u>.

2. The Industrial Revolution was an important phenomenon. ~~For~~ the growth
   of cities. Many people migrated from the countryside to urban centers. ~~In~~
   the eighteenth and nineteenth centuries. Urbanization led to many
   social troubles. Some common problems were child labor. ~~And~~ low
   wages.

3. During the Great Depression. ~~People~~ lost jobs and moved to the cities.
   Economic prosperity increased. ~~After~~ World War II. Today, most cities are
   prospering.

Teaching Tip:
Mention that although some professional writers may use fragments for effect, students should not use fragments in academic writing.

Teaching Tip:
Native and nonnative speakers often write sentence fragments. Emphasize how important it is to verify that all sentences in their writing express a complete idea. Students may need to review how to identify subjects and verbs. Refer them to Chapter 20.

Fragments with *-ing* and *to*

A fragment may begin with a **present participle,** which is the form of the verb that ends in *-ing* (*running*, *talking*). It may also begin with an **infinitive,** which is *to* plus the base form of the verb (*to run*, *to talk*). These fragments generally appear next to another sentence that contains the subject. In the examples, the fragments are underlined.

-*ing* fragment:	<u>Reacting to urban sprawl.</u> City planners started a new movement in the 1980s and 1990s.
to fragment:	Urban designers believe in the new urbanism. <u>To help people live better lives.</u>

How to Correct *-ing* and *to* Fragments

To correct an *-ing* or *to* fragment, add the missing words or join the fragment to another sentence. The following examples show how to correct the two previous fragments.

Join sentences:	Reacting to urban sprawl, **city** planners started a new movement in the 1980s and 1990s.
Add words:	Urban designers believe in the new urbanism. **They want** to help people live better lives.

> **Hint** **When the -*ing* Word Is the Subject**
>
> Sometimes a gerund (-*ing* form of the verb) is the subject of a sentence. In the example, *cycling* is the subject of the sentence.
>
> **Correct sentence:** <u>Cycling</u> is a great form of exercise in urban areas.
>
> A sentence fragment occurs when the -*ing* word is part of an incomplete verb string or when you mention the subject in a previous sentence. In the example, the fragment is underlined.
>
> **Fragment:** Many city dwellers get exercise. <u>Cycling on bike paths.</u>

Teaching Tip:
Nonnative speakers may confuse gerunds and progressive verb forms. Point out that gerunds function as nouns.

Teaching Tip:
Team Work
Ask students to generate the names of book, movie, and song titles. Write some of the titles on the board. Ask students to identify which titles are complete sentences. If all of the titles are fragments, then ask teams of students to create complete sentences out of the fragments.

PRACTICE 2   Underline and correct eight -*ing* and *to* fragments.
Answers will vary.

One principle is designing

EXAMPLE: The new urbanism movement has many principles. ~~Designing~~ <u>walkways in neighborhoods.</u>

1. New urbanism is a suburban planning movement. ~~To~~ <u>To create people-</u> *t* <u>friendly neighborhoods.</u> Urban planners design self-contained neighborhoods. ~~To~~ <u>To limit the use of cars.</u> *t* <u>Believing in the need to curtail</u> <u>urban sprawl.</u> ~~Architects~~ plan areas where people can walk to work. *, a*

2. The new urbanism movement is a reaction against older suburban areas. After World War II, architects designed suburbs that relied heavily on cars. <u>Living in traditional suburbs.</u> ~~Most~~ people must *, m* drive to the city centers to go to work. The commute causes traffic congestion and air pollution. Suburban dwellers waste a lot of time. ~~Traveling~~ <u>Traveling in their cars.</u> *t* Urban sprawl also creates problems for people who do not

, l
drive. ~~L~~imiting their daily activities. Nondrivers must find other means of

t
transport. ~~T~~o do errands downtown or at the mall.

3. Since 1990, the new urbanism movement has become very popular. City

t
planners design beautiful and functional areas. ~~T~~o improve the quality of

suburban life.

Teaching Tip:
Ask students to pay
particular attention
to explanatory
fragments, as they
are the most
common types of
fragments.

Explanatory Fragments

An **explanatory fragment** provides an explanation about a previous sentence and
is missing a subject, a complete verb, or both. These types of fragments begin
with one of the following words.

also	especially	for example	including	particularly
as well as	except	for instance	like	such as

In the examples, the explanatory fragment is underlined.

Fragment: Planners in the 1960s influenced the new urbanism movement.
For example, Jane Jacobs.

Fragment: New urbanism planners take into consideration many factors.
Especially reducing the use of the automobile.

How to Correct Explanatory Fragments

To correct explanatory fragments, add the missing words, or join the explanation
or example to another sentence. The following examples show how to correct the
previous explanatory fragments.

Add words: Planners in the 1960s influenced the new urbanism
movement. For example, Jane Jacobs **was an important
authority on urban planning**.

Join sentences: New urbanism planners take into consideration many
factors, **especially** reducing the use of the automobile.

PRACTICE 3 Underline and correct eight explanatory fragments.
You may need to add or remove words.   Answers will vary.

, such as
EXAMPLE: Some new urbanism towns are famous. ~~Such as~~ Celebration.

1. Seaside, Florida, became the first community built using new urbanism

principles. The town started in 1981 and became very famous.

For example, *The Atlantic Monthly.* ~~It~~ featured Seaside on its cover. The
developer Robert Davis hired experts in new urban planning. *, s* ~~Such as~~
architects and designers.

2. Seaside was easy to build because the area did not have traditional rules for
    there were
    developing land. For instance, no zoning regulations. The buildings in the
    , p
    town have uniform designs. ~~Particularly~~ the houses. They all have certain
    features. Porches, for example, must be sixteen feet from the sidewalk.
    Also, the streets. ~~They~~ must be made of bricks so cars cannot speed.
    , e
    Other towns are based on the same principles. ~~Especially,~~ Celebration,
    Florida.

3. Many people criticize such communities. *, p* ~~Particularly~~ the conformity of
    design. On the other hand, some people hope to live in an ideal locale.
    they would like
    For instance, no crime. However, critics point out that all communities
    have some social problems.

Dependent-Clause Fragments

A **dependent clause** has a subject and a verb, but it cannot stand alone. It
depends on another clause to be a complete sentence. Dependent clauses may
begin with subordinating conjunctions or relative pronouns. The following list
contains some of the most common words that begin dependent clauses.

Common Subordinating Conjunctions				**Relative Pronouns**
after	before	though	whenever	that
although	even though	unless	where	which
as	if	until	whereas	who(m)
because	since	what	whether	whose

In each example, the fragment is underlined.

Fragment: In the city, houses are close together. <u>Whereas in the suburbs, houses have large yards.</u>

Fragment: <u>Before William Levitt built Levittown.</u> Many people lived in congested neighborhoods.

How to Correct Dependent-Clause Fragments

To correct dependent-clause fragments, join the fragment to a complete sentence, or add the necessary words to make it a complete idea. You could also delete the subordinating conjunction. The following examples show how to correct the previous dependent-clause fragments.

Delete subordinator: In the city, houses are close together. In the suburbs, houses have large yards.

Join sentences: Before William Levitt built Levittown, many people lived in congested neighborhoods.

PRACTICE 4   Underline and correct eight dependent-clause fragments.   *Answers will vary.*

                                                                    because

EXAMPLE: William Levitt and his brother built Levittown. ~~Because~~ of a shortage of affordable housing.

1.   In 1948, developer William Levitt built a community on Long

                  that

    Island. <u>~~That~~ has been designated the first traditional suburb.</u> Levitt

    wanted to give returning soldiers the opportunity to participate in the

    American dream. He called his community Levittown. The town

                                                                that

    consists of similarly built single-family homes. <u>~~That~~ attracted young</u>

    <u>families.</u> People wanted to escape the crowds of big cities like New York

    and Philadelphia. The community grew to approximately 17,000

             , which

    houses. <u>~~Which~~ led to the beginning of urban sprawl.</u> Eventually, the

    Levitts built three more Levittowns.

because

2. Some people criticized the idea of Levittown. ~~Because~~ all of the houses

   looked similar. There were only four different house styles. Although it
   ,
   began with the premise of affordable housing for everyone~~.~~ Levittown

   initially did not permit nonwhites to buy houses in the community.

   Eventually, Levittown abandoned its "whites-only" policy. In 1957, the

   first African Americans to buy a house in Levittown, Pennsylvania, were
   , *who*
   Bill and Daisy Meyers. ~~Who~~ had rocks thrown at them by the other

   residents.

   , *it*
3. Because Levittown is getting older~~.~~ ~~It~~ has become a more attractive

   suburb. Many homeowners have remodeled their homes, and the saplings

   have grown into mature trees. Although many other suburbs have
   ,
   developed~~.~~ Levittown remains a model of traditional suburban living.

FINAL REVIEW

The following text contains the four types of fragments: phrase, *-ing* and *to*,
explanatory, and dependent clause. Correct twelve fragment errors.
Answers will vary.

EXAMPLE: The Alhambra fortress. ~~It~~ was the palace of the Muslim rulers of
Granada.

in
1. Muslims from North Africa invaded Spain. ~~In~~ 711 C.E. The conquerors
   that
   established a rich civilization. ~~That~~ was different

   from that of other medieval European countries.

   The North Africans, or Moors, called the territory

   Al-Andalus. The first emir was Abd-er-Rahman.
   , *he*
   Ruling wisely. ~~He~~ created a wealthy and cultured

The Alhambra

Teaching Tip:
You can use the final
review as a test.
Additional practice
and test material
appears in the
Instructor's
Resource Manual
and on
MyWritingLab.

empire. The Moors improved irrigation systems. ~~To~~ *to* help agriculture.

They introduced new crops. ~~Such~~ *,s* as saffron, figs, and rice. They

developed centers of learning. ~~In~~ *in* mathematics, science, and architecture.

2. Eventually, the Moorish empire deteriorated into small city-states. ~~Because~~ *b*

of political turmoil. Granada emerged as an influential city. By 1228, the

Nasrid family ruled Granada. ~~Establishing~~ *,e* a powerful dynasty. The

Nasrids supported the development of both arts and sciences. Architects

designed magnificent buildings. For example, *they built* the Alhambra Palace.

3. In the following centuries, Christian Spain fought to regain its lost

territory. In 1492, the Catholic monarchs, Isabelle and Ferdinand,

recaptured the Muslim regions. They expelled the Moors. ~~Especially~~ *,e* the

Nasrid rulers. Boabdil of Granada was the last Muslim king. According to

reports, he wept as he left the city. Seeing his tears, his mother said, "Don't

weep like a baby for what you could not defend as a man." Boabdil last

looked upon his beloved city from a hilltop. This spot later *was* known as *The*

Moor's Last Sigh.

The Writer's Room   Topics for Writing

Write about one of the following topics. Check that there are no sentence
fragments.

1. Define your ideal town. What characteristics would it have?

2. What are some similarities and differences between living in a city and living in a suburb?

Teaching Tip:
Pair Work
Each student can peer edit a partner's work. Ask them to look specifically for sentence fragments.

✔ **CHECKLIST: SENTENCE FRAGMENTS**

When you edit your writing, ask yourself this question.

☐ Are my sentences complete? Check for the next types of fragments.

- phrase fragments
- *-ing* and *to* fragments
- explanatory fragments
- dependent-clause fragments

Los Angeles and San Francisco are moving closer

because

together. ~~Because~~ of the San Andreas fault. The two cities will

if

make the largest urban area in the world. ~~If~~ the movement

continues.

Teaching Tip:
Writer's World Competition
Please advise students that they can submit their paragraphs and essays for possible publication to www .pearsonhighered .com/essayrewards/ writingrewards.html

my writing lab PEARSON

To check your progress in meeting this chapter's objectives, log in to **www.mywritinglab.com,** go to the **Study Plan** tab, click on **The Editing Handbook—Section 2** and choose **Fragments** from the list of subtopics. Read and view the resources in the **Review Materials** section, and then complete the **Recall, Apply,** and **Write** sets in the **Activities** section.

Run-Ons

LEARNING OBJECTIVES

1 What Are Run-Ons?
(p. 350)

2 Correcting Run-Ons
(p. 351)

Section Theme **URBAN DEVELOPMENT**

In this chapter, you will read about architects and architecture.

What Are Run-Ons?

A **run-on sentence** occurs when two or more complete sentences are incorrectly joined. In other words, the sentence runs on without stopping.

There are two types of run-on sentences.

1. A **fused sentence** has no punctuation to mark the break between ideas.

   Incorrect: Skyscrapers are unusually tall buildings the Taipei 101 tower is among the tallest.

2. A **comma splice** uses a comma incorrectly to connect two complete ideas.

   Incorrect: The CN Tower is located in Toronto, it is the world's tallest communication structure.

350

PRACTICE I   Write C beside correct sentences, FS beside fused sentences, and CS beside comma splices.

EXAMPLE: The White House contains 132 rooms and 35 bathrooms, it also has a tennis court and a jogging track.   _CS_

1. The White House is the official residence of the American president, the first president, George Washington, never lived in it.   _CS_

2. In 1790, George Washington moved the capital from New York to the District of Columbia he chose Pierre L'Enfant to plan the city.   _FS_

3. Washington and L'Enfant chose a site for the presidential residence, they held a competition for the best design.   _CS_

4. A young architect, James Hoban, won the competition he was inspired by a villa in Dublin, Ireland.   _FS_

5. The corner stone was laid in 1792, and many people came to watch the construction.   _C_

6. John Adams was the first president to live in the house he and his wife took up residence in 1800.   _FS_

7. During the War of 1812, the British set fire to the house, it was painted white to hide the damage.   _CS_

8. Originally, the residence was called the President's Palace, but Theodore Roosevelt started to call it the White House in 1901.   _C_

Teaching Tip:

Cooperative Learning (Jigsaw)
Place students in teams of three to five. Assign each team a grammar concept from the chapter. Teams are responsible for teaching the class about their topic. They should summarize key ideas, give examples, and prepare some practice sentences. Then each team can present a short lesson to the class. Another option is to ask students to number themselves from one to five. All of the ones get together, the twos, the threes, and so on. Students can take turns teaching others what they have learned.

Correcting Run-Ons

You can correct both fused sentences and comma splices in a variety of ways. Read the following run-on sentence, and then review the four ways to correct it.

> **Run-On:** Antoni Gaudí began his career as a secular architect he eventually became very religious.

1. Make two separate sentences by adding end punctuation, such as a period.

> Antoni Gaudí began his career as a secular architect. **He** eventually became very religious.

CHAPTER 24

2. Add a semicolon (;).

> Antoni Gaudí began his career as a secular architect**;** he eventually became very religious.

3. Add a coordinating conjunction such as *for, and, nor, but, or, yet,* or *so.*

> Antoni Gaudí began his career as a secular architect**,** **but** he eventually became very religious.

4. Add a subordinating conjunction such as *although, because, when, before, while, since,* or *after.*

> **Although** Antoni Gaudí began his career as a secular architect, he eventually became very religious.

PRACTICE 2   Correct the run-ons by making two complete sentences.

EXAMPLE: Antoni Gaudí designed very interesting works, he is considered to be a genius. *. He*

1. Antoni Gaudí was born in 1852 in Tarragona, Spain he is Catalonia's *. He*

   greatest architect.

2. Gaudí designed the Sagrada Familia he wanted to express his Catholic *. He*

   faith in his work.

3. Nature fascinated Gaudí, he incorporated nature's images into his *. He*

   creations.

4. Classical design used geometric shapes Gaudí's designs mimicked shapes *.*

   from nature.

5. Gaudí's style evolved from Gothic influences, he created intricate, flowing, *. He*

   asymmetrical shapes.

6. Businessmen in Barcelona commissioned Gaudí to design a modern

   neighborhood, he constructed many buildings like the Casa Milà. *. He*

Teaching Tip:
Remind students that run-ons are not necessarily long sentences. For the following sentences, ask students which one is the run-on:

The Eiffel Tower is in Paris, it's an impressive structure.

The Eiffel Tower, which is in Paris, is an impressive structure that is made of steel, and millions of people visit it every year.

Teaching Tip:
If you think the distinction between fused sentences and comma splices is not important, you could ask your students to identify both types of run-ons by writing "RO."

Teaching Tip:
To better understand how to correct run-ons, students may need to review types of sentences. Refer them to Chapter 21.

7. His work used the *trencadis* style ⌃ this style involves the use of broken tiles

   to decorate surfaces.

. This

8. Many people initially laughed at Gaudí's vision ⌃ eight of his creations are

   now recognized as World Heritage Sites.

. Eight

Teaching Tip:
Point out that the opening photo in this chapter is a Gaudí design.

CHAPTER 24

> ⟨*Hint*⟩ **Semicolons and Transitional Expressions**
>
> Another way to correct run-ons is to connect sentences with a transitional expression. Place a semicolon before the expression and a comma after it.
>
> **EXAMPLE:** The construction costs were too high**; therefore,** the town abandoned plans to build city hall.
>
> The design was beautiful**; nevertheless,** it was rejected.
>
> Some common transitional expressions are the following:
>
> | | | |
> |---|---|---|
> | additionally | meanwhile | of course |
> | furthermore | moreover | therefore |
> | however | nevertheless | thus |
>
> To practice combining sentences with transitional expressions, see Chapter 21.

PRACTICE 3   Correct the run-ons by joining the two sentences with a semicolon.   Answers will vary.

EXAMPLE: I. M. Pei has designed many famous buildings ⌃ the John F.
Kennedy Library is just one.

;

1. The Louvre Palace is one of the most recognized buildings in Paris ⌃ it was

   built in the Renaissance style for French monarchs.

;

2. The French Revolution abolished the monarchy ⌃ the Louvre became a

   museum.

;

3. I. M. Pei was born in China in 1917 ⌃ he immigrated to the United States to

   study architecture.

;

Teaching Tip:
You might ask students to try adding a transitional expression to each answer in Practice 3.

4. The French government commissioned Pei to enlarge the museum; he designed three pyramids for the entrance.

5. The main pyramid gives light to the underground entrance; it is made of many glass squares.

6. The pyramid is about seventy feet high; it has two smaller pyramids on each side.

7. The pyramids were completed in 1989; many people thought the entrance was unattractive.

8. I. M. Pei is an outstanding architect; his innovative designs have won many prizes.

Teaching Tip:
Tell students that people often use *coordinator* and *subordinator* as shortened forms of *coordinating conjunction* and *subordinating conjunction*.

PRACTICE 4   Correct the run-ons by joining the two sentences with a comma and a coordinator (*for*, *and*, *nor*, *but*, *or*, *yet*, *so*). Answers will vary.

EXAMPLE: Maya Lin's most famous design is the Vietnam Veterans
, but
Memorial Wall she has also created many other projects.

, but / yet
1. American soldiers fought courageously in the Vietnam War the war was controversial.

2. A Vietnam War veteran, Jan Scruggs, pressured Congress to build a
, for
memorial he wanted to recognize the valor of American soldiers.

, and
3. A competition for the best design was held in 1980 more than 2,500 people submitted ideas for the memorial.

, nor
4. The competitors could not be under eighteen could they be foreign citizens.

, but / yet
5. Maya Lin was only an undergraduate architect student she won the

    competition.

, but
6. Lin's parents came from China she was born in Ohio.

, and
7. Her design was a wall made of polished black granite the names of soldiers

    who lost their lives are etched on the wall.

, and / so
8. The wall, which juts out of the earth, is an unconventional memorial it initially

    caused controversy.

PRACTICE 5   Correct the run-ons by joining the two sentences
with a **subordinator.** Use one of the following subordinators: *because, before,
although, when, even though,* and *although.* If the dependent clause comes at
the beginning of the sentence, remember to add a comma. Answers will vary.

Even though   *,*
EXAMPLE: European ideas have influenced African architecture many
indigenous designs reveal beauty and practicality.

when
1. African architecture was influenced by Arabs they colonized North Africa.

Before   *,*
2. Europeans arrived in the sixteenth century Islam provided inspiration for

    architectural design.

3. Until the twentieth century, there were very few famous African
   because
architects African countries were controlled by European powers.

Even though modern   *,*
4. ~~Modern~~ African buildings are beautiful they are not appreciated as World

    Heritage Sites.

After the
5. ~~The~~ Aswan Dam, one of the most famous dams in the world, was constructed

    in Egypt in the twentieth century the Nile River no longer flooded

    each year.

6. The construction of the Aswan Dam was controversial *because* people were concerned about its impact on the environment.

7. *When the* ~~The~~ Eastgate Centre was built in Harare, Zimbabwe, it became the world's first modern building to use natural cooling methods.

8. Modern African architecture is gaining momentum *because* architects are considering the unique needs of Africa.

PRACTICE 6   Use a variety of methods to correct eight run-on errors. Add commas when necessary.   Answers will vary.

EXAMPLE: Many new buildings are being erected all over China, *and* modern building designs are very popular.

1. *When the* ~~The~~ Chinese Revolution dominated politics, China's government developed policies to minimize class differences. As a result, new buildings were designed for utility with no regard for beauty.

2. Now, China is industrializing at a great rate, *and* businesses are asking architects to design practical but beautiful buildings. The National Theatre building, for example, is controversial, *yet* it is also extremely intriguing. *Even though it* ~~It~~ was designed by French architect Paul Andreu, many people have criticized its design. It is shaped like an egg. It has three halls and a lake, *and* it has a bridge. Another highly discussed building in Beijing is the CCTV tower. *Because it* ~~It~~ looks like the letter *Z*, many Chinese think it is an eyesore.

3. The Beijing skyline has changed, *but* not everybody has liked the changes. In China, some people complain about the ugly architecture, ~~others~~ *. Others* believe the new buildings are beautiful. Average citizens are eager for Beijing to join the ranks of the most beautiful cities in the world.

FINAL REVIEW

Correct ten run-on errors.   Answers will vary.

and public
EXAMPLE: The construction industry is the largest in the world, ~~public~~ and
private buildings consume a lot of energy.

CHAPTER 24

1. When most people envision cities, they think about houses, roads, and

   ;
   skyscrapers built above ground they do not think about subterranean cities.

   However, many people use underground public and private buildings every

   day. In North America, there are at least five hundred public and private

   . For
   underground buildings ~~for~~ example, the Engineering Library at the

   University of Berkeley and the Vietnam Veterans Memorial Education

   Center are only two such subterranean structures. More and more

   underground structures are being built every day.

2. Some of the oldest underground cities are located in Cappadocia,

   . The
   Turkey the first underground city in that area was constructed around

   2000 B.C.E. Archaeologists believe that at one time, up to twenty

   because
   thousand people lived in those underground Turkish cities the early

   Christians used them as a means to escape persecution.

3. Montreal, Canada, contains an extremely large underground city.

   , and
   It was designed by I. M. Pei in the 1960s other architects have

   contributed to its expansion. It is located downtown and has around

   26 miles of tunnels with about 120 exterior access points. More than

   because
   500,000 people use the underground city each day they want to avoid

   Montreal's very cold temperatures in the winter.

Teaching Tip:
You can use the final
review as a test.
Additional practice
and test material
appears in the
Instructor's
Resource Manual
and on
MyWritingLab.

**Entrance to tunnels in
Cappadocia**

4. There are many reasons to build underground. First, underground buildings

   . Architects

   benefit from better climate control ~~architects~~ say that such buildings can

   be heated and cooled more efficiently than aboveground buildings. Also,

   building underground reduces the impact on the environment*;* forests and

   fields do not have to be cleared. Moreover, the wind, snow, and rain do not

   and

   erode the walls*,* well-constructed underground buildings are resistant to

   fire and earthquakes.

5. Perhaps in the future, there will be more underground public and private

   because

   buildings*;* they are more environmentally friendly and more energy

   efficient. Certainly it is time to rethink how urban planners design cities.

The Writer's Room   Topics for Writing

Write about one of the following topics. Edit your writing and ensure that there are no run-ons.

1. Give examples of any buildings or areas in your neighborhood, town, or country that you find attractive or unattractive. Describe these buildings and explain why you believe they are beautiful or unsightly.

2. Are there any changes or additions that you would make to the town or city where you live, such as adding a new park or a museum? What suggestions would you make to city planners?

Teaching Tip:

Cooperative Learning (Quick Review)
Divide the class into teams of three or four. Assign a part of the chapter to each team. Each team should review the information and generate three questions. Then ask teams to read the questions aloud. Anybody in the class can answer a question. Or, as an alternative, you can ask teams to exchange questions and to answer another team's questions.

CHECKLIST: RUN-ONS

When you edit your writing, ask yourself this question.

☐ Are my sentences correctly formed and punctuated? Check for and correct any fused sentences and comma splices.

One of the most successful architects in the world is Frank Lloyd ~~Wright. One~~

Wright. One

~~Wright one~~ famous house he designed, Fallingwater, is a national

monument.

CHAPTER 24

mywritinglab To check your progress in meeting this chapter's objectives, log in to **www.mywritinglab.com,** go to the **Study Plan** tab, click on **The Editing Handbook—Section 2** and choose **Run-Ons** from the list of subtopics. Read and view the resources in the **Review Materials** section, and then complete the **Recall, Apply,** and **Write** sets in the **Activities** section.

Teaching Tip:
Writer's World Competition
Please advise students that they can submit their paragraphs and essays for possible publication to www .pearsonhighered .com/essayrewards/ writingrewards.html

CHAPTER 25

Faulty Parallel Structure

Section Theme **URBAN DEVELOPMENT**

In this chapter, you will read about landscapes and gardens.

Teaching Tip:
Discuss the meaning of *parallel.* You could give the example of parallel bars used in gymnastics. The bars have the same size and shape and are a uniform distance apart.

What Is Parallel Structure?

Parallel structure occurs when pairs or groups of items in a sentence are balanced. Notice how the following sentences repeat grammatical structures but not ideas.

Parallel Nouns:	Books, stores, and catalogs give gardeners information.
Parallel Tenses:	Gardeners dig and plant in the soil.
Parallel Adjectives:	Kew Garden is large, colorful, and breathtaking.

360

Parallel Phrases: You will find the public garden down the road, over the bridge, and through the field.

Parallel Clauses: There are some gardens that have just trees, and some that have only flowers and plants.

CHAPTER 25

Correcting Faulty Parallel Structure

Use parallel structure for a series of words or phrases, for paired clauses, for comparisons, and for two-part constructions. If you see "//" or simply "faulty parallelism" on one of your marked essays, try the following tips for correcting those errors.

Teaching Tip:

Series of Words or Phrases

Use parallel structure when words or phrases are joined in a series.

Not Parallel: The English, the Chinese, and people from Japan create luxurious gardens.

Parallel Nouns: The English, the Chinese, and the Japanese create luxurious gardens.

Not Parallel: I like to read books about gardens, to attend lectures about gardening, and buying plants for my garden.

Parallel Verbs: I like to read books about gardens, to attend lectures about gardening, and to buy plants for my garden.

Paired Clauses

Use parallel structure with a series of dependent clauses.

Not Parallel: He designed a garden that was beautiful, that was well planned, and was unique.

Parallel *That* Clause: He designed a garden that was beautiful, that was well planned, and that was unique.

Not Parallel: We met a designer who was friendly, who had a lot of experience, and was available.

Parallel *Who* Clause: We met a designer who was friendly, who had a lot of experience, and who was available.

Cooperative Learning (Jigsaw) Place students in teams of three to five. Assign each team a grammar concept from the chapter. Teams are responsible for teaching the class about their topic. They should summarize key ideas, give examples, and prepare some practice sentences. Then each team can present a short lesson to the class. Another option is to ask students to number themselves from one to five. All of the ones get together, the twos, the threes, and so on. Students can take turns teaching others what they have learned.

Hint   Use Consistent Voice

When joining two independent clauses with a coordinating conjunction, use a consistent voice. For example, if the first part of the sentence uses the active voice, the other part should also use the active voice.

Not parallel:	_{active} The bees flew to the flowers, and then the nectar _{passive} was tasted by them.
Parallel active voice:	_{active} _{active} The bees flew to the flowers, and then they tasted the nectar.

Teaching Tip:
Ask students to describe a beautiful sight in nature and to include many nouns and adjectives in their sentences. Write them on the board. Then the group can ensure that the words are parallel.

PRACTICE I   Underline and correct the faulty parallel structure in each sentence.   Answers will vary.

EXAMPLE: The Hermitage, which was the Winter Palace of the Russian Tsars, has a collection of valuable

antique furniture
paintings, rare books, and furniture that is antique.

1. Tsar Peter the Great was cosmopolitan, educated, and
determined
he had great determination.

2. In 1703, Peter created plans and *ordered workers* workers were ordered to

build a new city.

3. The Tsar commissioned a summer palace and a *winter palace* palace for the winter.

4. The Tsar designed parks, flower gardens, and *arboretums* he was also creating

arboretums.

5. The summer garden contains trees that are exotic, flowers that are rare,
bushes that are beautiful
and beautiful bushes.

The Winter Palace

Teaching Tip:
Point out to students that they can remove the *that* clause in #5 (*The summer garden contains exotic trees, rare flowers, and beautiful bushes.*), and the *who* clause in #6 (*The Tsar was fussy, temperamental, and ambitious.*).

6. The Tsar was a man who was fussy, who was temperamental, and
   who was ambitious
   ~~was ambitious~~.

7. The landscaper, Domenico Trezzini, worked slowly, diligently,
   creatively
   and <u>he was creative</u>.

8. Tourists can stroll down paths, over bridges, and ~~walking~~ by marble statues.

9. St. Petersburg is called the "window to the west," "the city of the white

   nights," and <u>people also view it as</u> "the northern Venice."

Comparisons

Use parallel structure in comparisons containing *than* or *as*.

Not Parallel:	Designing an interesting garden is easier than to take care of it.
Parallel -*ing* Forms:	<u>Designing an interesting garden</u> is easier than <u>taking care of it.</u>
Not Parallel:	The rock garden looks as colorful as planting roses.
Parallel Noun Phrases:	<u>The rock garden</u> looks as colorful as <u>the rose garden.</u>

Two-Part Constructions

Use parallel structure for the following paired items.

either . . . or	not . . . but	both . . . and
neither . . . nor	not only . . . but also	rather . . . than

Not Parallel:	The lecture on landscaping was both enlightening and of use.
Parallel Adjectives:	The lecture on landscaping was both <u>enlightening</u> and <u>useful.</u>
Not Parallel:	I could either see the bonsai exhibit or going to a film.
Parallel Verbs:	I could either <u>see</u> the bonsai exhibit or <u>go</u> to a film.

PRACTICE 2 Correct ten errors in parallel construction.

EXAMPLE: City planners build parks to create green areas, to prevent
                                                          to develop recreational facilities
                    overcrowding, and <u>people can use them for recreation.</u>

1. During the Industrial Revolution, urban life changed rapidly and
   completely
   <u>with completion.</u> City planners realized that more people were moving to
                                                    immigrants
   the cities. Planners, politicians, and <u>people who immigrated</u> saw city life

   changing. Urban designers wanted to create green space rather than
   to fill
   <u>filling</u> cities with concrete buildings.

2. One of the most important advocates of city beautification was Frederick

   Law Olmsted. He was born in 1822, in Hartford, Connecticut. He not
                                            designed
   only promoted urban planning, but he also <u>was designing</u> beautiful city

   gardens. He and his collaborator Calvert Vaux designed New York's

   Central Park. Olmsted wanted the park to reflect his personal philosophy,
                                                    winding paths
   so in it he created open spaces, beautiful views, and <u>paths that wind.</u>

3. Olmsted and Vaux designed many other projects. An important design was

   the Niagara Falls project. At that time, the falls were not completely visible

   to tourists. Olmsted wanted to create a harmonious landscape, to allow
                                            to conserve the area.
   greater tourist accessibility, and <u>conservation of the area was important to</u>

   <u>him.</u> Such a park required a great deal of planning. Goat Island separates

   Canada from the United States. Either the landscapers could buy Goat
                                    could continue
   Island, or Goat Island <u>was continuing</u> to be an eyesore. Olmsted and Vaux

   bought the island and restored it.

4. For Olmsted, contributing to the community was more important than
having
~~to have~~ fame. He designed Mount Royal Park in Montreal, and the 1893
he planned
World Fair in Chicago ~~was also planned by him~~. He was known as much
for his respect of
for his sense of beauty as ~~respecting~~ the environment. Olmsted died in

1903, but thousands of people continue to enjoy his legacy.

CHAPTER 25

FINAL REVIEW

Correct ten errors in parallel construction.

EXAMPLE: Walking through a garden is more relaxing than ~~to read~~ a book.
reading

1. *Ikebana* is the ancient tradition of Japanese flower arrangement. During the

   seventh century, Chinese diplomats, monks, and ~~people who were~~ merchants

   came to Japan. They brought with them the idea of offering arranged

   flowers to Buddha. The Japanese adopted this tradition quickly, joyfully, and
   sincerely
   ~~with sincerity~~. Worshippers offered flowers to Buddha because they desired
   because
   tranquility, because they wanted to show their faith, and ~~they valued nature~~.

2. Ono-no-imoko was a courtier, a sculptor, and ~~he also painted~~.
   a painter
   He became both a devout Buddhist and ~~achieved expertise~~ on
   an expert
   Ikebana. He decided to leave the court to devote himself to

   Buddha. He traveled from the city, through the hills, and

   ~~he went~~ into a forest. He found a lake. He remained there
   aristocrats
   for the rest of his life. Many artisans, soldiers, and ~~people who~~

   ~~were aristocrats~~ came to learn Ikebana from him. His lessons on

   flower arrangement not only delighted the Japanese people but
   also influenced Japanese culture
   ~~Japanese culture was also influenced~~.

Teaching Tip:
You can use the final review as a test. Additional practice and test material appears in the Instructor's Resource Manual and on *MyWritingLab.*

3. Over the centuries, different Ikebana schools have developed. Poets,

    novelists

    essayists, and <u>people who write novels</u> have praised this form of flower

    arrangement. Today there are about 3,000 schools of Ikebana. People who

    satisfying

    study Ikebana find it inspiring, educational, and <u>it also satisfies them</u>.

The Writer's Room

Choose one of the following topics, and write a paragraph. Make sure your nouns, verbs, and sentence structures are parallel.

1. If you could be anywhere right now, where would you be? Describe that place. Include details that appeal to the senses.
2. What do you do to relax? List some steps.

✔ CHECKLIST: PARALLEL STRUCTURE

When you edit your writing, ask yourself this question.

☐ Are my grammatical structures balanced? Check for errors in these cases:

- when words or phrases are joined in a series
- when you write a series of dependent clauses
- when you make comparisons

English gardens

We saw Chinese gardens, Japanese gardens, and ~~gardens from England~~.

To check your progress in meeting this chapter's objectives, log in to **www.mywritinglab.com**, go to the **Study Plan** tab, click on **The Editing Handbook—Section 2** and choose **Faulty Parallel Structure** from the list of subtopics. Read and view the resources in the **Review Materials** section, and then complete the **Recall, Apply,** and **Write** sets in the **Activities** section.

Teaching Tip:

Cooperative Learning (Quick Review)
Divide the class into teams of three or four. Assign a part of the chapter to each team. Each team should review the information and generate three questions. Then ask teams to read the questions aloud. Anybody in the class can answer a question. Or, as an alternative, you can ask teams to exchange questions and to answer another team's questions.

Teaching Tip:

Writer's World Competition
Please advise students that they can submit their paragraphs and essays for possible publication to www .pearsonhighered .com/essayrewards/ writingrewards.html

Mistakes with Modifiers

LEARNING OBJECTIVES

1. Misplaced Modifiers (p. 367)
2. Dangling Modifiers (p. 370)

Section Theme **URBAN DEVELOPMENT**

In this chapter, you will read about pollution and other urban issues.

Misplaced Modifiers

A **modifier** is a word, a phrase, or a clause that describes or modifies nouns or verbs in a sentence. To use a modifier correctly, place it next to the word(s) that you want to modify.

> modifier   words that are modified
> <u>Trying to combat pollution</u>, **city planners** have launched an anti-littering campaign.

Teaching Tip:
Ask students how to correct the sentence with the misplaced modifier on page 368. The answer is "Waiting in the mayor's office, I saw a pamphlet about littering."

A **misplaced modifier** is a word, a phrase, or a clause that is not placed next to the word that it modifies. When a modifier is too far from the word that it is describing, the meaning of the sentence can become confusing or unintentionally funny.

I saw a pamphlet about littering waiting in the mayor's office.

(How could a pamphlet wait in the mayor's office?)

Commonly Misplaced Modifiers

As you read the sample sentences for each type of modifier, notice how the meaning of the sentence changes depending on where the modifier is placed.

Prepositional Phrase Modifiers

A prepositional phrase is made of a preposition and its object.

Confusing: Helen read an article on electric cars <u>in a cafe</u>.

(Who was in the cafe: Helen or the cars?)

Clear: <u>In a cafe</u>, Helen read an article on electric cars.

Participle Modifiers

A participle modifier is a phrase that contains an *-ing* verb or an *-ed* verb.

Confusing: Jamal Reed learned about anti-littering laws <u>touring Singapore</u>.

(Can laws tour Singapore?)

Clear: While <u>touring Singapore</u>, Jamal Reed learned about anti-littering laws.

Relative Clause Modifiers

A modifier can be a relative clause or phrase beginning with *who, whose, which,* or *that.*

Confusing: The woman received a $1,000 fine from the officer <u>who dropped a candy wrapper</u>.

(Who dropped the candy wrapper: the woman or the officer?)

Clear: The woman who dropped a candy wrapper received a $1,000 fine from the officer.

Limiting Modifiers

Limiting modifiers are words such as *almost, nearly, only, merely, just,* and *even*. In the examples, notice how the placement of *almost* changes the meaning of each sentence.

Almost all of the citizens took the steps that solved the littering problem.

(Some of the citizens did not take the steps, but most did.)

Teaching Tip:

Cooperative Learning (Jigsaw)
Place students in teams of three to five. Assign each team a grammar concept from the chapter. Teams are responsible for teaching the class about the concept. They should summarize key ideas, give examples, and prepare some practice sentences. Then each team can present a short lesson to the class. Another option is to ask students to number themselves from one to five. All of the ones get together, the twos, the threes, and so on. Students can take turns teaching others what they have learned.

All of the citizens **almost** took the steps that solved the littering problem.

(The citizens did not take the steps.)

All of the citizens took the steps that **almost** solved the littering problem.

(The steps did not solve the littering problem.)

Hint **Correcting Misplaced Modifiers**

To correct misplaced modifiers, follow these steps:

1. First, identify the modifier.
   Armando saw the oil slick **standing on the pier.**
2. Then, identify the word or words being modified.
   Armando
3. Finally, move the modifier next to the word(s) being modified.
   Standing on the pier, Armando saw the oil slick.

PRACTICE I Underline and correct the misplaced modifier in each sentence.

who was fined $500
EXAMPLE: The man ˄ forgot to flush the public toilet <u>who was fined $500</u>.

from the United Nations
1. Experts ˄ recognize Singapore as the cleanest city in the world <u>from the United Nations</u>.

who patrol city streets
2. Singaporean police officers ˄ will immediately arrest litterbugs <u>who patrol city streets</u>.

polluters receive
3. <u>After littering</u>, ~~officers give~~ a $1,000 fine ~~to polluters~~.

, wearing a bright yellow vest,
4. For a second littering offense, a polluter ˄ must clean a public area such as a park or school yard <u>wearing a bright yellow vest</u>.

in Parliament,

5. In 1992, Singapore politicians debated a new law that prohibited the
   importance, selling, or chewing of gum <u>in Parliament</u>.

6. <u>Because gum was stuck on them</u>, passengers could not close the doors to
   because gum was stuck on them.
   the subway trains.

   that has medicinal purposes
7. In 2004, the law was revised to allow gum into the country <u>that has</u>
   <u>medicinal purposes</u>.

   with no litter
8. Singaporeans <u>with no litter</u> are proud of their city.

Dangling Modifiers

A **dangling modifier** opens a sentence but does not modify any words in the sentence. It "dangles" or hangs loosely because it is not connected to any other part of the sentence. To avoid having a dangling modifier, make sure that the modifier and the first noun that follows it have a logical connection.

Confusing: <u>While eating a candy bar</u>, the wrapper fell on the ground.
(Can a wrapper eat a candy bar?)

Clear: <u>While eating a candy bar</u>, Zena dropped the wrapper on the ground.

Confusing: <u>To attend the conference</u>, a background in environmental work is necessary.
(Can a background attend a conference?)

Clear: <u>To attend the conference</u>, **participants need** a background in environmental work.

Teaching Tip:
Point out that the passive voice can cause many modifier errors. If students need more information, refer them to pages 396–397 in Chapter 28.

 Correcting Dangling Modifiers

To correct dangling modifiers, follow these steps:

1. First, identify the modifier.
   <u>When traveling</u>, public transportation should be used.
2. Then, decide who or what the writer aims to modify.
   Who is traveling? **People**
3. Finally, add the missing subject (and in some cases, also add or remove words) so that the sentence makes sense.
   <u>When traveling</u>, people should use public transportation.

PRACTICE 2 Underline the dangling modifier in each sentence. Then, rewrite the sentence keeping the meaning of the modifier. You may have to add or remove words to make the sentence logical. Answers will vary.

EXAMPLE: <u>Enjoying parks</u>, it is difficult when there is a lot of litter.

It is difficult for people to enjoy parks when there is a lot of litter.

1. <u>Believing it is not garbage</u>, cigarette butts are left on city streets.

   Believing it is not garbage, some people leave cigarette butts on city streets.

2. <u>With an unconcerned attitude</u>, the hamburger wrapper ended up on the ground.

   With an unconcerned attitude, the woman threw the hamburger wrapper on the ground.

3. <u>Unhappy with the garbage in the park</u>, a major cleanup took place.

   Unhappy with the garbage in the park, the public cleaned it up.

4. <u>Playing in the sand</u>, there were pieces of glass from broken bottles.

   Playing in the sand, the children found glass from broken bottles.

5. <u>To understand the effects of littering</u>, the cleanup costs must be examined.

   To understand the effects of littering, city councilors must examine the cleanup costs.

6. <u>Seeing no available trash can</u>, the cigarette butt can be wrapped up and carried.

   Seeing no available trash can, smokers can wrap up and carry cigarette butts.

7. <u>While walking barefoot on the grass</u>, a piece of glass cut Pablo's foot.

   While walking barefoot on the grass, Pablo cut his foot on a piece of glass.

8. <u>By thinking about litter</u>, parks can be kept clean.

   By thinking about litter, the public can keep parks clean.

Teaching Tip:
Students often make modifier mistakes by starting sentences with *Based on, Thankfully, Happily, Sadly,* or *Hopefully.* Ask students to correct the next sentence. *Hopefully, the train arrives on time.*

Teaching Tip:
Ask students to complete sentences that begin with the next modifiers: *Putting on her gloves; By refusing to enter; To leave the area clean; Searching for answers.* Tell them to generate a variety of sentences.

PRACTICE 3   Correct the dangling or misplaced modifiers. If the sentence is correct, write *C* next to it.   Answers will vary.

Keisha saw that

EXAMPLE: Walking by the sea, plastic bags were caught in the rocks.
                                        ^

   Using plastic bags, people create a lot of pollution.
1. Using plastic bags, a lot of pollution is created.

   Blown by the wind, plastic bags frequently litter sidewalks.
2. Blown by the wind, sidewalks are frequently littered with plastic bags.

3. Clogging drains, plastic bags often cause sewage to overflow.   *C*

   Birds are harmed because they can choke on plastic.
4. Choking on plastic, harm is caused to birds.

   With enthusiasm, DeShawn Bertrand teaches the public about
5. DeShawn Bertrand teaches the public about composting garbage with
   composting garbage.
   enthusiasm.

   Taking public transportation, people save gas costs and parking fees.
6. Taking public transportation, gas costs and parking fees are saved.

   Environmental activists who promote the green movement lobby oil
7. Environmental activists lobby oil industry managers who promote the
   industry managers.
   green movement.

8. Following a few rules, communities can reduce pollution.   *C*

FINAL REVIEW

Identify fifteen dangling or misplaced modifier errors in this selection. Then, correct each error. You may need to add or remove words to ensure that the sentence makes sense.   Answers will vary.

                                        Emilio discovered surprising results.
EXAMPLE: Working on his final project, ~~some surprising results were discovered.~~

   In his urban studies class,
1. Emilio discovered that there are many ways to help the environment
   ^   *Drinking coffee, he*
   ~~in his urban studies class.~~ He sat with his parents to discuss energy-saving
                                                            in their kitchens
   strategies ~~drinking coffee.~~ First, there are things people can do to help the
                                                            ^
   environment ~~in their kitchens.~~ When using freezer bags and aluminum foil,

people can   *to*
~~washing them can~~ reduce waste. Also, people should use cloth napkins and

dishtowels instead of paper products. ~~With airtight lids,~~ Emilio places
with airtight lids
leftover food in plastic containers.

2. Emilio and his parents also discussed tips for other areas of the home.
    who want to save energy
    Families can take measures in the bathroom ~~who want to save energy~~. For
    Emilio turns the faucet off as much as possible while he brushes
    example, people should take shorter showers. ~~While Emilio is brushing~~ his

    ~~teeth, it is important to leave the faucet turned off as much as possible.~~

    People can install a toilet dam to reduce water consumption.

                              With a smile,
3. ~~For their laundry room,~~ Emilio's parents bought energy-efficient
            for their laundry room
    appliances ~~with a smile.~~ After washing shirts, the family hangs them out to
                              Doing the shopping, they
    dry instead of using a clothes dryer. ~~They~~ also buy phosphate-free

    detergent ~~doing the shopping.~~

                                          near his house
4. When Emilio's father goes to the grocery store, he makes sensible

    decisions about products ~~near his house.~~ Trying to do fewer trips and
            the family has reduced
    buying in bulk, ~~its gas consumption is reduced.~~ He buys compact
            that save energy
    fluorescent lightbulbs at the local hardware store ~~that save energy.~~

                        , which is very old,
5. The family's furnace needs to be upgraded~~, which is very old.~~ ~~Based on~~

    ~~the latest technology,~~ Emilio's parents are planning to buy an
                based on the latest technology
    energy-efficient heater. Also, watching only one television, ~~there is a~~

    ~~reduction in energy consumption and~~ the family spends more time
            and reduces energy consumption
    together. Using the techniques mentioned above, Emilio's family has

    managed to reduce its energy consumption by nearly thirty percent.

Teaching Tip:
You could suggest that students research their topics.

CHAPTER 26

READING LINK

Urban Development

The following essays contain more information about urban issues.

"Friendless in North America" by Ellen Goodman (page 223)

"My African Childhood" by David Sedaris (page 546)

"Living Environments" by Avi Friedman (page 553)

"Nature Returns to the Cities" by John Roach (page 584)

Teaching Tip:

Writer's World Competition
Please advise students that they can submit their paragraphs and essays for possible publication to www .pearsonhighered .com/essayrewards/ writingrewards.html

 The Writer's Room

Write about one of the following topics. Proofread your text to ensure that there are no modifier errors.

1. What are some steps that your neighborhood or town could take to combat a littering or pollution problem?

2. What are some types of polluters? Write about three categories of polluters.

✔ CHECKLIST: MODIFIERS

When you edit your writing, ask yourself these questions.

☐ Are my modifiers in the correct position? Check for errors with the following:

- prepositional phrase modifiers
- participle modifiers
- relative clause modifiers
- limiting modifiers

   Wearing overalls, the
   ~~The~~ urban planner surveyed the garbage ~~wearing overalls~~.
      ^

☐ Do my modifiers modify something in the sentence? Check for dangling modifiers.
   Walking down the street, the childen dropped food wrappers.
   ~~Walking down the street, food wrappers were dropped.~~
      ^

mywritinglab To check your progress in meeting this chapter's objectives, log in to **www.mywritinglab.com,** go to the **Study Plan** tab, click on **The Editing Handbook—Section 2** and choose **Mistakes with Modifiers** from the list of subtopics. Read and view the resources in the **Review Materials** section, and then complete the **Recall, Apply,** and **Write** sets in the **Activities** section.

Subject–Verb Agreement

LEARNING OBJECTIVES

1. Basic Subject–Verb Agreement Rules (p. 375)
2. More Than One Subject (p. 377)
3. Special Subject Forms (p. 379)
4. Verb Before the Subject (p. 381)
5. Interrupting Words and Phrases (p. 382)

Section Theme **COMMERCE AND MARKETING**

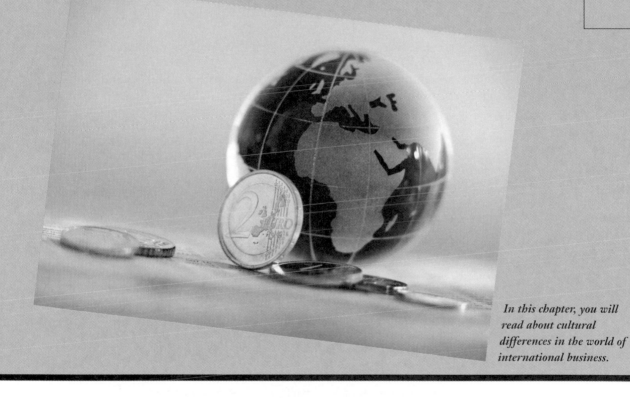

In this chapter, you will read about cultural differences in the world of international business.

Basic Subject–Verb Agreement Rules

Subject–verb agreement simply means that a subject and verb agree in number. A singular subject needs a singular verb, and a plural subject needs a plural verb.

Simple Present Tense Agreement

Writers use **simple present tense** to indicate that an action is habitual or factual. Review the following rules for simple present tense agreement.

Third-person singular form: When the subject is *he*, *she*, *it*, or the equivalent (*Mark*, *Carol*, *Miami*), add an *-s* or *-es* ending to the verb.

> **Maria Orlon** <u>works</u> as a marketing researcher.

GRAMMAR LINK

For more information about the present tense, see Chapter 28.

375

Base form: When the subject is *I, you, we, they,* or the equivalent (*women, the Rocky Mountains*), do not add an ending to the verb.

Many **businesses** <u>rely</u> on marketing research.

Agreement in Other Tenses

In the past tense, almost all verbs have one past form. The only past tense verb requiring subject–verb agreement is the verb *be,* which has two past forms: *was* and *were.*

I <u>was</u> tired. **Edward** <u>was</u> also tired. That day, **we** <u>were</u> very lazy.

In the present perfect tense, which is formed with *have* or *has* and the past participle, use *has* when the subject is third-person singular and *have* for all other forms.

The **travel service** <u>has raised</u> its booking fees. Other **agencies** <u>have not raised</u> their fees.

In the future tense and with modal forms (*can, could, would, may, might, must,* and *should*), use the same form of the verb with every subject.

I <u>will work</u>. **She** <u>should work</u> with me. **We** <u>can work</u> together.

CHAPTER 27

GRAMMAR LINK

For more information about using the present perfect tense, see Chapter 28.

ESL
Teaching Tip:
Some nonnative speakers may benefit from the information about *be, have,* and *do* because the verbs are used differently in other languages. For example, Spanish, Italian, and French speakers may say *I have twenty years old* instead of *I am twenty years old.*

> **Hint**   **Use Standard English**
>
> In casual conversations and in movies, you may hear people misuse the verbs *be, have,* and *do.* In professional and academic situations, use the standard forms of these verbs.
>
>   *is*   *has*   *doesn't*
> Karim ~~be~~ busy. He ~~have~~ a large family. He ~~don't~~ have free time.

PRACTICE 1   Underline the correct form of the verbs in parentheses.

EXAMPLE: Many businesses (<u>export</u> / exports) products to other nations.

1. Although several countries (<u>share</u> / shares) the English language, some

   linguistic details (be / is / <u>are</u>) different. For example, Americans and

   Canadians (<u>put</u> / puts) gas in their cars, whereas British citizens (<u>use</u> / uses)

petrol. In England, you (<u>do</u> / does) not phone people, you ring them.
Australians also (<u>use</u> / uses) interesting expressions. A "chalkie" (<u>is</u> / are) a
teacher, and a "mozzie" (<u>is</u> / are) a mosquito.

2. Spelling also (differ / <u>differs</u>) among English-speaking nations. The word
"flavor" (have / <u>has</u>) an *our* ending in Canada and Great Britain. Also, the
word "theater" (become / <u>becomes</u>) *theatre* in England and Australia.

CHAPTER 27

3. Business travelers (<u>need</u> / needs) to be aware of such differences. For
example, Jeremiah Brown (do / <u>does</u>) the marketing for an American
company. He (have / <u>has</u>) been with the company for two years. Last year,
he visited London, England. One day, he (<u>was</u> / were) with a client. They
(was / <u>were</u>) unable to agree on a price. When the client said, "That is too
much dosh," Jeremiah (<u>was</u> / were) confused. Then he learned that *dosh*
(<u>is</u> / are) a British slang word for "money."

ESL
Teaching Tip:
The rules for
agreement in
different verb tenses
are particularly
useful for nonnative
speakers. They may
apply certain
subject–verb
agreement rules to
tenses that don't
require them.

More Than One Subject

There are special agreement rules when there is more than one subject in a
sentence.

And

When two subjects are joined by *and*, use the plural form of the verb.

> <u>Colleges</u>, <u>universities</u>, and <u>trade schools</u> **prepare** students for the job
> market.

Or / Nor

When two subjects are joined by *or* or *nor*, the verb agrees with the subject that
is the closest to it.

> singular
> The layout artists or the <u>editor</u> **decides** how the cover will look.

> plural
> Neither the artist nor her <u>assistants</u> **make** changes to the design.

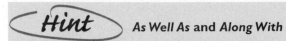

> **Hint**   As Well As and Along With
>
> The phrases *as well as* and *along with* are not the same as *and*. They do not form a compound subject. The real subject is before the interrupting expression.
>
> Japan, China, and South Korea **develop** high-tech computer products.
>
> Japan, as well as China and South Korea, **develops** high-tech computer products.

CHAPTER 27

Teaching Tip:

Cooperative Learning (Jigsaw)
Place students in teams of three to five. Assign each team a grammar concept from the chapter. Teams are responsible for teaching the class about their topic. They should summarize key ideas, give examples, and prepare some practice sentences. Then each team can present a short lesson to the class. Another option is to ask students to number themselves from one to five. All of the ones get together, the twos, the threes, and so on. Students can take turns teaching others what they have learned.

PRACTICE 2   Underline the correct verb in each sentence. Make sure the verb agrees with the subject.

EXAMPLE: Japan and China (<u>have</u> / has) interesting types of restaurants.

1. Tokyo and other Japanese cities (<u>have</u> / has) "Maid Cafés."

2. The hostess and the female servers (<u>dress</u> / dresses) in traditional maid uniforms.

3. Recently, in the Otome Road area of Tokyo, a businesswoman, along with her partner, (have / <u>has</u>) opened a Butler Café.

4. The coffee or the tea (come / <u>comes</u>) on a special tray.

5. The host and the waiters (<u>treat</u> / treats) the customers like British royalty.

6. "Mademoiselle" or "Your Highness" (<u>is</u> / are) said to each customer by the server in the butler uniform.

7. A crumpet as well as a large scone (appear / <u>appears</u>) on each table.

8. Every day, many young and old women (<u>try</u> / tries) to get a table at the Butler Café.

Special Subject Forms

Some subjects are not easy to identify as singular or plural. Two common types are indefinite pronouns and collective nouns.

Indefinite Pronouns

Indefinite pronouns refer to a general person, place, or thing. Carefully review the following list of indefinite pronouns.

Indefinite Pronouns				
Singular	another	each	nobody	other
	anybody	everybody	no one	somebody
	anyone	everyone	nothing	someone
	anything	everything	one	something
Plural	both, few, many, others, several			

Singular Indefinite Pronouns

In the following sentences, the verbs require the third-person singular form because the subjects are singular.

> Almost <u>everyone</u> **knows** about the Free Trade Agreement.

You can put one or more singular nouns (joined by *and*) after *each* and *every*. The verb is still singular.

> <u>Every</u> client **likes** the new rule. <u>Each</u> man and woman **knows** about it.

Plural Indefinite Pronouns

Both, few, many, others, and *several* are all plural subjects. The verb is always plural.

> A representative from the United States and another from Mexico are sitting at a table. <u>Both</u> **want** to compromise.

Collective Nouns

Collective nouns refer to groups of people or things. Review the following list of common collective nouns.

army	class	crowd	group	population
association	club	family	jury	public
audience	committee	gang	mob	society
band	company	government	organization	team

CHAPTER 27

Generally, each group acts as a unit, so you must use the singular form of the verb.

The <u>company</u> **is** ready to make a decision.

> ⟨ *Hint* ⟩ **Police Is Plural**
>
> Treat the word *police* as a plural noun because the word "officers" is implied but not stated.
>
> The police **have** a protester in custody.

Teaching Tip:
If your students have many problems with subject–verb agreement, suggest that they circle the subjects in each sentence and determine whether they are singular or plural.

PRACTICE 3   Underline the correct verb in each sentence.

EXAMPLE: The Executive Planet Web site (have / <u>has</u>) tips for business travelers.

1. Each large and small nation (have / <u>has</u>) its own gift-giving rules. For example, Singapore (have / <u>has</u>) strict rules against bribery, and the government (pride / <u>prides</u>) itself on being corruption-free. The police (<u>arrest</u> / arrests) officials who accept a bribe.

2. Specific rules (<u>apply</u> / applies) to gift-giving in Singapore. Certainly, everyone (love / <u>loves</u>) to receive a gift. Nobody (like / <u>likes</u>) to be left out while somebody else (open / <u>opens</u>) a present, so in Singapore, every businessman or businesswoman (know / <u>knows</u>) that gifts must be presented to a group. For example, if somebody (want / <u>wants</u>) to thank a receptionist, he or she (give / <u>gives</u>) a gift to the entire department. The group (accept / <u>accepts</u>) the gift graciously.

3. To be polite, most individuals (<u>refuse</u> / refuses) a gift initially. Some (<u>believe</u> / believes) that a refusal (make / <u>makes</u>) them appear less greedy.

If the gift-giver (continue / <u>continues</u>) to insist, the recipient will accept

the gift.

4. Singaporeans (<u>do</u> / does) not unwrap gifts in front of the giver. Such an

act (imply / <u>implies</u>) that the receiver is impatient and greedy. Everyone

(thank / <u>thanks</u>) the gift-giver and (wait / <u>waits</u>) to open the gift in

private. To avoid insulting their hosts, business travelers should learn

about gift-giving rules in other nations.

Verb Before the Subject

Usually the verb comes after the subject, but in some sentences, the verb is before the subject. In such cases, you must still ensure that the subject and verb agree.

There or Here

When a sentence begins with *there* or *here*, the subject always follows the verb. *There* and *here* are not subjects.

    V   S   V   S
   Here **is** the <u>menu</u>. There **are** many different <u>sandwiches</u>.

Questions

In questions, word order is usually reversed, and the main or helping verb is placed before the subject. In the following example, the main verb is *be*.

     V   S V   S
   Where **is** the <u>Butler Café</u>? **Is** the <u>food</u> good?

  In questions in which the main verb is not *be*, the subject agrees with the helping verb.

     HV   S V HV S   V
   When **does** the <u>café</u> **close**? **Do** <u>students</u> **work** there?

PRACTICE 4 Correct any subject–verb agreement errors. If there are no errors, write C for "correct" in the space.

    Have
EXAMPLE: ~~Has~~ you ever visited Turkey? _____

  Are
1. ~~Is~~ there etiquette rules about greetings? _____

ESL
Teaching Tip:
Nonnative speakers have particular problems with sentences beginning with *there* because they transfer structures from their other languages. Draw their attention to this rule.

ESL
Teaching Tip:
Nonnative speakers may add the *-s* ending to the main verb instead of the helping verb in question forms. They may need extra practice with verb agreement in questions.

CHAPTER 27

Teaching Tip:
If students have problems with Practice 4, suggest that they underline the subject.

     Does
2. D̶o̶ each nation have its own rules? _____

     are
3. There b̶e̶ specific rules in each country. _____

     greets
4. In Turkey, if someone enters a room, he or she g̶r̶e̶e̶t̶ the oldest person first. _____

     is
5. There b̶e̶ tremendous respect for elders. _____

     are
6. Why the two women a̶r̶e̶ holding hands? _____

7. In Turkey, handholding is a sign of respect and friendship. __*C*__

     has
8. In many companies, there h̶a̶v̶e̶ not been enough attention given to business etiquette. _____

Interrupting Words and Phrases

Words that come between the subject and the verb may confuse you. In these cases, look for the subject and make sure that the verb agrees with the subject.

      S   interrupting phrase   V

Some <u>companies</u> in the transportation sector **lose** money.

      S   interrupting phrase   V

The <u>manager</u> in my office never **wears** a suit and tie.

> ### *Hint*   **Identify Interrupting Phrases**
>
> When you revise your writing, place words that separate the subject and the verb in parentheses. Then you can check to see if your subjects and verbs agree.
>
>   S   interrupting phrase   V
>
> An <u>employee</u> **(**in my brother's company**) annoys** his co-workers.
>
> When interrupting phrases contain *of the*, the subject appears before the phrase.
>
>   S   interrupting phrase   V
>
> <u>One</u> **(**of the most common work-related ailments**) is** carpal tunnel syndrome.

PRACTICE 5   Identify the subject and place any words that come between each subject and verb in parentheses. Then underline the correct form of the verb. (Two possible verb choices are in bold.)

EXAMPLE: (One) (of the most controversial topics in business circles) **is** / **are** stress.

1. (People) in this nation **take** / **takes** very few vacation days. Other (nations),
   including France, England, and Sweden, **have** / **has** many vacation days.
   The average (employee) in France **have** / **has** about thirty-nine vacation
   days annually. The typical (American), according to numerous studies,
   take / **takes** only fourteen days off each year.

2. (Canada,) as well as England and France, **legislate** / **legislates** vacation
   days. (The United States,) unlike most industrialized countries, **do** / **does**
   not regulate benefits in the private sector. (One) of the problems caused by a
   lack of time off **is** / **are** stress-related illness.

3. Some (Americans), according to JobCircle.com, **is** / **are** beginning to
   rebel. (Workers) increasingly **call** / **calls** in sick when they really
   have / **has** family responsibilities or other reasons for missing work.
   (Alexia Williams,) for example, **work** / **works** in Houston as a
   receptionist. (Each) of the workers in her office **admit** / **admits**
   to using sick days for other purposes. (Most) of the workers
   have / **has** lied to the boss.

Interrupting Words—*Who, Which, That*

If a sentence contains a clause beginning with *who, which,* or *that,* then the verb
agrees with the subject preceding *who, which,* or *that.*

> A <u>woman</u> who **lives** in my neighborhood works as an executive.

Sometimes a complete dependent clause appears between the subject and verb.

> interrupting clause
> The <u>problem</u>, which we discussed, **needs** to be solved.

| **PRACTICE 6** | Correct nine subject–verb agreement errors. |

discusses
EXAMPLE: Jeff Geissler ~~discuss~~ maternity leave in an article for the Associated Press.

1. Elisa Elbert, who works for an accounting firm, is expecting a child. Elisa,
receives
like other Australian citizens, ~~receive~~ up to twelve months of paid leave.

   Madhuri Datta, a Canadian, is having her baby next month. Datta, who is
wants
due in November, ~~want~~ to share her paid leave with her husband. According
is
to a recent poll, one of the Canadian government's best laws ~~are~~ the one

   that permits parents to divide thirty-five weeks of paid parental leave.

2. The U.S. Family and Medical Leave Act, which only *covers* ~~cover~~ workers in
protects
large companies, ~~protect~~ new mothers from losing their jobs. The act,
provides
according to a Harvard study, ~~provide~~ for only twelve weeks of paid leave.

3. One of the Harvard researchers *thinks* ~~think~~ that the United States is out of step
have
with most nations. The study showed that 163 out of 168 nations ~~has~~ some

   sort of paid parental leave. The United States, along with Papua New
does
   Guinea and Swaziland, ~~do~~ not.

FINAL REVIEW

Correct fifteen errors in subject–verb agreement.

enjoys
EXAMPLE: The worker <u>enjoy</u> his afternoon nap.

Are
has
1. ~~Is~~ afternoon naps beneficial? In Spain, a siesta ~~have~~ been part of the

   culture for centuries. During a long afternoon break, employees return

ESL
Teaching Tip:
Nonnative speakers may question how *the United States* can be a singular noun. Point out that although the word is plural, it refers to one nation and is considered singular.

Teaching Tip:
You can use the final review as a test. Additional test material appears in the Instructor's Resource Manual and on *MyWritingLab*.

home and ~~has~~ *have* a siesta. However, this custom is changing. Now many multinational companies that operate in Spain ~~offers~~ *offer* a one-hour lunch. To give sleep-deprived Spaniards the siesta that they crave, a new type of business ~~have~~ *has* opened. There ~~is~~ *are* "Siesta Shops" throughout Spain.

Mario Carreno (b. 1913/Cuban) *La Siesta* 1946. Oil on canvas. © Christie's Images/ SuperStock.

2. José Luis Buqueras, as well as his wife, ~~work~~ *works* for a British multinational in Madrid. Each employee ~~have~~ *has* a one-hour lunch break. Luckily for Buqueras, there ~~be~~ *are* several siesta shops near his office. One of the best shops ~~charge~~ *charges* 15 euros, which is about 19 dollars, for a twenty-minute siesta. Either a chair or a bed ~~are~~ *is* in a small room. Somebody ~~massage~~ *massages* the customer's neck. Everybody ~~enjoy~~ *enjoys* the quiet music that plays in the background.

3. According to many medical professionals, a short afternoon nap helps reduce stress. There ~~is~~ *are* also studies showing that naps reduce heart disease. Everyone ~~benefit~~ *benefits* from a short rest during the day. Perhaps other nations can follow Spain's example.

CHAPTER 27

Teaching Tip:

Cooperative Learning (Question Cards) Place students in teams of three or four. Each team uses cards or cuts paper into six parts. Teams brainstorm questions about the chapter's key concepts. They write the question on one side of the paper and the answer on the other side. Teams should write about six questions. Then teams can exchange cards with another team. They can look at each question, answer it as a group, and then check the answer.

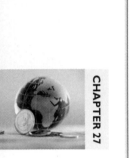

The Writer's Room

Write about one of the following topics. Proofread your text to ensure that your subjects and verbs agree.

1. Describe a visit that you made to a culturally different restaurant. What happened? Use language that appeals to the senses.

2. Do you have afternoon naps? Explain why or why not. Compare yourself to someone who has, or does not have, frequent naps.

✓ **CHECKLIST: SUBJECT–VERB AGREEMENT**

When you edit your writing, ask yourself these questions.

☐ Do my subjects and verbs agree? Check for errors with the following:

- present tense verbs
- *was* and *were*
- interrupting phrases

                                        are

The clients, whom I have never met, ~~is~~ unhappy with the
        is
new ad. It ~~be~~ too dull.

☐ Do I use the correct verb form with indefinite pronouns? Check for errors with singular indefinite pronouns such as *everybody*, *nobody*, or *somebody*.

                has

Somebody ~~have~~ to modify the photograph.

☐ Do my subjects and verbs agree when the subject is after the verb? Check for errors with the following:

- sentences with *here* and *there* before the verb
- question forms

    Does
~~Do~~ she watch commercials? There ~~is~~ many funny ads on
                                  are
television.

Teaching Tip:
Writer's World Competition Please advise students that they can submit their paragraphs and essays for possible publication to www.pearsonhighered.com/essayrewards/writingrewards.html

mywritinglab

To check your progress in meeting this chapter's objectives, log in to **www.mywritinglab.com,** go to the **Study Plan** tab, click on **The Editing Handbook—Section 3** and choose **Subject–Verb Agreement** from the list of subtopics. Read and view the resources in the **Review Materials** section, and then complete the **Recall, Apply,** and **Write** sets in the **Activities** section.

CHAPTER 28

Section Theme **COMMERCE AND MARKETING**

In this chapter, you will learn about advertising and marketing.

What Is Verb Tense?

Verb tense indicates when an action occurred. Review the various tenses of the verb *work*. (Progressive, or *-ing*, forms of these verbs appear at the end of this chapter.)

Simple Forms

Present	I <u>work</u> in a large company. My sister <u>works</u> with me.
Past	We <u>worked</u> in Cancun last summer.
Future	My sister <u>will work</u> in the Middle East next year.
Present perfect	We <u>have worked</u> together since 2001.
Past perfect	When Maria lost her job, she <u>had worked</u> there for six years.
Future perfect	By 2020, I <u>will have worked</u> here for twenty years.

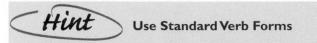

> ⟨*Hint*⟩   **Use Standard Verb Forms**
>
> **Nonstandard English** is used in everyday conversation and may differ according to the region in which you live. **Standard American English** is the common language generally used and expected in schools, businesses, and government institutions in the United States. In college, you should write using standard American English.
>
> **Nonstandard:**   He don't have no money.   She be real tired.
>
> **Standard:**   He <u>does not have any</u> money.   She <u>is really</u> tired.

CHAPTER 28

ESL
Teaching Tip:
Although your native speakers may benefit from the material in this chapter, it is particularly useful for nonnative speakers. They may make errors when they transfer patterns from their languages.

GRAMMAR LINK

For more information about subject–verb agreement, see Chapter 27.

ESL
Teaching Tip:
The visuals (tense time lines) are for the benefit of your nonnative speakers. In some languages such as Malay, the notion of verb tense does not exist.

Present and Past Tenses

Present Tense Verbs

The simple present tense indicates that an action is a general fact or habitual activity. Remember to add -*s* or -*es* to verbs that follow third-person singular forms.

Fact: Our fee **includes** mass mail-outs and pamphlet distribution.

Habitual Activity: Carmen Cruz **takes** drawing classes every Saturday.

PAST   Saturday   Saturday   Saturday   Saturday   FUTURE

          She draws.   She draws.   She draws.   She draws.

Past Tense Verbs

The past tense indicates that an action occurred at a specific past time. Regular past tense verbs have a standard -*d* or -*ed* ending. Use the same form for both singular and plural past tense verbs.

Yesterday morning, we **discussed** the campaign.

Yesterday morning   Today

We discussed the campaign.

PRACTICE I   Write the present or past form of each verb in parentheses.

EXAMPLE: Last year, Read Montague (publish) _____*published*_____ the results.

1. In the 1980s, the Pepsi Company (develop) _____*developed*_____ a very simple ad campaign. Ordinary people (taste) _____*tasted*_____ two drinks and (pick) _____*picked*_____ their favorite. Of course, most people (like) _____*liked*_____ Pepsi during that campaign. A young man, Read Montague, (wonder) _____*wondered*_____ about the ad. Why was Coke more popular if people actually (prefer) _____*preferred*_____ the taste of the competing drink? To find out, Montague (decide) _____*decided*_____ to become a neuromarketer.

2. Neuromarketers (study) _____*study*_____ the brain's responses to ads, brands, and logos. In 2003, Montague (repeat) _____*repeated*_____ the Pepsi challenge, and he (study) _____*studied*_____ participants' brains during the trials. He (discover) _____*discovered*_____ something interesting. Most Pepsi lovers (change) _____*changed*_____ their minds after learning which sample contained Coke. Their fond ideas about the Coke brand (seem) _____*seemed*_____ to override their initial preference for Pepsi! Montague's 2003 study (show) _____*showed*_____ that good marketing and branding is effective.

Teaching Tip:

Cooperative Learning (Jigsaw)
Place students in teams of three to five. Assign each team a grammar concept from the chapter. Teams are responsible for teaching the class about their topic. They should summarize key ideas, give examples, and prepare some practice sentences. Then each team can present a short lesson to the class.

Irregular Past Tense Verbs

Irregular verbs change internally. Because their spellings change from the present to the past tense, these verbs can be challenging to remember. For example, the irregular verb *go* becomes *went* when you convert it to the past tense.

The company **sold** the patent. (*sold* = past tense of *sell*)

Consumers **bought** the product. (*bought* = past tense of *buy*)

GRAMMAR LINK

See Appendix 2 for a list of common irregular verbs.

Be (Was or Were)

Most past tense verbs have one form that you can use with all subjects. However, the verb *be* has two past forms: *was* and *were*. Use *was* with *I, he, she,* and *it.* Use *were* with *you, we,* and *they.*

> The packing box **was** not sturdy enough. The plates **were** fragile.

PRACTICE 2   Write the correct past form of each verb in parentheses. Some verbs are regular, and some are irregular.

EXAMPLE: Long ago, John Pemberton (have) _____*had*_____ a great idea.

1. In 1884, John Pemberton (be) _____*was*_____ a pharmacist in Atlanta,

    Georgia. He (know) _____*knew*_____ about a successful French product

    called a "coca wine." Pemberton (make) _____*made*_____ his own version of

    the product and called it Pemberton's French Wine Coca. In 1885, Atlanta

    (pass) _____*passed*_____ prohibition legislation, so Pemberton created an

    alcohol-free version of his drink. He (mix) _____*mixed*_____ his syrup with

    carbonated water, and he (bring) _____*brought*_____ some samples to a local

    pharmacy. Customers (pay) _____*paid*_____ 5 cents a glass for the drink.

2. Pemberton's bookkeeper (be) _____*was*_____ a marketing wizard. Frank

    M. Robinson (think) _____*thought*_____ of a name for the drink. He also (feel)

    _____*felt*_____ certain that the drink required an interesting logo; thus,

    Robinson (develop) _____*developed*_____ the handwritten Coca-Cola logo. In

    1886, many stores (have) _____*had*_____ the red logo on their awnings.

3. In 1889, the Coca-Cola company (choose) _____*chose*_____ not to patent

    the formula for Coca Cola. Executives (do) _____*did*_____ not want

    competitors to know the secret formula of the soft drink. It remains

    one of the best-kept trade secrets in history.

Hint **Use the Base Form After *Did* and *To***

Remember to use the base form:

• of verbs that follow *did* in question and negative forms.

• of verbs that follow the word *to* (infinitive form).

        invent   *promote*

    Did he ~~invented~~ a good product? Pemberton wanted to ~~promoted~~ his soft drink.

ESL
Teaching Tip:
Nonnative speakers tend to incorrectly use the past tense with infinitives or with verbs that do not require it.

CHAPTER 28

PRACTICE 3   Correct twelve verb tense and spelling errors.

                        like

EXAMPLE: Consumer groups didn't ~~liked~~ the marketing campaign.

1. In past centuries, breastfeeding ~~be~~ [*was*] the most common method of feeding

   babies. At the end of the eighteenth century, some parents ~~feeded~~ [*fed*] their

   children cows' milk, but many infants could not digest it. Finally, in the

   1870s, the Nestle Company ~~maked~~ [*made*] the first infant formula. Consumers

   just had to ~~mixed~~ [*mix*] water with the formula.

2. In 1973, the Nestle Company wanted to ~~sold~~ [*sell*] the formula in Africa. The

   company ~~putted~~ [*put*] advertisements for the product in magazines and on

   billboards. Nestle also ~~gived~~ [*gave*] free samples to African women as soon as

   they had their babies. In hospitals, mothers ~~seen~~ [*saw*] their own breast milk dry

   up after they gave formula to their babies. When the women returned

   home, they did not ~~had~~ [*have*] enough money to continue buying enough

   formula. They added too much water to the formula, and the water ~~be~~ [*was*]

   often contaminated. Babies who ~~drinked~~ [*drank*] formula become malnourished. In

   many villages, the level of infant malnutrition and mortality ~~rised~~ [*rose*]. In the

1970s, the Nestle company faced a lot of criticism for its marketing

techniques in Africa.

Past Participles

A **past participle** is a verb form, not a verb tense. The past tense and the past participle of regular verbs are the same. The past tense and the past participle of irregular verbs may be different.

	Base Form	Past Tense	Past Participle
Regular verb:	talk	talked	talked
Irregular verb:	begin	began	begun

 Using Past Participles

You cannot use a past participle as the only verb in a sentence. You must use it with a helping verb such as *have, has, had, is, was,* or *were*.

	helping verb	past participle	
The company	**was**	founded	in 1863.
The products	**have**	become	very popular.

GRAMMAR LINK

For a list of irregular past participles, see Appendix 2.

Teaching Tip:
For the benefit of nonnative speakers, ask students to quiz each other about past participles. Students could open their books to Appendix 2, and then ask each other to spell irregular past participles. They should highlight the words that they misspell.

Teaching Tip:
You could ask students to identify the helping verbs by circling or underlining them.

PRACTICE 4 In the next selection, the past participles are underlined. Correct ten past participle errors, and write C above correct past participles.

                                                     met
EXAMPLE: The business ethics students have <u>meeted</u> many times to discuss the issue.

                C
1. Consumer groups have <u>expressed</u> concerns about online marketing
                                                                    come
   techniques. For example, the social networking site Facebook has <u>came</u>
                            earned
   under attack. Since its inception, Facebook has <u>earn</u> money through

   targeted advertising. The personal information of Facebook users can be
   C
   <u>viewed</u> by marketers.

                            launched
2. In 2007, Facebook Beacon was <u>launch</u>. At that time, when an online purchase
        made   *sent*
   was <u>maked</u> by a Facebook user, the information was <u>send</u> to the user's

friends. For example, Chad Reims bought movie tickets at Fandango.com

published

and the information was <u>publish</u> on his Facebook news feed without his

knowledge. In a well-known case, a man planned to propose to his

bought

girlfriend. After he had <u>buyed</u> an engagement ring online, the information

C   *seen*

was <u>distributed</u> to his Facebook friends. Of course, the news was <u>saw</u> by his

C

girlfriend. After a class-action suit was <u>filed</u>, Facebook allowed users to opt

out of the Beacon program.

been

3. Facebook's marketing practices have always <u>being</u> legal. Perhaps children

taught

should be <u>teached</u> to use privacy settings when they use social networking

sites.

ESL
Teaching Tip:
The present perfect tense is particularly difficult for nonnative speakers because many languages such as Russian and Spanish do not have an equivalent tense.

CHAPTER 28

ESL
Teaching Tip:
To practice the first usage of the present perfect, ask students questions that can generate either present perfect or simple past responses. For instance, you can ask the next questions. Student answers will shift from the present to the past to the present perfect.

• *Who is your best friend? When did you meet him or her?*

• *How long have you known your best friend?*

To practice the second usage of the present perfect, ask students the next questions.

• *Who has traveled to another country?*

• *How many countries have you visited?*

Present Perfect Tense

(*have* or *has* + past participle)

A past participle combines with *have* or *has* to form the **present perfect tense.**

> Kate **has been** a marketing manager for six years.

> Since 2001, the products **have sold** extremely well.

You can use this tense in two different circumstances.

1. Use the present perfect to show that an action began in the past and continues to the present time. You will often use *since* and *for* with this tense.

PAST
(5 years ago, the
factory opened)   NOW

The factory **has flourished** for five years.

2. Use the present perfect to show that one or more completed actions occurred at unspecified past times.

PAST   NOW
?   ?   ?   ?

Mr. Jain **has visited** China four times.
(The time of the four visits is not specified.)

> **Hint** — **Use Time Markers**
>
> When you try to identify which tense to use, look for time markers. **Time markers** are words such as *since, for,* or *ago* that indicate when an action occurred.
>
> **Simple past:** Three weeks **ago**, Parker launched her new perfume.
>
> **Present perfect:** **Since then**, her perfume has been selling very well.

CHAPTER 28

Choosing the Simple Past or the Present Perfect

Look at the difference between the past and the present perfect tenses.

Simple past: In 2002, Kumar Jain **went** to Shanghai.
(This event occurred at a known past time.)

Present perfect: Since 2002, Jain **has owned** a factory in China.
(The action began in the past and continues to the present.)

He **has made** many business contacts.
(Making business contacts occurred at unknown past times.)

Teaching Tip
Pair Work
Give students a topic such as *friends, sports,* or *hobbies,* and ask pairs of students to generate sentences that contain the simple past and the present perfect tenses.

> **Hint** — **Simple Past or Present Perfect?**
>
> Use the past tense when referring to someone who is no longer living or to something that no longer exists. Only use the present perfect tense when the action has a relationship to someone or something that still exists.
>
> designed
> Leonardo da Vinci ~~has designed~~ many products.

Teaching Tip:
As students do Practice 5, remind them to consider the context. If a series of events all occurred in the 1920s, they should use the past tense. If the event has a relationship with the present, and if they see key words such as *since* or *for,* they should use the present perfect.

PRACTICE 5 Write the simple past or present perfect form of the verb in parentheses.

EXAMPLE: For the last six years, my cousin Mike (be) ___*has been*___ a sales representative.

1. Since the beginning of the twentieth century, many companies (try)

   ___*have tried*___ to create memorable advertisements for their products.

   Before the 1920s, most ads (be) ___*were*___ on billboards and in

   magazines. Then, in 1922, companies (discover) ___*discovered*___ the potential of radio advertising. For example, the Lucky Strike Cigarette

Company (sponsor) _____*sponsored*_____ a music show. Since then,

many companies (sponsor) _____*have sponsored*_____ artistic and sporting

events.

2. In the mid-1920s, radio stations (decide) _____*decided*_____ to give short

time slots to advertisers so that they could promote their products as an

alternative to the sponsorship of shows. Ever since, commercials (be)

_____*have been*_____ an effective way for companies to market their products.

Most people (see) _____*have seen*_____ thousands of commercials.

Past Perfect Tense
(*had* + past participle)

The **past perfect tense** indicates that one or more past actions happened before another past action. It is formed with *had* and the past participle.

PAST PERFECT	PAST	NOW
▼	▼	▼

Mr. Lo **had spent** a lot on research when he launched the product.

Notice the differences between the simple past, the present perfect, and the past perfect tenses.

Simple past: Last night, Craig **worked** at Burger Town.
(The action occurred at a known past time.)

Present perfect: He **has owned** the restaurant for three years.
(The action began in the past and continues to the present.)

Past perfect: Craig **had had** two business failures before he bought Burger Town.
(All of the actions happened in the past, but the two business failures occurred before he bought the hamburger restaurant.)

Teaching Tip:

Cooperative Learning (Pair & Share)
Ask pairs of students to brainstorm sentences explaining how the world has changed since the 1950s. Write some of their sentences on the board and ask students to identify and form the present perfect verbs.

Teaching Tip:
Ask students to generate other sentences that require the simple past, present perfect, and past perfect tenses.

PRACTICE 6   Underline the correct verb form in each sentence. You may choose the simple past tense or the past perfect tense.

EXAMPLE: The Barbosas (were / <u>had been</u>) farmers for ten years when Alex Barbosa decided to sell organic beef.

1. Even though he (never studied / <u>had never studied</u>) marketing, Alex Barbosa decided to promote his organic beef.

2. He printed flyers, and then he (<u>distributed</u> / had distributed) them to private homes.

3. The flyer contained a picture that Barbosa (took / <u>had taken</u>) the previous summer.

4. The image of the meat carcass (<u>was</u> / had been) unappealing.

5. After Barbosa received negative feedback about his flyer, he remembered that his daughter (warned / <u>had warned</u>) him about the image.

6. Also, the neighborhood (<u>had</u> / had had) low-income families who could not afford the high price of the organic meat.

7. Finally, in 2005, Barbosa hired a business graduate who (learned / <u>had learned</u>) how to do effective marketing.

8. By December 2006, Barbosa's organic meat (found / <u>had found</u>) a niche in the marketplace.

Passive Voice
(be + past participle)

In sentences with the **passive voice,** the subject receives the action and does not perform the action. To form the passive voice, use the appropriate tense of the verb *be* plus the past participle. Look carefully at the following two sentences.

Teaching Tip:
To help students understand voice, you can write a sentence on the board such as *Workers make shoes in that factory.* Then write the word *shoes* under it, and ask students to generate a sentence that means the same thing as the first sentence, but uses *shoes* as the subject. The students will generate the passive form.

Active: The boss **gave** documents to her assistant.

(This is active, because the subject, *boss*, performed the action.)

Passive: Several documents **were given** to the assistant.

(This is passive because the subject, *documents*, was affected by the action and did not perform the action.)

> ## *Hint*   Avoid Overusing the Passive Voice
>
> Generally, try to use the active voice instead of the passive voice. The active voice is more direct and friendly than the passive voice. For example, read two versions of the same message.
>
> **Passive voice:**   No more than two pills per day should be ingested. This medication should be taken with meals. It should not be continued if headaches or nausea are experienced.
>
> **Active voice:**   Do not ingest more than two pills per day. Take this medication with meals. Do not continue taking it if you experience headache or nausea.

ESL
Teaching Tip:
Nonnative speakers—German speakers, for instance—overuse the passive form when they transfer sentence patterns from their own language. Remind students to use the passive voice sparingly.

Teaching Tip:
Mention that students should especially avoid the passive voice when writing documents such as résumés, medical labels, ads, leaflets, or instructions.

PRACTICE 7   Complete the following sentences by changing the passive verb to the active form. Do not alter the verb tense.

EXAMPLE: Each department *will be visited* by the supervisor.

The supervisor will visit each department.

1. A funny commercial *was created* by the advertising agency.

   The advertising agency created a funny commercial.

2. The ad *will be seen* by many people.

   Many people will see the ad.

3. A well-known comedian *was hired* by the company.

   The company hired a well-known comedian.

4. Many commercials *are created* by Pedro Guzman.

   Pedro Guzman creates many commercials.

5. Complaints about their commercials *are often ignored* by companies.

   Companies often ignore complaints about their commercials.

> When *Be* Is Suggested, Not Written
>
> In the passive voice, sometimes the verb *be* is suggested but not written. The following sentence contains the passive voice.
>
> A man **named** Harley Cobb complained about the car company's decision.
>   ↑
>   *(who was)*

CHAPTER 28

PRACTICE 8   Underline and correct eight errors with past participles.

EXAMPLE: A problem was <u>find</u> with the design.   *found*

1. When Apple Computer first released the Macintosh, a pull-down menu was <u>include</u> in the product. The computer also had a variety of icons for *included*

    different tasks. For instance, useless files were <u>drag</u> to a trash can icon. A *dragged*

    year later, Microsoft Corporation introduced its popular software program <u>name</u> Windows 2.0. The software, <u>modify</u> in 1988, looked a lot like *named* *modified*

    Apple's software. Apple sued Microsoft for copyright infringement and

    argued that Microsoft had copied the "look and feel" of Apple software.

2. There are strict rules about copyright. A unique product can be <u>patent</u>. *patented*

    However, people cannot copyright an idea. Therefore, Apple's decision to use specific icons could not be <u>protect</u>. Still, Apple argued that its original *protected*

    concept should not have been <u>copy</u>. The case, which lasted for four years, *copied*

    was <u>win</u> by Microsoft. *won*

Progressive Forms
(*-ing* verbs)

Most verbs have progressive tenses. The **progressive tense,** formed with *be* and the *-ing* form of the verb, indicates that an action is, was, or will be in progress. For example, the present progressive indicates that an action is happening right now or for a temporary period of time. The following time line illustrates both the simple and progressive tenses.

Every day, he **sells** leather wallets. (Simple present)

PAST   FUTURE

| sells | sells | sells | sells |
| Sunday | Monday | Today, he **is visiting** the stores on Main Street. (Present progressive) | Wednesday |

CHAPTER 28

To form the progressive, use the appropriate tense of the verb *be* with the *-ing* verb.

Present progressive:	Right now, I **am** <u>working</u>.
Past progressive:	We **were** <u>sleeping</u> when you phoned us.
Future progressive:	Tomorrow, at noon, I **will be** <u>driving</u>.
Present perfect progressive:	The receptionist **has been** <u>working</u> since 8:00 A.M.
Past perfect progressive:	She **had been** <u>speeding</u> when the officer stopped her.
Future perfect progressive:	Next year, when Enrique retires, he **will have been** <u>working</u> for thirty years.

Teaching Tip: Point out that the helping verbs show the tense.

Common Errors in the Progressive Form

- Do not use the progressive form when an action happens regularly.

  complains
  Every day he ~~is complaining~~ about his job.

- In the progressive form, use the correct form of the verb *be*.

  is
  Right now, Ron ~~be~~ talking with his manager.

- In the progressive form, always include the complete helping verb.

  is   *have*
  Right now, the manager discussing the problem. They been talking for hours.

- Only use the past progressive tense when an action was ongoing at a specific past time or was interrupted.

  agreed
  Yesterday, I ~~was agreeing~~ to meet the new client.

ESL

Teaching Tip:
Your nonnative
speakers may not
realize that certain
verbs should not
take the *-ing* form.
Draw their
attention to
this list.

CHAPTER 28

Nonprogressive Verbs

Some verbs do not take the progressive form because they indicate an ongoing state or a perception rather than a temporary action.

Examples of Nonprogressive Verbs

Perception Verbs	Preference Verbs	State Verbs	Possession
admire	desire	believe	have*
care	doubt	know	own
hear	feel	mean	possess
see	hate	realize	
seem	like	recognize	
smell*	look	suppose	
taste*	love	think*	
	prefer	understand	
	want		

*Some verbs have more than one meaning and can be used in the progressive tense. Compare the following pairs of sentences.

Nonprogressive	**Progressive**
He **has** a franchise. (expresses ownership)	He **is having** a bad day.
I **think** it is unethical. (expresses an opinion)	I **am thinking** about you.

ESL

Teaching Tip:
There are many
other examples of
names or slogans
that translate badly.
You might ask
students to go
to Web sites
containing bad
translations.
(Just type "bad
translations" in the
search engine, and
many sites will
appear.) Students
could work in
groups to repair the
poorly translated
sentences.

PRACTICE 9   Correct one verb error in each sentence.

      had
EXAMPLE: She been working in the store for ten years when she was fired.

1. Ellen Peters was producing and ~~give~~ *giving* away her own fragrances when her

    sister suggested that she try to market her perfume.

2. These days, Peters *is* negotiating with a cosmetics company that hopes to

    market her perfume internationally.

3. She *has* been looking for a product name for the last six months.

4. Last May, she ~~be~~ *was* planning to call it Golden Mist when someone told her

    that *mist* means "manure" in German.

5. While her friends were ~~brainstorm~~ *brainstorming* to help her, one of them suggested the

    name "Pete," which is a shortened form of Peters.

6. Unfortunately, *pété* ~~is meaning~~ *means* "release of gassy air" in French.

7. Often, companies ~~are having~~ *have* problems with bad translations.

8. For example, a Scandinavian vacuum cleaner company ~~was making~~ *made* a

   mistake when it created the slogan "Nothing sucks like an Electrolux."

9. Ellen Peters wants her product to sell internationally, so right now she is
   ~~work~~ *working* with a marketing firm to come up with a good product name.

FINAL REVIEW

Underline and correct fifteen errors in verb form or tense.

EXAMPLE: The book *Business Ethics* was <u>publish</u> *published* by Prentice Hall in 2006.

1. Since the 1930s, a clever sales technique <u>been</u> *has been* popular. The sales
   method is <u>call</u> *called* the "lowball technique." It is <u>use</u> *used* by car dealers and
   other salespeople. A customer is <u>offer</u> *offered* a product for less money
   than it seems to be worth. After the customer accepts the deal, the
   cost of the commitment increases.

2. For example, Carla and Wade <u>have needed</u> *needed* a new car last August.
   They went to a new car showroom. The cars in the showroom <u>was</u> *were*
   very appealing. After Carla and Wade <u>have</u> *had* chosen a car, the salesperson
   offered to reduce the price by $5,000. The couple <u>was agreeing</u> *agreed* to the deal.
   As they were <u>sign</u> *signing* the contract, the dealer announced that there would be
   a few extra charges. The floor mats, hubcaps, sound system, and a few
   other pieces of equipment were not <u>include</u> *included* in the price. Also, a

Teaching Tip:
You can use the final review as a test. Additional practice and test material appears in the Instructor's Resource Manual and on *MyWritingLab*.

agreed
"transportation" fee of about $2,000 was added. The couple had <u>agree</u> to

back
the initial deal, and they didn't <u>backing</u> out when the extra demands were

made
<u>maked</u>.

was
3. A few weeks later, Wade and Carla changed their minds, but it <u>be</u> too late.

signed
They had <u>sign</u> the contract, and they would have to buy the car.

Teaching Tip:

Cooperative Learning (Quick Review)
Divide the class into teams of three or four. Assign a part of the chapter to each team. Each team should review the information and generate three questions. Then ask teams to read the questions aloud. Anybody in the class can answer a question. Or, as an alternative, you can ask teams to exchange questions and to answer another team's questions.

▯ The Writer's Room

Write about one of the following topics. Proofread your writing and ensure that your verbs are formed correctly.

1. Describe a purchase you have made that you later regretted. Explain what happened. Why did you buy the product, and why did you regret buying it later?

2. What are the effects of advertising on consumers? How does the deluge of commercials, spam, billboards, and other advertising affect the population?

CHECKLIST: VERB TENSES

When you edit your writing, ask yourself these questions.

☐ Do I use the correct present and past tense forms? Check for errors in these cases:

- verbs following third-person singular nouns
- irregular present or past tense verbs
- question and negative forms

          were   *were*
The products that ~~was~~ defective ~~was~~ in his shop.

☐ Do I use the correct form of past participles? Check for errors in the following:

- spelling of irregular past participles
- present perfect and past perfect verbs
- passive and active forms

                           have made
Since the 1970s, some car companies ~~made~~ bad business decisions.

☐ Do I use *-ing* forms correctly? Check for the overuse or misuse of progressive forms. Also ensure that progressive forms are complete.

                         designing
In 1971, while engineers were ~~design~~ the Pinto, nobody
  wanted
~~was wanting~~ to make an unsafe car.

mywritinglab To check your progress in meeting this chapter's objectives, log in to **www.mywritinglab.com**, go to the **Study Plan** tab, click on **The Editing Handbook—Section 3** and choose **Verb Tenses** from the list of subtopics. Read and view the resources in the **Review Materials** section, and then complete the **Recall, Apply,** and **Write** sets in the **Activities** section.

Teaching Tip:
Writer's World Competition
Please advise students that they can submit their paragraphs and essays for possible publication to www.pearsonhighered.com/essayrewards/writingrewards.html

Problems with Verbs

Section Theme **COMMERCE AND MARKETING**

In this chapter, you will read about marketing campaigns, trademarks, and business innovations.

Verb Consistency

A verb tense gives your readers an idea about the time that an event occurred. A **faulty tense shift** occurs when you shift from one tense to another for no logical reason. When you write essays, ensure that your tenses are consistent.

Faulty tense shift: Jean Roberts traveled to Santiago, Chile, where she interviews a salon owner.

Correct: Jean Roberts traveled to Santiago, Chile, where she **interviewed** a salon owner.

ESL
Teaching Tip:
The error
mentioned in
the Hint box is
particularly
common among
nonnative speakers.

> ⬭ *Hint* **Would and Could**
>
> When you tell a story about a past event, use *would* instead of *will* and *could* instead of *can*.
>
> couldn't
> In 2001, Simon Brault wanted to be an actor. At that time, he <u>can't</u> find a good
>
> would
> acting job. To earn extra cash, he <u>will</u> deliver telegrams wearing a costume.

PRACTICE 1   Underline and correct ten faulty tense shifts in the next paragraphs.

EXAMPLE: In the 1990s, Gretta Zahn made a decision. She <u>decides</u> to work as
        a parts model. *(decided)*

1. In 1992, a modeling agent noticed seventeen-year-old Gretta Zahn's

   hands. He signed the young girl to a contract, and he said that he <u>will</u> *(would)*

   make her famous as a "hand model." During Zahn's modeling years, her

   jobs were diverse. She soaked her fingers in dishwashing liquid, <u>wear</u> *(wore)*

   diamond rings, and demonstrated nail polish.

2. In the 1990s, Zahn's modeling career was lucrative. In

   1994, at the height of her career, she <u>can</u> earn up to $1,500 *(could)*

   a day. In those days, she <u>will</u> wake up at 5:00 A.M., and *(would)*

   sometimes she <u>will</u> have to work for fourteen hours. At that *(would)*

   time, Zahn's agent told her that she <u>will</u> need to take *(would)*

   special care of her hands. From 1992 to 2000, she <u>cannot</u> *(could not)*

   wear jewelry because it would leave tan lines. Also, during

   those years, she <u>will</u> not do the dishes. *(would)*

3. In 2000, Zahn gave up modeling. Today, she enjoys gardening, and she

   likes to wear rings and bracelets. Her hands are no longer flawless, but she
   does
   <u>did</u> not mind. "I have a life," she says. "I no longer worry about getting a

   cut or scrape."

Teaching Tip:
Discuss with
students how the
two negative words
in the examples
cancel each
other out.

CHAPTER 29

Teaching Tip:

**Cooperative
Learning
(Jigsaw)**
Place students in
teams of three to
five. Assign each
team a grammar
concept from the
chapter. Teams are
responsible for
teaching the class
about the concept.
They should
summarize key
ideas, give examples,
and prepare some
practice sentences.
Then each team can
present a short
lesson to the class.

Avoiding Double Negatives

A double negative occurs when a negative word such as *no* (*nothing, nobody, nowhere*) is combined with a negative adverb (*not, never, rarely, seldom*, and so on). The result is a sentence that has a double negative. Such sentences can be confusing because the negative words cancel each other.

Double negative: Mr. Lee <u>doesn't</u> want <u>no</u> problems.
(According to this sentence, Mr. Lee wants problems.)

He <u>didn't</u> know <u>nothing</u> about it.
(According to this sentence, he knew something about it.)

How to Correct Double Negatives

There are two ways to correct double negatives.

1. Completely remove *one* of the negative forms. Remember that you may need to adjust the verb to make it agree with the subject.
   Mr. Lee **doesn't** want ~~no~~ problems.
   Mr. Lee ~~doesn't~~ wants **no** problems.
2. Change "no" to *any* (*anybody, anything, anywhere*).
   any
   Mr. Lee doesn't want ~~no~~ problems.

PRACTICE 2   Underline and correct five errors with double negatives. There are two ways to correct each error.

have no or don't have any
EXAMPLE: They <u>don't have no</u> trademark.

McDonald's corporation has been extremely zealous in protecting its
doesn't want anybody or wants nobody
trademark. The company <u>doesn't want nobody</u> to use a similar-sounding name.

For instance, in 1987, a couple of chefs decided to open a sushi restaurant in San

Francisco called McSushi. They printed menus and put up a sign. They

had nothing or didn't have anything

<u>didn't have nothing</u> left to do but to open their doors. Then they received a legal

letter from McDonald's Corporation. McDonald's had cornered the market on

had no or didn't have any

every McFood-type name. The sushi restaurant owners <u>didn't have no</u> money to

was nothing or wasn't anything

fight the huge hamburger chain. They decided that there <u>wasn't nothing</u> they

could do. They had to change their name, signs, and documents. McDonald's

argues that "Mc" suggests "fast" and other companies shouldn't copy it. These

don't want any or want no

days, if you <u>don't want no</u> problems, avoid creating a company name with "Mc"

in it.

Nonstandard Forms—*Gonna, Gotta, Wanna*

Some people commonly say *I'm gonna, I gotta,* or *I wanna.* These are nonstandard
forms, so avoid using them in written communication.

■ Write "going to" instead of *gonna.*

going to

The boss is ~~gonna~~ hire three new cashiers.

■ Write "have to" instead of *gotta* or *got to.*

have to

We ~~gotta~~ stay open until midnight.

■ Write "want to" instead of *wanna.*

want to

We ~~wanna~~ keep our jobs.

Teaching Tip:
Students often hear
these nonstandard
forms in movies and
on the street, but
remind them that
these are incorrect
forms.

PRACTICE 3 Underline and correct eight nonstandard verbs.

have to find

EXAMPLE: You and I <u>gotta find</u> a better job.

want to

1. If you <u>wanna</u> find work, there are many job-hunting sites on the Internet.

One of the oldest and most established sites is Monster.com. In 1994, Jeff

Taylor owned a job-recruitment agency, and he thought that an Internet site could help his business. He decided that his new site was ~~gonna~~ *going to* match job seekers with employers. That year, he created The Monster Board.

2. In 1995, Taylor sold his business because he didn't ~~wanna~~ *want to* pass up a great business offer. The new owners said that they were ~~gonna~~ *going to* change the name of the Web site. They didn't think that consumers would ~~wanna~~ *want to* associate "monster" and work. However, Taylor convinced them to keep the name.

3. In 1999, Monster Board joined with Online Career Center and became Monster.com. When you go on the site, you ~~gotta~~ *have to* find your region. Then you ~~gotta~~ *have to* choose the job category that interests you. If you go on the site, you are probably ~~gonna~~ *going to* find interesting jobs in your city or area.

Problems in Conditional Forms

In **conditional sentences,** there is a condition and a result. There are three types of conditional sentences, and each type has two parts, or clauses. The main clause depends on the condition set in the *if* clause.

First Form: Possible Present or Future

The condition is true or very possible. Use the present tense in the *if* clause.

> condition (*if* clause)   result
> If you **ask** her, she **will hire** you.

Second Form: Unlikely Present

The condition is not likely, and probably will not happen. Use the past tense in the *if* clause and use *would* or *could* in the result clause. In formal writing, when the condition contains the verb *be,* always use "were" in the *if* clause.

> condition (*if* clause)   result
> If I **had** more money, I **would start** my own business
>
> If Katrina **were** younger, she **would change** careers.

Third Form: Impossible Past

The condition cannot happen because the event is over. Use the past perfect tense in the *if* clause.

condition (*if* clause)   result

If the business **had closed** in 2002, many people **would have lost** their jobs.

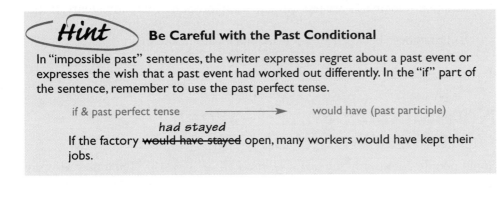

Hint **Be Careful with the Past Conditional**

In "impossible past" sentences, the writer expresses regret about a past event or expresses the wish that a past event had worked out differently. In the "if" part of the sentence, remember to use the past perfect tense.

if & past perfect tense   ⟶   would have (past participle)

                 had stayed

If the factory ~~would have stayed~~ open, many workers would have kept their jobs.

Teaching Tip:
Draw attention to this hint. Both native and nonnative speakers make errors with conditional forms.

PRACTICE 4 Write the correct conditional forms of the verbs in parentheses.

EXAMPLE: If they (patent) *had patented* the product, nobody else would have copied it.

1. If you search on the Internet, you (find) ____*will find (or can find)*____

   information about patents and trademarks. In 2004, Raul Lopez created an

   exercise machine. If he (patent) _____*had patented*_____ his invention,

   nobody else could copy it. So he paid a lot of money for a patent, and he

   named his machine "The Body Works." A few months later, someone else

   made a similar machine and called it Body Works.

2. Unfortunately, Lopez did not have a trademark. At the beginning,

   if he (ask) _____*had asked*_____ for a trademark, his idea (be)

   _____*would have been*_____ safer. Nobody could have used the same product name. Perhaps if he (speak) _____*had spoken*_____ with a

lawyer, he (save) _____*would have saved*_____ a lot of time and money.

If he (own) _____*had owned*_____ the Body Works name, nobody else

could have used it for a similar product. Tamara Monosoff, an inventor,

says that trademarks are less expensive and more useful than patents. If she

had to choose between a trademark and a patent, she (pay)

_____*would pay*_____ for a trademark.

Nonstandard Forms—*Would of, Could of, Should of*

Some people commonly say *would of, could of,* or *should of*. They may also say *woulda, coulda,* or *shoulda*. These are nonstandard forms, and you should avoid using them in written communication. When you use the past forms of *should, would,* and *could*, always include *have* with the past participle.

> Dominique Brown is a nurse, but she really loves real estate. She
> *should have*
> ~~should of~~ become a real-estate agent. She ~~woulda~~ been very successful.
> *would have*

Teaching Tip:
Both native and nonnative speakers make these types of errors because many native English speakers do not tend to pronounce the "have" clearly. Draw attention to this rule.

PRACTICE 5   Underline and correct nine errors in conditional forms or in the past forms of *could* and *should*.

have
EXAMPLE: The workers should ~~of~~ stayed home.

1. In 1943, seventeen-year-old Ingvar Kamprad did well in his studies, and
   could have
   his father gave him a gift of money. Kamprad <u>coulda</u> bought anything he
   should have
   wanted. His mother thought that he <u>shoulda</u> continued his studies. The

   young man had other ideas. He decided to create a company called IKEA.

2. In 1947, Kamprad decided to add furniture to his catalogue. One day, an

   employee from IKEA removed the legs from a table so that it would fit into his car trunk. Soon, the company created flat packaging designs. If the

employee woulda̲ owned a truck, perhaps IKEA would o̲f continued to sell
$\quad\quad\quad\quad$ *had* $\quad\quad\quad\quad\quad\quad\quad\quad\quad\quad\quad$ *have*

completely assembled furniture. If that had been the case, the company

would not o̲f been so successful.
$\quad\quad$ *have*

3. Kamprad's extreme youth helped him in his quest to take chances. Maybe

    if he woulda̲ been older, he woulda̲ been more conservative. If IKEA
    $\quad$ *had* $\quad\quad\quad\quad\quad\quad$ *would have*

    would not have̲ changed, perhaps it would o̲f remained a small company.
    $\quad$ *had not* $\quad\quad\quad\quad\quad\quad\quad\quad\quad$ *have*

Recognizing Gerunds and Infinitives

Sometimes a main verb is followed by another verb. The second verb can be a gerund or an infinitive. A **gerund** is a verb with an *-ing* ending. An **infinitive** consists of *to* and the base form of the verb.

> *verb + gerund*
> Edward finished̲ **installing** the carpet.

> *verb + infinitive*
> He wants̲ **to take** weekends off.

Some verbs in English are always followed by a gerund. Do not confuse gerunds with progressive verb forms.

Progressive verb:$\quad$ Julie is working now.

$\quad\quad\quad\quad\quad\quad\quad\quad\quad$ (Julie is in the process of doing something.)

Gerund:$\quad\quad\quad\quad$ Julie finished **working**.

$\quad\quad\quad\quad\quad\quad\quad\quad\quad$ (*Working* is a gerund that follows *finish*.)

**ESL
Teaching Tip:**
This section on gerunds and infinitives is especially relevant for nonnative speakers because their languages may just have one infinitive form.

Some Common Verbs Followed by Gerunds

acknowledge	deny	keep	recall
admit	detest	loathe	recollect
adore	discuss	mention	recommend
appreciate	dislike	mind	regret
avoid	enjoy	miss	resent
can't help	finish	postpone	resist
consider	involve	practice	risk
delay	justify	quit	

Some Common Verbs Followed by Infinitives

afford	decide	manage	refuse
agree	demand	mean	seem
appear	deserve	need	swear
arrange	expect	offer	threaten
ask	fail	plan	volunteer
claim	hesitate	prepare	want
compete	hope	pretend	wish
consent	learn	promise	would like

Some Common Verbs Followed by Gerunds or Infinitives

Some common verbs can be followed by gerunds or infinitives. Both forms have the same meaning.

> begin   continue   like   love   start

> Elaine likes **to read**. Elaine likes **reading**.
>
> (Both sentences have the same meaning.)

Stop, Remember, and *Used to*

Some verbs can be followed by either a gerund or an infinitive, but there is a difference in meaning depending on the form you use.

Term	Form	Example	Meaning
Stop	+ infinitive	He often stops to buy gas every Sunday.	To stop an activity (driving) to do something else.
	+ gerund	I stopped smoking five years ago.	To permanently stop doing something.
Remember	+ infinitive	Please remember to lock the door.	To remember to perform a task.
	+ gerund	I remember meeting him in 2004.	To have a memory about a past event.
Used to	+ infinitive	Jane used to smoke.	To express a past habit.
	+ gerund	Jane is used to living alone.	To be accustomed to something.

Prepositions Plus Gerunds

Many sentences have the structure *verb + preposition + object*. A gerund can be the object of a preposition.

> verb + preposition + gerund
> I dream **about** traveling to Greece.

Some Common Words Followed by Prepositions plus Gerunds

accuse of	be enthusiastic about	be good at	prohibit from
apologize for	feel like	insist on	succeed in
discourage <u>him</u> from*	fond of	be interested in	think about
dream of	forbid <u>him</u> from*	look forward to	(be) tired of
be excited about	forgive <u>me</u> for*	prevent <u>him</u> from*	warn <u>him</u> about*

*Certain verbs can have a noun or pronoun before the preposition.

PRACTICE 6   Complete the sentence with the appropriate verb. Underline either the gerund or the infinitive form.

1. Music devices are constantly changing. Do you remember (<u>listening</u> / to listen) to vinyl records? When my father was a child, he used (<u>to listen</u> / to listening) to Beatles albums. Later, everyone wanted (<u>to have</u> / having) cassette recordings. When CDs first came out, I

   looked forward (owning / to own / <u>to owning</u>) one. Later, when music was digitalized, I remember (to download / <u>downloading</u>) an Eminem song.

2. For my twentieth birthday, I dreamed (to receive / receiving / <u>of receiving</u>) an iPod. I stopped (to buy / <u>buying</u>) CDs because it was cheaper to download my favorite songs from iTunes. Today, some clever marketers have discovered that consumers enjoy (to touch / <u>touching</u>) LPs and record covers. Thus, Walmart and other stores have decided (<u>to sell</u> / selling) old-fashioned record players again.

3. A few years ago, Jack White, of the White Stripes, created a company called Third Man Records. As a child, he was excited (to hold / holding /

about holding) a new record in his hands. Now his company makes album

covers and presses vinyl records. He has succeeded (to sell / selling /

in selling) many albums. Many youths have caught on to the trend. Last

weekend when he was downtown, fifteen-year-old Alex Chen stopped

(to buy / buying) a record at a music store. Nowadays, he is used

(to listen / listening / to listening) to vinyl albums. In an interview with

Imprint Magazine, Chen said that he adores (to have / having) vinyl

albums. He has stopped (to download / downloading) most of his

music, and he buys albums instead. EBay executives say that users

manage (to buy and sell / buying and selling) a vinyl record every

ten seconds.

Teaching Tip:

Cooperative Learning (Ask & Learn)
Ask students to review the chapter and identify anything that they are not completely clear about. All students should write three questions on a paper. Then in teams, students can ask other members their questions and share answers.

FINAL REVIEW

Underline and correct fifteen errors with verbs and with double negatives.

EXAMPLE: Consumers <u>wanna</u> buy the best products.
                            want to

1. One of the biggest marketing mistakes is to fix something that is not

   broken. For example, in 1985, Coca Cola was the best-selling brand and

   had no or didn't have any
   the company <u>didn't have no</u> problems selling its product. Nevertheless,

   going to
   Coca Cola managers worried that Pepsi was <u>gonna</u> take too much market

   share. That year, Coke developers modified the original formula, and they

   made
   <u>make</u> the product much sweeter.

2. On April 23, 1985, at a press conference, Coca Cola's chairman introduced

   New Coke by calling it "smoother, rounder, and bolder." Executives hoped

   would
   the new formula ~~will~~ hurt sales of Pepsi. However, when New Coke hit

   complained   *want to*
   store shelves, consumers ~~complain~~ about the taste. They did not ~~wanna~~

   buy the new product. Three months later, the company pulled New Coke

   from the shelves and reintroduced the original product, calling it Coke

   have
   Classic. They should not ~~of~~ changed the original formula.

3. Another marketing mistake is to
                              is
   believe that a product ~~was~~ invincible.

   In the past, America's big three

   automakers thought consumers
                              driving
   would always enjoy ~~to drive~~ large

EV1 electric car

   American cars. However, tastes change, and companies ~~gotta~~ adapt. In

   have to

   1996, General Motors introduced the EV1 electric car. However, if
                                           would
   someone wanted to drive the car, he or she ~~will~~ have to lease it. The company
   did not sell it to anybody or sold it to nobody
   ~~did not sell it to nobody~~. Consumers in California loved the vehicle
                                           had
   because it was so fast, efficient, and quiet. If GM ~~would have~~ sold the
                              would have
   vehicles, many customers ~~woulda~~ bought them. For various reasons, GM
                                                       had
   crushed all of the electric cars in 2003. Perhaps if GM ~~woulda~~ considered

   the rising cost of oil, the company would not have stopped the electric car

   production.

Teaching Tip:
Writer's World
Competition
Please advise
students that they
can submit their
paragraphs and
essays for possible
publication to www
.pearsonhighered
.com/essayrewards/
writingrewards.html

The Writer's Room Topics for Writing

Write about one of the following topics. Ensure that your verbs are correctly formed.

1. If you had lived one hundred years ago, what job would you have done? Describe the job using details that appeal to the senses.

2. Examine this photo. What terms come to mind? Define a term or expression that relates to the photo. Some ideas might be *mindless work*, *balancing act*, *glass ceiling*, *success*, *a go-getter*, or *a "suit."*

READING LINK

International Trade

To find out more about the business world, see the following essays.

"Edison ...Wasn't He the Guy Who Invented Everything?" by Matt Richtel (page 89)

"College Students and the Challenge of Credit Card Debt" by Katie Earnest (page 212)

"Keep Your Roses" by Melonyce McAfee (page 243)

"Brands R Us" by Stephen Garey (page 564)

"The Rich Resonance of Small Talk" by Roxanne Roberts (page 567)

✔ CHECKLIST: OTHER VERB FORMS

When you edit your writing, ask yourself these questions.

☐ Are my verb tenses consistent? Check for errors with the following:

- shifts from past to present or present to past
- *can/could* and *will/would*

                                  would
When he drove trucks, he ~~will~~ drive when he was tired.

☐ Do I use the correct conditional forms? Check for errors in the following:

- possible future forms (*If I meet . . . , I will go . . .*)
- unlikely present forms (*If I met . . . , I would go . . .*)
- impossible past forms (*If I had met . . . , I would have gone . . .*)

                     had
If he ~~would have~~ sold shoes, he would have been successful.

☐ Do I use standard verbs? Do not write *gonna*, *wanna*, *gotta*, *shoulda*, etc.

                     want to
If you ~~wanna~~ know the truth about the Free Trade

                     have to
Agreement, you ~~gotta~~ do some research.

PEARSON mywritinglab To check your progress in meeting this chapter's objectives, log in to **www.mywritinglab.com,** go to the **Study Plan** tab, click on **The Editing Handbook—Section 3** and choose **Problems with Verbs** from the list of subtopics. Read and view the resources in the **Review Materials** section, and then complete the **Recall, Apply,** and **Write** sets in the **Activities** section.

Nouns, Determiners, and Prepositions

CHAPTER 30

LEARNING OBJECTIVES

1 Count and Noncount Nouns (p. 417)

2 Determiners (p. 418)

3 Prepositions (p. 420)

Section Theme **FORCES OF NATURE**

In this chapter, you will read about some unusual weather events.

Count and Noncount Nouns

In English, nouns are grouped into two types: count nouns and noncount nouns.

Count nouns refer to people or things that you can count such as *tree*, *house*, or *dog*. Count nouns have both a singular and plural form.

> She wrote three <u>articles</u> about global warming.

Noncount nouns refer to people or things that you cannot count because you cannot divide them, such as *sugar* and *imagination*. Noncount nouns have only the singular form.

> The <u>weather</u> is going to turn cold.

ESL
Teaching Tip:
Although your native speakers may benefit from the material in this chapter, it is particularly useful for nonnative speakers.

Here are some examples of common noncount nouns.

Common Noncount Nouns

Categories of Objects		Food	Nature	Substances	
clothing	machinery	bread	air	chalk	paint
equipment	mail	fish	electricity	charcoal	paper
furniture	money	honey	energy	coal	
homework	music	meat	environment	fur	
jewelry	postage	milk	heat	hair	
luggage	software	rice	ice	ink	
			radiation		
			weather		

Abstract Nouns

advice	education	health	knowledge	proof
attention	effort	help	luck	research
behavior	evidence	history	peace	speculation
creativity	extinction	information	progress	violence

 Latin Nouns

Some nouns that are borrowed from Latin or Greek keep the plural form of the
original language.

Singular	Plural	Singular	Plural
millennium	millennia	paparazzo	paparazzi
datum	data	phenomenon	phenomena

Determiners

Determiners are words that will help you determine or figure out whether a
noun is specific or general. Examples of determiners are articles (*a*), demonstratives
(*this*), indefinite pronouns (*many*), numbers (*three*), possessive nouns (*Maria's*), and
possessive adjectives (*my*).

Gabriel Daniel Fahrenheit manufactured <u>the</u> first mercury
thermometer in 1714. <u>Fahrenheit's</u> invention was <u>his</u> claim to fame.

Commonly Confused Determiners

Some determiners can be confusing because you can only use them in specific circumstances. Review this list of some commonly confused determiners.

a, an, the

A and *an* are general determiners and *the* is a specific determiner.

> I need to buy a new winter coat. The winter coats in that store are on sale.

Use *a* and *an* before singular count nouns but not before plural or noncount nouns. Use *a* before nouns that begin with a consonant (*a storm*) and use *an* before nouns that begin with a vowel (*an institute*).

Use *the* before nouns that refer to a specific person, place, or thing. Do not use *the* before languages (*He speaks Italian*), sports (*They watch tennis*), or most city and country names (*Two of the coldest capital cities in the world are Ottawa and Moscow*). Two examples of exceptions are *the United States* and *the Netherlands*.

many, few, much, little

Use *many* and *few* with count nouns.

> Many satellites collect weather information, but few forecasts are completely accurate.

Use *much* and *little* with noncount nouns.

> Much attention is focused on solar power, but North Americans use very little solar energy.

this, that, these, those

This and ***these*** refer to things that are physically close to the speaker or at the present time. Use *this* before singular nouns and *these* before plural nouns. ***That*** and ***those*** refer to things that are physically distant from the speaker or in the past time. Use *that* before singular nouns and *those* before plural nouns.

Near the speaker:
this (singular)
these (plural)

Far from the speaker:
that (singular)
those (plural)

> This **book** on my desk and those **books** on that **shelf** are about India. Did you know that in 1861, India had some very wet weather? In that **year**, Cherrapunji received 366 inches of rain. In those **days**, cities had trouble coping with so much rain, but these **days**, they are better equipped.

CHAPTER 30

Teaching Tip:

Cooperative Learning (Jigsaw)
Place students in teams of three to five. Assign each team a grammar concept from the chapter. Teams are responsible for teaching the class about their topic. They should summarize key ideas, give examples, and prepare some practice sentences. Then each team can present a short lesson to the class.

CHAPTER 30

PRACTICE 1   Underline the determiner in parentheses that best agrees with the noun after it. If the noun does not require a determiner, underline *X*.

EXAMPLE: (<u>The</u> / A / X) driest place on Earth is (the / a / <u>X</u>) Arica, Chile.

1. (Much / <u>Many</u>) people all over (<u>the</u> / a / X) world talk constantly about (<u>the</u> / a / X) weather. (<u>Few</u> / Little) phenomena are as exciting as extreme weather. For example, (the / <u>X</u>) tornadoes are seasonal in (the / <u>X</u>) North America. (<u>A</u> / The) tornado lasts about fifteen minutes. In 1967, there were around 115 tornadoes in (a / the / <u>X</u>) Texas. In (this / <u>that</u>) year, meteorologists believed (<u>a</u> / the / X) hurricane caused the numerous tornadoes in the state.

2. (<u>Many</u> / Much) people are fascinated with thunderstorms. (A / <u>An</u> / X) interesting fact about (a / <u>the</u> / X) Empire State Building is that it is struck by lightning around five hundred times per year. During thunderstorms, (the / <u>X</u>) golfers should be very careful. They should spend as (few / <u>little</u>) time as possible outdoors if there is lightning. (<u>A</u> / The) thunderstorm can produce a few hundred megawatts of electrical power.

3. (<u>The</u> / X) United States launched its first weather satellite in 1961. In (these / <u>those</u>) days, satellite pictures amazed weather researchers. Today, (<u>much</u> / many) research is being done by meteorologists about weather patterns. (<u>These</u> / Those) days, satellites gather (a / the / <u>X</u>) information about global weather systems.

Prepositions

Prepositions are words that show concepts such as time, place, direction, and manner. They show connections or relationships between ideas.

<u>In</u> 1998, northern New York State experienced nearly a week of freezing rain.

Freezing rain fell <u>for</u> a few days.

Prepositions of Time and Place

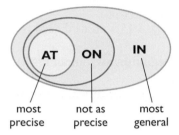

AT — most precise
ON — not as precise
IN — most general

Teaching Tip:
To practice using determiners correctly, ask students to write different sentences using as many different determiners as possible.

	Prepositions of Time	**Prepositions of Place**
in	in a year, month, or century (in February)	in a city, country, or continent (in Phoenix)
on	on a day of the week (on Monday) on a specific date (on June 16) on a specific holiday (on Memorial Day)	on a specific street (on Lacombe Ave.) on technological devices (on TV, on the radio, on the phone, on the cell phone, on the computer)
at	at a specific time of day (at 9:15) at night at breakfast, lunch, dinner	at a specific address (at 18 Oriole Crescent) at a specific building (at the hospital)
from . . . to	from one time to another (from 10:00 AM to 1:00 PM)	from one place to another (from Fort Lauderdale to Orlando)
for	for a period of time (for five hours)	for a distance (for two miles)

ESL
Teaching Tip:
Many nonnative speakers have difficulty with prepositions because they are not easily translated. For example, the Spanish word *en* can be translated as *in*, *on*, and *at*. Ask students to review the rules carefully.

Commonly Confused Prepositions

to Versus *at*

Use *to* after verbs that indicate movement from one place to another. Use *at* after verbs that indicate being or remaining in one place (and not moving from one place to another). Exception: Do not put *to* directly before *home*.

> Each day, Suraya **runs** to the office, and then she goes home and **sits** at the computer.

for, during, since

Use *during* to explain when something happens, *for* to explain how long it takes to happen, and *since* to indicate the start of an activity.

> During the summer, the restaurant closed for one week because of the heat.

> Since 2006, I have been taking skiing lessons during the winter.

CHAPTER 30

PRACTICE 2   Write the correct preposition in the blanks.

EXAMPLE: _____*At*_____ 5:15 A.M. we heard the news.

1. _____*Since*_____ the beginning of human history, people have been trying to predict the weather. Many writers have created almanacs to record weather-related events.

2. _____*In*_____ 1792, _____*during*_____ George Washington's second term as president, *The Old Farmer's Almanac* was published. Robert B. Thomas was its first editor. _____*From*_____ 8:00 A.M. _____*to*_____ 6:00 P.M., Thomas would work on his magazine. Sitting _____*at*_____ his desk, he developed a successful formula to forecast weather. He had over an 80 percent accuracy rate. Thomas died _____*in*_____ 1846, but people can go _____*to*_____ Dublin, New Hampshire, and view his secret formula _____*at*_____ the *Almanac*'s office.

3. *The Old Farmer's Almanac* has been published each year _____*since*_____ it was first established. _____*During*_____ World War II, the *Almanac* became notoriously associated with a German spy, whom the FBI captured _____*in*_____ New York. The spy had the *Almanac* _____*in*_____ his pocket. The U.S. government wanted to discontinue publishing the *Almanac* because it contained information that was useful _____*to*_____ the Germans. After discussing the issue _____*on*_____ the telephone, U.S. officials eventually allowed the *Almanac* to be published again.

Common Prepositional Expressions

Many common expressions contain prepositions. These types of expressions usually express a particular meaning. The meaning of a verb will change if it is used with a specific preposition. Examine the difference in meaning of the following expressions.

to turn on—to start a machine or switch on the lights

to turn off—to stop a machine or switch off the lights

to turn down—to decline something

to turn over—to rotate

to turn up—to arrive

The next list contains some of the most common prepositional expressions.

accuse (somebody) of	dream of	long for	satisfied with
acquainted with	escape from	look forward to	scared of
afraid of	excited about	participate in	search for
agree with	familiar with	patient with	similar to
apologize for	fond of	pay attention to	specialize in
apply for	forget about	pay for	stop (something) from
approve of	forgive (someone) for	prevent (someone) from	succeed in
associate with	friendly with	protect (someone) from	take advantage of
aware of	grateful for	proud of	take care of
believe in	happy about	provide (someone) with	thank (someone) for
capable of	hear about	qualify for	think about / of
comply with	hope for	realistic about	tired of
confronted with	hopeful about	rely on	willing to
consist of	innocent of	rescue from	wish for
count on	insist on	responsible for	worry about
deal with	insulted by		
depend on	interested in		

PRACTICE 3   Write the correct prepositions in the next paragraphs. Use the preceding list of prepositional expressions to help you.

EXAMPLE: Many people were upset ___*about*___ the damage from the storm.

1. In southern Asia, many people look forward ___*to*___ the monsoon. The word monsoon comes from the Arabic "mausin," which means "the season of the winds." During the wet season from June to September, India

receives an average of 12 inches of rain each month. During the monsoon,

people get tired ____*of*____ dealing with the rain.

2. Throughout the year, South Asians depend ____*on*____ the monsoon.

Farmers hope ____*for*____ adequate rainfall for their crops. Children love

the monsoon because it provides them ____*with*____ the opportunity to play

in the rain and the puddles. Although South Asians are often grateful

____*for*____ a good rainy season, they are also realistic ____*about*____ forces

of nature and think ____*about*____ possible flooding, transportation delays,

and malaria.

FINAL REVIEW

Correct fifteen errors in nouns, determiners, and prepositions.

EXAMPLE: ~~Much~~ *Many* geologists specialize ~~about~~ *in* glaciers.

1. The 2002 movie *Ice Age* was very popular. Modern audiences are familiar
   ~~of~~ *with* its subject because most students learn about glaciers in science class.

   About two hundred years ago, some ordinary people advanced their
   ~~theorys~~ *theories* that glaciers once covered the earth.

2. ~~On~~ *In* the nineteenth century, geologist Jean de Charpentier was going ~~at~~ *to*

   his cottage in rural Switzerland when he noticed ~~much~~ *many* unusual boulders

   lying near the path. A local woodcutter casually mentioned that the

   Grimsel glacier had moved the rocks from

   one place ~~in~~ *to* another. De Charpentier was

   shocked. He had been studying glaciers
   for
   ~~since~~ a long time. He participated ~~at~~ *in* a

Teaching Tip:
You can use the final
review as a test.
Additional practice
and test material
appears in the
Instructor's
Resource Manual
and on
MyWritingLab.

few

scientific meeting, but ~~little~~ scientists supported him. At ~~this~~ time, *that*

in

geologists did not believe ~~about~~ glaciers covering the Earth, yet an

ordinary woodcutter did.

little

3. James Croll had very ~~few~~ formal education when he received a job as a

janitor at a Scottish university. He convinced his brother to do the nightly

cleaning while Croll read science books in the library. Eventually, Croll

an   *weather*

sent ~~a~~ article on ~~weathers~~ to a scientific publication. He suggested that

ice

the advance and retreat of ~~ices~~ occurred because of a change in the Earth's

orbit. Other scientists soon proved his premise. By the twentieth century,

the Ice Age theory had become accepted.

The Writer's Room   Topics for Writing

Write about one of the following topics. Proofread your text to ensure that there are no errors in singular or plural forms, determiners, and prepositions.

1. What should people do to prepare for severe weather? List some steps.

2. Does the weather affect you emotionally? Write about the effects of weather on your mood.

CHAPTER 30

✓ **CHECKLIST: NOUNS, DETERMINERS, AND PREPOSITIONS**

When you edit your writing, ask yourself these questions:

☐ Do I use the correct singular or plural form of nouns? Check for errors with the spelling of regular and irregular plurals and count and noncount nouns.

      Many children   *in*   *snow*
    ~~Much childrens~~ love to play ~~on~~ the ~~snows~~.

☐ Do I use the correct determiners? Check for errors with *a*, *an*, *the*, *much*, *many*, *few*, *little*, *this*, *that*, *these*, and *those*.

      These   *much*   *the*
    ~~This~~ days, there is too ~~many~~ information about ~~a~~ impact of global warming.

☐ Do I use the correct prepositions? Check for errors with *in*, *on*, *at*, and *to*, with *for* and *during*, and with prepositional expressions.

      For   *on*
    ~~During~~ three months each winter, the town depends ~~of~~
                      at
    tourists who stay ~~to~~ the ski resorts.

mywritinglab To check your progress in meeting this chapter's objectives, log in to **www.mywritinglab.com,** go to the **Study Plan** tab, click on **The Editing Handbook—Section 4** and choose **Nouns, Determiners, and Prepositions** from the list of subtopics. Read and view the resources in the **Review Materials** section, and then complete the **Recall, Apply,** and **Write** sets in the **Activities** section.

Pronouns

LEARNING OBJECTIVES

Section Theme **FORCES OF NATURE**

In this chapter, you will read about nature's power.

Pronoun-Antecedent Agreement

Pronouns are words that replace nouns (people, places, or things) and phrases. Use pronouns to avoid repeating nouns.

> *They*
> Hurricanes are large tropical storms. ~~Hurricanes~~ commonly form in the Caribbean.

A pronoun must agree with its **antecedent,** which is the word to which the pronoun refers. Antecedents are words that the pronouns have replaced, and they always come before the pronoun. Pronouns must agree in person and number with their antecedents.

Sarah was late for **her** meeting because **she** drove slowly in the blinding rain.

Compound Antecedents

Compound antecedents consist of two or more nouns joined by *and* or *or*. When nouns are joined by *and*, use a plural pronoun to refer to them.

Davis and Reid wore **their** raincoats.

When singular nouns are joined by *or*, use a singular pronoun. When plural nouns are joined by *or*, use a plural pronoun.

Does the radio station or the TV station have **its** own weather channel?

Do environmentalists or activists have **their** lobby groups?

Collective Nouns

Collective nouns refer to a group of people or things. The group usually acts as a unit; therefore, most of the time, the collective noun is singular.

The company was fined for polluting. **It** had to pay a large sum of money.

GRAMMAR LINK

For a list of common collective nouns, see page 379 in Chapter 27.

PRACTICE I Circle the pronoun and underline its antecedent.

EXAMPLE: Although hurricane names used to be only female, now they may also be male.

1. Anna Petrowski and Colin Urban work for the World Meteorological Organization (WMO) where they help to select hurricane names.

2. Either citizens or politicians can add their choices to the WMO hurricane name list.

3. The WMO makes a list of distinctive names because they are easier to remember.

4. The WMO gives hurricanes English, French, or Spanish names because it wants to mirror the nationalities of people who may be affected.

5. In fact, when <u>hurricanes</u> become famous, the WMO retires (their) names.

6. In many countries, the <u>army</u> usually sends (its) personnel to help with

   emergency relief during a hurricane.

Indefinite Pronouns

Use **indefinite pronouns** when you refer to people or things whose identity is not known or is unimportant. This chart shows some common singular and plural indefinite pronouns.

Indefinite Pronouns				
Singular	another	each	nobody	other
	anybody	everybody	no one	somebody
	anyone	everyone	nothing	someone
	anything	everything	one	something
Plural	both, few, many, others, several			
Either singular or plural	all, any, half (and other fractions), none, more, most, some			

Singular

When you use a singular indefinite antecedent, also use a singular pronoun to refer to it.

> <u>Nobody</u> remembered to bring **his** or **her** raincoat.

Plural

When you use a plural indefinite antecedent, also use a plural pronoun to refer to it.

> The two men rushed into the street and <u>both</u> carried **their** own umbrellas.

Either Singular or Plural

Some indefinite pronouns can be either singular or plural depending on the noun to which they refer.

> Many meteorologists spoke at the conference. <u>All</u> gave important information about **their** research.
>
> (*All* refers to meteorologists; therefore, the pronoun is plural.)

Teaching Tip:
To help students remember singular indefinite pronouns, ask them to look at the word's ending. *Everyone, somebody,* and *nothing* end with singular nouns (*one, body, thing*); therefore, any verb or pronoun related to those words should also be singular.

Teaching Tip:

Cooperative Learning (Jigsaw) Place students in teams of three to five. Assign each team a grammar concept from the chapter. Teams are responsible for teaching the class about their topic. They should summarize key ideas, give examples, and prepare some practice sentences. Then each team can present a short lesson to the class.

I read <u>all</u> of the newspaper and could not find **its** weather section.

(*All* refers to the newspaper; therefore, the pronoun is singular.)

Hint **Avoid Sexist Language**

Terms like *anybody, somebody, nobody,* and *each* are singular antecedents, so the pronouns that follow must be singular. At one time, it was acceptable to use *he* as a general term meaning "all people." However, today it is more acceptable to use *he or she.*

Sexist:	<u>Everyone</u> should stay inside **his** house during a tornado.
Solution:	<u>Everyone</u> should stay inside **his or her** house during a tornado.
Better Solution:	<u>People</u> should stay inside **their** houses during a tornado.
Exception:	In the men's prison, <u>everyone</u> has **his** own cell.
	(If you know for certain that the subject is male or female, then use only *he* or only *she.*)

PRACTICE 2   Correct nine errors in pronoun–antecedent agreement by changing either the antecedent or the pronoun. If you change any antecedents, make sure that your subjects and verbs agree.   Answers will vary.

EXAMPLE: Some of the workers had ~~his~~ *their* own skis.

1. Everyone should know what to do if ~~they are~~ *he or she is* caught in extreme weather

   conditions. For example, people should be aware of lightning storms. All

   need to avoid open spaces, and ~~he~~ *they* should get inside a building. No one

   should remain in the open because ~~they~~ *he or she* could be struck by lightning. If

   lightning is nearby, each person who is outside should get into a crouching

   position but never lie down.

2. In the winter months, snowstorms can be dangerous. Somebody stranded

   in a blizzard should stay with ~~their~~ *his or her* car. Nobody should wander outside on

his or her
~~their~~ own during a blinding snowstorm. It is very dangerous if a car gets

stuck in a snowbank. One of the most common problems is carbon

monoxide poisoning, which happens when snow blocks the back of the car

its
and carbon monoxide gas backs up in ~~their~~ exhaust pipe. To solve this

his or her
problem, everyone should clear the snow from ~~their~~ exhaust pipe.

their
3. Many have heard ~~his or her~~ weather stations reporting on tornadoes.

During a tornado warning, everybody should go into a basement or

his or her
windowless room in ~~their~~ home. Knowing what to do during extreme

weather can save people's lives.

Vague Pronouns

Avoid using pronouns that could refer to more than one antecedent.

Vague: My father asked my brother where his umbrella was.
(Whose umbrella? My father's or my brother's?)

Clearer: My father asked my brother where **my brother's** umbrella was.

Avoid using confusing pronouns such as *it* and *they* that have no clear antecedent.

Vague: They say that thousands of people lost their lives during the 1995 earthquake in Kobe, Japan.
(Who are *they*?)

Clearer: **Government officials** say that thousands of people lost their lives during the 1995 earthquake in Kobe, Japan.

Vague: It stated in the newspaper that the scientific name for a thundercloud is "cumulonimbus."
(Who or what is *it*?)

Clearer: **The journalist** stated in the newspaper that the scientific name for a thundercloud is "cumulonimbus."

This, that, and *which* should refer to a specific antecedent.

Vague: My girlfriend said that the roads were icy. I was glad she told me <u>this</u>.

(What is *this*?)

Clearer: My girlfriend said that the roads were icy. I was glad she told me **this information.**

Teaching Tip:
Nonnative speakers may mistakenly use double subjects because, in many languages, the subject is repeated in the pronoun form.

> *Hint* ▸ **Avoid Repeating the Subject**
>
> When you clearly mention a subject, do not repeat the subject in pronoun form.
>
> Thunder ~~it~~ occurs when cold air collides with hot air.

CHAPTER 31

PRACTICE 3   The next paragraphs contain vague pronouns or repeated subjects. Correct the nine errors in this selection. You may need to rewrite some sentences.   Answers will vary.

                      The journalist reported
EXAMPLE: ~~They said~~ on television that most tornadoes occur in agricultural areas around the world.

1. Meteorologist Patricia Bowles told her friend Sheila that ~~her~~ *Sheila's* photo of the tornado would appear in the newspaper. ~~They~~ *Meteorologists* say that tornadoes are the most powerful storms on earth. Tornado winds ~~they~~ can often exceed 100 miles per hour. This *wind force* can cause property damage and sometimes kill people.

2. ~~It~~ *The science article* says that tornadoes form during thunderstorms when cool air moves downward and hot air rises very quickly, which creates a funnel effect. When this *funnel* touches the ground, it becomes a tornado. The United States ~~it~~ has a "Tornado Alley." This *area* consists of Texas, Oklahoma, Kansas, and Nebraska. These states ~~they~~ have more tornadoes than other parts of North America because cold air from Canada meets warm air from the Gulf of Mexico over the flat prairies.

Pronoun Shifts

If your essays contain unnecessary shifts in person or number, you may confuse your readers. They will not know exactly who or how many you are referring to. Carefully edit your writing to ensure that your pronouns are consistent.

Making Pronouns Consistent in Number

If the antecedent is singular, then the pronoun must be singular. If the antecedent is plural, then the pronoun must be plural.

> singular   *his or her*
> A **meteorologist** and ~~their~~ team spend years keeping meticulous records of weather patterns.

>   *plural   they*
> When there are storm **warnings**, ~~it~~ should be taken seriously.

Making Pronouns Consistent in Person

Person is the writer's perspective. For some writing assignments, you might use the first person (*I, we*). For other assignments, especially most college essays and workplace writing, you might use the second person (*you*), or the third person (*he, she, it, they*).

     Shifting the point of view for no reason confuses readers. If you begin writing from one point of view, do not shift unnecessarily to another point of view.

>   *They*
> **Many** tourists like to travel, but **they** should be careful. ~~You~~ never
>   *They*
> know when there will be bad weather. ~~You~~ should always be prepared for emergencies.

> **PRACTICE 4**   Correct five pronoun shift errors.

EXAMPLE: Many people were saddened when they heard that thousands of
                                     They
people had died in the 2001 Indian earthquake. ~~One~~ donated money, clothes, and blankets to the victims.

In 2010, we were traveling in Sumatra. We had just finished our breakfast
   we
when ~~you~~ felt the ground moving. Everything in our tenth floor apartment started
                                      we
to shake and fall. We knew we should not panic, but ~~one~~ really didn't know what
         we
to do. We knew ~~you~~ had to get out of the high-rise and onto the ground because
we
~~one~~ could never be certain that the building would remain standing. There were
            we
no guarantees that ~~you~~ could make it out in time.

Pronoun Case

Pronouns are formed according to the role they play in a sentence. A pronoun can be the subject of the sentence or the object of the sentence. It can also show possession. This chart shows the three main pronoun cases: subjective, objective, and possessive.

Pronoun			Possessive	
Singular	**Subjective**	**Objective**	**Possessive Adjective**	**Possessive Pronoun**
1st person	I	me	my	mine
2nd person	you	you	your	yours
3rd person	he, she, it, who, whoever	him, her, it, whom, whomever	his, her, its, whose	his, hers
Plural				
1st person	we	us	our	ours
2nd person	you	you	your	yours
3rd person	they	them	their	theirs

Subjective Case and Objective Case

When a pronoun is the subject of the sentence, use the subjective form of the pronoun. When a pronoun is the object in the sentence, use the objective form of the pronoun.

> subject   subject   object
> **He** left the umbrella at work, and **I** asked **him** to bring it home.

Possessive Case

A possessive pronoun shows ownership.

- **Possessive adjectives** come before the noun that they modify.

  She finished **her** <u>research</u> on the polar ice caps, but we did not finish **our** <u>research</u>.

- **Possessive pronouns** replace the possessive adjective and the noun that follows it. In the next sentence, the possessive pronoun *ours* replaces both the possessive adjective *our* and the noun *research*.

  > possessive adjective
  > She finished **her** <u>research</u> on the polar ice caps, but we did not
  >
  > possessive pronoun
  > finish **ours**.

Problems with Possessive Pronouns

Some possessive adjectives sound like certain contractions. When using the possessive adjectives *their*, *your*, and *its*, be careful that you do not confuse them with *they're* (they + are), *you're* (you + are), and *it's* (it + is).

GRAMMAR LINK

For more information about apostrophes, see Chapter 36.

> The book on clouds is ~~her's~~ *hers*. The weather almanac is ~~their's~~ *theirs*.

> (Hint)   **Choosing *His* or *Her***
>
> To choose the correct possessive adjective, think about the possessor (not the object that is possessed).
>
> If something belongs to a female, use ***her*** + noun.
>
>   Malina and **her** dog like to walk in the snow.
>
> If something belongs to a male, use ***his*** + noun.
>
>   Cliff used **his** new camera to photograph storm clouds.

CHAPTER 31

PRACTICE 5   Underline the correct possessive adjectives or possessive pronouns in each set of parentheses.

EXAMPLE: Dr. Jane Woody wondered whether (his / her) theories would be accepted.

1. Scientists study volcanoes and (its / it's / <u>their</u>) effects on weather patterns. When a volcano erupts and throws (his / <u>its</u> / it's) ash particles into the surrounding air, the explosion causes a lot of lightning and thunderstorms in the region nearby.

2. I have just joined the International Society on Volcanic Studies. The members and (there / they're / <u>their</u>) governments fund research into volcanic activity. A researcher and (their / <u>his or her</u> /its) assistants gather information about volcanic eruptions.

3. My assistant Judith, because of (<u>her</u> / hers) enthusiasm, is a wonderful colleague. We collect information on volcanic activity. (Our / <u>Ours</u>) is just one small part of this study.

4. One day, we would like to present (<u>our</u> / ours) research to climate scientists because we think it will be important to (they / <u>them</u>). Will you be in (you're / <u>your</u> / yours) office next Tuesday? Let's discuss (<u>our</u> / ours) work and (your / <u>yours</u>) when we meet.

Pronouns in Comparisons with *Than* or *As*

CHAPTER 31

Avoid making errors in pronoun case when the pronoun follows *than* or *as*. If the pronoun is a subject, use the subjective case, and if the pronoun is an object, use the objective case.

If you use the incorrect case, your sentence may have a meaning that you do not intend it to have. Review the next examples. Notice that when the sentence ends with the subjective pronoun, it is advisable to add a verb after the pronoun.

objective case

a) I like rainy days as much as **him.**

   (I like rainy days <u>as much as I like him.</u>)

subjective case

b) I like rainy days as much as **he** (does).

   (I like rainy days <u>as much as he likes rainy days.</u>)

> ### Hint   Complete the Thought
>
> To test which pronoun case to use, complete the thought.
>
> Eva understands him more than **I** [understand him].
> (Do I want to say that Eva understands him more than I understand him?)
>
> Eva understands him more than [she understands] **me.**
> (Or, do I want to say that Eva understands him more than she understands me?)

Pronouns in Prepositional Phrases

In a prepositional phrase, the noun or pronoun that follows the preposition is the object of the preposition. Therefore, always use the objective case of the pronoun after a preposition.

To **him**, global warming is not a big deal. <u>Between</u> **you** and **me**, I think he's misinformed.

Pronouns with *and* or *or*

Use the correct case when nouns and pronouns are joined by ***and*** or ***or***. If the pronouns are the subject, use the subjective case. If the pronouns are the object, use the objective case.

   She and I
~~Her and me~~ had to read about the causes of desertification, and then

       her and me
the instructor asked ~~she and I~~ to summarize the information.

     I
Frances or ~~me~~ could give the seminar on the rainforest. The

       me
students asked Frances or ~~I~~ to show a film on the Amazon.

Hint   **Finding the Correct Case**

To determine that your case is correct, try saying the sentence with either the subjective case or the objective case.

  Sentence: The professor asked her and (**I or me**) to research the topic.

  Possible answers: The professor asked **I** to research the topic.
                         (This would not make sense.)

                         The professor asked **me** to research the topic.
                         (This would make sense.)

  Correct answer: The professor asked **her** and **me** to research the topic.

PRACTICE 6   Correct any errors with pronoun case.

                                    I
EXAMPLE: Last summer, my friend and ~~me~~ visited China.

                                   I
1. Recently, my friend Larry Huang and me toured China.

   He and I
2. ~~Him and me~~ are interested in environmental issues.

                                                I did
3. He wanted to see the Three Gorges Dam more than ~~me~~ but convinced me

   to go along.

4. The guide told ~~we~~ ^{us} visitors that the completed dam would produce large

    amounts of electricity for China.

5. The guide asked Larry or ~~I~~ ^{me} to distribute some brochures about the

    dam.

6. Between you and ~~I~~ ^{me}, the guide should have explained some of the

    environmental problems caused by the dam.

Relative Pronouns

CHAPTER 31

Relative pronouns can join two short sentences. Relative pronouns include *who,
whom, whoever, whomever, which, that,* and *whose.*

Choosing *Who* or *Whom*

To determine whether to use *who* or *whom*, replace *who* or *whom* with another
pronoun. If the replacement is a subjective pronoun such as *he* or *she*, use **who**. If
the replacement is an objective pronoun such as *her* or *him*, use **whom**.

> I know a man **who** studies icebergs.
> (He studies icebergs.)

> The man to **whom** you gave your résumé is my boss.
> (You gave your résumé to him.)

**GRAMMAR
LINK**

For more
information about
relative pronouns,
see Chapter 22.

Teaching Tip:
Remind students
that they cannot use
"which" unless the
clause is set off
with commas.

PRACTICE 7   Underline the correct relative pronoun in the
parentheses.

EXAMPLE: People (<u>who</u> / which) live in the Arctic are used to harsh weather.

1. Ruth, (who / <u>whom</u>) I met in school, has been my best friend for twenty

    years.

2. Ruth, (<u>who</u> / whom) is a journalist, recently spent some time on Baffin

    Island.

3. The people on Baffin Island about (who / <u>whom</u>) Ruth is writing are

    mostly Inuit.

4. The Inuit, (<u>who</u> / whom) are accustomed to extreme weather, are active year round.

5. Ruth, (<u>who</u> / whom) loves the sun, sometimes feels depressed during the winter when there is very little daylight.

6. Many people (who / <u>whom</u>) Ruth has interviewed are worried about climate change.

Teaching Tip:
You can use the final review as a test. Additional practice and test material appears in the Instructor's Resource Manual and on MyWritingLab.

FINAL REVIEW

Correct the fifteen pronoun errors in the next paragraphs.

> their
> **EXAMPLE:** Many people around the world have lost ~~one's~~ relatives and
> property because of severe weather.

1. In 2009, wildfires raged in southern Australia.
Around 160 people died. Almost everybody in
his or her
the path of the fires had ~~their~~ home destroyed.
their
Police and firefighters had to use all of ~~they're~~

    training to fight the fires. Katrina Hobbart and
her
~~his~~ husband fled minutes before flames
who
engulfed the road. Ronald, ~~whom~~ is a reporter, stated that he had never
event
seen wildfires burn with such speed. This was a tragedy.
                                      ^

2. My friend Petra and ~~me~~ volunteered to help rebuild communities that
  I
    were destroyed. I directed traffic in my part of town, and Petra directed
hers   *whom*
    traffic in ~~her's~~. I also collected donations. Petra's boss, to ~~who~~ I sent the
it
    money, passed ~~them~~ to community organizers. Other volunteers were just
I was
    as committed to rebuilding as ~~me~~.

Scientists

3. Wildfires ~~they~~ are common in Australia. ~~They~~ say that it is the

its

driest continent on earth. Global warming and ~~their~~ consequences are

severe. For example, a rise in temperature might cause drought and heat

we are

waves. The forces of nature are more powerful than ~~us~~. Therefore, we

must work together to eliminate global warming. We must reduce our

we

carbon footprint so that ~~you~~ can prevent some of the natural disasters from

happening.

CHAPTER 31

Teaching Tip:

Cooperative Learning (Quick Review)
Divide the class into teams of three or four. Assign a part of the chapter to each team. Each team should review the information and generate three questions. Then ask teams to read the questions aloud. Anybody in the class can answer a question. Or, as an alternative, you can ask teams to exchange questions and to answer another team's questions.

The Writer's Room   Topics for Writing

Write about one of the following topics. Proofread your text to ensure there are no pronoun errors.

1. Describe a severe weather event that you or someone you know experienced. What happened? Try to use descriptive imagery.

2. Argue that bicycles should be the only type of vehicle allowed in city centers. Support your argument with specific examples.

✔ CHECKLIST: PRONOUNS

When you edit your writing, ask yourself these questions.

☐ Do I use the correct pronoun case? Check for errors with the following:

- subjective, objective, and possessive cases
- comparisons with *than* or *as*
- prepositional phrases
- pronouns following *and* or *or*

me

Between you and ~~I~~, my sister watches the weather reports

I (do)

more than ~~me~~.

☐ Do I use the correct relative pronouns? Check for errors with *who* or *whom*.

whom

My husband, ~~who~~ you have met, is a meteorologist.

☐ Do my pronouns and antecedents agree in number and person? Check for errors with indefinite pronouns and collective nouns.

> *its*
> The bad weather and ~~their~~ aftermath were reported on the news.

☐ Are my pronoun references clear? Check for vague pronouns and inconsistent points of view.

> *Scientists*
> ~~They~~ say the weather will change rapidly. I read the report,
>
> *I*
> and ~~you~~ could not believe what it said.

Teaching Tip:

Writer's World Competition

Please advise students that they can submit their paragraphs and essays for possible publication to www .pearsonhighered .com/essayrewards/ writingrewards.html

CHAPTER 31

mywritinglab To check your progress in meeting this chapter's objectives, log in to **www.mywritinglab.com,** go to the **Study Plan** tab, click on **The Editing Handbook—Section 4** and choose **Pronouns** from the list of subtopics. Read and view the resources in the **Review Materials** section, and then complete the **Recall, Apply,** and **Write** sets in the **Activities** section.

Adjectives and Adverbs

Section Theme **FORCES OF NATURE**

In this chapter, you will read about environmental issues and alternative energy sources.

ESL
Teaching Tip:
Because of first-language
transference errors,
many nonnative
speakers place
adjectives after the
noun. Remind them
that in English,
adjectives cannot
be placed directly
after a noun.

Adjectives

Adjectives describe nouns (people, places, or things) and pronouns (words that replace nouns). They add information explaining how many, what kind, or which one. They also describe how things look, smell, feel, taste, and sound.

> The **young** <u>students</u> convinced their **imposing** <u>principal</u> to start an **important** <u>project</u> on air quality in the schools.

Placement of Adjectives

You can place adjectives either before a noun or after a linking verb such as *be, look, appear, smell,* or *become.*

Before the noun: The **nervous** environmentalist gave a **suitable** speech.

After the linking verb: The biologist <u>was</u> **disappointed**, and he <u>was</u> **angry**.

Problems with Adjectives

You can recognize many adjectives by their endings. Be particularly careful when you use the following adjective forms.

Adjectives Ending in *-ful* or *-less*

Some adjectives end in *-ful* or *-less*. Remember that *ful* ends in one *l* and *less* ends in double *s*.

> The Blue Oceans Club, a **peaceful** environmental organization, has promoted many **useful** projects. Protecting the environment is an **endless** activity.

Adjectives Ending in *-ed* and *-ing*

Some adjectives look like verbs because they end in *-ing* or *-ed*. When the adjective ends in *-ed*, it describes the person's or animal's expression or feeling. When the adjective ends in *-ing*, it describes the quality of the person or thing.

> The **frustrated** but **prepared** lobbyist confronted the politician, and his **challenging** and **convincing** arguments got her attention.

 Keep Adjectives in the Singular Form

Always make an adjective singular, even if the noun following the adjective is plural.

> *year*
> Lucia was a forty-five-~~years~~-old woman when she sold her five-thousand-
> *dollar*
> ~~dollars~~ car and rode a bicycle to work.

ESL
Teaching Tip:
Many nonnative speakers make usage errors between *-ing* and *-ed* adjective endings. Draw their attention to this rule.

ESL
Teaching Tip:
In certain languages, adjectives agree in number and gender with the nouns they are describing. Remind students that adjectives are always singular in English.

Adverbs

Adverbs add information to adjectives, verbs, or other adverbs. They give more specific information about how, when, where, and to what extent an action or event occurred. Some adverbs look exactly like adjectives, such as *early*, *late*, *soon*, *often*, and *hard*. However, most adverbs end in *-ly*.

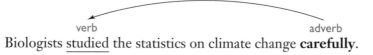

        verb   adverb

Biologists <u>studied</u> the statistics on climate change **carefully**.

       adverb adverb

They released the results **quite** <u>quickly</u>.

   adverb adjective

The **very** <u>eloquent</u> speaker was Dr. Ying.

Forms of Adverbs

Adverbs often end in *-ly*. In fact, you can change many adjectives into adverbs by adding *-ly* endings.

- If you add *-ly* to a word that ends in *l*, then your new word will have a double *l*.

                        professional + ly

    The journalist covered the story **professionally**.

- If you add *-ly* to a word that ends in *e*, keep the *e*. Exceptions are *true–truly* and *due–duly*.)

                    close + ly

    Scientists monitor the polar ice caps **closely**.

> ## *Hint:* Placement of Frequency Adverbs
>
> **Frequency adverbs** are words that indicate how often someone performs an action or when an event occurs. Common frequency adverbs are *always, ever, never, often, sometimes,* and *usually*. They can appear at the beginnings of sentences, or they can appear in the following locations.
>
> - Place frequency adverbs before regular present and past tense verbs.
>
>   Politicians **sometimes** <u>forget</u> the importance of the environment.
>
> - Place frequency adverbs after all forms of the verb *be*.
>
>   She <u>is</u> **often** an advisor for environmental agencies.
>
> - Place frequency adverbs after an initial helping verb.
>
>   They <u>have</u> **never** donated to an environmental group.

ESL
Teaching Tip:
Give students a list of adjectives and a noun, and ask them to put the words in the proper order. After students finish, explain about the order of adjectives: determiner (number, etc.); quality; size or shape; age; color; origin; type; noun. Suggestions: (1) wooden, box, beautiful, red, tiny; (2) earrings, Chinese, jade, two, stunning; (3) tall, prisoner, white, elderly, Spanish; (4) shy, girl, Greek, twenty-year-old.

PRACTICE 1   Correct eight errors with adjectives or adverbs.

> *quietly*
EXAMPLE: I entered the room ~~quiet~~ because the lecture had started.

> *frequently*
1. Many people ~~frequent~~ debate the issue of climate change. There are

    > *clear*
    two ~~clearly~~ sources that cause global warming: natural and human.

    > *often forget*
    People ~~forget often~~ that natural forces have contributed to climate change

    throughout the history of the world. Scientists know that ice ages have

    > *rapidly*
    developed and diminished ~~rapid~~.

    > *naturally*
2. Global temperature increases ~~naturaly~~ for several reasons. For instance,

    explosions in the Sun generate heat that causes the Earth's temperature

    > *abruptly*
    to rise ~~abrupt~~. Another natural source for global warming is volcanic

    eruptions. A strong eruption gives off smoke and gases. These elements

    > *sometimes act*
    may ~~act sometimes~~ as a shield preventing sunlight from entering the

    atmosphere. In addition, a minor change in the Earth's orbit may

    > *also affect*
    ~~affect also~~ the Earth's temperature. So when debating climate change, keep

    in mind the natural causes of temperature fluctuations.

Problems with Adverbs

Many times, people use an adjective instead of an adverb after a verb. Ensure that you always modify your verbs using an adverb.

> *really quickly*   *slowly*
The snowstorm developed ~~real quick~~. We had to drive very ~~slow~~.

PRACTICE 2   Underline and correct nine errors with adjective and adverb forms.

> *quickly*
EXAMPLE: Our world is consuming fossil fuels really ~~quick~~.

1. Presently, nuclear power generates about 14 percent

   of the world's electricity, but it is controversial.
   really quickly
   People's emotions rise ~~real quick~~ when they debate

   the issue.

2. Proponents believe that nuclear energy is not
   harmful
   ~~harmfull~~ to the environment, whereas burning fossil
   greatly   *safely*
   fuels contributes ~~great~~ to global warming. Nuclear energy can be used ~~safe~~.
   secure
   New storage methods have helped make nuclear waste more ~~securely~~.

3. Critics of nuclear energy say that reliance on nuclear power may have
   dangerous
   ~~dangerously~~ effects on human life, such as radiation poisoning. Some
   concerned
   ~~concerning~~ politicians argue that nuclear power plants invite terrorist acts.
   Fearful
   ~~Fearfull~~ opponents believe that nuclear power may lead to further nuclear

   proliferation.

Good and *Well* / *Bad* and *Badly*

Good is an adjective, and **well** is an adverb. However, as an exception, you can use *well* to describe a person's health (for example, *I do not feel **well***).

Adjective: We will have **good** weather tomorrow.

Adverb: She slept **well** even though the storm was noisy.

Bad is an adjective, and **badly** is an adverb.

Adjective: The **bad** weather remained during the past week.

Adverb: The meteorologist spoke **badly** during the nightly forecast.

Teaching Tip:
Point out to students that they may hear many people use *good/well* and *bad/badly* incorrectly, especially in spoken language. Emphasize that it is important to learn to use these words correctly.

PRACTICE 3   Underline the correct adjectives or adverbs.

EXAMPLE: Most people think it is a (good / well) idea to reduce greenhouse gases.

1. In 2006, the documentary film *An Inconvenient Truth* received (<u>good</u> / well) reviews at the Sundance Film Festival. The purpose of the documentary was to educate

the general public about the (<u>bad</u> / badly) effects of global warming on the environment. Former Vice President Al Gore narrated the documentary really (good / <u>well</u>). The film made a (<u>good</u> / well) case for reducing greenhouse gas emissions. The producers explained their ideas on global warming very (good / <u>well</u>).

2. However, there was some criticism of the documentary. Some analysts thought (bad / <u>badly</u>) of the film's message. They believed that it was biased because producers did a (<u>good</u> / well) job of exaggerating the reasons for global warming. The film's incomplete message might cause Americans to react (bad / <u>badly</u>) and panic. Some politicians also felt that the movie relied on (<u>bad</u> / badly) research. The documentary generated a lot of interest, and audiences all over the world debate the content of the film.

Comparative and Superlative Forms

Use the **comparative form** to compare two items. Use the **superlative form** to compare three or more items. You can write comparative and superlative forms by remembering a few simple guidelines.

ESL
Teaching Tip:
Remind your nonnative speakers that the comparative form is often followed by the word *than*.

Using -er and -est endings

Add -er and -est endings to one-syllable adjectives and adverbs. Double the last letter when the adjective ends in *one vowel + one consonant*.

| short | short**er** than | the short**est** |
| hot | hott**er** than | the hott**est** |

When a two-syllable adjective ends in -y, change the -y to -i and add -er or -est.

| happy | happ**ier** than | the happ**iest** |

Using *more* and *the most*

Generally, add *more* and *the most* to adjectives and adverbs of two or more syllables.

| beautiful | **more** beautiful than | the **most** beautiful |

Using Irregular Comparative and Superlative Forms

Some adjectives and adverbs have unique comparative and superlative forms. Study this list to remember some of the most common ones.

good / well	better than	the best
bad / badly	worse than	the worst
some / much / many	more than	the most
little (a small amount)	less than	the least
far	farther / further	the farthest / the furthest

PRACTICE 4   Fill in the blanks with the correct comparative and superlative forms of the words in parentheses.

EXAMPLE: The problems of global warming are (serious) __*more serious*__ than we previously believed.

1. The international community is trying to deal with one of the (urgent)

   _____*most urgent*_____ environmental problems the world is facing.

   Global warming is one of the (debated) *most debated*_____ issues

   in the scientific community. The Kyoto Protocol is an international

   agreement made under the United Nations. Countries agreed to reduce

   their greenhouse gas emissions and prevent the greenhouse effect from

   becoming (bad) *worse*_____ than in previous years.

CHAPTER 32

Teaching Tip:
There are some exceptions to the *more* and *most* rule, such as *gentle, simple,* and *narrow.* Explain that the rule applies to most adverbs and adjectives.

GRAMMAR LINK

Farther indicates a physical distance. *Further* means "additional." For more commonly confused words, see Chapter 34.

ESL
Teaching Tip:
Nonnative speakers may have difficulty with irregular forms. Suggest that they memorize irregular comparative and superlative forms.

2. Dr. Anif Mohammed is a famous climatologist. His presentation was

(short) _shorter_____ than other presentations, but it was also

the (clear) _clearest_____. In fact, he seemed to be the (little)

_least_____ nervous speaker at the conference.

Problems with Comparative and Superlative Forms
Using *more* and *-er*

In the comparative form, never use *more* and *-er* to modify the same word. In the superlative form, never use *most* and *-est* to modify the same word.

> The photographs of the tornado were ~~more~~ better than the ones of the rainstorm, but the photos of the huge waves were the ~~most~~ best in the exhibition.

Using *fewer* and *less*

In the comparative form, use *fewer* before count nouns (*fewer people, fewer houses*) and use *less* before noncount nouns (*less information, less evidence*).

> Diplomats have **less** time than they used to. **Fewer** agreements are being made.

Hint · Using *the* in the Comparative Form

Although you would usually use *the* in superlative forms, you can use it in some two-part comparatives. In these expressions, the second part is the result of the first part.

>   action   result
> The more you recycle, the better the environment will be.

PRACTICE 5 Correct the nine adjective and adverb errors in the next paragraphs.

EXAMPLE: If ~~less~~ *fewer* people drove cars, we would have ~~fewer~~ *less* air pollution.

1. The Amazon rainforest is the ~~most~~ largest in the world. It plays a vital role in regulating the global climate. Forests, such as the Amazon, create ~~more~~

ESL
Teaching Tip:
Native and nonnative speakers sometimes write *more* before a comparative that already has an *-er* ending. Draw their attention to this rule.

Teaching Tip:
Ask students if they should use *fewer* or *less* with the following nouns: *sugar, evidence, people, armies, furniture, beliefs,* and *snow.* Then point out that they can only use *fewer* with plural nouns such as *people, armies,* and *beliefs.*

GRAMMAR LINK
For a list of common noncount nouns, refer to page 418 in Chapter 30.

CHAPTER 32

better air quality for humans. Trees and plants remove carbon dioxide from the air and release oxygen into the air. The Amazon rainforest has been experiencing deforestation ~~real~~ *really* rapidly.

2. There are several reasons for the Amazon deforestation. The ~~most~~ biggest causes are cattle ranching and road construction. Roads provide ~~more~~ greater access for logging and mining companies. By clearing the forest, farmers obtain more land for their cattle.

3. The depletion of the Amazon rainforest is one of the ~~worse~~ *worst* problems for our global climate. ~~Less~~ *Fewer* politicians than environmental activists are concerned with this issue. The more humanity waits to tackle this problem, the ~~worst~~ *worse* it will become. Perhaps over time, governments and the general public will try ~~more~~ harder to save the Amazon rainforest.

FINAL REVIEW

Correct fifteen errors in adjectives and adverbs.

EXAMPLE: We need to find ~~more~~ better sources of renewable energy.

1. Our society has depended ~~economic~~ *economically* on oil for the past two hundred years. Oil is a nonrenewable energy source. Many politicians have reacted ~~bad~~ *badly* to the suggestion that we need to reduce our reliance on oil. They are

concerned about economic progress, which is presently fueled by oil. Yet,

worried

~~worrying~~ environmentalists believe that burning fossil fuels is causing

temperatures around the world to become ~~more~~ warmer. Because of the

threat of global warming, scientists are trying to develop alternative energy

really

sources ~~real~~ quickly.

                           powerful   *countless*

2. Wind energy is one ~~powerfull~~ alternative. Historically, ~~countles~~ efforts

have been made to use wind to power millstones for grinding wheat and

running pumps. Today, wind-powered turbines produce electricity 25

                                          strongly continually

percent of the time because winds might not blow ~~strong~~ or ~~continual~~.

Therefore, the wind is not a dependable source of energy.

Fewer

3. ~~Less~~ people use geothermal energy to heat homes in North America than

in some other parts of the world. Nevertheless, it is also one of the ~~most~~

best alternative energy sources. Steam and hot water from under the

                                        quickly

Earth's surface are used to turn turbines ~~quick~~ enough to create electricity.

There are a few areas, such as Iceland, that have steam close to the Earth's

surface. In such places, geothermal energy is cost-effective.

            preceding

4. The ~~preceded~~ energy sources are just a few of the alternative approaches

that researchers are working on perfecting. These alternatives do not

substitute completely for the versatility of oil. Scientists, government

                                    well

officials, and concerned citizens know ~~good~~ that our society must reduce

                                                  better

its dependence on oil. The more money we spend on research, the ~~best~~ the

chances will be to develop and promote energy alternatives.

Teaching Tip:

Cooperative Learning (Ask & Learn) Have students identify grammar points they find difficult. Then, in teams, students can ask each other questions to clarify anything they don't understand.

CHAPTER 32

READING LINK

Forces of Nature
The following essays contain more information about weather and climate issues.

"Weird Weather" by Pamela D. Jacobsen (page 571)

"The Rules of Survival" by Laurence Gonzales (page 573)

"Into Thin Air" by Jon Krakauer (page 578)

The Writer's Room Topics for Writing

Write about one of the following topics. Proofread your text to ensure that there are no adjective and adverb mistakes.

1. Compare two types of transportation that you have owned. Explain which one you prefer.

2. In 2010, there was a major oil spill off the coast of Louisiana. Should the government permit off-shore drilling? Explain why or why not.

✔ CHECKLIST: ADJECTIVES AND ADVERBS

When you edit your writing, ask yourself these questions:

☐ Do I use adjectives and adverbs correctly? Check for errors in these cases:

- the placement, order, and spelling of adjectives
- the placement of frequency adverbs, and the spelling of adverbs ending in -*ly*
- the adjective and adverb form
- the use of *good/well* and *bad/badly*

                   quietly   *interesting*
Magnus Forbes spoke very ~~quiet~~ about the ~~interested~~ article
                                        often
on El Niño at the news conference. He was asked about
                                  ^

environmental issues. The environmental lobbyist hid his
                really well
concern ~~real good~~.

☐ Do I use the correct comparative and superlative forms? Check for errors in these cases:

- *more* versus -*er* comparisons
- *the most* versus -*est* comparisons
- *fewer* versus *less* forms

The ~~most~~ quickest tornado trackers take the first photographs.
                       fewer   *less*
The organization has ~~less~~ members, but it also has ~~fewer~~ bad publicity.

Teaching Tip:
Writer's World Competition
Please advise students that they can submit their paragraphs and essays for possible publication to www .pearsonhighered .com/essayrewards/ writingrewards.html

my writinglab   To check your progress in meeting this chapter's objectives, log in to **www.mywritinglab.com,** go to the **Study Plan** tab, click on **The Editing Handbook—Section 4** and choose **Adjectives and Adverbs** from the list of subtopics. Read and view the resources in the **Review Materials** section, and then complete the **Recall, Apply,** and **Write** sets in the **Activities** section.

Exact Language

LEARNING OBJECTIVES

1 Using Specific and Detailed Vocabulary (p. 453)

2 Avoiding Wordiness and Redundancy (p. 455)

3 Avoiding Clichés (p. 457)

4 Using Standard English (p. 458)

Section Theme **PLANTS AND INSECTS**

In this chapter, you will read about plants.

Using Specific and Detailed Vocabulary

Effective writing evokes an emotional response from the reader. Great writers not only use correct grammatical structures, but they also infuse their writing with precise and vivid details that make their work come alive.

When you proofread your work, revise words that are too vague. **Vague words** lack precision and detail. For example, the words *nice* and *bad* are vague. Readers cannot get a clear picture from them.

Teaching Tip:

Cooperative Learning (Jigsaw)
Place students in teams of three to five. Assign each team a grammar concept from the chapter. Each team should present a short lesson about the concept to the class.

Compare the following sets of sentences.

Vague: The tree was big.

Precise: The 250-foot-tall giant sequoia seemed to touch the cloudless sky.

Vague: The gardener planted some flowers.

Precise: The gardener, Mr. Oliver, planted azaleas, hyacinths, and irises.

> *Hint* **Some Common Vague Words**
>
> The following is a list of some frequently used vague words. Try to find substitutes for overly familiar and vague words: *good, bad, nice, pretty, big, small, great, happy, sad, thing.*

CHAPTER 33

Creating Vivid Language

When you choose the precise word, you convey your meaning exactly. Moreover, you can make your writing clearer and more impressive by using specific and detailed vocabulary. To create vivid language, do the following:

- **Modify your nouns.** If your noun is vague, make it more specific by adding one or more adjectives. You could also rename the noun with a more specific term.

    Vague: the child

    Vivid: the angry boy   the tearful and frightened orphan

- **Modify your verbs.** Use more vivid, precise verbs. You could also use adverbs.

    Vague: talk

    More vivid: bicker   debate passionately

WRITING LINK
You can find more information about appealing to the five senses in Chapter 8, Description.

- **Include more details.** Add information to make the sentence more detailed and complete.

    Vague: Some plants are good for the health.

    Precise: Garlic has antibiotic properties that can fight bacteria and viruses.

PRACTICE 1   Underline vague words in the following sentences. Then replace them with more precise and detailed vocabulary.
Answers will vary.

EXAMPLE: Our town's garden is <u>pretty</u>.

> *The pond in our town's garden is filled with pink and white water lilies and*
> *surrounded by ferns and wild poppies that attract green frogs, mallard*
> *ducks, and cardinals.*

1. My neighbor likes to garden.
   _____

   _____

2. She has planted many flowers and plants.
   _____

   _____

3. There are also vegetables.
   _____

   _____

4. The herbs she has planted smell nice.
   _____

   _____

5. People come to see her garden.
   _____

   _____

Teaching Tip:
Group Work
Ask groups of students to use vivid language to describe the picture at the beginning of this chapter or to describe a photo in this book.

Teaching Tip:
Pair Work
Ask students to peer-edit each other's work.

CHAPTER 33

Avoiding Wordiness and Redundancy

Sometimes students fill their writing assignments with extra words to meet the length requirement. However, good ideas can get lost in work that is too wordy. Also, if the explanations are unnecessarily long, readers will become bored.

To improve your writing style, use only as many words or phrases as you need to fully explain your ideas.

The farm was big ~~in size~~.

(*Big* is a measure of size, so you do not need to say "in size.")

Correcting Wordiness

You can cut the number of words needed to express an idea by substituting a wordy phrase with a single word. You could also remove the wordy phrase completely.

because
I don't like gardening ~~due to the fact that~~ I spend most of the time just pulling out weeds.

CHAPTER 33

Some Common Wordy Expressions and Substitutions

Wordy	Substitution	Wordy	Substitution
at this point in time	now, currently	gave the appearance of being	looked like
at that point in time	then, at that time		
big / small in size	big / small	in order to	to
in close proximity	close or in proximity	in spite of the fact	in spite of
a difficult dilemma	a dilemma	in the final analysis	finally, lastly
due to the fact	because	past history	past or history
equally as good as	as good as	period of time	period
exactly the same	the same	still remain	remain
exceptions to the rule	exceptions	a true fact	a fact
final completion	end	the fact of the matter is	in fact
for the purpose of	for		

PRACTICE 2   Edit the following sentences by crossing out all unnecessary words or phrases. If necessary, find more concise substitutes for wordy expressions.

EXAMPLE: The Bodhi tree has grown to be big ~~in size~~.

1. Some trees around the world have become famous ~~due to the fact that~~ they
   because
   are associated with myths and legends.

2. A Bodhi tree, a large fig tree, is located ~~in close proximity~~ to the village of
   close
   Bodh Gaya, India.

3. Legend states that Siddhartha Gautama, the Buddha, overcame a ~~difficult~~ dilemma and attained spiritual enlightenment near the tree.

4. After he attained enlightenment, the Buddha spent many days in ~~exactly~~ the same spot to illuminate his disciples.

5. Many pilgrims visited the Buddha under the tree ~~in order~~ to hear his teachings.

6. The original Bodhi tree died, but ~~at this point in time~~ *now*, another tree is sprouting from the ancestor tree.

7. The Bodhi tree ~~still~~ remains an important destination for pilgrims who want to pay homage to the Buddha.

Avoiding Clichés

Clichés are overused expressions. Avoid boring your readers with clichés, and use more direct and vivid language instead.

clichés	direct words
<u>In this neck of the woods</u>, she is considered an expert on orchids.	In this area

Other Common Clichés

a drop in the bucket	death trap
add insult to injury	easier said than done
as luck would have it	go with the flow
axe to grind	in the nick of time
better late than never	keep your eyes peeled
between a rock and a hard place	at a loss for words
break the ice	under the weather
calm, cool, and collected	time and time again
crystal clear	tried and true

ESL
Teaching Tip:
If you have students who are nonnative speakers, you could discuss the meanings of these and other clichés with the class. You could also place native and nonnative speakers in mixed groups, and ask them to discuss the meanings of the expressions.

> ### Hint · Modifying Clichés
>
> To modify a cliché, change it into a direct term. You might also try playing with language to come up with a more interesting description.
>
> | | |
> |---|---|
> | **Cliché:** | She was as happy as a lark. |
> | **Direct language:** | She was thrilled. |
> | **Interesting description:** | She was as happy as a teenager whose parents had gone away for the weekend. |

Teaching Tip:

Pair Work

Ask students to do this practice with a partner.

PRACTICE 3 Cross out the clichéd expression in each sentence. If necessary, replace it with fresh or direct language. Answers will vary.

greatly impressed
EXAMPLE: I was ~~blown away~~ by my neighbor's garden.

CHAPTER 33

took a chance
1. My neighbor ~~threw caution to the wind~~ and planted some strange plants.

risked
2. She ~~was playing with fire~~ planting a ginkgo tree.

Ginkgo leaves

3. When I smelled something putrid, I was sure ~~beyond a shadow of a doubt~~ that it was the ginkgo tree.

She
4. ~~To add insult to injury, she~~ had also planted a corpse flower in her greenhouse.

did not know what to say
5. I ~~was at a loss for words~~ when she asked me how I liked her new plants.

My
6. ~~In the nick of time, my~~ boyfriend arrived, so I could avoid answering her question.

Using Standard English

Most of your instructors will want you to write using **standard English.** The word "standard" does not imply better. Standard English is the common language generally used and expected in schools, businesses, and government institutions in the United States. **Slang** is nonstandard language. It is used in informal situations to communicate common cultural knowledge. In any academic or professional context, do not use slang.

Slang: Me an' some bros wanted to make some dough, so we worked on a farm picking apples. We made a bit of coin, and our grub was included. It was real cool. On the weekends, we mostly chilled.

Standard American English: My friends and I wanted to make some money, so we worked on a farm picking apples. We were well paid, and our food was included. We had a memorable time. On the weekends, we mostly relaxed.

Hint ▸ **Reasons to Avoid Slang**

Slang changes depending on generational, regional, cultural, and historical influences. For example, one group might say "upset" whereas others might say "freaked out" or "having a fit." You should avoid using slang expressions in your writing because they can change very quickly—so quickly, in fact, that you might think that this textbook's examples of slang are "lame."

PRACTICE 4 Substitute the underlined slang expressions with the best possible choice of standard English.

EXAMPLE: Since ancient times people have eaten garlic even if it
             body odor
    causes <u>B.O.</u>

                           excitement
1. Recently, there has been a lot of <u>hype</u> about the medicinal properties of

   garlic.

                      felt sick
2. In the past, when people <u>were under the weather</u>, they believed the

   magical properties of garlic would help them heal.

                    desired
3. In Greek mythology, Circe <u>had the hots for</u> Ulysses, who ate garlic to

   protect himself from her advances.

                                         courage
4. Spanish bullfighters wore garlic necklaces so they would have the <u>guts</u> to

   fight bulls.

Teaching Tip:
Pair Work
Ask students to do
Practice 4 with a
partner. Go over
student answers to
make sure that they
have not simply
replaced one slang
word with another.

young women
5. Ancient Egyptian <u>chicks</u> would put garlic in their belly buttons to find out
    pregnant
    if they were <u>knocked up</u>.

    every day
6. In Eastern Europe, people wore garlic <u>24/7</u> to ward off evil spirits.

    extraordinary
7. Today, scientists believe that garlic is <u>awesome</u> because it may help fight

    cancer.

FINAL REVIEW

Edit the following paragraphs for twenty errors in wordiness, slang, clichés,
and vague language to make the text more effective.   Answers will vary.
Wordy, clichéd, and slang expressions are underlined.

Teaching Tip:
To help students
build vocabulary, ask
them to work in
pairs and come up
with a list of
possible
substitutions for
each slang term,
cliché, wordy
expression, or vague
term in the final
review.

Teaching Tip:
You can use the final
review as a test.
Additional practice
and test material
appears in the
Instructor's
Resource Manual
and on
MyWritingLab.

Currently   *upset*
1. <u>At this point in time</u>, many people are <u>freaking out</u> about genetically

    modified foods. Genetic modification (GM) is a technology that lets
                    experiment
    scientists <u>fool around</u> with the genetic composition of plants.

    Historically, people have always tried to change the characteristics of
                            to make
    plants <u>for the purpose of making</u> them more disease-resistant.

    That process has traditionally been done through hybridization,
                a reliable method
    <u>a tried and true method</u>. That is, two parent plants from the same genus
                                                            Hybrid
    are bred to create an improved hybrid plant. <s>One true fact is that</s> hybrid

    wheat is hardier than traditional wheat.

2. Today, in North America, hundreds of foods are genetically modified.
        Finally
    <u>In the final analysis</u>, there is great controversy about genetically modified
                                    repeatedly
    foods. Proponents of this technology say <u>time and time again</u> that food

will contain higher levels of nutrition, be resistant to disease, and produce

Despite or In spite of

higher yields. <u>In spite of the fact of</u> such arguments, opponents are

angry

<u>all fired up</u> about genetically modified foods because they say that there is

not enough knowledge about how such foods will affect human health.

unsafe

They believe such foods might be <u>a death trap</u>. For example, will

humans who are allergic to peanuts have a reaction if they are eating

tomatoes that have been genetically modified with a peanut gene?

Furthermore, opponents believe that the loss of diversity in crops

is alarming

and plants really <u>bites</u>. Another worry is that food production will

large

go into the hands of <u>super-sized</u> agricultural companies who will

prominent scientists

control growth and distribution of food. Moreover, <u>the bigwigs</u> in

worry

this debate <u>stress out</u> about the ethics of mixing genes from species to

species.

3. The genetically modified food industry is growing rapidly <s>in size</s>. But it is

important to have a healthy and open debate over this issue. Presently,

confused

consumers are faced with a <s>difficult</s> dilemma. Most people are <u>in a fog</u> and

are unknowingly buying genetically modified foods because such foods

lack complete labeling. For example, most cooking oil comes from

know

genetically modified grains. The public should <u>be in the know</u> about this

informed

technology. Consumers need to be <u>clued in</u> so that they make the right

choices.

CHAPTER 33

The Writer's Room Topics for Writing

Write about one of the following topics. Proofread your text to ensure that you have used detailed vocabulary and avoided wordiness, clichés, and slang.

1. Examine the photo below. What are some terms that come to mind? Some ideas might be *family farm*, *agribusiness*, *healthy living*, *back to basics*, *farm aid*, or *green thumb*.

2. Why are fast foods and other unhealthy foods so popular? Think of some reasons.

Teaching Tip:
Writer's World Competition
Please advise students that they can submit their paragraphs and essays for possible publication to www
.pearsonhighered
.com/essayrewards/
writingrewards.html

✓ CHECKLIST: EXACT LANGUAGE

When you edit your writing, ask yourself these questions.

☐ Have I used specific and detailed vocabulary? Check for errors with vague words.

Vague: My son likes to garden.

Detailed: My fifteen-year-old son, Kiran, is an enthusiastic gardener.

☐ Have I used exact language? Check for errors with wordiness, clichés, and slang.

now

Julian works in the garden center ~~at this point in time~~.

evident

It is ~~as plain as black and white~~ that many people like organic food.

easy

The biology exam was ~~a no-brainer~~.

mywritinglab   To check your progress in meeting this chapter's objectives, log in to **www.mywritinglab.com,** go to the **Study Plan** tab, click on **The Editing Handbook—Section 5** and choose **Exact Language** from the list of subtopics. Read and view the resources in the **Review Materials** section, and then complete the **Recall, Apply,** and **Write** sets in the **Activities** section.

CHAPTER 33

CHAPTER 34

Spelling and Commonly Confused Words

LEARNING OBJECTIVES

1 Spelling Rules (p. 464)

2 120 Commonly Misspelled Words (p. 467)

3 Look-Alike and Sound-Alike Words (p. 469)

Section Theme **PLANTS AND INSECTS**

In this chapter, you will read about insects.

Spelling Rules

It is important to spell correctly because spelling mistakes can detract from important ideas in your work. Here are some strategies for improving your spelling skills.

How to Become a Better Speller

- **Look up words** using the most current dictionary because it will contain new or updated words. For tips on dictionary usage, see page 531 in Chapter 40.

- **Keep a record of words that you commonly misspell**. For example, write the words and definitions in a spelling log, which could be in a journal or binder. See Appendix 6 for more information about your spelling log.

- **Use memory cards or flash cards** to help you memorize the spelling of difficult words. With a friend or a classmate, take turns asking each other to spell difficult words.
- **Write out the spelling of difficult words at least ten times** to help you remember how to spell them. After you have written these words, try writing them in a complete sentence.

Six Common Spelling Rules

Memorize the following common rules of spelling. If you follow these rules, your spelling will become more accurate. Also try to remember the exceptions to these rules.

1. **Writing *ie* or *ei***   Write *i* before *e*, except after *c* or when *ei* is pronounced as *ay*, as in *neighbor* and *weigh*.

i before *e*:	brief	field	priest
ei after *c*:	receipt	deceit	receive
ei pronounced as *ay*:	weigh	beige	vein

Here are some exceptions:

ancient	either	neither	foreigner	leisure	height
science	species	society	seize	their	weird

2. **Adding *-s* or *-es***   Add *-s* to form plural nouns and to create present-tense verbs that are third-person singular. However, add *-es* to words in the following situations.

- When words end in *-s*, *-sh*, *-ss*, *-ch*, or *-x*, add *-es*.

      noun   box–boxes   **verb**   miss–misses

- When words end in consonant *-y*, change the *-y* to *-i* and add *-es*.

      noun   baby–babies   **verb**   marry–marries

- When words end in *-o*, add *-es*. Exceptions are *pianos*, *radios*, *logos*, *stereos*, *autos*, *typos*, and *casinos*.

      noun   tomato–tomatoes   **verb**   go–goes

- When words end in *-f* or *-fe*, change the *-f* to a *-v* and add *-es*. Exceptions are *beliefs* and *roofs*.

      life–lives   wolf–wolves

Teaching Tip:

Cooperative Learning (Jigsaw) Place students in teams of three to five. Assign each team a grammar concept from the chapter. Each team should present a short lesson about the concept to the class.

CHAPTER 34

Teaching Tip:
Team Work
Put students into
teams and give them
the following
challenge. Ask them
to compete with
one another to
write as many
words as possible.
Each word must
have one of
the following
combinations of
letters: (1) an *ei*
vowel combination,
(2) an *lly* ending,
(3) a double *e*, or
(4) a *ght* ending.

ESL
Teaching Tip:
Many languages have
words that look
like English words
but are spelled
differently. You
might ask your
nonnative speakers
to keep a list of
such words. For
example, English:
occupation,
comfortable. Spanish:
ocupacion,
confortable. Also
point out that look-
alike words may
have different
meanings. For
example, in German,
the word *bald*
means *soon.*

3. **Adding Prefixes and Suffixes**   A **prefix** is added to the beginning of a word, and it changes the word's meaning. For example, *con-*, *dis-*, *pre-*, *un-*, and *il-* are prefixes. When you add a prefix to a word, keep the last letter of the prefix and the first letter of the main word.

im + **m**ature = i**mm**ature   mi**s** + **s**pell = mi**ss**pell

A **suffix** is added to the ending of a word, and it changes the word's tense or meaning. For example, *-ly*, *-ment*, *-ed*, and *-ing* are suffixes. When you add the suffix *-ly* to words that end in *-l*, keep the *-l* of the root word. The new word will have two *-l*s.

casua**l** + **l**y = casua**ll**y   factua**l** + **l**y = factua**ll**y

4. **Adding Suffixes to Words Ending in *-e***   If the suffix begins with a vowel, drop the *-e* on the main word. Some common suffixes beginning with vowels are *-ed*, *-er*, *-est*, *-ing*, *-able*, *-ent*, and *-ist*.

bak**e**–baking   creat**e**–created

Some exceptions are words that end in *-ge*, which keep the *-e* and add the suffix.

outrag**e**–outrag**e**ous   manag**e**–manag**e**able

If the suffix begins with a consonant, keep the *-e*. Some common suffixes beginning with consonants are *-ly*, *-ment*, *-less*, and *-ful*. Some exceptions are *acknowledgment*, *argument*, and *truly*.

sur**e**–sur**e**ly   awar**e**–awar**e**ness

5. **Adding Suffixes to Words Ending in *-y***   If the word has a consonant before the final *-y*, change the *-y* to an *-i* before adding the suffix. Some exceptions are *ladybug*, *dryness*, and *shyness*.

pretty–prett**i**est   happy–happ**i**ness

If the word has a vowel before the final *-y*, if it is a proper name, or if the suffix is *-ing*, do not change the *y* to an *i*. Some exceptions are *daily*, *laid*, and *said*.

employ–employed   apply–applying   Levinsky–Levinskys

6. **Doubling the Final Consonant**   Double the final consonant of one-syllable words ending in a consonant–vowel–consonant pattern.

ship–shi**pp**ing   swim–swi**mm**er   hop–ho**pp**ed

Double the final consonant of words ending in a stressed consonant–vowel–consonant pattern. If the final syllable is not stressed, then do not double the last letter.

refer–refe**rr**ed   occur–occu**rr**ed   happen–happened

120 Commonly Misspelled Words

The next list contains some of the most commonly misspelled words in English.

absence	curriculum	loneliness	reference
absorption	definite	maintenance	responsible
accommodate	definitely	mathematics	rhythm
acquaintance	desperate	medicine	schedule
address	developed	millennium	scientific
aggressive	dilemma	minuscule	separate
already	disappoint	mischievous	sincerely
aluminum	embarrass	mortgage	spaghetti
analyze	encouragement	necessary	strength
appointment	environment	ninety	success
approximate	especially	noticeable	surprise
argument	exaggerate	occasion	technique
athlete	exercise	occurrence	thorough
bargain	extraordinarily	opposite	tomato
beginning	familiar	outrageous	tomatoes
behavior	February	parallel	tomorrow
believable	finally	performance	truly
business	foreign	perseverance	Tuesday
calendar	government	personality	until
campaign	grammar	physically	usually
careful	harassment	possess	vacuum
ceiling	height	precious	Wednesday
cemetery	immediately	prejudice	weird
clientele	independent	privilege	woman
committee	jewelry	probably	women
comparison	judgment	professor	wreckage
competent	laboratory	psychology	writer
conscience	ledge	questionnaire	writing
conscientious	leisure	receive	written
convenient	license	recommend	zealous

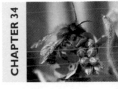

ESL

Teaching Tip:
Nonnative speakers may be confused as to why a word such as *beginning* doubles the *n* but *happening* doesn't. Say the following words out loud and ask students to guess which words require a double consonant: *preferred, offered, altered, opened, delivered, occurred.*

Teaching Tip:
Ask students to highlight words that they commonly misspell. Then ask them to exchange their lists with a partner. The partner can then ask the student to spell the difficult words.

PRACTICE I   Edit the next paragraphs for twenty misspelled words.

strength
EXAMPLE: Some insects have an incredible amount of ~~strenght~~.

1. Throughout history, humans have been either fascinated or repulsed by

   developed
   insects. In fact, humans have ~~developped~~ a close connection to insects and

   recognize the power and importance of insects for sustaining life. For

   example, insects pollinate plants and aerate soil. Without such help,

   environment
   the ~~enviroment~~ would suffer. Thus, human cultures have

   acknowledged
   ~~acknowleged~~ insects through art, literature, and religion.

2. First, the ancient Egyptians honored different insects. The dung beetle, or

   definitely
   scarab, was ~~definatly~~ an important religious symbol. The Egyptians called it

   believed
   Khepera, the god of virility and rebirth. They ~~beleived~~ that he was

   responsible
   ~~responsable~~ for pushing the sun along the horizon. To honor Khepera, the

   jewelry
   Egyptians wore scarab amulets as precious ~~jewlry~~ and buried the amulets in

   boxes
   pots and ~~boxs~~ with the dead. The ancients thought that the scarabs helped

   entering
   the dead who were ~~enterring~~ the afterlife.

3. Another insect, the cricket, was valued in Chinese culture. The Chinese

   especially
   kept both singing and fighting varieties. Singing crickets were ~~expecialy~~

   crucial to farmers. They knew it was time to plow when crickets and other

   ladies
   insects began to wake and sing. Wealthy ~~ladyes~~ and palace concubines

   kept crickets as pets in cages. Some experts believe that the crickets

   themselves
   represented the women ~~themselfs~~, who had very little status in the

   community. Fighting crickets were also very popular, and many people

   betting
   lost much of their savings ~~beting~~ on cricket fights.

4. Western artists are also fascinated with insects. There are many fables that

    feature different ~~speceis~~ *species* as the main characters. In modern literature,

    insects play a ~~noticable~~ *noticeable* role. For example, in Franz Kafka's *Metamorphosis*,

    the main character turns into a giant cockroach. Insects are common

    symbols in modern film. Jiminy Cricket is Pinocchio's ~~consceince~~ *conscience*. In the

    movie *The Fly*, a scientist is ~~unaturaly~~ *unnaturally* transformed into a six-foot human

    fly. ~~Flys~~ *Flies* and other insects can also symbolize human fear and repugnance.

5. Humans and insects have had a ~~truely~~ *truly* special relationship for many

    millennia. Different cultures have integrated insects into the fields of art,

    music, religion, and history. Indeed, some people say that the teeny creepy

    crawlers are survivors and will ~~surly~~ *surely* outlive humans.

Look-Alike and Sound-Alike Words

Sometimes two English words can sound the same but have different spellings and meanings. These words are called **homonyms.** Here are a few commonly confused words and basic meanings. (For more specific definitions for these and other words, consult a dictionary.)

accept	to receive; to admit	We must accept the vital role that insects play in our culture.
except	excluding; other than	I like all insects except ants.
allowed	permitted	We were not allowed to view the exhibit.
aloud	spoken audibly	We could not speak aloud, so we whispered.
affect	to influence	Pesticides affect the environment.
effect	the result of something	Scientists are examining the effects of pesticides on our health.

Teaching Tip: Ask students to look at the list and highlight the words that they commonly confuse.

been	past participle of the verb *to be*	He has <u>been</u> to the Imax film about caterpillars.
being	present progressive form (the *-ing* form) of the verb *to be*	She was <u>being</u> kind when she donated to the butterfly museum.
by	preposition meaning *next to*, *on*, or *before*	A bee flew <u>by</u> the flowers. <u>By</u> evening, the crickets were making a lot of noise.
buy	to purchase	Will you <u>buy</u> me that scarab necklace?
complement	an addition; to complete	The film about the monarch butterfly was a nice <u>complement</u> to the exhibit.
compliment	nice comment about someone	The film was informative, and the director received many <u>compliments</u>.
conscience	a personal sense of right or wrong	After spraying pesticides, the gardener had a guilty <u>conscience</u>.
conscious	aware; awake	He made us <u>conscious</u> of the important role insects play in our society.

PRACTICE 2   Underline the correct word in the parentheses.

EXAMPLE: Many people (by / <u>buy</u>) clothes made out of silk.

1. Silk has (<u>been</u> / being) produced (<u>by</u> / buy) the Chinese for at least four thousand years. The silkworm is actually a caterpillar that eats nothing (accept / <u>except</u>) mulberry leaves, grows quickly, and then encircles itself into a cocoon of raw silk. The cocoon contains a single thread around 300 to 900 yards in length, so it's not surprising that it takes about 2,000 cocoons to make one pound of silk. (Been / <u>Being</u>) very (<u>conscious</u> / conscience) of the long and intense silk-making process, most people (<u>accept</u> / except) the high cost of the material.

2. The Chinese valued silk and guarded the secret of its making carefully. In ancient China, only the emperor and his family were (<u>allowed</u> / aloud) to

wear silk garments. Sometimes, members of royalty wore the fabric as a (complement / compliment) to their regular clothes. Of course, less fortunate people admired the emperor's beautiful clothes and always (complimented / complemented) him.

3. By the fifth century, the secret of silk-making had been revealed to Korea, Japan, and India. How did the secret get out? Legend says that a princess with no (conscious / conscience) smuggled out silkworm larvae to Korea by hiding them in her hair. The emperor was outraged (by / buy) the actions of the princess, and there was great debate about her treachery.

everyday	ordinary or common	Swatting mosquitoes is an everyday ritual of camping.
every day	each day	Every day, I check my roses for aphids.
imminent	soon to happen	The journalist reported that the arrival of locusts in parts of Africa was imminent.
eminent	distinguished; superior	Professor Maurice Kanyogo is an eminent entomologist.
imply	to suggest	The entomologist implied that he had received a large grant.
infer	to conclude	His students inferred that they would have summer jobs because of the grant.
its	possessive case of the pronoun *it*	The worker bee went into its hive.
it's	contraction for *it is*	It's well known that the queen bee is the largest in the colony.
knew	past tense of *to know*	I knew that I should study for my test on worms.
new	recent or unused	But my new book on honey making was more interesting.

know	to have knowledge of	The beekeepers <u>know</u> that there has been a decline in bees in recent years.
no	a negative	There were <u>no</u> books on beekeeping in the library.
lose	to misplace or forfeit something	Do not <u>lose</u> the mosquito repellent.
loose	too baggy; not fixed	You should wear <u>loose</u> clothes when camping.
loss	a decrease in an amount; a serious blow	Farmers would experience a <u>loss</u> if there were no bees to pollinate crops.
peace	calmness; an end to violence	The <u>peace</u> in the woods was wonderful.
piece	a part of something else; one item in a group of items	The two <u>pieces</u> of amber had insects in them.
principal	director of a school; main	The <u>principal</u> of our school is an expert on beetles. They are his <u>principal</u> hobby.
principle	rule or standard	Julius Corrant wrote a book about environmental <u>principles</u>.
quiet	silent	The crickets remained <u>quiet</u> this evening.
quite	very	They usually make <u>quite</u> a noise.
quit	stop	I would like them to <u>quit</u> making so much noise.

CHAPTER 34

PRACTICE 3   Identify and correct ten word choice errors.

peace
EXAMPLE: I need some ~~piece~~ and quiet.

eminent
1. Professor Zoe Truger, an ~~imminent~~ entomologist, specializes in butterfly
   It's   *its*
   behavior. I am reading her book. ~~Its~~ very interesting. On ~~it's~~ cover, there
                                 Every day
   is a beautiful photograph of a butterfly. ~~Everyday~~, during the summer,

   thousands of monarch butterflies are found in southern Canada, their summer home. As autumn arrives, these butterflies know that migration to

imminent

warmer climates is ~~eminent~~.

principal

2. The ~~principle~~ of Jake's school took the students on a nature walk to look

quiet

for earthworms. The students were very ~~quite~~ when the guide told them

there are 2,700 species of earthworms.

know

3. Did you ~~no~~ that beekeeping is one of the world's oldest professions?

loose

Beekeepers wear ~~lose~~ clothing and protective gear. Some beekeepers must

quit

~~quiet~~ their profession because they are allergic to bee stings.

taught	past tense of *to teach*	I taught a class on pollination.
thought	past tense of *to think*	I thought the students enjoyed it.
than	word used to compare items	There are more mosquitoes at the lake than in the city.
then	at a particular time; after a specific time	He found the termite nest. Then he called the exterminators.
that	word used to introduce a clause	They told him that they would come immediately.
their	possessive form of *they*	They wore scarab amulets to show their respect for the god Khepera.
there	a place or location; an introductory phrase in sentences stating that something does or does not exist	The ant colony is over there. There is a beehive in the tree.
they're	contraction of *they are*	The ants work hard. They're very industrious.
to	part of an infinitive; indicates direction or movement	I want to hunt for bugs. I will go to the hiking path and look under some rocks.
too	also or very	My friend is too scared of bugs. My brother is, too.
two	the number after *one*	There were two types of butterflies in the garden today.

where	question word indicating location	<u>Where</u> did you buy the book on ladybugs?
were	past tense of *be*	There <u>were</u> hundreds of ladybugs on the bush.
we're	contraction of *we are*	<u>We're</u> wondering why we have this infestation.
who's	contraction of *who is*	Isabelle, <u>who's</u> a horticulturist, also keeps a butterfly garden.
whose	pronoun showing ownership	<u>Whose</u> garden is that?
write	to draw symbols that represent words	I will <u>write</u> an essay about the common earthworm.
right	the opposite of the direction left; correct	In the <u>right</u> corner of the garden, there is the compost bin with many worms in it.
		You are <u>right</u> when you say that earthworms are necessary for composting.

PRACTICE 4   Identify and correct fifteen word choice errors.

EXAMPLE: ~~Their~~ *There* are many different types of bees.

1. In 2007, ~~their~~ *there* were reports ~~than~~ *that* the honeybee population was mysteriously disappearing. According ~~too~~ *to* scientists at Pennsylvania State University, a large percentage of honeybee colonies ~~where~~ *were* dying. The demise of the honeybee population was worrisome because bees pollinate crops. People ~~who's~~ *whose* livelihoods depended on the agricultural industry worried about losing income. Records showed that, in 2007, honeybee populations declined at a greater rate ~~that~~ *than* at anytime in the past. Entomologists traveled to different countries ~~were~~ *where* they observed bee colonies. They ~~taught~~ *thought* parasites or a virus might be responsible for the deaths.

2. Presently, scientists are seeing some confusing statistics. ~~There~~ *They're* finding

that declines in honeybee populations vary in different countries. Annie

May Tricot, ~~whose~~ *who's* a specialist in bees, is studying this problem. She has

~~thought to~~ *taught two* courses on honeybee behavior. Her research shows that

honeybee populations in China and Argentina are increasing. Tricot will

~~right~~ *write* an article about this phenomenon. Scientists hope that the situation

will ~~write~~ *right* itself in the near future. ~~Were~~ *We're* looking forward to hearing what

Tricot has to say in her lecture on bees tonight.

FINAL REVIEW

Correct the twenty spelling errors and mistakes with commonly confused
words in the essay.

EXAMPLE: The bee ~~carrys~~ *carries* pollen grains from one plant to another.

1. Around the world, ~~unatural~~ *unnatural* causes such as climate change, pollution, and

human activities are threatening the ~~enviroment~~ *environment*. Forests are ~~expecialy~~ *especially*

vulnerable to these pressures because of ~~loging~~ *logging*, increasing pests, and

global warming. Conserving biodiversity is important to protect forests.

2. Biodiversity, a contraction of the words *biological diversity*, means that a

variety of plants, animals, and microorganisms coexist in an ecosystem.

Today, ~~imminent~~ *eminent* scientists concerned with species' extinction refer to

the ~~necesity~~ *necessity* of maintaining biodiversity on our planet. Scientists are

~~conscience~~ *conscious* of the value of each species. ~~Argueing~~ *Arguing* for conserving

Teaching Tip:
You can use the final
review as a test.
Additional practice
and test material
appears in the
Instructor's
Resource Manual
and on
MyWritingLab.

Teaching Tip:
Pair Work
Ask students to do
this activity in pairs.

biodiversity, scientists believe that if species become extinct, ~~than~~ *then* their

ecosystem will become unstable.

3. Insects are crucial to sustaining the biodiversity of an ecosystem and are

the most diverse life form on earth. Currently, there are approximately

800,000 identified species of insects, all of which are ~~usefull~~ *useful* in balancing

the ecosystem. For example, they pollinate plants, and they eat other

insects and plants. ~~Their~~ *They're* also important to the global economy. For

instance, insects are used for honey production, silk making, and

agricultural pest control. If an insect species becomes extinct, ~~they're~~ *there* will

be a variety of consequences for the remaining species in the ecosystem,

such as an increase in predatory insects or a ~~lost~~ *loss* of another species higher

on the food chain. Such a change in the ecosystem would have an ~~eminent~~ *imminent*

effect on all life forms.

4. Most people think that insects are troublesome and should be eradicated.
    Of course, insects such as ~~mosquitos~~ *mosquitoes* carry diseases, including malaria and
    West Nile virus, which are ~~harmfull~~ *harmful* to human health. But ~~its~~ *It's* important

to keep in mind that most insects provide important services for the

natural world, ~~to.~~ *too.* ~~Were~~ *Where* there are insects, there is a thriving ecosystem.

Extinction of an insect species will have a serious ~~affeet~~ *effect* on nature, so the

next time you are tempted to swat a fly or step on an ant, you might think

twice.

The Writer's Room **Topics for Writing**

Write about one of the following topics. Proofread your text to ensure there are no spelling and commonly confused word errors.

1. Discuss types of insects that are particularly annoying, repulsive, or frightening.

2. Are laws banning the use of pesticides on lawns a good idea? Explain your ideas.

✔ CHECKLIST: SPELLING RULES

When you edit your writing, ask yourself these questions.

☐ Do I have any spelling errors? Check for errors in words that contain these elements:

- *ie* or *ei* combinations
- prefixes and suffixes

> ~~Dragonflys~~ **Dragonflies** are ~~lovly~~ **lovely**. ~~There~~ **Their** wings are transparent, but
> ~~they're~~ **their** bodies are a variety of colors. They eat other
> insects such as ~~mosquitos~~ **mosquitoes**.

☐ Do I repeat spelling errors that I have made in previous assignments? I should check my previous assignments for errors or consult my spelling log.

READING LINK

Plants and Insects

The following readings contain more information on plants and insects.

"Living Among the Bees" by Lucie Snodgrass (page 128)

"Swamps and Pesticides" by Corey Kaminska (page 195)

"Songs of Insects" by Sy Montgomery (page 581)

"Nature Returns to the Cities" by John Roach (page 584)

CHAPTER 34

mywritinglab To check your progress in meeting this chapter's objectives, log in to **www.mywritinglab.com,** go to the **Study Plan** tab, click on **The Editing Handbook—Section 5** and choose **Spelling and Commonly Confused Words** from the list of subtopics. Read and view the resources in the **Review Materials** section, and then complete the **Recall, Apply,** and **Write** sets in the **Activities** section.

Teaching Tip:

Writer's World Competition Please advise students that they can submit their paragraphs and essays for possible publication to www .pearsonhighered .com/essayrewards/ writingrewards.html

Commas

Section Theme **HUMAN DEVELOPMENT**

In this chapter, you will read about life stages.

What Is a Comma?

A **comma (,)** is a punctuation mark that helps identify distinct ideas. There are many ways to use a comma. In this chapter, you will learn some helpful rules about comma usage.

Notice how comma placement changes the meanings of the following sentences.

The baby hits, her mother cries, and then they hug each other.

The baby hits her mother, cries, and then they hug each other.

Commas in a Series

Use a comma to separate items in a series of three or more items. Remember to put a comma before the final "and."

Unit 1	,	unit 2	,	and	unit 3
			,	or	

Canada, the United States, and Mexico have psychology conferences.

The experiment required patience, perseverance, and energy.

Some teens may work part time, volunteer in the community, and maintain high grades at school.

> **Hint** **Comma Before *and***
>
> There is a trend, especially in the media, to omit the comma before the final *and* in a series. However, in academic writing, it is preferable to include the comma because it clarifies your meaning and makes the items more distinct.

PRACTICE I Underline series of items. Then add fifteen missing commas.

EXAMPLE: Some psychological studies are <u>simple</u>, <u>obvious</u>, and <u>extremely important</u>.

1. Child development expert Mary Ainsworth worked in the <u>United States</u>, <u>Canada</u>, and <u>Uganda</u>. In an experiment called "The Strange Situation," she measured how infants reacted when <u>the primary caretaker left the room</u>, <u>a stranger entered</u>, and <u>the primary caretaker returned</u>. She determined that children have four attachment styles. They may be <u>secure</u>, <u>avoidant</u>, <u>ambivalent</u>, or <u>disoriented</u>.

2. Secure children may <u>leave their mother's lap</u>, <u>explore happily</u>, and <u>return to the mother</u>. Avoidant babies <u>are not upset when the mother leaves</u>, <u>do not look at the stranger</u>, and <u>show little reaction when the mother returns</u>. Ambivalent babies are <u>clinging</u>, <u>unwilling to explore</u>, and <u>upset by strangers</u>.

Teaching Tip:
Ask students who cries in each sentence. In the first sentence, the mother cries, and in the second sentence, the baby cries. Another example is the sentence *Jason watches plays and laughs.* Ask students to suggest how commas can change the meaning of the sentence.

CHAPTER 35

Teaching Tip:

Cooperative Learning (Jigsaw)
Place students in teams of three to five. Assign each team a grammar concept from the chapter. Each team should present a short lesson about the concept to the class.

Disoriented infants react oddly to their mother's return. They look fearful

avoid eye contact and slowly approach the returning mother.

Commas After Introductory Words and Phrases

Place a comma after an **introductory word** or **phrase.** Introductory words include interjections (*well*), adverbs (*usually*), or transitional words (*therefore*). Introductory phrases can be transitional expressions (*of course*), prepositional phrases (*in the winter*), or modifiers (*born in Egypt*).

Introductory word(s)	,	sentence.

Introductory word:	Yes, the last stage of life is very important.
Introductory phrase:	After the experiment, the children returned home.
	Feeling bored, he volunteered at a nearby clinic.

CHAPTER 35

PRACTICE 2 Underline each introductory word or phrase. Then add twelve missing commas.

EXAMPLE: Before leaving home adolescents assert their independence.

1. In *Childhood and Society* Erik Erikson explained his views about the stages of life. According to Erikson there are eight life stages. In his opinion each stage is characterized by a developmental crisis.

2. In the infancy stage babies must learn to trust others. Wanting others to fulfill their needs babies expect life to be pleasant. Neglected babies may end up mistrusting the world.

3. During adolescence a young man or woman may have an identity crisis. Confronted with physical and emotional changes teenagers must develop a sense of self. According to Erikson some adolescents are unable to solve

their identity crisis. <u>Lacking self-awareness</u>, they cannot commit themselves to certain goals and values.

4. <u>In Erikson's view</u>, each crisis must be solved before a person develops in the next life stage. <u>For example</u>, a person may become an adult chronologically. <u>However</u>, that person may not be an adult emotionally.

Commas Around Interrupting Words and Phrases

Interrupting words or phrases appear in the middle of sentences, and while they interrupt the sentence's flow, they do not affect its overall meaning. Some interrupters are *as a matter of fact*, *as you know*, and *for example*. Prepositional phrases can also interrupt sentences.

Sentence,	interrupter,	sentence.

The doctor, <u>for example</u>, has never studied child psychology.

Adolescence, <u>as you know</u>, is a difficult life stage.

The child, <u>feeling nervous</u>, started to laugh.

 Using Commas with Appositives

An appositive gives further information about a noun or pronoun. It can appear at the beginning, in the middle, or at the end of the sentence. Set off an appositive with commas.

beginning
<u>A large hospital</u>, the Mayo Clinic has some of the world's best researchers.

middle
Gail Sheehy, <u>a journalist</u>, has written about life passages.

end
The doctor's office is next to Sims Wholesale, <u>a local grocery store</u>.

Teaching Tip:
Pair Work
Ask students to do Practice 3 in pairs. By working together, they can share their understanding of the comma placement rules.

PRACTICE 3 REVIEW   The next sentences contain introductory words and phrases, interrupters, and series of items. Add the missing commas. If the sentence is correct, write C in the space provided.

EXAMPLE: Erik Erikson, a child development expert, wrote about identity crises. _____

1. Malidoma Somé, a West African, spent his childhood living at a Jesuit boarding school. _____

2. He returned to Dano, his parents' village, unable to speak his native language. _____

3. Feeling confused, twenty-year-old Malidoma wanted to reconnect with his tribe. _____

4. He convinced the elders to let him undergo a rite of passage, a ceremony usually done during puberty. __C__

5. Without initiation, a person is always considered a child. _____

6. The process involves living in the wilderness, finding food, and dealing with dangers. _____

7. Six weeks later, Malidoma emerged from the wilderness with a greater respect for nature. _____

8. The villagers, including the parents and elders, celebrated the return of the initiates. _____

9. Each initiate was greeted as an adult, a valuable member of the community. _____

10. Meaningful rite-of-passage ceremonies, in Malidoma Somé's view, should be created for North American adolescents. _____

Commas in Compound Sentences

In compound sentences, place a comma before the coordinating conjunction (*for, and, nor, but, or, yet, so*).

| Sentence | , and | sentence. |

Adulthood has three stages**, and** each stage has its particular challenge.

Carolina lives with her mother**, but** her sister lives on her own.

She goes to school**, yet** she also works forty hours a week.

(Hint) Commas and Coordinators

To ensure that a sentence is compound, cover the conjunction with your finger and read the two parts of the sentence. If one part of the sentence is incomplete, then no comma is necessary. If each part of the sentence contains a complete idea, then you need to add a comma.

No comma: Ben still lives with his parents **but** is very self-sufficient.

Comma: Ben still lives with his parents**, but** he is very self-sufficient.

PRACTICE 4 Edit the next paragraphs, and add twelve missing commas.

EXAMPLE: She is not an adult‚ yet she is not a child.

1. Adulthood is another stage in life‚ but the exact age of adulthood is unclear. Some cultures celebrate adulthood with high school graduation ceremonies‚ and others celebrate with marriage. Some people define adulthood as the moment a person has full-time work and is self-sufficient‚ yet many people only become independent in their thirties.

2. Are you an adult? Researchers asked this question to people in their thirties‚ and the results were surprising. Most did not feel fully adult until their late twenties or early thirties. Compared with previous generations‚ people today move into markers of adulthood slowly. They marry later‚ and they have children later.

Teaching Tip: Read the next sentences aloud, and ask students to identify the ones that require a comma. *The old man tumbled, and someone helped him up. The old man tumbled and broke his hip. The little mouse scampered into its hole but was unable to carry in some cheese. The little mouse tried to enter the hole, but he couldn't fit the cheese into the tiny space.*

3. Additionally, various cultures treat early adulthood differently. Adela Pelaez has a culturally mixed background. Her mother's lineage is British ` ` and her father's lineage is Spanish. At age nineteen ` ` she was encouraged to find an apartment. Today, twenty-one-year-old Adela pays her own bills ` ` and she does her own cooking. Alexis Khoury is thirty-one ` ` but she still lives with her parents. They are Greek immigrants ` ` and they want their daughter to stay home until she marries. Alexis will respect her parents' wishes ` ` and she will not leave home until she finds a life partner.

CHAPTER 35

Teaching Tip:
Read the next sentences aloud, and ask students to identify the ones that require a comma. *Although you are very sweet, I won't date you. Britney shaved her head even though she loved her glorious long hair. The thirty-year-old man moved into an apartment when he was able to afford it. When Latisha found a good job, she moved into a larger apartment.*

Commas in Complex Sentences

A **complex sentence** contains one or more dependent clauses (or incomplete ideas). When you add a **subordinating conjunction**—a word such as *because*, *although*, or *unless*—to a clause, you make the clause dependent.

dependent clause   independent clause

After Jason graduated from college, he moved out of the family home.

Using Commas After Dependent Clauses

If a sentence begins with a dependent clause, place a comma after the clause. Remember that a dependent clause has a subject and a verb, but it cannot stand alone. When the subordinating conjunction comes in the middle of the sentence, it is generally not necessary to use a comma.

Dependent clause,	main clause.

Comma: When I find a better job, I will move into an apartment.

Main clause	dependent clause.

No comma: I will move into an apartment when I find a better job.

PRACTICE 5   Edit the following sentences by adding or deleting commas.

EXAMPLE: Although thirty-year-old Samuel Chong lives at home ` ` he is not ashamed.

1. When he examined the 2001 census Mark Noble noticed a clear trend.

2. Although most people in their twenties lived on their own about 40 percent of young adults still lived with their parents.

3. In 1981, the results were different because only 25 percent of young adults lived at home.

4. After examining the statistics Noble determined several causes for the shift.

5. Because the marriage rate is declining fewer people buy their own homes.

6. When the cost of education increases people cannot afford to study and pay rent.

7. Other young adults stay with their parents because the rents are so high.

8. Because these conditions are not changing many young adults will probably continue to live with their parents.

Using Commas to Set Off Nonrestrictive Clauses

Clauses beginning with *who, that,* and *which* can be restrictive or nonrestrictive. A **restrictive clause** contains essential information about the subject. Do not place commas around restrictive clauses. In the following example, the underlined clause is necessary to understand the meaning of the sentence.

> **No commas:**   The local company <u>that creates computer graphics</u> has no job openings.

A **nonrestrictive clause** gives nonessential or additional information about the noun but does not restrict or define the noun. Place commas around nonrestrictive clauses. In the following sentence, the underlined clause contains extra information, but if you removed that clause, the sentence would still have a clear meaning.

> **Commas:**   Her book, <u>which is in bookstores</u>, is about successful entrepreneurs.

CHAPTER 35

GRAMMAR LINK

For more information about choosing *which* or *that*, see Chapter 22, Sentence Variety.

CHAPTER 35

> ## Hint · Which, That, and Who
>
> **Which**   Use commas to set off clauses that begin with *which*.
>
> The brain, **which is a complex organ**, develops rapidly.
>
> **That**   Do not use commas to set off clauses that begin with *that*.
>
> The house **that I grew up in** was demolished last year.
>
> **Who**   If the *who* clause contains nonessential information, put commas around it. If the *who* clause is essential to the meaning of the sentence, then it does not require commas.
>
> | | |
> |---|---|
> | **Essential:** | Many people **who have brain injuries** undergo subtle personality changes. |
> | **Not essential:** | Dr. Jay Giedd, **who lives in Maryland**, made an important discovery. |

PRACTICE 6   Edit the following sentences by adding twelve missing commas.

EXAMPLE: The neurologist, whom I have never met, made an exciting discovery.

1. Twenty years ago, scientists thought that the brain stopped changing in late childhood. They believed that after children reached twelve years of age, their brains would stop growing. In 1997, a team of doctors who specialized in brain research made an exciting discovery. Neuroscientist Dr. Jay Giedd, who works at the National Institute of Mental Health, realized that brain cells have a growth spurt just before puberty. Myelin, which connects brain cells, increases during adolescence. However, not all parts of the brain receive myelin at once, and the last region to receive it is the frontal lobe.

2. The frontal lobe, which is responsible for rational decision making, stops an individual from making impulsive choices. For example, imagine that you are driving your car. When another car cuts you off, the primitive part of

your brain wants to hurt the other driver. The frontal lobe helps you to think about alternatives and accept that everyone makes mistakes.

3. The delayed increase of myelin in the frontal lobe affects many teens and they may have trouble curbing their impulses. They may react quickly violently or irrationally. Youths become less impulsive after the frontal lobe has fully developed.

FINAL REVIEW

Edit this essay by adding seventeen missing commas and removing three unnecessary commas.

EXAMPLE: If people want to have longer lives they can exercise, eat well and avoid risky behavior.

Teaching Tip:
You can use the final review as a test. Additional practice and test material appears in the Instructor's Resource Manual and on *MyWritingLab*.

1. In 350 BC, Aristotle wrote an essay about life spans. Humans have a maximum life span and nothing can be done to prolong that span. Until recently scientists agreed with Aristotle. However a group of researchers believes that human life expectancy will increase significantly in the future.

2. Dr. James Vaupel a researcher at Duke University, believes that our life spans can be extended. He gives a concrete example. In 1840 the average Swedish woman lived to age forty-five. Today, Japanese women, who live to an average age of eighty-five have the world's longest life expectancy. This huge increase in life expectancy was partly due to the decrease in infant mortality. Surgery vaccines and antibiotics have helped to lower childhood death rates. Also,

CHAPTER 35

because they have access to new medical interventions people over age sixty-five are living longer. Still, only about 2 percent of the population lives to one hundred years of age.

3. According to Dr. Vaupel, today's babies will have much longer life expectancies than their parents had and half of all newborns could live to one hundred years of age. Dr. Aubrey De Grey, a professor at Cambridge University believes that human life expectancy will increase to five hundred years or more. Certainly, cures for cancer and heart disease could help increase life expectancy. Also, because so many women delay childbirth the period of human fertility may lengthen which could have an eventual impact on life expectancy.

4. Some experts disagree with Vaupel and De Grey. Leonard Hayflick discovered that human cells divide and reproduce about fifty times before slowing down and stopping. The longest average life span humans can attain in Hayflick's view is 120 years of age. However, some research labs are experimenting with ways of increasing the life spans of cells. For example scientists have isolated a part of the chromosome that shrinks with age. If scientists find a way to slow down cell aging the results could significantly increase life expectancies of all humans.

5. A very long life expectancy would force humans to rethink life stages. When would childhood end? Would you want to live to 150 years of age or more?

The Writer's Room Topics for Writing

Teaching Tip:
Writer's World Competition
Please advise students that they can submit their paragraphs and essays for possible publication to www .pearsonhighered .com/essayrewards/ writingrewards.html

Write about one of the following topics. After you finish writing, make sure that you have used commas correctly.

1. What problems could occur if the human life expectancy gets a lot longer? Think about the effects of an increased life expectancy.

2. Which life stage is the most interesting? Give supporting examples to back up your views.

✔ CHECKLIST: COMMAS

When you edit your writing, ask yourself these questions.

☐ Do I use commas correctly? Remember to use commas in the following situations:

- between words in a series of items
- after an introductory word or phrase
- around an interrupting word or phrase

> The conference will be in Santa Fe, San Francisco, or Phoenix.
>
> Beyond a doubt, many psychologists will attend.
>
> The key speaker, in my opinion, is extremely interesting.

☐ Do I use commas correctly in compound and complex sentences? Remember to use commas in the following situations:

- before the coordinator in a compound sentence
- after a dependent clause that starts a complex sentence
- around nonrestrictive clauses

> She will discuss brain development, and she will present case studies.
>
> When her presentation ends, participants can ask questions.
>
> The questions, which must be short, are about the brain.

CHAPTER 35

User Community:
"I use the text in my online writing class. I like how I am able to tie the MyWritingLab component into my online lessons. The videos and activities are engaging for students and really add another element to the lessons."
—Gwen Parsons, HOWARD COLLEGE

my writing lab To check your progress in meeting this chapter's objectives, log in to **www.mywritinglab.com,** go to the **Study Plan** tab, click on **The Editing Handbook—Section 6** and choose **Commas** from the list of subtopics. Read and view the resources in the **Review Materials** section, and then complete the **Recall, Apply,** and **Write** sets in the **Activities** section.

Apostrophes

Section Theme **HUMAN DEVELOPMENT**

In this chapter, you will read about artistic ability and creativity.

"Man Reclining," 1978, Fernando Botero, Private Collection.

What Is an Apostrophe?

An **apostrophe** is a punctuation mark showing a contraction or ownership.

Emma **Chong's** art gallery is very successful, and **it's** still growing.

Apostrophes in Contractions

To form a **contraction,** join two words into one and add an apostrophe to replace the omitted letter(s). The following are examples of common contractions.

1. **Join a verb with *not*.** The apostrophe replaces the letter "o" in *not*.

Teaching Tip:

is + not = isn't	has + not = hasn't
are + not = aren't	have + not = haven't
could + not = couldn't	should + not = shouldn't
did + not = didn't	was + not = wasn't
do + not = don't	were + not = weren't
does + not = doesn't	would + not = wouldn't

Exception: will + not = <u>won't</u>, can + not = <u>can't</u>

2. **Join a subject and a verb.** Sometimes you must remove several letters to form the contraction.

I + will = I'll	she + will = she'll
I + would = I'd	Tina + is = Tina's
he + is = he's	they + are = they're
he + will = he'll	we + will = we'll
Joe + is = Joe's	who + is = who's
she + has = she's	who + would = who'd

Exception: Do not contract a subject with *was, were, or did*.

Cooperative Learning (Jigsaw) Place students in teams of three to five. Assign each team a grammar concept from the chapter. Teams are responsible for teaching the class about their topic. They should summarize key ideas, give examples, and prepare some practice sentences. Then each team can present a short lesson to the class.

> ⟨ **Hint** ⟩ **Common Apostrophe Errors**
>
> Do not use apostrophes before the final *-s* of a verb or a plural noun.
>
>   *wants*   *galleries*
>   Mr. Garcia ~~want's~~ to open several ~~gallery's~~.
>
> In contractions with *not*, remember that the apostrophe replaces the missing *o*.
>
>   *doesn't*
>   He ~~does'nt~~ understand the problem.

CHAPTER 36

PRACTICE 1   Edit the next sentences for twelve apostrophe errors. You may need to add, move, or remove apostrophes.

EXAMPLE: Making a great work of art <u>isnt</u>ʼ a simple process.

    Who's
1. ~~Whos~~ a great artist? Why do some people have amazing artistic abilities

             don't
   whereas others ~~do'nt~~? Neurologists look inside the brain to answer

                    They've   *brain's*
   questions about creativity. ~~Theyve~~ said that the left portion of the ~~brains~~

ESL **Teaching Tip:** Nonnative speakers may incorrectly use apostrophes in past tense contractions of *be*. Draw their attention to the exception.

responsible for logical processing and verbal skills. The right ~~sides~~ *side's*

responsible for artistic, abstract thinking. In the past, neurologists ~~did'nt~~ *didn't*

believe that the left side of the brain had an impact on creative impulses,

but recent brain ~~sean's~~ *scans* have shown that both sides of the brain are used in

creative thinking.

2. ~~Whats~~ *What's* the source of creativity? Maybe ~~its~~ *it's* never going to be understood.
What everybody ~~know's~~ *knows* for certain is that artistic talent ~~isnt~~ *isn't* evenly
distributed. Some people ~~are'nt~~ *aren't* as talented as others.

> ⟨*Hint*⟩ **Contractions with Two Meanings**
>
> Sometimes one contraction can have two different meanings.
>
> **I'd** = I had *or* I would   **He's** = he is or he has
>
> When you read, you should be able to figure out the meaning of the contraction
> by looking at the words in context.
>
>   **Joe's** working on a painting. **Joe's** been working on it for a month.
>   (Joe is)   (Joe has)

CHAPTER 36

PRACTICE 2   Look at each underlined contraction, and then write
out the complete words.

EXAMPLE: They <u>weren't</u> ready to start a business.   *were not*

1. Rachel <u>Wood's</u> very happy with her sculpture.   *Wood is*

2. <u>She's</u> been a professional artist since 2002.   *She has*

3. <u>She's</u> an extremely creative woman.   *She is*

4. I wish <u>I'd</u> gone to art school.   *I had*

5. <u>I'd</u> like to be an artist, too.   *I would*

Apostrophes to Show Ownership

You can also use apostrophes to show ownership. Review the following rules.

Possessive Form of Singular Nouns

Add -'s to the end of a singular noun to indicate ownership. If the singular noun ends in s, you must still add -'s.

> **Lautrec's** artwork was very revolutionary.
>
> **Morris's** wife is a professional dancer.

Possessive Form of Plural Nouns

When a plural noun ends in -s, just add an apostrophe to indicate ownership. Add -'s to irregular plural nouns.

> Many **galleries'** Web sites contain images from their exhibits.
>
> The **men's** and **women's** paintings are in separate rooms.

Possessive Form of Compound Nouns

When two people have joint ownership, add the apostrophe to the second name. When two people have separate ownership, add apostrophes to both names.

> **Joint ownership:**   Marian and **Jake's** gallery is successful.
>
> **Separate ownership:**   **Marian's** and **Jake's** studios are in different buildings.

PRACTICE 3   Write the possessive forms of the following phrases.

EXAMPLE: the sister of the doctor   *the doctor's sister*

1. the brush of the artist   *the artist's brush*
2. the brushes of the artists   *the artists' brushes*
3. the rooms of the children   *the children's rooms*
4. the entrances of the galleries   *the galleries' entrances*
5. the photo of Ross and Anna   *Ross and Anna's photo*
6. the photo of Ross and the photo of Anna   *Ross's and Anna's photos*

CHAPTER 36

> ## Hint   **Possessive Pronouns Do Not Have Apostrophes**
>
> Some contractions sound like possessive pronouns. For example, *you're* sounds like *your*, and *it's* sounds like *its*. Remember that the possessive pronouns *yours*, *hers*, *its*, and *ours* never have apostrophes.
>
> its
> The conference is on ~~it's~~ last day.
> yours   hers
> The document is ~~your's~~ and not ~~her's~~.

PRACTICE 4   Correct nine errors. You may need to add, move, or remove apostrophes.

Botero's
EXAMPLE: ~~Boteros~~ paintings are exhibited around the world.

artists'
1. Many ~~artist's~~ paintings are unique. Have you ever heard of Fernando

Botero? His painting "Man Reclining" appears at the beginning of this

Botero's   *makes*
chapter. ~~Boteros~~ paintings usually contain images of people. What ~~make's~~ his

its
work unique is ~~it's~~ humor. He makes generals, religious figures, and dictators

They're
look like children. ~~Theyre~~ small and bloated. The images are very colorful.

It's
2. Another great artist is Georgia O'Keeffe. ~~Its~~ not difficult to recognize an

hers She's
artwork that is ~~her's~~. ~~Shes~~ known for her paintings of white bones, bull

you'll
skulls, and flowers. In many art galleries, ~~youll~~ find her artwork.

Teaching Tip: Botero's painting "Man Reclining" appears at the beginning of this chapter.

Apostrophes in Expressions of Time

If an expression of time (*year, week, month, day*) appears to possess something, you can add *-'s*.

Alice Ray gave two **weeks'** notice before she left the dance company.

When you write out a year in numerals, an apostrophe can replace the missing numbers.

The graduates of the class of **'99** hoped to find good jobs.

However, if you are writing the numeral of a decade or century, do not put an apostrophe before the final *-s*.

In the **1900s,** many innovations in art occurred.

PRACTICE 5 Correct ten errors. You may need to add or remove apostrophes.

wasn't
EXAMPLE: Jackson Pollock ~~wasnt~~ a conventional artist.

Teaching Tip:
Students may not
understand why
hours and *months*
take no apostrophe.
Point out both
words do not
modify another
noun, thus they are
not possessive.

1. In 1992, truck driver Teri Horton shopped for the *week's* ~~weeks~~ groceries, and then she passed by a thrift shop. She bought a painting for $5. She had planned to give it to a friend as a gag gift, but the large painting *wouldn't* ~~wouldnt~~ fit through the door of her *friend's* ~~friends~~ mobile home. A few *months* ~~month's~~ after that, Horton put the artwork in her garage sale.

2. Three *hours* ~~hour's~~ later, a local art teacher saw the painting and said, "Maybe *it's* ~~its~~ Jackson *Pollock's* ~~Pollocks~~ work!" Horton spent the rest of the *1990s* ~~1990's~~ trying to prove that *she'd* ~~shed~~ bought an original Pollock. Today, art *experts'* ~~expert's~~ opinions are still divided.

FINAL REVIEW

Edit the next paragraphs, and correct fifteen apostrophe errors. You may need to add, remove, or move apostrophes.

artist's
EXAMPLE: What is an ~~artists~~ motivation to create?

1. In 1982, Dr. Teresa Amabile made an interesting study in creativity. For *Amabile's* ~~Amabiles~~ study, she divided *schoolgirls* ~~schoolgirl's~~ into two groups. Both *groups'* ~~groups~~ rooms were filled with collage material, including colored paper, paste, and construction paper. The doctor chose collage-making because it *doesn't* ~~doesnt~~ require drawing skills.

Teaching Tip:
You can use the final
review as a test.
Additional practice
and test material
appears in the
Instructor's
Resource Manual
and on
MyWritingLab.

2. Both groups were invited to an "art party" in separate rooms. The first *group's* ~~groups~~ goal was to create art to win a prize, such as a toy. The doctor offered toys to the three best artists. Thus, the *children's* ~~childrens~~ motivation to

Donald Martin, after Van der Weyden
(20th Century American), "Portrait,"
Airbrush on wood. © Donald C. Martin/
SuperStock.

create was to win the exciting prize. The girls in the second

group ~~didnt~~ *didn't* have to compete for a prize. They were simply

told that three ~~name's~~ *names* would be randomly drawn for prizes.

3. The ~~doctors~~ *doctor's* hypothesis was that a ~~persons~~ *person's* creativity would

lessen if he or she were motivated by a reward. Amabile asked

local artists and art critics to judge the collages when the

children ~~werent~~ *weren't* in the room. The ~~judges~~ *judges'* scores for the first

group were consistently lower than those for the second

group. Thus, the ~~doctors~~ *doctor's* hypothesis was correct. A reward,

such as money or a prize, ~~isnt~~ *isn't* helpful to the creative process.

When people create art for ~~arts~~ *art's* sake, they tend to be more

imaginative.

The Writer's Room Topics for Writing

Write about one of the following topics. After you finish writing, make sure that you have used apostrophes correctly.

1. What are some jobs that require creativity? List examples of such jobs, and describe how they are creative.

2. Define a term or expression that relates to this photo. Some ideas might be *creativity, graffiti, art, vandalism,* or *beauty.*

Teaching Tip:

✓ CHECKLIST: APOSTROPHES

When you edit your writing, ask yourself these questions.

☐ Do I use apostrophes correctly? Check for errors in these cases:

- contractions of verbs + *not* or subjects and verbs
- possessives of singular and plural nouns (*the student's* versus *the students'*)
- possessives of irregular plural nouns (*the women's*)
- possessives of compound nouns (*Joe's and Mike's cars*)

> *shouldn't* *Wong's*
> You ~~should'nt~~ be surprised that Chris ~~Wongs~~ going to exhibit his paintings.
> *Chris's*
> ~~Chris'~~ artwork will be on display next week.

☐ Do I place apostrophes where they do not belong? Check for errors in possessive pronouns and present tense verbs.

> *looks* *its*
> It ~~look's~~ as though the gallery is moving ~~it's~~ collection to Houston.

Cooperative Learning (Quick Review) Divide the class into teams of three or four. Assign a part of the chapter to each team. Each team should review the information and generate three questions. Then ask teams to read the questions aloud. Anybody in the class can answer a question. Or, as an alternative, you can ask teams to exchange questions and to answer another team's questions.

CHAPTER 36

mywritinglab To check your progress in meeting this chapter's objectives, log in to **www.mywritinglab.com,** go to the **Study Plan** tab, click on **The Editing Handbook—Section 6** and choose **Apostrophes** from the list of subtopics. Read and view the resources in the **Review Materials** section, and then complete the **Recall, Apply,** and **Write** sets in the **Activities** section.

Teaching Tip:
Writer's World Competition Please advise students that they can submit their paragraphs and essays for possible publication to www.pearsonhighered.com/essayrewards/writingrewards.html

Quotation Marks, Capitalization, and Titles

Section Theme **HUMAN DEVELOPMENT**

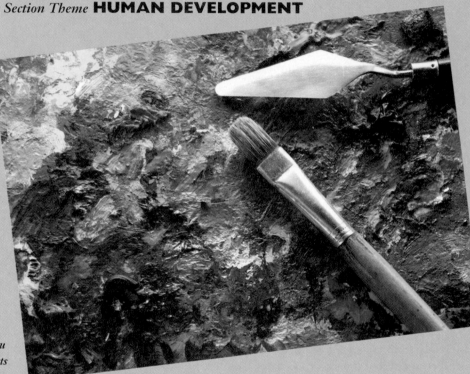

In this chapter, you will read about artists and musicians.

Quotation Marks (" ")

Use **quotation marks** to set off the exact words of a speaker or writer. When you include the exact words of more than one person in a text, then you must make a new paragraph each time the speaker changes. If the quotation is a complete sentence, punctuate it in the following ways.

- Capitalize the first word of the quotation.
- Place quotation marks around the complete quotation.

- Place the end punctuation inside the closing quotation marks.
- Generally, attach the name of the speaker or writer to the quotation in some way.

> Oscar Wilde declared, **"All art is useless."**

Review the following rules.

1. **Introductory Phrase**   When the quotation is introduced by a phrase, place a comma after the introductory phrase.

> Pablo Picasso said, "Art is a lie that makes us realize the truth."

2. **Interrupting Phrase**   When the quotation is interrupted, place a comma before and after the interrupting phrase.

> "In the end," says dancer Martha Graham, "it all comes down to breathing."

3. **End Phrase**   When you place a phrase at the end of a quotation, end the quotation with a comma instead of a period.

> "Great art picks up where nature ends," said Marc Chagall.

If your quotation ends with other punctuation, put it inside the quotation mark.

> "Who is the greatest painter?" the student asked.
> "That question cannot be answered!" the curator replied.

4. **Introductory Sentence**   When you introduce a quotation with a complete sentence, place a colon (:) after the introductory sentence.

> George Balanchine explains his philosophy about dance: "Dance is music made visible."

5. **Inside Quotations**   If one quotation is inside another quotation, then use single quotation marks (' ') around the inside quotation.

> To her mother, Veronica Corelli explained, "I am not sure if I will succeed, but you've always said, 'Your work should be your passion.' "

Hint   **Integrated Quotations**

If the quotation is not a complete sentence, and you simply integrate it into your sentence, do not capitalize the first word of the quotation.

> Composer Ludwig Von Beethoven called music "the mediator between the spiritual and the sensual life."

Teaching Tip:
If you teach research in your course, you may wish to add to this discussion by explaining how using quotations and documenting them properly will help students avoid plagiarism. They can find more information about summarizing and paraphrasing in Chapter 15.

CHAPTER 37

Teaching Tip:
Point out that a colon appears before a quotation only when the quotation is preceded by a complete sentence. Remind students to use commas after phrases.

Suzanne Valadon
(1867–1938
French) "Portrait
of Madam
Coquiot," 1915.
Oil on canvas.
Musée du Palais
Carnoles, Menton,
France. © Artists
Rights Society
(ARS), New York.

PRACTICE 1   In each sentence, the quotation is set off in bold.
Add quotation marks and periods, commas, or colons. Also, capitalize the
first word of the quotation, if necessary.

EXAMPLE: Professor Wayne Johnson asks ,"W where are the great female
artists?"

1. Art student Alex Beale says ,"T the lack of great female artists throughout
history is puzzling"

2. " One must consider the conditions for producing art " states Professor
Aline Melnor.

3. " Art schools did not accept women " she points out.

4. " Until a hundred years ago, the only alternative to family life for women
was the convent " proclaimed writer and feminist Germaine Greer.

5. " Suzanne Valadon " says historian Maria Sage " went from being an
artist's model to being an artist"

6. Historian Andre Villeneuve writes that sculptor Camille Claudel was " the
mistress of Auguste Rodin"

7. Germaine Greer shows the connection between female and male
artists :"T the painter Rosa Bonheur learned about art from her father,
who was also an artist"

8. Angel Trang told her mother " I know that I shouldn't have drawn on
the walls, but you always say 'Express yourself'"

PRACTICE 2   Correct ten punctuation errors in the next dialogue.

EXAMPLE: She told me, "Your future is in your hands."

Jamilla was concerned about her son. "I don't understand why you are leaving

college".

Omar looked at her and replied, "I need to try to make it as a musician."

"How will you make a living in the arts," she asked.

He replied, "I do not need to earn a lot of money to be happy."

"You're being very naïve," Jamilla responded.

Shocked, Omar said, "I'm simply following your advice. You always say, 'Find

work that you love.' "

"Perhaps you have to take some chances," his mother responded, "and learn

from your own mistakes."

M
Omar stated firmly, "my decision will not be a mistake!"

Using Quotations in Research Essays

Use quotations to reveal the opinions of an expert or to highlight ideas that are particularly memorable and important. When quoting sources, remember to limit how many you use in a single paper and to vary your quotations by using both direct and indirect quotations.

Direct and Indirect Quotations

A **direct quotation** contains the exact words of the speaker or writer, and it is set off with quotation marks.

> Amy Kurtz Lansing writes, "Connecticut has long been a center for the visual arts in America."

An **indirect quotation** keeps the author's meaning but is not set off by quotation marks. Note that an indirect quotation is also called a paraphrase.

> Amy Kurtz Lansing writes that Connecticut is one of America's artistic centers.

Integrating Quotations
Short Quotations

Introduce short quotations with a phrase or sentence. (Short quotations should not stand alone.) Read the following original selection, and then view how the quotation has been introduced using three common methods. The selection,

CHAPTER 37

written by Mary Lou Stribling, appeared on page 6 of her book *Art from Found Materials*.

Original Selection
Picasso is generally acknowledged as being the first major artist to use found objects in his paintings. About the same time, however, a number of other artists who were active in the Cubist movement began to make similar experiments. The collages of Braque and Gris, which were made of printed letters, newspapers, wallpaper scraps, bottle labels, corrugated cardboard, and other bits of trivia, are especially notable.

Teaching Tip: Point out that the page number is in parentheses.

Phrase Introduction
In *Art from Found Materials*, Mary Lou Stribling writes, "Picasso is generally acknowledged as being the first major artist to use found objects in his paintings" (6).

Sentence Introduction
In her book *Art from Found Materials*, Mary Lou Stribling suggests that Picasso was not the only artist to use found objects in his work: "About the same time, however, a number of other artists who were active in the Cubist movement began to make similar experiments" (6).

Integrated Quotation
In *Art from Found Materials*, Mary Lou Stribling reveals that artists incorporated everyday objects into their paintings, including "wallpaper scraps, bottle labels, corrugated cardboard, and other bits of trivia" (6).

 Words That Introduce Quotations

Here are some common words that can introduce quotations.

admits	concludes	mentions	speculates
claims	explains	observes	suggests
comments	maintains	reports	warns

The doctor **states**, "_____"

"_____," **observes** Dr. Hannah.

Dr. Hannah **speculates** that _____.

Teaching Tip: You can direct students to Chapter 16 for a discussion of MLA style.

Long Quotations

If you use a quotation in MLA style that has four or more lines (or in APA style, more than forty words), insert the quotation in your research paper in the following way.

- Introduce the quotation with a sentence ending with a colon.
- Indent the entire quotation about ten spaces (one inch) from the left margin of your document.
- Use double spacing.
- Do not use quotation marks.
- Cite the author and page number in parentheses after the punctuation mark in the last sentence of the quotation.

Review the next example from a student essay about art history that uses MLA style. The quotation is from page 132 of Germaine Greer's *The Obstacle Race*. The explanatory paragraph introduces the quotation and is part of an essay.

> Much great art has been lost owing to a variety of factors:
> Panels decay as wood decays. Canvas rots, tears, and sags. The stretchers spring and warp. As color dries out, it loses its flexibility and begins to separate from its unstable ground; dry color flakes off shrinking or swelling wood and drooping canvas. (Greer 132)

Teaching Tip:
Point out that the sample quotation would be double-spaced in a research essay.

> **Hint**   **Using Long Quotations**
>
> If your research paper is short (two or three pages), avoid using many long quotations. Long quotations will only overwhelm your own ideas. Instead, try summarizing a long passage or using shorter quotations.

Using Ellipses (. . .)

If you want to quote key ideas from an author, but do not want to quote the entire paragraph, you can use **ellipses.** These three periods show that you have omitted unnecessary information from a quotation. Leave a space before and after each period. If the omitted section goes to the end of the sentence or includes one or more complete sentences, add a final period (. . .). The original selection appeared on page 173 of the book *Crossroads* by Elizabeth F. Barkley.

Original Selection
The guitarist slides the steel bar across the strings, which are tuned to a single cord, and the steel bar changes the pitch of the chord by its location on the strings. The sliding of the bar gives the guitar a distinctive wavering timbre.

Quotation with Omissions
In *Crossroads*, Elizabeth F. Barkley writes, "The guitarist slides the steel bar across the strings. . . . The sliding of the bar gives the guitar a distinctive wavering timbre" (173).

Teaching Tip:
Point out that the ellipses are followed by a period in the example because the end of the first sentence was omitted.

PRACTICE 3 Read the quotation, and then answer the questions. The selection, written by Richard Paul Janaro, appeared on page 200 of *The Art of Being Human*.

Blues music is almost always about the empty aftermath of a once burning passion. The songs are written from either a male or a female point of view. Men sing of the faithlessness of women, and women return the compliment about men.

1. Write a direct quotation. Remember to introduce the title and author.
   Answers will vary.

   _____

   _____

2. Write a direct quotation with an omission. Remember to introduce the title and author.
   Answers will vary.

   _____

   _____

CHAPTER 37

Capitalization

Remember to capitalize the following:

- the pronoun *I*
- the first word of every sentence

   My brothers and **I** share an apartment.

There are many other instances in which you must use capital letters. Always capitalize in the following cases.

- **Days of the week, months, and holidays**

   Thursday   June 22   Labor Day

   Do not capitalize the seasons: summer, fall, winter, spring.

- **Titles of specific institutions, departments, companies, and schools**

   Microsoft   Department of Finance   Elmwood High School

   Do not capitalize general references.

   the company   the department   the school

- **Names of specific places such as buildings, streets, parks, cities, states, and bodies of water**

Eiffel Tower	Times Square	Los Angeles, California
Sunset Boulevard	Florida	Lake Erie

  Do not capitalize general references.

the street	the state	the lake

- **Specific languages, nationalities, tribes, races, and religions**

Greek	Mohawk	Buddhist	a French restaurant

- **Titles of specific individuals**

General Franklin	President Obama	Doctor Blain
Professor Sayf	Prime Minister Blair	Mrs. Robinson

  If you are referring to the profession in general, or if the title follows the name, do not use capital letters.

my doctor	the professors	Ted Kennedy, a senator

- **Specific course and program titles**

Physics 201	Marketing 101	Advanced German

  If you refer to a course without mentioning the course title, then it is unnecessary to use capitals. Also, do not capitalize the names of programs.

He is in his math class.	I am in the music program.

  Do not capitalize academic degrees when spelled out. Only capitalize the abbreviated form.

  Mike has a master of arts in literature, but his sister did not complete her **MA**.

  I have a doctorate in sciences, and Melissa has a **PhD** too.

- **The major words in titles of literary or artistic works**

The Miami Herald	*The Hangover*	*The Daily Show*

- **Historical events, eras, and movements**

World War II	Post-Impressionism	Baby Boomers

CHAPTER 37

> ## Hint — **Capitalizing Computer Terms**
>
> Always capitalize the following computer terms.
>
> Internet   Netscape   World Wide Web   Microsoft Office

PRACTICE 4   Add fifteen missing capital letters to the following paragraphs.

                                                    M
EXAMPLE: The musician was born on march 21.

1. The New York academy of Sciences has examined how people respond to

    music. The study, done in april 2005, examines whether musical training

    can make people smarter. The researchers found that listening to a song

    such as "in my life" can enhance brain functions.

2. Gordon Shaw, who passed away in 2005, earned his bachelor of science

    and later completed a doctorate in physics at cornell university. He was the

    co-founder of the Music intelligence neuronal development institute.

    He also wrote the book *Keeping Mozart in mind*. Shaw determined that

    music can enhance math abilities. I wish I had known that when I

    studied math 401 at Greendale high school. Maybe I will study music in

    college.

Titles

Place the title of a short work in quotation marks. Italicize the titles of longer documents, or underline such titles when the document is handwritten.

<u>Short Works</u>		<u>Long Works</u>	
short story:	"The Lottery"	**novel:**	*The Grapes of Wrath*
chapter:	"Early Accomplishments"	**book:**	*The Art of Emily Carr*
newspaper article:	"The City's Hottest Ticket"	**newspaper:**	*The New York Times*
magazine article:	"New Artists"	**magazine:**	*Rolling Stone*
Web article:	"Music Artists Lose Out"	**Web site:**	*CNET News.com*
essay:	"Hip-Hop Nation"	**textbook:**	*Common Culture*
TV episode:	"The Search Party"	**TV series:**	*Lost*
song:	"Mouths to Feed"	**CD:**	*Release Therapy*
poem:	"Howl"	**anthology:**	*Collected Poems of Beat Writers*

Capitalizing Titles

When you write a title, capitalize the first letter of the first word and all the major words.

> *To Kill a Mockingbird*   "Stairway to Heaven"

Do not capitalize the word ".com" in a Web address. Also, do not capitalize the following words, unless they are the first word in the title.

articles	a, an, the
coordinators	for, and, nor, but, or, yet, so
prepositions	of, to, in, off, out, up, by, . . .

Hint   **Your Own Essay Titles**

In essays that you write for your courses, do not underline your title or put quotation marks around it. Simply capitalize the first word and the main words.

Why Music Is Important

PRACTICE 5   Add ten capital letters to the next selection, and set off ten titles. Add quotation marks to the titles of short works. For long works, underline titles to show that they should be in italics.

                                           B   *W*
EXAMPLE: The magazine <u>business week</u> featured successful singers.

          S   "
  1. <u>Rolling stone</u>, a music magazine, published an article called The 500
          S   "
     Greatest songs of All Time. The first item on the list is the Bob Dylan

"   "

song Like a Rolling Stone. According to the magazine, the greatest album

                                        B

is <u>Sergeant Pepper's Lonely Hearts Club band</u>.

                              "   "

2. I heard my favorite song in a movie. The song Mad World was first

        B   A

recorded by the british band Tears for Fears. Released in august 1982 on

                    H

the album <u>The hurting</u>, the song was moderately successful. Then, for the

2001 movie <u>Donnie Darko</u>, the song was redone in a slower tempo with

piano music. The version by Gary Jules mesmerized filmgoers and helped

                                                    F

give the movie a cult following. In fact, last friday, when the movie played

            A   S

at a theater on arrow street in Cambridge, Massachusetts, the film sold

out. The song has appeared as background music in television shows such

                                            T

as <u>Third Watch</u> and <u>Without a trace</u>. Then, in 2009, Adam Lambert sang

it during an episode of <u>American Idol</u>. Once again, the song became a

great hit.

FINAL REVIEW

The following selection contains twenty-five errors. Correct fifteen errors
with capital letters. Correctly set off five titles by adding quotation marks or
underlining titles that should be in italics. Finally, correct five other
punctuation errors.

EXAMPLE: The marketing manager said, "Each generation is distinct."

1. Each generation is anointed with a title. F. Scott Fitzgerald described his

generation in his novel, <u>The Jazz Age</u>. Tom Brokaw, in his book *The*

        G

Greatest generation, discussed people who came of age in the 1930s. Born

                                                        D

between 1911 and 1924, they grew up during the Great depression. In her

Newsweek article, "Stepping Aside, Anna Quindlen describes her generation : "Born between 1946 and 1964, Baby Boomers take up more room than any other generation in American history."

2. Douglas Coupland, a comic strip artist for the magazine *Vista*, gave a name to his generation. His novel, *Generation X*, was published in March 1991. Coupland's book describes the generation that came of age in the 1970s and 1980s. Raised in Vancouver, he went to Sentinal Secondary School, which is on Chartwell Drive. The teenage Coupland listened to punk songs such as "London Calling" by The Clash. When he got older, he took Sculpture classes at Vancouver's Emily Carr Institute of Art and Design. Later, he received his master's degree in Italy. In an interview about his generation, Coupland said , "We grew up listening to the complaints of bitter ex-hippies." On page 27 of his book, a character has a mid-twenties breakdown that occurs because of "An inability to function outside of school or structured environments coupled with a realization of one's essential aloneness in the world," .

3. Political, social, and cultural events shape each generation. For example, the Millennials are people born in the late 1980s and early 1990s. They witnessed the aftermath of September 11, 2001, and came of age during the Iraq War. "Technology brings us together , " says DiAngelo Edwards, when asked to describe his generation. "We all watch YouTube , " he continues, "and we text our friends."

The Writer's Room **Topics for Writing**

Write about one of the following topics. Include some direct quotations. Proofread to ensure that your punctuation and capitalization is correct.

1. List some characteristics of your generation. What political events, social issues, music, and fashion bind your generation?

2. List three categories of art. Describe some details about each category.

3. Examine the photograph. What do you think the people are saying to each other? Write a brief dialogue from their conversation.

✔ **CHECKLIST: QUOTATION MARKS**

When you edit your writing, ask yourself these questions.

☐ Are there any direct quotations in my writing? Check for errors with these elements:

- punctuation before or after quotations
- capital letters
- placement of quotation marks

  "Art is making something out of nothing and selling it," said musician Frank Zappa.

☐ Do my sentences have all the necessary capital letters?

  War
  Munch's greatest works were painted before World ~~war~~ II.

☐ Are the titles of small and large artistic works properly punctuated?

  The Scream.
  Edvard Munch's painting was called ~~The scream.~~

CHAPTER 37

Teaching Tip:
Writer's World Competition
Please advise students that they can submit their paragraphs and essays for possible publication to www .pearsonhighered .com/essayrewards/ writingrewards.html

PEARSON **mywritinglab** To check your progress in meeting this chapter's objectives, log in to **www.mywritinglab.com,** go to the **Study Plan** tab, click on **The Editing Handbook—Section 6** and choose **Quotations Marks, Capitalization, and Titles** from the list of subtopics. Read and view the resources in the **Review Materials** section, and then complete the **Recall, Apply,** and **Write** sets in the **Activities** section.

Numbers and Additional Punctuation

LEARNING OBJECTIVES

1. Numbers (p. 511)
2. Additional Punctuation (p. 513)

Section Theme **HUMAN DEVELOPMENT**

In this chapter, you will read about photography and photographers.

Numbers

There are two basic styles for number usage. Business and technical documents use one style, and academic writing uses another. **In business and technical fields,** use numerals instead of words in charts, statistics, graphs, financial documents, and advertising. The numbers one to ten are written as words only when they appear in sentences.

Teaching Tip:
The rules presented about numbers apply to academic essays. The rules are not the same in fields such as business management, accounting, math, and so on.

Teaching Tip:

Cooperative Learning (Jigsaw)
Place students in teams of three to five. Assign each team a grammar concept from the chapter. Teams are responsible for teaching the class about the concept. They should summarize key ideas, give examples, and prepare some practice sentences. Then each team can present a short lesson to the class.

CHAPTER 38

However, **in academic writing,** numbers are spelled out more often. Review the rules for using numbers in academic writing.

- Spell out numbers that can be expressed in one or two words.

  We spent **eighteen** days in Mexico City.
  There were **forty-seven** people waiting for another flight.
  The airline had room for **four hundred**.
  That day, **thousands** of people cleared customs.

- Use numerals with numbers of more than two words.

  The manager booked rooms for **358** guests.

- Spell out fractions.

  Only **one-third** of the residents have their own homes.

- When the sentence begins with a number, spell out the number. If the number has more than two words, do not place it at the beginning of the sentence.

  Three hundred people were invited to the gallery.
  There were **158** guests.

- Use a numeral before million or billion, but spell out *million* or *billion*. (It is easier to read *20 million* than *20,000,000*.)

  The company hopes to sell about **14 million** units.

- Use numerals when writing addresses, dates, times, degrees, pages, or divisions of a book. Also use numerals with prices and percentages. Always write out *percent*. For prices, you can write *dollars* or use the $ symbol.

  A yearly subscription costs **$29**, which is about **15** percent less than the cover price.

> ## Hint Several Numbers in a Sentence
>
> When writing two consecutive numbers, write out the shorter number.
>
>   We used **two 35-mm** rolls of film.
>
> Be consistent when writing a series of numbers. If some numbers require numerals, then use numerals for all of the numbers.
>
>   The gallery guests consumed **300** appetizers, **8** pounds of cheese, and **120** glasses of wine.

PRACTICE I   Correct any errors with numbers in the next sentences.

nine
EXAMPLE: She was just ~~9~~ years old when she picked up a camera.

6
1. Photographer Moyra Davey has ~~six~~ cameras, 184 rolls of film, and
   33
   ~~thirty-three~~ different lenses.

   ten
2. She has worked professionally as a photographer for ~~10~~ years.

   twenty-five
3. A small art gallery exhibited ~~25~~ of Davey's photos.

   Forty
4. ~~40~~ people came to the opening.

   129
5. Davey would like to publish her photos and sell each book for ~~one hundred~~

   ~~and twenty nine~~ dollars.

   twenty
6. She wants to self-publish ~~20~~ 168-page books.

Additional Punctuation

Semicolon (;)

Use a semicolon

- between two complete and related ideas.

   The photograph was stunning; Sherman was very pleased.

- between items in a series of ideas, if the items have internal punctuation or are very long.

   Sherman's works were exhibited in Birmingham, Alabama; Fort Worth, Texas; Toronto, Ontario; and London, England.

Colon (:)

Use a colon

- after a complete sentence that introduces a quotation.

   The photographer Henri Cartier Bresson stated his view: "Photographers are dealing with things that are continually vanishing."

- to introduce a series or a list after a complete sentence.

   The new museum includes the work of some great photographers: Ansel Adams, Cindy Sherman, Edward Weston, Alfred Stieglitz, Dorothea Lange, and Annie Leibowitz.

Teaching Tip:
Because semicolons in a series are rarely used, and the semicolons can often be replaced by commas, this chapter introduces students to the idea but does not include related exercises. However, if you want students to practice using semicolons in a series, you can ask them to construct sentences that would need such semicolons. They can brainstorm sentences in pairs.

CHAPTER 38

GRAMMAR LINK

For practice using semicolons, see Chapters 21 and 24.

- to introduce an explanation or example

    The tiny sculpture is outrageously expensive: $2.5 million.

- after the expression "the following."

    Please do the following: read, review, and respond.

- to separate the hour and minutes in expressions of time.

    The exhibit will open at 12:30 P.M.

Hyphen (-)

Use a hyphen

- with some compound nouns. (Note that *compound* means "more than one part.") The following nouns always require a hyphen.

    sister-in-law   mother-in-law   show-off

- when you write the complete words for compound numbers between twenty-one and ninety-nine.

    twenty-five   ninety-two   seventy-seven

- after some prefixes such as *ex-*, *mid-*, or *self-*.

    self-assured   mid-December   ex-husband

- when you use a compound adjective before a noun. The compound adjective must express a single thought.

    one-way street   well-known actor   thirty-year-old woman

There is no hyphen if the compound adjective appears after the noun.

| The street is one way. | The actor was well known. | The woman is thirty years old. |

CHAPTER 38

Hint ▸ **Nonhyphenated Compound Adjectives**

Some compound adjectives never take a hyphen, even when they appear before a noun. Here are some common examples.

World Wide Web   high school senior   real estate agent

Dash (—)

You can use dashes to indicate long pauses or to dramatically emphasize words. Use dashes sparingly.

Ansel Adams waited until the sun was setting to capture the image—the perfect moment.

The gallery owner—hiding his excitement—offered to buy the rare photo.

Parentheses ( )

You can use parentheses to set off incidental information such as a date or abbreviation. Use parentheses sparingly.

> Lange's photo of the migrant mother, which was taken during the height of the Depression era (1936), has become an enduring image.

> The United Press Photographer's Association **(UPPA)** was founded in 1946.

 Using Abbreviations

An **abbreviation** is the shortened form of a word. Avoid using abbreviations in academic writing except for titles and time references.

Dr. = Doctor   Mr. = Mister   P.M. = post meridiem (after noon)

An **acronym** is formed with the first letters of a group of words. Many companies and organizations use acronyms. In an academic paper, give the complete name of the organization the first time you mention it and put the acronym in parentheses immediately after the full name. Use the acronym in the rest of the essay.

> The North Atlantic Treaty Organization (NATO) signed the agreement in 1949. Today, NATO's headquarters are in Belgium.

PRACTICE 2   Add any missing colons, hyphens, dashes, or parentheses.

ten-year-old
EXAMPLE: The ten year old truck broke down.

1. Florence Thompson and her husband, Cleo, were living in Merced Falls,
   — or :
   California, when there was a tragedy the Crash of 1929.

   thirty-two-year-old
2. In 1936, Florence, a thirty two year old woman, decided to keep her

   :
   children with her "I made a promise to Cleo to see his six kids raised, and

   by God I'm going to keep that promise!"

"Migrant Mother" by Dorothea Lange

3. In the back of her truck were Florence's possessions ꞉ a small stove, a few pieces of clothing, some blankets, and a canvas tent.

4. Florence and her children did many low wage jobs ꞉ they struggled and rarely had enough to eat.
   low-wage

5. One day, Florence was in a tent by the highway waiting for her son to return — a day that would make her famous.

6. That day, photographer Dorothea Lange was working for the Farm Security Administration (FSA) and was traveling around Nipomo Valley in California.

7. Lange described what happened ꞉ "I saw and approached the hungry and desperate mother, as if drawn by a magnet."

8. Sitting in her dust covered canvas tent, Florence Thompson was holding her baby, and her children were crowded around her.
   dust-covered

9. During a twenty minute session, Lange took many photos of the migrant mother.
   twenty-minute

10. The compassionate photographs of Dorothea Lange (1895–1965) have influenced modern documentary photography.

FINAL REVIEW

Identify and correct any errors in numbers, colons, hyphens, dashes, or parentheses.

EXAMPLE: Richard Avedon took large format photos.

1. Richard Avedon (1923–2004) was a great fashion photographer.

2. Before he joined the Merchant Marines, his father in law gave him a *father-in-law*

   camera a gift that changed his life. —

3. At the beginning of his career, he took photos with his ten year old *ten-year-old*

   Rolleiflex camera.

4. He became a staff photographer for *Vogue* he also worked for *Harper's* ;

   Bazaar.

5. Many of his photos featured three items a chair, a white backdrop, and a :

   face.

6. One of his greatest photos a masterpiece of shadow and light showed — —

   Audrey Hepburn's face.

7. He took 100s of photos of Hepburn, his favorite model. *hundreds*

8. His photographs have been exhibited at New York's Museum of Modern

   Art MOMA. ( )

9. He published the best selling book *Portraits*, and he co authored another *best-selling*   *co-authored*

   book, *The Sixties*.

10. His book has twenty-nine fashion shots, 125 portraits, and twelve war *29*   *12*

    images.

11. One of his photos—an iconic image of Marilyn Monroe has been —

    reproduced in 1000s of books and magazines. *thousands*

12. Avedon compared photography to music "The way I see is comparable to :

    the way musicians hear."

READING LINK

Human Development

Read more about human development and creativity.

"Out of Sight" by Ryan Knighton (page 108)

"On Genius" by Dorothy Nixon (page 164)

"The Dating World" by Naomi Louder (page 205)

"Medicating Ourselves" by Robyn Sarah (page 560)

"The Untranslatable Word 'Macho'" by Rose del Castillo Guilbault (page 587)

"Chance and Circumstance" by David Leonhardt (page 591)

"The Happiness Factor" by David Brooks (page 594)

"Guy" by Maya Angelou (page 598)

CHAPTER 38

Teaching Tip:

**Cooperative
Learning
(Ask & Learn)**
Ask students to
review the chapter
and identify anything
that they are not
completely clear
about. All students
should write three
questions on a
paper. Then in
teams, students can
ask other members
their questions and
share answers.

CHAPTER 38

Teaching Tip:
**Writer's World
Competition**
Please advise
students that they
can submit their
paragraphs and
essays for possible
publication to www
.pearsonhighered
.com/essayrewards/
writingrewards.html

The Writer's Room **Topics for Writing**

Write about one of the following topics. Proofread for errors in numbers or punctuation.

1. Describe a personal photograph that you cherish. When was the photo taken? What is in the photo? Why is it so compelling?

2. Compare two art forms. For example, you could compare a photograph and a painting or two pieces of music.

✔ **CHECKLIST: NUMBERS AND PUNCTUATION**

When you edit your writing, ask yourself these questions.

☐ Are there any numbers in my writing? Check that your numbers are consistently written, and verify that you have used words rather than numerals when necessary.

> *thousands*
> Lange took ~~1000s~~ of photographs.

☐ Are my semicolons, colons, hyphens, dashes, and parentheses used in a correct and appropriate manner?

> :   *well-used*
> She brought the following supplies, a camera, a ~~well used~~ chair, and a camera stand.

mywritinglab To check your progress in meeting this chapter's objectives, log in to **www.mywritinglab.com**, go to the **Study Plan** tab, click on **The Editing Handbook—Section 6** and choose **Numbers and Additional Punctuation** from the list of subtopics. Read and view the resources in the **Review Materials** section, and then complete the **Recall, Apply,** and **Write** sets in the **Activities** section.

Editing Practice

To conquer Mount Everest, climbers meet the physical and mental challenges through practice and training. To write good essays, students perfect their skills by revising and editing.

Why Bother Editing?

After you finish writing the first draft of an essay, always make time to edit it. Editing for errors in grammar, punctuation, sentence structure, and capitalization can make the difference between a failing paper and a passing one or a good essay and a great one. Editing is not always easy; it takes time and attention to detail. But, it gets easier the more you do it. Also, the more you edit your essays (and your peers' essays, too), the better your writing will be, and the less time you will need to spend editing!

Teaching Tip:
Practices 1 and 2 contain editing symbols and codes that are found at the back of the book. The practices can help students get used to more formal editing techniques. If you use different symbols or codes, tell your students about them before they begin these editing practices.

PRACTICE 1   Correct twenty errors in this essay. An editing symbol appears above each error. To understand the meaning of each symbol, refer to the revising and editing symbols on the inside back cover of this book.

1.   Since 1900, many products been defective. In his book *Business ethics*, Richard

       have been (vt)   *E* (cap)

T. De George discusses a famous product defect case. In the early 1970's, American

      1970s (p)

automakers was losing market share to smaller Japanese imports. Lee Iacocca, the

      were (agr)

CEO of Ford Motor Company wanted to produce a car that was inexpensive,

      , (p)

lightweight, and had an attractive look. Engineers developped the Ford Pinto.

      attractive (//)   *developed* (sp)

2.   Because Ford wanted the product on the market real quickly, the car was

      really (ad)

not test for rear-end impacts. After the Pintos been produced, they were put in

      tested (vt)   *had been* (vt)

collision tests, they failed the tests. When the Pinto was hitted from behind, a

      but (ro)   *hit* (sp)

bolt on the bumper will sometimes puncture the fuel tank. And cause an explosion.

      would (wc)   *tank and* (frag)

3.   Ford conducted a study and determined that a inexpensive baffle could be

      an (wc)

placed between the bumper and the gas tank. After conducting a cost–benefit

analysis, a decision was made. It was less expensive to fight lawsuits than inserting

      Ford made a decision (m)   *to insert* (//)

the baffle.

4.   In 1976, Pintos had thirteen explosions from rear-end impacts. Comparable

cars had less problems. When it be too late, the company realized that the lawsuits

      fewer (ad)   *was* (vt)

worse
ad
and the bad publicity were worst for the company than the cost of the repairs

would have been. After seven years and many deaths, the Pintos were recalled.

PRACTICE 2 EDIT AN ESSAY

Correct fifteen errors in this essay. An editing symbol appears above each error. To understand the meaning of each symbol, refer to the revising and editing symbols on the inside back cover of this book.

Climbing Everest

Tibetans
//
1   The Nepalese and Indians name it Sagarmatha, and people from Tibet call
M
cap
it Qomolangma. The rest of the world knows it as mount Everest, named

after surveyor Sir George Everest. With the highest peak in the world,
Mount Everest provides a challenge for climbers.
m
mountain climbers love the challenge.

its
P
2   In 1921, Tibet opened it's borders to the outside and gave climbers easy access

to Everest. The first Europeans to attempt to climb Everest were George Mallory
. U
ro
and Andrew Irvine in 1924, unfortunately, they both perished in the attempt.
attempts
pl
Many other unsuccessful attempt were made to reach the Everest summit. Then

in 1953, Edmund Hillary, a New Zealander, and Tenzing Norgay, a Nepalese

Sherpa, became the first climbers to reach the top of the world at 29,028 feet
heroes
sp
above sea level. Both men became world-famous heros.

3   Since 1921, around 2,200 mountaineers reached the summit; others have paid *(have reached / vt)* a great price. About 185 climbers have died in the attemt *(attempt / sp)*. There is a graveyard on

the ascent to the summit. Mountaineers see the remains of corpses and tents. The

dead remain on Everest. Even if climbers wanted to carry the corpses down, you *(they / shift)*

could not because of the altitude.

4   The popularity of climbing the world's ~~most~~ highest peak has become so great *(ad)*

that critics call Everest just another tourist trap. Many climbers set up businesses

as guides. A Nepalese businessmen is planning to develop a cyber café at the base *(businessman / pl)*

camp, some snowboarders want to surf down from the summit. There are also a *(; / ro)* *(is / agr)*

lot of trash on the summit trail. Nonetheless, Everest still catches the imagination

of persons all over the world. *(people / pl)*

PRACTICE 3   EDIT A FORMAL LETTER

Correct fifteen errors in this formal business letter.

George Bates

5672 Manet street west *(S   W)*

Lazerville, TX 76202

August 15, 2010

Customer Service

The Furniture store
                 S

1395 Division avenue
                A

Denton, TX 76205

Subject: Desk

Attention: Sales manager
                  M

I bought a desk from your store on august 13 2010, and the store delivers it
                                     A   *,*   *delivered*

thursday morning. After the delivery people had left, I discovered a large
T

scratch on the surface of the desk. Its also lopsided. Since I have always
                                    It's

found your products to be of excellent quality I would like to have a
                                              ,

replacement desk delivered to my home. If you do not have replacement
                                                          a

desk, then I would like to have a full reimbursement.

Thank you very much for your cooperation in this matter, I look forward to
receiving
receive my new desk.

        sincerely,
Yours sincerely,

George Bates

George Bates

PRACTICE 4   EDIT A WORKPLACE MEMO

Correct ten errors in the following excerpt from a memo.   Answers will vary.

To: Career development faculty members

From: Maddison Healey

Re: Internships

going to   *there*
I'm ~~gonna~~ take this opportunity to remind you that ~~their~~ are financial
            hire   *Development*
resources to ~~hiring~~ two new interns for the Career ~~development~~ Program.

If anyone wishes to participate in this collaboration, please let Danielle
        me
or ~~I~~ know. The current deadline for applying to the internship program is
                    April
the beginning of ~~april~~. The internship program/provides valuable
                              It is important to treat interns with
mentoring to college students. ~~Treating an intern with respect, it is very~~
respect.   *him or her*
~~important.~~ If you hire an intern, you are responsible for training ~~them~~.
                                        quickly
For those who are interested, please let me know as ~~quick~~ as

possible.

PRACTICE 5   EDIT A SHORT ARTICLE

Correct fifteen errors in the next selection.   Answers will vary.

Forget What Your Fifth Grade Teacher Taught You

                                            planets. On
1   The solar system no longer has nine ~~planets, on~~ August 24, 2006, the
                              Union
International Astronomical ~~union~~, which has a voting membership of about

2,500 scientists, met in Prague. It decided to demote Pluto from a planet to a dwarf planet. The astronomers said that Pluto does not exhibit the same characteristics as the other major planets. According to scientists, a planet must

must have
orbit the sun, it ~~must be having~~ a spherical shape, and it must have a clear orbit.

Unfortunately
~~Unfortunatly,~~ Pluto's orbit overlaps Neptune's orbit.

beginning   *many*
2   At the ~~begining~~ of the twentieth century, ~~much~~ astronomers suspected the possibility of another planet in the solar system. In 1930, while working for the Lowell Conservatory in Flagstaff, Arizona, astronomer Clyde Tombaugh took

ice
photographs of a sphere that was composed mainly of ~~ices~~ and rocks. It also had

Eventually   *ninth*
a satellite, Charon, orbiting it. ~~Evenutaly,~~ this sphere was named the ~~nineth~~ planet in the solar system.

excited
3   Scientists were very ~~exciting~~ about the discovery. People from all over the world suggested names for the new planet. The scientists from the observatory received so many suggestions that they had difficulty choosing one. An

year
eleven-~~years~~-old girl from Oxford, England, suggested the name Pluto.

4   The scientific community and the public have had a mixed reaction to the

Pluto as
declassification of ~~Pluto. As~~ a planet. Some refuse to accept it. But I wonder why

they are   *want to*
~~are they~~ resistant. Perhaps teachers don't ~~wanna~~ change astronomy textbooks.

Maybe humans feel particularly wary when the scientific community revises what

them
it once asked ~~us~~ to accept as fact.

mywritinglab   To check your progress in meeting this chapter's objectives, log in to **www.mywritinglab.com,** go to the **Study Plan** tab, click on **The Editing Handbook—Section 7** and choose **Editing Practice** from the list of subtopics. Read and view the resources in the **Review Materials** section, and then complete the **Recall, Apply,** and **Write** sets in the **Activities** section.

Reading Strategies and Selections

PART V

I n this chapter, the essays are organized according to the same themes used in the grammar chapters. The predominant writing pattern of each essay is shown in parentheses.

From Reading to Writing

Aspiring actors study ordinary people, psychological profiles, and the work of other actors to fully develop the characters they play. In the same way, by observing how different writers create their work, you can learn how to use those techniques in your own writing.

Reading Strategies

The reading strategies discussed in this chapter can help you develop your writing skills. They can also help you become a more active reader. You will learn about previewing, finding the main and supporting ideas, understanding difficult words, and recognizing irony. When you read, you expand your vocabulary and learn how other writers develop topics. You also learn to recognize and use different writing patterns. Finally, reading helps you find ideas for your own essays.

Previewing

Previewing is like glancing through a magazine in a bookstore; it gives you a chance to see what the writer is offering. When you **preview,** look quickly for the following visual clues so that you can determine the selection's key ideas:

- Titles or subheadings (if any)
- The first and last sentence of the introduction
- The first sentence of each paragraph
- The concluding sentences
- Any photos, graphs, or charts

Finding the Main Idea

After you finish previewing, read the selection carefully. Search for the **main idea,** which is the central point that the writer is trying to make. In an essay, the main idea usually appears somewhere in the first few paragraphs in the form of a thesis statement. However, some professional writers build up to the main idea and state it only in the middle or at the end of the essay. Additionally, some professional writers do not state the main idea directly.

Hint **Making a Statement of the Main Idea**

If the reading does not contain a clear thesis statement, you can determine the main idea by asking yourself *who, what, when, where, why,* and *how* questions. Then, using the answers to those questions, make a statement that sums up the main point of the reading.

Making Inferences

If a professional writer does not state the main idea directly, you must look for clues that will help you to **infer** or figure out what the writer means to say. For example, the next paragraph does not have a topic sentence. However, you can infer the main idea. Underline key words that can lead you to a better understanding of the passage.

> Algie Crivens III was 18 and fresh out of high school in 1991 when he was sentenced to twenty years in prison for a murder he did not commit. He spent the next eight-and-a-half years consumed with educating himself while his appeals crawled through the courts. Crivens is nothing if not energetic; he tends to speak in paragraphs, not sentences. While in prison, he channeled this energy into earning an associate's degree in social science and a bachelor's in sociology. He also took courses in paralegal studies and culinary arts. His fellow prisoners used to ask how he could spend so much time reading. But, to him, reading was a way to escape the boredom of prison life.
>
> —From "Righting a Wrong" by Liliana Ibara

PRACTICE I   Ask yourself the following questions.

1. What is the subject of this text?

   a young man who has been wrongfully convicted

2. What points can you infer that the writer is making?

   You can infer that the legal system sometimes makes mistakes, and that

   prisoners are not necessarily unmotivated, unintelligent, uneducated, or lazy.

Finding the Supporting Ideas

Different writers use different types of supporting ideas. They may give steps for a process, use examples to illustrate a point, give reasons for an argument, and so on. Try to identify the author's supporting ideas.

Highlighting and Making Annotations

After you read a long text, you may forget some of the author's ideas. To help you remember and quickly find the important points, you can highlight key ideas and make annotations. An **annotation** is a comment, question, or reaction that you write in the margins of a passage.

Each time you read a passage, follow these steps:

- Look in the introductory and concluding paragraphs. Underline sentences that sum up the main idea. Using your own words, rewrite the main idea in the margin.
- Underline or highlight supporting ideas. You might even want to number the arguments or ideas. This will allow you to understand the essay's development.
- Circle words that you do not understand.
- Write questions in the margin if you do not understand the author's meaning.
- Write notes beside passages that are interesting or that relate to your own experiences.
- Jot down any ideas that might make interesting writing topics.

Here is an example of a highlighted and annotated passage from an essay titled "Sprawl Fallout" by Patricia L. Kirk.

1   For suburbanites who spend hours in traffic each day commuting to city jobs, the concept of urban sprawl is more than a (euphemism) batted around by city planners. <u>Many commuters know the psychological tolls of their long, slow journeys—irritation, anxiety, less time at home—but the negative impacts might be broader than most realize.</u>   ◄ Euphemism?
◄ Background
Main point: urban
◄ sprawl is bad

2   Urban sprawl—a phenomenon that results in people living far from their workplaces—has been linked to asthma, obesity, and just plain foul   ◄ Definition of sprawl

Shows the effects of sprawl ➤

Traffic jams drive me crazy ➤

moods. In one study, people with long commutes reported more headaches, stomach problems, and fatigue than people with shorter drives. Irritability from long commutes was also shown to transfer to job performance, resulting in lower productivity.

Understanding Difficult Words

When you come across an unfamiliar word in a passage, do not stop reading to look up its definition in the dictionary. First, try using context clues to figure out the term's meaning on your own. If you still do not understand the word, circle it to remind you to look up its meaning in the dictionary when you have finished reading through the passage. You can keep a list of new vocabulary in the "Vocabulary Log" at the end of this book on page 614.

Using Context Clues

Context clues are hints in the selection that help to define a word. To find a word's meaning, try the following:

- **Look at the word.** Is it a noun, a verb, or an adjective? Knowing how the word functions in the sentence can help you guess its meaning.
- **Look at surrounding words.** Look at the entire sentence and try to find a relation between the difficult word and those that surround it. There may be a **synonym** (a word that means the same thing) or an **antonym** (a word that means the opposite), or other terms in the sentence that help define the word.
- **Look at surrounding sentences.** Sometimes you can guess the meaning of a difficult word by looking at the sentences, paragraphs, and punctuation marks surrounding it. When you use your logic, the meaning becomes clear.

In most cases, you can guess the meaning of a new word by combining your own knowledge of the topic with the information conveyed in the words and phrases surrounding the difficult word.

PRACTICE 2 Can you define the words *strewn, emanate,* and *haven*? Perhaps you are not quite sure. Looking at the words in context makes it much easier to guess the definitions of the words.

> When I arrived in my hometown, I was baffled by the changes in my old neighborhood. Garbage was **strewn** across front lawns, paint peeled on the graying wooden homes, and roofs sagged. The auto body shop on the corner **emanated** horrible fumes of turpentine and paint, forcing me to cover my nose when I passed it. I wondered what had happened to my former safe **haven**.

Now write your own definition of the words as they are used in the context.

strewn ___*scattered*___   emanated ___*gave off*___   haven ___*refuge*___

> ## Hint
> ### Cognates
>
> **Cognates** (also known as word twins) are English words that may look and sound like words in another language. For example, the English word *responsible* is similar to the Spanish word *responsable*, although the words are spelled differently.
>
> If English is not your first language, and you read an English word that looks similar to a word in your language, check how the word is being used in context. It may or may not mean the same thing in English as it means in your language. For example, in English, *sensible* means "to show good sense," but in Spanish, *sensible* means "emotional." In German, *bekommen* sounds like "become" but it really means "to get," and the German word *gift* means "poison" in English. If you are not sure of a word's meaning, you can always consult a dictionary.

ESL
Teaching Tip: Draw your nonnative speakers' attention to the cognates hint. Then, ask them to brainstorm a list of words in their native languages that look like English words. They should determine if the words have similar or different meanings in both languages. For example, some words that Spanish speakers may misuse—because the meanings in English and Spanish are different—are *actually, animator, embarrassed, costume, cruise, deception, resume,* and *sensible.* For instance, although *actual* means "real" or "genuine" in English, it means "current" or "present" in Spanish.

Using a Dictionary

If you cannot understand the meaning of an unfamiliar word even after using context clues, then look up the word in a dictionary. A dictionary is useful if you use it correctly. Review the following tips for proper dictionary usage:

- **Look at the dictionary's front matter.** The preface contains explanations about the various symbols and abbreviations. Find out what your dictionary has to offer.
- **Read all of the definitions listed for the word.** Look for the meaning that best fits the context of your sentence.
- **Look up root words, if necessary.** For example, if you do not understand the word *unambiguous*, remove the prefix and look up *ambiguous*.

Here is an example of how dictionaries set up their definitions:

Word-Break Divisions
Your dictionary may indicate places for dividing words with heavy black dots.

Stress Symbol (′) and Pronunciation
Some dictionaries provide the phonetic pronunciation of words. The stress symbol lets you know which syllable has the highest or loudest sound.

Parts of Speech
The *n* means that *formation* is a noun. If you do not understand the "parts of speech" symbol, look in the front or the back of your dictionary for a list of symbols and their meanings.

for•ma′•tion / for′mā shən/*n* 1, the process of shaping. 2, that which is shaped. 3, formal structure or arrangement, esp. of troops.

From *The New American Webster Handy College*, A Signet Book, 2000.

Determining Connotation and Denotation

A **denotation** is the literal meaning for a word that may be found in the dictionary. For example, the dictionary definition of *mother* is "a female parent." A **connotation** is the implied or associated meaning. It can be a cultural value

Teaching Tip:
Discuss how terms
such as *abandoned*
carry emotional
weight.

judgment. For instance, the word *mother* may trigger feelings of comfort, security, anger, or resentment in a listener, depending on that person's experience with mothers.

Authors can influence readers by carefully choosing words that have specific connotations. For example, review the next two descriptions. Which one has a more negative connotation?

Terry left his family.   Andrew abandoned his family.

Teaching Tip:
Ask students to
discuss how certain
words and phrases
show a bias. Also
ask them to rewrite
one of the passages
using a more neutral
tone.

PRACTICE 3   Read the next passages and underline any words or phrases that have strong connotations. Discuss how the words support a personal bias.   Answers will vary.

1. Furthermore, in too many states, <u>welfare keeps flowing while the kids are in jail</u>, or middle-class parents continue to claim children as tax deductions even as the state <u>pays for their upkeep</u> in detention facilities. We must demand that parents reimburse the state for housing their <u>failures</u>.

   from "Enough Is Enough" by Judy Sheindlin

2. There is no question about whom Ms. Politkovskaya held responsible in years of <u>unflinching</u> reporting from Chechnya: the Russian Army and Mr. Putin himself. When he <u>finally got around to acknowledging her death</u> yesterday, it was in a <u>cold-blooded statement</u> that the authorities "will take every step to investigate objectively the tragic death of the journalist Politkovskaya."

   from "Another Killing in Moscow" (*New York Times* editorial)

Teaching Tip:
To reinforce the link
between reading
and writing, you
might assign
students a particular
reading and have
them make an
outline of that
reading. Then point
out that all prose—
student essays,
research papers,
workplace
memos—also needs
clear writing plans.

3. Rohe could have chosen to give a substantive speech detailing why she believes "pre-emptive war is dangerous and wrong"—or as she so categorically put it, how she "<u>knows</u>" that it is. Instead she <u>took the easy way out by insulting the speaker and throwing out some leftist chestnuts</u> about the still missing Osama bin Laden and weapons of mass destruction. But the former would have required her to <u>grapple with ideas</u>; she chose to <u>take potshots</u>.

   from "The Real Meaning of Courage" by Linda Chavez

From Reading to Writing

After you finish reading a selection, you could try these strategies to make sure that you have understood it.

Summarize the reading. When you summarize, you use your own words to write a condensed version of the reading. You leave out all information except for the main points. You can find a detailed explanation about summaries in Chapter 15.

Outline the reading. An outline is a visual plan of the reading that looks like an essay plan. First, you write the main idea of the essay, and then write down the most important idea from each paragraph. You could make further indentations, and under each idea, include a detail or example.

Analyze the reading. When you read, look critically at the writer's arguments and evaluate them, point by point. Also analyze how the writer builds the argument and ask yourself questions such as *Do I agree? Are the author's arguments convincing?* Then, when you write your analysis, you can break down the author's explanations and either refute or agree with them, using your own experiences and examples to support your view.

Write a response. Your instructor may ask you to write about your reaction to a reading. These are some questions you might ask yourself before you respond in writing.

- What is the writer's main point?
- What is the writer's purpose? Is the writer trying to entertain, persuade, or inform?
- Who is the audience? Is the writer directing his or her message at someone like me?
- Do I agree or disagree with the writer's main point?
- Are there any aspects of the topic to which I can relate? What are they?

After you answer the questions, you will have more ideas to use in your written response.

Reading Selections

Theme: **Conflict**

READING 1

The CSI Effect
Richard Willing

> Richard Willing is a journalist for *USA Today*. In the next article, he discusses the impact of crime scene shows on courtrooms across the nation.

1   Television shows such as *CSI* (Crime Scene Investigation) are affecting action in courthouses by, among other things, raising jurors' expectations of what prosecutors should produce at trial. Prosecutors, defense lawyers, and judges call it "the *CSI* effect," after the crime-scene shows that are among the hottest attractions on television. The shows feature high-tech labs and gorgeous techies. By shining a glamorous light on a gory profession, the programs also have helped to draw more students into forensic studies.

2   The programs also foster what analysts say is the mistaken notion that criminal science is fast and infallible and always gets its man. That's affecting the way lawyers prepare their cases, as well as the expectations that police and the public place on real crime labs. <u>Real crime-scene investigators say that because of the programs, people often have unrealistic ideas of what criminal science can deliver.</u>

3   Many lawyers, judges, and legal consultants state they appreciate how *CSI*-type shows have increased interest in forensic evidence. "Talking about science in the courtroom used to be like talking about geometry— a real jury turnoff," says jury consultant Robert Hirschhorn of Lewisville, Texas. "Now that there's this obsession with the shows, you can talk to jurors about scientific evidence and just see from the looks on their faces that they find it fascinating."

4   But some defense lawyers remark that *CSI* and similar shows make jurors rely too heavily on scientific findings and unwilling to accept that those findings can be compromised by human or technical errors. Prosecutors also have complaints: They say the shows can make it more difficult for them to win convictions in the large majority of cases in which scientific evidence is irrelevant or absent.

5   Lawyers and judges note the *CSI* effect has become a phenomenon in courthouses across the nation. For example, in Phoenix, jurors in a murder trial noticed that a bloody coat introduced as evidence had not been tested for DNA. The jurors alerted the judge. The tests were unnecessary because, early in the trial, the defendant admitted his presence at the murder scene. The judge decided that TV had taught jurors about DNA tests but not enough about when to use them.

6   Juries are sometimes right to expect high-tech evidence. Three years ago in Richmond, Virginia, jurors in a murder trial asked the judge whether a cigarette butt found during the investigation could be tested for links to the defendant. Defense attorneys had ordered DNA tests but had not yet introduced them into evidence. The jury's hunch was correct—the tests exonerated the defendant, and the jury **acquitted** him.

acquitted: pronounced not guilty

7   The *CSI* effect is also being felt beyond the courtroom. At West Virginia University, forensic science is the most popular undergraduate major for the second year in a row, attracting 13 percent of incoming freshmen this fall. In June, supporters of an Ohio library drew an overflow crowd of 200-plus to a luncheon speech on DNA by titling it "CSI: Dayton." The Los Angeles County Sheriff's Department crime lab has seen another version of the *CSI* effect. Four technicians have left the lab for lucrative jobs as technical advisers to crime-scene programs. "They found a way to make science pay," lab director Barry Fisher says.

8   The stars of crime shows often are the equipment—DNA sequencers, mass spectrometers, photometric fingerprint illuminators, scanning electron microscopes. But the technicians run a close second. "It's 'geek chic,' the idea that kids who excel in science and math can grow up to be cool," says Robert Thompson, who teaches the history of TV programming at Syracuse University. "This is long overdue. . . . Cops and cowboys and doctors and lawyers have been done to death."

9   Some of the science on crime shows is state-of-the-art. Real lab technicians can, for example, lift DNA profiles from cigarette butts, candy wrappers, and gobs of spit, just as their Hollywood counterparts do. But some of what's on TV is far-fetched. Real technicians don't pour caulk into knife wounds to make a cast of the weapon. That wouldn't work in soft tissue. Machines that can identify cologne from scents on clothing are still in the experimental phase. A criminal charge based on "neuro-linguistic programming"—detecting lies by the way a person's eyes shift—likely would be dismissed by a judge.

10   Real scientists feel the main problem with crime shows is this: The science is always above reproach. "You never see a case where the sample is degraded or the lab work is faulty or the test results don't solve the crime," says Dan Krane, president and DNA specialist at Forensic Bioinformatics in Fairborn, Ohio. "These things happen all the time in the real world."

COMPREHENSION AND CRITICAL THINKING

1.   Find a word in paragraph 2 that means "cultivate or advance." __foster__

2.   What is the meaning of *exonerated* in paragraph 6?
     a. convicted   b. determined   c. exempted

3.   Underline the thesis statement; that is, find a sentence that sums up the main idea of the essay.

4.   In which paragraphs are there examples of the following:

     Anecdotes: _paragraphs 5, 6_

     Statistics: _paragraph 7_

     Expert opinions: _paragraphs 3, 7, 8, 10_

5.   What can you infer, or guess, after closely reading paragraph 6?
     a. The defendant left a cigarette butt at the crime scene.
     b. The defendant did not leave a cigarette butt at the crime scene.
     c. The DNA proved that the defendant was at the crime scene.

Teaching Tip:

Cooperative Learning (Jigsaw)
Ask students to read the text for homework or in class. Then divide the class into groups of three to four students. Ask some groups to list the main points of the text and write a summary. Ask other groups to list about ten difficult words and phrases from the text and to define them from the context. A third set of groups can answer the comprehension questions. Then ask students to share their information.

6.   What do lawyers and judges appreciate about crime-scene shows?

These days, jury members are interested in crime scene evidence, and

they like to hear about science in the courtroom. CSI-type shows have

helped create an interest in forensic evidence.

7.   What problems do crime-scene shows cause for lawyers? Think of at least two answers.

Juries expect crime scene evidence, even when it is not necessary or

possible to obtain. They trust crime scene evidence too much. They

don't realize that evidence can be flawed.

8.   Crime-scene shows glamorize forensic science. How might the reality of life as a forensic scientist be different from what is shown on TV?

TV shows make the job look exciting, but in reality, it is probably a very

depressing and gory line of work. Also, cases are not as easy to solve

as is shown on television. In real time, forensic results take longer to

obtain than on television.

9.   How are crime-scene shows great for science "geeks"?

The shows make people who are interested in science look attractive and

exciting.

10. Why do real scientists object to crime-scene shows?

The shows make the science look easy and "above reproach." In reality,

lab tests can be faulty or useless.

Teaching Tip:
The suggested
topics give students
the opportunity to
practice cause and
effect writing.
Specify whether
students should
write a paragraph
or an essay.

WRITING TOPICS

Write about one of the following topics. Remember to explore, develop, and revise and edit your work.

1.   Think about another type of television series or movie, and describe how it influences viewers. For example, you might choose soap operas, medical dramas, or mobster movies.

2.   What are the possible benefits of sitting on a jury? What effects could a criminal trial have on jury members?

READING 2

Types of Rioters
David Locher

Teaching Tip:
This classification essay also contains elements of narration, cause and effect, and argument.

David A. Locher is an author and college professor at Missouri Southern State College. The next excerpt about rioters is from his book *Collective Behavior*.

1   In March of 1992, Los Angeles was a city with a long history of conflict between racial groups. That year, a videotape of Rodney King being brutally beaten was shown over and over again on local, regional, and national television news reports. What almost no one realized at the time was that they were seeing an edited tape. KTLA, the Los Angeles television station that first acquired the videotape, edited out the first few seconds of the video because it was blurry. Most reporters, together with the public, saw only the edited, sixty-eight-second version of the video. They were not aware of the missing thirteen seconds, which apparently showed Rodney King charging at the police officers. The vast majority of Americans who saw the televised video believed that the beating had been totally unprovoked and that the officers were therefore guilty. The untelevised thirteen seconds were enough to convince many jurors that the beating was at least partially provoked. Legally, they believed that the beating was excessive but not sufficient grounds for conviction in a court of law.

2   The videotape created a presumption throughout the country that the officers would be found guilty. When the not guilty verdict was announced, it led to the South-Central Los Angeles riot, which was the bloodiest, deadliest, most destructive riot in modern American history. At the time the riots were beginning, no one blamed the prosecutors; most blamed the jury and the system itself. The generalized belief

The South Central riot

throughout much of the country and shared by the rioters was that guilty verdicts could not have been reached, no matter what. Participants believed that legal justice was beyond their reach, but revenge was right at hand.

3   In all riots, there are categories of participants. Five categories can be labeled ego-involved, concerned, insecure, curious spectators, and ego-detached exploiters. Each category of participant may be operating under

a different generalized belief, and possibly even a different set of structural strains.

Ego-Involved

4   Ego-involved participants feel a deep connection to the concerns expressed. In Los Angeles, the ego-involved participants were the ones who felt the most empathy for Rodney King, the most hatred for the LAPD, and the most outrage over the verdicts. They fully accepted the generalized beliefs and believed that it was up to them to do something. These individuals placed themselves into the position of responsibility. They threw bricks or started fires because they believed that doing so would produce real change and that their violent actions were the only way to produce that change. Ego-involved participants actually started the riot. Anger, outrage, and disappointment drove their actions. They believed that those actions were necessary, desirable, or unavoidable.

Concerned

5   Concerned riot participants are not so personally involved. They have a more general interest in the event. The concerned participants were those who took part in the rioting, but who focused their attention on following the lead of others. They accepted the generalized belief and engaged in riotous actions, but they did so as much out of empathy with the other rioters as empathy for Rodney King. These individuals helped the ego-involved start fires, break windows, and so on. Under only slightly different circumstances, they could just as easily have followed leaders in a peaceful march. In Los Angeles, the concerned participants were acting out of hatred of the system or of authority in general. They followed the lead of the ego-involved but did not choose the course of action themselves.

Insecure

6   Insecure participants just want to be a part of something or are afraid of missing out. They may not have any understanding of the riot's causes. In this sense, they may get confused. They see others throwing objects and smashing windows, and they engage in the same behavior themselves. However, it could be that the ego-involved and concerned participants are all attacking a particular building because of what it represents, while the insecure simply smash whatever is handy. Insecure riot participants revel in the power that they feel by taking part, and they seek safety in numbers.

7   In the South-Central riot, the insecure participants went along with the actions of the others because it made them feel powerful. They were standing up to authority, spitting in the eye of society, and all from the relative safety of a large and anonymous crowd. Individuals who would never think of talking back to a police officer suddenly felt secure enough to throw rocks at them. The meek became powerful; the tame became dangerous. These participants turned the violence away from symbols of authority and toward anyone or anything that stood in the path of the crowd.

Spectators

8   In any form of collective behavior, there may be those who want to watch the actions of participants but do not wish to get directly involved. Photographs and videotaped segments of the Los Angeles riots frequently reveal more people standing around watching the action than participants. At one point during the riot, Reginald Denny, a truck driver who was passing through the area, was pulled out of his truck and nearly beaten to death by rioters. There were many more people watching the attack on Denny than there were actually hitting him. For spectators, the riot was simply an exciting form of entertainment.

9   Spectators are important for several reasons. In a deadly riot, they can frequently become targets for the hostile participants. They may also get caught up in the excitement and decide to join the action. They may take the side of participants against police. Sometimes social control agents force them into action. Social control agents usually do not attempt to distinguish between spectators and active participants. Circumstances often make it impossible for them to do so. In Los Angeles, many spectators joined in the looting, and the police, soldiers, and guardsmen made no real attempt to distinguish between active participants and spectators. Everyone on the streets not wearing a uniform was perceived as a riot participant and treated accordingly. This sort of treatment sometimes outrages spectators to the extent that they become active in resisting social control.

Ego-Detached Exploiters

10   The ego-detached participant does not care about the issues that drive a riot. They do not accept the generalized belief shared by many other participants. They might not even know why the riot started in the first place. None of these issues matter to the ego-detached. They only want to exploit the conditions created by the riot for their own personal gain. An individual who throws a brick at a policeman might be driven by outrage over the verdicts (ego-involved), by a general hatred of the police

(concerned), or by a sense of power and group identity (insecure). An individual who throws a brick at a store window to steal a television is driven by the desire for a free TV. Looting is an act of exploitation by those who are detached from the strain and generalized belief of the riot. Looters use the circumstances created by the riot to gather as many material goods as possible for themselves. No deep sense of outrage over a legal injustice drives an individual to steal a freezer. The exploiter uses the chaos, confusion, and temporary lack of social control to acquire commercial goods for free. They carry out their own personal agendas under cover of the collective episode.

11   The Los Angeles riot was literally taken over by exploiters. The pattern of destruction reveals that the targets changed within the first few hours. Rioters first attacked buildings that symbolized authority or individuals who, through their race, symbolized those with authority. By nightfall, however, they started attacking liquor stores. Before long, any business was fair game. If it could be moved, it was stolen. If it couldn't be moved, it was destroyed. The actions of the exploiters are not difficult to pick out in Los Angeles: They removed any object with any potential value before setting fire to each building. This is not the action of social revolutionaries; it is the action of greedy individuals looking to score. The passion of the ego-involved and concerned participants may fade out within a brief period of time, but the greed of the exploiters does not go away. Only the return of effective social control or the absence of anything to steal ends looting.

12   By the time a riot as big as the South-Central riot has begun, the ego-involved participants may be dramatically outnumbered by those from other categories. This may make the entire event seem pointless or illogical to outside observers. "If they are so mad at the LAPD, why are they burning down their own houses?" was a common question asked by many Americans during the 1992 riot. These critics were overlooking the simple fact that many of the riot participants were not deeply concerned with the issues that caused the riot in the first place. Insecure participants blindly following the crowd and exploiters using the breakdown of social order for their own material gain can vastly outnumber those who actually care about the issues that caused the riot to begin in the first place. Spectators might outnumber all participants combined.

Teaching Tip:

Cooperative Learning (Pair & Share) Ask students to work with a partner to make a plan for this essay. Then students can join another pair and compare their essay plans.

COMPREHENSION AND CRITICAL THINKING

1.   What does Locher mean by a *generalized belief* in paragraph 4?

widely accepted belief that may or may not be based on facts

2. What is the meaning of *revel* as it is used in paragraph 6?
   a. feel drunk b. enjoy c. abuse

3. Which type of rioter simply wants to benefit materially from the riot?

   ego-detached exploiters

4. Using your own words, briefly sum up the main characteristics of each type of rioter.

   Ego-involved: *feel empathy and connected to the cause, have strong beliefs about the issue, believe they can change things*

   Concerned: *have a general interest in the cause, accept generalized belief, follow others, want to join in*

   Insecure: *don't want to miss something, confused, don't really understand the issues, want to feel powerful, might become violent*

   Spectators: *watch but don't want to get involved, might become targets, might join in*

   Ego-detached exploiters: *don't care about issues, want to steal or get something out of the riot, are motivated by greed*

5. Locher used emphatic order to organize his essay. Specifically, how does he organize the types of riot participants?

   from most involved in the issue to most destructive and self-involved

6. Does Locher feel that the riots were justified? You will need to infer, or read between the lines.   Answers will vary.

   No. The core reason to start the riots was based on incomplete media reporting, so the generalized belief may have been flawed.

7. Although this is mainly a classification essay, it also touches on causes and effects of the Los Angeles riot. Briefly sum up some of the main causes and effects.   Answers will vary.

   Causes: *a history of conflict among racial groups, faulty media reporting, and a sense in certain communities that justice cannot be obtained*

   Effects: *an underprivileged community was destroyed, an innocent bystander was nearly murdered, racial tensions increased, and exploiters and looters benefited*

Teaching Tip:
Ask students to discuss the first writing topic on page 542. They can divide the first writing topic into mainstream journalism, tabloid journalism, and specialty or highbrow journalism. They can categorize the ways in which news is transmitted: newspapers, magazines, Internet, and so on. Finally, they can choose to categorize a specific type of medium, such as magazines, according to its subject matter. For example, different magazines might focus on fashion, finance, music, or hard news.

8. The author starts this essay by telling an anecdote. Why is this anecdote crucial to the main focus of the essay?

It gives the reason for the subject of the essay. It links a theoretical

subject to a real event. It is the running example in the essay to explain

the types of rioters.

9. Who is the audience for this essay? Look closely at the tone and vocabulary.

It is an academic audience such as students in criminology.

WRITING TOPICS

Write about one of the following topics. Remember to explore, develop, and revise and edit your work.

1. What are some types of media reports? Divide media reporting into at least three categories.
2. When an event such as a celebrity divorce, a terrorist attack, or a sports scandal occurs, how do you react? Does one topic excite your interest more than others? Discuss at least three types of audiences for media reporting.

READING 3

Naming Good Path Elk
Kenneth M. Kline

Kenneth M. Kline, of African American and Lakota-Sioux descent, describes an initiation ceremony that he took part in during his adolescence. He looks back at the lessons he learned about giving.

1   I stand at the top of Morningside Park in New York City and stare down at Harlem's legendary brownstones. I come to this spot whenever I'm melancholy. Here, with the warm afternoon sun massaging my skin, I consider my life. Trying to survive as a freelance journalist has only meant that I am out of work. Six months ago, I lost my uptown apartment, and creditors are showing no mercy. My name is so tarnished I begin to think that my only escape is to change it. As far as I'm concerned, my good name is dead.

2   Just then, a strong wind blows up from the park, quenching the hot, humid afternoon. It takes me back to a summer I spent at Camp Flying Cloud in the remote mountains around Plymouth, Vermont. I was eleven in 1974 and one of fifty boys living in teepees and dressing in loincloths at the Native-American camp.

3   That was my first year at the camp, and I was eager to learn about the Native-American blood that flowed in my African-American veins, courtesy of both my grandmothers. I'd been at the camp for two weeks when Medicine Rainbow, the camp director, announced that we would begin our first naming ceremony of the summer at that night's powwow. In the tradition of the Lakota Sioux, those selected for the naming quest would trek into the wilderness and spend three days in strict silence at a place called Blue Ledges on the edge of a mountain. There we would meditate on the names we had been given and how they would shape our lives.

4   Everyone was excited about the ceremony—except me. I had something on my mind. Earlier that week, while playing stickball, I'd lost my balance trying to score and crashed into the goalie. "Look out, you moron!" he'd yelled, spewing derogatory comments about my dark skin. I dusted myself off and, before I could stop myself, drop-kicked him, the way I'd learned in karate school. He crumpled like a house of cards, then walked away crying. Ever since that scuffle, he'd become a target for teasing by other campers.

5   On the night of the powwow, I worried that the scuffle might have tarnished my reputation—that any name I received would reflect the fight. The evening began with the lighting of a large bonfire. <u>As the tall flames bowed</u> and flickered in the summer breeze, a camper named Running Bull Thunders marched in, holding a long Indian pipe. He was followed by four other campers in ceremonial garments. Bells around their ankles rang with each step as Running Bull Thunders offered a ritual in gratitude to <u>Mother Earth and the Four Winds for blessing us</u>. Then he seated himself before the drum at the fire's edge and began to beat softly: Boom-boom! Boom-boom! It was our signal to begin the powwow, our late-night dance around the campfire, singing traditional songs. Our voices and footsteps echoed in the night as <u>tall spruce and pine trees danced</u> alongside us in the firelight.

6   When the drumming stopped, we grew silent in anticipation. Suddenly a shadow broke away from the group. Known as the Stalker, he walked lightly to the fire and unrolled a red quilt with Native-American designs. Then, a shadow among shadows, he moved among us, an eagle feather between his fingers. He chose ten campers to be given names that night, and I was one of them.

7   The Stalker's strong hands clasped my arms as he whispered instructions in my ear. I was to take the eagle feather and sit cross-legged on the quilt. I held my breath as he came up behind me and daubed red paint on my temples. "Here is a boy who follows a good path like an elk crossing the woods," he told the gathering. "He is quiet and strong, always

Teaching Tip:

Cooperative Learning (Sharing Circle) Ask students to work in groups of three and share answers to the questions. They can also discuss the writing topics. Then take up the answers with the class.

giving and helping others, and is eager to learn. For this, he shall be known as Good Path Elk." Turning solemnly to me, he added, "You must never say your name unless you become lost. Speaking your Indian name will bring a power to help you find your way."

8   Had I heard right? Had he seen me earlier in the week fighting on the stickball field? Now a chill came into the night air, and it was time for the giveaway ceremony, in which a camper volunteers to give something in friendship. Burning Eagle, an older boy I admired for his skill with Indian crafts, got to his feet. He held a woolen vest decorated with leather and seashells. Stitched on the back was an elk. "To Good Path Elk," he said, walking up to me. "This is for your naming." I was overwhelmed. I couldn't say thank you because of the rule of silence, but I embraced him warmly.

9   The next morning, preparing to leave for Blue Ledges, I decided to take materials with me to make a pair of leggings. We newly named campers hiked over steep woodlands and crossed rivers until we came to a clearing of rocks beside a stream. From there we could see the mountains stretching into the distance. That was Blue Ledges.

Blue Ledges mountains

10   I felt on top of the world. I settled on a cool rock upstream from our campsite to work on my leggings. As I stitched, a gentle breeze from the mountainside seemed to whisper my Indian name: Good Path Elk. Good Path Elk. I looked up from my work to watch an eagle gliding high above the valley, and a strong sense of confidence filled me.

11   At the next naming ceremony, ten more campers were chosen, among them the goalie I had drop-kicked. His name was to be Forest Talker, because he liked to talk to the plants and the trees. As I thought about the quest he and the others would begin the next morning, I had an idea. I ran back to my teepee for the leggings I had made on my quest.

12   "I'd like to give my leggings to Forest Talker," I said as the giveaway ceremony began. "This is for your naming." The stillness of the night magnified the sound of wood crackling in the fire. I stared at Forest Talker: "With these I apologize for drop-kicking you."

13   A few days later, Forest Talker approached me. He said, "Thanks, Good Path Elk. Those were nice leggings. Want to play a game of stickball?"

14 Now, years later, I look out over Harlem, the sun polishing my skin as it did at Blue Ledges, the strong wind on my face reminding me of new beginnings. Suddenly I understand: There's no need to change my name. Instead I will find something to give, some way to use my life to help others. Through giving, I will find the strength to face all my challenges because in the end giving and receiving are the same. I take a deep breath of the wind as it climbs over the park, and in that moment I think I can still hear it—the wind at Blue Ledges, whispering my Indian name.

COMPREHENSION AND CRITICAL THINKING

1. Find an adjective in paragraph 4 that means "offensive" and "insulting."

    derogatory

2. What is the meaning of *daub* in paragraph 7?
    a. increase   b. remove   (c.) smear; apply

3. What is the author's mood at the beginning of the essay? Explain your answer.

    He feels upset about his lack of career success and his financial

    difficulties.

4. In paragraph 1, Kline says "As far as I'm concerned, my good name is dead." Why does he feel this way?

    He has no credit rating, and his name as a journalist is not valued.

5. Why did Kline drop-kick another boy?

    During the heat of a stickball game, the other boy had made derogatory

    comments about Kline's skin color.

6. Personification is the act of attributing human characteristics to something that is inanimate. Underline two examples of personification in paragraph 5.

7. Why was the author prepared to forgive the boy who had insulted him? You will need to infer, or read between the lines.

    He felt ashamed for using violence, and he saw that his actions

    resulted in the other boy being teased. Thus, he felt compassion for the

    other boy. He also believed he should live up to his native name.

8.   The author deviates from chronological order to recount his tale.
     Describe the order of events and explain how the order is significant.

     The time moves from the present, to the past, and back to the present.

     Because the author feels depressed in the present, he remembers a

     moment in the past that helps him to re-evaluate his present mood.

9.   How does the author change after remembering his naming ceremony?

     He felt lost and worthless. The memory reminds him that his native

     name implies "giving and helping others." This memory helps him focus

     on what he can do for others instead of focusing on what he hasn't

     done or doesn't have.

WRITING TOPICS

Teaching Tip:
The suggested
topics give students
the opportunity to
practice narrative
writing. Specify
whether students
should write a
paragraph or an
essay.

Write about one of the following topics. Remember to explore, develop, and revise
and edit your work.

1.   Write about your name. You could write about the following: the
     meaning of your name, the story of how your parents named you, the
     evolution of your feelings about your name, and so on.
2.   Have you ever done something that you feel ashamed about? Narrate
     what happened. Describe how you have changed since it happened.

Theme: **Urban Development**

READING 4

My African Childhood
David Sedaris

Teaching Tip:
This narrative essay
is also descriptive,
and it compares and
contrasts two
people's lives.

David Sedaris is an award-winning essayist and humorist. In the
following essay, excerpted from his collection *Me Talk Pretty One Day*,
Sedaris contrasts his own childhood with that of his friend who lived
in Africa.

1   When Hugh was in the fifth grade, his class took a field trip to an
Ethiopian slaughterhouse. He was living in Addis Ababa at the time, and
the slaughterhouse was chosen because, he says, "it was convenient."
This was a school system in which the matter of proximity outweighed
such petty concerns as what may or may not be appropriate for a busload
of eleven-year-olds. "What?" I asked. "Were there no autopsies scheduled

at the local morgue? Was the federal prison just a bit too far out of the way?"

2   Hugh defends his former school, saying, "Well, isn't that the whole point of a field trip? To see something new?"

3   "Technically yes, but . . ."

4   "All right then," he says. "So we saw some new things." One of his field trips was literally a trip to a field where the class watched a <u>wrinkled man fill his mouth with rotten goat meat and feed it to a pack of waiting hyenas</u>. On another occasion, they were taken to examine the <u>bloodied bedroom curtains</u> hanging in the palace of the former dictator. There were tamer trips, to textile factories and sugar refineries, but my favorite is always the slaughterhouse. It wasn't a big company, just a small rural enterprise run by a couple of brothers operating out of a low-ceilinged concrete building. Following a brief lecture on the importance of proper sanitation, a small white piglet was herded into the room, <u>its dainty hooves clicking against the concrete floor</u>. The class gathered in a circle to get a better look at the animal that seemed delighted with the attention he was getting. He turned from face to face and was looking up at Hugh when one of the brothers drew a pistol from his back pocket, held it against the animal's temple, and shot the piglet, execution-style. <u>Blood spattered, frightened children wept</u>, and the man with the gun offered the teacher and bus driver some meat from a freshly slaughtered goat.

5   When I'm told such stories, it's all I can do to hold back my feelings of jealousy. An Ethiopian slaughterhouse. Some people have all the luck. When I was in elementary school, the best my class and I ever got was a trip to Old Salem or Colonial Williamsburg, one of those preserved brick villages where time supposedly stands still and someone earns his living as a town crier. There was always a blacksmith, a group of wandering patriots, and a collection of bonneted women hawking corn bread or gingersnaps made "the old fashioned way." Every now and then we might come across a doer of bad deeds serving time in the stocks, but that was generally as exciting as it got.

6   <u>Certain events are parallel, but compared with Hugh's, my childhood was unspeakably dull</u>. When I was seven years old, my family moved to North Carolina. When he was seven years old, Hugh's family moved to the Congo. We had a collie and a house cat. They had a monkey and two horses named Charlie Brown and Satan. I threw stones at stop signs. Hugh threw stones at crocodiles. The verbs are the same, but he definitely wins the prize when it comes to nouns and objects. An eventful day for my mother might have involved a trip to the dry cleaner or a conversation with the potato chip deliveryman. Asked one ordinary Congo afternoon what she'd done with her day, Hugh's mother answered that she and a fellow

member of the Ladies' Club had visited a leper colony on the outskirts of Kinshasa. No reason was given for the expedition, though chances are she was staking it out for a future field trip.

7   Due to his upbringing, Hugh sits through inane movies never realizing that they're often based on inane television shows. There were no pokerfaced sitcom Martians in his part of Africa, no oil rich hillbillies or aproned brides trying to wean themselves from the practice of witchcraft.[1] From time to time a movie would arrive packed in a dented canister, the film scratched and faded from its slow trip around the world. The theater consisted of a few dozen folding chairs arranged before a bed sheet or the blank wall of a vacant hangar out near the airstrip. Occasionally a man would sell warm soft drinks out of a cardboard box, but that was it in terms of concessions.

8   When I was young, I went to the theater at the nearby shopping center and watched a movie about a talking Volkswagen. I believe the little car had a taste for mischief, but I can't be certain, as both the movie and the afternoon proved unremarkable and have faded from my memory. Hugh saw the same movie a few years after it was released. His family had left the Congo by this time, and they were living in Ethiopia. Like me, Hugh saw the movie by himself on a weekend afternoon. Unlike me, he left the theater two hours later, to find a dead man hanging from a telephone pole at the far end of the unpaved parking lot. None of the people who'd seen the movie seemed to care about the dead man. They stared at him for a moment or two and then headed home, saying they'd never seen anything as crazy as that talking Volkswagen. His father was late picking him up, so Hugh just stood there for an hour, watching the dead man dangle and turn in the breeze. The death was not reported in the newspaper, and when Hugh related the story to his friends, they said, "You saw the movie about the talking car?"

9   I could have done without the flies and the primitive theaters, but I wouldn't have minded growing up with a houseful of servants. In North Carolina, it wasn't unusual to have a once-a-week maid, but Hugh's family had houseboys, a word that never fails to charge my imagination. They had cooks and drivers, and guards who occupied a gatehouse, armed with machetes. Seeing as I had regularly petitioned my parents for an electric fence, the business with the guards strikes me as the last word in quiet sophistication. Having protection suggests that you are important. Having that protection paid for by the government is even better, as it suggests your safety is of interest to someone other than yourself.

[1]Sedaris is referring to *My Favorite Martian*, *The Beverly Hillbillies*, and *Bewitched*, popular television shows in the 1960s.

10   Hugh's father was a career officer with the US State Department, and every morning a black sedan carried him off to the embassy. I'm told it's not as glamorous as it sounds, but in terms of fun for the entire family, I'm fairly confident that it beats the sack race at the annual IBM picnic. By the age of three, Hugh was already carrying a diplomatic passport. The rules that applied to others did not apply to him. No tickets, no arrests, no luggage search: He was officially licensed to act like a brat. Being an American, it was expected of him, and who was he to deny the world an occasional tantrum?

11   They weren't rich, but what Hugh's family lacked financially they more than made up for with the sort of exoticism that works wonders at cocktail parties, leading always to the remark, "That sounds fascinating." It's a compliment one rarely receives when describing an adolescence spent drinking **Icees** at the North Hills Mall. No fifteen-foot python ever wandered onto my school's basketball court. I begged, I prayed nightly, but it just never happened. Neither did I get to witness a military **coup** in which forces sympathetic to the colonel arrived late at night to assassinate my next-door neighbor. Hugh had been at the Addis Ababa teen club when the electricity was cut off, and soldiers arrived to evacuate the building. He and his friends had to hide in the back of a jeep and cover themselves with blankets during the ride home. It's something that sticks in his mind for one reason or another.

Icees:
Iced drinks

coup:
attempt to overthrow a government (coup d'etat)

12   Among my personal highlights is the memory of having my picture taken with Uncle Paul, the legally blind host of a Raleigh children's television show. Among Hugh's is the memory of having his picture taken with Buzz Aldrin on the last leg of the astronaut's world tour. The man who had walked on the moon placed his hand on Hugh's shoulder and offered to sign his autograph book. The man who led Wake County schoolchildren in afternoon song turned at the sound of my voice and asked, "So what's your name, princess?"

13   When I was fourteen years old, I was sent to spend ten days with my maternal grandmother in western New York State. She was a small and private woman named Billie, and though she never came right out and asked, I had the distinct impression she had no idea who I was. It was the way she looked at me, squinting through her glasses while chewing on her lower lip. That, coupled with the fact that she never once called me by name. "Oh," she'd say, "are you still here?" She was just beginning her long struggle with Alzheimer's disease, and each time I entered the room, I felt the need to reintroduce myself and set her at ease. "Hi, it's me. Sharon's boy, David. I was just in the kitchen admiring your collection of ceramic toads." Aside from a few trips to summer camp, this was the longest I'd ever been away from home, and I like to think I was toughened by the experience.

14   About the same time I was frightening my grandmother, Hugh and his family were packing their belongings for a move to Somalia. There were no English-speaking schools in Mogadishu, so, after a few months spent lying around the family compound with his pet monkey, Hugh was sent back to Ethiopia to live with a beer enthusiast his father had met at a cocktail party. Mr. Hoyt installed security systems in foreign embassies. He and his family gave Hugh a room. They invited him to join them at the table, but that was as far as they extended themselves. No one ever asked him when his birthday was, so when the day came, he kept it to himself. There was no telephone service between Ethiopia and Somalia, and letters to his parents were sent to Washington and then forwarded on to Mogadishu, meaning that his news was more than a month old by the time they got it. I suppose it wasn't much different than living as a foreign-exchange student. Young people do it all the time, but to me it sounds

A pet monkey

fortitude:
strength

awful. The Hoyts had two sons about Hugh's age who were always saying things like "Hey, that's *our* sofa you're sitting on" and "Hands off that ornamental stein. It doesn't belong to you."

15   He'd been living with these people for a year when he overheard Mr. Hoyt tell a friend that he and his family would soon be moving to Munich, Germany, the beer capital of the world. "And that worried me," Hugh said, "because it meant I'd have to find some other place to live."

16   Where I come from, finding shelter is a problem the average teenager might confidently leave to his parents. It was just something that came with having a mom and a dad. Worried that he might be sent to live with his grandparents in Kentucky, Hugh turned to the school's guidance counselor, who knew of a family whose son had recently left for college. And so he spent another year living with strangers and not mentioning his birthday. While I wouldn't have wanted to do it myself, I can't help but envy the sense of **fortitude** he gained from the experience. After graduating from college, he moved to France knowing only the phrase "Do you speak French?"—a question guaranteed to get you nowhere unless you also speak the language.

17   While living in Africa, Hugh and his family took frequent vacations, often in the company of their monkey. The Nairobi Hilton, some suite of high-ceilinged rooms in Cairo or Khartoum: These are the places his people recall when gathered at a common table. "Was that the summer we spent in Beirut or, no, I'm thinking of the time we sailed from Cyprus and took the *Orient Express* to Istanbul."

18   Theirs was the life I dreamt about during my vacations in eastern North Carolina. Hugh's family was hobnobbing with chiefs and sultans

while I ate hush puppies at the Sanitary Fish Market in Morehead City, a beach towel wrapped like a hijab around my head. Someone unknown to me was very likely standing in a muddy ditch and dreaming of an evening spent sitting in a clean family restaurant, drinking iced tea and working his way through an extra-large seaman's platter, but that did not concern me, as it meant I should have been happy with what I had.

19   Rather than surrender to my bitterness, I have learned to take satisfaction in the life that Hugh has led. His stories have, over time, become my own. I say this with no trace of a **kumbaya**. There is no spiritual symbiosis; I'm just a petty thief who lifts his memories the same way I'll take a handful of change left on his dresser. When my own experiences fall short of the mark, I just go out and spend some of his. It is with pleasure that I sometimes recall the dead man's purpled face or the report of the handgun ringing in my ears as I studied the blood pooling beneath the dead white piglet. On the way back from the slaughterhouse, we stopped for Cokes in the village of Mojo, where the gas-station owner had arranged a few tables and chairs beneath a dying canopy of vines. It was late afternoon by the time we returned to school, where a second bus carried me to the foot of Coffeeboard Road. Once there, I walked through a grove of eucalyptus trees and alongside a bald pasture of starving cattle, past the guard napping in his gatehouse, and into the warm arms of my monkey.

kumbaya:
The title of a spiritual song popular in the 1960s that was thought to have African ties and symbolized peace, harmony, and unity among people.

Teaching Tip:

Cooperative Learning (Jigsaw)
Ask students to read the text for homework or in class. Then divide the class into groups. Ask some groups to list the main points of the text and write a summary. Ask other groups to list about ten difficult words and phrases from the text and to define them from the context. Then pair the different groups and ask them to share their information.

COMPREHENSION AND CRITICAL THINKING

1. What is the meaning of *inane* in paragraph 7?
   a. fascinating   b. serious   c. ridiculous

2. Find a word in paragraph 7 that means "to reduce" or "to stop."

   wean

3. Underline the thesis statement. Remember that it may not be in the first paragraph.

4. Look in paragraph 4 and underline examples of imagery that appeal to hearing and sight.   Answers will vary.

5. How were the writer's school field trips different from Hugh's?

   Hugh saw bloody and frightening things, such as animals getting
   slaughtered or the bloody curtains of a dictator. David's field trips were
   to American historical sites.

6. What nationality is Hugh? Look carefully at paragraph 10.

   He is American because his father worked for the U.S. State Department.

7. Briefly describe the writer's childhood. Give a few details.

   He had a typical middle-class upbringing that included having pets,

   going to movies, and watching television. His daily existence was safe

   and secure.

8. In paragraph 13, the writer describes the summer he spent with his grandmother, and in paragraph 14, he describes Hugh's year with the Hoyt family. What are some similarities and differences in their experiences?

   They both felt lonely, ignored, and perhaps neglected. They were both

   toughened by the experience. However, the narrator probably knew that

   his grandmother did care about him at one time, whereas Hugh was

   truly unimportant to the Hoyts.

9. In paragraph 4, the writer describes Hugh's trip to a slaughterhouse. In paragraph 8, he describes Hugh's trip to a theater, and in paragraph 11, he discusses a military coup that Hugh witnessed. What do the anecdotes about Hugh's childhood have in common?

   Each event has an undercurrent of horror and violence.

10. The writer uses humor to describe his friend's childhood. How does humor affect the reader's perception of events?

    By using humor, the writer makes Hugh's childhood seem exotic, but the

    events described are about death and violence.

11. On the surface, the writer appears to envy Hugh's childhood. What is he also suggesting?

    Hugh's childhood was often filled with violence and loneliness whereas

    the author's childhood, although dull, was filled with love and security.

12. Think about the title. Why does Sedaris call this essay "My African Childhood"?

    Sedaris appropriates his friend's childhood memories. He wishes that

    he had lived the African childhood.

WRITING TOPICS

Write about one of the following topics. Remember to explore, develop, and revise and edit your work.

1. Describe a particularly happy, exciting, or dangerous moment in your childhood. Where were you? What happened? Include imagery that appeals to the senses.
2. Reflect on how you were parented. How do you parent your own children, or how would you like to parent your future children? Compare and contrast your parenting style with the style of the people who raised you.

Teaching Tip:
The suggested topics give students the opportunity to practice narrative, descriptive, and comparison and contrast writing. Specify whether students should write a paragraph or an essay.

READING 5

Living Environments

Avi Friedman

Avi Friedman is a professor at the McGill School of Architecture. In the following article, which appeared in the *Montreal Gazette*, Friedman reflects on designing an appropriate house for the individual needs of families.

1   When invited to design a home, I first like to know what kind of dwellers my clients are. In our first meeting, I ask them to take me on a guided tour of their current residence and describe how each room is used—when and by whom. Walking through hallways, scanning the interior of rooms, peeping into closets, looking at kitchen cupboards, and pausing at family photos have helped me devise several common categories of occupants.

2   The "neat" household regards the house as a gallery. The home is spotless. The placement of every item, be it hanging artwork, a memento on a shelf, or furniture, is highly choreographed. The color scheme is coordinated and the lighting superb. It feels as if one has walked into an *Architectural Digest* magazine spread. Recent trends, professional touches, and carefully selected pieces are the marks of the place.

3   The "utilitarian" family is very pragmatic. They are minimalists, believing that they get only what they need. Environmental concerns play an important role in buying goods. The place, often painted in light tones, is sparsely decorated with very few well-selected items. Souvenirs from a recent trip are displayed and some photos or paintings are on the wall. They will resist excess consumption and will squeeze as much use as they can from each piece.

4   The home of the "collector" family is stuffed to the brim. It is hard to find additional space for furniture or a wall area to hang a painting. Books, magazines, and weekend papers are everywhere. Newspaper cutouts and personal notes are crammed under magnets on the fridge door. The collector family seems to pay less attention to how things appear and more to comfort. Stress reduction is a motto. Being an excessively clean "show house" is not a concern. Placing dirty breakfast dishes in the sink and the morning paper in the rack before leaving home is not a priority as long as things are moving along.

Teaching Tip:
This classification essay also includes elements of illustration and argument.

5   Of course, these are only a few household types, but at the end of a house tour, I have a pretty good idea about my clients. More than the notes that I take during a meeting, these real-life images tell me all about my client's home life and desired domestic environment. <u>When I began practicing, I quickly realized house design is about people more than architecture.</u> As hard as I might try, I will never be able to tailor a new personality to someone by placing them in a trendy style, one that does not reflect who they really are. I can attempt to illustrate options other than their current life habits and decorating choices. But in the end, when they move into their new place, they will bring along their old habits.

6   <u>My experience has taught me some homeowners have been trying hard to emulate lifestyles and décors that are really not theirs.</u> The endless decorating shows on television and the many magazines that crowd supermarket racks provide a tempting opportunity to become someone else. Some homeowners are under constant pressure, it feels, to undergo extreme makeovers and borrow rather than mature into their natural selves. They search for a readymade packaged interior style rather than discovering their own.

7   I am often at a loss when clients ask me what style I subscribe to, or solicit advice on the style they are to adopt. <u>I reply that styles are trendy and comfort is permanent, and that they should see beyond the first day of occupancy into everyday living.</u> Sipping a freshly brewed coffee on the back porch on a summer Sunday and letting the morning paper litter the floor while watching a squirrel on the tree across the yard is a treasured moment. It will never be able to fit into a well-defined architectural style. Home design needs to create the backdrop for such opportunities. It is these types of moments that make us enjoy life.

8   If someone wants to read, why not have a wall of books? Does someone love listening to music? Then a music room or corner should be created, even if it is not trendy. Does someone want to interact with the children? He or she might add a hobby space, even if it is outdated and cannot be found in most magazines.

9   Referring to technological advances, the renowned French architect Le Corbusier once described the home as a "machine for living." It is partially true. Home is the site where mundane and utilitarian activities take place. It is also where special moments, uniquely ours, are created and treasured.

Teaching Tip:

Cooperative Learning (Pair & Share) Ask students to work with a partner to make a plan for this essay. Then students can join another pair and compare their essay plans.

COMPREHENSION AND CRITICAL THINKING

1.   Find a four-word expression in paragraph 4 that means "completely filled."

    stuffed to the brim

2. Find a word in paragraph 6 that means "to copy."

    to emulate

3. Underline the thesis statement.

4. Underline the topic sentences in paragraphs 2–7.

5. Paragraph 8 is missing a topic sentence. Which sentence best expresses the main idea of that paragraph?
    a. People can create a music room in their homes.
    b. Everybody should think about his or her likes and dislikes.
    c. People should create spaces in their homes to accommodate their personal interests.
    d. Hobby rooms and bookshelves can help make a home feel very unique.

6. How does Friedman assess the needs of families when designing a house?

    He takes a tour of the house and asks family members how they use

    each room. He also looks in the closets and cupboards and looks at

    family photos to get an idea of the family's lifestyle.

7. What are the three categories of households that Friedman describes in this article?

    neat   *utilitarian*   *collector*

8. In your own words, describe the characteristics for each type of household.

    The neat household is highly organized and spotless. It looks as if it is

    a model for Architectural Digest. The utilitarian household has minimal

    possessions, and its objects are very practical. The collector household

    is usually very full of objects.

9. a. What influences families when they choose a design for their homes?

    They are influenced by television and magazine makeovers.

    b. Does Friedman think that such influences are positive or negative? Explain your answer.

    He thinks the influences might be negative because people feel pressured

    to do home makeovers. They emulate styles that are not really their own.

10. According to Friedman, what is the most important factor that home design should take into consideration?

    Home design should allow families to enjoy moments of leisure and

    relaxation, such as drinking coffee and reading the newspaper on a porch.

Teaching Tip:
The suggested topics give students the opportunity to practice classification writing. Specify whether students should write a paragraph or an essay.

WRITING TOPICS

Write about one of the following topics. Remember to explore, develop, and revise and edit your work.

1. Use a different classification method to describe types of living environments.
2. Friedman writes, "Home is the site where mundane and utilitarian activities take place. It is also where special moments, uniquely ours, are created and treasured." Write about different categories of special or memorable moments.

Teaching Tip:
"Slum Tourism" is a definition essay, but it also contains elements of argument, cause and effect, and comparison and contrast.

READING 6

Slum Tourism
Eric Weiner

Eric Weiner is author of *The Geography of Bliss: One Grump's Search for the Happiest Places in the World.* In his essay, he defines and analyzes slum tourism.

The Dharavi slum in Mumbai, India

1   Michael Cronin's job as a college admissions officer took him to India two or three times a year, so he had already seen the usual sites—temples, monuments, and markets—when one day he happened across a flier advertising slum tours. "It just resonated with me immediately," said Mr. Cronin, who was staying at the posh Taj Hotel in Mumbai where, he noted, a bottle of Champagne cost the equivalent of two years' salary for many Indians. "But I didn't know what to expect," he said.

2   Soon, Mr. Cronin, forty-one years old, found himself skirting open sewers and ducking to avoid exposed electrical wires as he toured the sprawling Dharavi slum, home to more than a million. He joined a cricket game and saw the small-scale industry, from embroidery to tannery, which quietly thrives in the slum. "Nothing is considered garbage there," he said. "Everything is used again." Mr. Cronin was briefly shaken when a man, "obviously drunk," rifled through his pockets, but the two-and-a-half-hour tour changed his image of India. "Everybody in the slum wants to work, and everybody wants to make themselves better," he said.

3   Slum tourism, or "poorism," as some call it, is catching on. From the shantytowns of Rio de Janeiro to the townships of Johannesburg to the garbage dumps of Mexico, tourists are forsaking, at least for a while, beaches and museums for crowded, dirty—and in many ways surprising—slums. When a British man named Chris Way founded Reality Tours and Travel in Mumbai two years ago, he could barely **muster** enough customers for one tour a day. Now, he's running two or three a day and recently expanded to rural areas.

muster:
gather together

4   Slum tourism isn't for everyone. Critics charge that ogling the poorest of the poor isn't tourism at all. It's voyeurism. The tours are exploitative, these critics say, and have no place on an ethical traveler's itinerary. "Would you want people stopping outside of your front door every day, or maybe twice a day, snapping a few pictures of you and making some observations about your lifestyle?" asked David Fennell, a professor of tourism and environment at Brock University in Ontario. Slum tourism, he says, is just another example of tourism finding a new niche to exploit. The real purpose, he believes, is to make Westerners feel better about their station in life. "It affirms in my mind how lucky I am—or how unlucky they are," he states.

5   Not so fast, proponents of slum tourism say. Ignoring poverty won't make it go away. "Tourism is one of the few ways that you or I are ever going to understand what poverty means," says Harold Goodwin, director of the International Center for Responsible Tourism in Leeds, England. "To just kind of turn a blind eye and pretend that poverty doesn't exist seems to me a very denial of our humanity." The crucial question, Mr. Goodwin and other experts say, is not whether slum tours should exist but how they are conducted. Do they limit the excursions to small groups, interacting respectfully with residents? Or do they travel in buses, snapping photos from the windows as if on safari?

6   Many tour organizers are sensitive to charges of exploitation. Some encourage—and in at least one case require—participants to play an active role in helping residents. A church group in Mazatlán, Mexico, runs tours of the local garbage dump where scavengers earn a living picking through trash, some of it from nearby luxury resorts. The group doesn't charge anything but asks participants to help make sandwiches and fill bottles with filtered water. The tours have proven so popular that during high season the church group has to turn people away. "We see ourselves as a bridge to connect the tourists to the real world," said Fred Collom, the minister who runs the tours.

7   By most accounts, slum tourism began in Brazil sixteen years ago, when a young man named Marcelo Armstrong took a few tourists into Rocinha, Rio de Janeiro's largest favela, or shantytown. His company,

Favela Tour, grew and spawned half a dozen imitators. Today, on any given day in Rio, dozens of tourists hop in minivans, then motorcycles, and venture into places even Brazil's police dare not tread. Organizers insist the tours are safe, though they routinely check security conditions. Luiz Fantozzi, founder of the Rio-based Be a Local Tours, says that about once a year he cancels a tour for security reasons.

8   The tours may be safe, but they can be tense. Rajika Bhasin, a lawyer from New York, recalls how, at one point during a favela tour, the guide told everyone to stop taking pictures. A young man approached the group, smiling and holding a cocked gun. Ms. Bhasin said she didn't exactly feel threatened, "just very aware of my surroundings, and aware of the fact that I was on this guy's turf." Still, she said, the experience, which included visiting galleries featuring the work of local artists, was positive. "Honestly, I would say it was a life-changing experience," Ms. Bhasin said. Saying she understood the objections, she **parried**, "It has everything to do with who you are and why you're going."

parried:
replied

9   Chuck Geyer, of Reston, Virginia, arrived for a tour in Mumbai armed with hand sanitizer and the expectation of human misery incarnate. He left with a changed mind. Instead of being solicited by beggars, Mr. Geyer found himself the recipient of gifts: fruit, and dye to smear on his hands and face, as people celebrated the Hindu festival of Holi. "I was shocked at how friendly and gracious these people were," Mr. Geyer said.

10   Proponents of slum tourism say that's the point: to change the reputation of the slums one tourist at a time. Tour organizers say they provide employment for local guides and a chance to sell souvenirs. Chris Way has vowed to put 80 percent of his profits back into the Dharavi slum. The catch, though, is that Mr. Way's company has yet to earn a profit on the tours, for which he charges 300 rupees (around $7.50). After receiving flak from the Indian press ("a fair criticism," Mr. Way **concedes**), he used his own money to open a community center in the slum. It offers English classes, and Mr. Way himself mentors a chess club. Many of those running favela tours in Brazil also channel a portion of their profits into the slums. Luiz Fantozzi contributes to a school and day-care center.

concedes:
acknowledges

11   But slum tourism isn't just about charity, its proponents say; it also fosters an entrepreneurial spirit. "At first, the tourists were **besieged** by beggars, but not anymore," said Kevin Outterson, a law professor from Boston who has taken several favela tours. Mr. Fantozzi has taught people, Mr. Outterson said, "that you're not going to get anything from my people by begging, but if you make something, people are going to buy it."

besieged:
overtaken

12   Even critics of slum tourism concede it allows a few dollars to trickle into the shantytowns, but say that's no substitute for development programs. Mr. Fennell, the professor of tourism in Ontario, wonders

whether the relatively minuscule tourist revenue can make a difference. "If you're so concerned about helping these people, then write a check," he said.

COMPREHENSION AND CRITICAL THINKING

1. In paragraph 3, what is the meaning of *forsaking*? Read the word in context before making your guess.

   <u>giving up; doing without</u>

2. In paragraph 4, find a word that means "staring."

   <u>ogling</u>

3. In your own words, define slum tourism.

   <u>Rich foreign tourists travel to third-world countries and go sightseeing</u>

   <u>in slums.</u>

4. How did slum tourism develop?

   <u>Marcelo Armstrong took a group of people to a Brazilian slum sixteen</u>

   <u>years ago.</u>

5. What are some criticisms of slum tourism?   Answers will vary.

   <u>It exploits poor people. It is voyeurism. It encourages Westerners to</u>

   <u>have a superior attitude about their own situation in life.</u>

6. What arguments support slum tourism criticism?   Answers will vary.

   <u>By going into a slum, people recognize that poverty exists. Most slum</u>

   <u>tour agencies get involved in helping people in the slum. It can also help</u>

   <u>slum dwellers become entrepreneurs.</u>

7. List two examples of how people's outlook was changed when they toured slums.

   <u>Mr. Cronin saw that poor people worked hard and wanted to better</u>

   <u>themselves. Chuck Geyer saw how friendly and gracious people in</u>

   <u>Dharavi were. Rajika Bhasin called her tour "a life-changing experience."</u>

8. What are some unwritten rules tourists should follow when they tour slums?

   <u>They should not stop in doorways and take photographs, they should</u>

   <u>not give money to beggars, they should be careful about their personal</u>

   <u>safety, and they should help the local economy by buying souvenirs.</u>

Teaching Tip:

Cooperative Learning (Sharing Circle) Ask students to work in groups of three and share answers to the questions. They can also discuss the writing topics. Then take up the answers with the class.

Teaching Tip: Engage students in a discussion about slum tourism and how they would feel about slum tourism in American cities. Also discuss tourism in wealthy areas. For examples, there are tours of stars' homes in Beverly Hills.

9.   According to the article, what is the best way to help slum dwellers?

People should buy items, show respect, and donate money to

development projects.

Teaching Tip:
The suggested
writing topics give
students the
opportunity to
practice definition,
comparison and
contrast, and
argument writing.

WRITING TOPICS

1.   What is the opposite of a slum? Come up with a new term for a wealthy neighborhood and define it. Use examples to support your definition.
2.   Compare two very different places that you have visited. You can compare two neighborhoods, two towns, or a rural area with an urban area.
3.   Is touring a slum *tourism* or *voyeurism*? Argue your point of view by using examples from your own city, state, or country.

Theme: Commerce and Marketing

READING 7

Medicating Ourselves
Robyn Sarah

Teaching Tip:
This argument essay
also contains
elements of process,
cause and effect,
and narration.

Robyn Sarah is a poet and a writer. Her work has appeared in *The Threepenny Review*, *New England Review*, and *The Hudson Review*, and she is a frequent contributor to the *Montreal Gazette*. In the next essay, Sarah reflects on society's overreliance on medication.

1   It is hard to pick up a magazine these days without finding an article attacking or defending some pharmaceutical remedy for syndromes of mood or behavior. These drugs are in vogue because they have shown themselves spectacularly effective for a range of conditions, though their exact workings are not well understood and their long-term effects are not known. Yet for all the noise we continue to hear about, say, Ritalin, for children with attention deficit disorders and related learning or behavior problems—or Prozac and the new family of anti-depressants prescribed to the stressed and distressed of all ages—the real debate on pharmaceuticals has yet to begin.

2   The enormous strides science has made in understanding brain chemistry have precipitated a revolution no less significant than the "cyber-revolution" now transforming our lives. The biochemical model has brought relief to many suffering individuals and families, removing devastating symptoms and lifting blame from parents whose contorted

anomalous:
unusual

responses to a child's **anomalous** behavior were once mistaken for its cause. But the very effectiveness of corrective pharmacology engenders an insidious imperative: we can, therefore we must. The realization that we

can chemically fine-tune personalities—that we may be able to "fix"
what were once believed innate flaws of character—has staggering
implications for our understanding of morality, our standards for
acceptable behavior, our mental pain threshold, and our expectations
of self and others.

3   The medication debate should not be a matter of "whether or not,"
but of where to stop. Mental illness is real and can be life-threatening.
But when is something truly a disorder, and when are we **pathologizing**
human difference, natural human cycles and processes? How do we
decide what needs fixing, and who should decide? These are not simple
matters.

pathologizing: making a disease of

4   During my own school years, the boy who today would be prescribed
Ritalin used to spend a lot of time standing in the hall outside the
classroom. His "bad boy" reputation dogged him year to year and became
part of his self-image. He learned to wheel-and-deal his way out of trouble
by a combination of charm and **subterfuge**; he learned to affect a rakish
persona to mask what anger he might feel about his **pariah** status. But in
spite of his often superior intelligence, anything else he learned in school
was hit-and-miss. Such "bad boys" rarely lasted beyond the second year of
high school.

subterfuge: evasion

pariah: outcast

5   Defenders of Ritalin point out that in making it possible for such
a child to focus and sustain attention, to complete tasks and take
satisfaction from them, the stimulant breaks a cycle of disruptive behavior,
punishment, anger, and acting out. Begun early, Ritalin can prevent the
battering of self-esteem such children undergo in school; introduced later,
it allows a child to rebuild self-esteem. These are powerful arguments
for a drug that, when it works, can effect what seems a miraculous
transformation in a "problem child," giving him a new lease on life in
a system that used to chew him up and spit him out.

6   But Ritalin is not a benign drug, and many are alarmed at the
frequency and casualness with which it is prescribed (often at the school's
prompting) for a disorder that has no conclusive medical diagnosis. Some
argue that children who may simply be high-spirited, less compliant, or
more physically energetic than the norm are being "drugged" for the
convenience of teachers and smooth classroom functioning. Others
wonder if the frequency of **ADD** and **ADHD** diagnoses says more about
the state of schools than it does about the state of children. Do our
schools give children enough physical exercise, enough structure and
discipline, or enough real challenge? A proliferation of troublemakers
can be an indication of something wrong in the classroom—witness
any class with an inexperienced substitute teacher. Pills to modify the
behavior of "disturbers" may restore order—at the cost of masking the
true problem.

ADD: attention-deficit disorder

ADHD: attention-deficit hyperactivity disorder

7   Something similar may be going on as diagnoses of depression and other disorders proliferate, especially among groups in the throes of life change (adolescent, mid-life, or geriatric). Just as physical pain is our body's way of alerting us to a problem, psychic pain can be a response to our changed position in the world. Psychic pain might indicate that we should reorient ourselves by reassessing and rebuilding our primary relationships. If I swallow a pill to conceal my existential problems—an "equanimity" pill—I may be easier to live with, but I may also be masking the need for some fundamental work to be done, some exercise of the spirit. Giving a boost to my brain chemistry might help me do this work, but it is just as likely to take away the urgency to do it.

8   I am myself no stranger to depression, but in eschewing the chemical solution, I have begun to sense I am swimming against the tide. For a while, I felt all the worse because so many of my peers, with lives no less complicated than mine, seemed to be handling mid-life pressures better than I was. Slowly it emerged that several had taken antidepressants at some point "to get over a rough spot." Some are still taking them.

9   The arguments are seductive. Why make things harder for ourselves, and why inflict our angst on others, when there is an alternative? One father I know, the stay-at-home parent of small children, told me he put himself back on Prozac (originally prescribed for migraines) because under stress he tended to be irritable, and things were more stressful with a new baby in the house. His irritability was not something he wanted to inflict on his children. Who could fault him for such a decision?

"Happy pills"

10   If we can really smooth our rough edges by popping a pill, why not make life pleasanter for our loved ones and associates by popping a pill? If a pill can make saints of us all, where is the virtue in resisting this pill? But the effect may be to mask how many people would otherwise be doing "badly," which not only induces the unmedicated to bash themselves for their human frailties, but blinds us all to societal ills that may explain why so many of us get depressed.

11   The new pharmaceutical culture could stigmatize the unmedicated. It could make us all less tolerant of our frailties and those of others. It could keep us reconciled to the values that have put us in the pressure cooker to begin with: the worship of youth and success, the pursuit of comfort and expediency, and a model of wellness based on uninterrupted productivity.

12   Shall we lose the sense of what it is to be unique, struggling, evolving souls in the world, and instead use designer drugs to make ourselves smooth-functioning cogs of an unexamined societal machine? Aldous Huxley predicted it in 1932, in his Utopian novel *Brave New World*. Remember the drug *soma*? It has "the advantages of Christianity and alcohol; none of their defects [. . .]. Anyone can be virtuous now. You can carry half your morality around in a bottle." Huxley's book, on the high school reading list a generation ago, enjoys that same place today. But I am beginning to think the satire may have been lost on us. Perhaps it was too late for the message even when he wrote it. With our complicity, his vision gets closer every day.

COMPREHENSION AND CRITICAL THINKING

1.   In paragraph 7, what does *proliferate* mean? _____*increase*_____

2.   Define the word *stigmatize* in paragraph 11. ____*brand, isolate, label*____

3.   In your own words, explain the essay's main point.

      The overuse of new medications influences our behavior, our values, and

      our expectations.

      _____

4.   In which paragraph(s) does the writer acknowledge an opposing viewpoint?

      paragraphs 2, 5, and 10

5.   Which strategies does the writer use to support her argument? There is more than one answer.
      (a.) fact   d. statistics
      (b.) anecdote   (e.) logical consequences
      c. quotations from informed sources

      For each type of support that you have identified, underline a sentence from the text.   Answers will vary.

6.   Using your own words, list at least four of the writer's main arguments.

      Behavior modification drugs may only hide the problem, not cure it.

      Perhaps children misbehave in schools because of the structure of the

      school day.

      Overprescribing drugs may not allow people to deal with the causes of

      their problems. Those who do not take any medication may feel deficient

      or even marginalized in a society that favors the use of medication.

      In certain circumstances, taking medication to modify behavior makes

      people less unique.

Teaching Tip:

Cooperative Learning (Jigsaw) Ask students to read the text for homework or in class. Then divide the class into groups of three to four students. Ask some groups to list the main points of the text and write a summary. Ask other groups to list about ten difficult words and phrases from the text and to define them from the context. A third set of groups can answer the comprehension questions. Then ask students to share their information.

Teaching Tip:
Ask students to
infer the answers to
questions 7 and 8.

7. The writer suggests some causes of overmedicating in our culture. What are they?

   It provides a simple solution for mental disorders, it lifts blame from parents, it controls children's behavior, and people have great confidence in science.

8. What are some of the effects of using medication to modify behavior problems?

   People do not examine their behavior; sightly eccentric behavior becomes unacceptable.

9. How does the writer conclude her essay?
   a. suggestion   b. prediction   c. call to action

10. Why does the writer quote Aldous Huxley in her concluding paragraph?

    Huxley predicted a world in which people use drugs to alter personality differences to control behavior.

Teaching Tip:
The suggested
topics give students
the opportunity to
practice argument
and process writing.
Topic 2 is a research
essay topic. Students
should review
Chapter 16.

WRITING TOPICS

Write about one of the following topics. Remember to explore, develop, and revise and edit your work.

1. Argue for the use of mood-altering drugs.
2. Argue that vaccinations should or should not be mandatory. You will have to do some research and support your points with the opinions of experts. See Chapter 16 for information about writing a research essay.
3. What are some of the mental and physical processes people go through to keep looking or feeling good?

READING 8

Brands R Us

Stephen Garey

Teaching Tip:
"Brands R Us" is an
argument essay, but
it also has elements
of cause and effect
and process.

Stephen Garey is a writer and a former advertising industry creative executive. He has published many articles about consumption and the environment. In the following essay, he makes a powerful argument about advertising.

1   Most people don't believe, don't remember, and don't think about advertising. Focus groups and other forms of testing have proven time and time again that the majority of ads are inefficient and ineffective. Indeed,

it's been estimated that some 80–85 percent of all advertising is neither consciously "seen" nor remembered by the consuming public. Within a few minutes after being exposed to an advertising message and brand, consumers have a hard time remembering the message or the brand that delivered it!

2   And yet, there's a direct connection between an individual's level of exposure to advertising and levels of product consumption. How can this be? If advertising is largely ineffective, if most advertising is neither seen nor remembered by most people, and if—two minutes after being exposed to a particular message or brand—consumers can't remember the brand or the message, then where's the connection? How does something so seemingly **benign** and banal impact consumption patterns and habits?

benign:
harmless

3   While we may not be paying much attention to each and every individual message that comes our way, the collective effect of all this advertising is quite powerful. All during our waking hours, some 3,000 to 5,000 messages per day *per individual* are instructing us to Buy, Buy, Buy and Buy Some More. Sometimes these messages are delivered quietly. Many times the advertisers shout them from the rooftops. But no matter how these messages are delivered to us—and as much as we might tend to consider advertising mere background or "wallpaper" in our day-to-day lives—there's little doubt that advertising *as a whole* strongly influences overall consumer behavior. In other words, by itself, the advertising for Hyundai automobiles has little effect upon one's personal life. But Hyundai ads combined with Apple Computer ads, Tide detergent TV commercials, Chivas Regal outdoor boards, GE television program sponsorships and Johnson's Floor Wax coupons in the Sunday newspaper—not to mention the specials down each and every aisle at the local department store or supermarket—have a very powerful *collective* effect indeed.

Advertisements in Times Square, New York

4   Because advertising is generally so lighthearted and entertaining, this collective messaging practically gives us permission to ignore the long-term consequences of our daily purchasing decisions. The almost comedic presentation of most advertising carries with it the underlying suggestion that we shouldn't take any of it too seriously.

5   But we should . . . and we must.

6   At one time, advertising's collective message to buy—and to replace what we have rather than repair what we have—served us well. When we were far fewer in numbers, when nations and communities were growing and businesses large and small were trying to build their customer base, consumption of goods in high volume was not only desirable, it was also respectable. But our population has exploded, and we're no longer

naïve about the hazards of our consumer culture. It's all too clear that advertising's collective power and our collective responses to it over time have had a profound, often adverse, impact upon people's lives and the planet we all share.

wanton:
unrestrained

7   **Wanton** consumption now presents serious dangers to our health and well-being. It's a way of life that has outlived its usefulness, and what needs to change is *us*, not the advertising that influences us. We need to change our view of advertising as a banal and benign medium and fully recognize its powerful, collective effect.

Teaching Tip:

Cooperative Learning (Pair & Share)
Ask students to work with a partner to make a plan for this essay. Then students can compare their plans with another pair of students.

8   We most certainly need to reduce consumption, and one of the first steps we can take towards consuming fewer unnecessary goods is to consume less advertising. Keep counters in the kitchen free of brand names; use unbranded containers. Take the roads less traveled: Use local streets at the edge of town and the old back highways as a way of avoiding exposure to commercial clutter. Steer clear of T-shirt advertising: Why should you be a walking, unpaid billboard? Watch less commercial television; listen to less commercial radio. Implementing just one or two of these suggestions can help you consume less advertising and, in turn, fewer products. And that's the whole idea.

COMPREHENSION AND CRITICAL THINKING

1.   What is the meaning of *adverse* in paragraph 6?

         negative or unfavorable

2.   Who is the audience for this essay?

         The general public

3.   There is no clear thesis in the opening paragraphs. Instead, the writer builds his argument. Using your own words, describe the main point, or thesis, of the essay.   Answers will vary.

Advertising, which inundates us and convinces us to constantly buy, is

dangerous for our health and the health of the planet.

4.   What is the main point of paragraph 3?

The numerous ads that consumers are exposed to influence them to

consume more.

5.   How does listing so many brand names in paragraph 3 help the writer's argument?

The brand names are universally recognized and reinforce the notion

that our exposure to brands is overwhelming.

6. The writer mentions that advertising in the past had a positive effect. What was it?

In the past, advertising helped economies grow.

7. In paragraphs 6 and 7, the writer says that overconsumption presents serious dangers to our health and our planet. Infer or guess what dangers he is referring to. Answers will vary.

There will be increasing pollution, depletion of resources, consumer debt, obesity, and so on.

8. List at least three steps that consumers should take to reduce the negative effect of advertising. Answers will vary.

Don't have brand names on your counters, avoid commercial areas, don't wear T-shirts with ads on them, and so on.

9. How does the writer conclude the essay?
   a. prediction   b. suggestion   c. quotation

WRITING TOPICS

Write about one of the following topics. Remember to explore, develop, and revise and edit your work.

1. Should advertising aimed at children be banned? Explain your answer.
2. Kalle Lasn, founder of *Adbursts* magazine, says, "Advertisements are the most prevalent and toxic of the mental pollutants." Agree or disagree with this statement. Develop your argument with specific examples.
3. Many brands have cult-like devotees. For example, Apple computers and Harley Davidson motorcycles have fanatic followers. Describe someone who is a "brand fan" and explain which brands that person loves. Another option is to choose some major brands, and describe the types of people who love those brands.

Teaching Tip:
The suggested writing topics give students the opportunity to practice argument, cause and effect, and definition writing.

READING 9

The Rich Resonance of Small Talk
Roxanne Roberts

Teaching Tip:
This process essay also has elements of narration, illustration, and argument.

Roxanne Roberts is a staff writer for the *Washington Post*. In the next article, she muses about the importance of small talk.

1   I talk too much. The good news is that I can enter a room full of strangers, walk up to anyone, and start yammering away. The bad news is . . . well, you can guess that I bore people. All things considered, this has worked out pretty well. In my sixteen years as a social reporter for a

newspaper, I've marched up to presidents, movie stars, and kings and felt unafraid to make small talk, otherwise known as the mother's milk of party coverage. I have an advantage, of course, in that I have a press pass and a notebook.

2   But small talk is a big deal for everyone; it is one of those essential social skills that separate the men from the boys. The ability to connect in short, casual conversations can make or break careers, friendships, and romances—it's how we gather information, and hopefully, make a favorable impression. <u>There are only three golden rules for small talk: First, shut up and listen; second, when in doubt, repeat Rule 1; third, get others to talk about themselves.</u>

3   First, Rule 1 and Rule 2 take a lifetime for the average extrovert or egomaniac to master. To listen that intently, to focus with every muscle, takes not only great skill but also great discipline, which is why mere mortals fall short. It is so easy to respond to a casual comment by unwittingly turning the spotlight back on yourself: "You're going to Italy? We stayed at this great little place outside of Florence." It seems so natural—your small talk might be helpful, witty, and even relevant, but you're nonetheless talking instead of listening—and you can never learn anything while talking, except that you talk too much.

4   In the meantime, there are a few other tricks for small talk with strangers and acquaintances. For example, introduce yourself by name, even if you think they know it. "I don't think we've met. I'm Queen Elizabeth II." It's gracious, it's efficient, and it's smart. It's very awkward when someone starts a conversation with "Remember me?" and you don't. Second, ask simple questions. "What do you think of the [party, conference, cheese puffs]?" Then listen. When you run into a casual acquaintance, ask what he or she has been doing lately. Then listen. Ask follow-up questions based on the answers. If you are genuinely interested, most people will be surprised and flattered. Resist the temptation to display your own special brand of brilliance, and when you catch yourself doing so, shift the focus back. Later on, when the relationship has evolved beyond small talk, you can strut your fabulousness.

5   Furthermore, mastering the art of small talk is important for drawing shy people into a conversation. If this is done right, they walk away thinking *you're* great. "A great small talker is someone who has three to four open-ended questions that make the person open up," says Ann Stock, former White House social secretary for the Clintons and currently the vice president of the Kennedy Center. "It ignites something in them that makes them start talking. After that, you ask leading questions."

6   Use your body language. There's nothing worse than chatting with people who simultaneously scan the room for someone more important.

Give someone your full and real attention during your conversation. Face him or her directly, and look in his eyes. Never underestimate small talk—even though many people dread it or think it's silly, boring, or superficial.

7   Once in a rare while, someone comes along who innately gets it and turns a brief, casual moment into a truly memorable encounter. Former president Bill Clinton is a genius at it. In the course of two minutes, he can lock eyes with a person, ask a seemingly simple question, and make a person feel as if she were the center of the universe. Clinton's remarkable memory for names and faces means he can meet someone and—months or years later—ask about his or her family or golf game. People are shocked and delighted.

8   Another legendary master at the art of small talk was the late Pamela Harriman, Democratic fundraiser, ambassador to France, and the woman once called the "greatest courtesan of the century"—a nod to her many high-profile lovers. What set her apart was her laser-like ability to make anyone feel as if he were the most important person in the room. She wanted to know everything about the people she met. She hung on to every word and seldom talked about herself. She made people feel as if they were brilliant, under-appreciated jewels. "She had the power to make people want to talk with her," William Pfaff wrote in the *International Herald Tribune* shortly after her death in 1997. "She was—or certainly made herself seem to be—interested in everyone with whom she spoke, and in what they had to say. She, in turn, had something intelligent to say to them." She was not, he wrote, an intellectual or particularly sophisticated in matters of international relations. She knew enough to ask the right questions. But mostly she let others do the talking: "The willingness to listen is seduction itself—certainly to vain men, and in the world in which she functioned, all men are vain."

9   Finally, consider the famous story about British Prime Minister Benjamin Disraeli and his great political rival, William Gladstone. Legend has it that a lady was taken to dinner one evening by Gladstone and the next by Disraeli. When asked her impression of the two men, she replied, "When I left the dining room after sitting next to Mr. Gladstone, I thought he was the cleverest man in England. But after sitting next to Mr. Disraeli, I thought I was the cleverest woman in England."

COMPREHENSION AND CRITICAL THINKING

1.   What is the meaning of *nod to* in paragraph 8?
        a. acknowledgment of
        b. an indication of agreement
        c. falling asleep

Teaching Tip:

Cooperative Learning (Sharing Circle) Ask students to work in groups of three and share answers to the questions. They can also discuss the writing topics. Then take up the answers with the class.

2. Underline the thesis statement.

3. Why does the author begin the introductory paragraph with the first-person pronoun *I*, but use third-person pronouns for the rest of the essay?

    The initial anecdote arouses the reader's interest.

4. Why does the author think that learning the art of small talk is important?

    Small talk allows people to advance their careers, make friends, and

    make a favorable impression on others.

5. Using your own words, list at least five pieces of advice the author gives to master the art of small talk.

    Introduce yourself, listen to others, get others to talk about

    themselves, ask open-ended questions, and let people know they are the

    focus of your attention.

6. According to Roberts, why is it difficult for people to follow the first rule of small talk?

    It is difficult because people have a tendency to bring the conversation

    around to themselves. People want to demonstrate their knowledge.

7. Why does the author use Bill Clinton and Pamela Harriman as examples to support her thesis?

    Both Clinton and Harriman were experts at small talk.

8. How are Clinton's and Harriman's strategies for making small talk similar?

    Both of them had the ability to make others feel "important"—as if

    they were "the center of the universe."

9. How are Clinton's and Harriman's strategies for making small talk different?

    Clinton impressed people with his ability to remember names and faces.

    He also remembered details about people. Harriman had the ability to

    make people feel valued, as if they were "under-appreciated jewels."

10. How is the anecdote in the concluding paragraph a good support for mastering the art of small talk?

    Disraeli made the lady feel as if she were the focus of his attention,

    thereby demonstrating that he had mastered the author's rule 3.

    Therefore, it is better to make people feel they are as important as,

    if not more important than, you are.

WRITING TOPICS

Write about one of the following topics. Remember to explore, develop, and revise and edit your work.

1. Explain steps that people can take to have better relationships with their life partners.
2. Describe a process people can go through to make their guests feel more comfortable. You can discuss houseguests, dinner guests, or party guests.

Theme: Forces of Nature

READING 10

Weird Weather
Pamela D. Jacobsen

Pamela D. Jacobsen is a journalist who writes for *The Christian Science Monitor*. In the next article, she reflects on some strange weather phenomena.

1   How's this for a weather forecast? "Temperatures in the low 70s tonight, with a slight chance of raining frogs. Thunderstorms tomorrow, with ball lightning and perhaps a few elves." Frogs from the sky? Ball-shaped lightning and elves? Can that be right? It can. There are several types of weird weather that confound us.

2   We've all heard the old saying "It's raining cats and dogs," yet we don't expect a downpour of small mammals. But frogs, fish, maggots, and even beer cans have fallen with rain. Falling frogs and fish can occur "with any tornado or waterspout that goes over a body of water with frogs and fish," says Marcin Szumowski. He's an assistant professor at the Desert Research Institute in Reno, Nevada. Swirling winds moving over bodies of water can suck up small creatures or light objects. They may be carried for many miles before falling as odd rain. On July 12, 1873, *Scientific American* reported that a storm in Kansas City, Missouri, had blanketed the city with frogs.

3   Another strange weather phenomenon is ball-shaped lightning. The ancient Greeks reported seeing strange glowing balls moving across the sky. The luminous globes are called ball (or globe) lightning. Sometimes ball lightning is the size of a baseball, but it can be up to six feet across. Dr. Szumowski says ball lightning is generally "red, or red and yellow, changing to white, and disappearing with a loud bang." It may also leave a bad smell behind. (The odor is believed to be caused by ozone.) It usually lasts for only twenty seconds or so, but it can linger for many minutes. Ball lightning travels in weird ways. Eyewitnesses describe it moving parallel to the ground. It may also descend vertically from clouds or bounce! It can

Teaching Tip: The suggested topics give students the opportunity to practice process writing. Specify whether students should write a paragraph or an essay.

Teaching Tip: This illustration essay also has elements of description and cause and effect.

Whirling dust

hiss, too. While it's very startling, it does little damage. Scientists don't exactly know what ball lightning is or why it acts the way it does. It may be glowing plasma (electrically charged gas) trapped in a series of magnetic fields.

4   Whirling dust and whirling fire are a third puzzling weather occurrence. Dust devils are swirling columns of air full of sand and debris. Columns can be 3,000 feet tall and from three to several hundred feet in diameter. They most often occur at midday in arid regions when the ground temperature is at least 68 degrees Fahrenheit hotter than the air directly above. When dust is picked up by the swirling air, a dust devil is seen. They are like mini-tornadoes but with important differences. Tornadoes develop underneath thunderstorms whereas dust devils form when the weather is clear, hot, and dry. Sometimes, a dust devil picks up more than sand. According to Szumowski at the Desert Research Institute, dust devils may also suck up flames from a nearby forest fire. It doesn't happen often, but when it does, it creates "a spectacular image of a rotating fire rope."

5   Elves are the latest of the strange weather phenomena to be documented. Elves look like huge bluish or white disks or cone-shaped light coming from the top of a thunderstorm. Some grow to be 250 miles or more in diameter, and they can extend 60 miles into the air. Elves may be produced when electromagnetic pulses move through the ionosphere, which is the atmospheric layer containing electrically charged air. The pulses could come from radio waves within the lightning flashes themselves. Elves last less than 1/1000th of a second. Like those impish creatures in fairy tales, they are gone <u>in the blink of an eye</u>!

6   The next time you look at the sky, consider the mysterious weather incidents that can occur. Sometimes reality is stranger than fiction.

COMPREHENSION AND CRITICAL THINKING

1.   Circle a word in paragraph 1 that means "mystify."

2.   Circle a word in paragraph 3 that is the opposite of "dull" or "dark."

3.   Underline a cliché in paragraph 5. Suggest a standard alternative for the cliché.

    quickly

4.   Underline the thesis statement.

5. List the four different types of weird weather phenomena described in this article.

   a rain of small mammals and fish; ball-shaped lightning; whirling dust

   and fire; and elves

6. How is it possible for living creatures to fall from the sky?

   According to the article, winds blowing over bodies of water can pick up

   fish and small mammals and carry them for many miles.

7. How can whirling fires occur?

   Dust devils suck up flames from forest fires.

8. What type of support does the author use to back her thesis? (You can choose more than one answer.)
   (a.) expert opinion   (b.) facts   (c.) examples   d. statistics

9. Throughout history, what have people probably attributed weird weather events to?   Answers will vary.

   Probably many people throughout history have attributed such events

   to supernatural powers.

10. Generally, what causes the weird weather events described in the essay?

    The events are always caused by a set of unusual natural occurrences.

WRITING TOPICS

Write about one of the following topics. Remember to explore, develop, and revise and edit your work.

1. How does the weather in different places affect people's lifestyles? Support your response with examples.
2. What are some inventions that humans have developed to deal with different types of weather? Give examples of specific inventions and the weather conditions that they deal with.

READING 11

The Rules of Survival
Laurence Gonzales

> Laurence Gonzales won the National Magazine Award in 2001 and 2002. His work has appeared in such publications as *Harper's*, *National Geographic Adventure*, and *Smithsonian Air and Space*, just to name a few. The next excerpt is from his latest book, *Deep Survival*.

Teaching Tip:
The suggested topics give students the opportunity to practice illustration writing.

Teaching Tip:
Some possible inventions could be air conditioners, fireplaces, humidifiers, fans, windshield wipers, umbrellas, insulation in walls, weather-specific clothing, and new types of heating sources such as geothermal energy.

Teaching Tip:
This process essay also explains causes and effects and contains examples of narrative and descriptive writing.

1   As a journalist, I've been writing about accidents for more than thirty years. In the last fifteen or so years, I've concentrated on accidents in outdoor recreation in an effort to understand who lives, who dies, and why. To my surprise, I found an eerie uniformity in the way people survive seemingly impossible circumstances. Decades and sometimes centuries apart, separated by culture, geography, race, language, and tradition, the most successful survivors—those who practice what I call "deep survival"—go through the same patterns of thought and behavior, the same transformation and spiritual discovery, in the course of keeping themselves alive. It doesn't seem to matter whether they are surviving being lost in the wilderness or battling cancer; the strategies remain the same.

2   Survival should be thought of as a journey or vision quest of the sort that Native Americans have had as a rite of passage for thousands of years. Once people pass the precipitating event—for instance, they are cast away at sea or told they have cancer—they are enrolled in one of the oldest schools in history. Here are a few things I've learned about survival.

Stay Calm

3   In the initial crisis, survivors are not ruled by fear; instead, they make use of it. Their fear often feels like (and turns into) anger, which motivates them and makes them feel sharper. Aron Ralston, the hiker who had to cut off his hand to free himself from a stone that had trapped him in a slot canyon in Utah, initially panicked and began slamming himself over and over against the boulder that had caught his hand. But very quickly he stopped himself, did some deep breathing, and began thinking about his options. He eventually spent five days progressing through the stages necessary to convince him of what decisive action he had to take to save his own life.

Lance Armstrong

Think, Analyze, and Plan

4   Survivors quickly organize, set up routines, and institute discipline. When Lance Armstrong was diagnosed with cancer, he organized his fight against it the way he would organize his training for a race. He read everything he could about it, put himself on a training schedule, and put together a team from among friends, family, and doctors to support his efforts. Such conscious, organized effort in the face of grave danger requires a split between reason and emotion in which reason gives direction and emotion provides the power source. Survivors often report experiencing reason as an audible "voice."

5   Steve Callahan, a sailor and boat designer, was rammed by a whale, and his boat sunk while he was on a solo voyage in 1982. Adrift in the Atlantic for seventy-six days on a five-and-a-half-foot raft, he experienced his survival voyage as taking place under the command of a "captain" who gave him his orders and kept him on his water ration, even as his own mutinous (emotional) spirit complained. His captain routinely lectured "the crew." Thus under strict control, he was able to push away thoughts that his situation was hopeless and take the necessary first steps of the survival journey: to think clearly, analyze his situation, and formulate a plan.

Celebrate Every Victory

6   Survivors take great joy from even their smallest successes. This attitude helps keep motivation high and prevents a lethal plunge into hopelessness. It also provides relief from the unspeakable strain of a life-threatening situation.

7   Lauren Elder was the only survivor of a light plane crash in the High Sierra. Stranded on a 12,000 foot peak, one arm broken, she could see the San Joaquin Valley in California below, but a vast wilderness and sheer and icy cliffs separated her from safety. Wearing a wrap-around skirt and blouse but no underwear, with two-inch heeled boots, she crawled "on all fours, doing a kind of sideways spiderwalk," as she put it later, "balancing myself on the ice crust, punching through it with my hands and feet." She had thirty-six hours of climbing ahead of her—a seemingly impossible task. But Elder allowed herself to think only as far as the next big rock. Once she had completed her descent of the first pitch, Elder said that she looked up at the impossibly steep slope and thought, "Look what I've done! Exhilarated, I gave a whoop that echoed down the silent pass." Even with a broken arm, joy was Elder's constant companion. A good survivor always tells herself, "Count your blessings—you're alive."

Enjoy the Survival Journey

8   It may seem counterintuitive, but even in the worst circumstances, survivors find something to enjoy, some way to play and laugh. Survival can be tedious, and waiting itself is an art. Elder found herself laughing out loud when she started to worry that someone might see up her skirt as she climbed. Even as Callahan's boat was sinking, he stopped to laugh at himself as he clutched a knife in his teeth like a pirate while trying to get into his life raft. And Viktor Frankl ordered some of his companions in **Auschwitz** who were threatening to give up hope to force themselves to think of one funny thing each day. Singing, playing mind games, reciting poetry, and doing mathematical problems can make waiting tolerable, while heightening perception and quieting fear.

Auschwitz: a Nazi concentration camp

Never Give Up

9   Yes, you might die. In fact, you will die—we all do. But perhaps it doesn't have to be today. Don't let it worry you. Forget about rescue. Everything you need is inside you already. Dougal Robertson, a sailor who was cast away at sea for thirty-eight days after his boat sank, advised thinking of survival this way: "Rescue will come as a welcome interruption of . . . the survival voyage." One survival psychologist calls that "resignation without giving up. It is survival by surrender."

10   Survivors are not easily discouraged by setbacks. They accept that the environment is constantly changing and know that they must adapt. When they fall, they pick themselves up and start the entire process over again, breaking it down into manageable bits. When *Apollo 13*'s oxygen tank exploded, apparently dooming the crew, Commander Jim Lovell chose to keep on transmitting whatever data he could back to mission control, even as they burned up on re-entry. Elder and Callahan were equally determined and knew this final truth: If you're still alive, there is always one more thing that you can do.

COMPREHENSION AND CRITICAL THINKING

1. What is the meaning of *precipitating* in paragraph 2?
   a. ending   b. unexpected   c. initiating or triggering

2. In paragraph 7, what is the meaning of *pitch*?
   a. throw   b. slope   c. tone

3. How does the author introduce the text?
   a. general background
   b. historical background
   c. anecdote
   d. contrasting position

4. In this process essay, the author describes the experiences of several survivors. Briefly explain what challenge the following people faced.

   Aron Ralston: _His hand was trapped in a boulder, and he had to decide how to free himself._

   Lance Armstrong: _He had to deal with cancer._

   Lauren Elder: _She survived a light plane crash and had to descend a snowy peak._

   Viktor Frankl: _He survived being incarcerated in a concentration camp._

Dougal Robertson: _He was cast away at sea for thirty-eight days._

5.   a. What do most of the stories of survival have in common? What kinds of threats were they surviving?

Most of the people were surviving a force of nature or a natural process

(cancer). They were dealing with a great physical or psychological threat.

   b. How is Frankl's journey different from those of the others mentioned in the essay?

Frankl had to survive a situation in which others (Nazis) were

deliberately trying to harm him and his companions at Auschwitz.

6.   This process essay also uses narration and cause and effect. What are some of the effects of positive thinking while in a dangerous situation?

When people keep their spirits up and refuse to give up hope, it helps them

deal with the issues they are facing. They think of creative solutions.

7.   What is the author's specific purpose?

He wants to inform readers about how others have survived, and teach

them about survival techniques.

8.   Who was probably the targeted audience for this essay?
   a. an academic or   b. children
      intellectual audience   c. a general audience
   Give some reasons for your choice.

The writing style appears too casual to be written for experts, and it

might scare children.

9.   What lessons does this essay have for the reader?

It shows how resilient the human spirit is. It reminds us that we can get

through our ordeals if we follow the survival steps of staying calm,

analyzing the situation, celebrating small successes, and so on.

10.   Using your own words, explain why it is important to enjoy the survival journey.

It helps make the situation tolerable and keeps people's spirits up.

WRITING TOPICS

Write about one of the following topics. Remember to explore, develop, and revise and edit your work.

1. Describe a difficult physical ordeal that you or someone you know went through. What happened? What steps were taken to get through the ordeal?
2. Explain the steps people should take when they have an emotional crisis. For example, how can they survive a breakup, a public humiliation, or the loss of a friend?

READING 12

Into Thin Air
Jon Krakauer

John Krakauer is a mountaineer and writer. In his memoir, *Into Thin Air*, Krakauer recounts the tragic tale of the 1996 Mount Everest climbing expedition in which he participated. During this expedition, many people who were Krakauer's climbing companions died when a sudden ferocious storm engulfed them. The next reading is an excerpt from Krakauer's best-selling book.

A mountain climber

1   The literature of Everest is rife with accounts of hallucinatory experiences attributable to hypoxia and fatigue. In 1933, the noted English climber Frank Smythe observed "two curious looking objects floating in the sky" directly above him at 27,000 feet: "[One] possessed what appeared to be squat underdeveloped wings, and the other a protuberance suggestive of a beak. They hovered motionless but seemed slowly to pulsate." In 1980, during his solo ascent, Reinhold Messner imagined that an invisible companion was climbing beside him. Gradually, I became aware that my mind had gone haywire in a similar fashion, and I observed my own slide from reality with a blend of fascination and horror.

2   I was so far beyond ordinary exhaustion that I experienced a queer detachment from my body, as if I were observing my descent from a few feet overhead. I imagined that I was dressed in a green cardigan and wingtips. And although the gale was generating a windchill in excess of seventy below zero Fahrenheit, I felt strangely and disturbingly warm.

3   At 6:30, as the last of the daylight seeped from the sky, I'd descended to within 200 vertical feet of Camp Four. Only one obstacle now stood between me and safety: a bulging incline of hard, glassy ice that I would have to descend without a rope. Snow pellets borne by 70-knot gusts stung my face; any exposed flesh was instantly frozen. The tents, no more than 650 horizontal feet away, were only intermittently visible through the whiteout. There was no margin for error. Worried about making a critical blunder, I sat down to **marshal** my energy before descending further.

marshal:
gather

4   Once I was off my feet, inertia took hold. It was so much easier to remain at rest than to summon the initiative to tackle the dangerous ice slope. I just sat there as the storm roared around me, letting my mind drift, doing nothing for perhaps forty-five minutes.

5   I'd tightened the drawstrings on my hood until only a tiny opening remained around my eyes, and I was removing the useless, frozen oxygen mask from beneath my chin when Andy Harris suddenly appeared out of the gloom beside me. Shining my headlamp in his direction, I reflexively recoiled when I saw the appalling condition of his face. His cheeks were coated with an armor of frost, one eye was frozen shut, and he was slurring his words badly. He looked in serious trouble. "Which way to the tents?" Andy blurted, frantic to reach shelter.

6   I pointed in the direction of Camp Four, and then warned him about the ice just below us. "It is steeper than it looks!" I yelled, straining to make myself heard over the tempest. "Maybe I should go down first and get a rope from camp—." As I was in midsentence, Andy abruptly turned away and moved over the lip of the ice slope, leaving me sitting there dumbfounded.

7   Scooting on his butt, he started down the steepest part of the incline. "Andy," I shouted after him, "it's crazy to try it like that! You're going to blow it for sure!" He yelled something back, but his words were carried off by the screaming wind. A second later he lost his purchase, flipped ass over teakettle, and was suddenly rocketing headfirst down the ice.

8   Two hundred feet below, I could just make out Andy's motionless form slumped at the foot of the incline. I was sure he'd broken at least a leg, or maybe his neck. But then, incredibly, he stood up, waved that he was O.K., and started lurching toward Camp Four, which at the moment was in plain sight, 500 feet beyond.

9   My backpack held little more than three empty oxygen canisters and a pint of frozen lemonade; it probably weighed no more than sixteen or eighteen pounds. But I was tired and worried about getting down the incline without breaking a leg, so I tossed the pack over the edge and hoped it would come to rest where I could retrieve it. Then I stood up and started down the ice, which was as smooth and hard as the surface of a bowling ball.

10   Fifteen minutes of dicey, fatiguing **crampon** work brought me safely to the bottom of the incline where I easily located my pack, and another ten minutes after that I was in camp myself. I lunged into my tent with my crampons still on, zipped the door tight, and sprawled across the frost-covered floor too tired to even sit upright. For the first time I had a sense of how wasted I was: I was more exhausted than I'd ever been in my life. But I was safe.

crampon: steel spikes attached to the soles of mountain-climbing boots to create a better grip on ice and prevent slipping.

Teaching Tip:

Cooperative Learning (Sharing Circle)
Ask students to work in groups of three and share answers to the questions. They can also discuss the writing topics. Then take up the answers with the class.

COMPREHENSION AND CRITICAL THINKING

1. In paragraph 1, *protuberance* means
    (a.) a bulge   b. a disturbance   c. a bird

2. In paragraph 3, what is the meaning of *blunder?*

    mistake

3. What type of narrator is telling this story?
    (a.) first-person   b. third-person

4. What can you infer or guess about his personality?   Answers will vary.

    He is courageous, reckless, and strong. He also has great mental

    endurance and physical endurance.

5. In your own words, sum up the story in a couple of sentences. Answer who, what, when, where, why, and how questions.

    In 1996, Krakauer, while descending to Camp Four on Mount Everest, got

    caught in a violent storm and nearly lost his life.

6. Describe the author's physical and mental state at the beginning of the essay.

    He was freezing cold and almost hypothermic. He was exhausted and

    hallucinating.

7. What were some obstacles that the narrator faced during his descent to Camp Four?

    He faced a lack of oxygen, fatigue, severe weather, mental exhaustion,

    hallucinations, and fear.

8. This excerpt contains examples of imagery (description using the senses). Give examples of imagery that appeal to touch, sight, and hearing.   Answers will vary.

    touch: ___*a windchill in excess of seventy below zero; hard glassy ice;*

    snow pellets . . . stung my face

    sight: ___*the tents . . . only intermittently visible through the whiteout;*

    his cheeks were coated with an armor of frost

    hearing: ___*he was slurring his words; his words were carried off by the*

    screaming wind

9. Which organizational method does the author use in this essay?
    (a.) time order   b. space order   c. emphatic order

10. The author uses dialogue in this essay. What is the purpose of the dialogue?

   The dialogue involves the reader in the author's experience by making the

   experience more vivid.

Writing Topics

Teaching Tip:
The suggested topics give students the opportunity to practice descriptive writing. Specify whether students should write a paragraph or an essay.

Write about one of the following topics. Remember to explore, develop, and revise and edit your work.

1. Have you or someone you know participated in a risky activity? What happened? Include descriptive details that appeal to the senses.
2. In Krakauer's story, he describes his reactions during a challenging moment from his past. Think about a time when you felt extremely excited, ashamed, or moved. Where were you and what were you doing? Describe what happened and include descriptive details.

Theme: **Plants and Insects**

Teaching Tip:
"Songs of Insects" has elements of illustration, description, and narration.

READING 13

Songs of Insects

Sy Montgomery

Sy Montgomery is a naturalist and writer. She has written many articles about animals and their environments. In the next article, Montgomery reflects on the methods of communication by insects.

1   In his poem "Conversational Insects," H. I. Phillips has a confession to make:

> I long to interview the little Insects,
>
> and get the drift of what they're driving at:
>
> To chat with Wasps and Crickets
>
> In bushes, trees and thickets
>
> And understand the language of the Gnat.

2   If you share this poet's sensibilities, now is the time to fulfill your longing. Though widely loved for its changing leaves and migrating birds, early fall is, in some circles anyway, yet more renowned for the sweetness of its insect voices.

3   The insects' songs tell of longing and pursuit, rivalry and battle. If the song of the autumn field cricket suddenly becomes louder, more rapid, and higher pitched, he's located a lady and is calling to her. If his calls soften, she has come to him and is ready to mate. (Unlike grasshoppers,

A cricket

entomologist:
a scientist who
specializes in
insects

orthopteran:
another term for
insects with
folded hind legs

the female cricket usually mounts the male.) If he encounters a
rival, he chirps more loudly, and the chirps get longer and less
rhythmic. A vicious battle may ensue—so vicious that cricket
fights were the entertainment extravaganza of the Sung dynasty
in 10th-century China. The victors earned the title *shou lip*—
"conquering cricket"—and were ceremoniously buried in little
silver caskets when they died of old age.

4   Some insect songs convey information people can use.
Because the insect's metabolism speeds up with the heat, the
hotter the weather, the faster the chirping. The male snowy tree
cricket, which begins singing in September and continues until
the killing frost, tracks temperatures so accurately that, in 1897,
Tufts College professor A. E. Dolbear developed a measurement
formula accurate to within one degree Fahrenheit: count the
number of chirps in 15 seconds and add 39.

5   Songs may have X-rated lyrics. Some species of
grasshoppers, for instance, explicitly announce the moment of copulation
with a distinct, sharp noise just before the male leaps onto the back of the
female—a sound that one **entomologist** interprets as the **orthopteran**
equivalent of "Oh, boy!" and terms it "the shout of triumph."

6   The autumn songs of these hopping insects are among the most
lovely and lyrical sounds of the natural world, appreciated around the
globe. For centuries, the Japanese have given one another gifts of singing
insects. These tiny pets were so popular around 1820 that fishermen and
peasants used to sell them in pushcarts door-to-door. Today, autumn
suzumushi (bell crickets) and *kirigirisu* (grasshoppers) are sold in nearly
every post office in Japan. In Africa, the songs of crickets are said to have
magic powers. And perhaps they do. Henry David Thoreau described the
song of one species as "a slumberous breathing," an "intenser dream."
Nathaniel Hawthorne, describing the autumn music of the snowy tree
cricket, wrote, "If moonlight could be heard, it would sound like that."

7   If it takes some effort for us to listen for insect song, it is because the
songs are not meant for us; they are meant for creatures that wear their
skeletons on their outsides and whose ears are on their elbows. Members
of the grasshopper family, including crickets, locusts, and katydids, hear
with small disks near one of the front leg joints. On the inside of the hind
leg, grasshoppers have a comb-like structure with a row of teeth. They rub
this comb against a ridge on the wing to produce a sound. And these songs
are perfect for their purposes. Over the relatively long distances that these
little animals must travel to find one another, looks mean nothing; songs
call out the identity of the musician. For this reason, entomologists can
sometimes better classify these insects by their songs than by their
appearance.

8   Most autumn-singing insects prefer to perform on warm mornings, afternoons, and early evenings. But if you listen carefully, you may be able to hear one or another singing almost anytime. The greenish yellow marsh meadow locust prefers to sing on hot, quiet forenoons from moist ditches and grassy banks. At night, in areas that have been spared aerial spraying, listen for the katydids. They'll be squawking from the lindens, elms, and maples where cicadas sang during summer days.

COMPREHENSION AND CRITICAL THINKING

1. What is the meaning of *pitch* as it appears in Paragraph 3?
    a. throw   b. slope   c. tone

2. Circle a word in paragraph 5 that means "overtly" or "clearly."

3. How is the author's introduction unusual?

    Sy Montgomery begins her essay with a poem.

4. According to the author, why is autumn the best season to appreciate singing insects?

    Singing insects make the most noise during the autumn.

5. In your own words, list some messages that singing insects communicate to each other.

    A singing insect can communicate when it has located a mate, when it is

    battling with a rival, and when it is procreating.

6. What useful information can singing insects communicate to humans?

    They communicate temperatures very accurately.

7. How do people in different cultures value singing insects?

    The Japanese give singing insects as gifts, and the Africans think the

    singing insects have magical powers. American writer Nathaniel

    Hawthorne, shows his appreciation for insects by comparing their songs

    to moonlight.

8. What type of singing insect is the author mainly describing?

    members of the grasshopper family

9. The author uses examples to support her main point, but she also describes a process. How do singing insects make their sounds?

    They rub a comb-like structure against a ridge on the wing to produce

    sound.

Teaching Tip:

Cooperative Learning (Jigsaw)
Ask students to read the text for homework or in class. Then divide the class into groups of three to four students. Ask some groups to list the main points of the text and write a summary. Ask other groups to list about ten difficult words and phrases from the text and to define them from the context. A third set of groups can answer the comprehension questions. Then ask students to share their information.

Teaching Tip:
If students are
unable to come up
with ideas for
writing topic 1, ask
them to think about
sunsets, a full moon,
a starry night, or a
thunderstorm. They
can also think about
places such as a
canyon, valley, lake,
river, or mountain.

10.   What is the main idea of this essay?

Not only are insect songs wonderful to hear, but they can also teach us

how some insects communicate with each other.

WRITING TOPICS

Write about one of the following topics. Remember to explore, develop, and revise and edit your work.

1.   List some elements in nature that inspire you or move you. Support your essay with examples.
2.   How is your personality similar to that of certain birds, mammals, or insects? Give examples to support your main point.

Teaching Tip:
The suggested
topics give students
the opportunity to
practice illustration
writing. Specify
whether students
should write a
paragraph or an
essay.

READING 14

Nature Returns to the Cities
John Roach

John Roach is a writer for *National Geographic*, and he has written many articles about nature. In the next essay, he describes animal life in our concrete jungles.

An urban raccoon

1   The concrete jungle isn't just for people anymore. Thirty years of good environmental stewardship combined with wildlife's innate ability to adapt has given rise to a resurgence of nature in America's urban centers. In New York City, raccoons have walked through the front door and into the kitchen to raid the refrigerator. In southern California, mountain lions have been seen cooling off under garden sprinklers and breaking into homes near Disneyland. In Chicago, beavers gnaw and fell trees and snarl traffic. In her book *Wild Nights: Nature Returns to the City*, Anne Matthews describes such incidents as she explores the resurgence of wildlife in New York and other cities. "Thirty years of environmental protection and absence of hunting [in cities] have allowed animal populations to soar," she notes.

2   The implications of the wildlife resurgence in cities vary. People may marvel at the presence of a falcon nest on the twenty-seventh floor of New York Hospital. On the other hand, some people were literally sickened to death in the fall of 2000 by the West Nile virus,

which had been carried to the city by migrating birds and transmitted to mosquitoes, which passed it on to humans.

3   Overcrowded cities and urban sprawl have put more people and wild animals in proximity than at any other time in American history, says Matthews. Encounters between these two groups are beginning to exceed what scientists call the cultural carrying capacity, defined in *Wild Nights* as "the moment humans stop saying 'Aww' and start calling 911." This change in the nature of the relationship between people and wildlife, says Matthews, is forcing people to reconsider their ethical and practical role as top predator.

4   Nature's return to U.S. cities has resulted in part from passage of the Clean Air Act in 1970 and the Clean Water Act in 1972. These laws of environmental protection that helped make air safer to breathe and water safer to drink also made cities more hospitable to wildlife, according to Matthews. After being cleaned up, New York Harbor is now home to booming populations of blue crabs and fiddler crabs, which in turn attract thousands of long-legged wading birds such as herons and egrets. With the air now cleaner, owls have flocked in growing numbers to the suburbs in search of easy prey: pets such as schnauzers, chihuahuas, and cats. In parts of the South and Midwest, forests that were logged in the nineteenth century have grown back over the last hundred years, allowing animal populations to recover. Car collisions with moose are now common along Interstate 95, the main East Coast traffic corridor. Crocodiles, who were all but erased by development pressure in Florida, are now breeding at four times their normal rate in the cooling canals of Florida's nuclear power plants.

5   Some creatures, such as rats, never really left the city. Today, an estimated 28 million rats—which are non-native, like much of the city's human population—inhabit New York. The greater New York area is home to eight million people, which means there are more than three rats to every person. Matthews explains how it happened. "Rats are smart," she writes. "Although a fast-forward version of natural selection has made rats in many big cities immune to nearly all conventional poisons, they still may press one pack member into service as a taster; if the test rat dies, the others resolutely avoid the bait."

6   Matthews says the strong adaptive ability of non-native species has begun to change the definition of wilderness. Rats were introduced into U.S. cities in the 1700s after arriving as stowaways on merchant ships. Zebra mussels, which have caused major problems in the Great Lakes by clogging intake pipes, were imported in the ballast water of international ships. "The most important thing is to realize that a city is wilder than we tend to imagine and the land we think of as untouched or wild really isn't,"

Teaching Tip: "Nature Returns to the Cities" is a cause and effect essay that also has elements of narration and argument.

Teaching Tip:

Cooperative Learning (Pair & Share) Ask students to work with a partner to make a plan for this essay. Then students can compare their essay plans with another pair of students.

says Matthews. "There has been so much human interference and reshaping that we really don't know what a pristine planet is." Matthews thinks people should not try to undo the effects of this increased interference with wildlife but to improve their understanding of it and continue to make room for nature in their lives.

7   Matthews says it's crucial that people consider what kind of world they want their grandchildren to inherit and act to ensure that such a world will exist. One immediate concern is what the impacts of global warming will be in fifty years. Citing the results of computer models showing future conditions if no action is taken to mitigate global warming, Matthews says much of New York will be under water, as sea levels rise three feet. New Orleans, Louisiana, already eight feet below sea level, might become the next Atlantis. What can we do? "What you can do is as small as don't use air conditioning as much, don't use your gas-guzzling [sport utility vehicle], walk more," says Matthews. "On the macro level, urge your congressperson to do something about environmental issues."

COMPREHENSION AND CRITICAL THINKING

1.   In paragraph 1, circle a word that means "reappearance."

2.   Define *prey*. Look in paragraph 4 for context clues.

      The animal that another animal kills, usually for food.

3.   Underline the thesis statement.

4.   What are at least two reasons the writer gives for animals returning to urban environments?

      Urban sprawl causes humans and wildlife to confront each other more

      often.

      The Clean Air and Clean Water Acts made cities more hospitable to wildlife.

      Some animals adapt well to city life (rats, for instance).

5.   What are at least three effects of wildlife in cities?

      New viruses such as the West Nile virus infect humans. People become

      afraid of the animals. The animals become a nuisance (rats and

      raccoons, for instance). Animals such as beavers damage structures.

      People have car collisions with animals.

6.   In paragraph 4, the writer implies that
      a.   The Clean Air and Clean Water Acts did not help the environment.
      b.   The Clean Air and Clean Water Acts were quite effective in helping to improve the quality of the air and water.

    c. Logging practices are much more detrimental to the environment today than they were in the past.

    d. Many dangerous predators such as crocodiles now roam the cities.

7. What is Matthews's opinion about abundant wildlife in the city?

She believes that people should accept the new reality because,

throughout history, humans and animals have interacted.

8. What is Matthews's definition of wilderness in paragraph 6?

She says that there is really no such thing as a pristine, untouched

wilderness because of human interference.

9. Although this is mainly a cause and effect essay, there are also elements of process. Which paragraph gives the readers clear steps to take to help the environment? ___7___

10. What incorrect assumption or belief do many people today have about the relationship between wildlife and cities?

People assume that humans and wildlife are distinct and do not really

interact, when in fact they have always been living together. There have

never been animal-free cities.

WRITING TOPICS

Write about one of the following topics. Remember to explore, develop, and revise and edit your work.

1. Describe your own experiences with wildlife in your home, yard, or neighborhood. What causes or caused the bird, animal, or insect to invade your area? How does it or how did it affect you and your neighbors?
2. Do you have a pet in your home? Why or why not? Describe the causes or effects (or both) of your decision about having pets.

Theme: **Human Development**

READING 15

The Untranslatable Word "Macho"
Rose del Castillo Guilbault

Rose del Castillo Guilbault is a journalist and the Editorial Director of the ABC affiliate station, KGO-TV, in San Francisco, California. In this essay, Castillo compares how two cultures define the term *macho*.

1   What is *macho*? That depends on which side of the border you come from. Although it's not unusual for words and expressions to lose their

Teaching Tip:
The suggested topics give students the opportunity to practice cause and effect writing. Specify whether students should write a paragraph or an essay.

Teaching Tip:
This comparison and contrast essay also contains elements of definition, narration, and argument.

subtlety in translation, <u>the negative connotations *of macho* in this country are troublesome to Hispanics.</u>

2   Take the newspaper descriptions of alleged mass murderer Ramon Salcido. That an insensitive, insanely jealous, hard-drinking, violent Latin male is referred to as macho makes Hispanics cringe. *"Es muy macho,"* the women in my family nod approvingly, describing a man they respect. But in the United States, when women say, "He's so macho," it's with disdain.

3   The Hispanic *macho* is manly, responsible, hardworking, a man in charge, and a patriarch. He is a man who expresses strength through silence, or what the Yiddish language would call a *mensch*.

4   The American *macho* is a chauvinist, a brute, uncouth, selfish, loud, abrasive, capable of inflicting pain, and sexually promiscuous. Quintessential *macho* models in this country are Sylvester Stallone, Arnold Schwarzenegger, and Charles Bronson. In their movies, they exude toughness, independence, and masculinity. But a closer look reveals their machismo is really violence masquerading as courage, sullenness disguised as silence, and irresponsibility camouflaged as independence.

5   If the Hispanic ideal of *macho* were translated to American screen roles, they might be Jimmy Stewart, Sean Connery, and Laurence Olivier. In Spanish, macho ennobles Latin males. In English, it devalues them. This pattern seems consistent with the conflicts ethnic minority males experience in this country. Typically, the cultural traits other societies value don't translate as desirable characteristics in America.

6   I watched my own father struggle with these cultural ambiguities. He worked on a farm for twenty years. He laid down miles of irrigation pipe, carefully plowed long, neat rows in fields, hacked away at **recalcitrant** weeds, and drove tractors through whirlpools of dust. He stoically worked twenty-hour days during harvest season, accepting the long hours as part of agricultural work. When the boss complained or upbraided him for minor mistakes, he kept quiet, even when it was obvious the boss had erred.

7   He handled the most menial tasks with pride. At home he was a good provider, helped out my mother's family in Mexico without complaint, and was indulgent with me. Arguments between my mother and him generally had to do with money or with his stubborn reluctance to share his troubles. He tried to work them out in his own silence. He didn't want to trouble my mother—a course that backfired because the imagined is always worse than the reality.

8   Americans regarded my father as decidedly un-macho. His character was interpreted as nonassertive, his loyalty as a lack of ambition, and his quietness as ignorance. I once overheard the boss's son blame him for

recalcitrant:
unmanageable

plowing crooked rows in a field. My father merely smiled at the lie, knowing the boy had done it, but didn't refute it, confident his good work was well known. But the boss instead ridiculed him for being "stupid" and letting a kid get away with a lie. Seeing my embarrassment, my father dismissed the incident, saying, "They're the dumb ones. Imagine, me fighting with a kid." I tried not to look at him with American eyes because sometimes the reflection hurt.

9 Listening to my aunts' clucks of approval, my vision focused on the qualities America overlooked. "He's such a hard worker. So serious, so responsible." My aunts would secretly compliment my mother. The unspoken comparison was that he was not like some of their husbands, who drank and womanized. My uncles represented the darker side of macho.

10 In a patriarchal society, few challenge their roles. If men drink, it's because it's the manly thing to do. If they gamble, it's because it's how men relax. And if they fool around, well, it's because a man simply can't hold back so much man! My aunts didn't exactly meekly sit back, but they put up with these transgressions because Mexican society dictated this was their lot in life.

11 In the United States, I believe it was the feminist movement of the early seventies that changed macho's meaning. Perhaps my generation of Latin women was in part responsible. I recall Chicanos complaining about the chauvinistic nature of Latin men and the notion they wanted their women barefoot, pregnant, and in the kitchen. The generalization that Latin men embodied chauvinistic traits led to this interesting twist of semantics. Suddenly a word that represented something positive in one culture became a negative prototype in another.

12 The problem with the use of macho today is that it's become an accepted stereotype of the Latin male. And like all stereotypes, it distorts truth. The impact of language in our society is undeniable. And the misuse of macho hints at a deeper cultural misunderstanding that extends beyond mere word definitions.

COMPREHENSION AND CRITICAL THINKING

1. Find a word in paragraph 2 that means "contempt." _____*disdain*_____

2. Underline the thesis statement.

3. What is the writer comparing and contrasting in this essay?
   She is contrasting the English-American view of macho with the
   Hispanic view of macho.

Teaching Tip:
Students can review the meaning of *connotation* on pages 531–532.

4. What connotations does the word *macho* have in Latin culture?

   It has positive connotations of somebody who is responsible,

   hardworking, and respected.

5. What connotations does the word *macho* have in American culture?

   It has negative connotations of someone who could be chauvinistic,

   uncouth, loud, or selfish.

6. According to the writer, why do men like Jimmy Stewart, Sean Connery, and Laurence Olivier better exemplify the word *macho* than men like Sylvester Stallone or Charles Bronson?

   The former are noble as in the Latin definition of macho, whereas the latter

   are sullen, irresponsible, and violent as in the American definition of macho.

7. In paragraph 8, the writer mentions that she tried not to look at her father "with American eyes." In her opinion, how did Americans view her father?

   They judged him as weak, nonassertive, and ignorant.

8. According to the writer, does the word *macho* in Latin cultures only have a positive connotation? Explain your answer.

   Macho also has a negative connotation. Macho men can behave badly by

   drinking too much or womanizing, and their wives cannot do anything

   about it.

9. How did the meaning of the word *macho* evolve in Latin communities in North America?

   It was initially positive. The feminist movement, as well as the

   generation of Latin women in the 1960s and 1970s, helped change the

   meaning of the word. The word became associated with chauvinism.

10. Although the predominant pattern in this essay is comparison and contrast, the writer also uses definition and narration. How do they help develop her central argument?

    She needs to define the terms to be able to compare adequately, and

    the narration provides examples to prove her point.

Teaching Tip:
The suggested topics give students the opportunity to practice comparison and contrast writing. Specify whether students should write a paragraph or an essay.

WRITING TOPICS

Write about one of the following topics. Remember to explore, develop, and revise and edit your work.

1. What are some stereotypes of your nationality, religion, or gender? Compare the stereotypes with the reality.

2. Compare and contrast two people in your life who have very different personalities.

READING 16

Chance and Circumstance

David Leonhardt

> David Leonhardt is a columnist for the *New York Times*. His columns focus on economics and society. In the following essay, he examines the theories of Malcolm Gladwell and ponders on the definition and the causes of success.

Teaching Tip:
"Chance and Circumstance" has three dominant essay patterns: definition, cause and effect, and argument.

1   In 1984, a young man named Malcolm graduated from the University of Toronto and moved to the United States to try his hand at journalism. Thanks to his uncommonly clear writing style and keen eye for a story, he quickly landed a job at the *Washington Post*. After less than a decade at the *Post*, he moved up to the pinnacle of literary journalism, the *New Yorker*. There, he wrote articles full of big ideas about the hidden patterns of ordinary life, which then became **grist** for two No. 1 best-selling books. In the vast world of nonfiction writing, he is as close to a singular talent as exists today.

grist:
useable material

2   Or at least that's one version of the story of Malcolm Gladwell. Here is another: In 1984, a young man named Malcolm graduated from the University of Toronto and moved to the United States to try his hand at journalism. No one could know it then, but he arrived with nearly the perfect background for his time. His mother was a psychotherapist and his father a mathematician. Their professions pointed young Malcolm toward the behavioral sciences, whose popularity would explode in the 1990s. His mother also just happened to be a writer on the side. So unlike most children of mathematicians and therapists, he came to learn, as he would later recall, "that there is beauty in saying something clearly and simply." As a journalist, he plumbed the behavioral research for optimistic lessons about the human condition, and he found an eager audience during the heady, proudly geeky '90s. His first book, *The Tipping Point*, was published in March 2000, just days before the **Nasdaq** peaked.

Nasdaq:
an electronic stock market started in 1971

3   These two stories about Gladwell are both true, and yet they are also very different. The first personalizes his success. It is the classically American version of his career, in that it gives individual characteristics— talent, hard work, **Horatio Alger**–like pluck—the starring role. The second version does not necessarily deny these characteristics, but it does sublimate them. The protagonist is not a singularly talented person who took advantage of opportunities. He is instead a talented person who took advantage of singular opportunities.

Horatio Alger:
American author (1832–1899) who wrote children's adventure novels

4   Gladwell's latest book, *Outliers*, is a passionate argument for taking the second version of the story more seriously than we now do. "It is not the brightest who succeed," Gladwell writes, "nor is success simply the sum of the decisions and efforts we make on our own behalf. It is, rather, a

To what degree is success due to good timing and luck?

gift. <u>Outliers are those who have been given opportunities—and who have had the strength and presence of mind to seize them.</u>"

5   He starts with a tale of individual greatness, about the Beatles, the titans of Silicon Valley, or the enormously successful generation of New York Jews born in the early twentieth century. Then he adds details that undercut that tale. So Bill Gates is introduced as a young computer programmer from Seattle whose brilliance and ambition outshine the brilliance and ambition of the thousands of other young programmers. But then Gladwell takes us back to Seattle, and we discover that Gates's high school happened to have a computer club when almost no other high schools did. He then lucked into the opportunity to use the computers at the University of Washington, for hours on end. By the time he turned twenty, he had spent well more than ten thousand hours as a programmer.

6   At the end of this revisionist tale, Gladwell asks Gates himself how many other teenagers in the world had as much experience as he had by the early 1970s. "If there were fifty in the world, I'd be stunned," Gates says. "I had a better exposure to software development at a young age than I think anyone did in that period of time, and all because of an incredibly lucky series of events." Gates's talent and drive were surely unusual. But Gladwell suggests that his opportunities may have been even more so.

anomaly:
peculiarity or strange quality

7   Gladwell explores the **anomaly** of hockey players' birthdays. In many of the best leagues in the world, amateur or professional, roughly 40 percent of the players were born in January, February or March, while only 10 percent were born in October, November or December. It's a profoundly strange pattern, with a simple explanation. The cutoff birth date for many youth hockey leagues is January 1. So the children born in the first three months of the year are just a little older, bigger and stronger than their peers. These older children are then funneled into all-star teams that offer the best, most intense training. By the time they become teenagers, their random initial advantage has turned into a real one.

8   At the championship game of the top Canadian junior league, Gladwell interviews the father of one player born on January 4. More than half of the players on his team—the Medicine Hat Tigers—were born in January, February or March. But when Gladwell asks the father to explain his son's success, the calendar has nothing to do with it. He instead mentions passion, talent and hard work—before adding, as an aside, that the boy was always big for his age. Just imagine, Gladwell writes,

if Canada created another youth hockey league for children born in the second half of the year. It would one day find itself with twice as many great hockey players.

9   *Outliers* is almost a political manifesto. "We look at the young Bill Gates and marvel that our world allowed that thirteen-year-old to become a fabulously successful entrepreneur," he writes at the end. "But that's the wrong lesson. Our world only allowed one thirteen-year-old unlimited access to a time-sharing terminal in 1968. If a million teenagers had been given the same opportunity, how many more Microsofts would we have today?"

10   After a decade—and, really, a generation—in which this country has done fairly little to build up the institutions that can foster success, Gladwell is urging us to rethink. Once again, his timing may prove to be pretty good.

COMPREHENSION AND CRITICAL THINKING

1. Find a word in paragraph 1 that means "height or peak." ____*pinnacle*____

2. Find a word in paragraph 2 that means "examined deeply." ___*plumbed*___

Teaching Tip:

3. What is the introductory style of the essay?
    a. definition   b. contrasting position   c. anecdote

4. Underline a sentence in the essay that defines *outliers*.

5. According to Gladwell, why is Bill Gates an outlier?

    His high school had a computer club when most other high schools did

    not. He had the opportunity to use computers at the University of

    Washington. He had clocked more than 10,000 hours on the computer

    at a very young age.

6. According to Gladwell, why is it luckier for hockey players to be born in the first three months of the year?

    These children are physically bigger and stronger than the other players,

    so they get more and better training opportunities. This gives them an

    advantage over other players.

7. How is Gladwell's perception of successful individuals different from how the general public views successful individuals?

    The public generally credits an individual's talents for his or her

    success whereas Gladwell believes success may be due to good timing

    and opportunity and dogged persistence.

8. In paragraph 9, the writer says that Gladwell's book is "almost a political manifesto." Explain.   Answers will vary.

    Gladwell believes that success is partly due to social context. Thus, all

    students should have access to good schools, high-quality computer

    labs, and so on.

9. What is the writer's opinion of Gladwell's thesis?

    In the conclusion, he says "Gladwell is urging us to rethink" and "his

    timing may prove to be pretty good." Thus, he has a positive opinion of

    Gladwell's thesis.

Teaching Tip:
The suggested
writing topics give
students the
opportunity to
practice definition,
cause and effect,
process, and
argument writing.
Ask students to
brainstorm ideas for
each of the writing
topics. Ensure that
they understand
what *blind ambition*
means.

WRITING TOPICS

Write about one of the following topics. Remember to explore, develop, and revise and edit your work.

1. What is *blind ambition*? Define the term and use examples to support your ideas.
2. Describe someone who you would consider "successful." What contributed to that person's success? How has success affected that person? Write about the causes or effects of the person's success.
3. Nowadays, more boys than girls drop out of school. Colleges and universities now have more female than male graduates in many of their programs. Explain what can be done to convince young men to stay in school and pursue higher education.

READING 17

The Happiness Factor
David Brooks

Teaching Tip:
This comparison
and contrast essay
also has elements
of argument and
narration.

David Brooks writes for the *New York Times*, *The Weekly Standard*, *Newsweek*, and the *Atlantic Monthly*. He is also a commentator on *The Newshour with Jim Lehrer*. In the following essay, Brooks makes an interesting comparison.

1   Two things happened to Sandra Bullock in 2010. First, she won an Academy Award for best actress. Then came the news reports claiming that her husband was an adulterous jerk. So the philosophic question of the day is: Would you take that as a deal? Would you exchange a tremendous professional triumph for a severe personal blow? On the one hand, an Academy Award is nothing to sneeze at. Bullock has earned the admiration of her peers in a way very few experience. She'll make more money for years to come. She may even live longer. Research by Donald A.

Redelmeier and Sheldon M. Singh has found that, on average, Oscar winners live nearly four years longer than nominees that don't win.

2   Nonetheless, if you had to take more than three seconds to think about this question, you are absolutely crazy. Marital happiness is far more important than anything else in determining personal well-being. If you have a successful marriage, it doesn't matter how many professional setbacks you endure, you will be reasonably happy. If you have an unsuccessful marriage, it doesn't matter how many career triumphs you record, you will remain significantly unfulfilled.

3   This isn't just sermonizing. This is the age of research, so there's data to back this up. Over the past few decades, teams of researchers have been studying happiness. Their work, which seemed flimsy at first, has developed an impressive rigor, and one of the key findings is that, just as the old sages predicted, worldly success has shallow roots while interpersonal bonds permeate through and through.

4   For example, the relationship between happiness and income is complicated, and after a point, tenuous. It is true that poor nations become happier as they become middle-class nations. But once the basic necessities have been achieved, future income is lightly connected to well-being. Growing countries are slightly less happy than countries with slower growth rates, according to Carol Graham of the Brookings Institution and Eduardo Lora. The United States is much richer than it was fifty years ago, but this has produced no measurable increase in overall happiness. On the other hand, it has become a much more unequal country, but this inequality doesn't seem to have reduced national happiness.

5   On a personal scale, winning the lottery doesn't seem to produce lasting gains in well-being. People aren't happiest during the years when they are winning the most promotions. Instead, people are happy in their twenties, dip in middle age and then, on average, hit peak happiness just after retirement at age sixty-five. People get slightly happier as they climb the income scale, but this depends on how they experience growth. Does wealth inflame unrealistic expectations? Does it destabilize settled relationships? Or does it flow from a virtuous cycle in which an interesting job produces hard work that in turn leads to more interesting opportunities?

6   If the relationship between money and well-being is complicated, the correspondence between personal relationships and happiness is not. The daily activities most associated with happiness are sex, socializing after work, and having dinner with others. The daily activity most injurious to happiness is commuting. According to one study, joining a group that meets even just once a month produces the same happiness

gain as doubling your income. According to another, being married produces a psychic gain equivalent to more than $100,000 a year.

7   If you want to find a good place to live, just ask people if they trust their neighbors. Levels of social trust vary enormously, but countries with high social trust have happier people, better health, more efficient government, more economic growth, and less fear of crime (regardless of whether actual crime rates are increasing or decreasing). The overall impression from this research is that economic and professional success exists on the surface of life, and that they emerge out of interpersonal relationships, which are much deeper and more important.

8   The second impression is that most of us pay attention to the wrong things. Most people vastly overestimate the extent to which more money would improve their lives. Most schools and colleges spend too much time preparing students for careers and not enough preparing them to make social decisions. Most governments release a ton of data on economic trends but not enough on trust and other social conditions. In short, modern societies have developed vast institutions oriented around the things that are easy to count, not around the things that matter most. They have an affinity for material concerns and a primordial fear of moral and social ones.

9   This may be changing. There is a rash of compelling books— including *The Hidden Wealth of Nations* by David Halpern and *The Politics of Happiness* by Derek Bok—that argue that public institutions should pay attention to well-being and not just material growth narrowly conceived. Governments keep initiating policies they think will produce prosperity, only to get sacked, time and again, from their spiritual blind side.

COMPREHENSION AND CRITICAL THINKING

Teaching Tip:

Cooperative Learning (Pair & Share)
Ask students to work with a partner to make a plan for this essay. Then students can compare their essay plans with another pair of students.

1.   In paragraph 4, what is the meaning of *tenuous*?
   a. unconvincing or questionable
   b. strong and convincing
   c. complete

2.   In your own words, what is the writer's main point?

   There is a greater correlation between interpersonal relationships and

   happiness than between increase in wealth and happiness.

   _____

3.   According to the essay, what factors are associated with increased levels of happiness?

   having enough money to cover basic necessities, being married, having a

   social network, and trusting your neighbors

4. In which paragraphs does the writer use expert opinion?

    1, 4, 6, 9

5. In paragraph 5, the writer states that people are happy in the twenties and after retirement, but not in their middle age. Why are people probably less happy in middle age?   Answers will vary.

    Middle-aged people are probably at their peak in income earning, but

    they might have the most career pressure. Thus, they may not spend

    enough time nurturing family bonds. For those who haven't succeeded

    financially, they might feel frustrated or depressed, which could lead

    to marital problems.

6. In paragraph 7, the writer mentions social trust but doesn't clearly define it. Infer or guess what social trust is.   Answers will vary.

    It is the ability to trust government officials, police, and neighbors.

7. In paragraph 8, the writer criticizes colleges because they don't prepare students to make social decisions. Think of ways that colleges could teach students to make moral and social decisions.   Answers will vary.

    Colleges could give credits for volunteer work. Business students could

    take ethics courses. Students could take anger-management courses.

    There could be a course on morals and ethics.

WRITING TOPICS

Write about one of the following topics. Remember to explore, develop, and revise and edit your work.

1. Compare two jobs. What elements in the jobs provided you with the most pleasure?
2. Define personal happiness and give examples to support your definition.
3. Define social trust. Break the topic down into categories and list examples for each category. For instance, you could write about trust in the government, trust in the police, and trust in one's neighbors.

Teaching Tip:
Questions 5, 6, and 7 require critical thinking. Ask students to discuss those questions in pairs or groups. You might give them some hints if they have problems coming up with ideas.

Teaching Tip:
The suggested writing topics give students the opportunity to practice comparison and contrast, definition, and classification writing.

Teaching Tip:
You might ask students to compare "Chance and Circumstance" and "The Happiness Factor." Both readings look at notions about success.

Teaching Tip:
"Guy" is a
descriptive essay,
but it also contains
elements of
narration, cause
and effect, and
comparison
and contrast.

READING 18

Guy
Maya Angelou

Maya Angelou is a poet, writer, director, and producer. Her best-known work, *I Know Why the Caged Bird Sings*, is a memoir of her life as a girl in Arkansas. In the next excerpt, taken from her autobiography *All God's Children Need Traveling Shoes*, Angelou recounts a personal tragedy that she experienced while in Ghana.

1   The breezes of the West African night were intimate and shy, licking the hair, sweeping through cotton dresses with unseemly intimacy, and then disappearing into the utter blackness. Daylight was equally insistent, but much more bold and thoughtless. It dazzled, muddling the sight. It forced through my closed eyelids, bringing me up and out of a borrowed bed and into brand new streets.

2   After living nearly two years in Cairo, I had brought my son Guy to enter the University of Ghana in Accra. I had planned to stay for two weeks with a friend of a colleague, settle Guy into his dormitory, and then continue to Liberia to a job with the Department of Information.

3   Guy was seventeen and quick. I was thirty-three and determined. We were Black Americans in West Africa, where for the first time in our lives the color of our skin was accepted as correct and normal.

4   Guy had finished high school in Egypt; his Arabic was good, and his health excellent. He assured me that he would quickly learn a Ghanaian language, and he certainly could look after himself. I had worked successfully as a journalist in Cairo and failed sadly at a marriage, which I ended with false public dignity and copious secret tears. But with all crying in the past, I was on my way to another adventure. The future was plump with promise.

5   For two days Guy and I laughed. We looked at the Ghanaian streets and laughed. We listened to the melodious languages and laughed. We looked at each other and laughed out loud. On the third day, Guy, on a pleasure outing, was injured in an automobile accident. One arm and one leg were fractured and his neck was broken.

6   July and August of 1962 stretched out like fat men yawning after a sumptuous dinner. They had every right to gloat, for they had eaten me up. Gobbled me down. Consumed my spirit, not in a wild rush, but slowly, with the obscene patience of certain victors. I became a shadow walking in the white-hot streets, and a dark spectre in the hospital.

solace:
comfort

7   There was no **solace** in knowing that the doctors and nurses hovering around Guy were African, nor in the company of the Black American expatriates who, hearing of our misfortune, came to share some of the slow hours. Racial loyalties and cultural attachments had become meaningless.

8   Trying utterly, I could not match Guy's stoicism. He lay calm, week after week, in a prison of plaster from which only his face and one leg and arm were visible. His assurances that he would heal and be better than new drove me into a faithless silence. Had I been less timid, I would have cursed God. Had I come from a different background, I would have gone further and denied His very existence. Having neither the courage nor the historical precedent, I raged inside myself like a blinded bull in a metal stall.

9   Admittedly, Guy lived with the knowledge that an unexpected and very hard sneeze could force the fractured vertebrae against his spinal cord, and he would be paralyzed or die immediately, but he had only an infatuation with life. He hadn't lived long enough to fall in love with this brutally delicious experience. He could lightly waft away to another place, if there really was another place, where his youthful innocence would assure him a crown, wings, a harp, ambrosia, free milk, and an absence of nostalgic yearning. (I was raised on the spirituals, which ached to "See my old mother in glory" or "Meet with my dear children in heaven," but even the most fanciful lyricists never dared to suggest that those **cavorting** souls gave one thought to those of us left to **moil** in the world.) My wretchedness reminded me that, on the other hand, I would be rudderless.

cavorting: having fun

moil: work hard

10   I had lived with family until my son was born in my sixteenth year. When he was two months old and perched on my left hip, we left my mother's house and together, save for one year when I was touring, we had been each other's home and center for seventeen years. He could die if he wanted to and go off to wherever dead folks go, but I, I would be left without a home.

COMPREHENSION AND CRITICAL THINKING

1. Find a word in paragraph 4 that means "a lot of." _____*copious*_____

2. What type of narrator is telling this story?
   (a.) first-person   b. third-person

3. Why were the writer and her son in Accra?
   Her son was going to the University of Ghana in Accra, and she wanted to help him settle in.

4. What causes the writer's plans to change?
   Her son has a serious accident. She must remain in Accra to help her son recuperate.

5. What type of relationship does the writer have with her son?
   They get along well. They laugh together, go places together, and so on.

Teaching Tip:

Cooperative Learning (Sharing Circle) Ask students to work in groups of three and share answers to the questions. They can also discuss the writing topics. Then take up the answers with the class.

6. Underline a simile in paragraph 6. (In a simile, two things are compared using *like* or *as*.) Then explain what paragraph 6 is about. What are the writer's emotions? Answers will vary.

    She was consumed with worry. Days seemed to slow down, and her concern deepened as the days blurred into each other.

7. Before the accident, what is the writer's attitude toward race?

    At the beginning of the story, she is happy to be in a country with black citizens because the color of her skin is "accepted as normal."

8. How does the writer's attitude about race change?

    After her son's accident, she only wants the doctors and nurses to fix him. She no longer cares what race they are.

9. How does the writer's definition of home change after her son's accident?

    She realizes that home is not a geographical location but an emotional state. Her son gives her comfort and a sense of belonging. If he died, she would be homeless.

Teaching Tip:
The suggested writing topics give students the opportunity to practice using description, definition, and narration.

Teaching Tip:
Writer's World Competition
Please advise students that they can submit their paragraphs and essays for possible publication to www .pearsonhighered .com/essayrewards/ writingrewards.html

WRITING TOPICS

1. This excerpt is from a memoir by Maya Angelou. Narrate a story about an important experience in your life. Explain what happened and use descriptions that appeal to the senses.
2. Define home. Give examples to support your definition.
3. Tell a story about a time that you moved from one place to another. What were your feelings and experiences? Use descriptive imagery in your essay.

 To check your progress in meeting this chapter's objectives, log in to **www.mywritinglab.com,** go to the **Study Plan** tab, click on **Reading Strategies and Selections** and choose **From Reading to Writing** from the list of subtopics. Read and view the resources in the **Review Materials** section, and then complete the **Recall, Apply,** and **Write** sets in the **Activities** section.

The Basic Parts of a Sentence

Parts of Speech	Definition	Some Examples
Adjective	Adds information about the noun.	small, pretty, red, soft
Adverb	Adds information about the verb, adjective, or other adverb; expresses time, place, and frequency.	quickly, sweetly, sometimes, far, usually, never
Conjunctive adverb	Shows a relationship between two ideas. It may appear at the beginning of a sentence, or it may join two sentences.	also, consequently, finally, however, furthermore, moreover, therefore, thus
Coordinating conjunction	Connects two ideas of equal importance.	but, or, yet, so, for, and, nor
Determiner	Identifies or determines if a noun is specific or general.	a, an, the, this, that, these, those, any, all, each, every, many, some
Interjection	Is added to a sentence to convey emotion.	hey, yikes, ouch, wow
Noun	Names a person, place, or thing.	singular: woman, horse, person plural: women, horses, people
Preposition	Shows a relationship between words (source, direction, location, etc.).	at, to, for, from, behind, above
Pronoun	Replaces one or more nouns.	he, she, it, us, ours, themselves
Subordinating conjunction	Connects two ideas when one idea is subordinate (or inferior) to the other idea.	although, because, even though, unless, until, when
Verb	Expresses an action or state of being.	action: look, make, touch, smile linking: is, was, are, become

Appendix 2
Irregular Verbs

Irregular Verb List

Base Form	Simple Past	Past Participle	Base Form	Simple Past	Past Participle
arise	arose	arisen	eat	ate	eaten
be	was, were	been	fall	fell	fallen
bear	bore	borne / born	feed	fed	fed
beat	beat	beat / beaten	feel	felt	felt
become	became	become	fight	fought	fought
begin	began	begun	find	found	found
bend	bent	bent	flee	fled	fled
bet	bet	bet	fly	flew	flown
bind	bound	bound	forbid	forbade	forbidden
bite	bit	bitten	forget	forgot	forgotten
bleed	bled	bled	forgive	forgave	forgiven
blow	blew	blown	forsake	forsook	forsaken
break	broke	broken	freeze	froze	frozen
breed	bred	bred	get	got	got, gotten
bring	brought	brought	give	gave	given
build	built	built	go	went	gone
burst	burst	burst	grind	ground	ground
buy	bought	bought	grow	grew	grown
catch	caught	caught	hang	hung	hung
choose	chose	chosen	have	had	had
cling	clung	clung	hear	heard	heard
come	came	come	hide	hid	hidden
cost	cost	cost	hit	hit	hit
creep	crept	crept	hold	held	held
cut	cut	cut	hurt	hurt	hurt
deal	dealt	dealt	keep	kept	kept
dig	dug	dug	kneel	knelt	knelt
do	did	done	know	knew	known
draw	drew	drawn	lay	laid	laid
drink	drank	drunk	lead	led	led
drive	drove	driven	leave	left	left

Base Form	Simple Past	Past Participle	Base Form	Simple Past	Past Participle
lend	lent	lent	slit	slit	slit
let	let	let	speak	spoke	spoken
lie[1]	lay	lain	speed	sped	sped
light	lit	lit	spend	spent	spent
lose	lost	lost	spin	spun	spun
make	made	made	split	split	split
mean	meant	meant	spread	spread	spread
meet	met	met	spring	sprang	sprung
mistake	mistook	mistaken	stand	stood	stood
pay	paid	paid	steal	stole	stolen
put	put	put	stick	stuck	stuck
prove	proved	proved / proven	sting	stung	stung
quit	quit	quit	stink	stank	stunk
read	read	read	strike	struck	struck
rid	rid	rid	swear	swore	sworn
ride	rode	ridden	sweep	swept	swept
ring	rang	rung	swell	swelled	swollen
rise	rose	risen	swim	swam	swum
run	ran	run	swing	swung	swung
say	said	said	take	took	taken
see	saw	seen	teach	taught	taught
sell	sold	sold	tear	tore	torn
send	sent	sent	tell	told	told
set	set	set	think	thought	thought
shake	shook	shaken	throw	threw	thrown
shine	shone	shone	thrust	thrust	thrust
shoot	shot	shot	understand	understood	understood
show	showed	shown	upset	upset	upset
shrink	shrank	shrunk	wake	woke	woken
shut	shut	shut	wear	wore	worn
sing	sang	sung	weep	wept	wept
sink	sank	sunk	win	won	won
sit	sat	sat	wind	wound	wound
sleep	slept	slept	withdraw	withdrew	withdrawn
slide	slid	slid	write	wrote	written

[1]*Lie* can mean "to rest in a flat position." When *lie* means "tell a false statement," then it is a regular verb: *lie, lied, lied.*

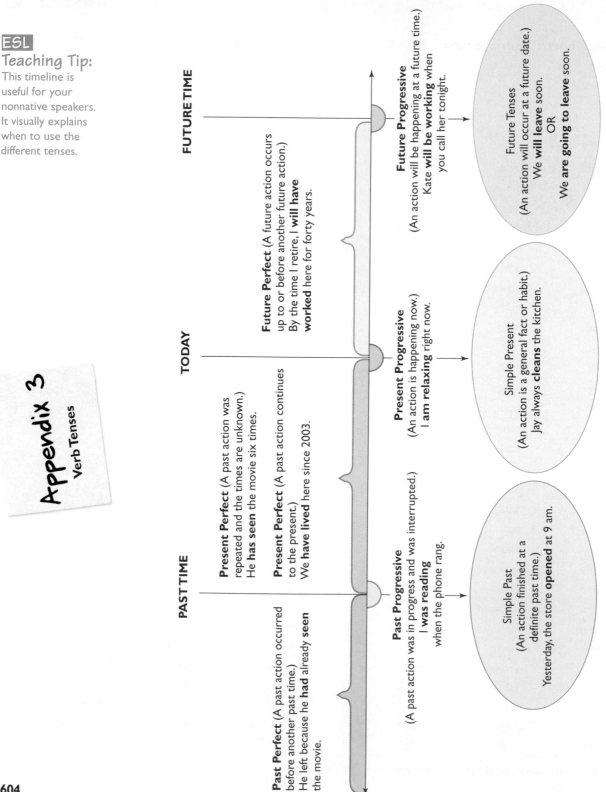

PAST TIME

TODAY

FUTURE TIME

Past Perfect (A past action occurred before another past time.)
He left because he **had** already **seen** the movie.

Present Perfect (A past action was repeated and the times are unknown.)
He **has seen** the movie six times.

Present Perfect (A past action continues to the present.)
We **have lived** here since 2003.

Future Perfect (A future action occurs up to or before another future action.)
By the time I retire, I **will have worked** here for forty years.

Past Progressive
(A past action was in progress and was interrupted.)
I **was reading** when the phone rang.

Present Progressive
(An action is happening now.)
I **am relaxing** right now.

Future Progressive
(An action will be happening at a future time.)
Kate **will be working** when you call her tonight.

Simple Past
(An action finished at a definite past time.)
Yesterday, the store **opened** at 9 am.

Simple Present
(An action is a general fact or habit.)
Jay always **cleans** the kitchen.

Future Tenses
(An action will occur at a future date.)
We **will leave** soon.
OR
We **are going to leave** soon.

604

Making Compound Sentences

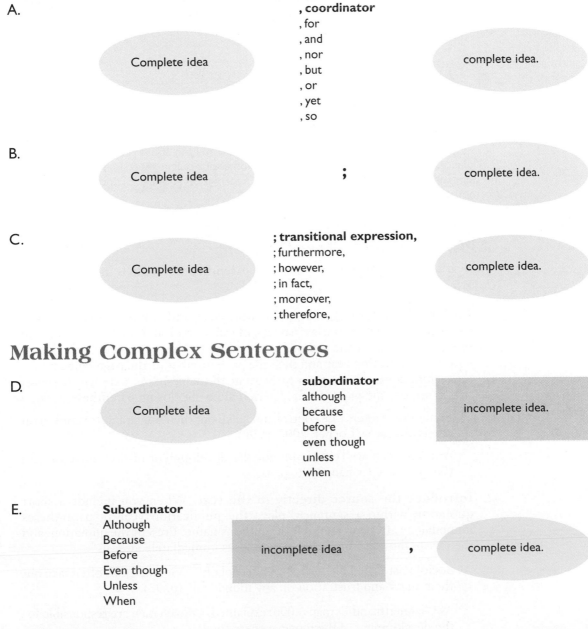

A.

Complete idea

, coordinator
, for
, and
, nor
, but
, or
, yet
, so

complete idea.

B.

Complete idea

;

complete idea.

C.

Complete idea

; transitional expression,
; furthermore,
; however,
; in fact,
; moreover,
; therefore,

complete idea.

Making Complex Sentences

D.

Complete idea

subordinator
although
because
before
even though
unless
when

incomplete idea.

E.

Subordinator
Although
Because
Before
Even though
Unless
When

incomplete idea

,

complete idea.

Appendix 5

Using APA Style

Teaching Tip:
These guidelines have been updated to follow the Sixth Edition of the *APA Publication Manual.* The main changes are:

• always include the abbreviated state, even when referring to a major city such as New York

• include the digital object identifier (DOI) when citing online journals

The American Psychological Association (APA) documentation style is commonly used in scientific or technical fields such as social sciences, economics, and nursing. Before you write a research essay for any course, ask your instructor which style he or she prefers.

> ## Hint APA Web Site
>
> To get some general information about some basic style questions, you can view the APA's Web site at www.apastyle.org. Use the menu on the left side of the page to direct you to specific style questions and answers.
>
> On the same Web site, there is a link to information about online or "electronic" sources. Because the information about online sources is continually being updated, the site has comprehensive information about the latest citation methods. Visit www.apastyle.org.

APA: Including In-Text Citations

Here are two basic options for inserting parenthetical citations in an APA-style research essay.

1. **Enclose the author(s), the publication year, and the page number(s) in parentheses.** Include the last name(s) of the source's author(s). For more than one author, separate the authors' names using & (the ampersand sign). Follow with the publication year and then the page number or the page range where the material appears, using *p.* or *pp.* Separate the names, date, and page references with commas, and place the final period after the closing parenthesis.

   > Sometimes rioters lose control and "take out their anger and frustration on any individual" (Locher, 2002, p. 92).

   > A dozen men are responsible for the development of the movie camera (Giannetti & Eyman, 2006, p. 4).

2. **Introduce the source directly in the text.** When you include a short quotation within a sentence, place the publication year in parentheses immediately after you mention the author's name. Present the quotation, and then write the page number in parentheses immediately after it.

   > Sociologist David A. Locher (2002) explains, "Violent mobs often take out their anger and frustration on any individual" (p. 92).

   > As Giannettti and Eyman (2006) explained, a dozen men are responsible for the development of the movie camera (p. 4).

606

APA: Making a References List

Similar to the MLA Works Cited list, the APA References list gives details about each source you have used, and it appears at the end of your paper. Follow these basic guidelines to prepare References using the APA format.

1. Write "References" at the top of the page and center it. Do not italicize it, bold it, underline it, or put quotation marks around it.
2. List each source alphabetically, using the last names of the authors.
3. Indent the second line and all subsequent lines of each reference one-half inch from the left margin.
4. Double-space the list.

 Writing the Author, Date, Title, and Place Using APA Style

Author
On the References page, write the complete last name and use the first and middle initials (if provided). Do not write complete first names.

Date of Publication
Put the date of publication in parentheses immediately after the name. If you do not have the author's name, then put the date immediately after the title. If no date is available, write (n.d.).

Title
Capitalize the first word of the title, the first word of the subtitle, and any proper nouns or adjectives in Reference lists. Do not add quotation marks or any other special marks around the titles of short works. Italicize titles of longer works such as books, newspapers, or magazines.

Place of Publication
Mention the name of the city and the postal abbreviation of the state or province.
Here is an example of a complete entry for a References list in APA style.

Brainard, S. (2006). *A design manual.* Upper Saddle River, NJ: Prentice Hall.

Books

Carefully review the punctuation of the following example.

Last name, Initial(s). (date). *Title of the book.* City, State of Publication: Publisher.

ONE AUTHOR   Reverse the name of the author. Put the complete last name and the first initial.

Krakauer, J. (1999). *Into thin air.* New York, NY: Random House.

TWO OR MORE AUTHORS   Reverse the name of each author.

> Ciccarelli, S. K., & Meyer, G. E. (2006). *Psychology*. Upper Saddle River, NJ: Prentice Hall.

BOOK WITH AN EDITOR INSTEAD OF AN AUTHOR   Put the editor's name followed by (Ed.).

> Koppleman, S. (Ed.). (1984). *Old maids: Short stories by nineteenth-century US women writers*. Boston, MA: Pandora Press.

TWO OR MORE BOOKS BY THE SAME AUTHOR   Include the author's name in all references. Arrange the works by year of publication, putting the earliest work first.

> Angelou, M. (1969). *I know why the caged bird sings*. New York, NY: Random House.

> Angelou, M. (2006). *Mother: A cradle to hold me*. New York, NY: Random House.

A WORK IN AN ANTHOLOGY

> Munroe, A. (2003). Boys and girls. In R. S. Gwynn & W. Campbell (Eds.), *Literature* (pp. 313–326). Toronto, ON: Pearson Longman.

ENCYCLOPEDIA AND DICTIONARY

> Democracy. (2005). In *Columbia encyclopedia* (6th ed.). New York, NY: Columbia University Press.

> Legitimate. (2003). In *The new American Webster handy college dictionary* (3rd ed.). New York, NY: Signet.

Periodicals

> Last name, Initials. (Year, Month and day). Title of article. *Title of the Magazine or Newspaper, Volume number*, Pages.

ARTICLE IN A MAGAZINE   When citing newspapers or magazines, write as much of the following information as is available.

> Shreeve, J. (2005, March). Beyond the brain. *National Geographic, 207*, 2–31.

ARTICLE IN A NEWSPAPER

> Dugger, C. W. (2006, December 1). Clinton helps broker deal for medicine to treat AIDS. *New York Times*, p. A9.

ARTICLE IN A JOURNAL

> Last name, Initials. (Year, Month). Title of article. *Title of Journal. Volume*(Issue), Pages.

> Seligman, M. (1998). The American way of blame. *APA Monitor, 29*(7), 97.

Electronic Sources

If the source was published on the Internet, include as much of the following information as you can find. Keep in mind that some sites do not contain complete source information.

> Last name, Initials. (date of most recent update). Title of article. *Title of Site* or *Online Publication*. Retrieved from http://site_address.html.

ARTICLE ON A PERSONAL WEB SITE

Krystek, L. (2006). Crop circles from outer space? *Museum of unnatural mystery*. Retrieved from http://www.unmuseum.org

ARTICLE IN AN ONLINE JOURNAL   If the article includes a DOI (digital object identifier), include it instead of the URL. A DOI is a special identification number that will lead you directly to the document on the Internet. If you cannot find the DOI, then go to *crossref.org* and do a DOI search.

Naremore, J. (2008). Films of the year, 2007. *Film Quarterly, 61*(4), 48–61. doi:10.1525/fq.2008.61.4.48

GOVERNMENT SITE (OR OTHER SITES WITHOUT AUTHOR INFORMATION)

If the author is not mentioned on the site, begin with the title followed by the date, and include as much information as you can find. Generally, you do not need to include date of retrieval unless your source is highly changeable such as Wikipedia.

Dangerous jobs. (1997). *US Department of Labor*. Retrieved May 28, 2006, from http://stats.bls.gov/iif/oshwc/cfar0020.pdf

Other Types of Sources

INTERVIEW THAT YOU CONDUCTED   In APA style, do not include a personal interview in your References list. In the actual text, just include the parenthetical notation along with the exact date of the communication. For example: (personal communication, June 15, 2008).

FILM OR VIDEO

Curtiz, M. (Director). (2003). *Casablanca* [DVD]. United States: Warner Bros. (Original movie released 1942)

SOUND RECORDING

Nirvana. (1994). About a girl. On *Unplugged in New York* [CD]. New York, NY: Geffen.

PRACTICE 1   Imagine that you are using the following sources in a research paper. Arrange the sources for a References page using APA style.

- An article by David Mamet in *Harper's* called "Bambi v. Godzilla." The article, published in the June 2005 issue, appeared on pages 33 to 37.

- A book by David Mamet called *Boston Marriage* that was published by Vintage Books in New York, in 2002.
- A book called *Flashback: A Brief History of Film* written by Louis Giannetti and Scott Eyman. The book was published by Prentice Hall in Upper Saddle River, New Jersey, in 2006.
- A book called *Cultural Anthropology* by Serena Nanda. The book was published by Wadsworth in Belmont, California, in 1991.
- An article called "Biography" on the Web site *Marilyn Monroe*. The site was created in 2006. The Web address is http://www.marilynmonroe.com/about /bio.html. You cannot find the author's name on the site.

References

Biography. (2006). Marilyn Monroe. 2006. Retrieved from http://
www.marilynmonroe.com

Giannetti, L., & Eyman, S. (2006). Flashback: A brief history of film. Upper
Saddle River, NJ: Prentice Hall.

Mamet, D. (2002). Boston marriage. New York, NY: Vintage Books.

Mamet, D. (2005, June). Bambi v. Godzilla. Harper's, 33–37.

Nanda, S. (1991). Cultural anthropology. Belmont, CA: Wadsworth.

Teaching Tip:
When students are writing a References list by hand, they should underline the titles that we show in italics here.

In the first few pages of your writing portfolio or copybook, try keeping three "logs" to help you avoid repeating errors and improve your writing.

Spelling Log

The goal of keeping a spelling log is to stop repeating errors. Every time you misspell a word, record both the mistake and the correction in your spelling log. Then, before you hand in a writing assignment, consult the list of misspelled words.

EXAMPLE:

Incorrect	Correct
finaly	finally
responsable	responsible

Grammar Log

The goal of keeping a grammar log is to stop repeating errors in sentence structure, mechanics, and punctuation. Each time a writing assignment is returned to you, identify one or two repeated errors and add them to your grammar log. Next, consult the grammar log before you hand in new writing assignments in order to avoid making the same errors. For each type of grammar error, you could do the following:

1. Identify the assignment and write down the type of error.
2. In your own words, write a rule about the error.
3. Include an example from your writing assignment.

EXAMPLE: Cause and Effect Essay (Mar. 10)   Fragment

Sentences must have a subject and verb and express a complete thought.

Also, an overbearing parent. That can cause a child to become controlling.

Vocabulary Log

The vocabulary log can provide you with interesting new terms to incorporate in your writing. As you use this book, you will learn new vocabulary. Keep a record of the most interesting and useful words and expressions. Write a synonym or definition next to each new word.

EXAMPLE: ubiquitous means widespread

Spelling Log

Grammar Log

Vocabulary Log

Credits

TEXT:

PHOTOS:

Index